TRIAL AND ERROR

CHAIM WEIZMANN

TRIAL AND ERROR

THE AUTOBIOGRAPHY
OF
CHAIM WEIZMANN

HAMISH HAMILTON
LONDON

First published in Great Britain, 1949
by Hamish Hamilton Ltd

PRINTED IN GREAT BRITAIN
BY WESTERN PRINTING SERVICES LTD., BRISTOL

ACKNOWLEDGMENT

These pages have been written over a long period of time and in a variety of places, in London, Rehovoth and New York. Book One was completed in 1941; Book Two in 1947. I have left the material unchanged and added an epilogue which was written in September 1948. In the preparation of these Memoirs I have had the assistance of three persons whose services and friendship I desire to acknowledge with deep gratitude: Miss Doris May, my faithful secretary for many years, to whom I dictated the first draft of almost the whole of Book One and much of Book Two; my friend, Meyer Weisgal, but for whose insistent prodding and continuous help this task might still be awaiting completion; last but not least I owe a deep debt of gratitude to my friend, the gifted writer and lecturer, Maurice Samuel, who worked with me in Rehovoth through the summer of 1947 on the drafting of Book Two and the final revision of the whole.

CHAIM WEIZMANN

FOR MY WIFE

MY COMRADE AND LIFE-COMPANION

CONTENTS

BOOK ONE

Book One

Book One

TRIAL AND ERROR

CHAPTER I

EARLIEST DAYS

*The Little Town among the Pripet Marshes—My People—My First Teachers
—The Pale of Settlement—Grandpa—The Timber Trade—My Father—
The Rafts—The Peasants and the Jews—The Two Worlds—First
Zionist Dreams—My Mother—Servants—Jewish Students, Zionists,
Assimilationists, Revolutionaries—Mother's Rôle in Our Lives and Her
Later Years—My Father's Influence*

THE little town of my birth, Motol, stood—and perhaps still
stands—on the banks of a little river in the great marsh area
which occupies much of the province of Minsk and the adjacent
provinces in White Russia; flat, open country, mournful and
monotonous but, with its rivers, forests and lakes, not wholly
unpicturesque. Between the rivers the soil was sandy, covered
with pine and furze; closer to the banks the soil was black, the
trees were leaf-bearing. In the spring and autumn the area was
a sea of mud, in the winter a world of snow and ice; in the
summer it was covered with a haze of dust. All about, in
hundreds of towns and villages, Jews lived, as they had lived
for many generations, scattered islands in a gentile ocean; and
among them my own people, on my father's and mother's side,
made up a not inconsiderable proportion.

Just outside Motol the river flowed into a large lake and
emerged again at the other end on its way to join the Pina;
that in turn was a tributary of the Pripet, itself a tributary of
the Dnieper, which fell into the Black Sea many hundreds of
miles away. On the further banks of the lake were some villages,
mysterious to my childhood by virtue of their general name—
'the Beyond-the-River.' For them Motol (or Motelle, as we
affectionately Yiddishized the name) was a sort of metropolis.

A very tiny and isolated metropolis it was, with some four or
five hundred families of White Russians and less than two
hundred Jewish families. Communication with the outside

world was precarious and intermittent. No railway, no metalled road, passed within twenty miles of us. There was no post office. Mail was brought in by anyone from the little town who happened to pass by the nearest railway station on his own business. Sometimes these chance messengers would hold on to the mail for days, or for weeks, distributing it when the spirit moved them. But letters played no very important part in our lives; there were few in the outside world who had reason to communicate with us.

There were streets of a kind in Motol—unpaved, of course— and two or three of them were Jewish, for even in the open spaces we drew together, for comfort, for safety, and for companionship. All the buildings were of wood, with two exceptions: the brick house of the 'richest Jew in town,' and the church. There were, naturally, frequent fires, the immemorial scourge of Russian villages; but since wood was plentiful, and stone prohibitively expensive, there was nothing to be done about it. Our synagogues, too, were of wood, both of them, the 'Old Synagogue' and the 'New Synagogue.' How old the first was, and how new the second, I cannot tell; but this I do remember: the Old Synagogue was for the 'better' class, the New for the poor. Members of the Old Synagogue seldom went to the New Synagogue; it was beneath their dignity. But occasionally my father (we belonged to the Old Synagogue) went there by special request. For among other gifts my father had that of a fine voice, and was an amateur *Chazan*, or prayer leader, much esteemed and sought after in Motol. On the Day of Atonement he would conduct perhaps half of the services— to the edification of his townsmen and the awe and delight of his children—and sometimes he was invited to perform this office in the New Synagogue, and would graciously accept.

Motol was situated in one of the darkest and most forlorn corners of the Pale of Settlement, that prison house created by czarist Russia for the largest part of its Jewish population. Throughout the centuries alternations of bitter oppression and comparative freedom—how comparative a free people would hardly understand—had deepened the consciousness of exile in these scattered communities, which were held together by a common destiny and common dreams. Motol was typical Pale, typical countryside. Here, in this half-town, half-village, I lived from the time of my birth, in 1874, till the age of eleven; and here I wove my first pictures of the Jewish and gentile worlds.

The life of the Jewish child in a Russian town of those times has been described over and over again in Jewish literature, and is not unfamiliar to the general reader. Like all Jewish boys I went to *cheder*, beginning at the age of four. Like nearly all *cheders*, mine was a squalid, one-room school, which also constituted the sole quarters of the teacher's family. If my *cheder* differed from others, it was perhaps in the possession of a family goat which took shelter with us in cold weather. And if my first *Rebbi*, or teacher, differed from others, it was in the degree of his pedagogic incompetence. If our schoolroom was usually hung with lines of washing, if the teacher's numerous children rolled about on the floor, if the din was deafening and incessant, that was nothing out of the ordinary. Nor was it anything out of the ordinary that neither the tumult nor the overcrowding affected our peace of mind or our powers of concentration.

In the spring and autumn, when the *cheder* was a tiny island set in a sea of mud, and in the winter, when it was almost blotted out by snow, I had to be carried there by a servant, or by my older brother. Once there, I stayed immured within its walls, along with the other children, from early morning till evening. We took lunch with us and consumed it in a short pause in the proceedings, often with the books still opened in front of us. On dark winter afternoons our studies could only be pursued by artificial light, and as candles were something of a luxury, and oil lamps practically unobtainable, each pupil was in turn assessed a pound of candles as a contribution to the education of the young generation.

In the course of my *cheder* years I had several teachers, and by the time I was eleven, or even before, considerable demands were made on my intellectual powers. I was expected to understand—I never did, properly—the intricacies of the Law as laid down in the Babylonian Talmud and as expounded and knocked into me by a *Rebbi* who was both ferocious and exacting, and certainly far from lucid in his expositions. He was always at a loss to understand why things needed to be explained at all; he felt that every Jewish boy should be able to pick up such things, which were as easy as they were sacred, by natural instinct, or at least just by glancing down the pages. I did not share his view, but was too badly terrorized to join issue with him as to his methods—if, indeed, I was at all aware of their inadequacy.

I did not relish the Talmudic teaching, but I adored that of the Prophets, for which I attended another *cheder*. There the teacher was humane and kindly, with a real enthusiasm for his subject. This enthusiasm he managed to communicate to his pupils, though here, too, school and surroundings were of the most depressing character. It is to this teacher, who became a lifelong friend of mine, that I am primarily indebted for my knowledge of the Hebrew Bible, and for my early and lasting devotion to Hebrew literature. He died in Poland not many years ago, and I was in correspondence with him till the end.

He was a man of the 'enlightened' type; that is, he had been touched by the spirit of the modernizing *Haskallah* (or Enlightenment) which was then abroad in the larger centres of Russian Jewry. Very surreptitiously he managed to smuggle into intervals in our sacred studies some attempts at instruction in secular knowledge. I remember how he brought into class, furtively and gleefully, a Hebrew text-book on natural science and chemistry, the first book of its kind to come into those parts. How this treasure fell into his hands I do not know, but without ever having seen a chemical laboratory, and with the complete ignorance of natural science which was characteristic of the Russian ghetto Jew, unable therefore to understand one scientific paragraph of the book, he gloated over it and displayed it to his favourite pupils. He would even lend it to one or another of us to read in the evenings. And sometimes—a proceeding not without risk, for discovery would have entailed immediate dismissal from his post—he would let us read with him some pages which seemed to him to be of special interest. We read aloud, of course, and in the Talmudic chant hallowed by tradition, so that anyone passing by the school would never suspect that we were not engaged in the sacred pursuits proper to a Hebrew school.

I have said that Motol lay in one of the darkest and most forlorn corners of the Pale of Settlement. This was true in the economic as well as in the spiritual sense. It is difficult to convey to the modern Westerner any idea of the sort of life which most of the Jewish families of Motol led, of their peculiar occupations, their fantastic poverty, their shifts and privations. On the spiritual side they were almost as isolated as on the physical. Newspapers were almost unknown in Motol. Very occasionally we secured a Hebrew paper from Warsaw, and then it would be a month or five weeks old. To us, of course, the news would be fresh. To tell the truth, we were not much interested in what was taking place in the world outside. It did not concern us particularly. If we were interested at all it was in the Hebrew presentation of the news. There were, from time to time, articles of general interest. No family in Motol could afford to subscribe to a newspaper regularly—nor would it have been delivered regularly. As it was, one copy would make the rounds of the 'well-to-do' families. When at last it reached the children it was in shreds, and usually illegible.

And yet Motol had two peculiar advantages, both deriving from its natural situation and its chief occupation, the timber trade. There was, in the Jewish population, a small layer which was more travelled than you would expect; and to some extent the effects of the general poverty were mitigated by the contact with nature.

My family was among the well-to-do, and it may help to give some idea of the standards of well-being which prevailed in Motol when I say that our yearly budget was probably seldom more than five or six hundred roubles (£50 or £60) in all. Even this income fluctuated widely, so that it could never be counted on with any degree of certainty. Out of it there were a dozen children to be clothed, shod and fed, and given a tolerably good education, considering our circumstances. On the other hand, we had our own house—one storey, with seven rooms and a kitchen—some acres of land, chickens, two cows, a vegetable garden, a few fruit trees. So we had a supply of milk, and sometimes butter; we had fruit and vegetables in season; we had enough bread—which my mother baked herself; we had fish, and we had meat once a week—on the Sabbath. And there was always plenty of fresh air. In these respects we were a great deal better off than the Jews of the city ghettos.

Our house stood next to that of my grandfather, who occupied all by himself what seemed to me then to be a mansion. I was greatly attached to grandpa, who was a good-natured, modest, simple soul, and at the age of five or six I went to live with him. I remember vividly those days—especially the winter mornings. Grandpa used to get up early, while it was still pitch dark, but the house was always beautifully warm, however severe the frost outside. First of all we said the long morning prayers; then came breakfast. At table grandpa used to tell me stories of the deeds of great Rabbis and of other mighty figures in Israel. I was particularly impressed by the visit of Sir Moses Montefiore to Russia—one of his innumerable journeys on behalf of his people. That particular visit had taken place only a generation or so before my birth, but the story was already a legend. Indeed, Sir Moses Montefiore was himself, though then still living, already a legend. He was to live on until 1885, to the fabulous age of one hundred and one years. On the occasion of which my grandfather used to tell me, Sir Moses came to Vilna, one of the oldest and most illustrious Jewish settlements in Russia, and the Jews of that community came out to welcome him. Grandpa told me how the Jews unharnessed the horses and dragged the carriage of Sir Moses Montefiore in solemn procession through the streets. It was a wonderful story, which I heard over and over again.

Grandpa died in 1882, when I was eight years old. I remember my grief, which I hardly understood myself. When they asked me why I was crying, I answered, 'Grandpa hurts me!'

The timber trade, the mainstay of Motol, played so large a part in our life, and is so closely bound up with my childhood and boyhood memories, that I must give it more than passing mention. To call even the more prosperous Jews of Motol real timber merchants would be somewhat of an exaggeration. They were at best subcontractors. But their connection with the basic trade of Motol did not give them any sense of security, for, as we shall see, it was hazardous and precarious in the extreme, and though it provided an all-year-round occupation, it was often far from providing an all-year-round income.

My father was what was called a 'transportierer.' He cut and hauled the timber and got it floated down to Danzig. It was a complicated and heartbreaking occupation. The forests stood on marshland, and except in times of drought and frost it was impossible to do any hauling. In the rainy seasons of spring and autumn the rivers overflowed, for there were no dykes and no attempt whatsoever at regulation. The rain came down and stayed there, till the summer dried it or the winter froze it. But sometimes it happened that between the rainfall and the dead of winter there intervened a heavy snowfall, which blanketed the soggy earth so that the frost could not penetrate. Unless a quick thaw intervened, and gave the following frost a chance to do its work, the forests and marshes remained impassable, and the season was ruined.

The cycle of work would begin in November, after the festival of *Sukkoth*, or Tabernacles. My father would set out for the heart of the forest, twenty or twenty-five miles away. His only communication with home was the sleigh road, which was always subject to interruption. He took along a supply of food and of warm clothing, and several bags of copper coins with which to pay the workers. We were never easy during father's absences in the forest, even during later years when my older brother Feivel went with him; for there were wolves in the forests and occasionally robbers. Fortunately there was, between my father and the fifty or sixty men he employed seasonally— *moujiks* of Motol and the neighbourhood—an excellent relationship, primitive, but warm and patriarchal. Once or twice he was attacked by robbers, but they were beaten off by his workmen.

It was hard, exacting work, but on the whole my father did not dislike it, perhaps because it called for a considerable degree of skill. It was his business to mark out the trees to be felled and he had to be able to tell which were healthy and worth felling. He had to supervise the hauling. The logs were roped and piled on the edge of the little river, to wait there for the thaw and the spring flood, which usually came between the festivals of *Purim* and Passover.

If the winter lingered we did not have father home for the Passover, for he could not leave to anyone else the responsible task of setting the timber afloat. When this happened it was a calamity which darkened the entire festival for us. But on the whole the thaw came in time, the stream broke up and flooded, and father would return on the last sleigh. He came home haggard, exhausted, and underfed; but it was an indescribably joyous home-coming. He brought the festival with him, as it were, and both would be with us for eight days.

After the Passover began the spring and summer work, the floating of the rafts to the sea. This too was a skilled and exacting occupation—really a branch of navigation. The rafts had to be fairly small to be able to negotiate the first streams; but they had to hold together strongly, against exceptional flood. The first job was to get them on the Pina and down to Pinsk, which they usually reached at *Shevuoth*, or Pentecost, seven weeks after Passover. There, instead of floating onward with the stream in a general southerly direction, which would have brought them to the Dnieper and the far-off Black Sea, the rafts were manœuvred in the opposite direction through a canal which connected the Pina with Brest Litovsk on the Boug, the main tributary of the Vistula, which flows into the Baltic Sea at the port of Danzig.

Now Brest Litovsk was on the edge of the marshes, and from there on the Boug ran through sandy soil. The country became undulating, and less monotonous. But as the river was never looked after, never dyked or dredged, it formed sandbanks, especially in the summer. If the rafts consisted of oak, or were unskilfully piled up and drew too much water, they often stuck fast. Then there was nothing to do but wait, and bake in the sun, and pray for rain, or for a fresh flow from the head-waters of the Boug in the Carpathians. Meanwhile, days, perhaps weeks, would pass, and you watched your slender profits being eaten up by the delay; for though you included this hazard in the price, you could not make it high enough to cover every contingency.

Sometimes scores of rafts, floating easily, would be held up by one or two heavier rafts which were stranded. To get round them was a ticklish job, and you usually had to bribe the officials—the river police—to be allowed to do it. When at last you floated on to the wide Vistula you were faced with troubles of another kind. The rains and freshets which you welcomed on the Boug were often a bane on the Vistula. The waters became swollen and turbulent, and the rafts might be torn to pieces. Then you would tie up to the shore, and watch the flood, and wait for it to subside. At Thorn, which was German, everything changed. The river was regulated, order prevailed. From Thorn to Danzig it was a peaceful journey.

This description of river navigation is from my personal

recollections, for when I was a schoolboy in Pinsk I used to spend much of my summers on the rafts. I had an uncle who was a great expert in this branch of the trade, and he would often take me on one of the journeys, which sometimes lasted for weeks. He used to have a very comfortable cabin, with bedroom and kitchen, on one of the rafts. He even had, as I remember, a mosquito net—an unheard-of innovation, though the air was sometimes black with insects. Those were jolly times for me. I did not go as far as Danzig, but got off on the nearer side of Warsaw, and took the train home.

The floating of the rafts lasted roughly from the Passover until the beginning of the great Jewish autumn festivals. Father would generally be back from Danzig for *Rosh Hashanah*, the New Year, and the Day of Atonement. Then, when the Feast of Tabernacles was past, and the heartache of collecting payments was over—and sometimes it wasn't—the annual cycle would begin again.

The friendly relations between my father and his workers were not unusual as between the individual Jew and individual gentile. In our particular corner of the world we lived on tolerable terms with our neighbours. They were a mild, kindly, hard-working lot. They had a fair quantity of land, they were not starved; some of them were even prosperous. They had— like the Jews—large families, and were always on the look-out for auxiliary occupations, one of which was the timber trade. From each peasant hut one of the men would hire himself out in the winter for the felling, and in the summer for the logging.

The language of the peasants in our part was an obscure dialect of Russian. Unlike the Ukrainian, it had no literature, and was not even written. Education was primitive in the extreme. There was, in every small town of the size of Motol, a government school, but attendance was not compulsory. Some of the peasants sent some of their children to school, irregularly; most of them grew up quite illiterate. By contrast the Jews, who did not make use of the government schools, and who had only the *cheders*, had a high degree of literacy. It is hard to remember a Jewish father whose sons, at least, did not attend a *cheder*. But there the education was entirely Hebrew and Yiddish. Those that wanted to give their children the beginnings of a Russian and modern education engaged a special teacher, usually of third-rate ability. I myself knew hardly a word of Russian till I was eleven years old.

Though personal contacts might generally be friendly, the economic structure of this part of the country and the history of its growth did not encourage good relations between Jews and peasants. There were many great estates, usually owned by Poles. The Polish landowners had about them numbers of Jews, who acted as their factors, bought their timber, rented some of the land or leased the lakes for fishing. The Poles constituted a *Junker* class, though in my time their wings were already being clipped by the Russians. Inherently they were hostile to the Jews, but under the common czarist oppression they assumed a kindlier attitude. The peasants, however, had no point of direct contact with the landed gentry; the Jews stood between the two classes. The Jews were therefore the only visible instrument of the exploiting nobility. Still, the exploitation did not produce the same disastrous effects as elsewhere, for this was a landed peasantry. I do not remember, in our district, any period of starvation such as we heard of from the Volga. With a piece of land, a few pigs, chickens and cows, and outside employment, the peasants could manage well enough, if they did not drink excessively. Except during the Christmas and Easter festivals, when they were roused to a high pitch of religious excitement by their priests, they were quite friendly towards us. At worst they never got wholly out of hand, and there were never any pogroms in Motol or the neighbouring villages. It is a melancholy reflection on human relationships when the absence of murder must be noted as a special circumstance which calls for gratitude.

The differences between the peasants and the Jews must not be minimized, for even in Motol we lived mainly apart. And much more striking than the physical separation was the spiritual. We were strangers to each other's ways of thought, to each other's dreams, religions, festivals, and even languages.

There were times when the non-Jewish world was practically excluded from our consciousness, as on the Sabbath and, still more, during the spring and autumn festivals, which were really great occasions for us. I do not know to whom they meant more, to the grown-ups or to the children. For them the festival represented a surcease from the turmoil of the working days, from their worries and depression. For us, it was freedom from the *cheder*, new clothes, games. For both there was a striking contrast with everyday life; there was an atmosphere of peace in our part of the village, and to usher in the sacred days the house itself was made to assume a solemn and festive appearance. Meals were more regular, more ceremonial; the family was united. Even the long hours of attendance at the synagogue—generally a bore on Sabbaths and weekdays— had their attraction, especially for the members of our family, for on such occasions father might be called upon to chant the prayers. Then people would come over from the other synagogue to listen, and the atmosphere became stifling; we youngsters watched and listened, and were filled with pride and happiness.

We were separated from the peasants by a whole inner universe of memories and experiences. In my early childhood Zionist ideas and aspirations were already awake in Russian Jewry. My father was not yet a Zionist, but the house was steeped in rich Jewish tradition, and Palestine was at the centre of the ritual, a longing for it implicit in our life. Practical nationalism did not assume form till some years later, but the 'Return' was in the air, a vague, deep-rooted Messianism, a hope which would not die. We heard the conversations of our elders, and we were caught up in the restlessness. But it was not for children; when one of us ventured a remark on the subject he was put down rather roughly. In particular I remember one *Rebbi*, himself an ardent nationalist, who thought it impious and presumptuous of a youngster to so much as mention the rebuilding of Palestine. He would say: 'You keep quiet. *You'll* never bring the Messiah any nearer. One has to do much, learn much, know much and suffer much before one is worthy of that.' He intimidated us so completely that we learned to keep our own counsel. Still, the dream was there, an ever-present background to our thoughts. And the *Rebbi*'s words, uttered so brusquely, have remained permanently in my mind.

As children we were left pretty much to ourselves, since father was away most of the time. Mother was of course the centre of the household, but in those years—and indeed, for a long time after—she was always either pregnant, or nursing an infant, so that she had little strength left for her growing brood. She bore my father fifteen children, of which three died in infancy and twelve grew into full manhood and womanhood. She did not think childbearing a burden. She wanted as many children as possible, and she went on having them happily and uninterruptedly from her seventeenth year until her forty-sixth. She was already a grandmother when my youngest brother was born, and two of my eldest sister's children rejoiced in the birth of an uncle. I remember that mother's constant childbearing was accepted in such a matter-of-fact way that when I was a schoolboy in Pinsk, and away from home, I saved up, kopeck by kopeck, enough to buy a new cradle, the old one having become very rickety; and I remember lugging it home on one of my visits, and proudly presenting it to mother for her 'next.'

We were luckier than most of our fellow-Jews in being able to afford 'servants,' if that is the real name for them. The first I remember was a combination charwoman, maid-of-all-work, adviser, family retainer—and family tyrant. She bossed all the children, and occasionally mother, too. She was a fixture in our lives, and could no more have been dismissed than a member of the family. The second, who outlived the first and was with us for something like thirty-five years, was a lovable peasant by the name of Yakim, who became as much a natural part of our world as the first. He was still with us when I left home for the West; and when I used to return, he would plead with me to let him come back with me and attend to my needs. He was very proud of my academic achievements, and even more of my Zionist activities. He had learned to sing, after a fashion, the Jewish national anthem, *Hatikvah*; and in moments of enthusiasm he would cry out: 'Come, little ones, let us sing *Tikvah*!'

It is perhaps an exaggeration to say that we were often left to ourselves. In father's absences, the *Rebbi* stood *in loco parentis*. And then there were uncles and aunts without number, in Motelle, in Pinsk, and in nearby villages. They took an active, loving and contentious interest in our welfare and our education, more especially in our religious education, which they frequently found deficient in the right degree of orthodoxy. One uncle in particular, Itchie Moshe, who was himself childless, was for ever admonishing us on our ungodliness. But as against him my uncle Jacob was the 'heretic' of the family. My father, I might mention, seldom preached at us.

Mother began to play a greater rôle in our lives after we had settled in Pinsk, and I was home only occasionally. She had passed beyond her childbearing years and she had a second blossoming of vitality. By then the house had become something like a public institution. The elder children were at the Gymnasium or at the university, the younger at the local school. During the vacations it was a pandemonium. Fellow-students were in and out at all hours; and they represented every shade of opinion in a student world given perhaps excessively to opinions and to loud exposition of them; there were Zionists, assimilationists, Socialists, anarchists, every variety of revolutionary. The discussions were interminable; and feelings often ran high, even between members of the family. There were times when brothers and sisters were not on speaking terms for months at a stretch. Amid this riot and clash of views mother moved imperturbably, ministering to all, whatever their shade of opinion. Most of the time she was in the kitchen. 'They've got to be fed,' she would say, 'or they won't have the strength to shout.' Herself orthodox—she said her prayers every day, and went to the synagogue every Sabbath—she was extraordinarily tolerant with regard to others. We children did not dream of imitating her piety; but there was no friction on this score, and none even on the score of the genuine danger which we created by our gatherings and by the harbouring of illegal literature. Herself alien to our views, mother co-operated loyally. She would bury our revolutionary pamphlets in the garden, and when a police raid took place—which happened more than once—she would confront the officers of the law with such dignity, and with such an air of innocence—which, for that matter, was not assumed—that she invariably disarmed the intruders.

It was a queer house over which her hospitable spirit presided. The bookcases contained probably as strange an assortment of literature as was ever assembled in a private home; the Talmud and the works of Maimonides cheek by jowl with Gorki and Tolstoy; text-books on chemistry, dentistry, engineering and medicine jostling the modern Hebrew romances of Mapu and the nationalist periodicals of the new Zionism. On the walls were pictures of Maimonides and Baron de Hirsch, of the Wailing Wall in Jerusalem and of Anton Chekhov. The disputes were carried on in three languages, Russian, Yiddish and Hebrew, and what they lacked in formality or logic they definitely made up in vehemence.

My mother was not a good housekeeper. It is very possible that she could have become one if the task, under those circumstances, had not been utterly hopeless. But she was wonderfully good—the kind of person to whom neighbours turn naturally in time of trouble. The earlier years of her marriage were hard on her; but from 1900 to 1912—the year of my father's death—she did know a certain amount of ease and comfort. Father then had an interest in the business of his first son-in-law, Lubin, who was a successful timber merchant on a large scale; this enabled my mother to go to Carlsbad and Kissingen for the summers. But even in the difficult days she was cheerful and optimistic. She would say: 'Whatever happens, I shall be well off. If Shmuel [the revolutionary son] is right, we shall all be happy in Russia; and if Chaim [myself] is right, then I shall go to live in Palestine.' I will not undertake to say who was right, but she spent her last years very happily in Palestine—with most of her family. But that was long afterwards. She was still in Pinsk when, two years after father's death, the First World War came, and with it the German invasion. From Pinsk mother fled to Warsaw, from Warsaw to Moscow. Already in her sixties, she passed through the storm of the Revolution and the civil war. In 1921 I was able to get her and my brother Feivel out of Moscow and send them to Palestine. I built a house for my mother on Hadar Ha-Carmel in Haifa, and there she lived until the day of her death, which occurred in 1939, in her eighty-seventh year. Till the end she was alert and in good spirits. She still said her prayers daily—reading without glasses—and she took an active interest in an old-people's home. I think that the moment of her greatest pride was when she sat with me and my wife on Mount Scopus on the day of the opening of the Hebrew University, April 1, 1925.

When I recall how seldom father was with us, and how preoccupied he was with the problem of a livelihood and yet how

large an influence he was in our lives, I am filled with genuine
wonder. He was a silent man, a scholarly spirit lost in the world
of business, and fired with deep ambitions for his children. He
did not believe in words of admonishment, and even less in
punishment. When he did say something, it carried great weight
with us. He was a natural aristocrat, an intellectual and something of a leader, too—the only Jew ever chosen to be the
starosta, or head man, of the town of Motelle. We loved him,
and tried to emulate his example. When he was home, and had
a few minutes free from the cares and worries of his daily life—
and how few those minutes were!—he usually read. His favourite
books were the works of Maimonides, and especially the *Guide
for the Perplexed*. The *Shulchan Aruch*, or *Code of Cairo*, he knew by
heart. On the Sabbath day he would sometimes call over the
older children and speak to them a little on the subject-matter
of his reading. He did it in the most casual way, so as not to
give the impression that there was any obligation on our part
to listen to him; this is probably why we all enjoyed these rare
conversations, and regarded it as a privilege to take part in
them.

Not particularly robust, he followed as long as he could a
hard and dangerous occupation. He worried overmuch for the
future of his children. A Jew of the lower middle class, he
aspired to give them the best education. There were twelve of
us ultimately, and with his and each other's help nine of us
went through universities—an unheard-of achievement in
those days. He belonged to the type familiar to old Russian
Jewry as the *Maskil*, the enlightened and modernized Hebraist;
and he took his part, as we shall see, in the Zionist movement.

Father's standing in the village of Motol and, later, in the
town of Pinsk, was very high; never by virtue of his economic
position, which even by the standards of Motol was only fair,
but because of his character and his scholarship. Motol, like
all little communities, was always filled with quarrels and
intrigues, especially in connection with the offices of Rabbi
and ritual slaughterer and synagogue cantor. There were
occasional scandals and on one or two occasions near-riots in
the synagogue. There lingers in my memory one vivid picture
of confusion, noise, hostility and raised fists, and father mounting the pulpit, striking the lectern, and lifting up his voice in

a rare outburst of anger: 'Silence!' I do not know what the occasion was. I do not know who had insulted whom, who was trying to push whom out of public office, or who had dared to break in on the reading of the Torah. I only remember the strange effect of that voice. It was as though a shot had been fired.

Father refused to take sides in public or private quarrels. If a man insisted on telling him his side of the story he would listen patiently to the end and say: 'From what you tell me, I can see that you are entirely in the wrong. Now I shall have to hear the other side; perhaps you are in the right after all." This sort of reception did not encourage litigants to come to him. Perhaps it was the undignified scenes he had witnessed in the synagogue which imbued my father with his lifelong hatred of clericalism, and of the exploitation of religion for a livelihood.

But he was, I need hardly say, a deeply religious man, respectful of tradition and of scholarship. He had an older brother, uncle Moshe, who was Rabbi of Lomzhe—a famous and distinguished position in Israel—and to whom he was greatly attached. I remember how, on a certain holiday, when I had come home from Pinsk, father entered the house in festive clothes, ready to sit down to the holiday meal, when a telegram was brought to the door. A telegram in Motol invariably meant calamity; for except in desperate circumstances no one would think of sending one to the village, where it had to be delivered from the nearest railway station, twenty miles away, by special messenger. And this telegram was no exception. It brought the news of the death of my uncle Moshe. My father gave no expression to his sorrow. But from that day on he never again led the prayers in the synagogue. He had completely lost his singing voice. I have noticed that I have inherited from father this curious and special vulnerability of the vocal chords.

He had a difficult life, and did not relax until his later years; but then he was too worn out to recuperate. He died at the age of sixty, which is young in our family. He left a number of Hebrew manuscripts, which I intended to look over, with a view to publishing some of them. But in her wanderings during the First World War my mother lost them.

I remember him best in my childhood days as he stood before

the Ark in the synagogue, leading the congregation in prayer. Many of the refrains have remained with me till this day, and they usually spring up in my mind when I am sad or solitary; and sometimes, on particularly solemn occasions, a few familiar bars of a synagogue melody will conjure up in my memory far-off pictures which I thought had faded from it for ever.

CHAPTER II

SCHOOLDAYS IN PINSK

I leave Home—The Russian 'May Laws' of 1882—Pogroms, Zionism and the Jewish Democratic Awakening—The Stampede to America— Educational Restrictions—My Brother Feivel—I Become Self-supporting —Russian Teachers—One Brilliant Exception—The Pinsk Community— My First Steps in Zionism—Pinsk in Zionist History—Primitive Practical Beginnings—Class Divisions on Zionism—Hebrew Renaissance—The Assimilationist Intelligentsia—Zionist Record of the Weizmann Family

THE first fundamental change in my life took place when, at the age of eleven, I left the small town of my birth and went out 'into the world'—that is, to Pinsk—to enter a Russian school: which was something not done until that time by any Motolite. From Motol to Pinsk was a matter of six Russian miles, or twenty-five English miles; but in terms of intellectual displacement the distance was astronomical. For Pinsk was a real provincial metropolis, with thirty thousand inhabitants, of whom the great majority were Jews. Pinsk had a name and a tradition as 'a city and mother in Israel.' It could not pretend to the cultural standing of great centres like Warsaw, Vilna, Odessa and Moscow; but neither was it a nameless village. The new *Chibath Zion* (Love of Zion) movement, the forerunner of modern Zionism, had taken deep root in Pinsk. There were Jewish scholars and Jewish public leaders in Pinsk. There was a high school—the one I was going to attend—there were libraries, hospitals, factories and paved streets.

The years of my childhood in Motol and of my schooling in Pinsk coincided with the onset of the 'dark years' for Russian Jewry; or perhaps I should say with their return. The reign of Alexander II had been a false dawn. For a generation the ancient Russian policy of repression of the Jews had been mitigated by the liberalism of the monarch who had set the serfs free; and therefore many Jews believed that the walls of the ghetto were about to fall. Jews were beginning to attend

28

Russian schools and universities, and to enter into the life of the country. Then, in 1881, came the assassination of Alexander, and on its heels the tide of reaction, which was not to ebb again until the overthrow of the Romanovs thirty-six years later. The new repression began with the famous 'Temporary Legislation. Affecting the Jews' enacted in 1882, and known as the May Laws. Nothing in czarist Russia was as enduring as 'Temporary Legislation.' This particular set of enactments, at any rate, was prolonged and broadened and extended until it came to cover every aspect of Jewish life; and as one read, year after year, the complicated ukases which poured from St. Petersburg, one obtained the impression that the whole cumbersome machinery of the vast Russian Empire was created for the sole purpose of inventing and amplifying rules and regulations for the hedging in of the existence of its Jewish subjects until it became something that was neither life nor death.

Parallel with these repressions, and with the general setback to Russian liberalism, there was a deep stirring of the masses, Russian and Jewish. Among the Jews this first folk-awakening had two facets, the revolutionary, mingling with the general Russian revolt, and the Zionist-nationalist. The latter, however, was also revolutionary and democratic. The Jewish masses were rising against the paternalism of their 'notables,' their *shtadlonim*, the men of wealth and influence who had always taken it on themselves to represent the needs of the Jew *vis-à-vis* the governmental authority. Theirs was, even in the best cases, a class view, characterized by a natural fear of disturbing the *status quo* or imperilling such privileges as they enjoyed by virtue of their economic standing. In the depths of the masses an impulse awoke, vague, groping, unformulated, for Jewish self-liberation. It was genuinely of the folk; it was saturated with Jewish tradition; and it was connected with the most ancient memories of the land where Jewish life had first expressed itself in freedom. It was, in short, the birth of modern Zionism.

By 1886, when I entered the high school in Pinsk, the atmosphere of Jewish life was heavy with disaster. There had been the ghastly pogroms of 1881. These had not reached us in Motol, but they had shaken the whole Jewish world to its foundations. I was a child, and I had lived in the separateness

of the Jewish life of our town. Non-Jews were for me something
peripheral. But even I did not escape a consciousness of the
general gloom. Almost as far as my memory goes back, I can
remember the stampede—the frantic rush from the Russian
prison house, the tremendous tide of migration which carried
hundreds of thousands of Jews from their ancient homes to far-
off lands across the seas. I was a witness in boyhood and early
manhood of the emptying of whole villages and towns. My own
family was once caught up in the fever—this was about the
time of the Kishinev pogrom of 1903—and though we finally
decided against flight, there were cousins and uncles and more
distant relatives by the score who took the westward path.
Many years later, in 1921, when I first visited America as the
President of the World Zionist Organization, and a mass
reception was held for me in the Manhattan Opera House in
New York, there were two entire sections of a balcony with a
big streamer across them: RELATIVES OF DR. WEIZMANN. I
have the impression that some of these relatives were very distant
indeed; but I can record that in Chicago there was until
recently—and perhaps there still is—a Motol synagogue; and I
met in Chicago the old keeper of the baths, the old prayer
leader, and other worthies I had known in childhood; I met
their children, too, the Americanized generation which still
remembered its origins dimly. In a sense, my childhood was
passed in a world which was breaking up under the impact of
renewed persecution. We did not have to live in the midst of
pogroms to experience their social effects, or to know that the
gentile world was poisoned. I knew little of gentiles, but they
became to me, from very early on, the symbols of the menacing
forces against which I should have to butt with all my young
strength in order to make my way in life. The acquisition of
knowledge was not for us so much a normal process of education
as the storing up of weapons in an arsenal by means of which
we hoped later to be able to hold our own in a hostile world.

I happened to belong to a 'lucky' transitional generation.
A few years after I entered the *Real-Gymnasium* of Pinsk came
the decree which limited the number of Jewish students in any
Russian high school to ten per cent of the gentile student body.
Since the Jewish people constituted only four per cent of the
Russian population this might not seem, at first sight, a very

unreasonable arrangement. But there was a catch; there always was in czarist legislation. The Jewish population was concentrated in, and *legally confined to*, the Jewish Pale of Settlement, which was only a very small fraction of the Russian Empire. Even within the limits of the Pale, the Jews were confined to urban areas, and were excluded from the country districts, so that within the Pale the Jewish inhabitants of the towns—i.e. the only places with schools—varied from thirty to eighty per cent of the total. Moreover, the non-Jewish population had not the same overwhelming thirst for knowledge as the Jews, who were always knocking at the doors of the schools. The result was that at the school entrance examinations, comparatively few non-Jewish candidates presented themselves, and it was *ten per cent of this small number* that was allotted to the Jews. It meant that in a Jewish population numbering perhaps tens of thousands, only four or five or six Jewish students would be admitted. Young children had to wait their turn for years, and this long, heartbreaking wait often ended in disappointment. The teachers and governing authorities of the schools within the Pale were typical Russian officials, and as such, not free from corruption. So the rich Jew would use his gold to pave the way for his boy to enter the school, while the poor boy, in spite of marked ability and brilliant success in the examinations, had to forgo the advantages which an education might have afforded him. This state of affairs produced very curious, tragi-comic results. There were occasions when a rich Jew would hire ten non-Jewish candidates (at times rather oddly selected) to sit for the entrance examination at the local school, and thus make room for one Jewish pupil—needless to say, his own son or a protégé.

Matters were infinitely more difficult at the universities, where the *numerus clausus* was three or four per cent. From certain higher institutions of learning Jews were excluded altogether.

I did not go to Pinsk alone. My brother, Feivel—older than I by three years—went with me, and we lodged together with some friends of the family. Feivel had not done so well at *cheder*. The *Rebbi* in Motol and my parents had come to the conclusion, wholly unwarranted I think, that he was not intellectual enough for a higher education, and it was decided to teach him a trade—he was the only one among us youngsters who learned a trade. He was clever with his hands, and an exceptionally good draftsman. He would as a matter of fact have made a good engineer. He was, however, apprenticed to a lithographer, to learn engraving, and did very well at it. But when he had been three years in Pinsk, he interrupted his apprenticeship and went back to Motol to help my father in the timber trade, thus interrupting his apprenticeship for several years. I imagine that this period was a bad one for the timber trade, or at least for my father's business; for just about then I made a special effort to become self-supporting, while continuing my studies at the *Real-Gymnasium*.

I had been aware from the beginning, that is, from my twelfth year on, that my schooling in Pinsk presented a serious economic problem to my parents. Board and lodgings probably did not come to more than two roubles—five shillings—a week; but that is a considerable proportion of an average weekly income of twelve roubles. And there was my brother, who was with me for the first three years. On top of board and lodging there was the question of clothes, not to mention school fees and books. In a town the requirements were higher than those of the simple village life of Motol. There was also the matter of prestige. In Pinsk I would come into contact with different classes and conditions of people, and my parents felt that their child must not lose caste. All in all, then, this was a great strain on the limited family resources. I knew that when I was eleven years old, and both Feivel and I had to be supported in Pinsk. I felt it more deeply when Feivel had to return home and I was left alone in Pinsk. I had tried even earlier to find a source of income to replace, at least in part, the maintenance allowance from my parents; I had not succeeded. But just when I was left alone, I was received as a kind of tutor into the household of a rich family. My task was to supervise the homework of the son, who was three forms below me in school. For this I received my board and lodging, and fifty roubles a year. The cash payment covered my fees, books and minor expenses, and from that time on I was no longer on my father's payroll.

My life was simple, arduous and, by the standards we apply to our children nowadays, rather grim. But I was by no means unhappy. I was adequately fed and clothed, and I had a room

—a cubbyhole, to be truthful—of my own. It was six feet by four, and contained, in addition to my bed, a big pot-bellied stove. It was a dusty, smelly sort of room, but the window gave on to a big courtyard, and I was not aware of being cramped. I did not have the time to worry about my comforts. In the morning I had to be at school at nine o'clock, and I stayed there until two-thirty in the afternoon. Then I had my homework, my daily Hebrew studies, which I pursued under the direction of a private teacher, and two or three hours with my pupil. I also did some general reading and took a certain part in the Zionist youth activities, such as they were then. But of these more later.

The school régime in Pinsk, and for that matter, I suppose, in all other Russian cities at that time, was very different from that of the Western world. There was no real contact between teachers and pupils, and little intercourse among the pupils themselves. As far as the Jewish boys were concerned, the teachers were looked upon as the representative of an alien and hostile power; they were more *tchinovniks* (officials) than peda-gogues, and in them human emotions and relationships were replaced by formalism and by the instinct for climbing inherent in the Russian official. With few exceptions—and there were some—the teacher had his eye not so much on the pupils as on the head of the school; the road to the good opinion of his chief, and therefore of promotion, was not the road of peda-gogics, but of strict adherence to the decrees and ukases issued by the higher authorities. These encircled pupil and teacher with a rigid framework of restrictions designed to impede the free growth of the mind. Our real intellectual interests—I am speaking of the Jewish boys—lay outside the school gates. Thus, we seldom borrowed books from the school library, as these were carefully chosen for their lack of interest; and though it was forbidden for a schoolboy to make use of the public libraries, we surreptitiously obtained books from them, at the risk of severe punishment.

There were, in our school, teachers who, without knowledge of their subject, without the slightest training in pedagogy, had obtained their positions through influential friends who prob-ably considered them unfit for any other office in the Russian bureaucracy, but good enough for a schoolteacher's job in a

B

provincial town like Pinsk. Even so, I still cannot understand how a man like our teacher of mathematics ever came to be appointed. Almost as far back as I can remember, our lessons with him really consisted of long wrangles between the teacher and the pupils—the latter having both a greater aptitude for the subject and a more solid knowledge of it than he. In geometry and algebra he could never follow our arguments, or explain the simplest theorem. The poor man coughed, spluttered, hemmed and hawed, and turned every colour of the rainbow; and we, with the natural ferocity of youth, continued to pester and torment him with questions which he could not answer. I am afraid this sport was one of the highlights of our school activity; still, the man had no business to be pretending to teach mathematics—or anything else.

Another source of amusement was our teacher of religion, who was, of course, a pope, or priest. We suspected that he did not always come into class quite sober; at all events, the intensity of the redness of his nose gave rise to considerable comment and speculation among his pupils. Jewish boys were not obliged to attend the courses in the Christian religion; but the classes in the Slavonic language, ancient and modern, were compulsory for all. Ancient Slavonic is rather difficult; I think the grammar is similar to that of classic Greek. This teacher did know something about his subject, but as a Christian and a Russian official he felt it beneath his dignity to assume that his Jewish pupils would ever succeed in learning or understanding anything of the language. Unfortunately for him they were the only ones who did. For, more to annoy him than for any other reason, we made a point of being well up on this subject. He was often compelled to fall back on us in the question period, and this invariably threw him into a rage. He used to set traps for us, but almost always we were ready for him, and the contests usually ended in his ignominious defeat. Thus Judaism triumphed in the midst of oppression.

There was one outstanding exception among my teachers, a man by the name of Kornienko, to whom, very possibly, I owe whatever I have been able to achieve in the way of science. He was a chemist, with a genuine love of his subject and a considerable reputation in the world at large. He was, in fact, the glory of our school, and this perhaps explains why he was able to do as much as he did without falling foul of the authorities. He had managed to assemble a little laboratory, a luxury which was then almost unknown in Russian high schools. His attitude towards his pupils was in wholesome contrast with that of the other members of the staff. He was a decent, liberal-minded fellow, and treated us like human beings. He entered into conversation with us, and did his best to interest us in the wider aspects of natural science. I need hardly say that most of us responded warmly, and there grew up a kind of friend-ship between pupils and teacher—a state of affairs unimaginably rare in the Russian schools of that day.

It was Kornienko who gave me my impulse towards chemistry. In the last, or seventh class—I was then in my eighteenth year—the students were allowed a certain amount of specialization. I had at least one hour of theoretical chemistry each day, and two or three whole mornings in the laboratory. Even so we did not get very far, for the poverty of the general standard could not but affect Kornienko's work. I found this out when I got to a German university where, in my first year, I had to learn, as entirely new, material which to the German students was merely a revision of the work they had been doing in their last high-school year. My equipment in mathematics and physics was of course still poorer. I have often wondered what would have been the course of my life if it had not been for the chance intervention of this gifted and fine-spirited teacher.

In spite of everything, one could not say that our school life was unpleasant; it may at times have dulled our wits, but we bore that quite cheerfully. I did well at the examinations, and generally received top marks, which was nothing to boast about in the circumstances. School and homework absorbed the minor part of my energies; and even when my Hebrew studies and my tutorial duties were thrown in, there was enough left for general activities, and from my fifteenth year on I was drawn more and more into the life of the city, and into the nascent Zionist movement.

Pinsk was not a pleasant town to live in, though I did not become aware of this fact until I had seen a little more of the world. Low lying, malarial, it was, like Motol, mud in the spring and autumn, ice in the winter, dust in the summer.

When the rains came the lower part of Pinsk was flooded, and from three sides could be approached only in boats. Of the streets, two or three were paved, or, rather, covered with cobblestones. As the floods retreated with the approach of summer, a miasmal mist went up out of the earth, and after it came a thick dust. Since all this belonged to the natural order of things, it did not occur to me that there was anything to complain about, and I cannot say that my boyhood was a time of discontent.

But I must not forget the happy interludes. There were the summer journeys on my uncle's rafts up the canal to Brest Litovsk and down the Boug to Warsaw. There were visits home in the summer, during the Christmas vacation, and for the Passover, and these trips were adventures in themselves. For though it was, as I have said, only twenty-five miles from Pinsk to Motol, the journey consumed at least twenty-four hours. In the winter the trip was made by sleigh; in the spring and summer—wind, weather and mud permitting—by cart. Of course I did not hire a cart for myself; that would have cost as much as three or four roubles. I waited for an opportunity. Usually it was a shopkeeper from Motol who came to Pinsk to replenish his stock. I would climb into the cart, make myself comfortable among the hay, straw, jars, barrels and bundles of provisions, and settle down for the journey. Sometimes we passed the night in the open air. The wagon was drawn to the side of the road and man and beast slept under the stars for a few hours. We might perhaps have made the journey in less than a day if we had dared to move a little faster. But the pace was regulated by the condition of the road, the structure of the wagon, and the amount of jolting which a human being could stand. We rattled along on those rutted tracks, the soul almost shaken out of our bodies, the wagon threatening to fall to pieces.

Sometimes I travelled alone, that is, with the merchant and the peasant driver; sometimes an uncle was with me, or father was returning home from Pinsk. And sometimes we did not pass the night under the open sky. There were two or three inns between Pinsk and Motol; there was also, halfway between the two towns, the estate of the powerful Count Skirmunt, a great landowner, and one of the fabulous figures of the vicinity. This estate contained immense gardens, woods, an entire village, Poretsche, and several small factories. Many, many years after I had left Motol and Pinsk behind me, I met the legendary Count Skirmunt. He was at that time the Ambassador of the liberated Poland to the Court of St. James; I sat next to him at a dinner. I told him how, in my boyhood, I used to steal apples from his—or his father's—orchard at Poretsche. He remembered two of my uncles, with whom he had done business.

In the winter the trip between Pinsk and Motol was shorter. The road was smooth, for snow had fallen, and the topmost layer had thawed and then frozen again to make a perfect surface for the sleigh. I remember that I used to be made sick by the monotonous whiteness of the roads and fields; so I would be bundled up in overcoats and rugs and dispatched all of a piece. I would fall asleep, and the first thing I knew we were in Poretsche.

The Jewish drivers were *sui generis*; jolly companions, full of worldly wit and wisdom. They might be without much book learning, but they were far from ignorant, and could while away the hours of the journey with wonderful stories. When they reached a good piece of road they would travel over it again and again, backward and forward—it was such a relief not to be jolted to pieces.

In Pinsk, as in Motol, I had no social contact with gentiles. They formed, indeed, a minority of the population, and consisted chiefly of administrators, railway officials and workers, those who managed the canal and a number of big landowners whose estates were in the vicinity but who maintained town houses. The Jewish population differed from that of other towns of the Pale in that it possessed, in addition to the usual overload of traders and shopkeepers, a comparatively large class of river and factory workers. Jews made up the majority of the porters, navvies and raft pilots. These last were a skilled class. It needed training and aptitude to manipulate the rafts upstream on the Pina and into the canal in such a fashion as not to damage the locks. Other Jews worked in the match factory and the sawmills.

Jewish Pinsk was divided into two communities, Pinsk proper and Karlin, each with its own set of synagogues, Rabbis, hospitals and schools. Karlin, where I lived, was considered, as they say in America, the right side of the tracks. It was here that I grew from boyhood into early manhood, here that I had my social and intellectual contacts, and here that I was inducted into the Zionist movement. Pinsk, then, set the double pattern of my life; it gave me my first bent towards science, and it provided me with my first experiences in Zionism.

These two fields of my life were sharply separated. Zionism was never tolerated as a political movement by the czarist régime, and practical Zionist work, primitive enough in those days, was carried on under the guise of philanthropy. In 1884, about a year before I came to Pinsk, there had taken place the famous Kattowitz Conference of the *Choveve Zion*—the Lovers of Zion—the first gathering of its kind. It marked, historically, the conscious, organized beginning of Zionism, and it followed closely the onset of the era of repression. Pinsk became one of the centres of the *Chibath Zion*. Rabbi David Friedman—who was known, according to the Jewish fashion, by the affectionate diminutive of Reb Dovidl, also as Reb Dovidl Karliner, from the name of his community—was a member of the Presidium of the Kattowitz Conference, and therefore the titular head of the movement in Pinsk. This Reb Dovidl was a remarkable figure, combining the highest traditions of old-world Jewish saintliness and scholarship with a feeling for the spirit of the times. He was a tiny, shrivelled-up wisp of a man, with a wonderful, transfigured face. He fasted every Monday and Thursday, and was considered even among pietists as exceptionally scrupulous in his observance of all the minutiæ of the Jewish ritual. He had a little synagogue attached to his house, and it was there that I attended services. The brother-in-law of Reb Dovidl was Reb Yechiel Pinnes (a name connected with Pina and Pinsk), one of the earliest settlers in Palestine hailing from our parts; he preceded, if I am not mistaken, the group of the *Bilus*, as they were called, who went out from Russia as the first modern colonizers in 1882. Several branches of the family also settled in America, and scores of their descendants are scattered throughout the United States. The name has been Americanized into Pines.

For a community of its size Pinsk contributed an unusually large number of workers and pioneers in Zionism. There was

Judah Berges, who married into a Pinsk family, a distinguished *Maskil* (a follower of the *Haskallah*, or new Enlightenment) and a man with a genuine gift of leadership. There was Aaron Eisenberg who went out to Palestine when I was still in Pinsk. His departure was a tremendous event and Pinsk gave him a great send-off. It was with a sense of awe that we assembled that evening and gazed with our own eyes on a man who was actually going to Palestine. He promised to write to us, and tell us what the land looked like; and afterwards we waited eagerly for every scrap of news about his movements and his adventures. Eisenberg settled in Rehovoth, became one of its most useful and most prosperous colonists, and contributed greatly to the development of the region. Forty years later I bought the land for our house in Rehovoth from the children of Aaron Eisenberg. George Halpern, who many years later became the manager of the Jewish Colonial Trust, likewise came from Pinsk, so did Isaac Naiditch, one of the founders— in 1920—of the *Keren Hayesod*, the Palestine Foundation Fund, an important instrument in the building of Jewish Palestine. The Shertoks, too, came from Pinsk; Moshe Shertok, of the younger generation of that family, brought up in Palestine, is a leading figure in the political life of modern Palestine. During my boyhood years in Pinsk, Zvi Hirsch Masliansky, the great folk orator, taught at a local Hebrew school. He was one of the most beloved and most influential of the *magidim*, or popular preachers. He settled afterwards in America, and was as beloved among the Yiddish-speaking masses there as he had been in Russia. He died a few years ago, an octogenarian, one of the last remaining links with the heroic early days of Zionism. These are names familiar perhaps only to Zionists; but they were the names of men who had a vision of redemption nearly sixty years ago, who transmuted the dream into tangible reality, and who, in the face of infinite discouragement on the part of practical people, sowed the seeds of that considerable achievement which is Jewish Palestine today.

We must not think of Zionism in Pinsk fifty-odd years ago, long before the coming of Theodor Herzl, in terms of the modern movement. Organized activity in the present-day sense simply did not exist. A youth organization was undreamed of. There were casual meetings of the older people, at which the

youngsters sneaked in, to sit in a corner. On rare occasions
when a circular was sent out, we were permitted to address the
envelopes. Our financial resources were comically limited; we
dealt in roubles and kopecks. One of the main sources of income
was the collection made on the Feast of Purim. Youngsters were
enlisted to distribute leaflets and circulars from house to house,
and modest contributions would be made by most of the householders. Not all, by any means. Not the very rich ones, for
instance, like the Lurias, the great clan of industrialists with
branches in Warsaw, Libau and Danzig, who owned the match
factory in Pinsk. For already, in those early days, the classic
divisions in Zionism, which have endured till very recent days,
manifested themselves. The Jewish magnates were, with very
few exceptions, bitterly anti-Zionist. Our supporters were the
middle class and the poor. An opposition—in the shape of a
labour movement—did not exist yet, for the Bund, the Jewish
revolutionary labour organization, was not founded until 1897
—the year of the first Zionist Congress.

Of course I took an active part in these money collections.
Because of my position as "tutor" in the home of a patrician
family, I used to be allotted not only the house of my patron,
but the houses of all the relatives, in-laws, sons- and daughters-
in-law. Purim always came in the midst of the March thaw, and
hour after hour I would go tramping through the mud of Pinsk,
from end to end of the town. I remember that my mother was
accustomed, for reasons of economy, to make my overcoats
much too long for me, to allow for growth, so that as I went I
repeatedly stumbled over the skirts and sometimes fell head-
long into the icy slush of the streets. I worked late into the night,
but usually had the immense satisfaction of bringing in more
money than anyone else. Such was my apprenticeship for the
activities which, on a rather larger scale, have occupied so
many years of my later life.

Another activity which engaged my attention—this was only
indirectly related to Zionism—was the agitation for the
modernized, improved *cheder*—the *cheder metukan*—which sprang
up about this time in Russian Jewry. A reform was badly
needed, not simply in regard to the accommodations, pedagogy
and curriculum, but in regard to the entire attitude towards
the elementary education of young children. It was extraordi-

nary that the Jews, with whom the education of their children was a matter of the profoundest concern, paid no attention to the first stages of that education. Any sort of luckless failure in the community was considered good enough to teach children their letters, and the word *melamed*, or teacher, was synonymous with *schlimihl*. Perhaps Jewish fathers had the notion that children would pick up the rudiments of reading and writing, of Hebrew and Bible, anyhow. So they did, I suppose; but at great cost in childhood happiness, and at the risk of acquiring a deep distaste for Jewish learning. The *cheder metukan* sought to introduce the element of humanism into early studies, with greater emphasis on Hebrew as a living tongue, on the secular aspects of the Jewish tradition, and on worldly subjects which were considered anathema by the old generation. My enthusiastic support of the new type of *cheder* got me into trouble with the ultra-orthodox, who threatened to denounce me to the police as an atheist, revolutionary, enemy of God and disturber of the peace.

Looking back from the vantage point of present-day Zionism, I can see that we had not the slightest idea of how the practical ends of the movement were to be realized. We knew that the doors of Palestine were closed to us. We knew that every Jew who entered Palestine was given 'the red ticket,' which he had to produce on demand, and by virtue of which he could be expelled at once by the Turkish authorities. We knew that the Turkish law forbade the acquisition of land by Jews. Perhaps if we had considered the matter too closely, or tried to be too systematic, we would have been frightened off. We merely went ahead in a small, blind, persistent way. Jews settled in Palestine, and they were not expelled. They bought land, sometimes through straw men, sometimes by bribes, for Turkish officialdom was even more corrupt than the Russian. Houses were built in evasion of the law. Between *baksheesh* and an infinite variety of subterfuges, the first little colonies were created. Things got done, somehow; not big things, but enough to whet the appetite and keep us going.

The obstinacy and persistence of the movement cannot be understood except in terms of faith. This faith was part of our make-up; our Jewishness and our Zionism were interchangeable; you could not destroy the second without destroying the

B*

first. We did not need to listen to propaganda. When Zvi Hirsch Masliansky, the famous folk orator, came to preach Zionism to us, he addressed the convinced. Of course we loved listening to him, for he spoke beautifully, and he invariably drew on texts from the book of Isaiah, which all of us knew by heart. But we heard in his moving orations only the echo of our innermost feelings.

This is not to deny that there was a wide assimilatory fringe in Jewish life. For that matter we, the Zionists, did not remain indifferent to Russian civilization and culture. I think I may say that we spoke and wrote the language better, were more intimately acquainted with its literature, than most Russians. But we were rooted heart and soul in our own culture, and it did not occur to us to give it up in deference to another. For the first time we fought the assimilationist tendency on its own ground, that is to say, in terms of a modern outlook. We had our periodicals, we had our contemporaneous writers, as well as our ancient traditions. We read *Ha-Zephirah* and *Ha-Melitz* and *Ha-Schachar*, the Hebrew weeklies and dailies; we read Smolenskin and Pinsker and Mohilever and Achad Ha-am, the protagonists of the *Chibath Zion*. There was a genuine renaissance in Hebrew, coinciding with the birth of the modern Yiddish classics, the works of Mendele Mocher S'forim, J. L. Peretz, Sholom Aleichem, which we also read eagerly. Hebrew was the pride and special symbol of Zionism, however. I, for instance, never corresponded with my father in any other language, though to mother I wrote in Yiddish. I sent my father only one Yiddish letter; he returned it without an answer.

The assimilationists in Pinsk—as in other Jewish towns—were drawn from the intelligentsia, which meant the professionals. They were the doctors, pharmacists, dentists and engineers. Once they had been opposed by nothing more than the inertia of the Jewish mass; now they were up against a conscious and enthusiastic countermovement, and they found the going difficult. A story was told in Pinsk of a typical assimilationist doctor who settled in the community and distinguished himself by refusing to talk anything but Russian to his Jewish patients. Not that he did not know Yiddish as well as any of them, but he considered Russian *bon ton*, and good business—one could charge higher fees in Russian. Shortly after him another doctor opened a practice in Pinsk, and this one, a Zionist, spoke Yiddish and even Hebrew with his patients. The competition made itself felt, so the assimilationist doctor rediscovered his mother tongue. Word was brought to the Zionist doctor: 'Your competitor is speaking Yiddish!' 'Wait,' was the answer, 'I'll have him speaking Hebrew before I'm through with him.'

These, then, were the beginnings of Zionism, in the midst of which I lived in my boyhood. They came from deep sources; and if the practical manifestations were rather pitiful at first, if a whole generation had to pass away and another take its place before action became planned and impressive, the significance of those who nurtured and transmitted the impulse must not be forgotten. It was because of them that Herzl found a movement ready for him. If other evidence of the significance of Russian proto-Zionism were needed, we need only look at the foundation layers of the present Jewish population of Palestine. Pinsk and Vilna and Odessa and Warsaw, and a hundred lesser-known Jewish communities are there, the first contributors of the human material of the Return.

Both by way of tribute to my parents, and as a part of this history, I must make note of the record of my family in relation to Palestine. It is symbolic of the reality that Zionism became for so many Russian Jewish families.

There were twelve of us who grew up, children of Oser and Rachel Weizmann, seven girls and five boys; I was the third child. Of the twelve, nine settled permanently in Palestine. All of them were, I think, useful to the country, constructive, each in his or her own way. In my mother's latter years, when we came together to celebrate the Passover in her home in Haifa, thirty-five of us, sons, daughters, sons-in-law, daughters-in-law, grandsons and granddaughters, sat down at table for the *seder*. My mother, presiding over the ceremony, always shed a few tears for those who were still dispersed. We brought not only our principles to Palestine, but our own population.

CHAPTER III

I TURN WESTWARD

*The Educational Dilemma—First Contact with the West—Germany and
German Jewry in the Nineties—Pfungstadt and Dr. Barness, the Assimilationist—German Anti-Semitism—I Return to Pinsk—My First Chemical
Job—Back to Germany—Berlin and the Russian Jewish Student Colonies
of the West—Russian Revolutionaries and Zionism—Revolutionary Assimila-
tionism—Zionist Leaders in the Making—Achad Ha-am, Philosopher,
Critic and Teacher—The Russian-Jewish Scientific Society—The Beginnings of Lifelong Friendships—Penniless Students—Endless Talk—Music
and Theatre—A Missionary among the Russian Marshes—Growing up*

My life, like the life of so many Russian Jews of my generation,
has been one marked regularly by important and fateful
decisions. The years did not run along prepared grooves. There
was not with us Jews, as with most peoples in that remote time,
the normal, natural development of one's career, the expected
thing, with only minor variations. Every division of one's life
was a watershed.

Here I was, eighteen years old, a graduate of the *Real-
Gymnasium* of Pinsk. What was to be the next step? That I was
to continue my studies was taken for granted. But where? In
Russia? Was I to try to break through the narrow gate of the
numerus clausus and enrol in the University of Kiev—as my
two brothers did some years later—or of Petrograd? I would
no doubt have succeeded. But the road was one of ceaseless
chicanery, deception and humiliation. I might pass the difficult entrance examination—Jewish students were given a special
set of more difficult papers—and still fail to obtain the necessary
'residential rights.' I would then have to go through the
mummery of enrolment as an artisan holding a fake job in one
of the forbidden cities. Then there would be years of bribery
and uncertainty; endless dodging of police roundups; constant
changes of address. I loathed the thought of all this furtiveness.
Moreover, I disliked Russia intensely, not Russia proper, that

44

is, but czarist Russia. All my inclinations pointed to the West, whither thousands of Russian Jewish students had moved by now, in a sort of educational stampede.

So I went West, and only the choice of the university was accidental. A friend of the family had a son attending a Jewish boarding school in the village of Pfungstadt, near Darmstadt in Germany. Learning that there was a vacancy on the staff for a junior teacher of Hebrew and Russian, he recommended me, and I was offered the position. I had no idea what the place was like—which was perhaps fortunate. All I cared was that I would get my board, lodging and three hundred marks —about seventy-five dollars—a year in exchange for two hours of tuition a day; that Pfungstadt was less than an hour away, by train, from Darmstadt, where there was a university; and that between my stipend and a little assistance from home I would be able to pay my fees, buy the necessary books and get through my courses. Afterwards? Well, I did not know. Perhaps I would return to Russia, in spite of the wretchedness of our lot there, and make the best of it under the czarist régime until the dawn of a brighter day. Perhaps I would go to Palestine. Perhaps I would remain in the West. In any case, I would not have to swindle my way through the higher education.

But my exit from Russia had its characteristic touch. Everybody in that country had a domestic passport, or identification card. One needed that in travelling from city to city. To go abroad one had to have a foreign passport, a rather expensive document. Since I had barely enough funds to get me to Pfungstadt fourth class, and to see me through the first month, I had to dispense with the foreign passport. I became, for the nonce, a raft worker, and as such entitled to make the round trip on the river to Danzig without a foreign passport. At Thorn, the first stop on German territory, I picked up my bundles and skipped.

It was a marvellous new world that I entered with a beating heart, a clean, neat, orderly world, which bewildered me for two reasons. First, it was so different from the gentile world I had been accustomed to. Second, my Pinsk Yiddish which, like most Russian Jews, I had taken to be next door to High German, turned out to be incomprehensible to the Germans— very much to my astonishment and resentment. However, even without the barrier of language, the country would have been strange enough. One trifling illustrative incident sticks in my mind. When I reached Frankfort-on-Main after a sit-up journey of some twenty-four hours on the fourth-class wooden benches, I went into a post office and sent a telegram to Pfungstadt. I counted out the money carefully and waited for a signed receipt. I waited and waited—it was unimaginable to me that one gave money to a government official and didn't get a receipt for it. The man behind the window managed to make me understand that in Germany government officials could be trusted with small change.

Pfungstadt was my introduction to one of the queerest chapters in Jewish history: that of the assimilated Jews of Germany, then in the high summer of their illusory security, and mightily proud of it. I was a boy of nineteen, naïve, ignorant and impressionable. I did not know then that Germany was in its great period of post-Bismarckian expansion, making gigantic strides forward among the world Powers. I did not know that German Jewry was exerting itself frantically to efface its own identity, to be accepted as German of the Germans. I did not see persons as types, and I did not think in terms of historic forces. My reactions were direct and personal. I saw different human beings, they aroused certain emotions in me; and this direct relationship was my sole guide to the world around me.

The small town of Pfungstadt was famous all over Germany for its brewery, and among the German Jews for its Jewish boarding school. The head of this school was a Dr. Barness, a man who in his own way was even more bewildering to me than the German gentiles. He was pious in the extreme, that is to say, he practised the rigid, formal piety of Frankfort Jewish orthodoxy. The school was *kosher*; it had in constant attendance a *Mashgiach*, or overseer of the ritual purity of the food. There were no classes on the Sabbath; no writing was done on that day; prayers were said three times daily, morning, afternoon and evening. But it was not the orthodoxy I had known and loved at home. It was stuffy, it was unreal, it had no folk background. It lacked warmth and gaiety and colour and intimacy. It did not interpenetrate the life of the teachers and pupils; it was a cold discipline imposed from the outside.

Dr. Barness was completely assimilated, and described himself as 'a German of the Mosaic persuasion.' He took his Judaism to mean that in all respects save that of a religious ritual he was as German, in culture, background and personality, as any descendant of the Cerusci. This philosophy he preached in and out of season, both at school and everywhere else, but especially at the meetings which he addressed on the subject of anti-Semitism. For anti-Semitism was eating deep into Germany in those days, a heavy, solid, bookish anti-Semitism far more deadly, in the long run, than the mob anti-Semitism of Russian city hooligans and the cynical exploitation of it practised by Russian politicians and prelates. It worked itself into the texture of the national consciousness. Even Dr. Barness could not ignore the evidence of Jew-hatred about him. But he regarded it as the result of a slight misunderstanding. If some Germans were anti-Semitically inclined, it was because they did not know the sterling qualities of the Jews, as exemplified in Dr. Barness and his like. They had to be told—that was all. A little enlightenment, judiciously applied, and anti-Semitism would simply vanish.

With all my youthful naïveté I just could not stomach Dr. Barness's rather fatuous and self-satisfied philosophy of anti-Semitism; and though it was shared by all the teachers in the school, I did not yet suspect that it was a characteristic of most of German Jewry. Naturally I did not know that I would come up against it repeatedly in later years, in contacts with German—and not only German—Jewish leaders, greater and wiser men than Dr. Barness, who on this subject were as trivial, as evasively blind, as he. At the time I only knew—when I began, with an increasing grasp of the language, to understand what he was talking about—that he caused me the acutest discomfort. Without a philosophy of history or of anti-Semitism, I felt clearly enough that Dr. Barness was an intellectual coward and a toady. Towards the end of my stay in Pfungstadt I got into an argument with him. Hearing him, for the hundredth time or so, say that if the Germans would only have their eyes opened to the excellent qualities of the Jews, etc., I answered desperately: 'Herr Doktor, if a man has a piece of something in his eye, he doesn't want to know whether it's a piece of mud or a piece of gold. He just wants to get it out!' Herr Doktor was speechless.

It was quite useless to argue with Dr. Barness, or with any of the teachers. Their conviction regarding the essential triviality and evanescent character of anti-Semitism was a complex which was related to their anxiety not to believe that a Jewish people existed. I remember how, shortly after my arrival, one of the teachers asked me what nationality I was; and when I answered, '*Ein Russischer Jude*' (a Russian Jew), he stared at me, then went off into gales of laughter. He had never heard of such a thing. A German, yes. A Russian, yes. Judaism, yes. But a Russian Jew! That was to him the height of the ridiculous.

The piety of the boarding school was to me utterly strange. I just did not feel any religion in it. Perhaps this effect was heightened by the wretchedness of the food, on which, I am afraid, some of the considerable profits of the institution were made. Moreover, I was lonely and desperately homesick for Pinsk, for my family, for Motol, for my friends, for the world I knew. My contacts with German life then, and later during my years as a student in Berlin, were few; but such as they were, they left me ill at ease. It was better in Pinsk, though Pinsk was Russia, and Russia meant czardom and the Pale and the *numerus clausus* and pogroms. In Russia at least we, the Jews, had a culture of our own, and a high one. We had standing in our own eyes. We did not dream that our Jewish being was something to be sloughed off furtively. But in Germany, surrounded by efficiency and power, the Jews were obsessed by a sense of inferiority which urged them ceaselessly to deny themselves and to regard their heritage with shame—and at the same time to sing their own praises in the ears of those who would not listen. It was here, in Germany, that I learned the full meaning of what Achad Ha-am expressed in his famous essay *Avdut betoch Cheruth*, 'Slavery in the Midst of Freedom,' addressed to the assimilatory Western Jews.

Darmstadt was a pleasant enough town, but I saw next to nothing of it. I had no time. On weekdays I got up at five, to take the train which arrived in Darmstadt at six-thirty. The university did not open until seven-thirty, so I had to walk the streets for an hour. I got back to Pfungstadt at half-past four, and taught Russian and Hebrew till half-past six. Since I had not the money for a regular meal in Darmstadt, I took with me a *brötchen* (roll) and a piece of cheese, or of sausage. That had to last me until suppertime, and supper, as I have indicated, was a wretched affair, though it was preceded by a solemn benediction and followed by a long grace. I had to work late into the night, learning German and trying to fill the gaps in my scientific and general education, which was far behind the standards of the German high schools. Between overwork, malnutrition and loneliness I had a rather cheerless time of it. I stuck it out for two terms and had something approaching a breakdown. My Pfungstadt experience left a permanent mark on my health; nearly fifty years later a doctor traced a lung hæmorrhage to the effects of my first eight months in Germany.

I left Pfungstadt without regrets, and remember it without pleasure. I have not retained a single permanent relationship as a result of my stay there, which is a rare experience for me. Many years later, when the school was in its decline, I came across one of its advertisements in a German Jewish periodical. It had taken to announcing that 'Dr. Chaim Weizmann taught here.' But apparently even this evidence of its one-time academic distinction was of no avail, for it ultimately closed its doors. Just before that happened the son of Dr. Barness wrote to me asking me to recommend him some pupils. My conscience would not let me. It was an obnoxious place.

The situation at home was bad. The family had moved to Pinsk, for a number of reasons. The younger children were growing up, and it was impossible to maintain them in school at Pinsk unless the home was there. Father could conduct his business from Pinsk as easily as from Motol; our only reason for staying in Motol had been the house. Pinsk was in one way better than Motol, because father's rafts all had to pass through Pinsk, which meant he would be at home oftener. But the first period of resettlement was a hard one. It was out of the question to send me back to the West. So I stayed in Pinsk for a year, working in a small chemical factory owned by one of the Lurias, and I took advantage of this interruption in my education to get rid of my military obligations, which had been hanging over me like a nightmare. It goes without saying that I had no intention of wasting four years serving Czar Nicholas. I appeared before the conscription board, was duly examined and duly pronounced fit. By a marvellous stroke of luck I managed to talk my way out of the army in a special interview with the local military commander, a decent and cultured Russian who thought it a pity to have my education interrupted.

At the end of a year father's business—he was already in partnership with his gifted and ambitious son-in-law—took a turn for the better. These two decided to finance my education between them: no jobs, and no provincial university this time. I was to go to Berlin and enrol in the *Polytechnicum*, which was considered one of the three best scientific schools in Europe. I was to have a hundred marks—twenty-five dollars—a month, not a munificent allowance, but one that would just about enable me to get along after paying for my courses; in any case, it was more than the majority of foreign students in Berlin had to live on. And so, in the summer of 1895, I set my face westward again.

The difference between Berlin and Darmstadt had to do with much more than academic rating. Darmstadt was a little place, without a foreign student body. I had chosen it as a *pis aller* because of the job in Pfungstadt. Berlin was a world metropolis, the first I learned to know. It was at the centre of the intellectual currents of the time. Above all, it had an enormous Russian-Jewish student colony, which was to play as important a rôle in moulding my life as the university itself.

These student colonies were an interesting and characteristic feature of Western Europe in the days of czarist Russia. In Berlin, Berne, Zurich, Geneva, Munich, Paris, Montpellier, Nancy, Heidelberg, young Russian Jews, driven from the land of their birth by persecution, by discrimination and by intellectual starvation, constituted special and identifiable groups. The women students were almost as numerous as the men. In some places they outnumbered the men. Medicine was the favourite study, for it offered the most obvious road to a livelihood; besides, it was associated with the idea of social service, of contact with the masses, of opportunity to teach, by precept and example. Engineering and chemistry came next, with law in the third or fourth place. Like myself, most of these students were vague about the future; were they to return to Russia, or were they to commit themselves to the West? They did not know. But whatever their choice of subject, whatever their plans, they were nearly all of a definite type. They belonged to the middle and lower-middle classes; for the rich Jews of

Russia—like the rich anywhere—could 'arrange' things, and seldom had to send their children to foreign universities. The Jewish students at the Western universities were 'rebels' in one sense or another; what else should they be under the circumstances? And they were, almost without exception, the children of *baalabatische* parents, solid, respectable, intelligent householders of the middle and lower-middle class, people steeped in Jewish tradition, instinctively liberal, ambitious—just like my father—for their children, eager to burst the bonds of the past. Many of these youngsters had received a good Jewish education. They spoke Yiddish, they read Hebrew, or at least were familiar with it.

The first westward tide of students had set in with the clamping down of educational restrictions in the early eighties. In my day the colonies were already well established; they had a tradition and a character. They were revolutionary in a peculiar sense, and in a specifically Russian setting involving for the Jews a complete denial of Jewish identity. It was an utterly anomalous situation. Jewish students in Western Europe could not become part of the revolutionary movement unless they did violence to their affections and affiliations by pretending that they had no special emotional and cultural relationship to their own people. It was a ukase from above. Also it was completely artificial; for these young men and women were not 'assimilated' ; they had not drifted away from the mode of life of their parents. On the contrary there was a deep and tender attachment to the ancient Jewish patterns. But the 'line,' as we should call it nowadays, forbade such a relationship; Zionism was 'counter-revolutionary.'

This extraordinary ukase was soon challenged. Long before the coming of Theodor Herzl, consciously Zionistic groups of Jewish students in the Western universities were already fighting the assimilationist-revolutionary movement, not on its revolutionary but on its assimilationist side. In Berlin there had been organized, five or six years before my arrival, the *Jüdisch-Russisch Wissenschaftliches Verein*—the Jewish-Russian Scientific Society. Its leaders were all destined to become prominent in the Zionist movement: Schmarya Levin, Leo Motzkin, Nachman Syrkin, Victor Jacobson, Arthur Hantke, Heinrich Löwe, Zelig Soskin, Willi Bambus, and many others. When I arrived in Berlin some of these had already graduated, or had left for other universities. Schmarya Levin, for instance—he developed into one of the great tribunes of Zionism, a man of fascinating personality and dazzling oratorical gifts—had gone to Koenigsberg to work on his doctorate thesis. Sooner or later I got to know all of them; and with most of them I developed enduring and lifelong relationships. I was to work with them in the course of the next twenty, thirty, forty years, in England, in America, in Palestine; I was to fight at their side, or against them, at the Zionist Congresses. I was to witness with them the development of the Zionist movement from what passed for a 'freak' phenomenon into a serious international force engaging the attention of statesmen.

In short, this was a world very different indeed from Pfungstadt and Darmstadt. Here, in Berlin, I grew out of my boyhood Zionism, out of my adolescence, into something like maturity. When I left Berlin for Switzerland, in 1898, at the age of twenty-four, the adult pattern of my life was set. Of course I learned a great deal in later years; but no fundamental change took place; my political outlook, my Zionist ideology, my scientific bent, my life's purposes, had crystallized.

Of my fellow-students who afterwards became my fellow-workers in Zionism I shall have much to say, in this and in succeeding chapters; for some of them became intimate and cherished friends; and the *Jüdisch-Russisch Verein* could, without derogating from the rôle played by similar student bodies in other Western universities, claim to have been the cradle of the modern Zionist movement. But I must speak first of a great man who was then living in Berlin, one whose influence on us, on Russian Jewry, and on the Zionist movement, was incalculable. Him, too, I was able to call, in later years, friend and comrade, though he was more—he was adviser and teacher, too; and I shall have much to say about him in later chapters of this narrative.

Asher Ginsburg, best, indeed almost exclusively, known under his pen-name of Achad Ha-am—'One of the People'—was the foremost thinker and Hebrew stylist of his generation. I was a boy of seventeen, a high-school student in Pinsk, when he first sprang into prominence with his article—a classic of Zionist history and literature—'Truth from Palestine.' He was a keen and merciless critic from the beginning, a man of unshakable intellectual integrity; but his criticisms sprang from a strongly affirmative outlook. For him Zionism was the Jewish renaissance in a spiritual-national sense. Its colonizational work, its political programme had meaning only as an organic part of the re-education of the Jewish people. A façade of physical achievement meant little to him; he measured both the organization in exile and in the colonies in Palestine by their effect on Jewry. His first concern was with quality. When he organized his society, the *Bnai Moshe*—the training school of many of the Russian Zionist leaders—he put the emphasis on perfection. The membership was never more than one hundred, but every member was tested by high standards of intelligence and devotion. As a writer, Achad Ha-am never put forth less than his best; he was precise and penetrating in his thoughts; he was sparing and exact in his style, which became a model for a whole school. As an editor he was not less exacting of his contributors. He criticized the early work of the *Chibath Zion* because it had placed the chief emphasis on the physical redemption of the Jewish people; he criticized the practical work of Baron Edmond de Rothschild because the latter, in coming to the rescue of the tottering colonies in Palestine, was animated—so it was thought, but somewhat mistakenly, as I shall show later—only by a spirit of old-fashioned philanthropy, which was less concerned with the remaking of the colonists than with immediate economic results; he criticized Herzl because he did not find in the new Zionist movement the proper attention to the inner rehabilitation of Jewry which had to precede, or at least accompany, the external solution of its problems.

It is not easy to convey to this generation of Jewry in the West the effect which Achad Ha-am produced on us. One might have thought that such an attitude of caution, of restraint, of seeming pessimism, would all but destroy a movement which had only just begun to take shape. It was not the case, simply because Achad Ha-am was far from being a negative spirit. Though essentially a philosopher and not a man of action, he joined the executive of the *Choveve Zion* Federation, the Odessa Committee as it was called, which supervised such practical work as was being done in Palestine. His criticisms were likewise exhortations. In his analysis of the spiritual slavery of 'emancipated' Western Jews he was forthright to the point of cruelty, and his arguments hurt all the more because they were unanswerable. The appearance of one of Achad Ha-am's articles was always an event of prime importance. We read him, and read him again, and discussed him endlessly. He was, I might say, what Gandhi has been to many Indians, what Mazzini was to Young Italy a century ago.

We youngsters in Berlin did not see much of him. At rare intervals we would drop in on him at his modest little home. But his presence in our midst was a constant inspiration and influence.

We held our regular Saturday night meetings at a café, and mostly it was the one attached to a certain Jewish hotel—the Hotel Zentrum on the Alexanderplatz, because there, during lean periods, we could get beer and sausages on credit. I think with something like a shudder of the amount of talking we did. We never dispersed before the small hours of the morning. We talked of everything, of history, wars, revolutions, the rebuilding of society. But chiefly we talked of the Jewish problem and of Palestine. We sang, we celebrated such Jewish festivals as we did not go home for, we debated with the assimilationists, and we made vast plans for the redemption of our people. It was all very youthful and naïve and jolly and exciting; but it was not without a deeper meaning.

At first I was greatly overawed by my fellow-students, among whom I was the youngest. Fresh from little Pinsk, with its petty Zionist collections and small-town discussions, I was staggered by the sweep of vision which Motzkin and Syrkin and the others displayed. There was also a personal detail which oppressed me at the beginning. I was only a student of chemistry; they were students of philosophy, history, economics, law and other 'higher' things. I was immensely attracted to them as persons and as Zionists; but gradually I began to feel that in their personal preparations for life they were as vague as in their Zionist plans. I had brought with me out of Russia a dread of the 'eternal student' type, the impractical idealist without roots in the worldly struggle, a figure only too familiar in the Jewish world of forty and fifty years ago. I refused to neglect the lecture hall and the laboratory, to which I gave at least six or seven hours a day. I worked at my subject, I studied consistently, I acquired a taste for research work. In later years I understood that even deeper motives impelled me in those days to attend strictly to the question of my personal equipment for the life struggle. For the time being it was enough for me to make up my mind that I was going to achieve independence.

However, I had my share of the social and intellectual life of the *Verein*, and of Jewish student life generally. It was a curious world, existing, for us Jewish students, outside of space and time. We had nothing to do with our immediate surroundings outside the university. In Berlin—and later when I was at Freiburg and Geneva—local politics, German and Swiss, did not exist for us. In part this was due to our tacit fear of destroying our own refugee opportunities. But it sprang mostly from the sheer intensity of our inner life. And there was a third factor. If we constituted a kind of ghetto—not a compulsory one, of course, and not in the negative sense—it was to a large extent because most of us were practically penniless. I, with my hundred marks allowance a month—that had to cover fees and books as well as living expenses—was among the well-to-do. But I think I can safely say that during all the years of my sojourn in Berlin I did not eat a single solid meal except as somebody's guest. We lived among ourselves because we could not afford to live separately.

Yet I need hardly say that we were thoroughly, sometimes even riotously, happy. Poverty loses most of its pangs when it loses its disgrace; and among us there was no stigma attached to poverty. Besides, the poorest of us were never completely destitute, the richest were never safe. Some, however, were definitely underfed. Nachman Syrkin, gifted, high-spirited, imaginative—he later became one of the founders of the Socialist Zionist party—was among these. At the beginning of every month he would turn up for a loan, and I pinched off what I could from my allowance. Towards the end of the month, when cash was scarce, he would ask for a 'pledge,' that is, for something which could be pawned. I had two pledges: one was a wonderful cushion, which my mother had made me take with me, and which brought a trifle from the pawnbroker; the other was my set of chemist's weights, which—I remember distinctly—was worth two marks and fifty pfennigs. At the end of the month I was generally without cushion and without weights.

Many of the friendships which I formed in those days lasted, as I have said, for the rest of my life. But there were figures which belong only to that period; they passed across the horizon and disappeared. What became of them I do not know.

There was a student called Kunin, who was reckoned among the well-to-do, for he lived, with two of his sisters, in a flat of his own. What he was studying, when he attended classes, no one really knew. We often visited him, for his sisters were charming girls, and one could count on an occasional meal there. All of us borrowed money from him, or else a 'pledge.' Kunin had a magnificent fur coat which became a tradition. He permitted us to pawn it, only on the strict condition that we redeem it before the summer vacation, because then he had to go home and take his coat with him to show his parents. Half of the winter Kunin went about shivering; but towards summer he would appear with his magnificent coat over his arm. As the swallows return for the spring, so Kunin's coat returned for the summer. If you saw Kunin coming down the street with his fur coat on his arm, you remembered that the long vacation was at hand.

Among the poorest of the students there was a certain Tamarschenko, who hailed from the Caucasus. Tamarschenko was working his way through college. Three months of the year he worked in a sugar factory—a device which served quite a number of students. One took a special six-months course in sugar chemistry, and then, at the time of the beet harvest, one got a job in a sugar factory, testing the sugar content of the beets, the mash and the finished product. Thus one lived for three months and saved something towards the expenses of the other nine. I imagine that Tamarschenko never finished his course; there was something too helpless about him. He became the symbol of ultimate *schlimihldom* in our student generation, and to his name was attached one of the legends of the time. Tamarschenko used to come, at noon, to the student restaurant, but could not afford fifty pfennigs for the regular meal. He would therefore order a glass of beer for ten pfennigs, and consume as many *brötchen* or rolls as he could lay his hands on. He had a technique of his own. In order not to make his depredations too conspicuous, he would sit down between two baskets and reach out in alternation on either side. One day, however, a waiter came over to him and said, very courteously: '*Herr Kandidat*, next time you are thirsty, please go to a bakery.'

For months at a stretch we would turn vegetarian. We argued that it was good for our health. It also happened to be cheaper. In addition to which, the vegetarian restaurant we frequented had the best collection of newspapers for its customers.

Our ghetto isolation was broken at two points: we loved music and the theatre, the former for its own sake, the latter because it also helped us to learn the language. There were special prices for students, and a row was reserved for them at all performances. On Sundays we got the theatre tickets for fifty pfennigs, so that was our favourite day; and if it happened that three performances were being given—morning, afternoon and evening, we would attend all three, eating our sandwiches between the performances, and returning at night sated with Shakespeare, Goethe and Ibsen. The opera and the concert hall were more expensive—a whole mark. But you could attend dress rehearsals for seventy-five pfennigs.

Felix von Weingartner was the premier conductor in Berlin in those days—and my hero. Nothing could keep me from his Beethoven concerts, one of which I remember for a particular reason. Spring was always the time for the Beethoven cycle, and sometimes it happened that the Ninth Symphony coincided with *Purim*, the jolliest of the Jewish half-festivals. On this particular *Purim* a dozen of us attended the dress rehearsal of the Ninth Symphony. We sat in the cheapest seats, of course, immediately under the roof. We followed the music passionately and applauded wildly. Towards the close of the symphony we stood up and, unable to restrain ourselves, sang along with the orchestra. Weingartner was curious to know who those queer individuals in the highest gallery could be, and after the performance he climbed up the stairs to investigate. We not only told him that we were his fervent admirers, we also reminded him that this was *Purim*, a day of joy and gaiety in the Jewish tradition; whereupon the famous conductor took us all to a *Bierhalle* and treated us to *Würstchen* and beer.

Towards the end of my Berlin period we had managed to establish a certain relationship with part of the Jewish community of the city. The German Jews, who had looked upon us Russian-Jewish students as wild men from the uncivilized East, learned to know us; and they developed a kind of liking for us —or perhaps merely a weakness. We were considered picturesque and interesting. The son of Hirsch Hildesheimer, the leading Rabbi of Berlin, joined our ranks. Steinschneider, the philosopher, dropped in now and again; once or twice he read a paper at a meeting. Professor Landau received some of us. And every year we gave a charity ball, which increasing numbers of the German Jews attended. But I cannot say that anything resembling real intimacy ever grew up between the Russian-Jewish student colony and the Jewish community of Berlin. The gap between the two worlds was almost unbridgeable.

In many ways it was our fault as much as theirs; and there were unfavourable circumstances of no one's making. We were in Berlin only when the university was open; for the vacations most of us scattered to our homes. During my student years in Berlin and Freiburg, as well as later on, when I was teaching at the University of Geneva, I invariably went back to Russia for my holidays. Nine months of the year I spent in the free Western world; but every June I returned to the East, and until the autumn I was the militant Zionist in the land where Zionism was illegal. In the East our opponents were the *Okhrana*, the Russian secret police. In the West it was an open fight, in the East a conspiracy. The West preached liberty, the East practised repression; but East and West alike were the enemies of the Zionist ideology.

It was in the fen and the forest area about Pinsk that I did my first missionary work, confining myself to the villages and small towns. In these forlorn Jewish communities it was not a question of preaching Zionism as much as of awakening them to action. I went about urging the Jews of places like Motol to enrol in the *Choveve Zion*; to send delegates to the first Zionist Congress, when that was called in 1897; to buy shares in the first Zionist bank, the Jewish Colonial Trust, when that was founded in 1898. Most of the meetings were held in the synagogues, where in case of a police raid I would be 'attending services' or 'preaching.' My dreams were opulent, my demands modest. It was a gala day for me when I managed to raise twenty or thirty roubles for the cause.

I remember being sent out, on a certain day shortly before *Yom Kippur*, the Day of Atonement, to a place called Kalenkovitch. It was a village widely known because of its scholarly and saintly Rabbi. He, like the famous Tana of old, Nahum Gimso, had lost both legs in an accident, and conducted his work from his bed. I left Pinsk at night and arrived at the Kalenkovitch station at three in the morning. There a peasant met me, and paddled me in his dugout through the marshes to the village proper. In the pre-dawn twilight some twenty Jews were assembled in the tiny wooden synagogue. The Rabbi had been carried to the meeting in his bed. He had heard of me, and before I addressed the meeting he blessed me and my work. I spoke of the great time at hand, of liberation, the Congress, the bank, the colonies, and persuaded my listeners to buy thirty roubles' worth of shares in the Jewish Colonial Trust. Later, while I was waiting for the peasant to row me back to the station, I got into conversation with an old Jew whom I had met before, Reb Nissan, an itinerant peddler of prayer-books, prayer-shawls, phylacteries and other religious objects. He had seemed to listen intently, and I was curious to know what he thought about it all. I said: 'Reb Nissan, did you understand what I was talking about?' He looked at me out of his old eyes under their bushy brows, and answered humbly: 'No, I didn't. I am an old man, and my hearing isn't very good. But this much I know: if what you spoke about wasn't true, you wouldn't have come here.'

With the years, the areas assigned to me by the local committee widened out. Mozyr was the first fair-sized town to which I was sent as an apostle. Mozyr had a large synagogue; it also boasted an intelligentsia. So, from the tiny communities of the marshlands I graduated to Vilna in the north, to Kiev and even Kharkov, with their large student bodies, in the south.

Here the missionary work was of a very different order. I no longer had just the folk to deal with. Among the Russian-Jewish assimilating intelligentsia, and among many of the

students, there was an ideological opposition to Zionism which
had to be countered on another level. These were not the
rich, orthodox Jewish families of Pinsk, obscurantist, reactionary. They were not, either, the *Shtadlonim*, the notables,
with their vested interests, their lickspittle attitude towards the
Russian Government, their vanity and their ancient prestige.
Nor were they like the German assimilating Jews, bourgeois or
Philistine. For these last strove, in their assimilationist philosophy, to approximate to the type of the German *Spiessbürger*,
the comfortable merchant, the *Geheimrat*, the professor, the
sated, respectable classes. Most of the Russian-Jewish intelligentsia, and above all the students, assimilated towards the
spirit of a Tolstoy or Korolenko, towards the creative and
revolutionary classes. It was, I think, a tragically erroneous
assimilation even so, but it was not base or repulsive. In Germany we were losing, through assimilation, the least attractive
Jewish groups. The opposite was the case in Russia.

For me, then, it was a time of threefold growth. I was
pursuing my scientific studies systematically, and to that
extent resisting the pressure of bohemianism in my surroundings. At the same time, within the Russian-Jewish Society, I
was working out, in discussion and debate, my political philosophy, and beginning to shed the vague and sentimental
Zionism of my boyhood. Thirdly, I was learning, one might
say from the ground up, the technique of propaganda and the
approach to the masses. I was also weaving the web of my
life's personal relationships.

CHAPTER IV

THE COMING OF HERZL

*' The Jewish State '—Herzl's True Historic Rôle—His Personality—
The First Zionist Congress called—Max Nordau—Zionists and Revolu-
tionaries at Berne University—Lenin, Plekhanov, Trotsky—Revolution
against the Revolutionaries—Russian Student Zionists and Herzl—Herzl's
Diplomacy—The Democratic Party—Western Zionism and Russian
Zionism*

I was in my second year in Berlin when, in 1896, Theodor
Herzl published his tract, now a classic of Zionism, *Der
Judenstaat—The Jewish State*. It was an utterance which came
like a bolt from the blue. We had never heard the name Herzl
before; or perhaps it had come to our attention, only to be
lost among those of other journalists and *feuilletonists*. Fundamentally, *The Jewish State* contained not a single new idea for
us; that which so startled the Jewish bourgeoisie, and called
down the resentment and derision of the Western Rabbis, had
long been the substance of our Zionist tradition. We observed,
too, that this man Herzl made no allusion in his little book to
his predecessors in the field, to Moses Hess and Leon Pinsker
and Nathan Birnbaum—the last a Viennese like Herzl, and
the creator of the very word by which the movement is known:
Zionism. Apparently Herzl did not know of the existence of
the *Chibath Zion*; he did not mention Palestine; he ignored the
Hebrew language.

Yet the effect produced by *The Jewish State* was profound. Not
the ideas, but the personality which stood behind them
appealed to us. Here was daring, clarity and energy. The very
fact that this Westerner came to us unencumbered by our own
preconceptions had its appeal. We of the Russian group in
Berlin were not alone in our response. The Zionist student
group of Vienna, *Kadimah*, was perhaps more deeply impressed
than we. There were also, as I have said, strong Zionist groups
at the universities of Montpellier and Paris and elsewhere. It

was from these sources that Herzl drew much of his early support.

We were right in our instinctive appreciation that what had emerged from the *Judenstaat* was less a concept than a historic personality. The *Judenstaat* by itself would have been nothing more than a nine days' wonder. If Herzl had contented himself with the mere publication of the booklet—as he originally intended to do, before it became clear to him that he was no longer his own master, but the servant of the idea—his name would be remembered today as one of the oddities of Jewish history. What has given greatness to his name is Herzl's rôle as a man of action, as the founder of the Zionist Congress, and as an example of daring and devotion.

I first saw Herzl at the second Congress, in Basle, in the summer of 1898, and though he was impressive, I cannot pretend that I was swept off my feet. There was a great genuineness about him, and a touch of pathos. It seemed to me almost from the beginning that he was undertaking a task of tremendous magnitude without adequate preparation. He had great gifts and he had connections. But these did not suffice. As I learned to know him better at succeeding Congresses, my respect for him was confirmed and deepened. As a personality he was both powerful and naïve. He was powerful in the belief that he had been called by destiny to this piece of work. He was naïve, as we already suspected from *Der Judenstaat*, and as we definitely learned from our contact with his work, in his schematic approach to Zionism.

His Zionism began as a sort of philanthropy, superior of course to the philanthropy of Baron de Hirsch, but philanthropy nevertheless. As he saw it, or seemed to see it, there were rich Jews and there were poor Jews. The rich Jews, who wanted to help the poor Jews, had considerable influence in the councils of the nations. And then there was the Sultan of Turkey, who always wanted money, and who was in possession of Palestine. What was more logical, then, than to get the rich Jews to give the Sultan money to allow the poor Jews to go to Palestine?

There were, again, two steps in the process. First, the rich Jews had to be persuaded to open their purses; second, the Great Powers had to be persuaded to put some pressure on

Turkey and to act as the guarantors in the transaction. In this connection the two leading Powers were Germany and England; Herzl began by putting the emphasis on Germany and the Kaiser; afterwards he shifted it to England. The whole of the Zionist Organization was merely an understructure for Herzl, whereby he would exert pressure on the rich Jews, and obtain the authority for his *démarches* among the Powers.

Young as I was, and totally inexperienced in worldly matters, I considered the entire approach *simpliste* and doomed to failure. To begin with, I had no faith at all in the rich Jews whom Herzl was courting. Even Baron Edmond de Rothschild, who had done considerable semi-philanthropic work in Palestine—he did a great deal more than that, later, when he achieved a deeper understanding of Zionism—regarded Herzl as a naïve person, who was completely overshooting the mark.

To me Zionism was something organic, which had to grow like a plant, had to be watched, watered and nursed, if it was to reach maturity. I did not believe that things could be done in a hurry. The Russian Zionists had as their slogan a saying of the Jewish sages: 'That which the intelligence cannot do, time [that is, work, application, worry] will do.' There was no lack of Zionist sentiment in the Russian-Jewish masses: what they lacked was will, direction, organization, the feeling of realities. Herzl was an organizer; he was also an inspiring personality; but he was not of the people, and did not grasp the nature of the forces which it harboured.

He had excessive respect for the Jewish clergy, born not of intimacy but of distance. He saw something rather occult and mysterious in the Rabbis, while he knew them and evaluated them as individuals, good, bad or indifferent. His leaning towards clericalism distressed us, so did the touch of Byzantinism in his manner. Almost from the outset a kind of court sprang up about him, of worshippers who pretended to guard him from too close contact with the mob. I am compelled to say that certain elements in his bearing invited such an attitude.

I remember (to run a little ahead of my story) a characteristic incident at one of the early Congresses. The committee which I liked most to serve on, and of which I was occasionally the chairman, was the *Permanenz-Auschuss*, a combined resolutions, steering and nominating committee. On the occasion to which

I refer, Herzl had intimated to us that he wanted us to nominate, as one of the Vice-Presidents of the Congress, Sir Francis Montefiore, of England, the nephew of the great Sir Moses Montefiore, who was a legendary name in Jewry because of his early interest in Palestine and his services to the Jewish people at large. We did not want Sir Francis as a Vice-President of the Congress. He was a very nice old English gentleman, but rather footling. He spoke, in and out of season, and in a sepulchral voice, of '*mein seliger Hoheim*'—'my sainted uncle.' He always wore white gloves at the Congresses—this in the heat of the Swiss summer—because he had to shake so many hands. Sir Francis was quite a decorative figure, and he was invariably called on to greet the Congress. We did not mind him as a showpiece, but we were rather fed up with his sainted uncle, and we wanted that particular Vice-Presidency to go to some real personality, like Ussishkin or Tschlenow. When Herzl pressed his point on me I said, 'But Dr. Herzl, that man's a fool.' To which Herzl replied, with immense solemnity: '*Er öffnet mir königliche Pforten*'—'he opens the portals of royalty to me.' I could not help grinning at this stately remark, and Herzl turned white. He was full of Western dignity which did not sit well with our Russian-Jewish realism; and without wanting to, we could not help irritating him. We were genuinely sorry, but it was an unavoidable clash of temperaments.

Most profound in its effect on the movement was Herzl's creation of the Zionist Congress. Having failed with the Jewish notables and philanthropists, he turned to the Jewish masses. He made contact with the leaders of the *Chibath Zion*. David Wolffsohn, who was to be his successor, came to him. The call for the first demonstration went out in 1897. It was not to be another Kattowitz Conference, a semi-furtive, internal Jewish affair. It was to be a public declaration, an address to the world, a manifesto of flesh and blood, the Jewish people itself reasserting its existence and confronting humanity with its historic demands.

That was how we felt about it, and that was what suddenly jolted us out of our old routine, and out of our daydreams. We resolved, in the spring of 1897, to devote the summer vacation to the propagation of the idea of the Congress. I myself was busy for months in the dim marshlands, persuading the communities to elect their delegates; I also received a mandate to the Congress from the community of Pinsk, a mandate which, I remember with warm gratitude, was renewed for every Zionist Congress that followed; other Zionists of Pinsk had to stand for election; about mine there was never any doubt. Three men who were particularly active among the Russian communities were Ossip Buchmiller, Boris Katzman and Moshe Margulis Kalvarisky. All three were taking the agricultural course at Montpellier, and all three settled in Palestine later. • For them, and for many others, the Congress was a far greater inspiration than the contents of the *Judenstaat*; and the truth is that Herzl's contribution to Zionism, apart from his personal example, was that of form. Conviction, devotion, persistence, tradition—all these things we had in ample measure. But we had no experience in parliamentary organization and action. It was here that Herzl shone, both by natural aptitude and by years of training as the correspondent of the *Neue Freie Presse* in the Chamber of Deputies in Paris.

Max Nordau, the famous author of *Degeneration* and *The Conventional Lies of Civilization*, was the other outstanding leader of early Western Zionism. Him I also saw for the first time at the second Congress, in 1898. The passionate devotion of selflessness which commanded respect in Herzl was lacking in Nordau, whom we found artificial, as well as inclined to arrogance. Nordau was, of course, a famous European figure; but what mattered to us was that he was an ardent Zionist only during the sessions of the Congresses. During the other three hundred and fifty odd days of the year we heard only occasionally of him within the movement; for then he attended to his business, which was that of a writer. He was not prepared, like Herzl and many others, to sacrifice his career for Zionism. Of Nordau's ability there was no doubt. His address at the first Congress was powerful, and made a deep impression. For the first time the Jewish problem was presented forcefully before a European forum. True, it was not done in our fashion; Nordau's concept of anti-Semitism was different from ours. But it was a bugle call sounded all over the world, and the world took note. Then came Nordau's main address at the second Congress, and it was a repetition, with variations, of the first. So it went on, from Congress to Congress, and the thesis lost its originality.

C

It is true that Nordau's occasional polemics with assimilated Jews had considerable value for us; but the fact remained that he did not pull his weight in the movement. For the movement was not, strictly speaking, his business. He was a *Heldentenor*, a prima donna, a great speaker in the classical style; spadework was not in his line.

The cleavage between East and West, between organic and schematic Zionism, was clarified in Nordau's development as a Zionist. In later years, after the First World War, he became the father of what is known as the Max Nordau Plan, if plan it can be called, which proposed the transfer of a million Jews to Palestine in one year, and the solution of the Jewish problem within a space of ten years. How this was to be done, and whether the Jews were prepared for such an immense dislocation, and whether Palestine could take them—all these questions were ignored. It was assumed that even if, of the million suddenly transplanted Jews, two or three hundred thousand perished, the remaining seven or eight hundred thousand would 'somehow' be established. One hardly knows how to characterize the whole proposal, which was taken seriously by a number of Jews, and which afterwards became part of the credo of the Revisionist Zionists.

I could not get away from the impression that Nordau's attitude towards the 'East-European' Jews was a patronizing one. His tone was supercilious. His talk sparkled with epigrams, but it betrayed no depth of feeling and perception. His Zionism was facile. There was latent in it from the beginning the irresponsibility of the Nordau Plan. It was easy for Nordau to believe in the possibility of a tremendous and miraculous leap forward in Zionist work; for me there was never a royal road, a shortcut—I shall have occasion to refer again and again, throughout this narrative, to my struggle against this false concept. Moreover, I held that Zionist progress could be directed only through Palestine, through tedious labour, every step won by sweat and blood. Nordau thought the movement could be directed from Paris—with speeches.

Nordau was no more successful than Herzl in winning over the notables and great philanthropists. While I was still teaching at Geneva—I am again anticipating—a deputation of Russian Zionists was organized to call on Baron Edmond de

Rothschild, to discuss with him the need for a reform in the administration of his colonies in Palestine. Achad Ha-am, Ussishkin, Tschlenow, Kohan-Bernstein (the last was a Herzlian Zionist) made up the deputation. In Paris they co-opted Nordau as their spokesman. I came up from Geneva to meet the deputation, and sat with it through a preliminary conference. I did not attend the interview with the Baron, but obtained an immediate first-hand report.

Nordau put the deputation's case before the Baron, whose reply was short and simple: 'These are my colonies, and I shall do what I like with them!' In those days Baron Edmond distrusted both the old Zionists and the new. He looked upon Herzl and Nordau as impractical agitators, on us as *schlimihls*. His attitude was a great shock to us; still, we did not break with him. After all, he was buying land in Palestine and settling Jews on it, and that was so much to the good. He was rich, autocratic and misguided, but he was animated by a fine and noble spirit. There was the hope that in time he would change—and this hope was finally vindicated.

In spite of my mandate from the Zionists of Pinsk I failed to attend the first Zionist Congress. I have always regretted it, not because it mattered much in the total, but because it is a gap in the record. That particular year things were not going well at home and I was painfully aware of the call that my education was making on the family resources. It happened that towards the end of my fourth term at Berlin I had made a little discovery in dyestuff chemistry, and my professor, Von Knorre—he was another teacher whom I remember with special gratitude—thought I might be able to sell it. He recommended me to a friend of his, one Ilyinsky, the manager of a dyeing plant in Moscow. The prospect of making some money, and relieving the strain on my father's budget, was a tempting one. But when I returned home for the summer vacation I threw myself into Zionist work, and kept putting off the visit to Moscow; and I did not accept Ilyinsky's invitation until the late summer.

Going to Moscow was not a simple business. I had no right to travel outside the Pale without a special permit, which I could not get. In Moscow I would not be able to register at a hotel; and anyone who put me up privately without reporting me to the police would himself be liable to arrest. So I had to make my arrangements carefully in advance. I found it necessary to stay in Moscow two days. The first night I slept at Ilyinsky's place, the second at Naiditch's. Naiditch had left Pinsk, and was already established as a successful merchant in Moscow, though he still continued, rather furtively, to contribute poetry to the Hebrew journals. I did not sell my chemical discovery; but for other reasons my stay in Moscow was a rather hateful experience. I loathed the necessity of dodging the police, and my loathing was transferred to the place. I did not see Moscow—I only caught a glimpse of the Kremlin from a distance; and I fled as soon as my business was transacted. Years later I sold the formula to a firm in Paris, while I was on a visit to the Zionist students of the Sorbonne. I remember that it brought me about six thousand francs, an enormous sum for me in those days.

The extra day's stay in Moscow made me late for the Congress. But I rushed from Moscow to Brest Litovsk, where my father was waiting for me. He had brought with him my renewed foreign passport—and ten roubles. That was all he could give me towards the expenses of my trip to Basle. I could have managed somehow, but I could not take the money from him. My lateness for the Congress, my disappointment in Moscow, and my father's financial condition, all took the heart out of me. I had the doleful satisfaction of learning, when I returned to Berlin in the autumn, that I had been missed at the Congress. Delegates from the communities I had visited and students from various universities had asked after me. My work in the movement was beginning to be known.

However, as I have already said, I did attend the second Zionist Congress, in Basle, a year later. My part in the deliberations was quite insignificant, but I followed the proceedings with profound respect—though I did not fail to make some mental reservations as to some of the methods and part of the machinery of the Congress. It was for me a time of undiluted joy and spiritual happiness; in these surroundings I felt at home, I felt welcome, and I felt myself to be needed. The people were congenial, and many of the older delegates were already experienced veterans in the movement. The inspiration generated at the Congress served as a powerful impetus to our work. We carried the message back to every corner of our vast ghetto, bringing a little light into the drab life of the Jewish communities.

The Zionist Congresses, at first annual and then biennial, became the tribune and the focus of the movement. The absorption of the old Zionist movement into the new, the story of the transfer of power, cannot be given here in detail; but it was Herzl's enduring contribution to Zionism to have created one central parliamentary authority for Zionism. Against the just criticisms which must be levelled at his leadership, this cardinal achievement must not be forgotten; and the criticisms cannot be understood except against the background of the world—or rather the worlds—in which I grew up and reached maturity.

If Russian Jewry was the cradle of my Zionism, the Western universities were my finishing schools. The first of these schools was Berlin, with its Russian-Jewish society; the second was Berne, the third Geneva, both in Switzerland. The second and third may be lumped together; and they differed radically from the first.

I finished my third year in Berlin; for the fourth—in 1898— I went to Freiburg to take my doctorate. My favourite professor, Bistrzcyki, a distinguished German chemist, of Polish origin, had moved from Berlin to Freiburg, and I followed him. There were very few Jewish students at Freiburg; but in the neighbouring university town of Berne—three-quarters of an hour away —there was a very large Russian-Jewish student colony, and here conditions were not at all like those which I had left behind me. Switzerland—and this meant chiefly Berne and Geneva—was, at the turn of the century, the crossroads of Europe's revolutionary forces. Lenin and Plekhanov made it their centre. Trotsky, who was some years younger than I, was often there. The Jewish students were swayed—it might be better to say overawed—by the intellectual and moral authority of the older revolutionaries, with whose names was already associated the glamour of Siberian records. Against them the tiny handful of Zionist students could make no headway, having no authority of comparable standing to oppose them.

Actually the fight was not of our choosing; it was thrust upon us. Our sympathies were with the revolutionaries; they, however, would not tolerate in the Jewish youth any expression of separate attachment to the Jewish people, or even special awareness of the Jewish problem. Yet the Jewish youth was not essentially assimilationist; its bonds with its people were genuine and strong; it was only by doing violence to their inclinations and upbringing that these young men and women had turned their backs, at the bidding of the revolutionary leaders, on the peculiar bitterness of the Jewish lot. My resentment of Lenin and Plekhanov and the arrogant Trotsky was provoked by the contempt with which they treated any Jew who was moved by the fate of his people and animated by a love of its history and its tradition. *They* could not understand why a Russian Jew should want to be anything but a Russian. *They* stamped as unworthy, as intellectually backward, as chauvinistic and immoral, the desire of any Jew to occupy himself with the sufferings and destiny of Jewry. A man like Chaim Zhitlovsky, who was both a revolutionary and a Jewish nationalist, was looked upon with extreme suspicion. And when the Bund was created—the Jewish branch of the revolutionary movement, national as well as revolutionary in character— Plekhanov sneered that a Bundist was a Zionist who was afraid of sea-sickness. Thus the mass of Russian-Jewish students in Switzerland had been bullied into an artificial denial of their own personality; and they did not recover a sense of balance until the authority of the 'old men' was boldly challenged and in part overthrown by the dissidents—that is, by us.

There were seven of us at first, including myself. Of the others I remember Chaim Chisin, S. Rappaport, Abram Lichtenstein, Nachman Syrkin and Zvi Aberson. Chisin and Rappaport were older men. The first had already lived in Palestine, and had come to Switzerland to learn medicine and return to Palestine. Rappaport, famous under the name of Ansky as the author of *The Dybbuk*, was not a Zionist, but he rather resented the overbearing attitude of the 'master people,' the Russians, towards Jewish nationalism. Lichtenstein, who later married my sister, and went with her to Palestine, was of my age. Of Nachman Syrkin I have already spoken; he came to us from the Berlin group; and of Aberson I shall speak further on.

These were the Zionists who issued their challenge to the dominant group; and it looked like a very uneven contest. We held our first organizational meeting in the back-room of the

Russian colony library; and we held it standing, for 'the others' had got wind of our projected meeting and had removed the furniture. But we founded, on our feet, a Zionist society, the first in Switzerland, under the name of *Ha-Schachar*, the Dawn; and we resolved to carry the fight into the open.

The mere proclamation of our existence created a scandal. The 'reactionary bourgeoisie' was on the march! The colony was in a turmoil, and attempts were made to browbeat us into submission. We refused to be browbeaten. Instead, we called a mass meeting of the Jewish student body for the purpose of increasing our membership, and the notices proclaimed that I was to read a paper and submit a resolution in favour of the Zionist programme.

I cannot help saying that this step called for a certain degree of moral courage. Lenin was not the world figure which he became later; but he already had a name. Plekhanov, an older man, was widely known. We on the other hand were nobodies. So if the founding of *Ha-Schachar* was a scandal, this step was revolution. The other side mobilized all its forces; we, for our part, invited down from Berlin two gifted young Zionist speakers, Berthold Feivel and Martin Buber. The meeting, which was held in a *Bierhalle*, expanded into a sort of congress, and lasted three nights and two days! It was before the dawn of the third day, at four o'clock, that the resolution was put to a vote, and we scored a tremendous triumph. A hundred and eighty students enrolled in the Zionist Society—a striking revelation of the true inclinations and convictions of a large part of the Jewish student body.

This was the first real breach in the ranks of the assimilatory revolutionists in Switzerland. I recall that Plekhanov was particularly outraged by our success. He came up to me after the close of the meeting and asked me furiously: 'What do you mean by bringing discord into our ranks?' I answered: 'But Monsieur Plekhanov, you are not the Czar!' There was already, in those days, something significant in the autocratic spiritual attitude of the revolutionaries.

Seen from this distance, and across a turbulent period of human history, that incident in a Swiss university may seem to be rather unimportant. It had, however, serious repercussions in our young world. The shock of the Berne rebellion was felt throughout the student body of the West, and Zionism was strengthened at a dozen different points. The struggle was on for the possession of the soul of that generation of young Russian Jews in the West. It must not be forgotten that of the thousands who were then preparing for a career in the West, a large proportion returned to Russia. The students who had been won for Zionism became influential cells in their home towns. I found them there later, carriers of the movement in the Jewish communities.

Of our battle against the dissolution of young Jewry in the Russian Revolution I shall speak again; but enough has been told here to indicate one set of reasons for the opposition to Herzl which took shape in the Democratic Faction at the early Zionist Congresses. We were not revolutionaries; but it would have been even more inaccurate to call us reactionaries. We were a struggling group of young academicians, without power, and without outside support; but we had a definite outlook. We did not like the note of elegance and pseudo-worldliness which characterized official Zionism, the dress suits and frock coats and fashionable dresses. On me the formalism of the Zionist Congresses made a painful impression, especially after one of my periodic visits to the wretched and oppressed Russian-Jewish masses. Actually it was all very modest, but to us it smacked of artificiality, extravagance and the *haut monde*; it did not bespeak for us the democracy, simplicity and earnestness of the movement; and we were uncomfortable.

Had we been other than we were, we could not have appealed to the student youth, which was later to constitute the leadership of the Zionist movement. Herzl had no access to it; he did not speak its language, just as, both figuratively and literally, he did not speak the language of the Russian-Jewish masses. If the Zionist movement became a factor in the great student colonies of the West, if it ceased to be a romantic 'sport' and compelled the serious attention of its opponents, it was because the young protagonists of the idea had found their way to the hearts of the Russian-Jewish student youth.

There were other, related reasons for our opposition. Herzl's pursuit of great men, of princes and rulers, who were to 'give' us Palestine, was the pursuit of a mirage. It was accompanied, most unfortunately, but perhaps inevitably, by a shift of the leadership to the right. Herzl played to the rich and powerful, to Jewish bankers and financiers, to the Grand Duke of Baden, to Kaiser Wilhelm II and to the Sultan of Turkey; later to the British Foreign Secretary. We, on the other hand, had little faith in the benevolence of the mighty. It was inevitable that the leadership should feel uneasy about the Democratic Faction, and about the left-wing section of the movement, the *Poale Zion*, which formed parallel with the right wing, the *Mizrachi*, or orthodox group. Official Zionism, as represented by the thoroughly respectable leadership, might have won the tolerance of the Russian authorities. Not so the young men, with their definitely leftist leanings. We began to represent a 'danger' to the movement. We were the 'subversives.'

A third set of reasons came into play. Herzl, as we have seen, relied on diplomatic activity to get Palestine for the Jews. At the first Congresses, Herzl's political statements, though always vague, did have a certain freshening and exhilarating effect. It seemed to us for a time that we had been romantics and dreamers, but that our visions had been little ones. Herzl spoke in large terms, of international recognition, of a charter for Palestine, of a vast mass migration. But the effect wore off as the years passed and nothing remained but the phrases. Herzl had seen the Sultan. He had seen the Kaiser. He had seen the British Foreign Secretary. He was about to see this or that important man. And the practical effect was nothing. We could not help becoming sceptical about these nebulous negotiations.

Side by side with the revolt of the Democratic Faction there was a more general revolt on the part of the Russian Zionists against the Western conception of Zionism, which we felt to be lacking in Jewishness, in warmth and in understanding of the Jewish masses. Herzl did not know Russian Jewry; neither did the Westerners who joined him—Max Nordau, Alexander Marmorek, the distinguished physician, Leopold Greenberg, the editor of the London *Jewish Chronicle*, and others. Herzl was quick to learn—not so the others. They did not believe that Russian Jewry was capable of furnishing leaders to the movement. Herzl, however, wrote, immediately after the first Congress:

And then . . . there rose before our eyes a Russian Jewry the strength of which we had not even suspected. Seventy of our

c*

delegates came from Russia, and it was patent to all of us that they represented the views and sentiments of the five million Jews or that country. And what a humiliation for us, who had taken our superiority for granted! All these professors, doctors, lawyers, industrialists, engineers and merchants stand on an educational level which is certainly no lower than ours. Nearly all of them are masters of two or three languages, and that they are men of ability in their particular lines is proved by the simple fact that they have succeeded in a land where success is peculiarly difficult for the Jews.

But Herzl discovered more. Of the Russian Jews, he said:

They possess that inner unity which has disappeared from among the westerners. They are steeped in Jewish national sentiment, though without betraying any national narrowness and intolerance. They are not tortured by the idea of assimilation, their essential being is simple and unshattered. They do not assimilate into other nations, but they exert themselves to learn the best that there is in other peoples. In this wise they manage to remain erect and genuine. And yet they are ghetto Jews! The only ghetto Jews of our time! Looking on them, we understood where our forefathers got the strength to endure through the bitterest times.

Yet, with all this intuitive perception, this generosity of understanding, Herzl could not remake his own approach to Zionism. How much less possible was this for the smaller men who surrounded him! The Zionism of the Westerners was to us a mechanical and so to speak sociological concept, based on an abstract idea, without roots in the traditions and emotions of the Jewish people. Excluded as we were from the leadership of the movement, we were expected to regard ourselves merely as its beneficiaries, and not, as we felt ourselves to be, the true source of its strength. We, the unhappy Jews of Russia, were to be sent to Palestine by them, the emancipated Westerners. And if Palestine was not available, well—some other territory would have to be found.

We were vindicated in our attitude towards the Western leaders when, at a crucial moment in Zionist history—following the Kishinev pogrom—Herzl attempted to substitute Uganda for Palestine, as a temporary palliative measure, he urged, failing to perceive that, with all their sufferings, the Jews of Russia were incapable of transferring their dreams and longings from the land of their forefathers to any other territory. It was thus made manifest that Palestine had, in fact, never been 'available' to the Western leadership. It had been a mirage, and when the mirage faded, Uganda—which as a matter of fact was even more of a mirage—was proposed in its place. The fact that the heart of Jewry was fixed, by every bond of affection and tradition, on Palestine, seemed beyond the understanding of the Westerners. The enormous *practical* significance of this fixation, its unique and quite irreplaceable power to awaken the energies of the Jewish people, escaped them.

We liked and admired Herzl, and knew that he was a force in Israel. But we opposed him within the movement because we felt that the Jewish masses needed something more than high diplomatic representatives, that it was not good enough to have two or three men travelling about interviewing the great of the world on our behalf. We were the spokesmen of the Russian-Jewish masses who sought in Zionism self-expression and not merely rescue. We must follow the example of the *Bilu* though on a far larger scale; this alone would encourage our youth, would release the forces latent in our people, would create real values. To Herzl all this was rather alien at first. But now that I have come to know and understand the Viennese milieu in which he grew up—so remote from all the troubles and vicissitudes of our life—and especially when I compare him with other Jewish Viennese intellectuals, of his time or a little later (Schnitzler, Von Hofmannsthal, Stefan Zweig—all men of talent), I am amazed at Herzl's greatness, at the profundity of his intuition, which enabled him to understand as much of our world as he did. He was the first—without a rival—among the Western leaders, but even he could not break the mould of his life. Within the limitations of that mould, and with his magnificent gifts and his complete devotion, he rendered incalculable service to the cause. He remains the classical figure in Zionism.

CHAPTER V

GENEVA YEARS

I Graduate, Begin to Teach and Sell my First Patent—Tug of War between Chemistry and Zionism—Crisis in East European Jewry and in Zionism—The Fourth Zionist Congress—Zionist Figures—Menachem Mendel Ussishkin—Yechiel Tschlenow—Lee Motzkin—Shmarya Levin—Vladimir Jabotinsky—Martin Buber—Berthold Feivel—Ansky—Zvi Aberson, the Luftmensch—The Spiritual Dilemma of the Zionist Youth—The Birth of the Idea of the Hebrew University—I meet my Future Wife—Vera Chatzman and Her Circle—A Glimpse into the Future

THE deep division of my life, or perhaps I should say its organic duality, manifested itself completely in the four years I spent in Geneva. Already in Berlin I had been aware of the double pull, towards science on the one hand, towards a public life in the Zionist movement on the other. There I had maintained the balance between the two forces; I still maintained it in Freiburg, while I was taking my doctorate. In Geneva the balance was disturbed, my scientific work suffered. Later on I emphasized my chemistry again, for a short period; and then again, in much later years, I abandoned it wholly for long periods.

My doctorate thesis was based on the dyestuff researches I had started in Berlin, and on the discovery which I had tried unsuccessfully to sell in Moscow. I managed to obtain with my doctorate the coveted top rating of *summa cum laude*, and the autumn following my graduation I was appointed *Privat Dozent* in chemistry at the University of Geneva. The nearest equivalent to this post in an English university is that of assistant lecturer. There is one important difference. The *Privat Dozent* received no fixed salary. He was paid by the pupil, at about fifty marks per term. The average enrolment gave the *Privat Dozent* something less than a very modest livelihood. But of course the title carried with it a certain distinction. It was the beginning of an academic career. It afforded opportunity for study and research. The next step was an assistant professorship, and after that came a full professorship. So, with all its poor pay, the post of *Privat Dozent* was much coveted.

I do not know how long I would have been able to retain the lectureship if it had not been for a great stroke of luck almost at the beginning. I was able to sell a patent to the *I. G. Farben-industrie* of Germany, and this provided me at once with a regular income of six hundred marks a month. That was a tremendous experience for me. I had become independent! What was more, I had achieved independence by my own efforts, and in my own field as chemist.

As to the actual contact with that gigantic enterprise, the *I. G. Farbenindustrie*, I paid little attention to it. Hardly anyone thought of it then as the focus of German military might and of German dreams of world conquest. But it gives me a queer feeling to remember that I too, like many another innocent foreign chemist, contributed my little to the power of that sinister instrument of German ambition. A little later I sold my earlier discovery to a Paris firm, and this windfall enabled me to repay my father some of the outlay on my education. I was quite startled by my initial success. I saw myself set up for life. I saw myself freed from all financial worries, and able to devote myself to my favourite pursuits. Actually, my income from the patent lasted four years, and then declined to zero. And the temporary liberation from the economic struggle was in the long run not as beneficial as it might have been. For though I continued in my scientific work, it was not with the concentration that I should have given it. I could have done a great deal more if I had not devoted by far the larger part of my time to Zionist activities.

It is easy to say that from the personal point of view this was a serious mistake; but I do not know if that is the right word for it. The tug-of-war between my scientific inclinations and my absorption in the Zionist movement has lasted throughout my life. There has never been a time when I could feel justified in withdrawing, except temporarily—and even then in a sort of strategic retreat only—from the Jewish political field. Always it seemed that there was a crisis, and always my conscience forbade me to devote more than a part of my time—usually the smaller—to my personal ambitions. The story of my life will show how, in the end, my scientific labours and my Zionist interests ultimately coalesced, and became supplementary aspects of a single purpose. It was not yet so in Geneva; at least, it did not seem to be so, and during the 1900 to 1904 period I suffered much because of the seeming division of my impulses.

It was not only a time of crisis in Jewry; it was also—and this continued for years—a time of crisis in the Zionist movement. I shall have a great deal to say about the evolution of the organization, about the internal stresses, about the false starts. Here I want to mention one of the Zionist Congresses—the fourth—that of 1900, held in London. Herzl had chosen London, rather than the Continent, for purposes of demonstration. He was interested more in the impression he might produce on English publicists and statesmen than in the internal strength of the movement. The speeches, or set platform pieces, were very fine indeed, and Nordau acquitted himself with the usual *eclat*. But the effect was spoiled by something beyond Herzl's, or anyone else's, control. At that time a great migration of Jews—practically an expulsion—had been set in motion by the Rumanian Government; and thousands of the wanderers were stranded in London. *They* staged a demonstration, at the doors of the Congress, which effectively undid any impression of strength that Herzl sought to produce. At one moment the delegates, who were assembled for the founding of a Jewish State, had to listen to a heart-rending appeal from Nordau for an impromptu collection on behalf of the migrants beleaguering the Congress. We all gave something, of course; but the contrast between the grandiose talk of a Jewish State and the pitiful eleemosynary gesture for the stranded wanderers was utterly disheartening. Moreover, in sheer honesty, I was forced to challenge the official report on the growth of the Zionist movement in Russia and to show, by cold analysis, that our progress was nothing like what the report would have it appear. I was forced to state, also, that the striving after external effect was leading to neglect of internal construction.

An incident of a personal nature added, for me, to the depressing effect of that Congress. One of my uncles, Berel, a sweet, gentle soul, was on his way to America, to join his children. There was no room for him in Russia. Once he had made a living in the villages, contracting for the delivery of hay and other fodder. Since the ukase driving the Jews from the villages, he had been lost. His children had established themselves in America—he was following them. I set out for the London Congress direct from Pinsk, and since I was in the eyes of my family a world traveller, I took uncle Berel with me as far as London, where he was to catch the boat. As I myself knew nothing about London, and spoke no English, it was a case of the halt leading the blind. However, I managed to get him down to the docks, and proceeded to the sessions. A few hours later he turned up at the hall, in tears. The poor man had lost his prayer-shawl and phylacteries and his small store of *kosher* food. He could not cross the Atlantic without them! I went with him to Victoria Station, the point of our arrival in London, and spent half a day looking for the basket with the precious comestibles and the appurtenances of Jewish orthodox prayer. We managed to get back to the boat in time, but those wretched few hours impressed me profoundly with the misery of the wanderers and the futility of the Congress.

I should mention, in connection with the history of our movement, that the London Congress was actually of some historic importance; but not as a demonstration. It was there that the Jewish National Fund, for the purchase of land in Palestine as the inalienable property of the Jewish people, was founded; founded in a very small way indeed, and as it were incidentally. It was destined to become one of our most important instruments in the building of the homeland, but its birth was obscure, and the attention paid to it was completely overshadowed by big talk of charters and international negotiations.

I went back to Geneva depressed, and more committed than ever to Zionist work. Geneva, too, was not exactly the place for withdrawal from the world's problems. The restlessness of Europe came to sharpest expression in the city of political refuge. At the Café Landolt, for example, expatriate students of many nationalities, either minorities suffering under foreign rule, or majorities suffering under native tyrannies, assembled daily and talked far into the night at their separate tables. The Zionists, too, the representatives of the classic oppressed minority, had their *Stammtisch*. Zionism was not yet a force, but it was no longer the queer, hole-in-the-corner movement it had been two or three years before. We were at least on the agenda of the political discussions.

The pressure towards participation in public life did not proceed entirely from the negative forces I have mentioned. I was attracted to it by the presence of the many strong personalities in the Zionist movement. I do not mean the 'great names'; I mean, much more, intrinsically interesting men and women who, giving themselves up as they did to political issues, would have made my abstention all the more difficult. Not all of them have left their impress in the history of Zionism, but I remember them for their individuality and attractiveness.

In the front rank of those whom the movement will remember stood Menachem Mendel Ussishkin, the practical leader of Russian Zionism, as Achad Ha-am was its spiritual leader. He was a powerful personality, eloquent, clear, logical and businesslike. He had exceptional executive ability, and carried on persistently and ably under difficult circumstances—among which was the illegality of the movement in Russia. He created Zionist cells in every important Jewish centre in his 'district' and was able to attract and inspire men of ability and character. Although he was a typical *Choveve Zion*, having been a member of Achad Ha-am's training group, the *Bnai Moshe*, and although he understood the shortcomings of Herzl's approach to the movement, he remained loyal to the latter as the central figure and mainstay of the Zionist Organization. It was only when Herzl brought up the Uganda proposal that his loyalty was stretched beyond the breaking point, and he prepared to lead a revolt against the leadership.

Ussishkin was a man of great energy, vast obstinacy and solid common sense. Perhaps his common sense was a little too solid. He had in him a strain of the autocrat, and was rather intolerant of younger people. Of the two academic centres of Zionism in the West, Berlin and Geneva, headed by Motzkin and myself respectively, he thought little; he called them 'the hot-air factories.'

Conservative by nature, he disagreed with Herzl's grand diplomatic manœuvres, but believed that we would get much further by haggling with the Turks direct. In his bearing Ussishkin suggested a mixture of a Turkish pasha and a Russian governor-general. But all his faults were outweighed by his sterling devotion to the cause. Nothing mattered to him but Zionism. He had the virtue of his defects, being utterly inflexible in his honesty and straightforwardness. His life harmonized with his character; so did his appearance. His skull was round and massive; you felt that he could break through a brick wall with it. His life was successful, clean, single-tracked, and in the finest Jewish tradition. He had the advantage of economic security—though that perhaps gives all the more point to his self-dedication to Zionism. His house was that of a Jewish patriarchal family. There was a joke current about Ussishkin, that whenever his wife was expecting a child, he would bang the table and say sternly: 'A boy! It's got to be a boy!' In this matter he had his way half the time, for his wife gave birth to one son and one daughter.

I got on well with Ussishkin, respecting his defects not less than his virtues. His egotism was impressive. He made people feel that they owed it to him to obey his orders. He was solid, bourgeois, even Philistine—and utterly dependable. Much was forgiven him because of his genuineness.

The first flaw in our relations appeared only in later years when he came to England during the First World War. He had had a bad time of it. Driven from Odessa, he had taken refuge in Istanbul. Thence he made his way circuitously to London, where he arrived in 1918. Somehow he managed to save part of his money from the Revolution. His Zionism was as deep-rooted as ever. This was after the Balfour Declaration, and Ussishkin arrived in London with the notion that a Jewish government was about to be established in Palestine. He had already drawn up a list of the cabinet members. When I explained to him that we were very far indeed from the necessity of setting up a Jewish cabinet in Palestine, he was deeply disappointed.

Intelligent and practical though he was, he sometimes betrayed these streaks of disconcerting naïveté. He was not only disappointed that we were not yet ready to form a Jewish cabinet for Palestine, but rather puzzled by the fact that the Allies should have won the war. He had been convinced that Germany was going to be the victor, for, like a great many Russians, non-Jewish as well as Jewish, he had been tremendously impressed by the German mind and by German achievement. For him Germany was the epitome of Western civilization. He had not known, till he came to England, of a West beyond the Spree. And when he did get to know England it was under circumstances inauspicious for himself. In the old ' a ys—that is, before the World War and the Russian Revolution—he had lived in Odessa, and from that city he had directed the affairs of the southern Zionist district. From that same vantage-point he had looked southward across the Black Sea towards Palestine, then in the hands of the barbarian Turk; and he had felt himself to be, by comparison, the European, the Westerner. But when England took Palestine it was he who was reduced to the status of barbarian, and it was as such, obscure, unheralded, that he arrived in London, and in a country whose ways and methods were strange to him. Besides, he had known me as a youngster at the first Congresses, and here I was, ensconced in the British capital, a 'native.' At times, when he was dealing in futures, he would give himself away with an innocent remark like: 'You know, *you* ought to stay in Europe, *I* will conduct Palestine's affairs.' It was a bit uncomfortable, but he was too much the Zionist, too deeply involved in the movement, to command anything but respect.

Not cast in the same large mould, but still of considerable stature, was Yechiel Tschlenow, another of the Russian leaders at the early Congresses. He too was under the influence of Achad Ha-am, and had belonged to the *Bnai Moshe* organization—Achad Ha-am's training school of Zionists. By profession he was a physician, and ranked high in his profession. There was something of the Russian about Tschlenow; he was slow, ponderous, excessively earnest, faithful and persistent. Like Ussishkin he was thrown out of his accustomed orbit by the Russian Revolution; but unlike Ussishkin he did not live long enough to remould his life in the Jewish homeland. He died towards the end of the First World War.

I have already spoken of the sacrifice, both in personal prospects and effectiveness of service, which was entailed by premature absorption in public life and consequent neglect of proper training. An outstanding instance was Leo Motzkin, a fellow-founder, with me, of the Zionist Democratic Faction. Motzkin was a gifted mathematician, whose abilities had attracted the attention of Professor Mandelstamm, of Kiev. Motzkin was sent to Berlin by the older man, who expected him to make a brilliant academic career. Nothing like that happened. Motzkin was an ardent Zionist, but with no sense of proportion in the distribution of his energies. He could have rendered much greater service to the movement in the long run if he had not let his public activity eat into his education. He became, almost from the first day, a *Vereins-Meier*, frittering away his days and nights in innumerable little student gatherings, and taking with tremendous seriousness every minor incident in student political life.

It is impossible to say how far Motzkin would have gone if he had given his great gift half a chance; but that he was a man of high ability was always clear. He became what we used to call a '*Privat-Gelehrter*,' a man who was muddling through his education in private. It hurt him in his Zionist work, for he never achieved complete independence. He was too fine a person to join the group of 'courtiers' who made a bodyguard around Herzl. He was in the opposition. But Herzl recognized Motzkin's qualities, and tried to win him over. He sent him, between the first and second Congresses, to Palestine, and at the second Congress Motzkin delivered an excellent report on the state of the colonies. It placed him under a certain obligation to Herzl; and though he remained part of His Majesty's Opposition, there was a little too much emphasis on 'Majesty's,' not enough on 'Opposition.'

The first place among the propagandists and leaders was occupied—practically without a rival—by Shmarya Levin, who in later years educated an American generation of Jews in Zionism. I had not met him in Berlin, where he had been a prominent member of the *Jüdisch-Russisch Wissenschaftliches Verein*, for he had already left for Koenigsberg. I met him at the early Congresses, beginning with the second or third. He was an extraordinarily gifted orator, of the intellectual rather than the emotional type. His speeches coruscated with brilliant phrases, Biblical and Talmudic quotations and penetrating analyses. Primarily a teacher rather than a politician, he was a man of the lobbies and of coteries, and took small part in the proceedings of the Congresses. Usually he would be seen in the midst of a group of cronies, whom he was entertaining with his biting characterizations of his opponents. If he was told: 'Dr. Levin, a vote is being taken, you are wanted in the Plenum,' he would answer, 'Wait, I must finish this game of chess.'

Chess was an obsession with him: a ruination, almost, according to his own account in his remarkable three-volume autobiography. He had no patience for detailed political action. Besides, he was, despite his savage wit, utterly innocent in worldly matters, and this was his charm. Outspoken, spontaneous, he made friends and enemies as he went along, without an eye either to personal consequences or the practical results for the movement. Nevertheless, on important issues he was instinctively in the right, and effectively so. In this he was like the great sailors of the Middle Ages who knew no navigational science, but by a combination of instinct and experience evaded the dangers of the sea.

He was both teacher and artist, with the skill of the first and the temperamental quirks of the second. I could always provoke him into a rage by asking, innocently: 'Shmarya, are you making a speech tonight?' He would answer hotly: 'I don't make speeches. I give lectures.' The word *Vortrag* has weight and importance: Shmarya was a lecturer, not just a speaker. But he was quite justified in making the distinction. Another trait of his which I remember well was his aversion to having in his audience anyone to whom he had already expounded the idea contained in his lecture. If I happened to be in town when he was lecturing, and threatened to come to hear him, he would offer me twenty marks to stay away.

Some of his retorts have become classics in the movement. On one of his visits to America. Shmarya had to listen, at a committee meeting, to a little speech by the anti-Zionist American Jewish philanthropist Jacob Schiff, in which the latter observed pompously, and in a heavy German accent: 'I am divided into three parts; I am an American, I am a German, and I am a Jew.' Shmarya rose immediately afterwards and wanted to know how Mr. Schiff divided himself; was it horizontally or vertically? And if horizontally, exactly which part had he left for the Jewish people? On the occasion of the language struggle around our technical school in Haifa, Shmarya carried on a bitter fight against Paul Nathan, the director of the German *Hilfsverein* (the Jewish philanthropic organization), also an anti-Zionist and a two hundred per cent German patriot, who demanded that the language of tuition in our new institute in Palestine should be German, while *we* would hear of nothing but Hebrew. Shmarya made deadly use of the parable with which the Prophet Nathan struck down the guilty King David for his crime against Uriah the Hittite. For Germany, said Shmarya, had all the schools and universities she could use, and the Jews of Palestine had but their one *Technikum*, the poor man's little ewe lamb, like Uriah's one possession, Bathsheba, whom David coveted. And rich Germany was prepared to rob poor Palestine of its sole possession. But this time it was *Nathan* who was on the side of the robber instead, as of old, on the side of the robbed.

The best of his speeches—or lectures—were filled with similar ingenious applications of Bible themes to contemporaneous problems. Shmarya was often called the great *Maggid*, or preacher, but he was more. He was gifted as a writer, too, as he showed in his occasional articles, and made evident beyond a doubt in his masterly autobiography. He was a good scholar, and wrote excellent Hebrew as well as Yiddish. Achad Ha-am properly criticized him for his lack of application. His great handicap was his natural ability, which encouraged him in habits of indolence. It was too easy for him to rise to the occasion unprepared.

An older generation of American Jews remembers Shmarya as the great teacher and dazzling personality. I remember him as the sterling collaborator and warm-hearted friend. We made many trips to America together, so that he and America were inextricably bound up in my mind. When, after his death, I had to visit that country alone, I felt orphaned.

One more 'youngster' of those days I must mention, the youngest of us all, Vladimir Jabotinsky. My contacts with him at the early Congresses were few and fleeting, but his part in the movement, and therefore in my life, assumed considerable proportions in later years. He came to us from Odessa as the boy wonder. In his early twenties he had already achieved a wide reputation as a Russian journalist, writing under the name of Altalina, and had attracted the attention of men like Maxim Gorki and the aged Leo Tolstoy. He, too, was a gifted orator, and became master of some half-dozen languages. But he is remembered as one of the founders of the Jewish Legion in the First World War, and as the founder of the Revisionist party, and of the so-called New Zionist Organization.

His speeches at the early Congresses were provocative in tone but left no very distinct impression, so that one did not know, for instance, whether he was for Uganda or against, whether he condoned Herzl's visit to Von Plehve, Russia's bitterly anti-Semitic Minister of the Interior, or condemned it. Some of this indistinctness or confusion may have been the effect of a certain exterior contradiction; for Jabotinsky, the passionate Zionist, was utterly un-Jewish in manner, approach and deportment. He came from Odessa, Achad Ha-am's home town, but the inner life of Jewry had left no trace on him. When I became intimate with him in later years, I observed at closer hand what seemed to be a confirmation of this dual streak; he was rather ugly, immensely attractive, well spoken, warm-hearted, generous, always ready to help a comrade in distress; all of these qualities were, however, overlaid by a certain touch of the rather theatrically chivalresque, a certain queer and irrelevant knightliness, which was not at all Jewish. I have mentioned that he came from Achad Ha-am's town because he was the antithesis of Achad Ha-am. The latter was pessimistic and supersensitive, always preaching limitation. Whatever you got was, in his eyes, much—or at any rate, big enough. Jabotinsky ran to the other extreme, and disliked Achad Ha-am who, as a person, did not fit into his scheme of things. Nordau was much nearer to the spirit of Jabotinsky; it was Nordau's plans and slogans that Jabotinsky adopted many years afterwards when he fought me in the Congress and, failing to win the Congress, left the Zionist Organization and, like Zangwill, founded his own. It was natural for Jabotinsky to think that Achad Ha-am had had an injurious influence on me, and was responsible for what the Revisionists called my 'minimal Zionism.'

Martin Buber and Berthold Feivel, inseparable friends, were of the Geneva colony for a time. Martin Buber is now a professor at the Hebrew University in Jerusalem; fifty years ago he was a young æsthete, the son of a rich father, a rather odd and exotic figure in our midst. In spite of his handsome allowance from home, he was usually in debt; for he was a connoisseur of the arts and a collector of expensive items. We were good friends, though I was often irritated by his stilted talk, which was full of forced expressions and elaborate similes, without, it seemed to me, much clarity or great beauty. My own inclinations were towards simplicity, and what I admired most was the ability to reduce a statement to its essential elements. Buber was only beginning to develop the incomparable German style which, many years later, produced his remarkable translation of the Bible. Berthold Feivel, his friend, who died in Palestine a few years ago, was also a writer, but natural, simple, sensitive and realistic. In his case particularly the style was the man; for Feivel rendered far greater service to Zionism than his more colourful friend. In a sense, it may be said that Feivel gave to Zionism, losing himself in it, and Buber took from it, using it as his æsthetic material.

Older than most of us, Ansky—author of *The Dybbuk*—was a sort of universal uncle. The Zionists liked him because of his tender Jewish understanding and his Jewish stories, for the telling of which he had a remarkable talent. The revolutionists found in him, despite his disagreements with them, a sympathetic soul. He had no very sharp political views, and was never really identified with any group.

The vast majority of the students in Berne and Geneva were as poor as church mice. Some received a tiny remittance from home, and eked this out with odd jobs, lessons, bookkeeping, translations—anything that came their way. Their survival was an eternal mystery. Queerest among these students was one to whom I became greatly attached, Zvi Aberson, of whom I write in part because our friendship remains a pleasant memory, and in part because he summed up in his person all the aspects of the Jewish spiritual and economic tragedy.

Aberson was the *Luftmensch par excellence*, gifted, rootless, aimless, untrained and well meaning, that type of lost soul which haunted me, filled me with dread for myself, and served as a terrifying example. Four years older than I, he was supposedly—and of course to some extent actually—a student. His field was 'the humanities,' the kind of material—history, philosophy, literature, 'things-in-general'—which one can take up, drop, take up again, vague and attractive subjects to which the bright type of 'eternal student' was usually drawn.

Typical, too, was the manner in which I got to know him. Coming home late one night, I made out a figure lying on the sofa in my living-room. Since friends were in the habit of dropping in and staying the night, I paid no attention to the sleeper. The next morning the unannounced visitor had disappeared. On the second night he was there again, and on the second morning gone again. Later that day I was introduced to Aberson among a group in the Café Landolt. Someone happened to ask him, in my presence, 'Aberson, where have you been these last two nights?' To which he answered, 'Oh, I slept in some Zionist fellow's home,' and I realized that this was my man.

I liked him from the first. Bohemian, homeless, living from hand to mouth, a true *Bettelstudent* or beggar student, and ugly as a monkey, he was a wonderful companion, gay, witty, sometimes however with a touch of mordant bitterness—a sort of beggar on horseback. Much of the time, I afterwards found out, he was hungry. He had a brilliant mind, but lacked all sense of application. He was hated by the Russian Marxists because he understood their philosophy, had its terminology at his fingertips, met them on their own ground and invariably routed them in argument. They hissed him, but he compelled their attention. The Bundists were terrified of him, and this man, who had so little to eat, was dubbed with unconscious irony, the *Bundistenfresser*, the gobbler-up of Bundists.

A few months after I learned to know him, Aberson, who had been a Bundist, but had never been able to stomach the Marxism of that time, definitely went over to Zionism. At the first conference of our Democratic Faction he delivered an address which became famous in the early history of our party. It was a devastating attack on the position of the Jewish Marxists and the assimilationists. In spite of their equalitarian principles, in spite of their quasi-humanistic attitude towards 'the Jewish problem,' the Jewish Marxists, said Aberson, were 'the usual bullying majority,' intolerant of the hunger for national freedom, the attachment to cultural traditions, which others felt. Liberators of the world, they repressed with ridicule and the weight of numbers those whom they called the minority, but who happened to represent the actual majority of the Jewish people—certainly in Russia; and if they lacked the oppressive instruments of the Czar, they were not less hostile than czarism to the inner demands of minority nationalities. And their doctrinaire brutality was all the more odious because it was turned against their own people.

At that time Aberson's point of view amounted to a tremendous intellectual discovery, for Eduard Bernstein's socialistic defence of minority nationalism was hardly known. It needed courage as well as imagination to apply the term 'oppressors' to the Socialist majority. But Aberson understood the spirit of the revolutionaries from within, grasped its essential spiritual weakness, and exposed it mercilessly.

We were so elated by the brilliance of Aberson's attack on the dominant group that we decided to commission him to develop his thesis and turn it into a book. A wealthy Jew of Baku, Shrirow, happened to be in town, and we persuaded him to back the enterprise. He placed a sum of money at our disposal for Aberson's use, and Aberson went off to Paris, on the generous stipend of fifty francs a week, to pursue his studies in the *Bibliothèque Nationale*. That was the last we heard of him for several months. Then suddenly he turned up in Geneva.

'Well?' we asked.

'I've been to all the museums and all the libraries,' was Aberson's happy answer. But he hadn't written a line.

We saw that the arrangement would not work, or, rather that Aberson would not work with this arrangement. So we changed it. I said: 'Now, you've had your fling. I'll take a room for you over mine, and you'll work here, in Geneva.' I hoped that under my watchful eye he would settle down to his task. The only effect of the new arrangement was that my collars, trousers, shirts and ties began to disappear. Aberson established a sort of commune, to which he contributed nothing—not even his writing. He read much; he accumulated a library of borrowed books, most of them on civic problems; but he never wrote his book. It was in him; he had the ideas, he had worked them into a system, but he could not get them down on paper.

He spent most of his time in the Café Landolt, and was always to be found there between four in the afternoon and midnight, talking, as a rule, to the oppressed nationalities, who came to look on him as their protector. Whenever he caught sight of me he would call me over, hand me his bill, and say: 'You'll have to ransom me.'

This man with the sharp analytical mind and the huge fund of knowledge had fallen, through lack of discipline and consistency, perhaps through hunger and privation, into complete unproductiveness. His daily life was one long fever of activity without purpose; and it was filled with all the dodges of poverty. Going out for a walk with Zvi was a highly complicated business. This street, that house, had to be avoided; he owed two francs here, three francs there, a laundry bill, a tailor's bill. One has to think not only of the energy he expended in evading his creditors, but the ingenuity he displayed in getting fresh credit. Now and again a windfall would enable him to carry out a cleaning-up operation and then the cycle would begin again. Occasionally we went on holiday together, usually during the Easter recess, which was not long enough to permit my return to Pinsk. We would stay at some cottage in a Swiss village, perhaps at the other end of the lake; we cooked our own meals, and we managed on as little as three or four francs a day. But if Zvi went alone, as sometimes happened, I would invariably get a telegram from him at the end of a week or two: CAN'T MOVE: SEND ME TWENTY-FIVE FRANCS.

This was Aberson, the good, quick-witted, warm-hearted, luckless *Bettelstudent*, with the penetrating mind and the silver tongue. In normal circumstances he would have gone far; but the circumstances of his life were distinctly abnormal; and though he was one of the extreme cases, he was illustrative of the dilemma of a whole generation. I, too, was trapped in it; I escaped it to some extent, but the experience left a permanent mark on my life.

I was to discover this in Berlin and Geneva; to confirm it later in England; to recognize it still later as an ineradicable feature of my inheritance. We Russian Jews, particularly those of us who devoted ourselves to the sciences, worked under frightful handicaps. Our primary education in Russia was a poor one. Most of us were poverty—stricken when we came to the Western universities. It so happens that my own personal experience with hunger and overwork—I am speaking of the year in Pfungstadt—was a brief one; even so it affected my health and lowered my vitality. What of those who never escaped from the condition? Much of their time was wasted on sheer drudgery, donkeywork, to eke out their means of subsistence; and all this in the midst of continuous undernourishment.

But this was not all. Our situation was complicated by the acute moral problem to which I referred earlier in this chapter. How could we devote ourselves to careers when conditions in Russia were so bitter? Was it not cowardly and selfish to pursue one's academic work in seeming deafness to the cry of one's people? I saw my closest friends, Leo Motzkin, Berthold Feivel, Shmarya Levin, Nachman Syrkin and others, the best and ablest, neglecting their university work. They plunged early into the Zionist movement, oscillating queerly between two incongruous rôles, that of the important public man and that of the bohemian student. They were not alone. Thousands of able young men and women were studying in Western universities; remarkably few of them ever became anything in science, art and literature. The dissipation of their energies, the drain on their nervous and even physical resources, made it impossible for them to concentrate on their studies. At best they managed to get their college diplomas, that is, their doctorates; and that was the end of it. They made no attempt at postgraduate work.

All this I saw and was part of; and it haunted me. I fought against it, but by no means with complete success. I still find myself under the necessity of filling out lacunæ in my education which should have been attended to forty and fifty years ago. And I look with envy on young colleagues whose scientific education is so much sounder than mine.

Of course there is the other side of the picture. During those years, 1895 to 1904, and particularly during the last four years, we laid the foundations of the Zionist movement among the educated Jewish classes, and inducted the future leadership of Zionism into its tasks. One may ask whether the movement would not have been better off in the long run if we had attended more closely to our personal equipment for the later struggle, whether it was not false economy to invest in the movement too much of our energy too early. Or one may have to recognize that the pressure of those times was bound to be too much for us. What remains true is that we did a great deal of Zionist work during the decade which linked two centuries.

It was in Geneva that we founded the first Zionist publishing house, *Der Jüdische Verlag*, with its periodical, *Der Jude*, which grouped about itself a number of men, some of them already well known, others with their mark still to make, like Feivel and Buber. Yechiel Tschlenow, of Moscow, Jacob Lestschinsky of Geneva, Micha Joseph Berdichevsky, the Hebrew writer, Abram Ittelson, the editor of the *Rassviet* in St. Petersburg, collaborated with us. This was the first cultural literary enterprise within the Zionist movement; it was sponsored and activated by the Democratic Faction, and it was a spontaneous expression of the feeling that the diplomatic activities of the Western Zionist leaders were not enough.

In Geneva, too, the idea of the Hebrew University in Jerusalem was first given form. It was not a new idea. It had already been discussed at the first Congress, in 1897. But we organized public opinion about it. The Hebrew University was also a response to a deep-seated need. The Russian-Jewish youth was being systematically excluded from the Russian schools. We felt the pressure in Germany and Switzerland; and part of the stream of migration was diverted to the south, to Italy. To us in Geneva it seemed logical to seek at least a partial solution for this homelessness of the young Jewish intellectual in a Hebrew University in Palestine. But only part of the impulse flowed from immediate practical considerations. It was also related to the general cultural programme and spiritual awakening which characterized the younger Zionist group and particularly the Russians, who had sat at the feet of Achad Ha-am.

We opened an office for the *Jüdische Hochschule*, or Jewish University, and carried out a referendum among the Jewish students. The revolutionary bodies greeted the proposal with derision. The Zionist youth was for it. But the Western Zionist leaders—Herzl alone excepted—considered the idea Utopian to the point of childishness. For them it was always political Zionism first, and practical work nowhere, until the charter for Palestine was obtained. They went on seeking important international contacts; they discouraged work in Palestine, which they considered premature and dangerous because it would antagonize Turkey and prejudice the chances of the charter. But we went ahead in the face of their opposition.

Yet it should be understood that we fought these problems

out internally, on the floor of the Zionist Congresses. For we always recognized that the Congress had come to stay; we, not less than Herzl, regarded it as the Jewish State in the making, and whatever our differences with the 'head of the State,' we were forever strengthening the 'State' itself, that is, the Zionist Organization and its parliament. It was within the Zionist Organization that the opposition which Motzkin and I headed, the Democratic Faction, sought to strengthen and deepen the spiritual significance of the movement, and to make the Organization the reflection of the forces of national Jewry. It took the Uganda incident—of which more later—to bring about a split, and then it was some of the Westerners, and not we of the East, who actually broke away, to found a separate organization.

In Switzerland, as in Berlin, the Russian-Jewish student body was self-contained and more or less isolated, and always for the same reasons; we could not afford to maintain social contacts; and the right of asylum was based on the tacit but rigid assumption that we foreigners would not take sides in local politics. Even so, we might have become more friendly with the Jewish population than we did. I had been a lecturer in Geneva for nearly three years before I found myself on calling terms with Geneva Jewry, or, to be more exact, with the Rabbi of Geneva and a few other Jewish families. One of these was the Flegenheimers, wealthy and rather kindly people. A son of theirs, Edmond, who shortened his name to Fleg, lived in Paris, where he achieved some standing as a writer. The Rabbi, Wertheimer, who had a chair at the local university, was a sweet, gentle old man.

Perhaps I would never have established even these contacts if it had not been for certain external causes. The great body of Jewish migrants from Russia passed through northern Europe, by way of Bremen and Hamburg, to America, always under the ægis of the German philanthropic organization, the *Hilfsverein der Deutchen Juden*. But a trickle came southward. A few emigrants discovered that any Russian Jew who got to Basle or Geneva would be helped on southward to Milan, and thence to Marseilles, where, one way or another, he might obtain the fare to America. I was already known to many Russian Jews as the leader of the Democratic Faction at the

Zionist Congresses, and the leader of the Zionist movement among the student youth in Switzerland. It was assumed that I had some local influence. So I was visited at regular intervals by recommended 'clients,' for whom I intervened with the Swiss-Jewish community.

A number of Russian Christians who wanted to get to America took advantage of the general confusion, and posed as Jews! One of them I caught red-handed because, in his innocence of the Jewish religion, he overdid his piety. He looked Jewish enough, and sported a very Jewish beard; if his Yiddish was not up to the mark, it was nothing unusual among certain Russian-Jewish communities outside the Pale. This man, whose name I have forgotten, was a wheelwright by trade, and to prove his bona fides he begged me to get him some kind of employment during his stay in Geneva, on the condition, naturally, that he would not have to work on the Sabbath. Rabbi Wertheimer sent me to a pious Calvinist, who, touched by the religious scruples of the emigrant, agreed to employ him on the basis of a five-day week. The Russian must have been chuckling heartily in his non-Jewish beard until one weekday I ran across him on the street and asked him if he had lost his job. To this he replied, quite shocked: 'But don't you know it's the festival of *Purim* today? Do you expect me to work on *Purim*?' To which I, equally shocked, but for a very different reason, said: 'This is the first time I've ever heard of *Purim* as a workless festival.' In the ensuing dispute I became exceedingly suspicious of the religious pretentions of my emigrant friend. A little inquiry uncovered the swindle, much to the disgust of the pietist.

I became acquainted with the Swiss Jews, good-natured, simple, middle-class people, whom I began to win over to the Zionist movement. It was the only Zionist work I did outside of academic circles, except at the Congresses and on my visits home. But by the time I left Switzerland in 1904 there were Zionist societies in Berne, Lausanne and Geneva.

Those were full, exciting years of growth, expansion and development. All in all they were happy years, in spite of the troubles that weighed on us, for it is not in the nature of youth to be unhappy for long stretches at a time, though, to be sure, I could hardly count myself as part of the youth by the time my Geneva period was ended. I left Russia for the West a boy of nineteen; I left Switzerland for England a man of thirty. The ways of my life were set; the instruments of my activities were forged. The Zionist Congresses had refashioned my Zionism on its practical side. I had a clear picture of the forces at work in the Zionist world. I knew the men and women who represented these forces. I was not the unsophisticated boy I had been when I left Pinsk. I was aware of the grimness and difficulty of the task ahead of us.

But Geneva may be said to have completed the pattern of the future because I established there the most important relationship of my life. It was in Geneva, in 1900—forty-seven years ago—that I first met my wife, in the company of a small group of Russian-Jewish girls who had been schoolmates of hers in her native city of Rostov-on-Don. Like so many others of her generation she had come to study medicine in Geneva because the schools of her own country were closed to her. But the small group of young women to which Vera Chatzman belonged differed in a marked way from the general run of Jewish girl-students in the Swiss universities of that time. Their looks, their deportment, their outlook on life, set them apart. They were far more attractive than their contemporaries from the Pale of Settlement; they were less absorbed in Russian revolutionary politics; not that they were indifferent; but they paid more attention to their studies, and less to the public meetings and endless discussions which took up so much of the time of the average Russian student abroad. Vera Chatzman was of a particularly quiet and retiring nature, inclined to be pensive, almost sad—so that she was set apart even among her companions. I used to call her affectionately *princesse lointaine*.

Rostov-on-Don, in southern Russia, is the gateway to the Caucasus; the Jewish community there was small, and though subject to all the disabilities which crippled Jewish life in the Pale, its material condition was on the whole easier. The district was wealthier, competition was less keen, and if a family belonged—as my wife's did—to the class of so-called 'guild merchants,' they enjoyed special privileges—for Jews, that is— and consequently a more comfortable existence. There was, moreover, little contact with the Jewish masses who dwelt chiefly in the south-western provinces of the vast Russian Empire.

All this had its effect on the bearing and manners of the group to which my future wife belonged, so that its members stood out in contrast from the majority of the Russian-Jewish students in Geneva, who for the most part seemed underfed, stunted, nervous and sometimes bitter—an easy prey to revolutionary propagandists. Student public opinion frowned on these girls, who were so different from the rest; but they paid little attention to whatever animosity or envy they aroused, and pursued their studies systematically, without permitting outside interests to deflect them.

Vera and I found our way to each other only slowly, partly because of the difference in our ages—about seven years— and our status; I was a lecturer, she a student—but chiefly because of the difference in our background and our approach to life, both of which meant, to me, Zionism and the Jewish problem. But there was a strong mutual attraction from the start, and as time went on we reached a tacit agreement that we must go through life together. We agreed, too, that we would have to wait for our marriage until Vera had finished her medical studies, and I could see clearly the road ahead of me.

Our first meetings were not very frequent, for we were both absorbed in our work, but as often as we met I would try to arouse her interest in the problems which preoccupied me so deeply. It seemed to me, at first, that she took things much more calmly than I, and in a sense she did, but I discovered in time that this was only on the surface. Much depth of feeling, character and understanding lay hidden beneath the calm surface; and these were qualities which not only attracted me in themselves, but gave me the assurance that I had found in her not only my future wife, but a helpmeet, comrade and support. The extent to which this assurance was justified will become evident throughout this narrative; here I will only say that throughout the vagaries of my rather complicated existence, it was my wife who so organized things as to give me a stable and tolerably safe background; if I have been able to carry on, to give my whole mind to my work, without taking much thought for financial or other practical matters, it has been entirely due to her forethought, her devotion and her savoir faire.

When we first met, my world of Zionist and Jewish affairs was for her more or less of a closed book. Had it not been for her innate sense of justice, and her desire to study things for herself before making up her mind, there might have been an unbridgeable gulf between us. But in her own quiet, studious and unassuming way, she began to absorb knowledge of this side of my life; during our Manchester days, which came soon after, she did a considerable amount of Zionist reading, which was none too easy for her at a time when, besides keeping house and looking after our first son, she worked for her English medical degree, and had to give most of her free time to her lectures and her clinics. Later she accompanied me to all of the Congresses and to Action Committee meetings; she got to know some of my Zionist friends and within a few years she acquired an expert understanding of our affairs.

At the outset I did not ask her whether she felt any sympathy for this world of mine, so new to her. Neither did I take it for granted. I left it to time and her own free decision. I was happy to watch her growing interest, and to see her becoming more and more attracted to the movement. From the first I felt that one day—not far distant—she would come to play a very great part not only in my personal life, but also in the life of the movement.

As the years passed, she accompanied me more and more frequently on the far-flung journeys which my Zionist affairs imposed on me. This not only gave me the privilege and advantage of her company in strange lands: it also gave her the chance of acquiring a shrewd insight into the problems of the movement and the characters of my Zionist friends and co-workers. Often she guarded me from pitfalls which her calm judgment detected before mine did. I was much more venturous, in a sense much more superficial, more happy-go-lucky, than she; so that I think we came to form a strong combination.

On one of my trips to Palestine closely following the First World War, we had to move in haste from a house in Addison Road (we were then living in London), which was being sold over our heads. My wife found another house, in Addison Crescent, but it was not to let, it could only be bought. She asked me, by letter, whether she should make the purchase, and I answered that I was content to be guided by her views in such matters. She acquired, decorated and furnished the house

D

—in her own exquisite taste—during my absence. That house was for thirty years the centre for all who were interested in, or connected with, Zionism and Palestine. Statesmen like Lord Balfour, General Smuts, Lord Cecil, Léon Blum, Mr. Philip Kerr, soldiers like Meinertzhagen, Macdonogh, Wyndham Deedes, T. E. Lawrence, Orde Wingate, Zionists like Bialik, Shmarya Levin, Feivel and Jacobson, American friends and supporters like Felix Warburg, Louis Marshall, Stephen S. Wise, Louis Lipsky, Morris Rothenberg, Ben Cohen and others, Palestinians visiting London, like Ruppin and Arlosoroff—all passed through Addison Crescent and all enjoyed my wife's warm and unobtrusive hospitality. In this home our boys grew up, here they spent their holidays and brought their friends; and here we stayed until the outbreak of the Second World War. By then my elder boy had married, and the younger was already in the R.A.F., so that we found ourselves alone in a house much too big for us. We decided with deep regret to give it up, consoled by the fact that we had by then made ourselves another home in Palestine. Of this I shall tell later, only noting here again that it is my wife's practical sense and exquisite taste which are everywhere in evidence in our Rehovoth home.

All this was in the far-off future when we became engaged in Geneva, shortly before my departure for England.

CHAPTER VI

END OF GENEVA DAYS

The Russian Tyranny—A Tour of the Russian Provinces—A Chief of Police—Nahum Sokolow in Warsaw—The Kishinev Pogrom—The Effect on the Zionist Movement and on Herzl—Herzl Visits Russia, Sees von Plehve—The Sixth Congress and Uganda—The Meaning of the Uganda Incident—Lord Percy and Sir Harry Johnston on the Uganda Offer—Sir Evans Gordon and the Aliens Bill—The El Arish Offer—The Crossroads in my Life

MY youth ended in Geneva; not by the strict count of years, according to which it had ended before, but rather by the division of my life. My last days in Geneva coincided with the great darkening of Jewish life in Russia, with the shock and disappointment of the Uganda incident in Zionism, with the death of Herzl. My youth did not close; it was closed for me. Then came a sort of interregnum, and a rebirth to new effort; but not in Geneva.

Early in 1903 I was hard at work both on chemistry and Zionism. I spent long days, and often whole nights, in the laboratory, engaged on a piece of research which was interesting in itself and which gave promise—a promise to be fulfilled—of new vistas in chemistry. It set the course of my investigations for many years to come, and formed the basis of several contributions to scientific journals. But only half of my energies were given to chemistry, and that half imperfectly; for while my scientific work never intruded on my preoccupation with the Jewish problem, the Jewish problem did pursue me into the laboratory. And it could not be otherwise. The times were tense, and the air was charged with disruptive forces. Russia was moving towards war with Japan, her reactionary rulers urged in that direction by the increasing pressure of social discontent and mounting revolution. The Jews within the Pale were ceasing to bear their sufferings passively. The younger generation was flocking to the ranks of the revolutionaries or else,

though to a smaller extent, to the Zionist movement. The Bund,
the Jewish revolutionary organization, was now a power,
counting its adherents in tens of thousands. The czarist bureaucracy, hostile at best to the Jews, began to retaliate with special
ferocity, and thousands of young Jews were thrown into prison
or sent to Siberia. There was hardly a Jewish family in Russia in
those days which had failed to pay its toll one way or another.

In March 1903, unable to endure any longer the seclusion
of Geneva, I broke off my scientific work, and returned to
Russia for a tour of the Russian-Jewish communities. It was the
longest journey of its kind I had ever undertaken, and, within
Russia, the last. It took me through the Pale and through
many cities of the north, the south and the south-east. The
immediate object of the journey was to spread the idea of the
Hebrew University; the more general object was Zionist
propaganda. I began with university towns like Kiev and
Kharkov—and everywhere I found an encouraging response,
both from nationally conscious students and from the communities at large. In Kiev, Professor Mandelstamm, the noted
oculist and ardent supporter of Herzl, took me to see Mr.
Brodsky, the sugar king of Russia. Mr. Brodsky was opposed to
Zionism, but he was keenly interested in the university project,
and promised us unqualified support. He was not alone in this
attitude. Then, as later, those wealthy Jews who could not
wholly divorce themselves from a feeling of responsibility
towards their people, but at the same time could not identify
themselves with the hopes of the masses, were prepared to
dispense a sort of left-handed generosity, on condition that their
right hand did not know what their left hand was doing. To
them the university-to-be in Jerusalem was philanthropy, which
did not compromise them; to us it was nationalist renaissance.
They would give—with disclaimers; we would accept—with
reservations.

Zionist propaganda in Russia was a ticklish business. It was
admittedly not as dangerous as revolutionary propaganda; but
it was not a straightforward business, either. I recall a diverting
incident which took place in the course of this tour. I went
from Kiev direct to Nikolaiev, a military and naval port on the
Black Sea. It had no importance as a Jewish centre, since Jews
could not settle there, and it contained only a small community,

dating from pre-proscription times. Of course I did not have a permit to visit Nikolaiev, and I went there because I was anxious to see an uncle of mine, a gifted Hebrew educator and a close friend.

I had not intended to do any propaganda work in Nikolaiev, but as I was already in the city the local Zionists could not let the occasion pass. A meeting was called, in the synagogue, naturally. There was no law against prayers. Unfortunately, the heavy attendance attracted the attention of the authorities, and while I was in the middle of my speech the building was surrounded by Cossacks, the police entered and marched off the whole congregation, including of course, the speaker, to the police station. I was brought before the chief of police, who subjected me to a long and searching interrogation. Since it was useless to pretend that we had been praying, I tried to explain what Zionism meant, and what the real object of my visit was. The subject was entirely foreign to the chief of police, who was good-natured, suspicious and very much convinced of his native shrewdness. As an official, he was down on every 'ism,' and Zionism sounded like socialism. He was convinced that we were engaged in subversive activities, dangerous to Russia and the Little Father. I made some headway with him until it occurred to him that we might be collecting money to send out of the country, which was also forbidden by law. Of this, too, I tried to disabuse his mind, and naturally he had no proof of our guilt. Then he asked me:

'Well, how do you finance your undertaking?'

'We have a bank in London,' I answered, meaning the Jewish Colonial Trust. This interested him at once, and he went on to inquire as to the amount of the money available in the bank, its management, organization and so on.

'It's a good idea,' he said, finally, 'to take all the Jews to Palestine. But why do you come to Nikolaiev, where there are so few of them. Why don't you go to Odessa?'

I explained that I was in fact on my way to Odessa, and that I had merely stopped off in Nikolaiev for a visit. Then suddenly, as if he had been keeping the question up his sleeve as a sort of *coup de grâce*, he said:

'How do you know there's any money in that bank of yours?'

'That is simple,' I said. 'They send us regular statements and accounts.'

Thereupon he leaned back in his chair and laughed uproariously.

'Young man, you are a dreamer—and a fool into the bargain. Look at those safes!' He waved a hand towards the locked cabinets that lined the walls. 'They're full of statements and accounts and receipts and checks. Every kopeck is there —on paper. But if you ask me where the *money* is'—he pursed up his lips and gave vent to a short, derisive whistle. 'I assure you, there isn't a kopeck in *your* bank, either! There can't be.'

He was immensely impressed with his own penetration. I played the innocent, which put him in high good humour. He even became polite, as well as compassionate.

'I'll let you off this time,' he said. 'But you'll have to take the next train to Odessa.'

I acceded promptly to the suggestion, thankfully submitted my passport to be stamped, and was preparing to leave the office when he called me back, got up, put his hand on my shoulder and said, with great kindliness:

'Look here! I see you're not a bad young man, really. Take my advice and have nothing more to do with those damn Jews. For if they ever get to this kingdom of theirs, the first man they'll string up to a lamp-post will be you!'

On this I parted from him and caught the next train to Odessa, very cheerful over what I regarded as an unusual piece of good luck.

My tour took me eastward to Rostov-on-Don, where I visited my fiancée's family for the first time, and southward to the remote Jewish community of Baku, on the Caspian Sea. Then I turned back north, and passed through Kishinev and Kherson, going as far as St. Petersburg. A curious circumstance which I noticed in those days was that the farther one travelled from the Pale of Settlement, the more normal were the relations between Jews and non-Jews. In Rostov, for example, the Jewish and Russian doctors and lawyers—the intelligentsia—mingled with little difficulty. But in the cities of the Pale, or in other cities with a large Jewish population, the infamous Black Hundreds organizations were at work. Krushevan's abominable anti-Semitic paper, *Bessarabetz*, was poisoning the air of Bessarabia. The Black Hundreds were composed mostly of a hooligan element, with some admixture of the local police and the clergy —a sinister combination, the aim of which was, of course, to create a diversion from the oncoming revolution, the Jews being used, in this classic manœuvre, as the lightning conductors. Perhaps no other paper sank to the level of Krushevan's, but *Novoye Vremya* of St. Petersburg and the *Grazhdanin* of Kiev were provocative and criminal in their attitude towards the Jews.

I noticed something else during this fairly thorough review of the Russian-Jewish communities, and that was the contrast between the Zionist and the revolutionary movements. We had made distinct progress; everywhere well-informed and able men and women were at work in the Zionist movement, preaching, organizing and hoping. There were young people among them, there were students and professional men, and large numbers were ready to pack up and go to Palestine; from their ranks were drawn the second *Aliyah*, or wave of immigration (the first *Aliyah* was that of the early eighties of the last century), that of 1905. But it could not be denied that we were making little headway against the tide of assimilatory revolutionary sentiment.

I was home again in Pinsk for the first days of Passover. It had been a great and enlightening experience for me. I had encountered difficulties, but I had also met, especially on the matter of the University, with encouragement and support. During the secular Passover interval I made a trip to Warsaw, to consult with Nahum Sokolow, who headed in the city an influential committee for the Hebrew University.

Sokolow, of whom I have not yet spoken, was among the older leaders in the Zionist movement, and in some ways one of the most remarkable. He was already famous in the Jewish world—at least, in the Hebrew-reading section of it—when Herzl appeared on the scene. He had been an *ilui* (boy genius), precocious in scholarship and in mastery of the Hebrew language, and he had developed into 'the European' among the Hebrew writers. He was extraordinarily versatile, particularly in the acquisition of languages. When I was a student in Berlin, and for many years afterwards, he was the editor of *Ha-Zephirah*, the leading Hebrew periodical of that time, and the principal organ of the Hebrew cultural renaissance. He lived in Warsaw, and any Jew with Hebrew cultural or Zionist political pretensions would always call on him when passing through the city. On my travels between Germany or Switzerland and Russia I made it a point to stop in Warsaw in order to visit his house. And a very strange house it was; it put one in mind of a railway station. People—mostly the youth—were forever coming and going, at the oddest hours. There was no cosiness about the house, but there was always someone interesting to be encountered. Sokolow himself was there only on occasion. He would show up at noon, or a little later, in his dressing-gown, and, in the afternoon disappear, to visit his favourite café, where he stayed until midnight. On his return home he would sit up until the small hours, preparing the next issue of *Ha-Zephirah*. He always had a dozen leading articles written in advance, and often filled an entire issue with his own material. He wrote on every conceivable subject and in every conceivable style, *feuilletons*, literary criticisms, dramatic reviews, political surveys and philosophic essays. *Ha-Zephirah* was always well written and well produced; its standards were high, its reputation without a rival. But the practical side of it rested on the shoulders of Mrs. Sokolow. Sokolow himself never took the slightest interest in the business management. Sometimes it seemed that, for the lack of a few hundred roubles, the paper would have to suspend publication. Always it was Mrs. Sokolow who rescued it. She carried the burden of the publication and of her household with skill and dignity.

Sokolow was always friendly towards young people, especially in their struggle to bring the cultural aspect of Zionism to the fore. But his support of us was mild, gentle, measured and without enthusiasm. The lack of practicality which he displayed in his management of *Ha-Zephirah* was carried over into other affairs. He had no idea of time, or of the meaning of a practical commitment. I remember that at one of the early Congresses he proposed the excellent idea of a Hebrew encyclopædia, and even said that he had obtained the funds for it. Of course he was just the man for such an enterprise, and we, the young people, were delighted when he asked us to collaborate with him. We waited until the excitement of the Congress was over, and went with him across the lake to Interlaken, for a quiet talk. He gave us a nice lunch and talked of everything under the sun—but the encyclopædia. We went away slightly dazed, and we never heard of the subject again.

From my earliest contacts with Sokolow I obtained a curious impression of over-diversification of opinions and convictions. In *Ha-Zephirah* he was a nationalist and Hebraist; but he also edited a Polish newspaper, *Israelita*, which catered in a general way to assimilated Jews, and in this periodical his nationalism was much less in evidence. This duality in his attitude was not repellent, for it was part of his nature to seek to harmonize extremes. We youngsters were intransigeant—and yet we were drawn to Sokolow. He felt that we were dogmatic, *bornes*, doctrinaire, and he tried to lead us on to understand the points of view of others, to temper what he considered our Jewish and Slavic intolerance. He was always in favour of compromise. 'The world will not go under,' he would say, 'if you yield an inch; and it makes life a little more bearable.' He was worldly in temperament and outlook, and he had a faculty, which most of us lacked, for the enjoyment of the good things of life.

Occasionally we were outraged by the Olympianism of his detachment—and in this connection I remember particularly my visit to him in that spring of 1903. It was during those Passover days that we got the news of the ghastly Kishinev pogrom. I lost my head, and was in something like a panic. Not so Sokolow. Telegrams were pouring into the office of *Ha-Zephirah*, with details of the butchery. In the midst of the universal horror Sokolow remained calm. Not that he lacked sympathy, but it was not in his nature to lose his balance. In that respect he was perhaps a corrective to youth—but we did not always find it easy to respect such philosophic objectivity.

A generation like the present, which has been steeped in tragedies far transcending the Russian pogroms, may wonder in retrospect at the thrill of horror which Kishinev sent through the Jewish world. I do not know whether Kishinev was the worst of those Russian outrages of the early 1900's. Certainly it cannot compete with what we have become accustomed to in the fourth and fifth decades of this century. Perhaps the key lies there: 'What we have become accustomed to.' In our memories Kishinev has remained the classic prototype of the pogrom. It was the first to take place in the twentieth century. It was the first—at a remove of nearly a generation—after the

D*

bloody series which had initiated the reign of Alexander III. Perhaps, again, we were moved by a half-conscious foreboding of what the new century had in store for us.

Forty-five men, women and children killed, more than a thousand wounded, fifteen hundred homes and shops destroyed and looted—this is the cold summary of the Kishinev pogrom. For twenty-four hours the Jews of Kishinev were delivered up to the fury of a mob drawn from the city riffraff and the countryside. It was only on the afternoon of the second day that, on the delayed order of the unspeakable Von Plehve, the Minister of the Interior, the military stepped in and halted the carnage and destruction.

The wave of indignation and despair which swept over the whole Jewish community, from one end of Russia to the other, was augmented by complex feelings of humiliation and impotence. The Kishinev pogrom was the reply of czarist Russia to the cry for freedom of its Jewish subjects. We knew intuitively that it was not to be the last, but was rather the signal for a whole series. The massacres were deliberately organized, carefully planned, and everywhere carried out under the eyes of the civil and military authorities, which stepped in only when they judged that the slaughter and pillage had gone far enough. The general Russian press was forbidden to tell the true story. The protests of Tolstoy and Korolenko were refused publication. Even we, the Jews, could speak of our misfortunes only in guarded tones. When our national poet Bialik wrote his flaming indictment of the pogrom, he had to disguise the allusion under a fictitious title—*The Burden of Nemirov*. For the general Russian public it was reported that there had been 'incidents,' drunken brawls of no particular importance.

Perhaps the most tormenting feature of the Kishinev pogrom was the fact that the Jews had allowed themselves to be slaughtered like sheep, without offering general resistance. In spite of the wild pogrom agitation of Krushevan, they had refused to believe in the possibility of a massacre carried out under the ægis of the Government; and the attack, which occurred in the midst of the last sacred days of Passover, overwhelmed them. The enemy, on the other hand, was well organized and the pogrom developed from section to section of the city with almost military effectiveness. There was no chance of improvising a defence. Here and there younger people who happened to be in possession of firearms put up a fight; they were at once disarmed by the military.

I had intended to proceed from Warsaw to Geneva. I abandoned my classes, such as they were, and returned to the Pale. Together with friends and acquaintances I proceeded to organize self-defence groups in all the larger Jewish centres. Not long afterwards, when a pogrom broke out in Homel, not far from Pinsk, the hooligans were suddenly confronted by a strongly organized Jewish self-defence corps. Again the military interfered, and did its best to disarm the Jews; but at least the self-defence had broken the first wave of the attack, which was not able to gather again its original momentum. Thus, throughout the Pale, an inverted guerrilla warfare spread between the Jews and the Russian authorities, the former trying to maintain order, the latter encouraging disorder. The Jews grew more and more exasperated, and our life therefore more and more intolerable.

I remember distinctly a time when a pogrom came as a positive relief to us. The tension, the constant alarms, the anomalous relations between us and our neighbours were harder to put up with than the actual attack. How could we be *quite* certain who would side with us, who would be neutral and who would join the attackers? At least when the attack took place we knew the worst, we could face up to our enemies and then, when the storm had passed, we might expect a period of comparative tranquillity. During the period of mounting suspense all normal activity seemed meaningless. We were at war. Our dreams of Palestine, our plans for a Hebrew University, receded into the background, or were blotted out. Our eyes saw nothing but the blood of slaughtered men, women and children, our ears were deaf to everything but their cries.

When at last I did return to Geneva, I found no peace in the laboratory or the lecture hall. Every letter I received from Russia was a lamentation. My spirits were depressed, my daily occupations seemed to be trivial; and yet I was powerless to help. I looked forward to the summer, and the Zionist Congress—it was to be the sixth—with mingled feelings of futility and of mystical hope.

It was clear to me that the Kishinev pogrom and the reign of terror which it opened boded no good for our movement. In a time of panic plans lose their shape, creative work becomes impossible, the stage is monopolized by wild and impossible schemes. The pressure of panic, while it became most manifest after the Kishinev pogrom, had been laid on the Zionist movement for years. 'The quick solution' had haunted us at every Congress, distracting us from sober planning and those unavoidably small beginnings which must precede larger achievement. It was in pursuit of a phantom diplomatic triumph that the official Zionist Organization had neglected the spiritual development of the movement, leaving that to us of the Democratic Faction.

When I returned to Geneva in the late spring of 1903, I addressed a memorandum to Herzl, in my name and Feivel's, in which I set forth the oppositional criticism of the Democratic Faction. I reported on conditions in Russia, on the spread of revolutionary sentiment among the Jewish youth, on the new repressive measures instituted by Von Plehve, and on the difficulties which beset the Zionist movement among the Jews themselves. Our progress, I said, was blocked there by the rightist attitude of the Zionist leadership and by its clericalist inclinations. As against this, Russian officialdom took its views of Zionism from Zionist publications which described the Democratic Faction as 'anarchistic, nihilistic, etc.' The Jewish youth of Russia was turning from us because it would have nothing to do with an official Zionism which it regarded as *Mizrachist* and petty bourgeois, while within the movement itself all other tendencies were stamped as atheistic and revolutionary. I pointed out to Herzl that this clericalist colouring arose from the fact that west European Zionism represented a passive nationalism, consciously or unconsciously influenced by assimilation, springing from a Judaism chiefly religious but not rooted in Jewish knowledge and folk experience. Meanwhile the continuous demand for practical work in Palestine was being ignored.

But Herzl, whatever he may have felt regarding the justice of our observations, was increasingly the prisoner of his line of action. He was driven to intensify and to emphasize his diplomatic activity. The calamities of Russian Jewry overwhelmed him; he foresaw the new tides of immigration which

Kishinev and its aftermath would set in motion, and he redoubled his efforts for 'the quick solution.' As the summer approached we heard vague rumours of political negotiations with England; but we did not learn of their character until the Congress met. Meanwhile another facet of Herzl's far-flung activities was made public. Herzl had managed to arrange an interview, in St. Petersburg, with Von Plehve, the man whose hands were stained with the blood of thousands of Jewish victims! And in the early part of August, shortly before the opening of the Congress, Herzl actually came to Russia to be received by the butcher of Kishinev.

There was a passionate division of opinion on this step. There were some who believed that the Jewish leader could not pick and choose his contacts, but had to negotiate even with a murderer if some practical good would come of it. Others could not tolerate the thought of this final humiliation. But there were still others—I was among them—who believed that the step was not only humiliating, but utterly pointless. Von Plehve, who had passed a series of decrees, shortly after the Kishinev pogrom, designed to render impossible any sort of Zionist activity, would not make any promises worth the recording; if he did, he would not keep them. It turned out that Herzl not only hoped to influence Von Plehve to suppress the activities of the Black Hundreds (it was an utterly fantastic hope since anti-Semitism was a necessary instrument of policy to Von Plehve, to Pobiedonostsev, the Procurator of the Holy Synod, and to the whole czarist clique), he even dreamed of enlisting Russian aid in persuading Abdul Hamid, the feeble ruler of Turkey, to open the gates of Palestine to us. Lack of realism could go no further; anti-Semites are incapable of aiding in the creation of a Jewish homeland; their attitude forbids them to do anything which might really help the Jewish people. Pogroms, yes; repressions, yes; emigration, yes; but nothing that might be conducive to the freedom of the Jews.

Such was the fathomless despair of masses of Russian Jews that Herzl's progress through the Jewish communities took on an almost Messianic aspect. In Vilna, especially, there was a tremendous outpouring of the Jewish population, and a great surge of blind hope, baseless, elemental, instinctive and hysterical, attended his arrival. Nothing came, naturally, of Herzl's 'cordial' conversations with Von Plehve, nothing, that is, except disillusionment and deeper despair, and a deeper division between the Zionists and the revolutionaries, for the latter were particularly furious at this concession to reaction. Herzl records his talks with Von Plehve in his memoirs. Many generalities were uttered, Von Plehve reiterated the stock accusation that the Jews were all revolutionaries, and made some vague promises which he had no intention of keeping. In exchange for these, Herzl, in an address to the Jewish leaders of St. Petersburg, warned the Zionists against harbouring radical elements in their midst! The memorandum which I had sent him had produced no results.

Worse was to follow at the Sixth Congress. It opened under the shadow of the Kishinev pogrom and Herzl's visit to Von Plehve; it closed with the Uganda episode.

The flurry of rumours regarding Herzl's negotiations with the British Government was put to rest only when the facts were submitted to the Congress. Before making these facts public, Herzl had already consulted the Action Committee—the cabinet—of the Congress, and had discovered that he would encounter strong opposition. How strong he was yet to learn. There was, among many of the Russian delegates, a deep resentment against Herzl in connection with his visit to Von Plehve. They could not speak out—though Nachman Syrkin did express bitter disapproval on the floor of the Congress—because they knew that even in Basle they were being watched by the Russian secret police, and that they would be held accountable, when they returned to Russia, for every incautious word. This repressed resentment was fortified when, having set the stage with his customary skill, Herzl read forth the famous letter from the British Government, signed by Lord Lansdowne, offering the Jews an autonomous territory in Uganda, in that part of it which is now British East Africa.

I remember one deeply significant detail of the stage setting. It had always been the custom to hang on the wall, immediately behind the President's chair, a map of Palestine. This had been replaced by a rough map of the Uganda protectorate, and the symbolic action got us on the quick, and filled us with foreboding. Herzl opened his address with a vivid picture of the situation of the Jews, which we, the Russian Jews, knew only too well. He deduced from it only one thing: the urgent necessity of bringing immediate, large-scale relief by emigration to the stricken people. Emergency measures were needed. He did not relinquish the idea of Palestine as the Jewish homeland. On the contrary, he intimated that Von Plehve's promises to bring Russian pressure to bear on Turkey had improved our prospects in Palestine. But as far as the immediate problem was concerned, something new, something of great significance had developed. The British Government had made us the offer of a territory in British East Africa. Admittedly British East Africa was not Zion, and never would be. It was only an auxiliary activity—but on a national or state foundation.

It was an extraordinary speech, carefully prepared—too carefully in fact, for its cautious, balanced paragraphs betrayed the essential contradictions of the situation. Herzl had already encountered deep opposition in the closed session of the Action Committee. But he had obtained a majority, and had enforced the unit rule, so that he could present the British offer in the name of the Action Committee. Knowing, then, that he would encounter similar opposition on the floor of Congress, he did not submit the proposition that the British offer be accepted; he cushioned the proposal by suggestion that the Congress send a commission of investigation to the territory in question, to report on its suitability.

The effect on the Congress was a curious one. The delegates were electrified by the news. This was the first time in the exilic history of Jewry that a great government had officially negotiated with the elected representatives of the Jewish people. The identity, the legal personality of the Jewish people, had been re-established. So much, then, had been achieved by our movement; and it meant much. But as soon as the substance of the offer, and Herzl's manner of announcing it, sank home, a spirit of disquiet, dejection and anxiety spread through the Congress. It was clear that Herzl's faith in Von Plehve's support of our hopes in Palestine was more or less put on. And again, it was all very well to talk of Uganda as an auxiliary and a temporary measure, but the deflection of our energies to a purely relief effort would mean, whatever Herzl's intentions were, the practical dismantling of the Zionist Organization in so far as it had to do with Zion.

How was it that Herzl could contemplate such a shift of objective? It was the logical consequence of his conception of Zionism and of the rôle which the movement had to play in the life of the Jews. To him, and to many with him—perhaps the majority of the representatives of the Jews assembled in Basle—Zionism meant an *immediate* solution of the problems besetting their sorely tried people. If it was not that, it was nothing at all. The conception was at once crude, naïve and generous. There is no *immediate* solution of great historic problems. There is only movement in the direction of the solution. Herzl, the leader, had set out with the contrary belief; and he met with disappointment. The *Judennot*—the Jewish need—was increasing hourly. Herzl had been in Russia and had cast a shuddering glance at the Pale and its miseries. Everywhere he had been received by a desperate people as its redeemer; it was his duty now to redeem. If Palestine was not, at the moment, feasible, he could not wait, for the flood of anti-Semitism was rising minute by minute and—to use his own words—'the lower strata of the Jewish edifice were already inundated.' If anything were to happen, then, there might not be enough Jews left to build Palestine; hence the offer of the British Government was providential; it had come just in the nick of time—a very present help in time of trouble. It would be cruel, heartless, un-Jewish and un-Zionistic to throw away a chance which might never again occur in the history of the Jewish people.

Herzl's statement to the Congress was cautious, dignified and guarded; off stage, in the lobbies of the Congress, he was less diplomatic, more human, more vehement. He, and those under his influence, little thought that what he was offering to Jews and Zionists was a snare and a delusion; there was no territorial project, however magnificent it might appear at first blush, which could possibly, within a short space of time, have relieved the tension and appreciably mitigated the disasters which had come upon us with the force of an avalanche. Jewish emigration from Russia, which before Kishinev had been rising steadily, reached the figure of one hundred thousand per annum after Kishinev. Those who spoke calmly of deflecting the stream of emigration to Uganda did not stop to reflect that Uganda was a country of which only one thing was known, namely, that it was a desolate wilderness populated by savage tribes; neither its nature, its climate, its agricultural nor its other possibilities corresponded—at the optimistic best—to the need of the hour. It is hard to tell to what extent Herzl was completely taken in by the Uganda proposal. In his tortuous diplomatic calculations he was also thinking of Uganda as a pawn. He wanted the Congress to accept Uganda in order to frighten the Sultan into action, as if to say: 'If you won't give us Palestine, we'll drop you completely and go to British East Africa.'

In any case, the proposal before the Congress was only that of an investigation committee. But no one was mistaken as to the symbolic significance of that proposal. A deep, painful and passionate division manifested itself on the floor of the Congress. When the first session was suspended, and the delegates scattered in the lobbies, or hastened to their caucuses, a young woman ran up on to the platform, and with a vehement gesture tore down the map of Uganda which had been suspended there in the place of the usual map of Zion.

I proceeded to the caucus of the Russian delegation, the largest at the Congress, for the discussion of our stand on the Uganda proposal. Ussishkin, the leader of the Russian Zionists —who was of course bitterly anti-Ugandist—was not at the Congress. He was in Palestine. The other Russian leaders, Kohan-Bernstein, Shmarya Levin, Victor Jacobson, were as implacably anti-Ugandist. The Polish delegates (they were a subgroup of the Russian delegation) were divided. Sokolow— characteristically—would not commit himself. My father, who was a fellow-delegate with me from Pinsk, was of the Russian minority which was pro-Uganda—so was my brother Shmuel —and for the only time in our lives there was a coolness between us. I should mention that among the Russian Zionists there was a certain type of respectable middle-class householder who had always been sceptical of the feasibility of the rebuilding of Palestine. There were practical men, merchants, men of affairs, who argued that Herzl's efforts for Palestine had reached an impasse. 'What's the good of pursuing a phantom?' they said. And then again: 'What have we to lose by accepting Uganda?' Or else it was: 'The British are a great people. It is a great government which makes the offer. We must not offend a great government by refusing.'

All of these arguments, it seemed to me, were informed by a

curious inferiority complex. In the session of the Russian delegation, I made a violent speech against the Uganda project, and swung to our side many of the hesitant. In the confusion of the offer, which Herzl had flung so dramatically at the Congress, many of the delegates had lost their bearings. I myself, I admitted, had for a moment looked upon the incident as a party manœuvre, but it had become clear to me that it was much more fundamental. It was an attempt to give a totally new character to the Zionist movement. The very fact, I said, that the *Mizrachi*—the religious Zionists—were mostly for Uganda, and the Democratic Faction mostly against it, revealed the nature of the move.

'The influence of Herzl on the people is very great,' I said. 'Even the opponents of Uganda cannot get away from it, and they cannot make up their minds to state openly that this is a departure from the Basle programme. Herzl, who found the *Chibath Zion* movement already in existence, made a pact with it. But as time passed, and the idea of Palestine did not succeed, he regretted the pact. He reckoned only with external conditions, whereas the forces on which we base ourselves lie deep in the psychology of our people and in its living impulses. We knew that Palestine could not be obtained in short order, and that is why we do not despair if this or that particular attempt fails.' And I closed my speech with these words: 'If the British Government and people are what I think they are, they will make us a better offer.' This last sentence became a sort of slogan for the anti-Ugandists at the Congress.

The debate on the Uganda proposal had opened at the first session of the Plenum with a speech in the affirmative by Max Nordau. It was not a convincing speech, for Nordau himself was not thoroughly convinced, and had yielded only to pressure. It was then that he coined the famous phrase *Nachtasyl*—night shelter; Uganda was to be colonized, nationally, as a sort of halfway station to Palestine. As the debate unfolded, the first flush of excitement over the recognition of the Zionist Organization by a great government died away. The feeling against the proposal began to crystallize.

The debate was resumed after the separate sessions of the caucuses, and was closed by a second address from Nordau. The Congress was in a high state of tension. Family bonds and lifelong friendships were shattered. The vote on the resolution was by roll-call. Every delegate had to say 'Yes' or 'No.' The replies fell, in a deathly silence, like hammer blows. We felt that the destiny of the Zionist movement was being decided. Two hundred and ninety-five delegates voted 'Yes,' one hundred and seventy-five 'No.' About a hundred abstained. I remember vividly Herzl calling Sokolow's name. 'Herr Sokolow.' No answer. 'Herr Sokolow!' No answer. And a third time, 'Herr Sokolow!' With the same result. To indicate the excitement under which all of us laboured, I record a minor incident which took place afterwards, in the train which was taking a group of us from Basle towards Russia. Tschlenow turned to Sokolow and said:

'If I, or Weizmann here, had abstained from voting, it would have mattered little; but how could you, the editor of the most important Hebrew paper in Eastern Europe, to which thousands of readers look for guidance, abstain? You must have an opinion one way or the other on a fundamental question like this!'

To which Sokolow replied, with unwonted heat:

'I could write you a dozen articles on this issue, and you would not find out whether I am *pro* or *con*. . . . And here you dare to ask me to my face for a definite reply. That's more than I can stand!'

Now the extraordinary feature of the vote was that the great majority of the negatives came from the Russian delegation! The delegates from Kishinev were against the Uganda offer! It was absolutely beyond the understanding of the Westerners. I recall how, after the vote, Herzl came up to a group of delegates in the lobby, and in the course of a brief interchange of views exclaimed, apropos of the recalcitrant Russians: 'These people have a rope around their necks, and still they refuse!'

A young lady, the one who had torn down the map of Uganda from the wall behind the dais, happened to be standing by. She exclaimed, vehemently: '*Monsieur le Président, vous êtes un traître!*' Herzl turned on his heel.

Technically, Herzl had a majority for the Uganda proposal, but it was quite clear that acceptance of the British offer would be futile. The vote had been too close. Besides, the people *for* whom British East Africa was to be accepted, the suffering, oppressed Russians, did not want it. They would not relinquish Zion.

When the result of the roll-call was announced in the Plenum the Russian members of the Action Committee who had been against the proposal at the closed session compelled Herzl to exonerate them from responsibility for the unit vote. They then left the dais and marched out from the hall, followed by the great majority of the Russian delegates. It was an unforgettable scene. Tschlenow, Kornberg and others of the older statesmen wept openly. When the dissidents had assembled separately, there were some delegates who, in the extremity of their distress, sat down on the floor in the traditional ritual mourning which is observed for the dead, or in commemoration of the destruction of the temple on the ninth of Ab. I remember that not long afterwards Achad Ha-am wrote an article *Ha-Bochim* ('The Weepers'), in which he mournfully recalled his consistent criticism of the lack of folk Zionism in the Western leaders; this defection from Palestine, he declared, had been implicit in the Western leadership from the beginning; it had first declared itself in Herzl's *Judenstaat*, in which Zion had not even been mentioned; then in his *Altneuland*, his Utopian novel which had described a Jewish homeland of the future without a Jewish culture; and now came the dénouement, the substitution of a remote, unknown African territory for the glory of the historic Jewish homeland.

Meanwhile, as we sat in caucus, depressed, our hearts filled with bitterness, a message was brought in that Herzl would like to speak to us. We sent back word that we would be glad to hear him. He came in, looking haggard and exhausted. He was received in dead silence. Nobody rose from his seat to greet him, nobody applauded when he ended. He admonished us for having left the hall; he understood, he said, that this was merely a spontaneous demonstration and not a secession; he invited us to return. He reassured us of his unswerving devotion to Palestine, and spoke again of the urgent need for finding an immediate refuge for large masses of homeless Jews. We listened in silence; no one attempted to reply. It was probably the only time that Herzl was thus received at any Zionist gathering; he, the idol of all Zionists. He left as he had entered; but I think that at this small meeting he realized for the first time the depth of the passion which linked us with Zion. This was the last time that I saw him except from a distance, on the platform. He died in the following year, at the age of forty-four.

Nothing came of the Uganda offer. The year after Herzl's death, at the seventh Zionist Congress, in 1905, it was definitely rejected, and Israel Zangwill and others seceded from the Zionist Organization in order to found the Jewish Territorial Organization, which for years looked for another territory on which to settle large numbers of Jews in a homeland of their own, but never, never found one.

The sixth Congress, with its dramatic focalization of the Jewish problem, taught me much. In particular, two of the issues there presented illustrated the principle of organic growth in which I have always believed. Nothing good is produced by panic. It was panic that moved Herzl to accept the Uganda offer uncritically: it was panic that prevented us from making good use of another proposal—that of El Arish, which was presented to the sixth Congress. I believe that the exposition of both offers belongs to this record.

Shortly after the sixth Congress I decided to go to England to find out for myself, if I could, what there was in the Uganda offer, which was to come up for a final decision at the seventh Congress. I knew a few English Jews; one was Leopold Greenberg, the editor of the London *Jewish Chronicle*, but I could not go to him. He had been instrumental in bringing Herzl together with Joseph Chamberlain and Lord Lansdowne and Arthur James Balfour, who was then Prime Minister. My opposition to the Uganda offer had made Greenberg my enemy, and we never established friendly relations again. When I settled permanently in England, Greenberg did his best to keep me out of the movement; he succeeded, certainly, in preventing me for a long time from developing close contact with the London Zionists, and the *Jewish Chronicle* remained consistently hostile to me. I also knew Dr. Moses Gaster, the *Haham*, or head of the Sephardic Communities, who had been one of Herzl's earliest supporters in England. I was to know him much better in later years. He was a good Zionist but suffered, I believe, from jealousy; he considered himself more fitted than Herzl for the position of President of the Zionist Organization, but never rose higher than a Vice-Presidency of the Congress.

It was to Gaster that I turned, and he gave me a letter to Lord Percy, who was then in charge of African affairs. Lord Percy was the first English statesman I met. He was a man in the middle thirties, with the finely chiselled features of his family, courteous and affable in manner, and obviously well informed. He asked me a great deal about the Zionist movement, and expressed boundless astonishment that the Jews should ever so much as have considered the Uganda proposal, which he regarded as impractical on the one hand, and, on the other, a denial of the Jewish religion. Himself deeply religious, he was bewildered by the thought that Jews could even entertain the idea of any other country than Palestine as the centre of their revival; and he was delighted to hear from me that there were so many Jews who had categorically refused. He said: 'If I were a Jew I would not give a halfpenny for this proposition!'

I was so impressed by Lord Percy's views that immediately on leaving him I sat down in an adjoining room, and on the stationery of the Foreign Office wrote a report of the conversation to my fiancée. The substance of the letter I communicated to the *Neinsager*—the Nay-sayers or opponents of Uganda—in Russia. I believe that this contributed not a little to the final defeat of the Uganda proposal.

From Lord Percy I went to Sir Harry Johnston, the famous explorer, who knew Uganda well. He too was of the opinion that the practical value of the offer was nil. He added that the few white settlers, mostly English, who were already in Uganda, would fight against a Jewish influx into their territory, which could not accommodate more than a very limited number. I came to the conclusion that Greenberg had indoctrinated Herzl with the idea, which lacked—apart from its ideological and moral shortcomings—any solid foundation and which Herzl had grasped at in the panic of pressure.

Johnston also sent me to see an English gentleman whose name was widely and unfavourably known to the Jewish people —Sir William Evans Gordon—the father of the Aliens Bill. He was generally regarded as responsible for all the difficulties placed in the way of Jewish immigrants into England. I had

met him some years before, when he had been making a tour
of the Jewish Pale of Settlement in Russia. Looking back now,
I think our people were rather hard on him. The Aliens Bill
in England and the movement which grew up around it were
natural phenomena which might have been foreseen. They
were a repetition of a phenomenon only too familiar in our
history. Whenever the quantity of Jews in any country reaches
saturation point, that country reacts against them. In the early
years of this century Whitechapel and the great industrial
centres of England were in that sense saturated. The fact that
the actual number of Jews in England, and even their proportion to the total population, was smaller than in other countries
was irrelevant; the determining factor in this matter is not the
solubility of the Jews, but the solvent power of the country.
England had reached the point when she could or would
absorb so many Jews and no more. English Jews were prepared
to be absorbed in larger numbers. The reaction against this
cannot be looked upon as anti-Semitism in the ordinary or
vulgar sense of that word; it is a universal social and economic
concomitant of Jewish immigration, and we cannot shake it
off.

Sir William Evans Gordon had no particular anti-Jewish
prejudices. He acted, as he thought, according to his best lights
and in the most kindly way, in the interests of his country. He
had been horrified by what he had seen of the oppression of
the Jews in Russia, but in his opinion it was physically impossible for England to make good the wrongs which Russia
had inflicted on its Jewish population. He was sorry, but he
was helpless. Also, he was sincerely ready to encourage any
settlement of Jews almost anywhere in the British Empire, but
he failed to see why the ghettos of London or Leeds or Whitechapel should be made into branches of the ghettos of Warsaw
and Pinsk. I am fairly sure he would equally have opposed the
mass influx of any foreign element; but as it happened, no
other foreign element pressed for admission in such numbers.
It requires a good deal of imagination to think of newly created
ghettos in terms of the second or third generations, which will
have adapted themselves with incredible rapidity and skill
to the structure of the new life, and will have lost their identity
almost beyond recognition; to foresee them, under changed

names, figuring in the honours lists of Oxford and Cambridge, and making genuine contributions to English life. It is too much to expect the ordinary, well-meaning citizen to look so far ahead. It is too much to expect him to view a strange and often—as he thinks—disturbing element without that natural prejudice which a settled, firmly rooted citizen of a country with an age-long tradition must feel in the presence of a homeless wanderer, assumed to be continually on the lookout for a home, a country to adopt. Evans Gordon gave me some insight into the psychology of the settled citizen, and though my views on immigration naturally were in sharp conflict with his, we discussed these problems in a quite objective and even friendly way.

Uganda was one lesson in the dangers of panic policy. El Arish was another.

During the sixth Congress we learned that, side by side with the Uganda offer, there was another in the making. Herzl had been negotiating with His Majesty's Government on something much nearer home, namely, the possibility of Jewish colonization in the strip of territory between the present southern boundary of Palestine and Egypt commonly known as El Arish. Apparently discussions had been going on for some considerable time, but the general body of Zionists did not know how these discussions had arisen, or anything else about them beyond the fact that an expedition had been sent out to El Arish to survey the ground, and that the expedition had brought back an unfavourable report. We were informed at the Congress that His Majesty's Government, always mindful of the Jews, and desirous of ameliorating their lot, had given every facility to representatives of the Zionist movement to conduct an investigation on the spot. The commission had discussed the situation fully with Lord Cromer, who had received them sympathetically, but the project had been found to be impracticable owing to the lack of water in this part of southern Palestine.

Irrigation possiblities had been discussed, but all these depended on the utilization of water from the Nile, and to this the Egyptian Government was naturally opposed. On a careful analysis of the report, and with the scanty information made available to us at the Congress, one could not help feeling that the commission's attitude was largely dictated by the ever-present desire of the Zionist leaders at that time to undertake colonization only on a very large scale; for only such colonization, they felt, could do anything to lighten the sufferings of the Jewish people. If large-scale colonization was not possible, they preferred to drop the entire matter. In my opinion it was this view, and this view alone, which was responsible for bringing the El Arish project—a very tangible reality—to naught. The expedition was not satisfied with the thin strip of land along the coast of southern Palestine on which it was fairly certain that colonies could have been established, since there was good prospect of subterranean water. (There are, in fact, settlements in El Arish today.) But that was too small a task for the great ideas which then prevailed in the circles of the Zionist leadership. It was too modest a beginning. It did not appeal to the vision and imagination either of the leaders or of the masses, before whose eye the word 'solution' was constantly dangled. So the commission felt obliged to include in its investigation the 'Pelusian Plain' (Sinai Desert); and this did not lend itself to colonization unless water was found. The project was abandoned in its entirety, and no attempt made to examine in detail the smaller strip of territory where colonization was possible. It might have made, I think, a very considerable difference to the present fate of Palestine if we had then concentrated on making a beginning, however small, along the coast of southern Palestine.

Kishinev, Uganda, El Arish and the sixth Zionist Congress brought a deep crisis into my life. I perceived the utter inadequacy of the Zionist movement, as then constituted, in relation to the tragedy of the Jewish people. Kishinev had only intensified in the Jews of Russia the ineradicable longing for a Jewish homeland in Palestine—in Palestine, and not elsewhere. Elsewhere meant for them only a continuation of the old historic rounds of refuge. They wanted Palestine because that meant restoration in every sense. But the Zionist movement could not give them Palestine there and then; and a spirit of falsification and self-betrayal had crept into the movement. The substitute project of Uganda was chimerical; and it did not even speak the language of the ancient hope and memory. Zionism was at the crossroads; it would either learn patience and endurance, and the hard lesson of organic growth, or it would disintegrate into futility.

I felt that I too was at the crossroads, and that I had to take a decisive step to signalize my realization that a new start had to be made. On July 4, 1904, Herzl died in Vienna; and on the day when a delegation of students set out for Vienna to attend the funeral, I closed the first chapter of my Zionist life, and set out for England, to begin the second.

CHAPTER VII

NEW START IN ENGLAND

Why England?—Zionism in England Half a Century Ago—I Settle in Manchester—Professor Perkin—Fixing up a Laboratory—First Lessons in English—Tom, the Lab Boy—First Research Work in England—I Lecture in English—My Students—My Tactful Japanese Colleague—The Insistent Call of Zionism—A Zionist Meeting in Manchester—I Put My Foot in it—English Zionism Recovers from Uganda—The Manchester Centre Crystallizes—Achad Ha-am in England

My flight to England, in 1904, was a deliberate and desperate step. It was not, to be sure, real flight; it was in reality a case of *reculer pour mieux sauter*. I was in danger of being eaten up by Zionism, with no benefit either to my scientific career or to Zionism. We had reached, it seemed to me, a dead point in the movement. My struggles were destroying me; an interval was needed before the possibilities of fruitful work could be restored. Achieving nothing in my public effort, neglecting my laboratory and my books, I was in danger of degenerating into a *Luftmensch*, one of those well-meaning, undisciplined and frustrated 'eternal students' of whom I have already written. To become effective in any sense, I had to continue my education in chemistry and wait for a more propitious time in the Zionist movement.

I chose England for various reasons, chiefly intuitive. My position in Geneva and my income from my patent were both petering out. There was little scope for an alien in a small country like Switzerland, which was already overcrowded with émigrés from other countries, especially my own. I knew little of France, and Paris had never attracted me. Germany was out of the question. England presented itself to me as a country in which, at least theoretically, a Jew might be allowed to live and work without let or hindrance, and where he might be judged entirely on his merits.

My Zionist views, too, led me to look upon England as the

one country which seemed likely to show a genuine sympathy for a movement like ours; and the history of the relations between England and Zionism, even at that time, bore witness to this probability. There were no other reasons that I can recall, except my profound admiration for England. There was certainly nothing of any material value in England to attract me. I had no prospects whatsoever. In that sense it was a leap in the dark. I took with me no impedimenta: I had none. My assets consisted of a certain amount of chemical experience and many good intentions—to work hard, to withdraw for a time from all public activity, and to devote myself wholeheartedly to building up a new life in new surroundings. I had no knowledge of the language, my circle of acquaintances in England was very limited. I had no preference for one part of the country over another. London, the first city I came to, inspired me—as it had done on the occasion of my previous visits—with awe; its size, its buildings, its climate terrified me. Among its crowds I was a solitary, setting out on uncharted seas in a derelict boat, without rudder or compass.

In London I lodged for a few weeks with a tailor in Sidney Street, a sweet, gentle fellow, a Zionist like myself, but of the left wing. I paid very little for my board and lodgings—certainly not enough to more than cover the expense I caused him. There was a curious spirit of isolation about this intelligent, well-read host of mine. He would walk the streets of London with me, to teach me something about the city. But he would not accompany me beyond the Bank. There he would stop and say, solemnly: 'I never go beyond this point.' For some obscure reason I was terribly impressed by this touch of the hermit.

I saw Gaster, met Sir William Evans Gordon again and re-established contact with some of the Zionists who had attended the Congresses. Zionism in England reflected the general critical condition of the movement at its worst. Zangwill was leading, or attempting to lead Jewry into East Africa, and it was regarded as something very near treason against Zionist ideals to permit oneself to criticize the East African project, and to insist that the Zionist movement must always have as its primary object the upbuilding of Zion. Zionism at this time was acquiring a peculiar savour; it tended to be transformed into a rather low-grade British patriotism—a British patriotism based on an imaginary attachment to an imaginary country which nobody had seen and nobody knew, a remote dependency of the British Empire populated by savages. But the mere fact that it was within the orbit of the British Empire was sufficient to fire the imagination of many of the superpatriots. In their enthusiasm they forgot the Biblical motto of the Zionist movement: 'If I forget thee, O Jerusalem, let my right hand forget her cunning.'

I found myself isolated, socially, intellectually and morally. There was a certain bitterness among many Zionists, who attributed the untimely death of Herzl to the stubbornness of the anti-Ugandists; the opposition had killed him. I was handicapped in my efforts to widen my circle of acquaintances by my ignorance of the language; and most of my so-called Zionist friends, captured by the idea of a great Jewish State in Uganda, gave me the cold shoulder. At that time they were still awaiting a report on the offered territory; but they were certain that it would be good: otherwise, they argued, the offer would never have been made. I was helpless in the face of such naïveté.

My isolation grew deeper and more complete, and I came to the conclusion that in the circumstances the best thing I could do was to keep away from the unpleasant and unprofitable strife which was being waged around ideas which meant little or nothing to me. This state of mind was the determining factor in my choice of a provincial city in which to begin my work. I was more determined than ever to keep out of Zionist politics for a time, to be by myself and to devote myself to study and thought. I felt instinctively that if I stayed in London I should be dragged, against my will, into the vortex of futile discussion.

I picked Manchester as my place of exile—for exile it really was. I was no longer a youngster—I was in my thirtieth year. I had achieved some standing both in the academic world and in public life. Manchester was to be a complete if temporary eclipse. I was beginning all over again. No job was waiting for me. The best I could look forward to was the privilege of a small laboratory in the University, for which I would pay. The rest would depend on my work—and my luck.

In Manchester I knew just one person, Joseph Massel, the Zionist, who was a printer by trade and a Hebrew poet by avocation, and he turned out to be a veritable angel. He met me at the station, when I arrived on an August Bank Holiday, and took me to his house, a dark, moth-eaten place, half of which was occupied by his printing plant. But it was a sweet, wholesome Jewish home, and during my first few months in Manchester my Friday evenings with the Massels were the high-lights of my life. It was Massel, again, who found lodgings for me near the University, and who introduced me to Charles Dreyfus, the chairman of the Zionist group in Manchester, and director of the Clayton Aniline Works, where I later obtained part-time employment as research worker.

Two factors entered into my choice of Manchester. It was a big centre of the chemical industry, and it possessed a great University, the chemical school of which, familiar to me from scientific literature, had a particularly high reputation. And I had, among my letters of introduction, one to Professor William Henry Perkin, of Manchester University.

It was Professor Graebe, of Geneva, who had given me this letter, and here again I cannot help pausing on the curious way in which the strands of my life have been woven together. It so happened that the work I had been doing under Graebe had been on similar lines to that which the father of Professor Perkin, Sir William Henry Perkin, had done nearly half a century before. Very few people know that it was an English-man—namely William Henry Perkin—who was the founder of the coal-tar dye industry. As a boy of eighteen he had produced, chemically, the colouring matter which subsequently became known as aniline blue, or mauve—and which, incidentally, gave its name to the 'mauve decade.' It was Germany, how-ever, in that tremendous expansion of her industries which accompanied the dream of world conquest, which exploited the discovery. Of the manner in which Germany and her imperialism crossed the path of my Zionist and scientific interests I shall have much more to say later. Here, at any rate, was another premonitory contact, to which I paid little atten-tion at the time. I only knew that Professor Perkin was rather touched that I should have been working in the same field as his father, and perhaps his kindness to me was due primarily to this quite fortuitous sentimental factor. Whatever the reason, I was very warmly received. As a former pupil of Adolph von Bayer, of Munich, Perkin spoke excellent German. He kept me in conversation for about an hour, inquired into my work, explained the mechanism of the Manchester Chemical School, and immediately arranged to let me have the use of a laboratory, for which I was to pay a fee of six pounds. Then he said good-bye! He was leaving for his holiday, and he paused long enough to describe, with happy anticipation, the villages and inns in the Dolomites which he intended to visit. He shook hands with me and left, accompanied by my warmest gratitude and keenest envy.

The six pounds I had to pay for the laboratory made a considerable hole in my resources; and when I paid the money to the bursar I made an unspoken vow: 'This is the last *you* get out of me.' I had saved up a little in Geneva out of my patent royalties; and I had a small income—I think it was ten pounds a month—from the Baku oil man, Shrirow (the same one who had provided the funds for the disastrous experiment with Zvi Aberson) for whom I was doing some research. But that was not going to last very long. It was therefore with a high spirit of determination that I plunged into my work.

The beginning was not encouraging. The laboratory in which Professor Perkin had bidden me make myself at home was a dingy basement room which had evidently not been used for many months. It was dark, grimy and covered with many layers of dust and soot; the necessary apparatus was there, but a great deal of cleaning and rearranging had to be done before it could be made habitable. As far as I could see, I was alone in the building, and I had no idea where to find the paraphernalia to fit up a laboratory. The first thing I did was to set to work to scrub the tables, clean the taps and wash up the dirty apparatus which stood about in picturesque disorder. This occupied my first day. It was not exactly a scientific occupation, but it kept my thoughts busy till evening when, very tired, and suffering from housemaid's knee, I stumbled back to my lodgings.

The following morning I returned very early to the laboratory, and to my great joy found it inhabited by another living being. This was Edwards, the chief steward of the laboratories, an all-powerful person who was responsible not only for the charwomen and lab boys, but also for all chemical and glass stores. I realized at once that here was, from my point of view, the most important man in the place. He did not look at all like the laboratory stewards I had known in Berlin and Geneva; he was perhaps more like a churchwarden; anyhow, he was unctuous and exceedingly polite, his language always cautious and diplomatic. Unfortunately, our conversations in the early days were rather slow and disconnected, since my English was practically non-existent and he knew no other language. The first morning I spoke with pencil and paper, drawing for him most of the apparatus I wanted. I also wrote out the formulæ of the chemicals. He brought me an English chemistry text-book, and going through it I pointed to the pictures, and he was kind enough to read out to me several passages. In this way we got on tolerably well, and by the end of the morning I had collected a fairly good outfit and had been given access to the Holy of Holies—the storeroom where the fine chemicals I needed for my work were kept. Edwards also placed at my disposal a lab boy. His language, too, was entirely incomprehensible to me, but he possessed a peculiar gift which I had never encountered before: he had learned how to play football with every piece of apparatus which came into his hands. He was something of an artist in this way, and could kick pieces of glassware about without actually smashing them. He never handed me anything in the ordinary way, but was for ever performing some sleight of hand, either throwing the piece of apparatus up into the air and catching it, or slinging it at a nicely calculated angle to fall on a definite spot on my desk. But he was kindly and jolly. He talked mostly with his hands, and at the top of his voice, being probably under the impression that the more loudly one speaks the more easily the foreigner understands.

Tom proved to be a great asset, and did well by me, even showing an inclination to procure various luxuries for my laboratory. Thus, without any prompting from me, he produced some matting for the stone floor, and gave me an elaborate explanation—mostly by gesticulation—to the effect that every worker in this room had invariably finished up with rheumatism, so that the matting was an essential prerequisite for one's bodily welfare. He also expressed the hope that I would not be staying long in this room, but would shortly be moved upstairs. Foreign gentlemen usually began in the basement, but if they did well they went up. I took careful note of Tom's wise remarks, which were based on wide experience and careful observation. He went on to give me, in his sketchy way, some characteristics of the *dramatis personæ* in the laboratories, so that when they arrived I might find them more or less familiar. Tom was blessed with remarkable common sense and receptiveness; he was a keen and reliable observer of the people around him. We soon became firm friends, so much so that he repeatedly offered to 'pinch' some special chemical for me from stores not accessible to ordinary mortals. I did my best to discourage this idea, because I thought it was still too early for me to embark on attempts of this kind. But Tom did not quite agree with me. Everybody did it, he said; and it wasn't really 'pinching' because of course you could always sign a receipt for any chemical you took. It appeared that every worker in the labs had his own little private store of chemicals laid up in his own special hiding place; it saved their running about and wasting time; and anyway, explained Tom, it was always well to be prepared.

I fitted myself out as best I could, and in company with my lab boy, set up my first experiments. . . . It had been a rather difficult beginning, but the creation of a laboratory in a strange town, especially during the vacation, when the place is half dead, and in the hands of charwomen, plumbers and workmen of all kinds, is usually a heartbreaking task. Mine was made easier by the consistent kind-heartedness which I encountered from the workmen around me. Not only were they most considerate in not invading my quarters at inconvenient times, but they showed great sympathy, tried to supply me with whatever information I needed, and spared no effort to produce any piece of apparatus or furniture that I asked for.

I settled down to work, and while my experiments were cooling or simmering I had ample time to yield myself up to contemplation of the world around me. My thoughts wandered towards the future, and then swung back to the past. What struck me first was the profound difference between the turbulent years I had left behind me and the placid and peaceful atmosphere of this basement laboratory in Manchester. But I did not let my mind run idle for too long. From the first week on I spent several hours a day in the systematic study of English. I learned whole pages of my chemistry text-book by heart. The

E

technical language was fairly easy to follow, but what I did to the pronunciation, reading aloud to myself, is now beyond my imagination. However, I must have made some progress, for I found myself gradually opening up lines of communication with my fellow-workers in the laboratory building.

About six weeks passed in this way. I lived, except for the contacts I have mentioned, almost *incommunicado*. I used to bring my lunch to the lab and work solidly from nine o'clock in the morning till seven or eight at night, or even later; and I continued to fill in my time with the reading of chemical text-books and articles in chemical reviews.

With this almost complete absence of distraction, my work progressed rather well, and when Professor Perkin returned, about six or seven weeks after our first interview, I was glad to have something to show him. He seemed pleased, and was most encouraging; he placed at my disposal two research men, whom I could employ on special subjects. They were not the best men available, but they were pleasant people and willing workers. Later I had as my assistant a young demonstrator by the name of Pickles, a Lancashire boy with a massive north-country accent. He was an extremely likeable fellow, whose only defect was his illusion that he could speak German.

I have special reason to remember the first work I did in England, for in a curious way it came up again in scientific circles after à lapse of over three decades. The subject is perhaps not without interest for the general reader. We established a reaction between magnesium organic compounds and phthalic anhydrides, leading to a new class of compounds which in turn can be converted into derivatives of anthracene, the basis of certain important dyestuffs. The scientific value of the discovery lay in the fact that the chemical structure of the anthracene derivatives so produced was, unlike those produced by previous methods, unambiguous. Nothing much was done with our method until the thirties, when research work on synthetic carcinogenous (cancer-producing) substances set in, prompted by the discovery that coal tar owes its carcinogenic action on the skin to the presence of a hydrocarbon which is also an anthracene derivative and can be made synthetically. This aroused interest in methods for the synthesis of such somewhat complicated hydrocarbons, and with the group of my co-workers which formed the Rehovoth team (concerning which I shall have much to tell later) in Palestine, we made investigations in greater detail and extended our earlier observations in various directions. In the hands of Professor Fieser of Harvard, and his pupils, our method became a valuable tool in their well-known research on the relations between molecular structure and cancer-producing activity. Professor Dufraisse of Paris made use of our reaction for his studies on photo-oxidation, and actually investigated a number of new substances which we sent him from Rehovoth.

There was one brief interruption in my work of which I shall tell later. The term began at the University, and my laboratory was enlivened from time to time by invasions of young students and senior research men. I began to make the acquaintance of my colleagues. By this time I was speaking English of a sort, and my relations with the college folk were such as to make me desire to stay in the laboratory and become part of their world. Indeed I cherished this ambition, but I was so far from dreaming that it could come true that I did not speak of it to anyone.

Three months had passed, and I was face to face with the problem of how to continue my existence in Manchester. My savings and my income from Shrirow had given out. I reflected that if there was anything at all in my secret ambition, a year or two at least would have to pass before it could be realized and I would be given employment in the school of chemistry. I was at an impasse.

Two things happened, almost simultaneously, to resolve my difficulties. First, Charles Dreyfus invited me to do some research for his firm. It was a type of work that would not interfere with my college programme, and in fact I would not have to leave my laboratory, to which I had by now become very much attached. After obtaining the permission of Professor Perkin, I agreed to combine the two duties, and in this wise obtained the bare minimum required to support me in Manchester. So, from November 1904 on, I was more or less secure from the material point of view. My budget was a very modest one; it did not exceed £3 a week, all told—board, lodging, laboratory expenses, books, everything. I even had a small sum to send my sister who had just begun her studies in Zurich.

I was so engrossed in my work that, had it not been for my weekly visit to the Massels, I would never have known any other street than the one which led from my lodgings to the college. I was living with a Jewish family, who had probably originated on Cheetham Hill, but who pretended to have nothing to do with it. In fact they pretended to know nothing about the Jewish community generally, and to be entirely innocent of Yiddish. I had my suspicions regarding the accent of the older members of the family, but it was hinted to me that it was Australian; my knowledge of English did not extend to the niceties of colonial pronunciation so I could not challenge the claim. However, they were kindly people, and made me feel at home with them. I saw little of them for I went out early in the morning, and came home late. My room was never invaded by members of the family, and I could live alone with my books, my letters and my thoughts.

I was slowly accustoming myself to Manchester life. My greatest difficulty was with the fogs, which depressed me terribly. They seemed always to be thickest in my basement laboratory; my eyes suffered and I was tormented by a permanent cold. Tom thought that such colds could be cured by inhaling chemical fumes, but though I thought highly of Tom's worldly wisdom I did not feel I could extend this good opinion to his medical knowledge, and I declined his advice. Towards Christmas I found myself feeling unusually tired and depressed. I was overworked; I was homesick for my European surroundings; I was cut off from Zionist work; and I had seen my fiancée only once since my departure from Geneva. And then, with complete unexpectedness, came my second stroke of good fortune, and my gloom was dispelled miraculously by a conversation I had with my professor just before we parted for the Christmas vacation (he went away, I stayed in Manchester); he said that when the next term began I might try to deliver a weekly lecture on some branch of chemistry with which I was most familiar; and he urged me not to be discouraged by the linguistic difficulties I would experience in the beginning. He himself, he said, had passed through this stage when he delivered his first lectures in a German university. He would advise his senior men to come to my lectures, and I would find them, he assured me, 'well behaved.' He also suggested that he would propose my name for a research scholarship, to begin with the year.

I was in heaven.

I devoted the entire three weeks of the Christmas vacation to the preparation of my lectures, and in January 1905 I delivered my first lecture on chemistry in English. I went into the lecture theatre with a beating heart. I was used to public speaking. I had addressed large audiences in many towns in Russia, Switzerland and Germany; but no political speech I ever delivered, no matter how important and critical the issue, has ever affected me as deeply as this first lecture at an English university. I did not yet know the English students. In the short time I had spent in Manchester I had had little opportunity of getting near them. They seemed to me, from a distance, to be terribly young, and terribly boisterous. I thought that they took their studies less seriously than the heavy-weight German students to whom I was accustomed. They gave an impression of flippancy and superficiality. In all this, I discovered, I was seriously mistaken.

When I came into the lecture theatre they received me with a friendliness which encouraged me to put my case before them as well as I could. I was a foreigner, I said, and had been in the country only a few months; I was consequently at their mercy. I would do my best, but I would certainly perpetrate many howlers. They could make all the jokes they wanted at my expense—after the lecture. The effect of this little introductory appeal was remarkable. They listened to the lecture with the closest attention; when the hour was over, they did not leave the theatre, but stayed on and surrounded me, putting a great many questions to me which showed they had understood the main points of the lecture, and were genuinely interested. So the first ordeal passed triumphantly; the next lecture, a week later, was already routine.

When about a month had passed, Professor Perkin suggested that I take a special tutorial class in connection with his own lectures on organic chemistry. I jumped at the offer, and again put my best into the preparation. The 'tuts,' which were voluntary and informal, became very popular. Between these and my regular lectures I found myself in intimate contact with the students, and the experience was one of the finest I can look back on. We established a cordial relationship from the outset, but I did not hesitate to subject my students to a discipline and a schedule of work to which they were not at all accustomed. I insisted on great cleanliness in the laboratory —not an easy thing to achieve under local climatic conditions, aggravated as they were by the smoke of many factories. I insisted also on neat records. I followed up the work of each student, having set myself the ambition of taking over the whole course in organic chemistry. I concentrated, in particular, on making the work as interesting as possible, introducing material that did not appear in the text-books. I watched my men. I used to tell the class that if a man worked well during the year, but did badly in the examinations, it would not weigh much with me, and he could depend on me to defend him before the visiting examiners. On the other hand, if a bad student happened, by fluke, to do well in the examination, he could count only on the strict minimum of credit. These Lancashire students, who had a keen sense of justice, agreed with me tacitly, and after a sojourn of a year or two in Manchester, I was completely at home with them.

A curious incident out of those days, in no way connected with my student contacts, comes to my mind, shedding an indirect light on the spirit of hospitality which was the pride of Manchester University. I arrived in England at the height of the Russo-Japanese War, and shortly after Perkin's return from Europe a Japanese student was sent to share my basement lab. He took me for a Russian, and was, of course, very careful to allude neither to the war nor its causes. Now and again he would bring a newspaper into the lab; so would I. We read the war reports with close attention, and when we discussed— each in his own variety of English—the day's news, it was always in relation to some quite trivial incident. Listening to us, you would have thought the war did not exist. In actual fact we were both rejoicing in the progress of events—but for different reasons. I saw in this wretched war the possibility of the discrediting of czarism, perhaps even its overthrow. The Jap was an ardent patriot and prayed silently for the triumph of his country's arms. When the news of the battle of Tsushima, in which the Russian armada was completely annihilated, was reported, we sat at opposite ends of the laboratory, each eagerly devouring the special edition of the evening papers. The Jap could no longer contain his feelings: after he had finished reading, he came over and silently pressed my hand in condolence. I was fully aware of the misunderstanding, but my English was not equal to an explanation. I accepted his sympathy in silence and went on with my work. We never got round to a discussion of the war.

A few months later I was astounded to read in the Annual Report of the Director of Laboratories a paragraph referring proudly to the international character of the Manchester Chemical School, and rejoicing over the unifying influence of science which bridged the gulf between nation and nation, and made it possible for a Japanese and a Russian to work side by side during the tragic period of the Russo-Japanese War. It was not until some years later that I felt able to explain to my acquaintances what my real feelings had been about the Russian defeats.

Parallel with this process of adjustment to English university life there was going on in me a deep inner struggle round the repression of my Zionist activities—a repression which was only partial at best. The perpetual problem of 'the proper course of action' returned to haunt me. Here I was, quietly ensconced in Manchester, pursuing an academic career, while 'over there,' in the Zionist world, in the Jewish world, in the world at large, issues clamoured for attention. In September 1904, before Professor Perkin returned from his vacation, I interrupted my work to make a dash for Vienna, where the Action Committee held its first meeting after the death of Herzl. It was a depressing affair; the helplessness of those on whom the leadership had devolved was painfully obvious. The best they seemed to hope for was some sort of an attempt to keep in existence the work which had been initiated by the departed leader. I saw some of my old Zionist friends on this trip, and, of course, I saw my fiancée. I returned to Manchester with my sense of frustration deepened. Letters continued to reach me, describing the condition of the movement abroad. I was out of things. The fact that I had, in a sense, planned this did not make the condition more acceptable.

I had little affinity with the Zionists in England, who were still concentrating, for the larger part, on the possibilities of Uganda. Many of them even thought that if Uganda was found to be unsuitable then all we had to do was start looking for another territory. Only a few still adhered to those tenets which were the soul of the movement. Zionism as such was in a state of stagnation, and Zionist activity was limited to the usual clichés and claptrap performances of Jewish societies in English provincial towns. I felt no incentive to associate myself with this sort of thing. Moreover, I was still regarded with suspicion as an opponent of the views being propagated by the leaders in London. In one way, then, it was not hard for me to hold myself aloof; but the discouragement from the outside did nothing to lessen my own feeling of isolation and futility.

My first contact with the Manchester Zionist Society of those days was rather disastrous. I went with my friend Massel to a meeting for which there had been announced a lecture. The title was: 'Stray Observations of a Wandering Jew.' I thought I would meet in the lecturer a fellow-wanderer who had perhaps gone through much the same experiences as myself before my arrival in England.

To my utter astonishment and dismay, the wanderings of the lecturer proved to have covered nothing more than a trip from London to Brussels. He described in great detail how he had bought his ticket at Cooks', how he had crossed the Channel, how he had landed at Calais, and how he had travelled on to Brussels. I listened patiently, waiting at least for some description of the Jews and Jewish life he had met on his very brief pilgrimage. My patience was not rewarded even to this limited extent. Only towards the end of his paper did the speaker mention, quite casually, a synagogue in Brussels, which he had visited and found wanting. I failed to see what all this talk had to do with Jews or Jewish wanderings, and was puzzled to find a roomful of people listening with deference to the speaker, and apparently taking his remarks as real spiritual sustenance for Zionists.

At the conclusion of the meeting, the chairman was inspired by someone—probably my friend Massel—to call on me to move a vote of thanks. I was too new to the country and its usages to know what this meant—namely, that I was expected to approve the lecture, and add a number of compliments. I only realized that I was being asked to say something, and I took my responsibility literally and seriously. I felt that the lecture had been, in intellectual content, beneath criticism, and I gave vent to my feelings in no uncertain terms. The consternation of the good Zionists of Manchester may be better imagined than described. I had committed something worse than a *faux pas*; I had confirmed all the evil reports which were current about me as an obstreperous fellow, a natural rebel and a born obstructionist. It took me months to live the incident down.

The setback only served to convince me that sustained abstention from Zionist work was psychologically impossible for me. I went back to my laboratory and my classes, but the pressure of events, or rather of their report, broke in on my academic retreat, destroyed my peace of mind, and finished by paralysing my scientific work. My new English acquaintances sometimes spoke of Russia with me; but they spoke of it as of a curiosity, a survival from a past quite inconceivable to them, with which they had no real concern. I never liked these conversations; for to me all these questions were matters of bitter and intimate concern, to my friends they were abstract subjects for discussion. It was apparently impossible for them to realize that these were things affecting vitally the everyday life of people like themselves—their contemporaries in another country.

My hatred of the Russian régime grew as I contrasted life in Russia with life in England, where freedom of speech and thought were things taken for granted, like the air one breathed. The hopes which were born of the impending defeat of Russia made it harder than ever for me to bear with my self-imposed exile from public affairs. A great struggle was going on over there; the will of the Russian people was beginning to manifest itself, a desperate and tottering bureaucracy was striking back with the last remnants of its forces. The people emerged with a partial victory. A parliament (with very limited powers, it is true, but still a parliament) was brought into being, and if its legislative actions were cancelled by imperial ukases, at least a tribune had been created from which the Russian people could address the world. We naturally hoped that, in the fundamental changes which were taking place, Jewry, which had given its full share to the toll of victims in the struggle, would also receive its share of the benefits. Perhaps the era of savage oppressions was over, perhaps the intolerable laws which

E*

hedged in the life of the Jewish community would be rescinded. All these hopes were doomed to disappointment. A few Jewish deputies were elected to the Duma, and there they had the opportunity of speaking up on behalf of the inarticulate millions which they represented. But the Russian Imperial Government had already chosen the path which was to lead, a decade later, to its irretrievable ruin. The Revolution was liquidated amid Jewish pogroms; the Duma was repressed, the ancient tyranny returned.

These bloody developments had a direct bearing on the character of the Zionist movement. At first they had resulted in the panic mood which had expressed itself in the Uganda and other territorial proposals. As the utter impracticability of Uganda was revealed, the deeper strength of Zionism reasserted itself. The movement was more than a relief organization; it was the source of endurance of the Jewish people. During the preponderance of the Herzlian view, Palestine had been merely an incidental part of the plan; now it was beginning to be realized that the cementing of an intimate bond between the movement and Palestine was in itself a source of moral comfort, hope and rehabilitation. The stage was being set for the resolution of the conflict between 'political Zionism' and 'practical Zionism.' The actual synthesis did not take place for some years, but the change of heart in the Zionists was beginning—and it was this that made possible my gradual resumption of activities.

The Manchester Zionist Society abandoned their 'syllabus,' as they called it (it was a hodgepodge of random subjects covered by random speakers) in favour of a more serious programme of lectures in Zionism and Zionist aspirations. The change attracted numbers of the younger members of the community, who for the first time heard something of real Jewish life. As my anti-Ugandist sins and my shocking *faux pas* at the lecture receded into the background, I ceased to be the sinister figure of my early Manchester days. I was invited to speak at the Zionist Society. I answered questions, I encouraged discussion; it was discovered that the exchange of views was interesting as well as instructive.

Slowly Manchester became a centre of Zionist thought which was destined, after months and years of laborious effort, to spread its influence through the surrounding towns and to

leave its impress on English Zionism as a whole. The details of
this growth belong to later pages of this story. They were
bound up, naturally, with a gradual extension of my contacts.
I found out that Manchester was not the Jewish intellectual
wilderness I had imagined it to be. I formed many friendships
there, friendships which were not only of a personal character,
but which grew into lifelong comradeship in Zionist work. I
met, soon after my arrival, Charles Dreyfus, who was the
chairman of the Manchester Zionist Society. About that time
I also became acquainted with Harry Sacher, who was then
beginning his distinguished career in journalism and law, and
who was to play an important rôle in the Zionist movement.
Simon Marks and Israel Sieff, who have rendered long years of
service to Zionism, came into the orbit of the movement some
years later. Of these friends I shall speak again.

The beginnings of my integration with English Zionism
belong to the 1905 to 1906 period. One fortuitous circumstance
helped to make that transition time easier for me: Achad Ha-am
came to live in London and, though journeys to London were
luxuries I could ill afford, I managed now and then to go
down and spend a week-end with him in his modest house in
Hampstead.

I had known Achad Ha-am for many years, first as a name,
then personally when I was a student in Berlin, and later in
occasional contacts. He had been one of the formative forces in
my early life. Now he became, though nearly twenty years my
senior, a friend, and I observed at closer range this personality
which has left such a mark on the Jewish thought of the last
generation. It has often been thrown up at me that I have not
been as critical of Achad Ha-am as of the other Zionist personalities. The truth is that I thought of him always as the
philosopher, not as the man of action. A music critic does not
have to play an instrument, but his criticism is not the less
valid. I did not expect from Achad Ha-am what I expected
from Herzl; my approach was altogether different.

In the days when I, as little more than a youth, had already
become critical of Herzl and the 'Western' outlook on Zionism,
I felt myself particularly drawn towards Achad Ha-am. He,
the clear thinker and mature man, understood the significance
of the cleavage between East and West better than I, though

he carried his distrust too far; for he attended only the first Zionist Congress, and could never be induced to attend another. If there were some who acclaimed Herzl with uncritical and unbalanced enthusiasm, Achad Ha-am was over-cautious in his appraisal of the man and of the instrument he had created, the Congress. At the first festive gathering in Basle, he sat (as he reported later) 'like a mourner at a wedding.' He trembled for the moral values of the movement. Jewish dignity, Jewish freedom, Jewish self-emancipation, were not to be won by public demonstrations, but by inner discipline and self-mastery. As he had criticized the 'Lovers of Zion' and the administration of the Rothschild colonies in Palestine, so he criticized the Congress for what he thought was the essential emptiness of its programme.

The Zionist movement stood for a time under the double sign of Herzl and Achad Ha-am. There was Herzlian Zionism, with its great political vistas and its deferment of the practical work; there was the Zionism of Achad Ha-am, concentrating on the qualitative progress of the resettlement in Palestine. It was only in later years that the two views were synthesized, and much of my thought and work was given to the achievement of this synthesis. But as between the two men, there had always been a feeling of mutual respect. Achad Ha-am was impersonal and impartial in his criticism; he was guided by a deep-rooted intellectual probity; and the Russian Zionists in particular took his strictures to heart.

On the personal side, Achad Ha-am was of a quiet, reserved and retiring nature. Though primarily a thinker he had a strong streak of practicality; the great tea firm of Wissotzky had sent him to London to manage the English branch, and he did this extremely well. Very certainly Wissotzky would not have employed him otherwise. With all his high qualities, or because of them, Achad Ha-am was modest, and had an aversion to the limelight. His pen-name, Achad Ha-am—'One of the People' —was chosen without affectation. In his habits as in his systematic thinking, he was exact to the point of pedantry. I remember how on one occasion he was two minutes late for an appointment with us, and was so distressed that I had to assure him that our watches were wrong by exactly two minutes.

I have never understood why this self-effacing individual was singled out by the anti-Semites as the leader of that mysterious and melodramatic conspiracy which goes under the name of 'The Elders of Zion.' They were for ever alluding to 'Usher Ginsburg,' the man behind the sinister Jewish plot for world domination. Perhaps it was because the famous 'Protocols' started somewhere in south Russia, and Achad Ha-am was the secretary of the old Odessa Committee for Palestine in the days of the *Chibath Zion*. Whatever the reason, a more absurd juxtaposition surely never existed than the one between the arch-plotter against Western civilization who was supposed to head 'The Elders of Zion,' and the academic and rather prim little man whose mind was filled with philosophic concepts, and who never meddled in non-Jewish affairs. But then, it may be rather absurd on my part to look for rhyme or reason in the weird workings of the anti-Semitic mind.

CHAPTER VIII

TAKING ROOT

My First Meeting with Arthur James Balfour—Marriage—Doubling in Science and Zionism—Our Elder Son is Born—My Wife Doubles in Housekeeping and Medicine—Zangwill and Territorialism—Working the Provincial Communities—Manchester University—Arthur Schuster—Samuel Alexander—Ernest Rutherford—The Great City of Manchester

PERHAPS this is the best point to place on record a memorable encounter which symbolized for me the far-off beginnings of a new chapter in the relationship between England and Zionism. It also has a special place in my life. It was about this time that I had resumed my Zionist activities in the new and limited setting of Manchester and the English provinces; and my meeting with Arthur James Balfour has set a stamp on the entire period.

Charles Dreyfus, whom I have mentioned as managing director of the Clayton Aniline Works, and chairman of the Manchester Zionist Society, was also a member of the Manchester City Council and chairman of the Conservative party in Manchester. In spite of the fact that he was an ardent Ugandist, and was for ever arguing the issue with me, we developed friendly relations with each other which lasted many years—in fact, until his death, which occurred at a very advanced age. Early in 1906 a general election took place in England, and Balfour was chosen to contest the Clayton division of North Manchester. In the midst of the confusion and hullabaloo of the campaign Balfour, at Dreyfus's suggestion, consented to receive me. He was interested in meeting one of the Jews who had fought against the acceptance of the Uganda offer made by his Government. That I was anxious to meet Balfour goes without saying. Dreyfus's interest in the matter was to have Balfour convince me that I had been wrong in my attitude; it did not occur to him that the upshot of the interview would be in the contrary sense.

I was taken to Balfour in a room in the old-fashioned Queen's Hotel, in Piccadilly, which served as his headquarters. The corridors were crowded with people waiting for a word with the candidate. I surmised that Mr. Balfour had consented to see me for a few minutes—'a quarter of an hour,' Dreyfus warned me—simply to break the monotony of his routine. He kept me for well over an hour.

I had been less than two years in the country, and my English was still not easy to listen to. I remember how Balfour sat in his usual pose, his legs stretched out in front of him, an imperturbable expression on his face. We plunged at once into the subject of our interview. He asked me why some Jews, Zionists, were so bitterly opposed to the Uganda offer. The British Government was really anxious to do something to relieve the misery of the Jews; and the problem was a practical one, calling for a practical approach. In reply I plunged into what I recall as a long harangue on the meaning of the Zionist movement. I dwelt on the spiritual side of Zionism, I pointed out that nothing but a deep religious conviction expressed in modern political terms could keep the movement alive, and that this conviction had to be based on Palestine and on Palestine alone. Any deflection from Palestine was—well, a form of idolatry. I added that if Moses had come into the sixth Zionist Congress when it was adopting the resolution in favour of the Commission for Uganda, he would surely have broken the tablets once again. We knew that the Uganda offer was well meant, and on the surface it might appear the more practical road. But I was sure that—quite apart from the availability and suitability of the territory—the Jewish people would never produce either the money or the energy required in order to build up a wasteland and make it habitable, unless that land were Palestine. Palestine has this magic and romantic appeal for the Jews; our history has been what it is because of our tenacious hold on Palestine. We have never accepted defeat and have never forsaken the memory of Palestine. Such a tradition could be converted into real motive power, and we were trying to do just that, struggling against great difficulties, but sure that the day would come when we would succeed.

I looked at my listener, and suddenly became afraid that this appearance of interest and courtesy might be nothing more than a mask. I felt that I was sweating blood and I tried to find some less ponderous way of expressing myself. I was ready to bow myself out of the room, but Balfour held me back, and put some questions to me regarding the growth of the movement. He had heard of 'Dr. Herz'—a very distinguished leader, who had founded and organized it. I ventured to correct him, pointing out that Herzl had indeed placed the movement on a new footing, and had given the tradition a modern political setting; but Herzl had died young; and he had left us this legacy of Uganda, which we were trying to liquidate.

Then suddenly I said: 'Mr. Balfour, supposing I were to offer you Paris instead of London, would you take it?'

He sat up, looked at me, and answered: 'But Dr. Weizmann, we have London.'

'That is true,' I said. 'But we had Jersualem when London was a marsh.'

He leaned back, continued to stare at me, and said two things which I remember vividly. The first was: 'Are there many Jews who think like you?'

I answered: 'I believe I speak the mind of millions of Jews whom you will never see and who cannot speak for themselves, but with whom I could pave the streets of the country I come from.'

To this he said: 'If that is so, you will one day be a force.'

Shortly before I withdrew, Balfour said: 'It is curious. The Jews I meet are quite different.'

I answered: 'Mr. Balfour, you meet the wrong kind of Jews.'

Before I go on to relate the more immediate consequences of this interview, let me mention an odd episode which came like an echo, at the end of three decades, to my last remark. Balfour was maintaining, at the time of our meeting, a correspondence with Mrs. Leopold de Rothschild, the mother of Anthony and Lionel de Rothschild, and soon after our conversation he wrote her a letter in which he said: 'I had a most interesting conversation with a young Russian Jew, a lecturer at the university.' Now Mrs. de Rothschild was a bitter anti-Zionist. When Mrs. Blanche Dugdale, Balfour's niece, who had become his literary executrix, was collecting material for his biography, she wrote to Mrs. de Rothschild asking if she could use any of her uncle's letters to her. Mrs. de Rothschild sent them all, with the exception of this one, which her son read out to me—quite inadvertently, of course—after her death. I had said to Balfour: 'You meet the wrong kind of Jews.' Of course, I did not set eyes on the Rothschilds until years later.

I return to the narrative. The conversation with Balfour taught me two important things. The first was that, in spite of years of Zionist propaganda in England, both in the press and by word of mouth, a leading British statesman like Mr. Balfour had only the most naïve and rudimentary notion of the movement. The second was that if someone had been found to present the case of Palestine to the British authorities, it would not have been difficult to enlist their sympathies and perhaps, in certain circumstances, their active support. Mr. Dreyfus's plan for my re-education had gone awry; for I was now more convinced than ever that instead of going off on the wild goose chase that was Uganda, we should have made our position clear to England from the outset.

There followed a period in my life on which I look back with not a little astonishment at my powers of physical endurance. At a time when I undertook the responsibility of marriage, and when it was of the utmost importance for me to establish myself firmly in my academic career, I was drawn again into Zionist activity by my feeling that the time was ripe for a thorough-going change in the character of the movement. We were about to move beyond the Uganda deadpoint, and I could no longer abstain from work. The conversation with Balfour—about which I published nothing until many years later—was like a tocsin or alarm. I was not free to choose my course of action.

I must, however, put developments more or less in their chronological order.

My fiancée had stayed on in Geneva to complete her medical course. In the summer of 1906 she graduated, returned to Rostov to visit her family and obtain certain necessary marriage papers, and then came up to Danzig, to meet me. We were married in the near-by town of Zopott, with only four members of my family present, my father and mother, my elder brother Feivel and my sister Miriam. Immediately after the marriage we went to Cologne, where a meeting of the Action Committee, under the chairmanship of David Wolffsohn, Herzl's successor, was being held, and there, for a week, my young bride practically lost sight of me.

The sessions of the Action Committee were long and stormy. We—that is, the younger group of the Democratic Faction—were trying to unseat Wolffsohn, whom we considered unfit for the Presidency. He was a well-meaning and devoted Zionist, generous and hard-working, but without personality or vision. He did his best to imitate his idol, Herzl, but he had neither Herzl's personality nor his organizing ability. At bottom Wolffsohn was a businessman, and his passion was the Zionist bank—the Jewish Colonial Trust. He looked upon us younger men as something like desperadoes, quite unfit to be entrusted with responsibilities. We got him out somewhat later, and substituted for the Presidency a general Presidium, or Council, with Professor Otto Warburg as chairman.

But concerning those Cologne sessions I remember chiefly my wife's extraordinary patience and understanding, and my feelings of guilt. I remember coming home—to the hotel, that is—at five o'clock one morning, with a great bouquet of flowers and a basket of peaches as a peace offering. It wasn't necessary, but it made me feel a little better. Such was our honeymoon.

When the sessions of the Action Committee closed, we took a trip down the Rhine to Switzerland, spent a week there, and returned to Manchester. We arrived at Victoria Station late one night, with one shilling in our possession. During the last hour of the trip we debated whether we ought to spend the shilling on sandwiches or try to get a cab to the lodgings which I had arranged for before leaving Manchester. Fortunately we were met at the station by a friend of mine, a chemist from the Clayton Works, so we had the sandwiches and the cab.

The first autumn and winter in Manchester was a really horrid time for my wife. My choice of lodgings had not been a very fortunate one. The landlady was a slattern, who spent the whole day with curling pins in her hair, reading detective novels. The house was dirty, the food tasteless, the surroundings indescribably drab and dismal. Most of the time my wife was alone; I stayed late in the laboratory, and when I did have a free evening I was as likely as not to devote it to a Zionist meeting. The wives of my colleagues were extraordinarily kind to us, but in my wife's case there was, as there had been for me at the beginning, the barrier of language. Here she was, in a gloomy, foggy, northern city, cut off from the world she had known, and married to a struggling young scientist who had, as a sideline, a full-time political interest. I recall that winter with something less than pleasure.

The period that followed saw a gradual improvement. In the spring, when we were expecting our first child, we moved to a tiny house in Birchfield Road. This was quite a desperate undertaking. My salary at the university was then, I think, about £250 a year. I was earning another hundred and fifty a year as research chemist for the Clayton Works. But of this total I was sending an average of two pounds a week to two sisters and a brother who were now studying in Zurich. To furnish our home—which we did on the instalment plan—I undertook the marking of chemistry papers for Oxford, Cambridge and South Kensington colleges. The payment was a shilling for the lower papers, half a crown for the higher papers. I had to mark one thousand papers to pay off Kendal Milne's, the furniture dealers; and it was stone-breaking, heartbreaking work. I did it at odd hours, day or night, very often with my new-born son, Benjy, on my lap. I held him there partly out of affection and partly to give my wife an occasional rest. Now and again he set up a great wailing, as infants will, and I can only hope that I was never driven to do any injustice to my unfortunate examinees.

My wife began her duties as housekeeper and mother under great handicaps. She had taken a brilliant medical degree, she spoke four languages, she played the piano excellently, but having left home in her early youth to pursue her medical studies, she knew nothing at all of housekeeping. She likes to recall how, one morning, the maid came in and announced that the butcher was at the door. 'What does he want?' she asked. 'He wants to know what you want,' answered the maid. 'I want meat,' was my wife's reply. It did not occur to her that one had to specify the animal and the anatomical section of the animal.

However, she learned quickly, in part with the help of two ministering angels. The first was Mrs. Benfey, the wife of a colleague of mine at the Clayton Works, and the second was Mrs. Schuster, the wife of Professor (afterward Sir) Arthur Schuster, one of my senior professors, of whom I shall have more to tell. Mrs. Schuster took a tremendous liking to my wife. She admired her spirit, her charm and her ability. In particular she was rather astonished that a young woman who had taken her medical degree at a European university should be both beautiful and smart.

Before long our house became organized, simply, modestly and in the fine taste that was innate with my wife. We were able to receive as well as to pay visits. My income grew slowly. Our son was a great source of joy to us, and in time we were able to engage a nurse, so that my wife could resume her studies. That was in 1909, and in 1911 she graduated, and obtained a position as medical officer for a number of city clinics and municipal schools for mothers, under the direction of the health officer, Dr. Niven, a senior wrangler, a man of high intelligence and advanced views. By then we were solidly settled, my income at the university had risen to six hundred a year, my wife was making three hundred and fifty, and, with some other earnings, we had about a thousand a year between us, a considerable sum in those days. We were in clover. Out of this, however, I was helping my brothers and sisters through their university courses in various parts of Europe, to the extent of about two hundred and fifty a year. At one time my brother Shmuel came to live with us, and studied at Manchester University; at another time it was my sister Anna. We were, and have remained, a rather clannish family.

But I have anticipated, and I must return to the period when we were counting our pennies and living on short rations— rations considerably shortened, I should say, by the constant diversion of my energies into the Zionist movement. The Uganda issue had faded out. Zangwill, who had been a determining influence in English Zionism, had definitely left the movement, to attend to his own newly formed Jewish Territorial Organization. Although his committee included some very distinguished and high-sounding names—chiefly of English Jews who objected to Zionism in its pure form—the organization was doomed to failure from its birth.

It was in effect a sort of geographical society which scoured the world to find an empty territory in which to plant the Jews, and it laboured under the same fallacy which had led astray some of the originators of the modern Zionist movement: namely, that it was possible, by any kind of territorial project, to cure, as if with a magic wand, the evils from which Jews suffered in congested areas, and to deflect the stream of immigrants pouring into highly industrialized Western countries towards some waste and desolate place such as could only be rendered habitable after decades of work and the expenditure of untold wealth. The territories usually discovered were either too hot or too cold. However, the formation of the J.T.O. had one important advantage; it served to isolate this particular fallacy, and to concentrate its adherents in one place, leaving the rest of Zionism to go back to its original programme, to revise its position in the light of the experience gained in the recent controversy, and to set to work accordingly.

In these circumstances, my contact with the English Zionists became, with a few exceptions, more intimate and friendly. They no longer regarded me as revolutionary, and some of them began to realize that there are times when 'the longest way round is the shortest way home.'

The leadership of the Manchester Jewish Community rested between Charles Dreyfus and Nathan Laski, father of Harold Laski. Mr. Laski was of Russian origin, and his interest in the Zionist movement was therefore more natural. The great majority of German Jews in Manchester were dissociated from their people, and many of them were converts to Christianity. Dreyfus and the other members of his family, who came from Geneva, were honourable exceptions. There was also in Manchester a considerable settlement of Sephardic Jews, important because of the rôle they played in the cotton trade with India and Egypt. But by far the largest part of the community was made up of Russian Jews who were, as usual, very poor, very Jewish and, to me, very attractive. With them I felt most at home.

In the other towns—that is, in Leeds, Halifax, Liverpool, Glasgow, Edinburgh, Bradford—to which I travelled increasingly on Zionist missionary work, I found communities modelled very much on the Manchester pattern: a handful of devotees to the cause among the lower-middle classes, indifference or hostility among the upper classes, whether of British, German or Russian origin, but with the largest number of exceptions in the last. With some of the well-to-do Russian Jews one could at least talk, though they, like the others, displayed their Jewish interest chiefly in the founding of hospitals and orphan asylums, and in other local philanthropies—visible and tangible enterprises which redounded to the credit of the communities and the glory of the patrons. The Rabbis and Hebrew teachers were friendly to us; so was the Jewish press—what there was of it. The old English-Jewish families might just as well have belonged to another world.

On the whole the communities were sombre and drab. There was rarely a decent hall to hold meetings in; usually we gathered in an ill-lit room in some gloomy building. I remember how I used to arrive in Manchester at midnight on Sunday, after a week-end visit to Edinburgh or Leeds, and had to make the long walk home through the dreary streets all the way to Withington; for there were no trams after midnight, and if a cab was obtainable it was beyond my means. And at home my wife would be waiting for me with the fire burning and something warm to eat, for I invariably came home half dead with fatigue and hunger. She looked sad and lonesome, but never reproachful. I think I would have felt better if she had made a bit of a scene.

I liked those poor Jewish communities. They learned to forgive me for my opposition to Herzl, and I worked hard with them. I taught, I explained, I invited discussion. I felt that they were my sort. And in spite of the drudgery, I was on the whole happy—or I would have been, if there had not hovered over all of us the shadow of the great Jewish tragedy in the East. But at least there was a sense of progress now. The movement had swung back into its proper orbit, and the little we were doing had meaning and relevance.

London I visited only to see Achad Ha-am, Herbert Bentwich, and a group of younger Zionists, Harry Sacher, Leon Simon and others. I was not invited to address any meetings there. The road was still barred by Greenberg of the *Jewish Chronicle*. I am afraid that in addition to his recollection of my opposition to Herzl, he also felt resentment at the rôle I was beginning to play among the provincial Zionists. I am sorry to say that we never became reconciled, but I do not think the fault was mine.

Side by side with my Zionist activity in England, I resumed more sustained contact with European Zionism, so that all in all that pre-war period 1906 to 1914 was one of the most fruitful, as well as one of the most exacting, in my life. But an account of the general progress of Zionism during those years must be deferred while I try to complete the picture of our Manchester life.

I feel I cannot too often stress the kindness which my wife and I encountered from my colleagues at the university. They were a remarkable group of men, and made up, I believe, as distinguished a faculty as was then to be found anywhere in any English or European school. Outside of my own department I became acquainted very early with the physicist, Arthur Schuster. He was a converted Jew, probably baptized in childhood, and came of a prominent Frankfort banking family. There were three brothers, all of whom made fine careers, but by far the ablest was Arthur, a contemporary of J. J. Thomson, and a great physicist. He was extremely intelligent, an excellent student, and kind-hearted to a degree—but possessed of biting wit. Among the many visitors of the Schusters—they kept open house—was Marie Stopes, famous in later years as a leader of the birth-control movement. She was at that time a graduate student, doing research, if I remember rightly, on botany. She was an ebullient young woman, who held forth endlessly and vigorously on a great variety of subjects, while Schuster was the typical savant, restrained and cautious. One day, asking Miss Stopes how she was getting along in her work, he received the cheerful reply: 'Oh, wonderfully! I make a new discovery every day!' Whereupon Professor Schuster inquired courteously: 'Dr. Stopes, if you discover on Tuesday that your discovery of Monday was all wrong, do you count that as one or as two discoveries?'

The Schusters were accounted liberals, or even radicals, by the standards of those days. Mrs. Schuster, who was active in university and civic affairs, was the friend and patroness—as she still is, in her gracious old age—of all young academicians and people of promise generally. The Schuster house was very close to ours, in Victoria Park, and it is not easy to express what that proximity—and propinquity—came to mean for us. Nearly forty years have passed since then, and we have not had a birthday in all that time which has not brought us a letter of greetings from Lady Schuster. With her daughter, Nora, we were, as younger people, on an even more intimate footing, and my wife and I treasure among our most precious memories that of a great mountain-climbing tour of Switzerland in the summer of 1913, with Nora Schuster and Harry Sacher as our companions. The daughter of an English clergyman, Mrs. Schuster took a keener interest in Jewish affairs than did her husband, and she reproached her children—who were, of course, only half-Jewish—for their indifference to the Zionist movement! Lady Schuster and Sir Arthur attended, in 1925, the opening of the Hebrew University in Jerusalem, Sir Arthur in a double capacity as representative of Manchester University and as Secretary of the Royal Society. Him I could not get to take an active part in Zionism, but he did become a regular contributor to the Zionist funds, and left part of his splendid library to the Hebrew University.

Another man with whom we became very close was Professor Samuel Alexander, the author of *Time, Space and Deity*, and one of the great philosophers of our generation. When we left our little house in Birchfield Road, and moved to more commodious quarters in Brunswick Road—this was, I think, in 1913—we were practically next-door neighbours of Alexander's. I had an enormous admiration for him. He, too, after a time, began to take an interest in the affairs of his people and became, within his very modest means, a contributor to the Zionist funds. He used to come, now and then, to Jewish meetings, and lecture on Spinoza, but he stayed aloof from public affairs. He followed closely the development of the Hebrew University, and sent us one of his best men, Professor Roth, to occupy the chair of philosophy. I tried hard to get Alexander to go to Jerusalem himself, but it could not be managed; for in his later years he became rather deaf, and had to be looked after.

His personality was as attractive as his appearance was arresting. He looked like some ancient Jewish prophet. He was very tall and had a vast beard and a magnificent dome of a forehead; and he went about in the shabbiest of clothes. He was shockingly absent-minded. He was a rather odd sight

when he mounted his bicycle and rode to or from the university
—the more so as he would be riding on the pavement as often
as on the road, to the delight of passers-by, who all knew him
well, and the great distress of the local police.

A third man with whom I stood on a very friendly footing
was Ernest (afterwards Lord) Rutherford, and this too was a
friendship which survived years of separation. Rutherford
succeeded Schuster, whose departure to London, to take up the
secretaryship of the Royal Society, was a great blow to us.
Rutherford was the very opposite of Schuster. Youthful,
energetic, boisterous, he suggested anything but the scientist.
He talked readily and vigorously on every subject under the
sun, often without knowing anything about it. Going down to
the refectory for lunch I would hear the loud, friendly voice
rolling up the corridor. He was quite devoid of any political
knowledge or feelings, being entirely taken up with his epoch-
making scientific work. He was a kindly person, but he did not
suffer fools gladly. Also he was rather contemptuous of persons
who spoke a few languages. 'You can express yourself well in
one language, and that should be English,' he used to say. Any
worker who came to him and did not prove to be a first-class
man was out in short order. Thus, to be allowed to work with
Rutherford was soon recognized as a distinction, and a galaxy
of famous young physicists and chemists issued from his school.
Nils Bohr, the Danish Nobel Prize winner, was among them;
so was the brilliant Moseley, whose promising life was cut short
at the age of twenty-seven by a Turkish bullet at Gallipoli;
E. N. da C. Andrade, Wilson, Geiger and others of note, were
also of Rutherford's school.

With all this, Rutherford was modest, simple and enormously
good-natured. When he went to Cambridge I lost sight of him
for a time. He later became, at my prompting, a friend of the
Hebrew University, and presided once or twice over dinners
in its behalf.

I cannot help linking my memories of Rutherford with those
of a closer friend, Albert Einstein. I have retained the distinct
impression that Rutherford was not terribly impressed by
Einstein's work, while Einstein on the other hand always spoke
to me of Rutherford in the highest terms, calling him a second
Newton. As scientists the two men were strongly contrasting

types—Einstein all calculation, Rutherford all experiment. The personal contrast was not less remarkable: Einstein looks like an etherealized body, Rutherford looked like a big, healthy, boisterous New Zealander—which is exactly what he was. But there is no doubt that as an experimenter Rutherford was a genius, one of the greatest. He worked by intuition, and whatever he touched turned to gold. He seemed to have a sixth sense in his tackling of experimental problems. Einstein achieved all his results by sheer calculation. Rutherford was considered the greatest chemist of his day. He obliterated the line of demarcation between chemistry and physics and discovered the transmutation of the elements, turning chemistry back to alchemy. But he knew no chemistry in our accepted sense of that science and method. Nor was he a great mathematician, in which he again stood in contrast to Einstein.

Rutherford greatly enjoyed pulling my leg about Zionism. 'What's wrong with England?' he used to ask me, uproariously, and laugh loudly enough to be heard halfway across the university. One morning, when I came into the common room, he thrust the London *Times* under my nose: 'Look at that!' he roared. Israel Gollancz had been appointed professor of Old English literature at Queen's College, London. 'You see!' shouted Rutherford. 'I understand that Gollancz's grandfather came here from Galicia! Not chemistry, or physics, mind you, but literature, something of national significance,' and he finished up with a great burst of laughter.

'You know, professor,' I said, 'if I had to appoint a professor of Hebrew literature at the Hebrew University in Jerusalem, I would not take an Englishman!'

'There you are!' shot back Rutherford. 'I always said you were narrow-minded, bigoted and jingoistic.'

'For England,' I explained, 'it doesn't matter much. Your culture is too well established. Gollancz may even bring a new note into the teaching of English literature, and England will profit by it. But if you had ten chairs of English literature, and ten Jews got them, what would you think of it?'

'Oh, that!' roared Rutherford, 'that would be a national calamity.'

None of the men at Manchester had so much as heard of Zionism before they met me. Yet it is extraordinary, to say the least, that, whether or not they became Zionists, they were all willing to help along. Even Rutherford, with all his banter, was taken by the idea of the Hebrew University.

With such men about me—and I have described just a few of them—how could I do otherwise than develop a deep attachment to the university? It is true that I suffered one deep disappointment in the course of my academic career: I never got my full professorship. But the disappointment has not dimmed my affection for Manchester, and the years I spent there make up one of the brightest and warmest periods in my recollection. Nor was it the university alone. Perhaps it is not easy for a stranger to get to know Manchester, but when my wife and I did get to know it, we realized that my almost random choice of this provincial city had been an inspired one. Manchester boasted—as so many other cities do, in their own way—that 'what Manchester thinks today, England thinks tomorrow.' In this case the boast was not empty. Apart from its great university, Manchester was a true metropolis of culture. It had in those days the Horniman Repertory Theatre, a pioneer in its time; it had, and still has, the Hallé Concerts, deservedly famous in the world of music, and the *Manchester Guardian*, as distinguished a newspaper as is to be found anywhere. The municipality was a model of liberalism and intelligence. All in all, we found ourselves at one of the centres of intellectual activity. It was in Manchester that my wife and I became British subjects. I only regret that my wandering life forced me, after twelve years of residence there, to break my contact with Manchester so completely.

CHAPTER IX

RETURN TO REALITIES

'Political Zionism' and 'Practical Zionism'—Their Synthesis—The Genesis of the Homeland—My First Visit to Palestine—Dream and Reality—The Old Colonies and Baron Edmond de Rothschild—The New Zionist Enterprises—Joshua Chankin—Lost Opportunities—The Challukkah Spirit—Arthur Ruppin, the Great Colonizer—The Sand Dunes Which Became Tel Aviv—Samuel Pevsner—Disappointment in Jerusalem—Quiet Growth of the Homeland—Harry Sacher, Simon Marks and Israel Sieff— My Scientific Work—Synthetic Rubber and Fermantations—I Almost Settle in Berlin

THE condition of the Zionist movement in 1906, the year I turned back from my imperfect and fitful seclusion to give it again its proper rôle in my life, may be summarized thus: the controversy between the Ugandists and the 'classical' Zionists had transformed itself into the controversy between 'political' and 'practical' Zionism; and this in turn was yielding to a fusion of the two schools. The political Zionists argued: 'Palestine belongs to Turkey. The purchase of land is forbidden by law. We can do nothing now but work for the charter, and use the Great Powers, like England and Germany, to help us obtain the charter.' It was a view shared by the German and Austrian Zionist organizations, and by most of the Westerners. A small group in England, headed by Dr. Gaster and Herbert Bentwich, opposed them. Gaster's opposition, however, was not very useful. I had the highest respect for his scholarship and his Jewish feeling, but I could not escape the impression that his Zionist point of view was tainted by an ingrained personal opposition to Herzl. My chief source of strength was Achad Ha-am and the group that gathered about him.

The second, or practical school—ours—took what I have repeatedly called a more organic view of Zionism, and of historical process. In reality the 'cultural' and 'practical' Zionists were not opposed to Zionist political activity, as has often been represented; they only sought to impress upon the Zionist world the obvious truth that political activity alone is not enough; it must be accompanied by solid, constructive achievement, the actual physical occupation of land in Palestine, which in turn would be accompanied by the moral strengthening of the Jewish consciousness, the revival of the Hebrew language, the spread of the knowledge of Jewish history, and the strengthening of the attachment to the permanent values of Judaism.

I repeat that the process of fusion of the two schools was not a simple matter. Such was the fascination of phrases, such the force of prejudices once they were given sway over the mind, that the first resumption of real colonizing activity ran up repeatedly against obstinate opposition. It was as if people felt that bringing Jews into Palestine, founding colonies, beginning industries, in a modest way, was not the real business of Zionism. *That* was quite different; that consisted of the repetition of our intention to create a Jewish commonwealth in Palestine; and until such a commonwealth was created in a charter no progress of any importance would be achieved.

The deadlock was broken, I believe, at the eighth Zionist Congress, held at The Hague in the summer of 1907. I made there an ardent plea for the views which I had been propagating since my entry into the movement. I said, in effect: 'Our diplomatic work is important, but it will gain in importance by actual performance in Palestine. If we achieve a synthesis of the two schools of Zionism, we may get past the dead point. Perhaps we have not done very much till now. But if you tell me that we have been prevented by local difficulties, by the Turkish authorities, I will not accept it. It is not wholly the fault of the Turks. Something can always be done.' I pleaded that even if a charter, such as Herzl had dreamed of, were possible, it would be without value unless it rested, so to say, on the very soil of Palestine, on a Jewish population rooted in that soil, on institutions established by and for that population. A charter was merely a scrap of paper; unlike other nations and governments, we could not convert it into a reality by force; we had nothing to back it with except work on the spot. It was, of course, necessary for us to keep our case before the tribunals of the world, but the presentation of our case could only be effective if, along with it, there was immigration, colonization, education.

To carry my point, I coined the phrase 'synthetic Zionism,' which became a slogan among the practical Zionists. It was with this rallying cry that we managed to effect a change in the Executive, and in the programme. David Wolffsohn was displaced from the Presidency. A Presidium was formed, to which the younger men were admitted—Victor Jacobson and Shmarya Levin among others—together with some of the 'practical' Zionists, like Ussishkin and Tschlenow. Professor Otto Warburg, the distinguished botanist, a definite exponent of 'practical' Zionism, was elected chairman of the Presidium. Dr. Arthur Ruppin, who was to become our foremost colonizing expert, was invited to go out to Palestine and organize a Colonization Department, doing the best he could in the political circumstances then prevailing.

For those who are interested in the genesis of things, for whom an existing community is not something self-understood, but an organism which had a beginning, and a period of first growth, the early history of Jewish Palestine will have a special fascination. Today a strong, well-knit and vigorous Jewish nation in the making, numbering over six hundred thousand souls, exists in Palestine, with its agriculture, its cities, industries, schools, hospitals and university. Today the acquisition of a few thousand acres of land at a single purchase is a commonplace. We have seen—and I trust we shall again see—tens of thousands of Jewish immigrants drawn annually into Palestine and integrated with its economy and culture. But in the years of which I am speaking a few hundred acres of land was a vast territory; the arrival of a handful of immigrants was an event; a single little industry was a huge achievement. Capital was not yet tempted to seek out Palestine. A powerful workers' movement did not exist because there was no working class yet in Palestine. Seen in retrospect our outlook of those days was not merely modest; it was almost pitiful. Yet the pre-war years 1906 to 1914 were decisive in a sense. The stamp of their work is still visible in Palestine. For we accumulated a body of experience which was to stand us in good stead in the years that followed the First World War. We anticipated many of the problems which were to confront us in the days of larger enterprise. We laid the foundations of institutions which are part of the recreated Jewish National Home. Above all, we got the feel of things so that we did not approach our task after the Balfour Declaration like complete beginners.

It was not an accident that my own first contact with Palestine itself should have been made in the year 1907, the year in which the movement recovered the sober sense of reality. When the change was effected in the Zionist Executive, Johann Kremenetzky, of Vienna, one of the old Herzlian Zionists, not as deeply set in his ways as the Marmoreks and Fischers, was won to our view. Kremenetzky, like many others passed over hastily in these records, deserves, both as a person and a Zionist, much more generous treatment than can be given him here. He had migrated to Vienna from Odessa as a boy and had become a successful industrialist. He owned, at that time, a factory making electric bulbs, and had made it a model of its kind. The friendship we established lasted till long after the First World War, for he lived to a ripe old age—eighty-five, I think. He used to visit me in London, a gallant, beautifully groomed figure of a man, with undimmed vigour and undiminished faculties, devoted to Palestine to the end. Kremenetsky it was who made my first visit to Palestine possible. He challenged me, during the course of the Congress, to put into practice what I was preaching, to go out to the country and to investigate, as an industrial chemist, the prospects of establishing an industry there. In particular, he suggested the possibility of the manufacture of essential oils. As it happened I was engaged in working out a process for the synthetic production of camphor which stands in near relation to that part of chemistry which deals with essential oils. I may as well say at once that nothing direct came of this particular project. But like many another experiment in those days it had great value in that it began the search for practicalities. Something was indeed to come, much later, of the application of my chemical training to the problem of the upbuilding of Palestine, and this first visit of mine to the country, in 1907, might have been made much later had it not been for the shift of emphasis which took place at the Hague Congress.

Thus it came about that, instead of returning to Manchester, where I had left my wife and our six-weeks-old baby, I set out at the end of the Congress for Palestine, travelling down first to

Marseilles and taking a boat there. I had two companions on the journey, Manya Wilbushevitch Shochat, one of the great women pioneers, and a Dr. Klimker, a pioneer of the oil and soap industry of Palestine. All the way from Marseilles to the eastern shores of the Mediterranean I kept preparing myself for the shock of the first contact. I damped my hopes down, suppressed my excitement. I said to myself: 'You must free yourself entirely from your romanticisms, from all the associations with which you have bound up the name of Palestine since your childhood. You will find a derelict country ravaged by centuries of Turkish misrule. You must look at things soberly and critically, with the eyes of the chemist rather than those of the Zionist.' And thus the chemist and the Zionist were at constant war within me during the sea voyage. I was so anxious to be detached and objective that I denied myself the advantage of my emotions. Yet I knew then, and I have confirmed since, that while a cool, matter-of-fact estimate of the possibilities of Palestine is an absolute essential, the normal element of our historical and psychological attachment to the country is an invaluable ally in the struggle to overcome those material and moral difficulties which seem so formidable to the chemist and physicist. To ignore the force of sentiment in the name of practicality is to cease being practical.

However, if I was determined to find the minimum of encouragement, circumstances were not less determined to give my hopes no foothold. The journey took much longer than we anticipated. The last lap took us from Alexandria to Beyrouth, and there we were clapped into quarantine for ten days. The building in which we were interned was dignified by the name of 'hospital.' It was a dilapidated military barracks, with the most primitive sanitary arrangements, very poor food, and no attendance at all. If there had been any diseases about, this would have been the place to catch them. Fortunately there weren't any diseases about, either in Egypt, or on our boat, or in Syria; the quarantine had been instituted chiefly as a source of revenue for the local pasha and his henchmen. Cramped as I was for time, I would have been glad to give them their cut and get out; but that would have been a blow to the institution. So we sat it out. Manya Shochat and Klimker—both of whom had been in Palestine before—utilized the time to instruct me in the ways of the country, and to describe general conditions. Victor Jacobson, who was in Beyrouth as the director of the local branch of the Anglo-Palestine Bank, came to see us, and it was from him that I first heard something of the nascent Arab national movement.

Released at last from quarantine, I proceeded from Beyrouth to Jaffa by boat, and set foot on the land which had been such an integral part of my thoughts ever since my childhood. I was face to face at last with the reality, and as always happens in such cases, the encounter was neither as bad nor as good as I had anticipated.

A dolorous country it was on the whole, one of the most neglected corners of the miserably neglected Turkish Empire. Its total population was something above six hundred thousand, of which about eighty thousand were Jews. The latter lived mostly in the cities, Jerusalem (where they formed a majority of the population), Hebron, Tiberias, Safed, Jaffa and Haifa. There were twenty-five colonies on the land. But neither the colonies nor the city settlements in any way resembled, as far as vigour, tone and progressive spirit are concerned, the colonies and the settlements of our day. The dead hand of the *Challukkah* lay on more than half the Jewish population. That institution, historically significant in its time, calls for a word of description. For many generations pious European Jews had made it a practice to migrate to Palestine in their old age, so that they might die on holy soil. They were supported by a system of collections in the European communities. Their sole activity was the study of sacred books. They had never intended to take up gainful occupations, nor were they, as a rule, young enough to do so if they had had the intention. A few of them went into business in a small way. Historically speaking, they had been the expression of the undying Jewish attachment to Palestine; but in an age which was to witness the reconstruction of the Jewish Homeland, they were a useless and even retarding element.

The colonies were, with very few exceptions, in not much better case. When I was a boy in Motol and Pinsk the first wave of modern colonizers—the *Bilus*, as they were called—had set out for Palestine, under the impulse of the *Chibath Zion* movement. They had been ardent, romantic, devoted, full of noble

F

purposes and high dreams. But they had been inexperienced and impractical. They too had fallen into the grip of a kind of *Challukkah* institution, but the funds for them came, not from public collections, but from the never-ending generosity of Baron Edmond de Rothschild. They had not even started out with intelligent plans. They had not envisaged a process of national development, in which Jewish workers and Jewish landowners would form harmonious parts of a larger programme. The colonies were more in the nature of businesses than agricultural enterprises. The settlers dealt in oranges as they had dealt in other commodities back in Russia. Most of the labour was Arab, and the Jews were overseers. There was no pioneering spirit. Moreover, the few colonies were detached and scattered; they did not form blocks of territory. All this was particularly true about Petach Tikvah, Rishon-le-Zion and Ness Zionah in the south, of Rosh Pinah, Mishmar Ha-Yarden and Metullah in the north. I found Achad Ha-am's criticisms, his observations on the paralysing effect of the Baron's well-meant paternalism, thoroughly justified. Though there was an agricultural school at Mikveh Israel, there was no real scientific study of soil conditions, of crops, of the care of cattle. There existed no system of agrarian credits. There was no system for training newcomers.

The picture was not all dark. Our Zionist type of enterprise was to be found in a few places like Merchaviah, Ben Shemen and Huldah. The young men and women who had come out of Russia in the last few years were establishing their first foothold in the Jewish colonies, competing, by superior intelligence and organization, with the cheaper Arab labour. There was a Jewish high school—the *Gymnasium*—in Jaffa; and the Bezalel Arts and Crafts School had been established in Jerusalem the year before I came out. Enough had been started to show that more could be done.

Joshuah Chankin, one of the famous original pioneers, was my guide on my first visit to Palestine. He accompanied me through the length and breadth of the country. We travelled mostly by carriage, for the only railway then in existence ran —if that is the word—between Jaffa and Jerusalem, and took four or five hours to cover a distance which we now make in less than an hour by car.

I could not have had a better guide. He knew every nook and corner of the land; he knew the history and development of all the colonies, and spoke of them informatively as well as amusingly. We began our tour from Jaffa, and worked our way as far as Metullah, which is today on the Syrian border. I remember Nazareth vividly. We arrived there on a hot afternoon, riding southward, and from the hilltop we looked down on the wide stretch of the Valley of Jezreel, spreading at our feet like a vast carpet framed by the hills of Samaria and Ephraim, with Mount Tabor to the left. It was a superb sight, though the countryside was parched with the late summer heat, and there was hardly a patch of green anywhere for the eye to rest on. How different that panorama looks today, with countless Jewish colonies covering the valley from end to end! Chankin told me how a part of the Emek—that is the Jezreel Valley—had been bought, long before, by the *Choveve Zion*, for a comparatively small sum, and how, because of the lack of funds, the instalments were discontinued, so that the first payments were lost and, with them, the opportunity. He said: 'Of course we shall have to buy it again,' and we did, later, paying ten to fifteen times the original price, because of the land values we ourselves had created. But I remember thinking how right I had been when I had told the Congress that, in spite of restrictions and difficulties, much more could be done in Palestine than had actually been done.

I spoke long and earnestly with Chankin about the disheartened and disheartening state of the colonies. New blood had to be brought into the country; a new spirit of enterprise had to be introduced. Once there had been a stream of immigration, the *Bilus* of the 'eighties, more than twenty years before; but there had been no follow-up. The pioneers that had once been so young, so full of energy and will-power, had become old, tired, decrepit. The Baron's régime had helped to undermine them. They had come to rely on his bounty; a bad harvest, a cattle plague, or any other calamity, sent them to him for help. Their initiative had been destroyed by the dictatorial bureaucracy of the Baron's administration. They had lost hope; and they saw their children, born to them in Palestine, leaving the land and going to the cities, or, what was worse, returning to the exile from which they themselves had once fled in order to build a homeland for the coming generations.

The primary object of my visit, the establishment of a factory for essential oils, receded into the background of my thoughts. I was preoccupied with larger issues. Over and over again it was borne in on me that from a distance I had sensed the actual state of affairs; in spite of all political and administrative obstacles, there were great possibilities. Only the will was lacking. How was that to be awakened? How was a cumulative process to be set in motion? Our means were miserably small. The Jewish National Fund, created for the purchase of land as the inalienable property of the Jewish people, was little more than a charity-box collection. The Palestine office of the Zionist Organization, which Ruppin now headed, was no better off. When Ruppin demanded, in those days, that a land-development company be founded with the modest capital of one million marks—£50,000—the Organization placed at his disposal exactly one-tenth of that sum; and when we reflected that Baron Rothschild had sunk in the country something like fifty million marks, with the results I have described, we might well have been discouraged. If we were not, the fact must be ascribed to our feeling that a great source of energy was waiting to be tapped—the national impulse of a people held in temporary check by a misguided interpretation of historic method.

I made up my mind that I would go back to Europe to press with redoubled energy for immediate practical work in Palestine; and it was then, I think, that I laid out the programme of my Zionist work for the next eight years. How, it will be asked, did we actually get past the dead point? The answer is: simply by getting past it! I have said that between 1906 and 1914 we accumulated a body of experience, anticipated our future problems and laid the foundations of our institutions. But it must not be thought that these were merely token achievements. They had substance. By 1914 we had increased the Jewish population from eighty thousand to one hundred thousand, our agricultural workers from five hundred to two thousand. The turnover of the Palestine office had grown thirty-fold. We had founded the Jewish National Library, and the *Technikum* of Haifa; our *Gymnasium* was attracting large num-

bers of Jewish students from abroad, who were bringing
considerable sums annually into the country. These evidences
of growth were, however, less important than the change of
spirit which had come over the entire community. Apart from
founding new colonies, like Kinereth and Deganiah, we had
penetrated the old colonies, creating among them annexes of
young people. The existence of two thousand Jewish land-
workers acted as an attraction for young Jews from abroad.
There was an instrument for them to turn to, an instrument
which could absorb them into the new life. The transformation
which was wrought in the old European Palestine communities
by the influx of young European Jews began to affect the old
Sephardic, or Eastern, communities, and led to an influx of
Yemenite Jews from Arabia. The *Challukkah* spirit of Palestine
was at last being attacked—though it yielded very slowly. The
Hebrew language had, thanks in part to the magnificent work
of Eliezer ben Yehudah, been revived, and was the natural
medium of converse for the majority of the Palestinian Jews,
and wholly so for the young. The flow of emigration from Palestine had fallen considerably.

Perhaps I can best sum up the progress of those years in a
remark made to me by Baron Rothschild. Shortly before the
First World War he paid a visit to Palestine, and saw for
himself the change that had been wrought. I met him, soon
after, in Paris, when I went to see him in connection with my
work for the Hebrew University. I asked him for his impressions of Palestine, and he answered me simply and honestly:
'Without me the Zionists could have done nothing, but without
the Zionists my work would have been dead.' The *rapprochement*
between the Baron and the Zionist movement dates from that
period; he had become convinced at last that the Zionists were
not simply idealistic agitators; they were capable of getting
things done.

The man who during those years—and indeed throughout
the quarter-century following the First World War—played a
decisive part in the colonization of Palestine was Arthur Ruppin.
I suppose it was wholly fitting that I should have met this
eminently practical Zionist during my first visit to Palestine,
when I was establishing my own contact with realities. I had
heard something of him, for it was the seventh Zionist Congress

—that of The Hague—which decided to engage him as the director of the newly founded Palestine Department; and when I was introduced to him in Haifa I was somewhat taken aback. I saw before me a young German—I would almost have said Prussian—correct, reserved, very formal, seemingly quite remote from Jewish and Zionist problems. I was told that he was an assessor, or assistant judge, that he had had a successful business career, and that he had come out to Palestine in the spring of 1907, and spent several months there studying the land. All that one perceived on first meeting Ruppin was a German statistician and student of economics, but beneath that cool exterior there was a passionate attachment to his people, and to the building up of Palestine. I learned this in the course of the years.

Ruppin was a man of brilliant mind, and of absolute integrity. His practical gifts were reinforced by equal gifts as a theoretician, and his books on Jewish sociology deservedly take a front rank in their field. His coolness misled people into thinking him an easy-going sort of person. Actually, whatever he said and wrote and did was the result of deep thought and a solid sense of responsibility. I remember few errors of judgment on his part, and when he differed with me—as for example in 1922, on the question of the minimum costs of colonization— he was usually right. In all disputes he used to disarm opposition by his imperturbability, and in a movement which had its very excited moments, he would never let himself be provoked into anger or abuse. He would answer quietly, with a kindness which killed opposition. I do not think I ever saw him angry, although, God knows, he had reason enough on occasion.

There was one case in which he was treated with the grossest unfairness. In 1919 he came to England from Palestine, and produced two hundred thousand pounds out of moneys which he had handled for the Zionist Organization. This large sum, totally unexpected, was a godsend. It helped to fill up the deep cavity formed in the capital of the Jewish Colonial Trust by the losses sustained in Russia in consequence of the Revolution, losses which made the position of the bank, at the beginning of our new period of work, rather precarious. But Ruppin was bitterly abused, and suspicion was cast on his integrity. This is how he had come by the money: during the war he had been receiving, from America, twenty-five thousand dollars a month, for work in Palestine. The money was sent to him via Constantinople, and he had paid out in Turkish pounds. As the war dragged on, the Turkish pound sank in relation to the American dollar, and Ruppin saved a considerable sum each month. He carried out his instructions to the letter, and the saving was not of his own making. This, on top of the dislike which he had occasioned by the socialist tendency of his colonization work, precipitated a bitter attack, and he was accused of being a speculator. I do not know of a more ridiculous and more unjustified accusation ever levelled at a man of absolute devotion and honesty. Curiously, the attack did not seem to touch him. His friends were furious, but he remained quite unmoved.

I have not had a better collaborator in my Zionist work than Arthur Ruppin. I received from him not only splendid service, but constant encouragement in enterprises which, without his support, would have lacked reality. He assured us all, in the old days, that Palestine was capable of absorbing large numbers of Jews in agriculture, and that we must not let ourselves be frightened off by the smallness of the country. One incident, which occurred during our first meeting in Palestine, illustrates the daring of his vision, concealed by his quiet, almost frigid exterior. I was staying in Jaffa when Ruppin called on me, and took me out for a walk over the dunes to the north of the town. When we had got well out into the sands—I remember that it came over our ankles—he stopped, and said, very solemnly: 'Here we shall create a Jewish city!' I looked at him with some dismay. Why should people come to live out in this wilderness where nothing would grow? I began to ply him with technical questions, and he answered me carefully and exactly. Technically, he said, everything was possible. Though in the first years communication with the new settlement would be difficult, the inhabitants would soon become self-supporting and self-sufficient. The Jews of Jaffa would move into the new, modern city, and the Jewish colonies of the neighbourhood would have a concentrated market for their products. The *Gymnasium* would stand at the centre, and would attract a great many students from other parts of Palestine and from Jews abroad, who would want their children to be educated in a Jewish high school in a Jewish city.

Thus it was Ruppin who had the first vision of Tel Aviv, which was destined to outstrip, in size and in economic importance, the ancient town of Jaffa, and to become one of the metropolitan centres of the eastern Mediterranean. Perhaps I should say that the most important consequence of the shift from purely political to 'synthetic' Zionism was the introduction into Palestine, in those early years, of a number of first-class men who did excellent work then and in the post-war years. Ruppin was foremost among them. Not altogether in his class, but of high value nevertheless, was Samuel Pevsner, in whose house I met Ruppin. Pevsner had belonged to our Berlin Zionist group, and we had been friends nearly a decade before. He was a man of great ability, energetic, practical, resourceful and, like his wife, highly educated. For such people, going to Palestine was in effect going into a social wilderness—which is something to be remembered by those who, turning to Palestine today, find in it intellectual, cultural and social resources not inferior to those of the Western world. The Jewish community of Haifa was a tiny one, and nine-tenths of it was Sephardic. The bridge of Hebrew which was to unite Oriental and Occidental Jewry had not yet been created. So Pevsner and his wife lived almost in isolation. But Pevsner was a tremendous optimist, and though he died young, he lived long enough to see his optimism vindicated. He practically built up modern Jewish Haifa, that is to say, the splendid quarter of Hadar Ha-Carmel on the slopes above the old city.

During the first visit to Palestine I came across scattered reminders of my childhood days in Pinsk. The Eisenbergs were settled in Rehovoth. The Gluskins were in Rishon-le-Zion. And others, whose names escape me, were taking root in the cities and colonies, tiny advance guards, the 'Pilgrim Fathers' of the new Palestine to be.

My most unhappy experience during the three-weeks tour of the country—it would have been five weeks but for the quarantine episode—was Jerusalem. I went up from Jaffa, not without misgivings. Jaffa already had the small beginnings of a new life, and the promise of a new society; Jerusalem was the city of the *Challukkah*, a city living on charity, on begging letters, on collections. Here the reality turned out to be as bad as the anticipation. From the Jewish point of view it was a miserable ghetto, derelict and without dignity. All the grand places belonged to others. There were innumerable churches, of every sect and nationality. We had not a decent building of our own. All the world had a foothold in Jerusalem—except the Jews. The hotel to which we were directed was a dilapidated and verminous ruin, with nondescript people pouring in and out all day long, and all of them engaged apparently in wasting their own and each other's time. It depressed me beyond words, and I left the city before nightfall. I remained prejudiced against the city for many years, and even now I still feel ill at ease in it, preferring Rehovoth to the capital.

But I was struck, as everyone must be, by the glorious surroundings of Jerusalem; and I thought then that there was only one place where, in time to come, we might erect some building worthy of the Jewish community; there was one hill still uncrowned by monastery or church—the Scopus, on which stood then only the small villa of Lady Grey Hill, and on which now stands the Hebrew University.

Those were unsensational years which preceded the First World War, a time of hard work and quiet growth. The modest progress which we were achieving in Palestine was mirrored in the steady evolution of the Zionist movement towards the serious appraisal of factual problems. When, in September 1913, Ruppin, addressing the eleventh Zionist Congress in Vienna, said: 'We have come to terms with the fact that we must achieve our object not via the charter, but via practical work in Palestine,' he expressed the prevailing sentiment of the movement: we had not given up the hope of a charter, but we had come to terms with the conditions created by the lack of it. In short, the Zionist movement had become serious and realistic. We were not neglecting opportunities simply because they were for the time being limited ones.

In such an atmosphere I had every incentive to Zionist activity. It would take me too far afield to tell in detail of my Zionist labours in those years; and except for the story of the founding of the *Technikum* in Haifa, and of the beginnings of the Hebrew University in Jerusalem, I shall dismiss the period in a paragraph. I was once more as deeply involved in political activity as in the old Geneva days. My wife and I attended all the Congresses in Europe, and went to meetings of the Action

F*

Committee. I toured the English provinces. I took part in the
expanding Zionist programme of the Manchester community.
Here, by 1914, a strong group had formed. Harry Sacher had
returned from London, to become one of the leader writers on
the *Manchester Guardian*. Two young businessmen of great
ability and a sense of social responsibility, whom I have already
mentioned, Simon Marks and Israel Sieff, had been drawn
into the movement. They were not Zionists at first, but they
had heard me speak at one of the Manchester meetings, their
interest had been aroused, and they wrote to me—this was in
1913—asking if they might come to see me and discuss the
movement with me. From that time on we worked together, in a
friendship which has meant much to me and to Zionism. For
Zionism became increasingly the *leitmotif* of their lives, and
they brought to it qualities of which we stood greatly in need.
They were young and energetic. They were practical, and knew
that work could not be done without a budget. They were not
hampered by ancient Zionist dissensions, nor were their lives
scarred by recollections of persecution. They were jolly and
they loved the good things of life. They helped me, in later
years, to put some sort of organization into my rather disorganized life. And they were, like Harry Sacher, a great
spiritual find. Here were people with whom problems could
be discussed, with whom I could check and verify my ideas,
and gauge how they would impress others. Not knowing the
great difficulties in our way, they were readier for action than
I, who was often hesitant and overcautious. In short, they
helped to make Manchester, the city to which I had come as
a stranger, and had considered a place of exile, a happy place
for me.

The reader may by now have forgotten that I was not only
a Zionist worker, but a teacher at a university, and a research
chemist. The fact is that my two lives ran side by side in a sort
of counterpoint. Where I found all the time and energy is
something of a puzzle; but I know that between 1906 and 1914
I enjoyed my chemical researches more than I had ever done
before, or have done since. I enjoyed teaching no less. I published a considerable number of papers, and these in time
brought me a Doctorate of Science from the university. Around
1912 I was put in charge of the course in chemistry for medicine,

and some of the advanced medical students came to my laboratory. Thus I gradually built up a special section, and was promoted to a readership in biochemistry. I had a laboratory of my own and was completely independent—that is to say, I was no longer attached to the chair in organic chemistry, and could begin to hope for a full professorship of my own.

My interest in biological chemistry and in bacteriology as a special branch of organic chemistry began some years after I had settled in Manchester. Facilities for this work were lacking at the university, where biochemistry did not form part of the curriculum at that time, while the study of bacteriology was confined to the medical school. I began to pay frequent visits to the Pasteur Institute in Paris, where I worked in the bacteriological and microbiological departments. For a time I devoted most of my holidays, Christmas, Easter and summer, to these interests, making use of the trips to attend Zionist Congresses and Conferences. In Paris I learned something more than chemistry; I became acquainted with French civilization and the French way of life. My wife and I usually stayed in the Latin Quarter, with her sister and her brother-in-law, Joseph Blumenfeld, a gifted chemist. Urbain, Perrin, Langevin, liberals and thinkers as well as first-rate scientists, brilliant men who combined the qualities of the research student with those of the artist, were then at the Sorbonne. I worked for a time in Perrin's laboratory, learning something of colloidal chemistry, a part of biochemistry.

During one of our holidays in Switzerland I gave two or three months to research on milk bacteriology with a very distinguished man by the name of Burri. The rest of my training in biochemistry I supplemented with my own reading and work in Manchester. It was during this period, too, that I began the study of fermentations. I was led to this subject by its relation to the production of synthetic rubber, which was already then—around 1910 or 1911—a burning question. The use of rubber was growing enormously, prices were going up, and there was a clamour for an artificial product.

The obvious approach to the problem was to find a method for the synthetic production of isoprene and for its polymerization to a rubber. The easiest raw material I could think of was isoamyl alcohol, which is a by-product of alcoholic fermenta-

tion, but as such was not available in sufficiently large quantities. I hoped to find a bacterium which would produce by
fermentation of sugar more of this precious isoamyl alcohol
than does yeast—one was not yet aware of the fact that isoamyl
alcohol is not a fermentation product (of sugar), but is formed
by degradation of the small amounts of protein invariably
present in a fermenting mash. In the course of this investigation I found a bacterium which produced considerable amounts
of a liquid smelling very much like isoamyl alcohol. But when
I distilled it, it turned out to be a mixture of acetone and butyl
alcohol in very pure form. Professor Perkin advised me to
pour the stuff down the sink, but I retorted that no pure
chemical is useless or ought to be thrown away. A later chapter
will have to describe how right I was in my attitude towards
this interesting fermentation process. At this stage of my
chemical research I decided that it was worth while seeing
whether butadiene, which could be made from butyl alcohol
in the same way as isoprene from isoamyl alcohol, could not
be polymerized to a rubber-like substance exactly like isoprene.
We studied the preparation of butadiene, its purification, for
which we discovered a very nice method, viz. the formation
of a crystalline addition product with liquid sulphur dioxide,
and its polymerization which we found was catalysed by small
amounts of metallic sodium.

The question of synthetic rubber, however, very soon ceased
to be urgent as the price of natural rubber dropped again, and
the whole subject was forgotten until the Germans, during and
especially after the First World War, took it up again, and until
the Second World War brought it into the foreground of
technical and strategic interest. As still no good technical method
for the production of isoprene existed, the idea of replacing it
by butadiene was taken up, and the first polymerization
process used our sodium method (hence the German name,
Buna, from *bu*-tadiene-*na*trium, the latter being the German for
sodium). Even the purification of butadiene with sulphur
dioxide has recently been advocated again. In order to round
off the narrative, I may add that we succeeded eventually in
finding a simple method for making isoprene—but this belongs
to another period.

My work centred primarily on two subjects. The first was

the elaboration of a reaction which I had discovered in Geneva, and which led to the comparatively easy production of polynuclear compounds; the second was the investigation of anthraquinone derivatives. These are the mother substances for the making of dyestuffs and some pharmaceuticals. As far as the latter were concerned, I had to feel my way slowly, and do a good deal of reading, for I was a stranger in this domain. It was only during the war that I achieved a certain familiarity with the subject.

One rather disagreeable incident out of those years I must set down, less for what it meant than for what it might have come to mean. I had been hoping, as I have told, for a full professorship at the university. In 1913 a vacancy was created. I had been doing a great deal of work outside my regular schedule, conducting classes which should properly have been taken by my senior, Professor Perkin. I had reason to believe that my abilities as a teacher, as well as my natural liking for that sort of work, would be rewarded by the final promotion. However, the appointment went elsewhere and I must confess I was very much put out. It happened that at this time the development of the Zionist movement abroad made urgent the introduction of new forces into the various departments. Palestine was growing. In Germany there was an upswing in the movement, and Kurt Blumenfeld, one of the leading spirits in German Zionism, was effectively organizing the new academic youth. He, Shmarya Levin and others urged me insistently to give up my post at Manchester University, come out to Berlin, and head one of the departments of the Organization. In the pique of my disappointment I actually began to consider the proposal seriously.

Whether, left to my own counsel, I would actually have taken this step, I do not know. But it was my wife who put her foot down. She disliked Germany. So, for that matter, did I. She had, after years of hard work, established herself in her profession in a new country; she was winning golden opinions from her superiors in the municipality; and here I was suggesting that we pull up stakes and begin all over again. That was too much. She understood my disappointment; she felt it as keenly as I. But a new start—and in Germany, of all places—was out of the question. She could not face the prospect of taking her medical degree for the third time, 'And,' she added, 'our road to Palestine will not be via Berlin.' I cannot help thinking that she was guided by something more than personal considerations, either for herself or for me. In any case, I shudder to think of the possible results if I had yielded to the importunity of my friends and my own momentary impulse.

CHAPTER X

THE EVE OF THE WAR

*Progress Towards the Hebrew University—Baron Edmond de Rothschild—
His Zionist Philosophy—Paul Ehrlich and the Hebrew University—The
Haifa Technikum and the Battle of the Languages—The First World
War Begins*

THE dream of a Hebrew University in Jerusalem was born almost simultaneously with the Zionist movement. Professor Herman Shapira of Heidelberg had given voice to it when I was still a student in Berlin. The Jewish student youth which was the banner-bearer of Zionism in the West was deeply stirred by the idea, and I was a warm protagonist of it during the Geneva period. Herzl, convinced though he was that practical work in Palestine must wait for the political triumph of the charter, showed himself less intransigent than most of his lieutenants—a situation not unusual in political history—and encouraged the young men in this instance. I discussed the question with him in 1901, and he promised to try to obtain from the Sultan a special 'firman' authorizing the establishment of the university; but when I visited him in Vienna in 1902, he stated that there was no hope of such a 'firman,' and that the project would have to be abandoned for the time being.

Our group, the Democratic Faction, would not take no for an answer. In 1902 Martin Buber, Berthold Feivel and I published the first pamphlet on the subject. It was entitled *Die Jüdische Hochschule*, and in it we gave a rough outline of the practical side of the project, including an approximate budget. The response to the pamphlet was extraordinarily encouraging; not only students, but men prominent in artistic and scientific circles wrote to us, offering their support. At about the same time Israel Abrahams, of Cambridge University, wrote an article in support of the idea in the London *Jewish Chronicle*. Our group in Geneva received hundreds, perhaps thousands, of warm commendatory letters from every part of the world. And the reader will perhaps remember that when the series of pogroms beginning with Kishinev broke upon us, I was touring the Russian cities agitating for the Hebrew University.

Kishinev, Uganda, the death of Herzl, the temporary immobilization of the Zionist movement, all served to eclipse the work for the Hebrew University. But in the intervening years the need which existed for such an institution, and the appeal which it made to academic groups, went on increasing. However, it was not until the Vienna Congress of 1913 that the Organization placed the university on its agenda. I read a paper on the project, and at the close of the discussion David Wolffsohn made the first substantial contribution towards its fulfilment, and his example was followed by others. Wolffsohn's gift of one hundred thousand marks—£5,000—was earmarked for the University and National Library, which was not built until the end of the First World War. Meanwhile I was charged with the task of organizing the University Committee, and Ruppin, the head of the Palestine Department, was instructed to look around for a suitable site.

To anticipate a little: Ruppin actually secured, some time later, the piece of land on Mount Scopus on which I had set longing eyes in 1907. The money for this purchase came from Isaac Goldberg, a Russian Zionist. Ruppin also obtained an option on the Grey Hill House, which we finally acquired in 1916. The oddity of this last circumstance lies in the fact that in 1916 the war was going full blast, and Palestine was in the hands of the enemy Turks. I still remember the astonishment of the Grey Hill family when they were told that there was a buyer for their estate on the Scopus. Lady Grey Hill, in particular, was so moved by this evidence of our faith in the ultimate victory of the Allies that she agreed to cede the property to us in advance of the formal arrangements for its transfer. She told us, when we had sealed the bargain, that this act of ours had done more than anything else to convince her that England was going to win the war. I could not help thinking of the ancient Romans, coolly buying and selling suburban parcels of land which the victorious armies of Hannibal, then besieging Rome, still occupied.

It was in the winter of 1913 that I first made the personal

acquaintance of Baron Edmond de Rothschild of Paris, whose name, long a household word in Jewry, recurs so frequently in these pages. M. Gaston Wörmser, the Baron's secretary and friend, having been approached on the subject of the university by an old Zionist colleague of mine, wrote me that the Baron was deeply interested in the project. The news was unexpected, for we still thought of the Baron as the rich autocrat interested exclusively in the philanthropic aspects of the Jewish problem, and disdainful of political Zionism. We were quite mistaken, but through no fault of ours, for the Baron was not a man to explain himself. In part he would not, for that went against his dictatorial temperament; in part he could not, for I doubt whether he really understood himself. Throughout the years that followed I obtained, as I think, some insight into that curious and complex personality, one of the most interesting I have ever encountered. I cannot help breaking the narrative at this point in order to set down my impressions of him.

When I first met Baron Edmond he was a man in the sixties, very much alert, still something of a dandy, but full of experience and *sagesse*. Everything about him was in exquisite taste, his clothes, his home—or rather his homes—his furniture and his paintings, and there still clung to him the aura of the *bon vivant* which he had once been. In manner he could be both gracious and brutal; and this was the reflex of his split personality; for on the one hand he was conscious of his power, and arrogant in the possession of it; on the other he was rather frightened by it, and this gave him a touch of furtiveness. To his family he was, with his tremendous interest in the Jewish problem, an enigma and a wild man; but when, in later years, other Rothschilds began to show an interest in Palestine, and were ready to give us a little money for the work, he forbade me peremptorily to apply to them. 'What!' he said, furiously. 'After I've spent tens of millions on the project, while they made fun of me, they want to come in now with a beggarly few hundred thousand francs and share the glory? If you need money, you come to *me*!' Which I often did, and rarely in vain. I remember, for instance, how when the movement was in a very tight corner for lack of funds (this was in 1931, when I had been thrown out of office) I set out on one of my *schnorring* expeditions and arrived in Paris, only to be struck down by a bad attack of grippe. The Baron heard of my condition, and came to the hotel—to the bewilderment, indeed almost the panic, of its personnel—with a cheque for forty thousand pounds. He put this into my hand with the remark: 'This should help to bring your temperature down.' It did.

His interest in Zionism was, *au fond*, as deeply political as ours. The manner in which (years before I met him, at the time when he was being bitterly criticized by the Zionists) he bought the colonies, with some attempt at strategic placement, indicates that he was thinking far ahead, in political and national terms. But he was nationalist with a distrust of the national movement, and of the people. He did not understand that it was not enough to give money, and not enough to settle Jews in Palestine. They had to be encouraged in the development of independence, initiative and inner growth. The Zionist movement as such had to be strengthened, for it was the matrix of all achievement. This he could not see. He wanted everything to be done quietly, by order, without a national movement. He disliked the paraphernalia of the organization. On one occasion he said to Ussishkin and myself: 'Why must you people go around making speeches and attracting attention?' To which Ussishkin answered, half seriously: 'Baron Edmond, give us the key to your safe and we promise not to make any more speeches.' He accused me once of being a Bolshevik, by which he meant, of course, a 'wild man' generally. I said: '*Monsieur le Baron, on est toujours le Bolshevik de quelqu'un*'—'One is always somebody's Bolshevik.' He understood the allusion.

However, he was not a man to be jested with, not even when in his national purposes he overshot the mark, going sometimes beyond the Zionists themselves. At a certain time, I remember, he financed a series of excavations on the Mount of Zion, where some seven ancient cities lie one on top of another. His purpose was to uncover the Ark of the Covenant, which he believed to be buried there. I asked him, very seriously, what he hoped to achieve with the Ark. He answered: '*Les fouilles, je m'en fiche: c'est la possession*'—'Excavations be damned, it's possession that counts.'

These revelations, this insight into the man, came later. In 1913, at our first meeting, I only knew that the Baron was indicating a wider range of interest in Palestine than we had credited him with, or that he had learned from experience what he would not learn from argument.

Chiefly we talked, of course, about the University, and on this subject he expressed himself with force and clarity. He saw the University-to-be as a great centre of light and learning, from which knowledge would radiate out to the uttermost ends of the earth, reflecting credit on Jerusalem and on the Jewish community. But here, too, he showed himself the autocrat, having, like all rich men, very decided views on subjects entirely outside his competence. He was of the opinion that the Hebrew University should be devoted exclusively to the humanities, for it would never be able to compete with the scientific schools of England, France and Germany. Shmarya Levin used to say that a rich man always put him in mind of the fat and the lean cows of Pharaoh's dream; the rich man will give you a fat donation, and then follow it up with a lean philosophy which eats up the fat donation. I thought the Baron's views quite absurd; to me a university is a university. However, I had his support for the general idea. His second condition, though a hard one, was more reasonable. I had to get Paul Ehrlich to head the University Committee.

Ehrlich was then at the very height of his phenomenal career, and utterly unapproachable by ordinary mortals. I had heard, moreover, that he took little interest in Jewish matters, and indeed in any matters outside the scope of his medical research. I was at a loss for a means of contact, until I bethought myself of an old friend in Berlin, Professor Landau, who was related to Ehrlich by marriage. In March of 1914 I made a special journey to Berlin, sought out Landau and said, in effect, that I would be grateful to him for the rest of my life if he would telephone his illustrious relative in Frankfort and arrange an interview for me.

Professor Landau acceded to the request, very doubtful though he was of the feasibility of my plans. I would be lucky, he said, if Ehrlich gave me five minutes of his time; and luckier still if I could persuade him to detach his thoughts from his scientific affairs long enough to get him to understand what I was talking about; for Ehrlich was utterly impervious to outside influences, especially in his laboratory, where I proposed to visit him.

I was not in a very sanguine state of mind when I mounted the steps of the Speyer Institute, in Frankfort. In spite of my public activities, I was by nature shy, and hanging about in the antechambers of the great was not in my line. Not that on this occasion I had much hanging about to do. The difficulty turned out to be of another character, for the rather extra-ordinary interview which Ehrlich granted me quite promptly nearly turned out to be a piece of propaganda for Ehrlich's scientific theories rather than for the Hebrew University.

I have retained an ineradicable impression of Ehrlich. His figure was small and stocky, but he had a head of great beauty, delicately chiselled; and out of his face looked a pair of eyes which were the most penetrating that I have ever seen—but they were eyes filled with human kindness.

Ehrlich knew that I was a chemist, but he did not know what I was coming to see him about. He therefore plunged at once into the subject of his researches. He introduced me to some of his assistants (since become famous) and especially to his rabbits and guinea pigs. Then he took me on a fairly com-prehensive, if rapid, tour of his laboratory, talking all the time and performing test-tube experiments as we went along.

It was fascinating; but it would have been more so if I had not been wondering how I could switch the conversation to the purpose of my visit. I listened respectfully while he unfolded part of his theory of chemistry—for he was a great chemist as well as a great medical man. He spoke of chemistry as of a weapon with which one could shoot at diseases. He put it this way: if you have your chemistry properly applied, you can aim straight at the cause of a sickness. By 'properly applied' he meant the creation of a certain group in a compound with a specific affinity for certain tissues in the human body. Such a compound, injected into the body, unites with those tissues only. He gave me an instance: if one injected a certain dyestuff called methylene blue into an animal—say a mouse—and after-wards cut open the body, one would find that the whole nervous system had been stained blue, while the rest of the body had remained unaffected. In methylene blue the grouping of the atoms makes it a specific for the nervous tissues. But suppose methylene blue had a curative value for certain nervous diseases; you could then, as it were, aim for the nerves without

affecting the rest of the body. He developed this theory to me—
it is obsolete now, but was new then—with great eloquence and
excitement as I followed him about the laboratory.

At last I took my courage in my hands, and steered the conversation cautiously in my direction: I mentioned that I had
come to see him, at the suggestion of Baron Edmond de Rothschild of Paris, on the subject of a Hebrew University in Jerusalem. He listened for a few moments, and then exclaimed:
'But why Jerusalem?' I was off at last! I set out with considerable energy to explain why Jerusalem was the one place
in all the world where a Hebrew University could and ought
to be established. Somehow I caught his interest, and my excitement rose as I saw that he was following my argument with
increasing attention. It was perhaps twenty minutes before he
interrupted me, saying: 'I am sorry, we must stop now. After
I have seen my patients, we shall go home and continue.'

Then, excitedly, he pulled out his watch and exclaimed:
'You have kept me nearly an hour. Do you know that out
there, in the corridor, there are counts, princes and ministers who
are waiting to see me, and who will be happy if I give them ten
minutes of my time.' He said it good-naturedly, and I replied:
'Yes, Professor Ehrlich, but the difference between me and
your other visitors is that they come to receive an injection
from you, but I came to give you one.'

We continued our conversation later that evening at his
house, where I met Mrs. Ehrlich, a typical, sweet German
Hausfrau, who was always scolding her husband for his untidi-
ness, and for his ceaseless smoking. Ehrlich was literally never
without a cigar in his mouth, and I think it was this habit that
killed him. By the time I left him he promised to see Baron
Edmond on his next visit to Paris, which was to take place in
a few days, and to give him his answer.

I stayed on for a little while in Germany, and got back to
Manchester for the first day of Passover. I found waiting for me
an enthusiastic telegram from Ehrlich. He was in Paris; he
had talked to the Baron; and he had consented to serve on the
University Committee. It was a tremendous scoop for me.

In the months that followed I organized the rest of the committee. Baron Edmond delegated his son, James de Rothschild,
of London—concerning whom I shall have much more to say—

to serve as his representative. Professor Otto Warburg of Berlin joined. Professor Landau of Berlin persuaded his son, the mathematician, then at Göttingen, and later professor at the Hebrew University, to accept a place. Martin Buber and Achad Ha-am also became members. After a good deal of discussion and correspondence it was agreed that our first official meeting should be held in Paris—on August 4, 1914.

That meeting was postponed *sine die*.

A few pages back I said that those years—1906 to 1914—made up a period of tranquil and unsensational development in Zionism. One exception should be made, for it was shortly before the war that a bitter and significant struggle was waged about the second of our higher institutions of learning in Palestine, the Haifa *Technikum*, between the Zionists and the leaders of German Jewry.

Actually the *Technikum*, or Technical College, was the first to be built, though the University—the foundation of which was laid in the midst of the war, and the opening of which did not take place until 1925—had been spoken of long before. The *Technikum* was the child of Achad Ha-am and Shmarya Levin. The first considerable sum of money towards the institution was given by Mr. Wissotzky, the Russian tea magnate, a man of immense wealth, devoted to Jewish causes, and something of a Hebrew scholar. He was the main support of *Ha-Shiloach*, the Hebrew monthly, and the Mæcenas of Achad Ha-am. Wissotzky's contribution was one hundred thousand roubles, then about £10,000, and with this the building could be put up and the necessary equipment purchased. Wissotzky, who was advanced in years, and could not often attend the meetings of the Curatorium, or Board of Directors, which were held in Berlin, appointed Achad Ha-am a member.

When Achad Ha-am and Levin chose Haifa as the site of the new educational institution, they showed vision of a high order. The infant town of Tel Aviv was piqued by the choice, but Haifa was destined to be the industrial heart of the new Palestine, and the proper place for a technical college. Of greater service, however, was the fight which Levin put up around the question of the language of instruction.

To understand the significance of this struggle we must recall that those were the days of the 'capitulations' in Turkish territory. Every foreign institution in the corrupt and feeble Turkish Empire placed itself under the protection of a foreign country, and the European Powers vied with each other for influence and prestige within Turkish territory. The Jews in particular were used as catspaws in this game of intrigue, and the little community which we were struggling to weld into a creative unit was torn apart by its 'benefactors' and 'protectors.' There was one system of Jewish schools supported by the *Alliance Israelite Universelle* of Paris: there the language of instruction was naturally French. The Germans used the *Hilfsverein der Deutschen Juden* with *its* system of schools as *their* instrument of intrigue in the Near East. There the language of instruction was German. England was very much behind in the general competition, having under its ægis only the Evelina de Rothschild School in Jerusalem, where the language was English. At school Jewish children in Palestine therefore spoke French, English or German according to their foreign 'protectors.' It was a strange and rather pathetic fact that when they mingled with each other outside the schools they took to Hebrew as the common denominator. It apparently occurred to no one that the proper language for Jewish children in the schools of Palestine was their own Hebrew.

The Haifa *Technikum* had placed itself under the protection of Germany, and Dr. Zimmerman, then German Under-Secretary for Foreign Affairs, had obtained from the Turkish Government the permission for the purchase of the land and the erection of the building, which was completed in 1913. The Curatorium consisted at first of representatives of the *Hilfsverein* and of Mr. Wissotzky; later, when he sensed that a crucial point would be reached in the struggle about the language, Achad Ha-am obtained a place for me on the board. Achad Ha-am himself did not wish to be brought into too open conflict with his old friend Wissotzky, who, though a Hebraist, was weakening on the question under the pressure of the majority.

The decisive meeting took place in Berlin, in June 1914. Ranged against us were James Simon, the Cotton King, and Paul Nathan, his right-hand man, directors of the *Hilfsverein* and the undisputed heads of German Jewry. They were the

usual type of *Kaiser-Juden*, like Albert Ballin and Max Warburg, more German than the Germans, obsequious, super-
patriotic, eagerly anticipating the wishes and plans of the
masters of Germany. *They* would not hear of Hebrew as the
language of instruction in the *Technikum*. They had three
arguments against it and in favour of German, in a sort of
crescendo. First, German was the great language of science and
technology, while Hebrew was practically useless in this respect.
As a concession they were willing to have gymnastics and drawing taught in Hebrew! Second, the school was under the
German flag. Third—the climax—Dr. Zimmerman wanted
German! Dr. Zimmerman had gone to all this trouble in
obtaining the concessions for the school on the tacit understanding that German would be the language of instruction
and that it would be a German institution. In fact, Dr. Zimmerman was—according to an indirect remark made by Mr.
Simon—anxiously awaiting the result of this meeting. It would
be a feather in Dr. Zimmerman's cap if he could point to
another foothold of German influence in the Near East. At
this point I blew up and asked hotly: 'What the devil has
Dr. Zimmerman got to do with *our* Technical College in
Palestine?' I saw genuine grief and terror on the faces of the
German Jews seated at the table. I went on, however, to warn
them that if German was voted, nobody in Palestine would pay
the slightest attention to the decision, since it would be entirely
contrary to the spirit of the new Palestine, and possibly also to
the original intentions of the donor. (The donor, though present,
preferred to remain silent.) The vote was taken, and I found
myself in a minority of one.

I escaped from the meeting and telegraphed a digest of the
proceedings to Shmarya Levin, who was conducting the struggle
at the Palestinian end. Within twenty-four hours the teachers
of the *Technikum* had gone out on strike. The German *Hilfsverein*
withdrew its support from its schools, which the Zionist
Organization had to take over. This was the first time that we
had been charged with the support and direction of an educational system; it was, in a sense, the beginning of our Hebrew
school system in Palestine. Dr. Levin set out at once for
America, to enlist the help of American Jewry, and obtained
it in generous measure.

This fight of ours against Zimmerman had wide bearings on our political status, and stood me in good stead in time to come. Our enemies in England did not hesitate to point out, during the First World War, that we were a German organization because the headquarters of the Zionist Executive were in Berlin. The incident just recorded provided one clear refutation of the baseless accusation. It was we, the Zionists, who found the courage, weak and outnumbered as we were, to refuse to become the catspaws of the Germans in Palestine. We were neither German nor French, we said, but Hebrew, and those that would support our Hebrew culture would obtain our support in return. It was an argument which Shmarya Levin used with great effect in America.

The meeting of the Curatorium in June 1914, insignificant as it was in the scale of international affairs, made it clear to me that war was inevitable. Not there and then, of course; not immediately—it never *is* immediately—but at some time in the future. This minor manifestation of the bitter German determination for the extension of its power at any and anybody's cost—perhaps because it was minor, perhaps because it showed Germany's vigilance at every point—made a deep impression on me. From Berlin I went straight to Paris, with the intention of inducing Baron Rothschild to buy up the Haifa *Technikum*, lock, stock and barrel. But the Baron hesitated; not because he did not see, and sympathize with, my point of view, but because he too felt obscurely that we were standing on the threshold of great and tragic events, and that it would be a useless gesture to acquire the institute at that time, since many years might pass before we would be able to make use of it.

It is a strange thing to remember how these premonitions of ours never crystallized into an actual belief. Yes, there would be a war somewhere, sometime; war was inevitable, but it had nothing to do with the here and now. Or as far as the here and now was concerned, the catastrophe would always be averted, the unbelievable inevitable would not come to pass. Thus, in spite of many signs of impending storm, the end of July found my wife, my little son, Benjy, and myself making our usual preparations for a short holiday in Switzerland. We left Manchester according to plan on July 28, after making the necessary inquiries about trains, and finding that everything was 'normal.' We broke our journey in London and spent a few hours at Achad Ha-am's home. He too was anxious to believe that the storm would prove to be no more than diplomatic, and that the exchanges of telegrams and conversations between the Great Powers would smooth things over. I remember calling at Cook's office to ask about trains to Paris, and being told again that everything was 'perfectly normal.' Later it became clear that even then the British Expeditionary Force was being transported secretly and in all haste across the Channel.

We arrived in Paris on the evening of July 31. The pandemonium which reigned in the Gare du Nord was sufficient to show us the difference in temper between the French and the British people. Here things were decidedly not normal. We could not leave the train, and decided to continue by the 'Paris Ceinture' to the Gare de Lyon, the point of departure for the south. The brief trip took an interminable time, with constant stops, and frequent incursions of excited passengers, who filled up every available inch of space in compartments and corridors, to the point of suffocation. From fragments of conversation we gathered that Jaurès had been assassinated that evening in a boulevard café, and everybody thought that with him had died the last chance of peace. He alone might effectively have appealed to the workers of Europe not to march, and his appeal alone might have moved his German friends.

At the Gare de Lyon, the train was practically taken by assault. By great good luck we managed to keep our seats, and after a ghastly night found ourselves in Switzerland. Two days later Germany declared war against France.

CHAPTER XI

SHOCK AND RECOVERY

Caught in Switzerland—Paris in the First World War—Hope Born of Catastrophe—Back in Manchester—I Meet C. P. Scott—I am Introduced to Lloyd George—Herbert Samuel's Pro-Zionist Stand—Asquith's Attitude —Obstacles Loom—Reintroduction to Balfour—Jewish Opposition to Zionism

WHEN the shock of the incredible had passed, when we managed to absorb the fact of the war, the instinct of life reasserted itself. In spite of what I recall now in the way of premonitions, it must be remembered that the First World War, unlike the Second, was not preceded by a long series of absolutely unmistakable warnings. The diplomatic 'incidents' had been as it were in the tradition. War was inevitable; but it had looked inevitable after Fashoda; it had looked inevitable again after the Agadir incident. Aggressive, pushful, arrogant —Germany had been all that; but she had lacked the shamelessness of nazism, and she had not given her game away by a preliminary series of monstrous misdeeds. There was a profound difference in our approach to the two wars. When the Second World War finally 'broke'—I am reminded of the days when we used to wait for pogroms in Russia—we knew at last, all of us, where we stood. It was not thus with the First World War, the actual descent of which produced an effect of stupefaction. Besides, there was an excuse in 1914, after nearly half a century of comparative peace, for refusing to entertain the thought of an immediate general war. It came, and it overwhelmed us with horror. Then the horror receded. Its place was taken by a deep resentment—and by hope. The war was here and it had to be won; and after it was won a better world had to be built on the ruins of the old.

Switzerland, where my wife, my seven-year-old son and I were marooned, was, of course, in a state of considerable excitement. We reached the Rhône Valley, climbed up to the village where we had reserved rooms, and arrived to find that everyone from the small *pension* had been mobilized, and that the prospects of food and of service were of the smallest. Still, we were there. We were 'on holiday.' We promised our landlord that we would try our best to substitute for the absent help, and we settled down for a few days to see how events would shape before taking steps to return to England. The few days lengthened into a fortnight before we succeeded in joining up with a party of other stranded British citizens.

Again I recall some queer circumstances connected with that state of indecision, of belief and disbelief, which preceded the First World War. In Manchester the railway office had told us that everything was normal. All the same we had taken a passport with us. What last-minute impulse was it that moved me to arm myself with a passport—in those days when no one thought of carrying such a document about? Was it some echo of my youth in Russia? I had also taken a supply of money in gold. With my name—not to mention my appearance—I might have had the devil of a job convincing the British Consul at Montreux that I was a British citizen, with a perfect right to proceed to England with my family.

Another three weeks passed before we found ourselves on a train headed for Paris. The trip, which should have taken less than twelve hours, lasted two nights and two days. At the French frontier, and at several points within France, the passengers had to go to the *Mairie*, or town hall, to have their papers examined. But it was not this alone which made the passage through France indescribably depressing.

In one little town in the Juras, Dôle—the birthplace of Pasteur—we were held up for several hours, while train after train came westward with German prisoners, French wounded and French refugees, and train after train went eastward with fresh troops. The French were retreating from Alsace, and the Battle of the Marne was in full swing.

There was one spectacle so horrible, so devastating, that it has haunted me ever since. As one of the trains drew in from the front there looked out of a window some four or five women, dishevelled, bedraggled, with contorted and obscene faces, utterly inhuman in appearance, so that we started back from the sight in horror. I asked an officer who descended from the train who these terrifying creatures were. He answered: 'These harpies are Frenchwomen who were caught on the field of battle robbing the dead!' My little boy was frightened out of his wits by the awful sight, and the image sank deep into my mind.

This was what we saw, and yet we said to ourselves the war was going to be won. During those first few weeks of the precipitate French and British retreat the issue was by no means obvious. We reached Paris at last, a Paris more beautiful than we had ever known it before, with every house beflagged and beflowered, but a Paris that was pathetic, too, with its atmosphere of partings, of absent menfolk, and of many women in mourning. The city was proud and collected, but almost disturbingly quiet. We could not help comparing Paris with the powerful and self-confident German capital which we had seen only a few weeks before. The contrast was disheartening. And yet, behind the dread, for no reason I could put my finger on, without a genuine argument to offer, we had begun to feel that the French would not give way. They had been caught unawares; they were unprepared and disorganized; but they would come to. What they lacked in preparation and organization they would make up in courage and improvisation.

With this resurgence of hope came the longing for, the belief in, something better after the war. We were afraid, my wife and I, to utter this hope at first; and it was with diffidence that we mentioned to each other the possibility that after the war, in a sensible reordering of the world, we too, the Jews, would find our lot made a little easier, and that our need to rebuild our homeland would be recognized as part of the world's need. I found old Baron Edmond in Paris, in his magnificent home, very sad, but very calm. Both his sons were away, in the army. With real astonishment I heard him reiterate my own half-formulated views. Yes, he said, things looked black, but we would win the war. And this was the time for us to act, so that we might not be forgotten in the general settlement. He urged me, immediately on my return to England, to get in touch with British statesmen. It was his opinion—and I agreed with him—that the war would spread to the Middle East, and there things of great significance to us would happen.

Thus hope begets action and tends to justify itself. There

was a short period of preliminary fumbling. We got back to London, where we were somewhat staggered to find the city still 'absolutely normal'—it was that queer, significant 'business-as-usual' phase of the war, corresponding in a way with the 'phony war' period of a quarter of a century later (and perhaps the cue for it in Hitler's mind). I went to see my friends, Achad Ha-am, Leon Simon, Samuel Landman—the last one was the secretary of the Zionist Organization—and the Zionists of the East End. We talked vaguely of great possibilities now opening, but no concrete plan of action emerged. I cut my stay in London short and proceeded to Manchester, arriving at the beginning of the university term.

It was a dolorous home-coming. Many of the students and younger instructors had gone into the army—as volunteers, of course, for conscription was (characteristically for England) only beginning to be spoken of. There was an atmosphere of uncertainty; and I went about with my hopes, waiting for my chance.

It came very soon, and, it would seem, by accident. Some two months after my return I made the acquaintance of a man who was to be of incalculable value to the Zionist movement— C. P. Scott, the famous editor of the *Manchester Guardian*. Very possibly, if we had not met thus, I might have gone to see him, for his sympathy with Jewish ideals was widely known, and his personal and public influence was enormous. As it was, the meeting occurred at a party in Withington, ·at one of the big German half-Jewish homes which took an interest in my wife's work in the Schools for Mothers—an enterprise later adopted by the municipality, with my wife as a medical officer. When I was presented to Mr. Scott, I saw before me a tall, distinguished-looking gentleman, advanced in years, but very alert and attentive. He was inquisitive about my origin and work, and also interested in the Polish question.

He asked me: 'Are you a Pole?'

I answered: 'I am not a Pole, and I know nothing about Poland. I am a Jew, and if you want to talk to me about that, Mr. Scott, I am at your disposal.'

He did want to talk to me about it, and in a few days I received an invitation from him to visit him at his home. He was so unaffected, so open, so charming that I simply could not help pouring out my heart to him. I told him of my hatred for Russia, of the internal conflicts of the Jews, of our universal tragedy, of our hopes and aspirations for Palestine, of the little we had already done there, and of our almost Messianic dreams—such as they appeared then—for the future. He listened with the utmost attention, and at the end of the rather one-sided conversation he said:

'I would like to do something for you. I would like to put you in touch with the Chancellor of the Exchequer, Lloyd George.' Then he added: 'You know, you have a Jew in the Government, Mr. Herbert Samuel.'

At this I exclaimed, almost rudely: 'For God's sake, Mr. Scott, let's have nothing to do with this man.' I thought, on general grounds, that Herbert Samuel was the type of Jew who by his very nature was opposed to us. It will be seen that I was mistaken.

Nor did I guess with what thoroughness Mr. Scott would go into our problems. He began to read literature on Palestine, and I provided him with a map of the country showing our settlements. On November 12, I wrote to him: 'Don't you think that the chance for the Jewish people is now within the limits of discussion at least? I realize, of course, that we cannot "claim" anything, we are much too atomized for it; but we can reasonably say that should Palestine fall within the British sphere of influence, and should Britain encourage a Jewish settlement there, as a British dependency, we could have in twenty to thirty years a million Jews out there, perhaps more; they would develop the country, bring back civilization to it and form a very effective guard for the Suez Canal.'

Early in December 1914, the interview with Lloyd George took place. Lloyd George, in his *War Memories*, dates his acquaintance with me, and his interest in our movement, from the time (1917) when I came to work for the Ministry of Munitions, and centres the relationship on the subject of my chemical work for the Government during the second half of the war. His narrative makes it appear that the Balfour Declaration was a reward given me by the Government when Lloyd George became Prime Minister, for my services to England. I almost wish that it had been as simple as that, and that I had never known the heartbreaks, the drudgery and the uncertainties which preceded the Declaration. But history does not deal in Aladdin's lamps. Actually, Lloyd George's advocacy of the Jewish homeland long predated his accession to the Premiership, and we had several meetings in the intervening years, as will be seen below.

It became a practice with me, whenever I happened to be in London, and Mr. Scott came up on the night train, to meet him at Euston Station for breakfast. His usual greeting to me was: 'Now, Dr. Weizmann, tell me what you want me to do for you,' and breakfast would pass in conversation on Zionist affairs. On this morning of December 3, however, his greeting was: 'We're going to have breakfast at nine o'clock with Mr. Lloyd George.'

There were present at this meeting, besides Lloyd George, Mr. Scott and myself, Herbert Samuel, then President of the Local Government Board under Asquith, and Josiah Wedgwood, then to me an unknown figure. I was terribly shy and suffered from suppressed excitement, knowing how much depended on this meeting. At first I remained a passive listener. They talked about the war in a way that seemed to me extraordinarily flippant.

I was very, very serious-minded, did not quite appreciate English humour, and did not understand at first that behind this seeming flippancy there was a deadly seriousness. Lloyd George began to fire questions at me, about Palestine, about our colonies there, about the number of Jews in the country and the number who could go there. I answered as best I could. Then I had the surprise of my life when Herbert Samuel interposed some helpful remarks. I had been frightened out of my wits by his presence. It became clear that every person in the room was favourably disposed, and an atmosphere was created which warmed and encouraged me.

Lloyd George pointed out that I ought to talk with Balfour, as well as with the Prime Minister, Mr. Asquith. At this point Herbert Samuel said—I could hardly believe my ears—that he was preparing a memorandum on the subject of a Jewish State in Palestine, to present to the Prime Minister.

How differently our dreams and plans impressed different people! Here is what Asquith wrote in his diary on January 28, 1915:

I received from Herbert Samuel a memorandum headed 'The Future of Palestine.' He goes on to argue at considerable length and with some vehemence in favour of the British annexation of Palestine, a country of the size of Wales, much of it barren mountain and part of it waterless. He thinks we might plant in this not very promising territory about three or four million European Jews and that this would have a good effect on those who are left behind. It reads almost like a new edition of 'Tancred' brought up to date. I confess I am not attracted to this proposed addition to our responsibilities, but it is a curious illustration of Dizzy's favourite maxim, 'Race is everything,' to find this almost lyrical outburst from the well-ordered and methodical brain of Herbert Samuel. [He added, a few weeks later]: Curiously enough, the only other partisan of this proposal is Lloyd George, and I need not say he does not care a damn for the Jews or their past or their future, but thinks it will be an outrage to let the Holy Places pass into the possession or under the protectorate of 'agnostic and atheistic' France.

This last bit is in queer contrast to a comment from a very different quarter. I was in Paris again at the end of 1914, and Baron Edmond proposed that I see Lord Bertie, the British Ambassador, who was a friend of his—at least, he used to get very good dinners at the Baron's house. Lord Bertie received me rather coolly. What he thought of the interview he tells in his diaries, which, like Asquith's memoirs, were published ten years later:

Edmond de Rothschild sent a co-religionist established in Manchester to 'talk' about what I think an absurd scheme, though they say it has the approval of Grey, Lloyd George, Samuel and Crewe: they did not mention Lord Reading. It contemplates the formation of Palestine into an Israelite State, under the protectorate of England, France or Russia, preferably of England. . . . What would the Pope, and Italy, and Catholic France with her hatred of Jews, say to the scheme?

Lord Bertie himself was, by the way, a Catholic. I do not know what his subsequent attitude towards Zionism was. Asquith's remained cold. He visited Palestine in 1924-5, and wrote:

There are less than a million people in the country . . . of whom about one-tenth are Jews, the remainder Christians and Arabs, the Arabs being three-fourths of the whole. I suppose you could not find

G

anywhere a worse representation of any one of the three religions—
especially the Christians. The Jews are increasing (mainly from the
less civilized parts of Eastern Europe) as a result of the Zionist
propaganda, and no doubt are much better looked after and happier
here than they were in the wretched places from which they were
exported. But the talk of making Palestine a Jewish National Home
seems to me just as fantastic as it has always been.

Very odd indeed is the contrast between this report and Balfour's on *his* visit to Palestine, which took place a few months
later, on the occasion of the opening of the Hebrew University.

This gives only a hint of the obstacles we were to encounter—
obstacles based on the most contradictory grounds, irreconci-
lable with each other or with realities. Bertie cited the Catholi-
cism and the anti-Semitism of the French, Asquith attributed
Lloyd George's interest to the latter's dislike of 'French
atheism'; Asquith implies that our human material was of the
wretchedest kind, unfit to build a land; we were to hear before
long that we threatened to build too well. Some of the opposition, internal and external, I knew well; some of it I guessed
at; some came from utterly unexpected sources, but as to that,
some of our help came from quarters equally unpredictable.

Meanwhile, the interview with Lloyd George had gone off
extraordinarily well. The Chancellor promised to give the
matter serious thought. He noted that there would undoubtedly
be strong opposition from certain Jewish quarters, and he fore-
told, very accurately, that Edwin Montagu, later Secretary of
State for India, would be one of our bitterest opponents. I
made no attempt to conceal from Lloyd George or the others
the fact that the rich and powerful Jews were for the most part
against us; and I did not mention my talk with Balfour in
1906. I thought that old history.

I heard nothing about the effects of the interview until months
later, and then indirectly. Lloyd George gave Mrs. James de
Rothschild a description of the meeting, and made two remarks
which stuck in her mind. He said: 'When Dr. Weizmann was
talking of Palestine he kept bringing up place names which were
more familiar to me than those on the Western Front.' Then
he repeated what he had said in an aside to Herbert Samuel:
'When you and I are forgotten, this man will have a monument
to him in Palestine.' I do not know how reliable a prophecy

this will turn out to be, but should anyone ever take the fancy to put up a monument to me, I hope he will be told that Palestine is the only place where I should like to have it.

I followed up at once Lloyd George's suggestion about seeing Balfour. Professor Alexander, with whom Balfour was acquainted as a brother philosopher, sent him a note reintroducing me and received in reply a postcard on which Balfour had scribbled: 'Dear Sam: Weizmann needs no introduction, I still remember our conversation in 1906.' When I walked into Balfour's office in London—he was then First Lord of the Admiralty—he hailed me with: 'Well, you haven't changed much since we met.' And, almost without a pause, 'You know, I was thinking of that conversation of ours, and I believe that when the guns stop firing you may get your Jerusalem.'

I was thrilled to hear him say this, nonchalantly on the surface, but, in the British way which I was beginning to understand, quite seriously. I did not follow up this opening; the time and place were not propitious. He invited me to his home in Carlton Gardens and there, a few days later, we had a tremendous talk which lasted several hours.

It was not a practical conversation. It developed about abstract ideas and principles. Mr. Balfour mentioned that, two years before, he had been in Bayreuth, and that he had talked with Frau Cosima Wagner, the widow of the composer, who had raised the subject of the Jews. I interrupted Mr. Balfour and offered to tell him what Frau Wagner had said. He agreed, and I told him that, in Frau Wagner's opinion, the Jews of Germany had captured the German stage, press, commerce and universities, and were putting into their pockets, only a hundred years after emancipation, everything the Germans had built up in centuries. Frau Wagner, I ventured to guess, resented very much having to receive so much moral and material culture at the hands of the Jews, and there were many like her. It was quite possible that Frau Wagner did not even know the full extent of the services which Jews had rendered Germany, particularly in the field of science; to what degree they had been responsible for the growth of the German chemical industries, to take only one field. (Later in this book I shall deal at some length with the extraordinary chapter of Germany's use of Jewish scientific genius for power purposes which the scientists had never contemplated.) I went on to say that I might be in agreement with Frau Wagner as to the facts, but I was in entire disagreement as to the conclusions to be drawn from them. The essential point which most non-Jews overlook, and which forms the crux of the Jewish tragedy, was that those Jews who were giving their energy and their brains to the Germans were doing it in their capacity as Germans, and were enriching Germany, and not Jewry, which they were rapidly abandoning. There was no contact whatsoever between the Jewish grandees in Germany and the Jewish people. Indeed, they had to hide their Judaism in order to be allowed to place their gifts at the disposal of the Germans. Frau Wagner, however, did not recognize them as Germans, and we stood there as the most exploited and misunderstood of peoples. To escape from this intolerable situation a definite status for the Jewish people, in a Jewish homeland in Palestine, and under normal conditions, was necessary. Those conditions were, primarily, the rebirth of the language of the Jews and their culture.

And I went on to tell Balfour of the struggle, in 1914, against the introduction of a foreign language into the Haifa Technical College.

We talked of the war, of course, and I spoke openly of my feelings towards Russia. Mr. Balfour wondered how a friend of England could be so anti-Russian when Russia was doing so much to help England win the war. I gave him a description of what was taking place behind the Russian lines, especially when the Russians advanced into new territory—the pogroms, and the expulsions which made every Russian victory a horror for the Jews—this while hundred of thousands of Jews were fighting in the Russian Army. It was news to him! Then I spoke again of our Zionist hopes. At the close of our talk Balfour said: 'It is a great cause you are working for. You must come again and again.'

Not long after this talk I met Balfour again at a lunch given by Lady Crewe, and the discussion turned on Russia and the Jews. Balfour heckled me on my opinions, and I said then that the hopes reposed in Russia were mostly vain. Russia was corrupt and rotten, and her contribution to victory would be small in the long run. Lady Crewe—who was a Rothschild—

told James de Rothschild, subsequently, that I seemed to be pro-German, and this of course simply terrified James de Rothschild. I might say that it was always easier to speak frankly to non-Jews than to Western Jews; there was less likelihood of being misunderstood. Mrs. Blanche Dugdale, Balfour's niece and biographer, herself an ardent, lifelong friend of Zionism, made some very pertinent remarks in this connection, regarding one of our bitterest Jewish opponents of those days. 'Mr. [Edwin] Montagu could not extend to his own people the sympathy he evinced later for nationalism in India. He saw the spectre of anti-Semitism in every country if its Jews permitted themselves to dream of a territorial centre or a national political existence outside their present citizenships. Such aspirations in English Jews he looked upon as traitorous disloyalty to their native land. In the case of Jews living under less happy conditions he believed that their relations with the countries of their birth would only be worsened. This was not a point of view which ever appealed with great force to the non-Jewish populations of the British Empire, many of whom as, for example, the Scotch, are perfectly accustomed to combining strong separate racial consciousness with a wider loyalty.'[1]

I was to find this point of view confirmed again and again in my dealings with non-Jews; not only with members of minority 'races' in the British Empire—the Balfours were Scotch, of course—but with the English themselves; and not only in Britain, but in America and in other lands. Those contacts with C. P. Scott, Lloyd George and Balfour were only the beginnings of our discoveries of friends. They were enormously important, but hardly more so than those we established with a host of lesser-known men inside and outside of governmental circles. Among non-Jews there existed, as we have seen, opposition to, perhaps even contempt for, our dreams, which might be challenged on grounds of practicality, or of policy. I have not heard them challenged on grounds of incompatibility with good citizenship except among Westernized Jews of a certain class pursuing a dream which is infinitely less practical than ours—that of placating the anti-Semites. The opposition of

[1] From *Arthur James Balfour, First Earl of Balfour*, by Blanche E. C. Dugdale (London, 1936).

these Jews turned out to be costlier by far to us than the reasoned objections of non-Jews; besides, being psychological rather than reasonable, it was implacable. If my prophecy to Mr. Scott of a million Jews in Palestine at the end of twenty-five or thirty years has fallen short by some forty per cent, much of the blame is directly attributable to the internal obstructionism of a small but influential group of Jews. I shall have to deal with it at some length, for it is an instructive part of our history, and it repeated itself at another crucial period.

CHAPTER XII

ASSIMILATIONISTS AND ZIONISTS

Seeking a United Jewish Front—Assimilationist Jews and Mr. Lucien Wolf—Their Active Obstructionism—Lord Reading—General Smuts—Zangwill's Aloofness—The Rothschilds Divided on Zionism

I T was with a heavy heart, with a premonition of failure, that I undertook, in the latter part of 1914, to negotiate with the representatives of assimilated English Jewry for a United Jewish Front on the problem of Palestine. I wrote at about that time to Dr. Judah Magnes, who was playing a leading part in American Zionism: 'I am not sure yet whether we shall succeed in having a United Jewish Front and a united Jewish action, but we are certainly trying our utmost to secure it, and we are prepared to go a long way towards meeting our opponents.'

The trouble was that our opponents would not go an inch towards meeting us. Two years of negotiation produced from the anti-Zionist Jews of England the following official statement of principle:

In the event of Palestine coming within the spheres of influence of England or France at the close of the war, the Governments of these powers will not fail to take account of the historic interest that country possesses for the Jewish community. The Jewish population will be secured in the enjoyment of civil and religious liberty, equal religious rights with the rest of the population, reasonable facilities for immigration and colonization, and such municipal privileges in the towns and colonies inhabited by them as may be shown to be necessary.

In effect, this statement means, at its generous best, that in view of the historic connection between the Jews and Palestine, Jews in that country ought not to be treated worse than the rest of the population. If that represented a compromise with the Zionists, from what original position had the British anti-Zionist Jews advanced?

At that time there existed in England what was known
as the 'Conjoint Committee,' composed of representatives of
the Anglo-Jewish Association (presided over by Dr. Claude
Montefiore) and the Board of Deputies (presided over by Mr.
David L. Alexander). Both of these bodies consisted of old-
fashioned, well-to-do assimilationist Jews, who looked upon
Judaism as a collection of abstract religious principles, upon
Eastern European Jewry as an object of compassion and philanthropy, and upon Zionism as, at best, the empty dream of a few
misguided idealists. Their religious leader was Dr. Montefiore,
a high-minded man who considered nationalism beneath the
religious level of Jews—except in their capacity as Englishmen. Their secular representative, the secretary of the Conjoint Committee, was Mr. Lucien Wolf, a man of considerable
distinction, a historian of note, in whom the opposition to
Zionism was a mixture of principle and of personal idiosyncrasy.
Mr. Wolf was a gifted but embittered man. He had good
relations with the Foreign Office, where he was considered the
spokesman of the Jews, that is, the Jew who came to ask for
favours for his co-religionists in other countries. He resented the
rise of what he called 'foreign Jews' in England, looked upon
the Foreign Office as his patrimony—he was of an old Anglo-
Jewish family—and put me down as a poacher, though I kept
my contacts among government figures quiet, and did not
parade them even in front of my Zionist colleagues. It was hard
for Wolf, who knew how to handle the Foreign Office, to look
on while Zionists came along and established connections in his
preserve; the more so as Zionism was in his view a purely East
European movement, with a certain following in the East End
of London, and beneath the notice of respectable British Jews.
It was still harder, in fact impossible, for him to understand that
English non-Jews did not look upon his anti-Zionism as the
hallmark of a superior loyalty. It was never borne in on him
that men like Balfour, Churchill, Lloyd George, were deeply
religious, and believed in the Bible, that to them the return of
the Jewish people to Palestine was a reality, so that we Zionists
represented to them a great tradition for which they had
enormous respect. Certainly it could not get home to Lucien
Wolf that those English statesmen had no respect at all for the
rich anti-Zionist Jews. I remember Lloyd George saying to me,

a few days before the issue of the Balfour Declaration: 'I know that with the issue of this Declaration I shall please one group of Jews and displease another. I have decided to please your group because you stand for a great idea.' The same spirit animated men like Smuts and Milner, but not Reading or Montagu; and not Lucien Wolf, to whom, for all his intelligence, it was quite incomprehensible.

To give Mr. Wolf credit, he did realize that common work on the part of the Conjoint Committee and the Zionists was impossible. He gave three reasons, in a letter to Mr. Sokolow dated June 15, 1915. They were:

(1) That the Zionists do not consider civil and political emancipation as a sufficiently important factor for victory over the persecution and oppression of Jews, and think that such a victory can only be achieved by establishing a 'legally secured home for the Jewish people.'

(2) The Conjoint Committee considered as dangerous and provoking anti-Semitism the 'national postulate' of the Zionists, as well as special privileges for Jews in Palestine.

(3) The Conjoint Committee could not discuss the question of a British protectorate with an international organization which included different, even enemy, elements.

None of these objections—and I emphasize the last one—ever occurred to the many Englishmen who were encouraging us so generously in those days. But it is not easy to argue with a complex. Towards the end of 1914, I had written to James de Rothschild: 'I am afraid I differ from my colleagues who think or who thought that it would be possible to establish co-operation between the Zionists and the Conjoint Committee. After having heard once Mr. Wolf's views, it was clear to me that such co-operation was impossible.' And not much later I put the case fully to Dr. Moses Gaster:

'There is no doubt these two bodies [the Conjoint Committee and the *Alliance Israelite* of France] work together, and they pursue an almost identical policy as far as our movement is concerned; this policy can be summed up in one word: "opposition." Of course, we cannot object to their position, much as we may deplore it. They have a perfect right to hold anti-national opinions, but the objectionable feature in their policy —and it is this which fills me with great anxiety—is, that

G*

whereas they themselves don't do anything to further the Zionist cause, or even the Palestinian cause, they will try their utmost to hamper us in our work when the decisive moment comes. Of course their opposition is illogical; if people say that they are not nationalist Jews, they have no right to prevent other people from acting as nationalist Jews, especially as they are a small minority living in the West, detached from the masses in the East, from the joys and sorrows of those masses, from their aspirations and ideals.'

My premonition that these men would become obstacles in the decisive moment was only too well founded. They were directly responsible, as we shall see, for that ambiguity of phrasing in the Balfour Declaration which was to plague us for more than a quarter of a century. If they had been content with withholding their financial support, we on our side would have been content to forget them. But they discouraged others, by precept as well as example. They went out of their way to influence British public opinion against us. They created in Jewish life a tradition, as it were, of active obstructionism which often came to life at critical moments of world and Jewish history. There has, happily, been a profound change in the attitude of this group in the last few years—it began with the formation of the mixed Jewish Agency with which I deal in the second book. Two men, Louis Marshall and Felix Warburg, of the United States, had no little share in bringing about this change. Also, Palestine has ceased to be a matter for theoretical debate. It is a living reality which it is impossible to oppose now.

There were some exceptions even in the early days. Here and there the opposition softened. Some who fought the Balfour Declaration or were averse to it accepted it later as a *fait accompli*. Not Edwin Montagu (at that time Financial Secretary to the Treasury, and later Secretary of State for India), or Claude Montefiore, or Lucien Wolf. But Lord Reading did. He did not become what might be called enthusiastic; he was half won over by the practical achievements which followed in later years.

My first meeting with Reading, which took place in the middle of the war, was a chilly one, and its effect on me was all the more painful by its contrast with another first encounter on the

same day. I had been introduced in the morning to General
Smuts, or, rather, I had gone into his office with a letter of
introduction. Utterly unknown to him, I was received in the
friendliest fashion, and given a most sympathetic hearing. A
sort of warmth of understanding radiated from him, and he
assured me heartily that something would be done in connection with Palestine and the Jewish people. He put many searching questions to me, and tried to find out how sincerely I
believed in the actual possibilities. He treated the problem with
eager interest, one might say with affection. The same morning,
in the same government building, I was introduced to Reading.
It was as if I had run into an iceberg. Frosty, remote, detached,
indifferent, he seemed to resent my talking to him on such
subjects as Palestine and a Jewish homeland. But, as I have said,
he accepted the Balfour Declaration, and thawed a little towards the movement. Later he became friendly with Sir Alfred
Mond, who after the war was one of our most generous
collaborators. Reading's son, the present Marquis, married
Mond's daughter, and Reading was induced to become the
chairman of the Palestine Electric Corporation. Their younger
generation, today, is with us heart and soul.

There were a few English 'leading Jews,' however, who stood
with us from the beginning: Herbert Samuel, for instance, who
was, indeed, very effective. To begin with, he had the rank of
statesman, and helped to a considerable extent to offset Edwin
Montagu. More than that, however, he guided us constantly,
and gave us occasional indications of the way things were
likely to shape. He was discreet, tactful and insistent. He made
the mistake of assuming that Asquith was friendly, but a
similar assumption in the case of Sir Edward Grey was correct,
and led to useful results.

Zangwill was, or had been, a Zionist. In the early days of the
movement Herzl had leaned heavily on him, and he had made
a great impression at one of the first Congresses by his brilliant
attack on the 'grand dukes' of the I.C.A.—the Jewish Colonization Association—which was spending millions of pounds on
futile attempts to settle masses of Jews on the soil elsewhere than
in Palestine. I remember how, at one of the Congresses, Zangwill participated in the debate though he was not a delegate.
When his status was challenged Herzl, who was then presiding,

declared: 'When we have a genius in our midst, we will not take into consideration the usual political formalities.' Zangwill's understanding of Zionism was subtle, his devotion substantial. Yet, as we have seen, he broke away from the movement, at the time of the Uganda split, to found his Jewish Territorial Organization which, while dividing our forces, achieved nothing in its search for another territory than Palestine.

I tried hard to enlist his co-operation. We conferred in the autumn of 1914, and on October 4 I wrote to him:

'Whatever the differences which, I am afraid, are still in existence, I am nevertheless convinced that at the present critical moment we must try to find the possibility for working together and save what can be saved from this débâcle which has befallen our people. . . .

The time has come to put forward our claim for the establishment of an organized, autonomous Jewish community in Palestine. Nobody doubts our intellectual achievements, nobody can doubt now that we are capable of great physical efforts and that, were all the mental, moral and physical forces of Jewry concentrated on one aim, the building up of a Jewish community, this community would certainly not lag behind, and could stand comparison with any modern, highly civilized state. . . .'

My offer evoked no response. Zangwill never got over his rift with us. In 1917 he indicated the possibility of a *rapprochement*, and in December of that year he spoke at the public meeting in the London Opera House to celebrate the Balfour Declaration. His territorial organization had become meaningless, and he dissolved it that year. However, there was one fortunate result to our negotiations—the accession to our forces of Dr. M. D. Eder, the distinguished psychiatrist. Zangwill himself remained outside, his attitude critical and unhelpful. The House of Rothschild, perhaps the most famous family in Jewish exilic history, was divided on the issue of Zionism. Of Baron Edmond, of Paris, I have already spoken at some length. His son James, an Englishman, and a member of Parliament, was friendly to our idea and I had met him when he joined the Hebrew University Committee as his father's representative. But in 1914 he was in the army, and came to London only at rare intervals. His wife Dorothy, however, was won over, and proved enormously helpful. She was a close friend of Lady Crewe's, who maintained a political salon in her wonderful house on Curzon Street. Her husband, Lord Crewe, was a prominent politician, a great Liberal, and a friend of Asquith and Lloyd George.

Old Leopold de Rothschild, whom I never met, was, like his wife, furiously anti-Zionist, and remained so to the end. Sir Philip Magnus, who was also anti-Zionist in his views, was interested for a time in Palestinian colonization as pure philanthropy; he tried to make a dent in Leopold de Rothschild's out-and-out opposition but without success. Of Mrs. de Rothschild's almost pathological anti-Zionism I gave some indication when I told of her suppression of Balfour's letter about me. Another incident will help to illustrate her implacable hostility to us. When one of her sons was killed in Palestine in the course of the war, she went to the trouble of writing a letter to the Zionist Organization, forbidding us peremptorily to 'make a case of it,' i.e. have it appear that her son had died fighting for the liberation of Palestine! It had never occurred to us to capitalize on her son's death. But such was her horror of Zionism that she trembled at the thought that we might besmirch the name of her dead son with it. Her attitude never changed; and in part she transmitted it to her surviving sons, Anthony and Lionel. They, in time, lost some of their hostility, and made their peace with the Balfour Declaration. But they did not become friendly or particularly helpful.

A third branch of the family was that of Nathaniel, *the* Lord Rothschild of England. His two sons, Walter and Charles, were friendly to us. It was to Walter, the second Baron, that Balfour addressed the Declaration. Charles might have been as helpful to us as his elder brother, but he was inclined to melancholy, and took no part in London life. He, however, often visited us in London and was eager to learn the background of Zionism. His wife, Jessica, like Mrs. James de Rothschild, did much to help us to widen our contacts and enable us to place our views before Englishmen of influence.

My contact with the English Rothschilds began in the flurry of activity which followed our recovery from the shock of the war. In November 1914, Baron Edmond had gone to Bordeaux;

James de Rothschild was away in the army. I drew a bow at a venture and wrote to Mrs. James de Rothschild asking if I might see her. She replied at once. I called, and we had a long conversation, which was resumed the following day. She was interested, ready to help, but utterly innocent of any knowledge of the subject. To her, whom I suspected of being more interested than appeared, as to her sister-in-law, Mrs. Charles de Rothschild, and their relative, Lady Crewe, I had to explain our viewpoint, our philosophy, our hopes, in the most elementary terms.

I wrote to Lady Crewe: 'We who come from Russia are born and bred in an aspiration towards a new and better Jewish life. It must not only be a comfortable life, but a *Jewish* one, a normal Jewish life, just as the Englishman leads a normal English life. . . . We who come from Russia, where a most modern and perfect machinery is set up to crush the Jewish body and soul, are least afraid of so-called anti-Semitism. We have seen too much of it. But we are convinced that as long as the Jew will be considered only as an appendix to someone else (sometimes desirable and tolerated, sometimes, mostly perhaps, undesirable) there will be trouble. We have the right to be treated as normal human beings, capable of entering into the family of nations as an equal, and to be masters of our own destiny. We hate equally anti-Semitism and philo-Semitism. Both are degrading. We are conscious of the fact that we have contributed our share towards progress and shall continue to do so in a higher degree when we can live as free men in our own, free country.'

This educational work bore fruit. To what extent it wrought a change in the basic Jewish outlook of these men and women I cannot say; but they were willing to listen, and they did not recoil from some degree of self-identification with the natural impulses of the Jewish masses. Kindliness and sympathy often had to do duty for integral understanding, for the gulf was too wide, economically, socially, culturally, to be completely bridged. The degrees of interest in the Jewish problem varied, of course. With some it was a matter of concern, with some, at least for a time, a genuine preoccupation. With one, alone, was it a passion, and that was Baron Edmond of Paris. A dozen men of his stamp and his capacity to help would have changed the

history of Palestine, would have overcome completely the handicap of the anti-Zionist Jews and the hesitancies and the
oppositions in the non-Jewish world. We did not get them.

A great source of help, in those days, was the Manchester
group of English-born Zionists of whom I have already spoken.
Harry Sacher, as leader writer on the *Manchester Guardian*, was
an excellent link with C. P. Scott. It was Sacher who put me in
touch with Herbert Sidebotham, the prominent journalist and
publicist who was associated with the *Manchester Guardian* and
later (as 'Scrutator') with the *Sunday Times*. Sidebotham was
interested in our ideas from the British strategic point of view,
always believing that a Palestine built up by the Jews would be
of importance for the British Commonwealth of nations. Leonard
Stein, who later became the very able secretary of the World
Zionist Organization, joined us after the war. I had heard of
him as a brilliant Oxford student (he had been President of the
Union), and as a potential Zionist; but the army swallowed him
up. I did not get to him until 1918 when, returning from
Palestine, I found him in a rest camp in Taranto, Italy, undergoing a cure for a bad case of trench feet.

Then there were, of course, Israel Sieff and Simon Marks,
with whom I became increasingly intimate, and whose collaboration became more and more important. With these young
men it was possible to speak more intimately than with the men
and women in high places, and the need to let off steam after
'high' diplomatic negotiations was sometimes overwhelming.
If it was pleasant to find among some of the Rothschilds a
generous degree of sympathy, it was correspondingly difficult
to put up with the blind, immovable and utterly unprovoked
hostility of the 'pure' philanthropists in a matter which, on
their own showing, was actually none of their business. I wrote
to Sacher and Simon in December 1914:

'The gentlemen of the type of Lucien Wolf have to be told
the candid truth and made to realize that *we* and not *they* are
the masters of the situation, that if we come to them it is only
and solely because we desire to show to the world a *united Jewry*
and we don't want to expose them as self-appointed leaders.

'If anyone of their tribe had done the amount of work I did
for the University there would be no end of trumpet blowing.
Starting with nothing, I, Chaim Weizmann, a Yid from Motelle

and only an *almost* professor at a provincial university, have organized the flower of Jewry in favour of the prospect. . . .'

If there was some bitterness in this and in occasional other outbursts of the kind, it had to do chiefly with the thought of how much more others might have achieved if they had been willing.

CHAPTER XIII

INTERNAL ZIONIST STRAINS

Russian Zionists and the First World War—The Copenhagen Bureau—Shmarya Levin in America—Brandeis and the American Provisional Zionist Executive—Vladimir Jabotinsky and the Jewish Legion—Pinchas Rutenberg

THOSE ancient Zionist dissensions from which my young English friends were so happily free were of many kinds. There was, for instance, the ghost of the old Uganda quarrel. It was no more than a ghost, but it was troublesome. Zangwill remained alienated from us because of it. Greenberg never forgot or forgave me my opposition to Herzl. Quarrels which had lost their substance went on existing as habits in men who could not adapt themselves to new conditions. There was, again, the recollection of the division between 'cultural' and 'practical' Zionism. That, too, had created hostilities which outlived their meaning, but continued to plague us.

But a new internal division now appeared in the ranks of the old European Zionists, numbers of whom began to turn up in England during the course of the war. They were all, like myself, under the influence of Achad Ha-am; and again like myself, they were all anti-Russian, that is, against czarist Russia. I have already told how my own anti-Russian feelings were constantly getting me into hot water. But apart from hating Romanov Russia, I did not have any faith in it as a military ally, and whenever my university friends talked about 'the great Russian steam-roller' which was going to crush the Germans and lumber through to Berlin, I freely indicated my scepticism. It is true that the rôle of Russia in the First World War was, despite the corruption of the régime, considerable if brief. It neutralized for a time a part of the German Army, and thus helped to prevent the capture of Paris. But I held the idea that Russia was capable of bursting through into Germany to be quite ridiculous.

In spite of all this I believed, as did Achad Ha-am, that the Allies were going to win; and it was here that the division arose. The Zionists who were arriving in England from the Continent were not only anti-Russian, but believed, for the greater part, in the inevitability of a German victory. This was not a result of wishful thinking. As in the case of Ussishkin, their conviction flowed from very deep sources. For the Jews and the intellectuals generally of Russia, the West ended at the Rhine, and beyond that boundary there was only an unknown world. They knew Germany, they spoke German, and they were vastly impressed by German achievement, German discipline and German power. They knew, as I did, that Russia was rotten through and through, eaten up by graft, incompetence and indolence, and in their eyes Russia did not deserve to win. Of course in this they were influenced by the ghastly history of the Jews in Russia. Germany, it is true, was also anti-Semitic, but German anti-Semitism did not show as much on the surface. It bore a milder aspect. My friends did not look deeply enough, and failed to read the trends in the country. Their views were not shared, be it noted, by Jewish thinkers like Achad Ha-am and the historian Dubnow. But into the attitude of my friends there also entered the Polish-Russian disbelief in the power of the democracies to stand up against mighty Germany.

The practical issue of this false reading of historic forces was that the Zionists insisted on the neutrality of the Zionist Organization, and they discouraged my first tentative steps to get in touch with the British statesmen. To give expression to this neutrality the old Action Committee, whose headquarters were in Berlin, called a conference in Copenhagen, which was neutral territory, and proposed to establish new headquarters there.

I was sharply opposed to leaving power in the hands of the old Executive. Shmarya Levin, then in America, had participated in the formation of the American Provisional Executive Committee for Zionist Affairs, with Mr.—soon after Justice— Brandeis at its head; and I supported him without reserve. I wrote to him on October 18, 1914:

'I consider the activities of the old Action Committee impossible and even dangerous for the future of our cause. Taking into account the present political situation, I cannot help thinking that the conference at Copenhagen would prove absolutely useless for our movement, and actually harmful for the future. The American Provisional Executive Committee should be given full power to deal with all Zionist matters, until better times come.' I believed that our destiny lay with the Western democracies. I wrote further to Levin: 'It is in the interests of the peoples now fighting for the small nationalities to secure for the Jewish nation the right of existence. Now is the time when the peoples of France, Great Britain and America will understand us. . . . The moral force of our claims will prove irresistible; the political conditions will be favourable to the realization of our ideal. But we must be ready for this moment when it comes. We must unite the great body of conscious Jews in Great Britain, America, Italy and France.'

When the bureau in Copenhagen was actually opened, I cut myself off from the European Zionists, even though they had transferred themselves to neutral territory. I wrote to the bureau asking that no mail be sent to me. I had to break with some of my closest friends, like Motzkin and Victor Jacobson. They had, it is true, one tremendous but short-sighted argument against me—Russia! Day after day, reports came to us of the pogroms which accompanied the advance of the Russian armies, pogroms which made the Jews in the small towns and villages long for the coming of the Germans as liberators! Today it seems inconceivable that such a situation should ever have existed. So deep were the anti-Russian feelings of the old Executive, that when the Balfour Declaration was published and we arranged to celebrate the triumph with a public meeting in the London Opera House, Tschlenow, then in London, objected to it as a breach of Zionist neutrality! I was looked upon as a crank and an Anglo-maniac. Oddly enough, this attitude continued among certain groups, even after the war. That the Bolsheviks in Moscow should accuse me of being a British agent was part of the day's work; but that Zionists should accuse me of being ready to sell out the movement to England was rather hard to bear.

My dissociation of myself from the Copenhagen Bureau had interesting and far-reaching results. One of the officials of the Copenhagen Bureau was Martin Rosenblüth, who was in England, in the employ of the Organization, at the beginning of the Second World War, some twenty-five years later, and was interned as an enemy alien. As the President of the Zionist Organization I was asked to appear before the judge who examined the case. The judge was friendly and reasonable; he said that one of the things that weighed against Rosenblüth was the fact that during the First World War he had been employed in the Copenhagen office of the Zionist Organization, and in touch with German officers. I suggested that Rosenblüth, being a German officer, was of course loyal to his native country, but he would certainly not have let himself be used in his Zionism by the Germans, whereupon the judge said: 'But Dr. Weizmann, you couldn't have known what was happening then.' I asked what made him say that, and he answered: 'Why, you cut yourself off from the Copenhagen Bureau as soon as it opened!' The record of my letter had, it seems, been kept by Scotland Yard, and the action protected me for decades. It must have weighed a great deal with the authorities when I was invited to work for the Admiralty in the course of the First World War.

All my common sense had told me that I had to set myself completely right from the outset, whatever misinterpretation might be put on my action by the Zionists. I could not help thinking of a story out of my boyhood in Pinsk. We had in the city a *feldsher*—a licensed healer without a medical degree—to whom our servant went one day with a badly cut finger. The first thing he did was to give her a big dose of castor oil. 'Come what may,' he explained, 'let's at least be sure that we have to do with a clean stomach.' In breaking with the Copenhagen Bureau I wanted to make sure of a clean record; for though I was violently anti-Russian, I was just as violently anti-German and pro-British.

Tschlenow and Ussishkin were typical instances of unhappy Russian Zionists who did not believe, until the last moment, that England would win the war. But there were exceptions, and the most notable among them were Vladimir Jabotinsky and Pinchas Rutenberg. Of the former I have already written; of both of them I shall have much to say when I come to deal with the reconstruction of Palestine, and with cleavages in the Zionist movement far deeper than the fortuitous political ones arising from the war—cleavages going down to the basic ethos of Judaism and Zionism, of State building, of social ideals and social concepts. My personal relationship with both Jabotinsky and Rutenberg has been generally misunderstood in Zionist circles, and the misunderstanding has served to obscure issues of more than personal importance.

The opening of the war found Jabotinsky in Alexandria, as the correspondent of the *Russkiya Vyedomosti*, and there, together with Trumpeldor, he conceived the idea of forming, out of several hundred young Jews who had fled to Egypt from Pale-stine, a Jewish battalion to fight on the side of the Allies. This was the beginning, in fact, of the famous Zion Mule Corps which served so brilliantly in Gallipoli. However, before the corps was formed, Jabotinsky was already in France, Italy and England, with the larger ambition of forming several Jewish regiments. He came to me, too, and I thought his idea good, and in spite of the almost universal opposition I decided to help him.

It is almost impossible to describe the difficulties and disap-pointments which Jabotinsky had to face. I know of few people who could have stood up to them, but his pertinacity, which flowed from his devotion, was simply fabulous. He was dis-couraged and derided on every hand. Joseph Cowen, my wife, who remained his friend until his death, and I were almost alone in our support of him. The Zionist Executive was of course against him; the non-Zionist Jews looked on him as a sort of portent. While he was working for the Jewish Legion we invited him to stay with us in our London house, to the discontent of many Zionists.

We became very friendly in those days. Some time before I established myself permanently in London, I used to share rooms with him in a little street in Chelsea—3 Justice Walk—and we had a chance now and again to talk at length, and to indulge in some daydreaming. We had one memorable con-versation which opened my eyes. We were beginning our work, and I said: 'You, Jabotinsky, should take over the propaganda of the movement, oral and literary. You are a genius in that field.' He looked at me almost with tears in his eyes. 'Now, Dr. Weizmann,' he said, 'the one thing I am fitted for is political work, and here you are trying to shove me into the entirely wrong path.'

It startled me beyond words, for political work was precisely
what he was unfit for; and above all he was unfit to negotiate
with the British. In spite of his extreme pertinacity, he was
impatient in expression. He lacked realism, too. He was immensely optimistic, seeing too much and expecting too much.
Nor did all his disappointments on behalf of the Jewish Legion
ever cure him of these qualities.

Jabotinsky succeeded in building up his Jewish regiments and
came out with one of them to Palestine when I was there, in
1918. He was promoted to the rank of captain. At the end of
that year, when I was leaving the country, he became the political officer of the Zionist Organization. I was of course not at
all easy in my mind about this appointment, but Dr. Eder
was there with him, and I thought the combination would not
be too bad.

Pinchas (or Peter) Rutenberg, too, first came to me in connection with the founding of a Jewish Legion in the First
World War. He turned up at our house, in Manchester, in the
late autumn of 1914. It was a dark night, the lights were all
out, and, since house service had already been cut short, we
had made ourselves a little supper in the kitchen. The bell
sounded, and when I went to open the door I saw standing in
the doorway a dim, bulky figure from which issued, in a low,
deep voice, greetings in Russian. I had no idea who the man
was, and even when he told me his name it conveyed nothing
to me. I was not well versed in the history of the Russian
Revolution. I did, of course, know of the famous affair of Father
Gapon, the *agent provocateur* of the first Russian revolution of
1905, who had been caught by the revolutionaries and strangled;
but I did not know of the part which Rutenberg had played in
it. So when this strange, bulky man came to my house in the
darkness, speaking Russian in a low, conspiratorial voice, I
was uneasy. After I had read the letter of introduction from
Marcel Cachin, the French Socialist, who was then, I think, in
the government, I was somewhat reassured. But I was still on
my guard. I was known as an anti-Russian, and strange Russians
were not in my line.

He came in, and began to unfold his views, speaking of
Russia, of the Jewish people, of a Jewish army and of Palestine.
He impressed me at once as genuine, but his views on the

Jewish problem and on Palestine were superficial; he had obviously not given much thought to the subject. In the midst of the conversation he made a remark which afterwards recurred to me as odd in the extreme. He said he was in a hurry, and was anxious to get back to London in time for *Yom Kippur*. Why a revolutionary should have *Yom Kippur* on his mind I did not understand. However, it happened that I was going up to London shortly after *Yom Kippur*, so we decided to meet at the house of Achad Ha-am. Arriving there a little before him, I learned something of his antecedents.

When I got to know Rutenberg a little better, I was impressed by his energy and by his ardent desire to do something for the improvement of the Jewish position; but though I appreciated his genuineness, I was depressed by his lack of insight into our problems. His great work for Palestine, the harnessing of the Jordan for electricity, came in later years. For the time being his activity was concentrated on the Jewish army. In the interim he disappeared. He had gone back to Russia, and ranged himself with Kerensky, and we heard of him as the governor of Petrograd. Then he disappeared again when the Bolsheviks came into power. He was heard of in Odessa, where he was helping to evacuate anti-Bolsheviks. Finally, after the war, he turned up again in London. It is my impression that if Kerensky had remained in power, Rutenberg would not have come back to Jewish life. He was a revolutionary by nature, and the Revolution always beckoned to him.

However, he did come back, and set about his tremendous plan for the electrification of Palestine. But the early picture would not be complete if I did not mention that when he came to us he was completely devoid of any contacts with Jewish life. The Zionists were the only ones who listened to him—and that in connection with his plans for the harnessing of the Jordan. Had it not been for the Zionists he would not have obtained his first couple of thousand pounds for the preliminary survey work in Palestine.

Rutenberg was a man of immense energy, tact and ability in dealing with the many Jewish factors he encountered, which was the more surprising in view of his lack of Jewish background. As a type he, the practical engineer, stood midway between Jabotinsky and Achad Ha-am. He saw the difficulties before him, but he did not suffer from explosive repressions, like Jabotinsky, or from excessive proneness to criticism, like Achad Ha-am. He came from the revolutionary school, and had been trained in adversity. But his single-mindedness was what captured people, and as his contacts increased he grew into them. He himself made the impression of a tremendous turbine harnessed to a single great purpose. Not being acquainted with Jewish ways, he often mistook natural scepticism for indifference, and, being centred on his one idea, he did not realize that the Zionists were weighed down with many worries, that they were entering on a course of action in Palestine for which they had had little preparation.

During the first period of my collaboration with Rutenberg and Jabotinsky, that is during the formation of the Jewish Legion, as it came to be called, they did have to face the opposition of the official Zionist bodies, but they could always count on Cowen, myself and one or two others. The Russian Zionists, with whom we kept in touch, were solidly against them. The Copenhagen Bureau, the centre of our neutrality, denounced the plan, and forbade all Zionists to take an active part in it. My support of the army took on, to my distress, an aspect of rebellion at a time when, seeking—though without much hope —unity in the Jewish world, I was breaking it in the Zionist world.

This was added to the burden of my sin of 'unneutrality,' already heavy enough in the eyes of some Zionists. Samuel Pevsner, who was at that time in America, wrote me: 'We are following your activity with the greatest sympathy'; but Shmarya Levin and Dr. Judah Leib Magnes considered my political activity in England, discreet as it was, responsible for the persecutions of the Jews in Palestine, and required me to stop it immediately. I wrote to Magnes on January 1, 1915: 'In all I did, I did not commit our Zionist Organization, did not pledge myself or any other Zionist to any definite course without the sanction of the Executive. . . . The fact that British statesmen are favourable to Zionist ideals, the fact that British statesmen would like to see Palestine occupied or protected by England, is, of course, very well known and is discussed in the press, has been for the last three months, and I cannot hold myself or anybody responsible for it.'

At the same time, in order to obtain official sanction for my activities, I was urging that all available members of the Inner Action Committee should come over to London as soon as possible.

To conduct internal Zionist politics during the First World War was to walk on eggs.

CHAPTER XIV

WORKING FOR THE GOVERNMENT

*A Much-needed Change—Mr. Churchill Places a Large Order—I Leave
Manchester University—We Move to London—Our Second Son, Michael,
is Born—Science and Zionism Mingle*

My life had become extremely complicated, for my manifold
Zionist activities were carried on side by side with an increasingly heavy schedule at the university. The young instructors
were gone, and I had to do part of their work. On top of everything else I enlisted in a training corps, and learned to form
fours. I had to go to Paris occasionally, and to London quite
often. My means were limited, and I was torn between conflicting duties. I would return from an afternoon visit to
London late in the night, and snatch a few hours' sleep before
proceeding to my classes; or else I would take the night train,
sit up all the way to Manchester, and take up my daily tasks
immediately on my arrival. Much of the time, what with the
travel, the interviews, the conferences, the correspondence, the
laboratories and the lecture rooms, I moved about in a sort of
dreamlike trance. It was threatening to become more than I
could stand.

Then, suddenly, a drastic change came into my life, and the
source of it was my scientific and not my political work. On my
return from Switzerland at the end of August 1914, I found a
printed circular on my desk, from the War Office, inviting
every scientist in possession of any discovery of military value
to report it. I promptly offered the War Office my fermentation process, without remuneration. I received no reply. I
nevertheless continued my studies on fermentation, without
feeling that they had any immediate practical application.
One day, in the spring of 1916, I received a visit from Dr. Rintoul, the chief research chemist of Nobel's, the big explosive
manufacturers, located at Ardeer, in Ayrshire. What the
original purpose of his visit was I do not know. We gossiped

about the war, and then the conversation turned to my researches, which I described to him in detail. When I had ended, he said to me, thoughtfully: 'You know, you may have the key to a very important situation in your hands.' Still in the dark as to what he had on his mind, I merely replied: 'Dr. Rintoul, excuse me, you happen to be leaning against the situation!'

Dr. Rintoul turned to inspect the apparatus, then asked for my laboratory notebooks. He seemed pleased with the results described in them, and there and then offered to acquire the process on behalf of his firm. I was rather staggered—and very much delighted; for Nobel's was one of the biggest firms in England. Again it was like something in a dream. For the offer was a good one, and it promised to bring much-needed relief into a situation which had become almost impossible. It was not the physical and mental strain alone which was wearing me down; it was a feeling of frustration. I felt out of things in Manchester. The centre of my Zionist work was London. My Manchester friends were enormously helpful, but they could not, with the best will in the world, substitute for the capital. And here was an offer which opened big vistas for me.

That same day Dr. Rintoul telephoned to Scotland and asked the director of the plant, a Mr. Rogers, to come down to Manchester, together with two or three other chemists. My experiments were repeated, the results found satisfactory. Then followed a discussion of the terms of the contract, which were excellent. I did not, by the way, even have the patent on my process, for I had never appreciated its technical importance. Nor did I publish anything on it until much later.

The dazzling contract never went into effect. Very soon after it was negotiated, there was a big explosion in the Ardeer plant, and my hopes went up with most of the buildings. It was going to take them a long time, they wrote me, to reconstruct their factories, and they had such a heavy backlog of orders that it would be impossible for them to undertake anything new. They asked me to release them, which I did at once. Some time later they brought the matter to the attention of the Government.

So it came about that one day in March 1916 I returned from a visit to Paris to find waiting for me a summons to the British Admiralty, where I was to see Sir Frederick L. Nathan, the head of the powder department. He explained to me that there was a serious shortage of acetone, which was the solvent in making cordite. Without this solvent it would be necessary to make far-reaching changes in the naval guns. I was invited to work on this problem. For a few months I had to carry the double responsibility of teaching in Manchester and putting up a pilot plant in London. My week was split into two parts: four days at the university, three in London. I travelled backwards and forwards by night, to save time. It was nerve-racking, and not too productive. And so the university was requested to relieve me of most of my teaching work, and I was engaged by the Government. To finish the business, my new employers brought me into the presence of the First Lord of the Admiralty, who was at that time Mr. Winston Churchill.

Mr. Churchill was brisk, fascinating, charming and energetic. Almost his first words were: 'Well, Dr. Weizmann, we need thirty thousand tons of acetone. Can you make it?' I was so terrified by this lordly request that I almost turned tail. I answered: 'So far I have succeeded in making a few hundred cubic centimetres of acetone at a time by the fermentation process. I do my work in a laboratory. I am not a technician, I am only a research chemist. But, if I were somehow able to produce a ton of acetone, I would be able to multiply that by any factor you chose. Once the bacteriology of the process is established, it is only a question of brewing. I must get hold of a brewing engineer from one of the big distilleries, and we will set about the preliminary task. I shall naturally need the support of the Government to obtain the people, the equipment, the emplacements and the rest of it. I myself can't even determine what will be required.'

I was given a *carte blanche* by Mr. Churchill and the department, and I took upon myself a task which was to tax all my energies for the next two years, and which was to have consequences which I did not then foresee.

I had to start by building up what is now called a pilot plant, something quite new of its kind. It meant a great deal of pioneering in a field in which I had had no experience whatsoever. First, then, we found a place where we could carry out our first large-scale experiment. It was the Nicholson gin factory in Bromley-by-Bow. We ran into a lot of trouble trying to find shortcuts and over-simplify the process. For instance, we thought we might be able to dispense with aseptic conditions, which were costly and time-consuming. Then we discovered this to be impossible. It took us six or seven months to apply the process on a half-ton scale fairly regularly and with consistently satisfactory results. From that point we reached out for a larger scale, and the Admiralty decided on a twofold plan. It would build a new factory in one of its arsenals, at Holton Heath, near Poole, Dorsetshire, and it would take over the large distilleries and adapt them, wherever possible, to our process.

The double plan entailed an enormous amount of work. The distilleries were scattered throughout England, Scotland and Ireland. A group of chemists had to be trained in the process. I took over the laboratory of the Lister Institute in Chelsea, and there I began to train a number of young people in this branch of chemistry. From Chelsea I sent them out to the various distilleries. The young English scientists were excellent men to work with, but the distilleries were neither very happy about the conversion of their plants, nor particularly helpful. However, this was not all. When the process was in full swing, we were almost forced to suspend operations because of the grain shortage. The food controller could not let us have what we needed—nearly half a million tons of maize. All maize had to be imported from America, and this was the time of the unrestricted U-boat campaign. I tried to substitute chestnuts as the source of the starch, and in part succeeded. The results were not as satisfactory, nor was the supply of chestnuts large enough. We tried wheat, of course, but its yield was lower than that of maize, and since wheat, though grown in England, was not very plentiful either, we were again confronted with the importation problem. Under the pressure of these conditions the production of acetone was shifted to Canada and America —America had by this time entered the war. Some was manufactured in France, some in India, from rice. In Canada the process was particularly successful under the direction of a former pupil of mine, Herbert Speakman, now professor of biological chemistry at the University of Toronto. Speakman organized the work with great skill. He had good material to work with and excellent men. The first American plant for this method of producing acetone was built at Terre Haute, Indiana.

I received, later on, a number of lucrative offers from the Admiralty, and, again, from the Ministry of Munitions when it was headed by Lloyd George. I refused them, and asked instead for a salary about equal to what my wife and I had been earning till then in Manchester, for it soon became evident that I would have to give up my university work altogether and move permanently to London. It was in the middle of 1916 that I severed my connections with Manchester, temporarily as I then thought, but, as it turned out to be, permanently.

After the war my patents were released and taken over by Commercial Solvents, one of the great chemical concerns of America. The Government gave me a token reward for my work, amounting to about ten shillings for every ton of acetone produced, a total of ten thousand pounds. The decision was reached by a committee under the chairmanship of Reginald McKenna.

The Government built a laboratory for me in 1916, and we came to London. I had to leave my wife, with my son, in Manchester, as she was still medical officer of the Infant Clinic, and owing to the shortage of medical help could not be released. She joined me early in 1917. We took a house at 67 Addison Road, and my wife made a charming and attractive home of it. It was in this house that our second boy, Michael, was born on November 16, 1917. It was not a large place, but it soon became a centre not only for the Zionists, but for a great many British political figures. My work brought me into touch with all sorts of people, high and low, in the British Government. Balfour succeeded Churchill in the Admiralty, Lloyd George became Minister of Munitions, and I had much to do with his board, for a great many problems not directly connected with acetone flowed into my laboratories. When the first period of experiment and construction was over, I had a certain amount of leisure, as well as more opportunity to see British statesmen than had been the case when I lived in Manchester. The centre of gravity of my life shifted once again towards my Zionist interests, and from this point on the tide of events moved rapidly towards one of the climactic points in the history of the movement and, I believe, in the history of the Jewish people —the issue of the Balfour Declaration.

CHAPTER XV

TOWARDS THE BALFOUR DECLARATION

The Deeper Meaning of Zionism—Hesitancy of British Statesmen—Jewish Palestine in the Second World War—British Statesmen and Jewish Anti-Zionists—England's Pro-Zionism in First World War—Colonel Meinertzhagen—Sir Mark Sykes—We Publish Zionism and the Jewish Future—Herbert Sidebotham—Our Propaganda Widens

THE reader will remember that from the beginning I had looked upon Zionism as a force for life and creativeness residing in the Jewish masses. It was not simply the blind need of an exiled people for a home of its own. I could not agree with Herzl that the *Judennot*, the tragedy of Jewish homelessness, persecution and poverty, was sufficient to account for the Zionist movement, and was capable of supplying the necessary motive power for the creation of a Jewish homeland. Need alone is negative, and the greatest productions of man spring from an affirmation. Jewish homelessness was not just a physical discomfort; it was also, and perhaps in larger measure, the malaise of frustrated capacities. If the Jewish people had survived so many centuries of exile, it was not by a biological accident, but because it would not relinquish the creative capacities with which it had been entrusted.

For assimilated Jews all this was a sealed book; in their complete alienation from the masses, the source of inspiration, they had not the slightest concept of the inner significance, the constructive moral-ethical-social character of Zionism. They looked upon it—Lucien Wolf, for instance—as a primitive tribalism. They felt themselves, when they were men of an ethical turn of mind like Claude Montefiore, called upon to 'rescue' Judaism from Zionism, or to rescue it just so. It is worth noting, in this connection, that in the Second World War the only part of the entire Mediterranean basin on which the United Nations could count without reservation for full co-operation in the war against nazism and fascism was Jewish

Palestine. It would be wrong to ascribe this to the peculiar position of the Jews, who could never hope to come to terms with Hitlerism. The reverse is equally true; it was Hitlerism which could not come to terms with fundamental Jewish democracy. The character assumed by Jewish Palestine was a projection of the Jewish national, ethical and social content. In a war for the assertion of world democratic principles, a Jewish Palestine could not have played any other rôle, whatever the attitude of the anti-democratic forces towards the Jewish people.

The deeper meaning of Zionism must not be lost sight of in the record of practical steps, of day-to-day strategic adjustments, which led up to the granting of the Balfour Declaration, and which accompanied future developments. I am reverting now to the common accusation that Zionism was nothing but a British imperialistic scheme, the Balfour Declaration a *quid pro quo*, or rather payment in advance, for Jewish service to the Empire. The truth is that British statesmen were by no means anxious for such a bargain. I wrote to Mr. C. P. Scott, in March, 1915:

'The British cabinet is not only sympathetic towards the Palestinian aspirations of the Jews, but would like to see these aspirations realized. I understand Great Britain would be willing even to be the initiator of a proposal to that effect at the peace conference. But at the same time Great Britain would not like to be involved in any responsibilities. In other words, they would leave the organization of the Jewish commonwealth as an independent political unit entirely to the care of the Jews. At the same time there is a view prevalent that it is not desirable that Palestine should belong to any great power.

'These two views are in contradiction. If Great Britain does not wish anyone else to have Palestine, this means that it will have to watch it and stop any penetration of another power. Surely, a course like that involves as much responsibility as would be involved by a British protectorate over Palestine, with the sole difference that watching is a much less effective preventative than an actual protectorate. I therefore thought that the middle course could be adopted . . . viz. the Jews take over the country; the whole burden of organization falls on them, but for the next ten or fifteen years they work under a temporary British protectorate.'

In effect, this is an anticipation of the mandate system. Indeed, had the original idea, or the mandate system, been fully implemented, the service which Jewish Palestine, alone among the Mediterranean peoples, rendered to the cause of democracy in the Second World War would have been proportionately greater. I wrote, in the same letter, of the bond which such a Palestine would create between England and the Jewish people, and added: 'A strong Jewish community on the Egyptian flank is an efficient barrier for any danger likely to come from the north.' There was a time, in the Second World War, when this danger was very real. If it did not materialize, it does not cancel the value of the thirty thousand Jewish soldiers who volunteered from Palestine for service with the United Nations armies of the Near East and Europe, or of the considerable rôle which Palestine played in the war as a minor arsenal of democracy.

I wrote further: 'England . . . would have in the Jews the best possible friends, who would be the best national interpreters of ideas in the Eastern countries and would serve as a bridge between the two civilizations. That again is not a material argument, but certainly it ought to carry great weight with any politician who likes to look fifty years ahead.' As to what actually happened I refer the reader to the second part of this book.

From part of the foregoing it is clear that England's connection with Palestine rested on the idea of a Jewish Homeland in Palestine; but for the idea of a Jewish Homeland, England would not have entertained the thought of a protectorate—or later of a mandate—over Palestine. In short, England felt she had no business in Palestine except as part of the plan for the creation of the Jewish Homeland. Always (as we have already seen in the case of Asquith) there was a shying away from the assumption of 'responsibility' bound up with Palestine as such. I wrote to Mr. Scott at about that time:

'Sir E. Grey is in full sympathy with the Jewish national ideals, as connected with the Palestinian scheme, but would not like to commit himself as to the advisability of establishing a British protectorate over Palestine. He thinks that such a step

H

may lead to difficulties with France and, secondly, may go
against the opinion of a certain school of liberals in this
country. He would, therefore, be inclined to look for a scheme
by which the Jews would not lay any additional burden on
England.'

These hesitancies, as we know, were later to introduce a note
of uncertainty into the British attitude towards the Jewish
Homeland. How was it that the decision was actually made,
and why was the pledge actually given? One factor, perhaps the
decisive one, was the genuine appeal which the idea itself made
to many of the leaders of Britain. One of the differences between that time and ours is in the approach to State problems.
The so-called realism of modern politics is not realism at all,
but pure opportunism, lack of moral stamina, lack of vision,
and the principle of living from hand to mouth. Those British
statesmen of the old school, I have said, were genuinely religious.
They understood as a reality the concept of the Return. It
appealed to their tradition and their faith. Some of them were
completely baffled by the opposition to our plan on the part of
assimilated Jews; others were actually rubbed the wrong way
by it. Lord Milner was a great friend of Claude Montefiore,
the spiritual leader of the anti-Zionists; but on this point he
would not be influenced. Milner understood profoundly that
the Jews alone were capable of rebuilding Palestine, and of
giving it a place in the modern family of nations. He said,
publicly: 'If the Arabs think that Palestine will become an
Arab country, they are very much mistaken.' Wickham Steed,
the editor of *The Times*, expressed intense annoyance to me at
the action of the anti-Zionists—we shall come to the incident
later—in publishing a series of letters against the plan in his
paper. Philip Kerr, afterwards Lord Lothian, an enlightened
imperialist, saw in a Jewish Palestine a bridge between Africa,
Asia and Europe on the road to India. He, like many others, was
taken aback by the anti-Zionism of the 'leading' British Jews;
but the measure of understanding which I expected from him—
he was then secretary to Lloyd George—and from others may
be gauged by the frankness of the following letter, which I
wrote to him at the height of the Jewish anti-Zionist opposition, in 1917:

'There is another aspect of the question which troubles me.

It seems as if the cabinet and even yourself attach undue importance to the opinions held by so-called "British Jewry." If it is a question of the Jews who have settled in Great Britain, well, the majority of these Jews are in favour of Zionism. If, on the other hand, by British Jews one understands the minority of wealthy, half-assimilated Jews who have been living in this country for the last three or four generations, then, of course, it is true that these people are dead against Zionism. But here is the tragic misunderstanding. Zionism is not meant for those people who have cut themselves adrift from Jewry, it is meant for those masses who have a will to live a life of their own and those masses have a right to claim the recognition of Palestine as a Jewish National Home. The second category of British Jews will fall into line quickly enough when this declaration is given to us. I still expect a time, and I do so not without apprehension, when they will even claim to be Zionists themselves. Some Jews and non-Jews do not seem to realize one fundamental fact, that whatever happens we will get to Palestine. . . . No amount of talk by Mr. Montagu or people like him will stem the tide.'

There were, at that time, alike in the highest Government posts and in those of secondary importance, men with a real understanding both of the moral implication of the Zionist movement and of the potentialities of Palestine. To some extent before my moving to London, but much more afterwards, I set myself to discovering these men, guided almost always by the indefatigable Mr. Scott. Some of them I met in the course of my work at the Admiralty and with the Ministry of Munitions. In the one department of the war where they really dealt with political problems—the War Office—there were men of first-rate political capacity and of deep appreciation of the Zionist movement, even if they did not always agree with all of its phases. There was a general atmosphere of sympathy, all the way from General Wilson, the Chief of Staff, who was a great friend of Lloyd George, to the lower ranks of the department, which were responsible for the detailed work. In the Foreign Office, too, there was a predisposition to look favourably on the Zionist problem. The tone of public opinion at large, as far as we could ascertain it, was one of interest, and not unfriendly. The *Manchester Guardian* was with us; *The Times* was favourably inclined. There was an eager desire to win over the Jewish public opinion of the world. In this respect, too, there is a fundamental difference between then and now: Hitler taught the world not to attach too much importance to public opinion in general and to Jewish public opinion in particular.

In another sense, too, it was easier to work then than now because most of the discussions were in the realm of the abstract. The great difficulties, like the Arab problem, had not yet come to the fore. There were only doubts of the usual kind, such as one hears even now: 'Are the Jews capable of building up a country? Isn't Palestine too small?'—although at that time the eastern boundary of Palestine went as far as the Hedjaz Railway and included Transjordan—'Will the Jews go to Palestine? Is not Zionism the dream of a few intellectuals and of a handful of poor Jews living in the ghettos of Poland and Russia?' But these doubts were without great weight. What mattered was the readiness of people to listen and be convinced; and I pleaded the cause of Palestine wherever I could obtain a hearing.

My Zionist work thrust itself insistently into my labours at the Admiralty. As the pressure of the first stages in the training of chemists and the creation of plants relaxed, I found myself caught up again in the maze of personal relations. There is not room enough in this record for more than a passing allusion to most of the thoroughly interesting, sometimes rather extraordinary, personalities who played a part in that phase of Zionist history. Some of them, however, it is impossible to dismiss offhand.

Very soon after the beginning of my association with the Admiralty I made the acquaintance of Colonel Richard Meinertzhagen, a member of an important Danish family which had long been settled in England, and which had given the country a large number of able men. Meinertzhagen, a nephew of Mrs. Sidney Webb (later Lady Passfield) had had a magnificent career. He was a man of lion-hearted courage, and had fought on almost every front. He was repeatedly wounded and sent home; I met him during one of these leaves, in the office of the D.M.I. (Director of Military Intelligence). At our first meeting, he told me the following story of himself: he had been an anti-Semite, though all he had known about

Jews had been what he had picked up in a few casual, anti-Semitic books. But he had also met some of the rich Jews, who had not been particularly attractive. But then, in the Near East, he had come across Aaron Aaronson, a Palestinian Jew, also a man of great courage and of superior intelligence, devoted to Palestine. Aaronson was a botanist, and the discoverer of wild wheat. With Aaronson, Meinertzhagen had many talks about Palestine, and was so impressed by him that he completely changed his mind and became an ardent Zionist—which he has remained till this day. And that not merely in words. Whenever he can perform a service for the Jews or Palestine he will go out of his way to do so.

The men with whom I had most to do, apart from Meinertzhagen, were Colonel Gribbon and Professor C. K. Webster, both of whom were under the orders of General Macdonogh, Chief of Intelligence. They were both exceptionally gifted. Webster had been lent to the War Office by Liverpool University, where he occupied the chair of History; later he became Professor of International Relations at Aberystwyth. He had travelled much in Japan, India and Asia Minor, and knew the Near East well. He was a devoted friend of the Zionist movement.

One of our greatest finds was Sir Mark Sykes, Chief Secretary of the War Cabinet, a very colourful and even romantic figure. He was a devout Catholic, a great landowner in the Hull district, a breeder of racehorses, and a widely travelled man intimately acquainted with the Middle East. His family had given many explorers, soldiers and foreign representatives to the country. He was not very consistent or logical in his thinking, but he was generous and warm-hearted. He had conceived the idea of the liberation of the Jews, the Arabs and the Armenians, whom he looked upon as the three downtrodden races *par excellence*. Sykes was brought into touch with Zionist affairs and myself through Dr. Moses Gaster—which was somewhat unusual, for Gaster had a tendency to keep his 'finds' to himself, and to play a lone hand. Thus, for instance, Gaster did not tell me until after I had met Sir Herbert Samuel that the latter, though not a member of the Zionist Organization, had long been interested in the idea of a Jewish State in Palestine! And when I went to meet Samuel—this was in November

1914—Gaster looked at me with a mixture of roguishness and distrust, and said: 'Ho-ho! So you are going to negotiate with Herbert Samuel!' I never understood the meaning of this queer streak in him.

Still odder, in this general connection, was the fact that Gaster was so furiously anti-Russian that he appeared almost pro-German, and definitely at any rate he felt that all our negotiations with British statesmen and officials were pointless. It was Gaster who had first won Sykes over to Zionism, yet on the occasion of a crucial conference with Sykes and others, held in Gaster's house, Gaster began to air his views on England's dark prospect in the war. The situation was painful, to say the least, and it speaks well for the tolerance and large-mindedness of Sykes that he did not walk out of the room. Harry Sacher, who was present, and who felt, like the rest of us, that Gaster had never pulled his weight in the movement, interrupted him curtly and said: 'Now, now, Dr. Gaster, the spadework will be done by Dr. Weizmann and Mr. Sokolow.'

Gaster's views on the Germans and the outcome of the war underwent an abrupt change one day when an air raid took place and a number of bombs dropped in front of his house. I happened to call on him, and when I asked him how he felt about the air raid, he said, furiously: 'I'm through with them!' —meaning the Germans.

I cannot say enough regarding the services rendered us by Sykes. It was he who guided our work into more official channels. He belonged to the secretariat of the War Cabinet, which contained, among others, Leopold Amery, Ormsby-Gore and Ronald Storrs. If it had not been for the counsel of men like Sykes and Lord Robert Cecil we, with our inexperience in delicate diplomatic negotiations, would undoubtedly have committed many dangerous blunders. The need for such counsel will become evident when I come to tell of the complications which already, at that time, surrounded the status of the Near East.

Sir Ronald Graham, who was a senior official in the Foreign Office, also took a great interest in our work. He was desirous of seeing something done for the Jewish people, but he was more sedate and less imaginative than Sykes, and lacked his warm and urgent temperament. I do not know how deep his sympathies were, but he was of considerable help in bringing about the Balfour Declaration. I rather think that to him it was more a propaganda matter than an attempt to solve a difficult problem.

Of larger stature and superior abilities was Leopold Amery, later Colonial Secretary. Amery got his enlightened imperialist principles from Milner. He was the most open-minded of all that group. He realized the importance of a Jewish Palestine in the British imperial scheme of things more than anyone else. He also had much insight into the intrinsic fineness of the Zionist movement. He gave us unstinted encouragement and support. He, in particular, was incensed when the leading Jews attacked the scheme openly in 1917.

It was gradually borne in on me, even before I had settled in London—that is, before this network of relationships had been created in full—that a decisive period was approaching. Early in the spring of 1916 I called together the Manchester Zionists in a little room on Cheetham Hill and put the situation before them. I told them of my talks with Edmond de Rothschild, with Achad Ha-am, with Herbert Samuel and, above all, with the British statesmen. With the support of the Manchester Zionists I went to London, and there talked with Joseph Cowen, the chairman of the English Zionist Federation. We decided, as a first step, to publish a little book on Zionism. For, apart from a few pamphlets, mostly out of date, and some reports of the Congresses, there was nothing that could be put into the hands of British statesmen.

The obstacle to the first step was—money. We had not a penny in our treasury. I had to go to Paris and ask Baron Edmond for the money. He favoured the idea and gave me two hundred and fifty pounds, which I turned over to Leon Simon, who undertook the production and publication of the book. It appeared under the title of *Zionism and the Jewish Future*. A number of men collaborated, and I wrote the foreword.

It was a small book, but it was up to date and it contained some sober and factual information on Palestine. Much to our astonishment, it was soon out of print, and a second printing had to be put out. Nor was it bought, by any means, only by Jews. There was a considerable general interest in the subject. In part, the success of the book was due to the review, by Lord

Cromer, which appeared in the *Spectator*. Lord Cromer said, among other things: 'The British public will have much more to do with this subject than is apparent now. . . . Before long politicians will be unable to brush it aside as the fantastic dream of a few idealists. . . .'

The time taken by these *démarches* and by the volume of my correspondence crowded closely on my exacting official and professional duties. I had no office and no secretary. We were continuously receiving people in our little house. My wife answered all the telephone calls, helped me to the limit of her strength with my visitors and my correspondence, and did what she could, and more, to lighten my burden. But the situation, becoming increasingly difficult and complicated, was beyond her strength. The office of the English Zionist Federation was useless for our purpose. It was out in Fulborne Street, in the East End. After much consideration and heart-searching we decided to open an office at 175 Piccadilly, and Simon Marks, who was released from military service for this purpose, took charge of it. From that time on our work assumed more organized and systematic form. The little office in Piccadilly became an important centre towards which gravitated every-thing in Zionist life. A great many people from neutral countries passed through London. A small group crystallized which gradually constituted itself a political committee. To it came those members of the Zionist Executive who passed through London. We had with us Achad Ha-am, Harry Sacher (who was now living in London), Israel Sieff, some Palestinians like Aaron Aaronson, Tolkowsky and Dr. Oettinger, who were extremely valuable because of their knowledge of Palestine and of its economic and agricultural possibilities and problems. Although the committee was entirely unofficial—the only member of the Zionist Executive on it was Mr. Sokolow—it was a close-knit group, animated by one purpose, and harmonious in its working methods. It was sufficiently represen-tative to give us the feeling that we were speaking for the move-ment as a whole, but it was not cumbersome, and the discussions were fruitful. From time to time we had the benefit of the advice of Herbert Samuel, of James de Rothschild, and of other members of the House of Commons. Later we had the help of Sir Alfred Mond.

Sokolow appeared in London some time in 1916. He took up his quarters in the Regent Palace Hotel, and kept his office in his suitcase. He was particularly useful because of his connections with the clerical world. He interviewed a number of Anglican bishops, among them, I believe, the Archbishop of Canterbury. He liked this sort of work, being himself more or less of the archiepiscopal type. Later he conducted negotiations with the French and Italian authorities and with the Vatican. He too had feared, at the beginning of the war, that Germany would be victorious; but he changed his views later, and like myself began to see an era of liberation and hope in the prospect of an Allied victory.

Our first official political committee was formed in January 1916, and at the beginning contained, besides Sokolow and myself, Joseph Cowen, Dr. Gaster and Herbert Bentwich, as the representatives of the English Zionist Federation. The committee worked in close consultation with the Rothschilds, Herbert Samuel and Achad Ha-am.

Sokolow took a leading hand in the preparation of the first memorandum which we presented to Sir Mark Sykes.

In 1916, Herbert Sidebotham, then of the *Manchester Guardian*, helped us to found the British Palestine Committee, which played an important rôle in the moulding of public opinion in our favour. A small weekly, edited by Sidebotham, was put out; it contained serious, informative articles aimed at the more thoughtful type of reader, and was often quoted in the general press. It also carried on propaganda in the larger cities somewhat on the model of the Phil-Hellenic Societies. Mr. Sidebotham was one of the first prominent English publicists to perceive the coincidence of the interest between Great Britain and a Jewish Palestine. Through the Palestine Committee, consisting largely of non-Jews, and *Palestine*, he constantly urged this view upon the British public, and in 1918, after the issue of the Balfour Declaration, published his book, *England and Palestine*, conceived in the same spirit.

Thus the work went on steadily throughout the period from 1914 to 1917. In the provinces the Zionists co-operated, drawing the attention of their M.P.'s to our cause. The young people, too, were of assistance. The stage was being set for the final struggle.

H*

CHAPTER XVI

FROM THEORY TO REALITY

Zionism Becomes an International Factor—The Amateur State-builders—
First Memorandum to the British Government—The Two Fundamental
Principles—The International Tangle—The Secret 'Sykes-Picot' Treaty
—French and Italian Ambitions—A Condominium for Palestine?—
Difficulties with France—Lord Robert Cecil—Mobilizing World Jewish
Opinion—Justice Louis D. Brandeis

ZIONISM was rapidly passing from the preliminary stage of propaganda and theoretical discussion to that of practical realities. Our contacts had become firm enough, public opinion was sufficiently developed for the transition. We had travelled a long way from the tentative 'feelers,' the scattered individual sympathies, of 1914. The picture of the forces for and against us had clarified. We knew who was with us and who against us in the Jewish world. We had discovered, in the English political world, a heavy preponderance of opinion in our favour. As early as March 1916, the subject was being mooted in the European chancelleries. Sir Edward Buchanan, the British Ambassador to Russia, was instructed by Sir Edward Grey to sound out the Russian Government on 'the question of Jewish colonization in Palestine.' The French Government or, more exactly, the Foreign Minister, M. Pichon, sent Professor Victor Guillaume Basch to America to assure American Jewry that in the disposition of Turkey's Asiatic territories after the war, the interests of the Jewish colonies in Palestine would be protected by the French and British. Perhaps the most interesting evidence of the seriousness with which the Zionist movement was being taken was the effort of imperial Germany to make use of it for her own ends. The German Zionist leaders were approached with the request to offer their services as intermediaries for peace negotiations. Their reply was that they would make an effort only if they received from the German Government a written undertaking to conclude peace on the basis of no annexations and no indemnities (this was at a time when German arms were successful). I communicated the move confidentially to Sir Ronald Graham. After some vague *pourparlers* the German Government dropped the offer.

The time had come, therefore, to take action, to press for a declaration of policy in regard to Palestine on the part of the British Government; and towards the end of January 1917 I submitted to Sir Mark Sykes the memorandum prepared by our committee, and had several preliminary conferences with him.

This memorandum, the first we submitted—in unofficial form, it is true—to the British Government is, I think, of some interest independently of its place in this narrative. It represents the efforts of a group of amateur state builders, members of a people which had for many centuries been separated from this type of activity. None of us had had any experience in government and colonization. We had no staff of experts to lean on, no tradition of administration, no civil service, no means of taxation, no national body of land workers. We were journalists, scientists, lawyers, merchants, philosophers. We were one or two generations removed—if that—from the ghetto. Nevertheless, in retrospect, the memorandum does seem to have anticipated the shape of things to come.

The document was called: 'Outline of Programme for the Jewish Resettlement of Palestine in Accordance with the Aspirations of the Zionist Movement.' Its first point had to do with national recognition:

The Jewish population of Palestine (which in the programme shall be taken to mean both present and future Jewish population) shall be officially recognized by the Suzerain Government as the Jewish Nation, and shall enjoy in that country full civic, national and political rights. The Suzerain Government recognizes the desirability and necessity of a Jewish resettlement of Palestine.

The second point laid down a principle which, on the practical side, was not less fundamental than the principle of recognition on the theoretical side. A repudiation of this principle—and it has been repudiated—is a denial of the whole plan.

The Suzerain Government shall grant to the Jews of other countries full and free right of immigration into Palestine. The Suzerain

Government shall give to the Jewish population of Palestine every facility for immediate naturalization and for land purchase.

The history of our efforts to build Palestine since the Balfour Declaration is in part a history of the struggle to obtain the application of the foregoing principles.

The third point dealt with instrumentalities.

The Suzerain Government shall sanction a formation of a Jewish Company for the colonization of Palestine by Jews. The said Company shall be under the direct protection of the Suzerain Government. The objects of the Company shall be: (*a*) to support and foster the existing Jewish settlement in Palestine in every possible way; (*b*) to aid, support and encourage Jews from other countries who are desirous of, and suitable for, settling in Palestine by organizing immigration, by providing information, and by every other form of material and moral assistance. The powers of the Company shall be such as will enable it to develop the country in every way, agricultural, cultural, commercial and industrial, and shall include full powers of land purchase and development, and especially facilities for the acquisition of Crown lands, building rights for roads, railways, harbours, power to establish shipping companies for the transport of goods and passengers to and from Palestine, and every other power found necessary for the opening up of the country.

In case the Suzerain Government shall appoint a Governor and a body of officials to govern Palestine, such appointment shall be made with due regard to the special requirements of the Jewish population.

The fourth and fifth points were directed towards the development of local autonomy and the recognition and development of the institutions already created by us in Palestine.

The contents of the memorandum may be seen under two aspects. One is the external, bespeaking our expectations and needs *vis-a-vis* the Government of Palestine. The other is internal, and bespeaks the duties and tacit promises of the Jewish people. There have been difficulties, throughout the years, in regard to both aspects; and there has been a constant functional interrelation between the two. If the Government of Palestine fell short in respect of the external expectation, the Jewish people, seen as a unit, fell short in respect of the internal. Before and since the issue of the Balfour Declaration the recognition of the nationhood of a Palestinian Jewry met with the obstinate resistance and denial of the assimilationist Jews. Time and again the Zionist movement has been 'asked' to relinquish both sets of principles; the principle of nationality and the principle of free immigration. The first request came from the assimilationist Jews, the second from various groups in the Government controlling Palestine. In both instances we have been told that such a renunciation would be for our own good. In both instances the argument was nonsense. The national principle was the source of our internal strength; the principle of free immigration the only conceivable instrument of expansion. No doubt the discussion will go on until, with the fulfilment of our aspirations, it becomes irrelevant.

However, there the document was—the first draft of our charter, the first approach to the integration of Zionism with the complex of realities. And now our discussions took on a new character. We were, so to speak, in the world arena; we had taken the plunge into international politics. We found ourselves in the midst of crosscurrents of national purposes, vested interests and contradictory forces within individual countries. Thus, though France had made some gestures of friendship towards the Zionist movement, such as the Basch mission to America, she had plans of her own with regard to the Near East. Italy and the Vatican had interests, too. Of course, we had never been so naïve as to imagine that nothing more was needed than England's consent. As far back as 1915 I had discussed the question with Mr. C. P. Scott, and a letter of mine to him, written on February 11 of that year, reads in part: 'Firstly as for France, I don't think that she should claim more than Syria, as far as Beirut. The so-called French influence, which is merely spiritual and religious, is predominant in Syria. In Palestine there is very little of it—a few monastic establishments. The only work which may be termed civilizing pioneer work has been carried out by the Jews. From the point of view of justice, therefore, France cannot lay claim to a country with which it has no connection whatsoever.'

It will be remembered that the sharp intramural Jewish struggle round the Haifa Technical College had, in fact, been the reflex of contending claims or ambitions on the part of various Powers with regard to Palestine. This was familiar ground to us. What we did not know in the early stages of our practical negotiations was that a secret tentative agreement, which was later revealed as the 'Sykes-Picot Treaty,' already existed between France and England! And the most curious part of the history is this: although Sir Mark Sykes, of the British Foreign Office, had himself negotiated this treaty with M. Georges Picot of the French Foreign Office, Sir Mark entered into negotiations with us, and gave us his fullest support, without even telling us of the existence of the tentative agreement! He was, in effect, modifying his stand in our favour, seeking to revise the agreement so that our claims in Palestine might be given room. But it was *not* from him that we learned of the existence of the agreement, and months passed—months during which we carried on our negotiations with the British and other authorities—before we understood what it was that blocked our progress.

The first full-dress conference leading to the Balfour Declaration took place at the home of Dr. Gaster on the morning of February 17, 1917, Dr. Gaster presiding. There were present, besides Dr. Gaster, Lord Rothschild, Herbert Samuel, Sir Mark Sykes, James de Rothschild, Sokolow, Joseph Cowen, Herbert Bentwich, Harry Sacher and myself. Sir Mark attended, as he told us, in his private capacity.

The discussions touched on several points which were to constitute the heart of the problem in the ensuing months. First, we were determined that there was to be no condominium or internationalization in Palestine, with all the complications, rivalries, inefficiencies, compromises and intrigues which that would entail, to the detriment or perhaps complete paralysis of our work. What the Zionists wanted was a British protectorate with full rights according to the terms of the memorandum. These arguments did not, however, apply to the Holy Places, which we wanted internationalized. Second, the term 'nation,' as applied to the emergent Jewish homeland in Palestine, referred to the Jewish homeland *alone*, and in no wise to the relationship of Jews with the lands in which they lived. So much was made clear by Herbert Samuel. To this I added that the Jews who *went* to Palestine would go to constitute a Jewish nation, not to become Arabs or Druses or Englishmen.

We reviewed the international situation. It was the consensus of opinion that the Jews everywhere, in so far as they were

interested in a Jewish homeland in Palestine, held the views we
were putting forward. Of one country we could speak with
official authority. Mr. Brandeis, the head of the Zionist movement in America, and adviser to President Wilson on the Jewish
question, was in favour of a British protectorate, and utterly
opposed to a condominium. This was true, also, of the Russian
Zionists. We anticipated no objection on this score from any
Zionist group; not even the German. Not so simple, however,
was the external international situation, that is to say, the attitude
of the other Powers. On this subject Sir Mark Sykes talked at
some length. He spoke with the utmost freedom of the difficulties
which confronted us. I may say, in fact, that he placed all his
diplomatic skill at our disposal, and that without it we should
have had much heavier going than we did. There is, of course,
no doubt in my mind that, on the Sykes-Picot agreement, he
was, like Georges Picot, bound to secrecy by his Government.

Sir Mark began by revealing that he had long considered the
question of Palestine and the Jews, and that the idea of a Jewish
Palestine had his full sympathy; moreover, he understood
entirely what was meant by 'nationality,' and there was no
confusion in his mind on that point. His chief concern, at the
moment, was the attitude of the Powers. Sir Mark had been in
Russia, had talked with the Foreign Minister, Sazonov, and
anticipated little difficulty from that quarter. Italy, he said,
went on the principle of asking for whatever the French
demanded. And France was the real difficulty. He could not
understand French policy. The French wanted all Syria and a
great say in Palestine. We (the Zionists) would have to discuss
the question very frankly with the French—and at this point
we interrupted to say that 'we' did not at all relish having to
conduct such negotiations: that was the business of the British
Government. Mr. James de Rothschild pointed out very
correctly that if British Jews approached the French Government, the latter would get French Rabbis to press for a French
Palestine.

Sir Mark then went on to speak of the Arab problem, and of
the rising Arab nationalist movement. Within a generation, he
said, the movement would come into its own, for the Arabs
had intelligence, vitality and linguistic unity. But he believed
that the Arabs would come to terms with us—*particularly if*

they received Jewish support in other matters; Sir Mark anticipated the attitude of the greatest of the Arabs, the Emir Feisal.

This, in brief, was the substance of our first 'official' conference. Upon it followed a lively activity. Sokolow was entrusted with the task of modifying the attitude of the French, and of winning the consent of Italy and the Vatican—a task which he discharged with great skill. Georges Picot, the French official who had negotiated the secret agreement with Sir Mark, was not particularly helpful. His first suggestion was that the Jews of Eastern Europe should be content with equal rights on the spot, and should use them for the purpose of settling on the land; his second was that if a Jewish State was to be created in Palestine, the French should have the protectorate. His first point, which had no foundation in knowledge, ignored the very essence of the Jewish problem, and the *raison d'être* of the Zionist movement. The second did not suit our book, because we were convinced that as colonizers and colonial administrators the British were superior to the French; but this was not something one could exactly state. There were three-cornered conversations between Sokolow, Picot and Sykes, between Picot, Sykes and myself—and at no time was the secret agreement mentioned! When the ground had thus been explored in England, Sokolow left for Paris and Rome, where he continued his work, always, like myself, blindfolded, knowing nothing of the Sykes-Picot agreement. In Italy his task was extremely delicate because of the Vatican.

Although the Vatican had never formulated any claims in Palestine, it had a recognized interest in the Holy Places. But then practically all Palestine could be regarded as a Holy Place. There was Galilee, because of the roads on which Christ had walked; there was the Jordan Valley, because of the river in which Christ had been baptized. There were Jerusalem and Bethlehem and Nazareth. On such principles, very little of Palestine was left.

From now on our preoccupation was not with obtaining recognition for the Zionist ideal, but with the fitting of its application into the web of realities, and with preventing its frustration by unwise combinations and concessions. The chief danger came always from the French. I had a long talk with Balfour on March 22, 1917—he had become Foreign Minister,

replacing Sir Edward Grey—and the situation then looked so
serious that Balfour made a rather startling suggestion: if no
agreement could be reached between England and France, we
should try to interest America, and work for an Anglo-American
protectorate over Palestine. It was an attractive if somewhat
far-fetched idea, but, as I wrote to C. P. Scott, 'it is fraught with
the danger that there always is with two masters, and we do
not know yet how far the Americans would agree with the
British on general principles of administration.'

It was again the attitude of the French which came to the
fore in my talk with the Prime Minister, Mr. Asquith, on April 3.
In spite of what we have seen, from private notes published
years later, of Asquith's personal unfriendliness to the Zionist
ideal, his official attitude was helpful. Neither he nor Mr. Balfour, however, mentioned the Sykes-Picot treaty. I learned of
its existence on April 16, 1917, from Mr. Scott who had obtained
the information in Paris. The arrangement was: that France was
to obtain, after the war, not only northern Syria, but Palestine
down to a line from St. Jean d'Acre to Lake Tiberias, including
the Hauran; the rest of Palestine was to be internationalized.

This was startling information indeed! It seemed to me that
the proposal was devoid of rhyme or reason. It was unjust to
England, fatal to us, and not helpful to the Arabs. I could easily
understand why Sykes had not been averse to the abrogation
of the treaty and why Picot had not been able to defend it
with any particular energy.

On April 25 I went into the matter thoroughly with Lord
Robert Cecil, the Assistant Secretary for Foreign Affairs, one
of the great spirits of modern England, and a prime factor in
the creation of the League of Nations. Like Balfour, Milner,
Smuts and others, Lord Cecil was deeply interested in the
Zionist ideal; I think that he alone saw it in its true perspec-
tive as an integral part of world stabilization. To him the
re-establishment of a Jewish Homeland in Palestine and the
organization of the world in a great federation were comple-
mentary features of the next step in the management of human
affairs.

We did not talk openly of the Sykes-Picot treaty. I alluded
only to 'an arrangement which is supposed to exist,' and which
dated from the early days of the war. According to its terms

Palestine would be cut arbitrarily into two halves—a 'Solomon's judgment,' I called it—and the Jewish colonizing effort of some thirty years wiped out. To make matters worse, the lower part of Palestine, Judea, would not even pass under a single administration, but would become internationalized: which in effect meant—as I had recently written to Philip Kerr—an Anglo-French condominium. What we wanted, I said to Lord Cecil, was a British protectorate. Jews all over the world trusted England. They knew that law and order would be established by British rule, and that under it Jewish colonizing activities and cultural development would not be interfered with. We could thus look forward to a time when we would be strong enough to claim a measure of self-government. Lord Cecil then asked what were the objections against a purely French control. I answered that of course a purely French control was preferable to dual control, or internationalization, but the French in their colonizing activity had not followed the same lines as the English. They had always interfered with the population and tried to impose on it the *esprit français*. Moreover, I did not think the French administration as efficient as the British, and I ventured the opinion that the Zionist Organization had—even then—done more constructive work in Palestine than the French in Tunis.

Lord Cecil then raised the subject of my going out to Palestine and Syria. I answered that I was prepared to make the trip—if my work at the Admiralty would permit it—but only with the understanding that I was to work for a Jewish Palestine under a British protectorate. Lord Cecil agreed to this view. He saw the difficulties of the situation, but suggested that it would help a great deal if the Jews of the world would express themselves in favour of a British protectorate; to which I answered that the task of mobilizing this opinion was exactly what I was prepared to undertake; and it would be in pursuance of such a task that I would go to Palestine. (My trip to Palestine did not come off until after the Balfour Declaration.)

There are two points in this interview which have been raised before in these memoirs, but which I feel I ought to stress again. The first is the value which was placed on Jewish public opinion. The second is the relationship which would exist between the British protectorate in Palestine and the creation of the Jewish

Homeland. It was the Jews who gave substance and reality to the idea of a British protectorate—which afterwards took the form of a mandate—over Palestine. It was our movement, the labour, the capital and the sacrifice we put into it, which made the proposal attractive and, in fact, purposeful. The progress which Palestine has made in these years is due to our efforts, as one commission after another has testified; and I believe that certain consequences flow from all these facts.

We had long pointed out to the British, and I repeated it again in my interview with Lord Cecil, that a Jewish Palestine would be a safeguard to England, in particular in respect to the Suez Canal. Our foresight had larger bearings than we ourselves understood. It is proper to ask, after this interval of a quarter of a century, with the Second World War fresh in our memories, what the position would have been in the Near East, not for England alone, but for the world democratic cause, if we had not provided in Palestine a foothold for England; if, instead of the bulwark thus constructed, Palestine had been as open as Syria and Iraq to a Nazi drive after the fall of France. It is, I think, permissible to say that there was something providential in our insistence on the arrangement which we put through, and the exertions by which we gave it effect.

Nor can it be objected that all this is merely wisdom after the event. We were always seeing decades ahead. When I found Sykes somewhat hesitant about our plans, I wrote to Scott—this was March 20, 1917: 'I cannot help feeling that he considers the Zionist scheme as an appendage to the bigger scheme with which he is dealing, the Arab scheme. Of course, I understand that the Arab position is, at present, much more important from the point of view of the immediate prosecution of the war than the Jewish question, which requires a rather long view to appreciate its meaning; but it makes our work very difficult if, in all the present negotiations with the Arabs, the Jewish interests in Palestine are not well defined.'

I believe it is also proper to ask what would have been left today of Arab rights not only in Palestine, but in Syria, Iraq and even in Saudi Arabia, if Zionist foresight had not created the British foothold in the Near East, and strengthened it with a vigorous Jewish settlement whose loyalty to the democratic cause was not merely verbal, but expressed itself in action.

In the mobilization of Jewish public opinion, undertaken, as we have just seen, at the instance of the British Government, we had in mind England, South Africa, Russia, France, Italy, Canada and America—but by far the greatest emphasis was placed on America. Of America's rôle in the movement I shall have much to say. At this point, one aspect of her immense services is relevant. Mr. Louis D. Brandeis was at the head of the movement then, and I was in constant touch with him. On April 8, 1917, I sent him a report on the general position, which I could say was developing very satisfactorily. 'The main difficulty,' I wrote, 'seems to be the claims of the French. . . . We look forward here to a strengthening of our position, both by the American Government and American Jews, and on that point I had a conversation with Mr. Norman Hapgood in the presence of Mr. Herbert Samuel, Mr. Neil Primrose, Mr. James de Rothschild and Commander Wedgwood, M.P. An expression of opinion coming from yourself and perhaps from other gentlemen connected with the Government in favour of a Jewish Palestine under a British protectorate would greatly strengthen our hands.'

Before long, Mr. Brandeis was able to throw the full weight of his remarkable personality into the scales. America had entered the war in March of that year. On April 20, Mr. Balfour arrived in America on a special mission, and almost immediately met the Justice at a party at the White House. Mrs. Dugdale, Balfour's biographer, reports that Balfour's opening remark to Brandeis was: 'You are one of the Americans I had wanted to meet,' and continues: 'Balfour remarked to Lord Eustace Percy, a member of his Mission, that Brandeis was in some ways the most remarkable man he had met in the United States. It seems, from such notes of these conversations as survive, that Balfour pledged his own personal support to Zionism. He had done it before to Dr. Weizmann, but now he was British Foreign Secretary. Mr. Justice Brandeis seems to have become increasingly emphatic, during the course of the British Mission's visit, about the desire of American Zionists to see a British Administration in Palestine.'

My letter of April 8 must have reached Mr. Brandeis about the time of Balfour's arrival on the twentieth. I wrote again, on April 23: 'Both Russia and America are at present proclaiming anti-annexationist principles. . . . I need not dwell on the fact that Jewish National Democracy and the Zionist Organization which essentially represents this Democracy trust implicitly to British rule, and they see in a British protectorate the only possibility for a normal development of a Jewish common-wealth in Palestine. Whereas, in my opinion, Great Britain would not agree to a simple annexation of Palestine, and it does not desire any territorial expansion, it would certainly support and protect a Jewish Palestine. This is why American support for this scheme is so valuable at the present stage.'

Mr. Brandeis did more than press the idea of a Jewish Pale-stine under a British protectorate. He carried on a general work of clarification. In America as in England, then as later, Jewish opposition to Zionism was confined to minority groups. Mrs. Dugdale records further: 'As late as January, 1918, our Am-bassador in Washington reported, on the authority of Mr. Justice Brandeis himself, that the Zionists were violently opposed by the great capitalists, for different reasons,' and she adds, in passing: 'this in itself shows how baseless was the idea, once very prevalent, that the Balfour Declaration was in part a bargain with American financiers.'

But the most important feature of American help at that time issued from the policy proclaimed by President Wilson in repudiation of secret treaties. The Sykes-Picot arrangement was not a full treaty; but it was sufficiently official to create the greatest single obstacle to our progress. The proclamation of the Wilsonian principle of open covenants openly arrived at com-pelled the Powers to put their cards on the table. The Sykes-Picot arrangement, or semi-official treaty, faded into the back-ground.

From all the foregoing it will be seen that our work was carried on harmoniously and systematically. As Mrs. Dugdale puts it, succinctly: 'A Jewish national diplomacy was in being.' She adds: 'By the end of April [1917] the Foreign Office recognized, with some slight dismay, that the British Govern-ment was virtually committed.'

The final struggle round the issue of the Balfour Declaration was, however, still before us; and it was preceded by an 'incident' which is, I think, worth recording for other reasons than historic importance.

CHAPTER XVII

OPERA BOUFFE INTERMEZZO

Mysterious Cable from Mr. Brandeis—Intrigues About Turkey—Ex-Ambassador Henry Morgenthau—Secret Mission to Gibraltar—Meeting with Professor Frankfurter—Vagueness and Confusion

ONE morning early in June of that year (1917) I received a cable from Mr. Brandeis to the effect that an American commission was travelling to the East and that I should try to make contact with it somewhere. Who the members of the commission were, what its purpose was, to what point of the East it was travelling, and where I could establish contact, were details not mentioned. That it had something to do with us was obvious; I would not have received the cable otherwise. Everything else was a complete mystery. I immediately consulted Sykes and Ormsby-Gore. From them I learned that attempts were being made to detach Turkey from the Central Powers. America was taking the lead in the move, with the cognizance of the other Powers. Ex-Ambassador Henry Morgenthau would be leaving New York shortly for Switzerland, to be met there by French and English groups.

The Foreign Office did not attach much importance to the manœuvre. I did—at first. There was, I thought, the possibility that the negotiations might be conducted on the basis of an integral Turkey, leaving the Jews, the Arabs and the Armenians in the lurch. I put this question point-blank to the Foreign Office; they replied that it was axiomatic that no arrangements with Turkey could be arrived at unless Armenia, Syria and Arabia were detached from Turkish rule.

I was not satisfied. A fortnight later I learned that Mr. Morgenthau was to be accompanied on his mission by 'some Zionists!' Nor was I reassured by the names suggested as the English envoys. They did not seem to me to be the proper persons for such a mission. It seemed to me that the only man by whom the British Government could be adequately represented, who thoroughly understood the Near East, and enjoyed the full confidence of the representatives of the Arabs, Jews and Armenians, was Sir Mark Sykes, the man who had had this particular question in his hands for the last three years. I knew that there were influences in the Foreign Office working against Sir Mark precisely because of the views he held and because, as I wrote to the ever-helpful Mr. Scott, 'he is much more broadminded than some bureaucrats.'

A few days later I was asked to call on Balfour. He took up the subject of the commission, but seemed to be almost as much in the dark as myself with regard to its exact purposes and plans. However, Mr. Morgenthau had obviously obtained President Wilson's blessing for his scheme, whatever it was, and the French were apparently keen on it. The British did not like the smell of it, and they wanted Mr. Morgenthau to be turned back before he reached Egypt. But how was this to be done without making a bad impression on President Wilson? I looked rather blank, suspecting that Mr. Balfour already had some plan in mind, but quite unable to guess at it. Then, to my complete astonishment, he suggested that, without giving the affair an official character, I was to be sent to Gibraltar as the British representative. I was to talk to Mr. Morgenthau, and keep on talking till I had talked him out of this mission.

By this time it was becoming clear to me that the whole matter was not by any means as serious as I had feared. I accepted Mr. Balfour's offer, obtained leave of absence from the Admiralty, and set out to catch Mr. Morgenthau.

The Foreign Office armed me with a formidable set of credentials and attached to me, as intelligence officer, Kennerley Rumford, a great singer—he was the husband of Clara Butt—and a delightful companion, though somewhat unsuited for a secret mission. We travelled through France to Spain, and at Irun were met by a lady intelligence officer and conducted to San Sebastian. The lady was very smart, and exceedingly well dressed; she arrived in a big luxury car. From that point on we moved, as it were, with a cortège of German spies. Rumford, though in mufti, looked every inch a British officer; and his methods of preserving secrecy were not exactly subtle. At San Sebastian we took two sleeping compartments for Madrid, and bought up the adjacent compartments on either side. An instant before we started a man boarded the train and claimed loudly and insistently that he had a prior reservation on one of the adjacent compartments. Rumford, losing his patience in the ensuing argument, finally drew a revolver and brandished it in the face of the intruder who, probably unaccustomed to such public demonstrations on the part of a secret-service agent, hastily withdrew. In Madrid our baggage was rifled, a procedure which we expected and in fact facilitated by leaving our bags unlocked. We seemed to have got rid of our pursuers when we left Madrid by car, taking the train at Seville for Algeciras.

Before leaving England I had asked whether I might visit Max Nordau, who, being an Austrian, had been expelled from France as an enemy alien, and was in Madrid. I knew Nordau to be staunchly pro-Ally, and I was anxious to see him. The Foreign Office said: 'We have nothing against your visiting Dr. Nordau, but you had better consult the British Ambassador in Madrid.' I anticipated all sorts of difficulties. Immediately on my arrival I proceeded to the Embassy, to pay my respects and to arrange my visit to Nordau; but before I could proffer my request I was informed that I was expected to lunch, and that Dr. Nordau would be there.

We arrived in Gibraltar on July 3, a day or so before the Americans were expected in Cadiz, whither an intelligence officer was sent to escort them to Gibraltar. The party consisted of Mr. and Mrs. Morgenthau, Professor Felix Frankfurter—then assistant to Secretary of State Baker—Lewin-Epstein, a veteran Zionist, and an Armenian, whose name now escapes me. The commission brought with it, through the submarine-infested waters, eighteen trunks and four hundred thousand dollars in gold. The money had been entrusted to Lewin-Epstein by the Joint Distribution Committee for relief work in Egypt and the Near East.

Lewin-Epstein I knew; of the brilliant Professor Frankfurter, and of his services to Zionism, I had heard, and also, of course, of Mr. Morgenthau, the former Ambassador to Turkey. But the gentleman who was Mr. Morgenthau's secretary, guide and adviser was new to me, and to him I took an instantaneous, cordial and enduring dislike. It appeared he had left Turkey only some six weeks before the conference, and was, therefore, Mr. Morgenthau's expert on conditions in that country.

On the fourth the French representative arrived. He was a Colonel Weyl, a charming and well-informed man who had been for many years the head of the Turkish tobacco monopoly, knew the country, and spoke Turkish. The French, it soon transpired, were taking the American mission seriously. After all, here was an ex-Ambassador, who had come across the ocean with the blessings of the President, and accompanied by a whole suite. Besides, the wish may have been father to the thought: the French were prepared to consider a separate peace with Turkey, on the basis of the inviolability of the Turkish Empire. I, for my part, soon came to the conclusion that the whole business was a *canard*.

Mr. Morgenthau had had an idea. He felt that Turkey was on the point of collapse, sick of the war, and sicker still of German domination. It had occurred to him that perhaps Talaat Pasha might be played off against Enver Bey, and a peace move encouraged. I put two simple questions to Mr. Morgenthau. First, did he think the time had come for the American Government to open up negotiations of such a nature with the Turkish authorities; in other words, did he think Turkey realized sufficiently that she was beaten, or likely to lose the war, and was, therefore, in a frame of mind to lend herself to negotiations of that nature? Second, assuming that the time was ripe for such overtures, did Mr. Morgenthau have any clear ideas about the conditions under which the Turks would be prepared to detach themselves from their masters?

Colonel Weyl was particularly anxious to obtain a precise answer from Mr. Morgenthau. But Mr. Morgenthau was unable to furnish one. In fact, as the talks went on, it became embarrassingly apparent that he had merely had a vague notion that he could utilize his personal connections in Turkey to some end or other; but on examining the question more closely, he was compelled to admit that he did not know the position and was not justified in saying that the time had arrived for negotiations. Nor had he received any definite instructions from President Wilson. In short, he seemed not to have given the matter sufficiently serious consideration. I asked Mr. Morgenthau several times why he had tried to enlist the support of the Zionist Organization. To this question, too, he had no clear answer. I therefore thought it necessary to state clearly to Mr. Morgenthau that on no account should the Zionist Organization be compromised by these negotiations. When I asked Frankfurter, informally, what *he* was doing on this odd mission, he answered that he had come along to keep an eye on things!

It was no job at all to persuade Mr. Morgenthau to drop the project. He simply persuaded himself, and before long announced his intention of going to Biarritz instead of Egypt. In Biarritz, he said, he would communicate with General Pershing, and await further instructions from President Wilson.

We talked in this vacuum for two whole days. It was midsummer, and very hot. We had been given one of the casements in the Rock for our sessions, and the windows were kept open. As Mr. Morgenthau did not speak French, and Colonel Weyl did not speak English, we had to fall back on German. And the Tommies on guard marched up and down outside, no doubt convinced that we were a pack of spies who had been lured into a trap, to be court-martialled the next morning and shot out of hand. I must confess that I did not find it easy to make an intelligible report to Sir Ronald Graham.

We all travelled back through Spain together, on a wonderful train which was placed at our disposal, and parted company amicably, if somewhat sheepishly. This was the last of the 'commission.' I can only offer a surmise on the origins of it. America had entered the war, and Morgenthau had been withdrawn from Turkey. He had returned to find all his friends with big jobs, and himself rather out of things. It would have been only natural for him to go to Wilson, and to say: 'Look here, Mr. President: I know the Turks, I know Enver Bey, Talaat Pasha and the others. If I could only get to see them, I could persuade Turkey to quit.' I can imagine Mr. Wilson replying: 'All right, go ahead.' No other explanation will fit the picture.

I never saw Mr. Morgenthau again, but I did come across Mrs. Morgenthau years later at a great garden party which Samuel Untermyer gave at Greystone. Taken off my guard I exclaimed rather clumsily: 'Oh, Mrs. Morgenthau, I haven't seen you since Gibraltar!' Mrs. Morgenthau said, coldly, 'Yes!' and turned her back on me.

How the story of this mission got out I do not know, and it

hardly matters now. But get out it did. When the Lodge
Committee brought its resolution before the American Congress, in support of the Jewish Homeland in Palestine, in 1922,
and a Senate committee looked into its merits, someone—I
think it was Senator Reed—objected strongly to its passage. He
said that the leaders of the Zionist movement were unworthy
men, and that I in particular had prolonged the war for two
years by scuttling the Morgenthau Mission!

CHAPTER XVIII

THE BALFOUR DECLARATION

*The Enemy from Within—A Destructive Jewish Minority—The London
Times Sides with Us—First Draft of Proposed Declaration—Montagu's
Attack in Cabinet Meeting—Brandeis Helps from America—The Com-
promise Document—Balfour Declaration is Issued*

IT was an extraordinary struggle that developed within English
Jewry in the half-year which preceded the issue of the Balfour
Declaration—a struggle which probably had no historic parallel
anywhere. Here was a people which had been divorced from
its original homeland for some eighteen centuries, putting in a
claim for restitution. The world was willing to listen, the case
was being sympathetically received, and one of the great Powers
was prepared to lead in the act of restitution, while the others
had indicated their benevolent interest. And a well-to-do, contented and self-satisfied minority, a tiny minority of the people
in question, rose in rebellion against the proposal, and exerted
itself with the utmost fury to prevent the act of restitution from
being consummated. Itself in no need—or believing itself to
be in no need—of the righting of the ancient historic wrong,
this small minority struggled bitterly to deprive the vast
majority of the benefits of a unique act of the world conscience;
and it succeeded, if not in baulking the act of justice, at least
in vitiating some of its application.

The assimilationist handful of upper-class British Jews were
aware that the Zionist cause was making great headway in
Government circles and in general public opinion. But it was
only in the spring of 1917 that they felt the critical moment to
be approaching, and I knew that action could be expected. On
May 20, a special conference of delegates from all the constituent Zionist societies of Great Britain was held in London. I
had been the President of the Zionist Federation for about a
year, and in my official address to the assembly I issued a note
of warning against the impending attack. We were already so

far advanced in our path to recognition that I could speak of the dangers which attended success.

I said: 'One reads constantly in the press, and one hears from friends, both Jewish and non-Jewish, that it is the endeavour of the Zionist movement immediately to create a Jewish State in Palestine. Our American friends have gone further, and they have even determined the form of this State, by advocating a Jewish Republic. While heartily welcoming all these demonstrations as a genuine manifestation of the Jewish national will, we cannot consider them as safe statesmanship. . . . States must be built up slowly, gradually, systematically and patiently.' At that time the whole world—and the Jews more than anyone else—had been thrilled by the overthrow of the czarist régime in Russia, and the establishment of the liberal Kerensky régime. This, too, was a danger of a sort. 'Some of us—some of our friends even, and especially some of our opponents,' I told the conference, 'are very quick in drawing conclusions as to what will happen to the Zionist movement after the Russian Revolution. Now, they say, the great stimulus of the Zionist movement has been removed. The Russian Jews are free; they do not need any places of refuge outside Russia—somewhere in Palestine. Nothing can be more superficial, and nothing can be more wrong than that. The sufferings of Russian Jewry never were the cause of Zionism. The fundamental cause of Zionism was, and is, the ineradicable national striving of Jewry to have a home of its own—a national centre, a national home with a national Jewish life. And this remains now stronger than ever. A strong and free Russian Jewry will appreciate more than ever the strivings of the Zionist Organization.'

I was speaking the simple truth. The great outburst of enthusiasm with which the Balfour Declaration was received in Russia, the great revival of the Zionist movement, before its final extinction by the Bolshevik régime, was a stirring demonstration of the Jewish national will to live. But I reserved for the end of my address to the conference what weighed most heavily on my mind. I said: 'It is a matter of deep humiliation that we cannot stand united in this great hour. But it is not the fault of the Zionist Organization. It is, perhaps, not the fault of our opponents. It must be attributed to the conditions of our life

in the Dispersion, which have caused in Jewry a cleavage difficult to bridge even at a time like this. It is unfortunate that
there still exists a small minority which disputes the very existence of the Jews as a nation. But there need be no misgivings
on that account; for I have no hesitation in saying that if it
comes to a plebiscite and a test, there can be no doubt on which
side the majority of the Jews will be found. And I warn you
that this test is bound to come—and come sooner, perhaps,
than we think. . . . We do not want to offer to the world a
spectacle of a war of brothers. We are surrounded by too many
enemies to be able to afford this luxury. But we warn those who
will force an open breach that they will find us prepared to
stand up united in defence of the cause which is sacred to us.
We shall not allow anybody to interfere with the hard work
which we are doing, and we say to all our opponents: "Hands
off the Zionist movement!"'

As I suspected, the attack had been prepared. Four days
later, on May 24, the Conjoint Committee—or at least the two
principal officers of the Conjoint Committee, Mr. David L.
Alexander, President of the Board of British Jews, and Mr.
Claude G. Montefiore, President of the Anglo-Jewish Association—published a long statement in *The Times*, violently
repudiating the Zionist position, and urging the Government
against favourable action on our demands. All the old arguments that I had learned to expect since the time of my
encounter with Western assimilation in the person of Dr.
Barness of Pfungstadt were there. The Jews were a religious
community, and nothing more. The Jews could not claim a
National Home. The utmost that could be demanded for the
Jews of Palestine was enjoyment of religious and civil liberty,
'reasonable' facilities for immigration and colonization, and
'such municipal privileges in towns and colonies as may be
shown to be necessary,' and so on, and so on.

There were some interesting anomalies in the situation which
would have amused us if the matter had been less serious.
Messrs. Alexander and Montefiore repudiated the Zionist
philosophy on the ground that Judaism was nothing more than
religion. The Chief Rabbi of the British Empire, Dr. Hertz,
and the *Haham* of the Portuguese and Spanish communities,
Dr. Gaster, rebutted the attack! Messrs. Alexander and Monte-

fiore—and with them, of course, the group to which I have alluded, Mr. Lucien Wolf, Mr. Edwin Montagu (by then Secretary of State for India) and others—were afraid of having their patriotism challenged. *The Times*, in a rather remarkable leading article, answered: 'Only an imaginative nervousness suggests that the realization of territorial Zionism, in some form, would cause Christendom to turn round on the Jews and say "Now you have a land of your own, go to it."'

This leading article was written by Wickham Steed, after various letters by Dr. Hertz, Dr. Gaster, Lord Rothschild and myself had appeared in *The Times*. I went to see Steed in order to hand him my own letter. He received me with the utmost cordiality. I found him not only interested in our movement, but quite well informed on it. He had known Herzl in Vienna; he had known Leopoldstadt and the Viennese Jews. He was not only glad to publish the Zionist statements but expressed downright annoyance with the heads of the Conjoint Committee. For a good hour or so we discussed the kind of leader which was likely to make the best appeal to the British public, and when it appeared, on the twenty-ninth, it caused something like consternation among the assimilationists. It was a magnificent presentation of the Zionist case. I cannot refrain from quoting two more sentences, aimed directly at the arguments of the Conjoint Committee heads. 'We believe it [Zionism] in fact to embody the feelings of the great bulk of Jewry everywhere. . . . The importance of the Zionist movement is that it has fired with a new ideal millions of poverty-stricken Jews cooped up in the ghettos of the Old World and the New.'

The bringing of the fight into the open had made it imperative that the Government take action, and thus settle the issue. On June 13, before I left on my Gibraltar 'mission,' I wrote to Sir Ronald Graham: 'It appears desirable from every point of view that the British Government should give expression to its sympathy and support of the Zionist claims on Palestine. In fact it need only confirm the view which eminent and representative members of the Government have many times expressed to us, and which have formed the basis of our negotiations throughout the long period of almost three years.' And a few days later I went, with Sir Ronald and Lord Rothschild, to see Mr. Balfour (this visit had nothing to do with the Gibraltar

mission) and put it to the Foreign Secretary that the time had
come for the British Government to give us a definite declaration of support and encouragement. Mr. Balfour promised to
do so, and asked me to submit to him a declaration which would
be satisfactory to us, and which he would try and put before
the War Cabinet.

While I was absent in Gibraltar, the Political Committee,
under the chairmanship of Sokolow, busied itself with the
preparation of the draft. A number of formulæ were devised;
in all of them we were careful to stay within the limits of the
general attitude on the subject which prevailed among the
leading members of the Government. This is something to be
borne in mind for the reconstruction of the complete picture.
The final formula on which we agreed, and which Lord Rothschild handed to Mr. Balfour on our behalf on July 18, 1917,
ran as follows:

His Majesty's Government, after considering the aims of the
Zionist Organization, accept the principle of recognizing Palestine
as the National Home of the Jewish people and the right of the
Jewish people to build up its national life in Palestine under a protection to be established at the conclusion of peace, following upon the
successful issue of the war.

His Majesty's Government regard as essential for the realization
of this principle the grant of internal autonomy to the Jewish
nationality in Palestine, freedom of immigration for Jews, and the
establishment of a Jewish National Colonizing Corporation for the
re-establishment and economic development of the country.

The conditions and forms of the internal autonomy and a Charter
for the Jewish National Colonizing Corporation should, in the view
of His Majesty's Government, be elaborated in detail and determined with the representatives of the Zionist Organization.

It is only fair to note that the Jewish opposition to Zionism
was mitigated by opposition within the ranks of the non-
Zionists themselves. It transpired that the heads of the Conjoint Committee had acted without the knowledge and consent
of the constituent bodies, the Board of British Jews and the
Anglo-Jewish Association, in issuing the anti-Zionist statement
to *The Times*. A vote of censure of those bodies actually
forced the resignation of Mr. Alexander and a number of his
colleagues. Small as the non-Zionist body of sentiment was, the

active opposition was even smaller. And yet it was capable of working great harm, and we waited with much concern for the response of the Government.

On August 17, I was able to write to Felix Frankfurter, in the United States: 'The draft has been submitted to the Foreign Office and is approved by them, and I heard yesterday, it also meets the approval of the Prime Minister [Lloyd George].'

It remained, of course, to be approved by the War Cabinet —but from the individual expressions of opinion which had come from its members, there cannot be the slightest doubt that without outside interference—*entirely from Jews!*—the draft would have been accepted early in August, substantially as we submitted it.

About September 18, I learned that our declaration had been discussed at a Cabinet meeting from which both Mr. Lloyd George and Mr. Balfour were absent, and that the sharp intervention of Edwin Montagu had caused the withdrawal of the item from the agenda. The same day I received a letter from Lord Rothschild, in which he said: 'I have written to Mr. Balfour asking him for an interview Thursday or Friday. . . . Do you remember I said to you in London, as soon as I saw the announcement in the paper of Montagu's appointment, that I was afraid we were done?'

I did not feel as desperate as Lord Rothschild, but the situation was unpleasant. We saw Balfour separately, I on the nineteenth, Lord Rothschild on the twenty-first. I received the utmost encouragement from Balfour. He told me that his sympathies had not been changed by the attitude of Montagu. I was able to send the following cable to Brandeis on the same day:

Following text declaration has been approved Foreign Office and Prime Minister and submitted War Cabinet: 1. His Majesty's Government accepts the principle that Palestine should be reconstituted as the National Home of the Jewish people. 2. His Majesty's Government will use its best endeavours to secure the achievement of this object and will discuss the necessary methods with the Zionist Organization.

I added that the opposition of the assimilationists was to be expected and that it would be of great assistance if the text of

I

this declaration received the support of President Wilson and of Brandeis.

To Lord Rothschild, Balfour expressed the same unwavering firmness on the issue as to me. Lord Rothschild wrote to me, after his interview with Balfour on September 21: 'I said I had evidence that a member of the Cabinet was working against us. He [Balfour] hastily said: "He is *not* a member of the Cabinet, only of the *Government*, and I think his views are quite mistaken."'

On the twenty-first I had another talk with Smuts—a member of the War Cabinet—and obtained from him the expected reiteration of his loyalty. At the same time we were doing our best to counteract the activities of the assimilationists, who were attacking us in a series of pamphlets, in the press, and in person-to-person propaganda, as well as in the Cabinet. On the twenty-eighth I talked again with Lloyd George, who put our memorandum on the agenda of the War Cabinet for October 4. And on the third I wrote to the Foreign Office, for transmission to the War Cabinet:

'We cannot ignore rumours which seem to foreshadow that the anti-Zionist view will be urged at the meeting of the War Cabinet by a prominent Englishman of the Jewish faith who does not belong to the War Cabinet. We are not in a position to verify these rumours, still less to criticize the fact should these rumours prove to be true; but we must respectfully point out that in submitting our resolution *we entrusted our national and Zionist destiny to the Foreign Office and the Imperial War Cabinet* in the hope that the problem would be considered in the light of imperial interests and the principles for which the Entente stands. We are reluctant to believe that the War Cabinet would allow the divergence of views on Zionism existing in Jewry to be presented to them in a strikingly one-sided manner. . . . Where there is a human mass claiming recognition as a nation there the case for such recognition is complete. We have submitted the text of the declaration on behalf of an organization which claims to represent the national will of a great and ancient, though scattered, people. We have submitted it after three years of negotiations and conversations with prominent representatives of the British nation.'

Whether these sharp expostulations reached the members of

the War Cabinet the next day I do not know. But the meeting of the War Cabinet to deal with the declaration was to be held, according to advice given me, on the fourth. That day I came to the office of Mr. Kerr, Lloyd George's secretary, and I had the temerity to say: 'Mr. Kerr, suppose the Cabinet decided to ask me some questions before they decide the matter. Would it not be well for me to stay here and be in readiness?' To this he replied, kindly, even compassionately: 'Since the British Government has been a Government no private person has been admitted to a session of the Cabinet. So you go back to your laboratory, Dr. Weizmann, and everything will be all right.'

I did not go back to my laboratory. I could not have done any work. I went, instead, into the office of Ormsby-Gore, close by, and waited. There was nothing I could do, of course, but I should have had to be more—or less—than human to have occupied myself during those hours with the routine of my laboratory. I learned too late that I might have done something.

When the Palestine item was laid before the War Cabinet, Edwin Montagu made a passionate speech against the proposed move. The tenor of his arguments will be gathered from the general propaganda of the anti-Zionists, given on the foregoing pages. There was nothing new in what he had to say, but the vehemence with which he urged his views, the implacability of his opposition, astounded the Cabinet. I understand the man almost wept. When he had ended, Balfour and Lloyd George suggested that I be called in, and messengers were sent for me. They looked for me high and low—and I happened to be a few doors away in the office of Ormsby-Gore. I missed a great opportunity—and this was entirely due to Philip Kerr. Perhaps, however, it was better so. I might, in that setting, with Montagu in front of me, have said something harsh or inappropriate. I might have made matters worse instead of better. Certain it was that Montagu's opposition, coupled with the sustained attacks which the tiny anti-Zionist group had been conducting for months—their letters to the press, the pamphlets, some of them written pseudonymously by Lucien Wolf, their feverish interviews with Government officials—was responsible for the compromise formula which the War Cabinet submitted to us a few days later.

It was on the seventh of October that I wrote to Kerr the letter quoted on pages 226-7, expressing my chagrin and bewilderment at the attention paid by the British Government to a handful of assimilated Jews, in their opposition to what was the deepest hope of millions of Jews whom we, the Zionists, represented. On October 9, I could cable as follows to Justice Brandeis:

The cabinet after preliminary discussion suggested following amended formula:

'His Majesty's Government views with favour the establishment in Palestine of a National Home for the Jewish race and will use its best endeavours to facilitate the achievement of this object; it being clearly understood that nothing shall be done which may prejudice the civil and religious rights of the existing non-Jewish communities in Palestine, or the rights and political status enjoyed in any other country by such Jews who are fully contented with their existing nationality and citizenship.'

Most likely shall be asked to appear before the cabinet when final discussion takes place in about a week. It is essential to have not only President's approval of text, but his recommendation to grant this declaration without delay. Further your support and enthusiastic message to us from American Zionists and also prominent non-Zionists most desirable to us. Your support urgently needed.

A comparison of the two texts—the one approved by the Foreign Office and the Prime Minister, and the one adopted on October 4, after Montagu's attack—shows a painful recession from what the Government itself was prepared to offer. The first declares that 'Palestine should be reconstituted as the National Home of the Jewish people.' The second speaks of 'the establishment in Palestine of a National Home for the Jewish race.' The first adds only that the 'Government will use its best endeavours to secure the achievement of this object and will discuss the necessary methods with the Zionist Organization'; the second introduces the subject of the 'civic and religious rights of the existing non-Jewish communities' in such a fashion as to impute possible oppressive intentions to the Jews, and can be interpreted to mean such limitations on our work as completely to cripple it.

I was not given a chance to present our views to the War Cabinet, and the anti-Zionists alone had their say at the

October 4 session. The Cabinet actually did not know what to do with the obstructionist Jews. Sykes, Amery, Ormsby-Gore were nonplussed. In the end it was decided to send out the text to eight Jews, four anti-Zionists and four Zionists, for comments and suggestions, with a covering letter in which it was stated that 'in view of the divergence of opinion expressed on the subject by the Jews themselves, they [the Government] would like to receive in writing the views of representative Jewish leaders, both Zionist and non-Zionist.'

We, on our part, examined and re-examined the formula, comparing the old text with the new. We saw the differences only too clearly, but we did not dare to occasion further delay by pressing for the original formula, which represented not only our wishes, but the attitude of the members of the Government. In replying to the letter of the Government I said: 'Instead of the establishment of a Jewish National Home, would it not be more desirable to use the word "re-establishment"? By this small alteration the historical connection with the ancient tradition would be indicated and the whole matter put in its true light. May I also suggest "Jewish people" instead of "Jewish race".' (This last suggestion actually came from Mr. Brandeis.)

It goes without saying that this second formula, emasculated as it was, represented a tremendous event in exilic Jewish history—and that it was as bitter a pill to swallow for the Jewish assimilationists as the recession from the original, more forthright formula was for us. It is one of the 'ifs' of history whether we should have been intransigent, and stood by our guns. Should we then have obtained a better statement? Or would the Government have become wearied of these internal Jewish divisions, and dropped the whole matter? Again, the result might have been such a long delay that the war would have ended before an agreement was reached, and then all the advantage of a timely decision would have been lost. Our judgment was to accept, to press for ratification. For we knew that the assimilationists would use every delay for their own purposes; and we also knew that in America the same internal Jewish struggle was going on—complicated by the fact that President Wilson, who was wholeheartedly with us, considered the publication of a declaration premature, in view of the fact that no state of war existed between America and Turkey. Brandeis's intention was to obtain from President Wilson a public expression of sympathy. In this he was not successful. But on October 16, Colonel House, acting for President Wilson, cabled the British Government America's support of the substance of the declaration. This was one of the most important individual factors in breaking the deadlock created by the British Jewish anti-Zionists, and in deciding the British Government to issue its declaration.

On November 2, after a final discussion in the War Cabinet, Balfour issued the famous letter known as the Balfour Declaration. It was addressed to Lord Rothschild. In an earlier talk with Balfour, when he had asked me to whom the forthcoming declaration should be addressed, I suggested Lord Rothschild rather than myself, though I was President of the English Zionist Federation. The text read:

His Majesty's Government view with favour the establishment in Palestine of a National Home for the Jewish people, and will use their best endeavours to facilitate the achievement of this object, it being clearly understood that nothing shall be done which may prejudice the civil and religious rights of the existing non-Jewish communities in Palestine or the rights and political status enjoyed by Jews in any other country.

While the Cabinet was in session, approving the final text, I was waiting outside, this time within call. Sykes brought the document out to me, with the exclamation: 'Dr. Weizmann, it's a boy!'

Well—I did not like the boy at first. He was not the one I had expected. But I knew that this was a great event. I telephoned my wife, and went to see Achad Ha-am.

A new chapter had opened for us, full of new difficulties, but not without its great moments.

Book Two

CHAPTER XIX

THE ZIONIST COMMISSION

ANTICIPATION AND REALITIES

What the Framers of the Balfour Declaration Intended—Appointment of the Zionist Commission—Preparations, Including Reception by the King—Small Beginnings of Great Troubles—I am Presented to King George V—Leonard Stein in Taranto—War-time Cairo, 1918—Arrival in Palestine—Military Indifference Toward and Disregard of Balfour Declaration—Causes Behind this Attitude—General Wyndham Deedes Introduces me to Protocols of Elders of Zion—The Helpfulness of General Deedes—General Allenby's Attitude—Establishing Myself with G.H.Q.—Hammer and Anvil—Hostile Military Administrators—Natural Difficulties and Unnecessary Ones—Allenby Becomes Friendly—Damage Already Done

A GENERATION has passed since the Balfour Declaration became history. It is not easy to recapture, at this distance, the spirit of elation which attended its issue—a spirit shared by non-Jews and Jews alike: on the Jewish side the expectation of imminent redemption, on the non-Jewish side the profound satisfaction awakened by a great act of restitution. Certainly there were dissident voices on both sides, but they were overborne by numbers and by moral authority. The foremost statesmen of the time had collaborated in the declaration. Balfour was to say later that he looked upon it as the great achievement of his life; Viscount Cecil, one of the founders of the League of Nations, considered the Jewish Homeland to be of equal importance with the League itself. And in spite of the phrasing the intent was clear. President Wilson declared: 'I am persuaded that the Allied nations, with the full concurrence of our Government and our people, are agreed that in Palestine shall be laid the foundations of a Jewish Commonwealth.' Speaking for Balfour and himself, Lloyd George tells us in his memoirs:

As to the meaning of the words 'National Home' to which the Zionists attach so much importance, he [Balfour] understood it to mean some form of British, American or other protectorate, under which full facilities would be given to the Jews to work out their own salvation and to build up, by means of education, agriculture and industry, a real centre of national culture and focus of national life. . . . There can be no doubt as to what the [Imperial War] Cabinet then had in their minds. It was not their idea that a Jewish State should be set up immediately by the Peace Treaty without reference to the wishes of the majority of the inhabitants. On the other hand, it was contemplated that when the time arrived for according representative institutions to Palestine, if the Jews had meanwhile responded to the opportunity afforded them and had become a definite majority of the inhabitants, then Palestine would thus become a Jewish Commonwealth. The notion that Jewish immigration would have to be artificially restricted in order that the Jews should be a permanent minority never entered the head of anyone engaged in framing the policy. That would have been regarded as unjust and as a fraud on the people to whom we were appealing.

It will be, among other things, my painful duty to retrace to their beginnings the steps which have placed such a gap between the promise of the declaration and the performance; and those beginnings, I regret to say, coincided with the first efforts to translate policy into actuality.

Early in 1918, His Majesty's Government decided to send a Zionist Commission to Palestine to survey the situation and to prepare plans in the spirit of the Balfour Declaration. The Commission was to be representative of the Jews of all the principal Allied countries; but as America was not at war with Turkey, she did not feel able to appoint representatives, and the Russian members, though duly appointed, were unable for 'political reasons' to leave in time to join us. There came to join us, then, the Italians and the French.

The Italian Government sent us Commendatore Levi Bianchini, who proved to be a most devoted worker, collaborating closely with every aspect of our work in Palestine; but one soon got the impression that his devotion had an Italian rather than a Palestinian bias. In the light of subsequent developments it is easy to understand the deep interest evinced by the Italians in Zionist activities in Palestine even in those early days. Already the Jewish National Home was viewed with a certain jealousy and suspicion as tending to strengthen British influence in 'Mare Nostrum'; and every effort was made to offset this by encouraging Italian participation in Palestine's economic development. It was repeatedly suggested to us that we might make use of Italian firms, Italian workers, Italian supplies for the execution of our preliminary work.

The French sent us Professor Sylvain Lévi, an avowed anti-Zionist! He was forced upon us by the French Government—which had made strong representations to the British—and by Baron Edmond de Rothschild, who felt that the presence of Sylvain Lévi on the commission, in spite (or even because) of his known views, would help us to combat certain opposition currents in French Jewish opinion; this with especial reference to the anti-Zionist *Alliance Israelite*, of which Sylvain Lévi was the distinguished President. Like Commendatore Bianchini, Lévi was a devoted worker in the field—and in the same spirit. He seemed to feel that it was his business to keep the French end up. He showed great interest, of course, in the settlements of the P.I.C.A. (Palestine Jewish Colonization Association) founded by Baron Edmond de Rothschild long before the Zionist Organization was in a position to take up practical work in the country. Sometimes one could not help feeling that M. Lévi looked a little askance at the growth of Zionist influence as an infringement on the virtual monopoly enjoyed till then by the P.I.C.A.

Mr. James de Rothschild, Baron Edmond's son, acted as a kind of liaison officer between ourselves and the P.I.C.A. interests in Palestine, and was naturally somewhat biased in favour of the settlements created by his father. Mr. de Rothschild was and was not a member of the Zionist Commission. He attended all our meetings, but did not wish to be officially identified with us. Occasionally this state of things would create an awkward situation, which would usually be relieved by the diplomatic talents of Major Ormsby-Gore (now Lord Harlech), our liaison officer with the British military authorities.

The representatives of English Jewry on the Commission were, besides myself, Mr. Joseph Cowen, Dr. David Eder, Mr. Leon Simon and Mr. I. M. Sieff (secretary).

Our departure was set for Monday, March 8, 1918. A few days before that date Sir Mark Sykes, who was responsible for collecting and organizing us, and making our travelling arrangements—no easy task in wartime—suddenly had the idea that it would be useful for the prestige of the Commission if I, as its chairman, were to be received by His Majesty the King before we left. I was deeply appreciative—as we all were—of the honour, but I had some misgivings as to the wisdom of the step. I knew that we were setting out on a long and difficult road, and I felt that it would be better to defer the audience until we had something substantial to our credit in Palestine, and could report progress. But the authorities whom we consulted thought otherwise, and naturally I fell in with their views.

Here the first of those incidents occurred which were to make the Zionist Commission a sort of prelude or thematic overture to the future. Arrangements were made for me to be taken to the Palace on the Saturday morning preceding the departure. I bought, and put on, my first and last top hat, and came to the Foreign Office at the appointed hour, to find a very confused and apologetic Sir Mark Sykes, who informed me that he had just received some 'very disquieting' telegrams from Cairo, to the effect that the Arabs were beginning to ask uncomfortable questions. . . . He was inclined to think that it might be better to cancel the audience.

In a sense this did no more than vindicate my first instinctive reaction to the suggested audience; but at this point I simply could not agree to the cancellation, and certainly not on the ground specified. The audience had, of course, not been given any publicity; but it was known in the narrow circle of my colleagues, and they would be deeply distressed by what they would regard both as a serious setback and a bad augury for the future. I told Sir Mark what I felt on this point and urged him to arrange another audience in spite of the shortness of time available. Sir Mark, while underlining his personal sympathy for our position, felt unable to do this, and so we stood in a corridor of the Foreign Office engaged in heated and at times painful discussion. We were joined by Major Ormsby-Gore, who was inclined to take my view of the subject. I remember maintaining with much emphasis and warmth that if we were going to be deflected from a considered line of action by such things as telegrams vaguely indicating some stirrings of the Arab world, our work in Palestine would be utterly impossible, and we had better not go out at all.

The argument went on for what seemed a long time; and eventually we decided that the best thing to do would be to put the position to Mr. Balfour, who happened at this moment to come into view mounting the Foreign Office stairs. Sir Mark suggested that I should see him; I preferred to have Sir Mark put the case, knowing he would present it in the fairest possible light. Major Ormsby-Gore and I waited outside the room for half an hour or so, and then Sir Mark emerged to say that Mr. Balfour thought that the audience should take place, and was at that moment telephoning to the Palace to explain that the whole misunderstanding had arisen through his own late arrival at the office! A second audience was fixed there and then for the following Monday morning—the very day of our departure for Palestine.

And so I was presented to His Majesty King George V. The first thing he said on greeting me was: 'You know, Mr. Balfour always *does* come late to the office. I quite understand.' He then turned the subject to Palestine, and showed great interest in our plans. Knowing me to be of Russian birth he also spoke at some length on the Russian Revolution—then front-page news —saying at one point: 'I always warned Nicky about the risks he ran in maintaining that régime; but he would not listen.' He then returned to the purpose of the audience and wished us success in our endeavours.

The same evening we set out on our journey. Our land itinerary was Paris-Rome-Taranto. In Taranto we were to take ship through the submarine-infested waters of the Mediterranean to Alexandria, and there we spent seven days waiting for an escort. It was a desolate place, short of food and destitute of any occupation or distraction. The only civilized spot was the British rest camp for soldiers and sailors travelling to and from the Middle East. Towards the end of my stay, when I was getting desperate with boredom, I discovered that my old friend Leonard Stein was also among the marooned at Taranto. I had not seen him since the outbreak of the war, and I had much to tell him. We went together to Taranto's one small hotel and took a room. It was a steaming hot day. He lay on one bed, I on the other. And for hours I talked, recounting the story of the last four years and the negotiations leading up to the Balfour Declaration, all of which he heard for the first time.

The only relief from the tedium of Taranto town was a stroll. on the beach, whence there was a good view of the magnificent array of Italian battleships, destroyers and other fighting craft, securely locked up behind double bars in Taranto port. It seemed odd that with all that naval force lying idle a substantial British transport should be kept waiting seven days for lack of escort (to be provided, eventually, by the solitary Japanese destroyer which plied between Taranto and Alexandria). Innocently, I inquired of a British Vice-Admiral who was among my fellow-travellers why the Italian destroyers could not act as escorts, and thereby unleashed an outburst of fury which staggered me: 'These Italians are fit for nothing but to sit behind double locks in port! They *like* it! Once I had dire need of a destroyer—not for escort, for real work—and I only got it by threatening to ram their blasted gates!'

Finally we set out on our nine-day zigzag for Alexandria. Most of the passengers were soldiers or sailors on leave, but there was a sprinkling of important Egyptian or Levantine civilians, looking to my eyes very like divers, or Michelin tyre advertisements, owing to the extraordinary assortment of life-belts, inflatable waistcoats, and so on, in which they bedecked themselves.

The Commission reached Alexandria just before the Feast of Passover, and spent about three weeks there. This was my first contact with the great Sephardic community of Egypt, and also with the innumerable Arab coteries in which Egypt abounded at this time. The latter were organized—if that is the right word—into separate political groups, all busy pulling wires in different directions. Wartime Cairo was one vast labyrinth of petty intrigues, and we should have been rather helpless without the skilful guidance of Major Ormsby-Gore and Sir Reginald Wingate. Sir Reginald, in particular, had had great experience with Arabs and Arab mentality, and was generous with his advice.

Curiously enough, and in spite of the telegram received by Sir Mark Sykes, we observed no hostility, even in circles dominated by people like Nim'r, the famous editor of *Mokattam*. This was possibly due to our inexperience; we were still unable to read between the lines. We were repeatedly warned by our official friends, as well as by the few members of the Jewish community who came to our assistance—most of them, I regret to say, instead of providing us with a bridge between East and West, remained as remote as the Arabs—never to attack any problem directly. The Arab is a very subtle debater and controversialist—much more so than the average educated European—and until one has acquired the technique one is at a great disadvantage. In particular, the Arab has an immense talent for expressing views diametrically opposed to yours with such exquisite and roundabout politeness that you believe him to be in complete agreement with you, and ready to join hands with you at once. Conversations and negotiations with Arabs are not unlike chasing a mirage in the desert: full of promise and good to look at, but likely to lead you to death by thirst.

A direct question is dangerous: it provokes in the Arab a skilful withdrawal and a complete change of subject. The problem must be approached by winding lanes, and it takes an interminable time to reach the kernel of the subject. Towards the end of our stay in Egypt we began to penetrate a little way behind the veil of words, and occasionally to catch a glimpse of the real meaning covered by what at first seemed to be a mass of irrelevant verbiage.

It was not easy for us to get at the temper of Egypt with regard to the war, which had then been going on for nearly four years. There was still no definite outcome. A great coalition of nations seemed unable to batter down the Central Powers, and German armies, in their last desperate push—as it turned out to be—were even threatening Paris and the Channel ports. On the whole we decided that the Egyptian atmosphere was not entirely friendly to the Allied cause.

From the confusion of Egypt the Commission drifted piecemeal into Palestine. First went Mr. James de Rothschild, as a kind of advance guard. He was invited by Allenby to stay at G.H.Q. where he had many friends, and a cousin, Dalmeny (now Lord Rosebery), acting as A.D.C. to the Commander-in-Chief. It was my feeling that he preferred to go alone, and not be identified with us too closely on his arrival in Palestine. A little later I received an invitation to stay at G.H.Q. for a few days. My colleagues, accompanied by Major Ormsby-Gore (now installed with us as our liaison officer), followed shortly after.

Within a week we found ourselves assembled in Palestine, settled in Tel Aviv in the house of David Levontin, who was then absent from the country. Tel Aviv at this time was a little seaside town consisting of perhaps a hundred houses and a few hundred inhabitants. It was quiet, almost desolate, among its sand dunes, but not unattractive, though it had been cut off from the outside world for nearly four years, and had suffered under both the German and Turkish occupations.

G.H.Q. was in Ramleh—or rather in Bir Salem—in a building formerly a small German hospice, standing on a hill surrounded by orange groves, and visible from our present home in Rehovoth. It was a modest house but, for the prevailing conditions, quite comfortable. On my arrival I found myself at once in the war atmosphere, an abrupt and startling change from Cairo. At breakfast the first morning I was wedged in between General Allenby and General Bols, who talked war across me—casualties, attacks, retreats—and I could not but sense a certain strain in the atmosphere. In fact, I felt we could hardly have descended on G.H.Q. at a more inopportune moment. The news from the Western front was bad; most of the European troops in Palestine were being withdrawn to reinforce the armies in France. The train which had brought me from Cairo had been promptly loaded with officers and men being rushed to the West. Allenby's own advance was completely checked; he was left with a small Indian Moslem force, and the Arabs, quick to sense the weakening in the British position, were showing signs of restiveness. Our arrival was definitely no accession of strength or comfort, especially as Arab agitators lost no time in proclaiming that 'the British had sent for the Jews to take over the country.'

This was only the beginning of our difficulties. I soon discovered that the Balfour Declaration, which had made such a stir in the outside world, had never reached many of Allenby's officers, even those of high rank. They knew nothing about it, and nothing about the sympathy shown at that time to our aims and aspirations by prominent Englishmen in every walk of life. They were cut off from Europe; their minds were naturally concentrated on the job in hand, which meant winning the war or—more precisely at the moment—holding their own on their particular front, and not being rolled back by the Turks under Liman von Sanders. Unfortunately this was not all; there were deeper and so to speak more organic obstacles in the mental attitude of many of Allenby's officers. The scanty Jewish population, worn out by years of privation and isolation, speaking little English, seemed to them to be the sweepings of Russian and Polish ghettos. And Russia at this time was hardly in the good books of the Allies, for it was soon after the Bolshevik revolution, which on the whole they identified with Russian Jewry; Russians, Jews, Bolsheviks were different words for the same thing in the minds of most of the British officers in Palestine in those days, and even when they were not entirely ignorant of developments, they saw little reason to put themselves out for the Jews—Declaration or no Declaration.

This peculiar situation had not, however, developed of itself. In an early conversation with General (now Sir Wyndham) Deedes (he was one of the few men who *did* understand our position), I learned of at least one of the sources of our tribulations. Suddenly, and without introduction, he handed me a few sheets of typewritten script, and asked me to read them carefully. I read the first sheet and looked up in some perplexity, asking what could be the meaning of all this rubbish. General Deedes replied quietly, and rather sternly: 'You had better read all of it with care; it is going to cause you a great deal of trouble in the future.' This was my first meeting with extracts from the Protocols of the Elders of Zion.

Completely baffled, I asked Deedes how the thing had reached him, and what it meant. He answered, slowly and sadly: 'You will find it in the haversack of a great many British officers here—and they believe it! It was brought over by the British Military Mission which has been serving in the Caucasus on the staff of the Grand Duke Nicholas.'

It would be a mistake to imagine that the views of the whole British army were tainted by the ideas expressed in the Protocols of the Elders of Zion; but at a time when the horrors of the Bolshevik revolution were fresh in everyone's mind the most fantastic rumours and slanders—operating frequently on existing backgrounds of prejudice—gained credence, and the extracts from the Protocols which I then saw had been obviously selected to cater to the taste of a certain type of British reader.

But even without this unpredictable blow at us our position

was difficult enough. On meeting Allenby I had of course handed over my credentials and letters of introduction from Mr. Lloyd George, Mr. Balfour and others; but warm though their terms were, I saw that they made little impression. Almost his first remark was: 'Yes, but of course nothing can be done at present. We have to be extremely careful not to hurt the susceptibilities of the population.' He was polite, even kind, in manner, but not at all forthcoming when we got down to the purposes of the Commission. One felt that this was a military world, and in it only soldiers had a right to exist. Civilians were a nuisance. But here we were—a very motley group of civilians —injected into the military organism like a foreign body. . . . The messianic hopes which we had read into the Balfour Declaration suffered a perceptible diminution when we came into contact with the hard realities of G.H.Q.

I stayed three days at Bir Salem. Rightly or wrongly, I felt that those days were in the nature of a period of probation. Authority wanted to see a little more of me, and find out what kind of fellow had been inflicted on them by the politicians in London, before they let me loose in Palestine. I had no chance of communicating with various friends of mine in Rishon or Rehovoth, who had been eagerly awaiting my arrival. I was little more than a mile away from them, but there was no bridge leading from G.H.Q. to the surrounding villages. I spent an anxious three days. I had to mind every word I said, and suppress a great many ideas I had brought out with me, putting them into cold storage for the time being. Major James de Rothschild was of course on much more intimate terms with the staff than I was; many of them were old friends of his. But his contribution towards raising my morale was confined to repeated warnings not to say anything and not to do anything: 'Remember, walls have ears!'

'It was always a relief to go into Deedes's tent; with him I could speak freely, dream freely. He it was who initiated me into the habits of military camps, and eventually put me in touch with General Clayton, the political officer of the army in Palestine, in whose charge the Commission had been officially placed. The second night of my stay in Bir Salem I spent entirely in Deedes's tent. We talked of the present and of the future, and I told him of my hopes and plans. He listened patiently and benignly to it all; both critical and sympathetic, he warned me of the many obstacles I should have to overcome, but ended by reminding me that faith could move mountains. We talked until we were exhausted, and eventually he had a camp bed put up for me and I passed the remainder of the night—a short two hours!—under canvas with him. We awoke to find that the 'latter rains' had come upon us while we slept, and the whole floor of the tent was covered with spring flowers. We took them as a happy omen.

That morning, as I stood in front of my tent, which was near the main road, I saw Allenby driving past. He stopped, and after a friendly greeting motioned me to get into the car with him, saying that he was going up to Jerusalem and thought I might like to go up with him. He was right: I was devoured by the desire to 'go up to Jerusalem.' But something within held me back. I remembered the rather curious reticence of the last couple of days, and after a minute I said: 'I would like to come; but in the circumstances don't you think it would be better for me to go a little later, and in my own time? It might be embarrassing for you to be seen entering the capital with me.' Allenby got out of the car and stood by me for a minute or two, apparently deep in thought; then he smiled and held out his hand to me: 'You are quite right—and I think we are going to be great friends.' From that time I felt that, with the Commander-in-Chief anyhow, the ice was broken. Eventually we did go up to Jerusalem together, but that was in July—just before the laying of the foundation stones of the Hebrew University.

After those three days I was, so to say, released from G.H.Q.; my colleagues and I were given free passes, a car, petrol, and— greatest favour of all—our own telephone. We were, I believe, the only civilians in Palestine to be so privileged. I was determined that no action of mine should destroy the tender plant of confidence which had begun to grow up between G.H.Q. and ourselves. And this—though mercifully I did not know it at the time—was the beginning of the hard road which I have had to tread for practically the rest of my life. I was placed between the hammer and the anvil—between the slow-moving, unimaginative, conservative and often unfriendly British administration, military or civil, and the impatient, dynamic Jewish people, which saw in the Balfour Declaration the great promise of the return to them of their own country, and contrasted it resentfully with the administrative realities in Palestine.

There were, of course, notable and noble exceptions in those early days, like Wyndham Deedes and Gilbert Clayton and the Commander-in-Chief himself. But they were not the men in daily contact with the population; they were immersed in the conduct of the war, and had to leave the details of administration to men of lower rank in the military hierarchy; and these were, almost without exception, devoid of understanding, or vision, or even of kindness.

The Governor of Jaffa—and thus of Tel Aviv—was at this time a Colonel Hubbard. Under him he had, if not the largest, then certainly the most active Jewish community in Palestine. But in all his actions and utterances, trivial as most of them were, he went out of his way to discourage the Jews and encourage the Arabs, in so far as it was possible for him to do so. A typical instance, taken from a note made at the time, was his reception of a small committee of Jewish agricultural engineers, surveyors, and so on, who had occasion to visit Nablus (under official Government auspices) to inspect some *Jiftlik* (State) land in the neighbourhood. Colonel Hubbard told them—jokingly, perhaps, but if so it was a bad joke—that if they did not leave immediately they ran the risk of being half-killed by the excited populace. He added a contemptuous reference to President Wilson, 'who meddles too much with Palestine,' and concluded by saying that if the committee wished to travel through the *Jiftlik* it would have to take a regiment of soldiers along. In conversation with friends he was wont to say that if 'trouble' should occur in Jaffa, he would take no responsibility for it, and would not interfere, or allow troops under his command to interfere.

Then there was Colonel Ronald Storrs, in Jerusalem. He was much more subtle in his approach. He was everyone's friend; but, try as he might, he failed to gain the confidence of his Jewish community. The chief administrator, General Money, had on his staff several advisers and officials who, from the first moment, felt it to be their duty to impress upon the Jewish communities under their charge that, whatever the politicians in London might have been fools enough to say or do, *here* we were in a quite different world: '*Nous allons changer tout cela.*'

With the best will in the world those early days in Palestine would have been difficult enough. The Jewish community was depleted, derelict and disorganized. Most of its leading figures had been banished by the Turkish authorities, either to Damascus or to Constantinople. Ruppin, our able colonization expert, was in Constantinople. We missed equally Meir Dizengoff, the distinguished mayor of Tel Aviv. He was a moderate, practical, level-headed man who served the city for nearly three decades after the period of which I am writing. He attended conscientiously to his duties and to the needs of the *Yishuv*, unbiased by party feeling. His opinions were respected by everyone, and almost universally accepted. Deprived of him and a few others like him, the Jews of wartime Palestine hardly knew which way to turn. The German and Turkish occupations had exhausted and disrupted the Jewish settlements, and numbers of Jews had fled to Egypt as refugees. After the occupation by the British Army they began to drift back. There was, of course, a great scarcity of commodities, and as soon as the road to Egypt was opened people began to press for permits to go and replenish their stocks. This became a source of much trouble for the Commission, for we were the official intermediaries between the Jewish population and the military authorities. Only one railway line connected Palestine with Egypt, and there was only one train daily in each direction. The limited accommodations were badly needed for military purposes, and it was not possible to obtain permits for civilians except for the most urgent reasons. With great reluctance I found myself obliged to forward applications to the transport officer from time to time, though I kept them down as far as possible. Even with a friendly attitude on the part of British officers such necessary restrictions were bound to become a source of grievance both against the Commission and the British authorities.

But the attitude of far too many of the British officers towards the Jews could by no stretch of the imagination be called friendly, and this was particularly the case in the district of Jaffa. And in that atmosphere of tension and expectation the reasonable and the unreasonable restrictions were often lumped together; trivial things assumed the importance of affairs of

State; and there were instances of discrimination which I did not consider trivial at all. I did my best to smooth over the rough places, but my assurances to the Jews that these frictions and inconveniences were inevitable in a period of transition went unheeded in the face of the realities of daily life. It was no use telling them that it was far-fetched to draw ultimate conclusions from the attitude of this or that officer, and that the men who really counted understood our troubles and were with us, not against us. The fact was, after all, that though Generals Deedes and Clayton gave much of their time and diplomatic skill to easing the situation, the general relations between the British authorities on the spot and the Jewish population grew more and more strained, and there were only a few points where normal friendly relations existed and where the indispensable good will was actively being fostered.

And then an incident occurred which made it necessary for me to bring the whole matter to the attention of the Commander-in-Chief.

Some time in May 1918, we heard that the colony of Petach Tikvah (one of the premier settlements established by Baron Edmond de Rothschild in the early 1880's) would have to be evacuated for military reasons. Regrettable as this was from the point of view of the settlers, no reasonable person could raise any objection to it if military exigencies required it. The military authorities on the spot promised me that, should the suggested evacuation be definitely decided on, due notice would be given and the Zionist Commission would be allowed to help in the arrangements; that is to say, we would provide housing for the evacuees, in Tel Aviv and elsewhere, we would see to it that their plantations were looked after, and we would let them have reports from time to time. I had already informed the colonists of this understanding between us and the military, and they had naturally accepted it. Suddenly, on the eve of the Feast of Pentecost, a messenger came to us posthaste from Petach Tikvah, saying that orders had been given to evacuate the colony the next morning, and that all our careful preparations had apparently gone for nothing. What made matters worse was that there were two Arab villages nearer to the front than Petach Tikvah, and they had received no evacuation orders. For this, of course, there may have been military reasons, but it was very hard to understand just the same. Deductions —not pleasant ones—were naturally made from these developments: Jews were not trusted, and had to be turned out; Arabs, who were known to cross the enemy lines repeatedly, were left unmolested. It was difficult for me, inexperienced as I was, to appreciate the true position, and after a great deal of heart-searching I decided to go to the fountainhead, and asked for an interview with the Commander-in-Chief.

I was invited to dinner with General Allenby the same evening. I had not seen him since my first days in Palestine. After dinner, the General suggested that we find a quiet place to talk, as he had all the night before him: there would probably be some sort of skirmish before dawn, and he could not in any case expect any sleep. I began by explaining to him the Petach Tikvah tangle, about which he naturally knew little, since the orders had been given by the divisional officer and G.H.Q. was not yet informed of them. He agreed, however, that the matter ought to be looked into, and asked his A.D.C. to make inquiries there and then and report back to him immediately. The result was that the evacuation was postponed for a few days, and the arrangements previously made for it were upheld.

There was, however, more to our talk. The General asked me for a more detailed report on the relations between the Jewish population and his administration. This gave me my opening, and I proceeded to explain that, while we understood that matters of high policy could not at the moment be implemented, and that the Balfour Declaration could not find practical application till after the war, the continuance of strained relations between the Jewish population and the British military authorities was doing no good to anyone at present, and might seriously prejudice the future. It was not simply a matter of relations between the Jews and the British, nor was it the immediate question of the particular rebuffs or setbacks. It was rather the effect on the Arab mind. The Jews were anxious to help the British; they had received the troops with open arms; they were on the best of terms with the Anzacs. But it seemed as though the local administration was bent on ignoring the Home Government's attitude towards our aspirations in Palestine, or, what was worse, was going out of its way to show definite hostility to the policy initiated in London. The outlook for later relations between Jews and Arabs was, in these circumstances, not a promising one.

This was my first opportunity of discussing at length with General Allenby questions of policy and our future. Like most of the Englishmen at that time in Palestine, the Commander-in-Chief, though not hostile, was inclined to be sceptical, though not because he feared trouble from the Arabs; it was rather that, in his view, Palestine *had* no future for the Jews. Indeed, the Arab question at that time seemed to give no grounds for anxiety. Such prominent Arab spokesmen as there were had more or less acquiesced in the policy; at any rate, they made no protest. With some of them—like the old Mufti of Jerusalem, and Musa Kazim Husseini—we had established very friendly relations; and, as will be seen in the next chapter but one, the titular and actual leader of the Arab world, the Emir Feisal, was even enthusiastically with us. What I had to overcome in the Commander-in-Chief, then, was a genuine scepticism as to the intrinsic practicality of the plan for the Jewish Homeland.

I pointed out to him that there were untapped resources of energy and initiative lying dormant in the Jewish people, which would be released by the impact of this new opportunity. These energies, I believed, would be capable of transforming even a derelict country like Palestine. I reminded him of the villages founded by Baron Edmond de Rothschild, which even in those days were oases of fertility in the surrounding wastes of sand—in startling contrast to the Arab villages, with their mud hovels and dunghills. I tried with all my might to impart to the Commander-in-Chief some of the confidence which I myself felt—in part because I had come to have a great personal regard for him, and also because I felt that his attitude might be crucial when the time came to get down to practical problems. I remember that towards the end of the long talk, when I felt his resistance yielding a little, I said something like this:

'You have conquered a great part of Palestine, and you can measure your conquest by one of two yardsticks: either in square kilometres—and in that sense your victory, though great, is not unique: the Germans have overrun vaster areas—or else by the yardstick of history. If this conquest of yours be measured by the centuries of hallowed tradition which attach to every square kilometre of its ground, then yours is one of the greatest victories in history. And the traditions which make it so are largely bound up with the history of my people. The day may come when we shall make good your victory, so that it may remain graven in something more enduring than rock—in the lives of men and nations. It would be a great pity if anything were done now—for instance by a few officials or administrators—to mar this victory.'

He seemed at first a little taken back by this tirade; but when I had finished he said: 'Well, let's hope it will be made good.'

After this interview relations between ourselves and the administration underwent a certain improvement; but on the whole the spirit governing officialdom was not conducive to co-operation between ourselves and the British or between ourselves and the Arabs. There were constant changes of governors under the military occupation, with constant set-backs. Whether the Arabs got positive encouragement to oppose the Allied policy from one or two of the British officials, or whether they just drew their own conclusions from the day-to-day conduct of these gentlemen, it is impossible to say, much less to prove. Nor does it much matter. The fact was that Arab hostility gained in momentum as the days passed; and by the time a civil administration under Sir Herbert Samuel took over, the gulf between the two peoples was already difficult to bridge.

CHAPTER XX

THE ZIONIST COMMISSION

CHALLUKKAH JEWRY

*A Picturesque Old Community—Our Good Intentions Misunderstood—
Dr. M. D. Eder and the Challukkah Jews—Jabotinsky as Political
Liaison Officer—The Other-worldliness of Challukkah Jews—Myrtles for
the Feast of Tabernacles—The Commander-in-Chief Provides Them*

THERE was a second Jewish community in Palestine, which was
equally the concern of the Zionist Commission—an old, quaint,
picturesque and appealing community which long antedated
the coming of the elements which were concerned with the
building up of the Jewish Homeland. Perhaps one ought to say
a 'first' Jewish community, since it was such in point of time,
and certainly in point of numbers. This was *Challukkah* Jewry,
a settlement which for generations had been supported by
charitable contributions collected among pious and orthodox
Jews in the great communities of Poland, Russia, Hungary,
Germany and the United States.

The *Challukkah* Jews were for the most part elderly, strictly
religious men and women who devoted their last years to
prayer, sacred study and good deeds generally. They lived in a
strange world of their own, fantastically remote from present-
day realities, and the majority of them were hardly conscious
of the crisis through which the world was passing or of its implications for their own future and for that of their people. All
they knew definitely about the war was that it had dried up the
source of most of their income, since no money could now reach
them from their European benefactors. Even the life of abject
poverty to which they were accustomed threatened to become
impossible. And then the American Jewish Joint Distribution
Committee stepped in, and charged the Zionist Commission
with the distribution of funds among the various organizations
and individuals which had hitherto been the recipients of

Challukkah moneys. This brought us into close contact with the old *Yishuv* (or settlement) of the existence of which most of our members had till then been completely ignorant.

We found that there existed a number of 'institutions' of one kind or another—schools, hospitals, homes for the aged and the like. Some were little more than names and decorative letterheads, but some were genuine if rather primitive organizations engaged in charitable work. Their management, and the conditions obtaining in them, came as a severe shock to members of the Commission, whose standards were those of Western Europe; and they rebelled against the idea of handing over funds to institutions whose standards of hygiene and administration were those of a medieval Oriental world. But the first attempts to introduce some reasonable change ran up against a stone wall of resistance and unleashed a storm of outrage and indignation: such suggestions were not only anathema, they were heathen, impious, heartless, ignorant and malevolent. We did our utmost to persuade the *Challukkah* Jews that the furthest thing from our minds was to interfere with their religious views and observances; and we assured the 'administrators' that we were only anxious to make conditions a little modern and comfortable for their charges. Our well-meant efforts led to tremendous and interminable discussions in which we, being unversed in Talmudic logic and dialectic, invariably came off second best. Our only effective weapon was that we *were* in control of the Joint Distribution Committee's fund; but the effectiveness of this weapon was weakened by two circumstances, so that we had to use it with great circumspection.

First, we disliked very much forcing our point of view on others. We preferred to use persuasion; and we could only regret that we had been created such a stiff-necked, stubborn people.

Second, our friends had, of course, the right of appeal to the military authorities, who always had a soft spot in their hearts for picturesque inefficiency and who, as between the dignified, sacerdotal presence, the flowing robes and the courtly manners of Rabbi X of Hebron, and the go-ahead, unromantic, practical common sense of Dr. Y of the Commission, infinitely preferred the former. He was—perhaps here lies the point!—the nearest approach provided by the Jewish community to the Arab sheik! So we always knew that, in case of trouble with one of our old gentlemen, leading to an appeal to the Military Governors, we were, to put it mildly, 'for it.'

The burden of this side of our work—and it was a heavy one —fell almost entirely on Dr. David Eder. Superficially you would have said that there could hardly have been found a less suitable man for the job. He was Western by birth and upbringing, a scientist, Western in outlook, leftist in politics, and entirely, or almost entirely, ignorant of any of the languages in current use in the old *Yishuv*. But these handicaps were purely superficial, and he overcame them. What mattered were his real kindness, his tolerance and humanity, his eagerness to understand the other's point of view: and these qualities soon gained for him the deep respect and affection of even the most recalcitrant among them. To nobody but Eder would they open up; he seemed possessed of some sort of intimate personal magic which charmed away their fears and suspicions. Eder's office was always full of these 'clients.' An interpreter was present—he was, indeed, indispensable—but most of the conversations seemed to be conducted in the most peculiar mixture of languages I have ever met: broken German and Yiddish, the few words of Hebrew which Eder had picked up since his arrival in Palestine and the fewer words of English which the old gentlemen had acquired—these, with a little Ladino, resulted in a dialect which often defied the best efforts of the interpreter, but somehow served to establish not only communication, but confidence and understanding, between Eder and his interlocutors. It may be imagined, indeed, that the progress was slow; the remarkable thing was—when I look back on all the difficulties—that there was any progress at all.

I must digress here to tell the later story of Dr. Eder. When I left Palestine, in September of that year, he took charge of the Commission. Although nominally our relations with the military administration were in the hands of Jabotinsky, it was Eder's authority which expressed itself in the Commission, and whenever difficulties arose, either with the Jewish community or with the military, it was he who was called upon to straighten matters out. It is remarkable that though in private he was at times temperamental, and affected a gruff manner, he remained to the outside world a model of patience and forbearance. He always gained his point by persuasion, and never resorted to threats or bluster.

Unfortunately the same could not always be said of his political colleague. Jabotinsky shared few of Eder's external handicaps; he was familiar with all the necessary languages, speaking fluent French, English, Hebrew and German; he possessed great eloquence and a high degree of intelligence; but he seemed to be entirely devoid of poise and balance and, what was worse, of that mature judgment so urgently required in that small but very complex world. Actually every member of the Commission was required to stand between two worlds, as different from each other as could be imagined, and to serve as a bridge: a difficult rôle, unless the bridge rests on solid pillars and has at the same time enough resilience to withstand the shock of large and excited crowds.

Jabotinsky took over from me—theoretically—a few days before I left the country, so that I had an opportunity of watching, from a distance, his zeal and ardour, of which General Clayton, the political officer, was an early victim. When I came into Clayton's tent to take leave of him on the eve of my departure, he very quietly remarked to me that he thought it might be useful if I would impress upon Captain Jabotinsky that things would be much easier if he would fix definite hours each day at which to call upon him to transact business, and not to walk in on him at all hours of the day and night! Coming from Clayton, whom I knew to be so well disposed towards us, this remark did not augur well for my successor. I tried to impress on Jabotinsky the need for caution, and naturally warned Eder, who shared my anxiety. He promised to keep an eye on things, and he did, with his usual conscientiousness and devotion.

Eder was a tower of strength to us in those days. He understood the British better than most of us, was always able to reason matters out, to explain difficulties, and to advise. He was a newcomer, not only to Palestine, but also to Zionism; it took a little time before the Palestine community came to appreciate to the full his personality and his work, but at the end of his two years' stay he had greatly endeared himself to the *Yishuv*. His departure left a large gap, and we were deeply sorry to see him return to the outside world and to his neglected profession, distinguished authority though we knew him to be in it.

One of the thorniest problems with which Eder had to deal, in connection with the old *Yishuv*, rose from the following circumstances: recruiting for the Jewish battalions was still going on in Palestine at the time of our arrival; our able-bodied men from the settlements had already gone, but we were trying to provide reserves, and this entailed an appeal to the old *Yishuv*. We asked them either to join the army or, if they could not do that, to try and replace the men who had enlisted from the colonies. There were of course relatively few young men among the *Challukkah* Jews, and most of those few were either physically unfit for the army or had conscientious objections. About a hundred of them, however, agreed to go to the settlements to do agricultural work.

Well then, we made arrangements with the farmers who were to employ them to provide them with strictly *kosher* food, and with transportation back to Jerusalem every Friday afternoon before the Sabbath set in; for it was utterly unthinkable that, war or no war, any religious Jew should be expected to keep the Sabbath elsewhere than in the Holy City. They had other various needs which it was not easy to meet in time of war, but we did our best to ensure their satisfaction. The wages paid them were, of course, far above the meagre dole they received from charity. But neither this fact, nor our careful arrangements to provide for their comfort and satisfy their scruples, could persuade them to stay in the settlements for more than a very short time. It must be admitted that they were quite unfitted for agricultural labour, physically as well as mentally. Mostly they regarded it as a 'worldly' occupation, liable to distract a man from the proper purposes of existence, which were prayer and Talmudic study. As to the financial side of it, one of them very seriously explained to me that physical exertion entailed the consumption of more food, as well as greater wear and tear of clothes, so that he preferred less money and a sedentary and pious life.

It is difficult for the Western mind to understand how completely divorced from reality the old *Yishuv* in Palestine was at that time. Its members lived immured behind the walls of a medieval ghetto—but a ghetto of their own making and stronger than any which an enemy could have erected around them. We did all we could to break through to them, and knew we were not having too much success. Nevertheless, we were rather horrified to discover how remote from them we had remained, even towards the end of 1918, with half a year of patient work behind us. The discovery came when Oliver Harvey, then chief censor of Palestine, asked me to help him with the censorship of Hebrew letters, of which he handed over a sackful. They were almost all from the Jews of the old *Yishuv* to their contributors in America and other accessible countries. Quite ninety per cent of them were devoted to complaints about the hardships which the writers were enduring at the hands of the Zionist Commission, with frequent hints of maladministration of funds. The military censors suggested that we confront the writers—the majority of them well known to us— with these accusations, but we decided that on the whole it was better to forward the letters, since we were certain that the addressees were pretty familiar with the methods of their correspondents. In this view events proved us to have been entirely justified.

A curious incident out of that time has stayed vividly in my memory, perhaps because it was so typical of this side of our work. It occurred just as I was leaving Palestine for England at the end of September 1918. My train was due to pull out of Lydda in a couple of hours; my luggage was packed, and was being taken out to the car. I was following it when I noticed two venerable gentlemen—their combined ages must have been in the neighbourhood of one hundred and eighty years—bearing down upon me. What struck me at first, apart from their great age, was that I had not seen them before. By this time I was under the impression that I had met every man, woman and child in the Jewish community of fifty thousand, most of them several times. Slowly and with dignity they advanced to meet me, pausing to give close scrutiny to the car, the luggage and the other indications of departure. Then they turned to me and said: 'But you are not really going away? You can't go yet. There are still some matters of importance to be settled here.'

I was only too conscious that there *were* matters of importance still unsettled—many of them to remain so for many years—

but I did not at once grasp what was meant. Sensing my ignorance, the elder of the two gentlemen proceeded to enlighten me:

'Do you not know that the Feast of Tabernacles is almost upon us, and we have no myrtles?' (At the Feast of Tabernacles certain prayers are said by orthodox Jews while they hold a palm branch adorned with myrtles in one hand and an ethrog, or citron, in the other.)

Though I was familiar enough with the need for myrtles at *Sukkoth*, it had somehow slipped my mind, and it had not occurred to me to include this particular job among the many chores of the Zionist Commission, operating in the midst of a bloody war.

A little startled, I said: 'Surely you can get myrtles from Egypt.'

My friends looked pained. 'For the Feast of Tabernacles,' one of them answered, reproachfully, 'one must have myrtles of the finest quality. These come from Trieste. In a matter of high religious importance, surely General Allenby will be willing to send instructions to Trieste for the shipment of myrtles.'

I explained carefully that there was a war on, and that Trieste was in enemy territory.

'Yes, they say there is a war,' replied one of the old gentlemen. 'But *this* is a purely religious matter—a matter of peace. Myrtles are, indeed, the very symbol of peace. . . .'

The conversation showed every sign of prolonging itself indefinitely; I thought of my train from Lydda—the only one that day—and steeled myself to firmness. 'You will have to make do,' I said, 'with Egyptian myrtles.'

At this stage my interlocutors brought out their trump card. 'But there is a quarantine imposed on the importation of plants from Egypt; the military authorities do not permit it.'

We seemed to have reached a deadlock. I had to go, and with some misgivings handed the two Rabbis over to my colleagues, assuring them with my parting breath as I climbed into the car that every possible effort would be made to secure the myrtle supply in time for Tabernacles, by some means or other. (By what means, I would have been hard put to it to explain.)

I travelled down to Egypt genuinely worried over this
question of myrtles and the quarantine; and even more worried
by the responsibility for some thousands of people living, like
these two old gentlemen, in a world of their own so remote
from ours that they seemed as unreal to us as the war did to
them. By the time I fell asleep in the train I was no longer sure
what was, in fact, real, the war or the Feast of Tabernacles.

The business of renewing contacts in Cairo—there were
many of them—drove the myrtles from my mind. But when I
went to take leave of General Allenby just before my boat
sailed, and we had finished our business talk, he suddenly said:
'By the way, about those myrtles!' He pulled a letter out of
his pocket, glanced at it, and added: 'You know, it is an
important business; it's all in the Bible; I read it up in the
Book of Nehemiah last night. Well, you'll be glad to hear that
we have lifted the quarantine, and a consignment of myrtles
will get to Palestine in good time for the Feast of Tabernacles!'

CHAPTER XXI

THE ZIONIST COMMISSION

THE POSITIVE SIDE

King Feisal, Leader of the Arabs—The Journey to Akaba with Ormsby-Gore—Circumnavigating the Sinai Peninsula—Echoes of Exodus—Feisal's Friendliness—Lawrence of Arabia—Return to Palestine to Lay Foundation Stones of Hebrew University—An Act of Faith in the Midst of War—Return to London—Lunch with Lloyd George, November 11, 1918

Two achievements may, I think, be written down to the credit of the Zionist Commission of 1918. They were of very different orders; the first was in the political field, the second in the spiritual; the first has been almost forgotten—though the day will come when its significance will be revived—the second has gathered volume and importance with the passing years. They were: the understanding reached with King Feisal and the laying of the foundation stones of the Hebrew University.

It was in June 1918, some three months after our arrival, that the Commander-in-Chief suggested that we attempt to approach King Feisal for at least a tentative agreement on the Zionist programme. Feisal was, in Allenby's opinion, as in that of most informed people, the only representative Arab whose influence was of more than local importance. By virtue of his personal qualities, and of his position as Commander-in-Chief of the Arab Army, he carried great weight in Arabia—then in revolt against the Turks—and with the British authorities. We fell in readily with this suggestion, which seemed to us to be a real sign of Allenby's desire to pave the way for future good relations between ourselves and the Arab world; coming from the head of the British in Palestine it did something to compensate us for the difficulties we encountered with his subordinates.

It was accordingly arranged that I set out with Major Ormsby-Gore for Akaba, and proceed thence up the Wady Araba into Transjordan. The Turks still held the Jordan Valley;

the only way to reach Feisal's headquarters was to go down by rail to Suez, thence by boat to Akaba, circumnavigating the Sinai Peninsula, and from Akaba northwards to Amman by such means of locomotion as might offer themselves. Thus the journey, which today can be made in a couple of hours by car from Jerusalem, took upwards of ten days, and in the heat of June it was no pleasure jaunt.

The boat which took us through Suez and the Gulf of Akaba was a small, grimy, neglected vessel in which some of our fellow-passengers professed to recognize the former yacht of the German Embassy in Constantinople. But we found it diffi-cult to accept this story; it seemed incredible that any ship could, in four short years, have accumulated so many coats of filth and such a variety of vermin. She was manned by a Greek crew, and the six days we spent aboard her seemed the longer for the insecurity which was added to our discomfort. The heat was unbearable; food, clothes, sheets, everything one touched was covered, permeated, with fine dust particles, clouds of which blew across our decks from the shores. The bathroom was long since *hors de combat*, and we devised what substitutes we could.

Whether from the bad food, the intense heat or the vermin, Major Ormsby-Gore fell ill with dysentery before we reached Akaba, and I was only too thankful to get him ashore there and into the care of a British doctor. He was not fit to continue the journey, and reluctantly we decided that I had better go on alone. Hubert Young was encamped at Akaba and he made the arrangements for the next stage, providing me with a British officer and an Arab guide. We set off by car up the Wady Musa —on that day not easily-distinguishable from the 'burning fiery furnace' of the Bible. There was no trace of vegetation, no shade, no water, no village wherein to rest; only the mountains of Sinai on the horizon, bounding a wilderness of burning rock and sand. The car stood it for perhaps three hours and then gave up. We continued on camels, and finally on foot, till we reached the R.A.F. station at the foot of the so-called Negev mountain, where we found hospitality and good friends to give us shelter for the night. They sent us off the next morning with a fresh car and an English driver, who was to take us up the mountain by a rough and ready track made for army lorries.

The car made about half the slope when it too gave up, and we again continued on foot to the top of the Transjordan plateau, feeling by now extremely tired and rather sorry for ourselves.

But on the top of the plateau we were in a different world. A fresh breeze replaced the sultry heat of the lower slopes; the countryside, though already parched in places, showed many pleasant green stretches threaded with brooks and rivulets; one or two villages were surrounded with trees and bushes. A British camp crowned the hilltop, and from this we obtained a third car. A metalled road continued forward, and in a few hours we were in sight of the headquarters of the Arab Army.

There came out to meet us Arab officers on camels, bearing gifts of water and fruit, with greetings from the Emir Feisal bidding us welcome to his camp. On reaching G.H.Q. I was received by Colonel Joyce, who advised me to take a good rest and not to attempt to see the Emir until the next day. So that evening found me wandering about the camp. It was a brilliant moonlit night—Palestinian moonlight—and I looked down from Moab on the Jordan Valley and the Dead Sea and the Judean hills beyond. I may have been a little lightheaded from the sudden change of climate, but as I stood there I suddenly had the feeling that three thousand years had vanished, had become as nothing. Here I was, on the identical ground, on the identical errand, of my ancestors in the dawn of my people's history, when they came to negotiate with the ruler of the country for a right of way, that they might return to their home. . . . Dream or vision or hallucination, I was suddenly recalled from it to present-day realities by the gruff voice of a British sentry: 'Sorry, sir, I'm afraid you're out of bounds.'

My talk with the Emir took place the following morning. I found him surrounded by his warriors, a forbidding-looking band engaged, when I arrived, in performing some sort of fantasia. Among them moved T. E. Lawrence, famous afterwards as 'Lawrence of Arabia,' chatting to various chiefs, and probably making arrangements for the night, when they would go forth on their destructive mission to blow up a few kilometres more of the Hedjaz railway. To my astonishment I saw English gold sovereigns—already a rarity to most of us—being distributed, and then I remembered the several heavy cases which had travelled with us, under strong guard, on our boat through the Red Sea.

I spent half an hour or so watching the army exercises, and was then invited to follow the Emir into his tent, where I was offered tea—instead of the inevitable coffee. There was little difference, either in consistency or flavour, both being nothing more than highly concentrated sugar solutions.

With the help of an interpreter we carried on a fairly lengthy and detailed conversation. After the usual exchange of politenesses, I explained to him the mission on which I had come to Palestine, our desire to do everything in our power to allay Arab fears and susceptibilities, and our hope that he would lend us his powerful moral support. He asked me a great many questions about the Zionist programme, and I found him by no means uninformed. At this time, it must be remembered, Palestine and Transjordan were one and the same thing, and I stressed the fact that there was a great deal of room in the country if intensive development were applied, and that the lot of the Arabs would be greatly improved through our work there. With all this I found the Emir in full agreement, as Lawrence later confirmed to me by letter.

The war was at that time—June 1918—still at a critical stage. One could perhaps have said that the whole conversation seemed to the Emir rather less than real; one could have added that he was only indulging in the elaborate Arab courtesy of which I have already spoken. Time was to prove that this was not the case, and in the sequel the reader will find ample evidence that the Emir was in earnest when he said that he was eager to see the Jews and Arabs working in harmony during the Peace Conference which was to come, and that in his view the destiny of the two peoples was linked with the Middle East and must depend on the good will of the Great Powers.

Our conversation lasted over two hours, and before I left he suggested that we be photographed together. Occasionally, during our talk, he fell into French; he did not speak it fluently, but could make himself understood quite well, and this to some extent relieved the strain of a long conversation through an interpreter.

The Emir promised to communicate the gist of our talk to his father, the Sherif Hussein, who was, he said, the ultimate judge of all his actions, and carried the responsibility for Arab policy. From subsequent events it was clear that his father raised no objections to the views expressed to me by his son.

This first meeting in the desert laid the foundations of a life-long friendship. I met the Emir several times afterwards in Europe, and our negotiations crystallized into an agreement, drawn up by Colonel Lawrence and signed by the Emir and myself, which has been published several times, both in British and in French diplomatic papers. Thus the leader of the Arab world against Turkey, who by his leadership initiated a new period of Arab revival, came to a complete understanding with us, and would no doubt have carried this understanding into effect if his destiny had shaped as we at that time expected it would. Unfortunately, for reasons beyond his control, he was unable to realize his ambitions; he did not unite the Arab world, but was forced out of Syria and given the throne of Iraq. Then followed the rise of Ibn Saud, and the practical annihilation of the Hashimite family. Arab unity receded once more into an unfulfilled dream.

I anticipate part of my narrative to say that this circumstance reflected most unfavourably on our relations with the Arabs, since among the many difficulties facing us in this field perhaps the paramount trouble is the lack of any single personality or group of personalities capable of representing the Arab world and of speaking on its behalf. It will be seen, when I come to tell of the Paris Peace Conference, during which Feisal was the recognized spokesman of the Arab world, that the under-standing reached with him was a matter of great importance. Events—and politicians—have conspired to push it into the background, but fundamental realities—and I hold the ultimate identity of Arab and Jewish interests to be a fundamental reality —have a way of reasserting themselves, and this one, I believe, will some day be recognized again for what it is.

I would like at this point to pay tribute to the services which T. E. Lawrence rendered our cause, and to add something regarding his remarkable personality. I had met Lawrence fleetingly in Egypt, with Allenby, and later in Palestine. I was to meet him quite often later, and he was an occasional visitor to our house in London. His relationship to the Zionist move-ment was a very positive one, in spite of the fact that he was strongly pro-Arab, and he has mistakenly been represented as anti-Zionist. It was his view—as it was Feisal's—that the Jews would be of great help to the Arabs, and that the Arab world stood to gain much from a Jewish Homeland in Palestine.

His personality was complex and difficult. He was profoundly shy; his manner was whimsical, and it was difficult to get him to talk seriously. He was much given to the Oxford type of sardonic humour. But when one did manage to get him into a serious vein he was frank and friendly, and his opinions, especially regarding the affairs of the Near East, were really worth having.

The second entry on the credit side of the Zionist Commission may have looked much less impressive at the time; no one today denies its value. Before leaving London I had secured from Mr. Balfour his consent in principle to our trying to lay the foundation stones of the Hebrew University on the plot of land acquired for that purpose on Mount Scopus—subject, of course, to the consent of the military authorities on the spot. In May 1918 we approached General Allenby on the subject and found him at first—not surprisingly, perhaps—very much taken aback. He exclaimed: 'But we may be rolled back any minute! What is the good of beginning something you may never be able to finish?' My reply was: 'This will be a great act of faith—faith in the victory which is bound to come, and faith in the future of Palestine. I can think of no better symbol of faith than the founding of the Hebrew University, under your auspices, and in this hour.' He was not unimpressed, but he repeated: 'You have chosen almost the worst possible time. The war in the West is passing through a most critical phase; the Germans are almost at the gates of Paris.' I said: 'We shall win this war. The present crisis is only one episode.' In the end Allenby agreed to send a telegram to the Foreign Office asking for advice, and after a short interval received an affirmative reply.

And so, in July 1918, a modest but memorable ceremony took place. On the afternoon of the twenty-fourth the foundation stones of the Hebrew University were laid on Mount Scopus, in the presence of General Allenby and his staff, of representatives of the Allied armies co-operating with him, of Moslem, Christian and Jewish dignitaries from Jerusalem, and of representatives of the *Yishuv*.

The physical setting of the ceremony was of unforgettable and sublime beauty. The declining sun flooded the hills of Judea and Moab with golden light, and it seemed to me, too, that the transfigured heights were watching, wondering, dimly aware perhaps that this was the beginning of the return of their own people after many days. Below us lay Jerusalem, gleaming like a jewel.

We were practically within sound of the guns on the northern front, and I spoke briefly, contrasting the desolation which the war was bringing with the creative significance of the act on which we were engaged; recalling, too, that only a week before we had observed the Fast of the Ninth of Ab, the day on which the Temple was destroyed and Jewish national political existence extinguished—apparently for ever. We were there to plant the germ of a new Jewish life. And then I spoke of our hopes for the University—hopes which at that moment seemed as remote as the catastrophe of the Roman conquest, but which, at the time of writing, are in process of realization.

The ceremony did not last longer than an hour. When it was over we sang *Hatikvah* and *God Save the King*. But no one seemed anxious to leave, and we stood silent, with bowed heads, round the little row of stones, while the twilight deepened into night.

What we—my friends of the Hebrew University Committee and I—felt at the time was best expressed in a letter which I received some weeks later from Achad Ha-am, who had encouraged us, in our student days in Switzerland, when we first mooted the idea of a Hebrew University in Palestine nearly two decades before the Balfour Declaration was dreamed of.

London
12th August 1918

MY DEAR WEIZMANN,

. . . I feel it my duty to express to you my deep satisfaction and heartfelt joy on the occasion of this historical event. I know that, owing to present conditions, the erection of the building will have to be postponed, so that for a long time—heaven knows how long—the laying of the foundation stones will remain an isolated episode without practical consequences. Nevertheless I consider it a great historical event. . . .

Since the beginning of our national movement in connection

with the colonization of Palestine we have always felt, some of us unconsciously, that the reconstruction is possible only on spiritual foundations, and that the laying of these foundations must be taken in hand simultaneously with the colonization work itself. In the first embryonic period when the whole work in Palestine was still of very small dimensions, and in a very precarious condition, the spiritual effort was concentrated in the then very popular Hebrew school in Jaffa, which was as poor and unstable as the colonization itself. In the following period, the colonization work having been enlarged and improved, the need for laying spiritual foundations made itself felt more vividly, and found its expression in the 'Hebrew Gymnasium' at Jaffa—an institution incomparably superior to its predecessor. Now we stand before a new period of our national work in Palestine, and soon we may be faced with problems and possibilities of overwhelming magnitude. We do not know what the future has in store for us, but this we do know: that the brighter the prospects for the re-establishment of our national home in Palestine, the more the need for having the spiritual foundations of that home on a corresponding scale, which can only be conceived in the form of a Hebrew University. By this I mean—and so, I am sure, do you—not a mere imitation of a European University, only with Hebrew as the dominant language, but a University which, from the very beginning, will endeavour to become the true embodiment of the Hebrew spirit of old, and to shake off the mental and moral servitude to which our people has been so long subjected in the Diaspora. Only so can we be justified in our ambitious hopes as to the future influence of the 'Teaching' that 'will go forth out of Zion.'

It became clear to me soon afterwards that there was little practical work which the Commission could do in Palestine for the time being. The country was under military administration, the army was preparing for another push, and underneath it all I had the feeling that the war was working up to its crisis and that I ought to get back to London to report. When I consulted Allenby, I found him of the same opinion; he added that it might possibly be of use, politically, if I were in fact to give it out that I was leaving Palestine as a result of my disappointment

K*

at not being able to do anything constructive while the military fate of the country remained undecided. He wished me good luck and a speedy return.

In October 1918 I found myself in London again, reporting to the authorities, and to English and American Zionist friends, on our work in Palestine and our hopes and fears for the future. I informed the Prime Minister, Mr. Lloyd George, of my return, and was invited to lunch with him on November 11. The date naturally had no particular significance for anyone at that time. When the day came, and with it the news of the armistice, I assumed that the lunch would be off, since it was pretty obvious that Mr. Lloyd George would have much more important things to attend to. So I telephoned his secretary, Philip Kerr (later Lord Lothian), and asked whether I was still expected. I was surprised and delighted to receive an affirmative reply, and still more so to be told that we would be alone.

The problem was then how to make my way to Number Ten Downing Street. The streets were packed with joyous crowds, it seemed impossible to reach an assigned place, and least of all the Prime Minister's residence. However, I set off from our house in Addison Road at midday, allowing myself plenty of time to walk, for I could expect no conveyance. By about one-thirty (the hour of my appointment), I was in Green Park, just outside the little iron gate that leads into Downing Street. So were a great many other people. The gate was closely guarded by several policemen. Timidly I approached one of those on our side with a request to be let through, which was of course promptly refused. 'But,' said I, 'I have an appointment with the Prime Minister for lunch.' The policeman looked at me. 'So several other people have already informed me,' he remarked dryly. I then produced a visiting card, and asked if he would show it to his colleague on the inside of the gate, who might then inquire from the porter at Number Ten whether I was telling the truth. After some hesitation he agreed to do this, and in a few minutes returned all smiles to let me through.

I found the Prime Minister reading the Psalms; he was moved to the depths of his soul and was, indeed, near to tears. The first thing he said to me was: 'We have just sent off seven trains full of bread and other essential food, to be distributed by Plumer in Cologne.'

When at length we settled down to lunch, I had my opportunity of reporting on events in Palestine. But it was a hurried and confused visit; I was conscious of the Prime Minister's preoccupation with other matters, and felt that I must take up as little of his time, and even of his attention, as I could. At three o'clock he had to be at a Thanksgiving service in the Abbey, and at a quarter to the hour I watched him emerge from the door of Number Ten, to be overwhelmed immediately by a cheering crowd and borne, shoulder-high, from my view.

POSTWAR

THE end of the war brought such fundamental changes in the structure of the world—and more particularly of the Jewish world—that for a while we could see little but the external difficulties which towered in our path. By comparison with the cataclysms of the Second World War the changes wrought by the First in the condition of the Jewish people may seem to have been of manageable proportions. But they were profound enough, and in their time unprecedented. It was some months before we could draw breath again, achieve some sort of general view, and decide where lay our best prospects.

The very conditions which had brought about the Balfour Declaration had also been responsible for a disastrous weakening of the Jewish people as a whole. There was also the separate German peace with Russia, and the Bolshevik revolution, which had virtually eliminated Russian Jewry as a factor to be reckoned with in our reconstruction plans. Between the Balfour Declaration and the accession of the Bolsheviks to power, Russian Jewry had subscribed the then enormous sum of thirty million roubles for an agricultural bank in Palestine; but this, with much else, had now to be written off; and though a few refugees, mostly orphans, did eventually trickle through to Palestine (where some of them were settled with money from South Africa at Kfar Noar), they were too few to make an impression on the country. Polish Jewry had suffered so severely in the general war, with the backward and forward movement of armies, and was still suffering so much in the separate Russo-Polish War, that it was incapable of making any appreciable contribution to the tasks which lay ahead of us. So our eyes turned westward to the one great Jewish community which had remained intact, though we knew that the American Jews were by no means as deeply permeated with the Zionist ideal as the European.

In the first few months after the war, the world at large, and the Jews perhaps more than the rest, lacked everything: food, gold, clothes, shelter, medicine. It was swept by epidemics, which in some areas decimated the populations. Even in well-organized and relatively wealthy States the work of reconstruction presented an enormous problem. How much more difficult was it for us, a small and scattered people, without a country, without a government, without executive powers, without forces, without funds. And we had to begin our colonization work in an old exhausted country, with a small Jewish population whose social stratification up to that time had made them, to say the least, unsuited to such a task.

Then there were problems which arose within our own ranks as a result of a failure to understand the external problems. In Palestine itself our political difficulties were increasing rather than diminishing as the months went by; but the Continental Zionists were for the large part under the illusion that all political problems had been solved by the issue of the Balfour Declaration! My own experience in Palestine during 1918, and my contacts with the British military authorities and the Arabs, had taught me one hard lesson, namely, that we stood only on the threshold of our work, politically and in every other way. What struck me as curious was that the American Zionists, under Justice Brandeis, though fully aware of what was going on in England and in Palestine, none the less shared the illusions of our Continental friends; they too assumed that all political problems had been settled once and for all, and that the only important task before Zionists was the economic building up of the Jewish National Home.

It was a misunderstanding which, as I shall relate, was to haunt us for many years and to have serious consequences for the movement; it was to produce dangerous internal tensions, and to affect the whole course of Zionist history. It began to

manifest itself at the very first postwar meeting of the Zionist
Action Committee (General Council), which took place in
London in February 1919. To me fell the thankless task of
explaining the realities of the situation to my Zionist friends
from the Continent—an American delegation arrived later, for
the June meeting—some of whom had come to the meeting
with ready-prepared lists of names for the 'Cabinet' which,
they assumed, would soon be elected in Jerusalem! Brought
down to earth by the cold facts, they could not conceal their
disappointment; some of them went at once to the other
extreme, and concluded that the Balfour Declaration was a
meaningless document. It was my job—then and for many
years after, and in many places—to preach the hard doctrine
that the Balfour Declaration was no more than a framework,
which had to be filled in by our own efforts. It would mean
exactly what we would make it mean—neither more nor less.
On what we could make it mean, through slow, costly and
laborious work, would depend whether, and when, we should
deserve or attain statehood.

Twelve years later, and speaking of the League of Nations
Mandate in which the Balfour Declaration was incorporated, I
still had to tell a Zionist Congress: 'Like all people and groups
without the tradition of political responsibility, the Jews are
apt to see in the printed text of a document the sole and
sufficient guarantee of political rights. Some of them have clung
fanatically to the letter of the Mandate and have failed to
understand its spirit. Practical politics, like mechanics, are
governed by one golden rule: you can only get out of things
what you put into them.' If such admonitions were necessary—
as indeed they were—after more than a decade of practical
experience, how much more so were they at the very outset
of the work! At that small gathering in 1919 I found myself
face to face with a highly critical opposition. Alas, I understood
them far better than they understood me. They felt the threat
of pogroms hanging low over their countries, and they yearned
for a sure refuge. The Balfour Declaration had seemed to
promise them that, and to some of them the arguments which
I conceived to be so reasonable must have sounded like bitter
mockery of their cherished hopes. I should have felt their
criticism less deeply if I had not understood the impulses behind

it, if the intensity of the feelings expressed had not been for me
an indication of the stark tragedy which even then—this was
1919, not 1945—had overwhelmed the Eastern European
Jewish communities—a tragedy which the Zionist movement
was at the moment powerless to relieve. Some of the critics,
too, were close personal friends of my youth.

It was in this atmosphere that we had to make a modest
beginning, accepting the hard facts and fortified by the conviction that this small start would grow and blossom into something
not unworthy of our age-long hopes. The first thing was to
reorganize and strengthen the Zionist Commission in Jerusalem. Then we had to make the Home Government understand
just what the peculiarly hostile attitude of the administration
on the spot meant to us, and ask that measures be taken to
remedy the situation. Telegrams were in fact sent to Palestine
from the Home Government, indicating in no uncertain terms
that the Balfour Declaration was the considered policy of His
Majesty's Government, and the gist of these telegrams was
communicated both to Jews and Arabs by the military
authorities, Palestine being still under military occupation.
But the comments attached to them by Sir Ronald Storrs,
Military Governor of Jerusalem, and others, were such as to
deprive them of most of their effect.

We were engaged, also, in the preparation of our case for the
Peace Conference then sitting in Paris. A preliminary draft
had been produced by an advisory committee under Sir Herbert
Samuel, with Maynard Keynes, Lionel Abrahams and James
de Rothschild as members. Simon Marks took this draft to
Paris to consult with Ormsby-Gore on it, and returned, as I
recall, rather crestfallen: Ormsby-Gore had given him some
kindly but unpalatable advice about 'coming down to earth,'
'adjusting oneself,' 'revising one's ideas,' and so on. All the
same, the draft which Ormsby-Gore had considered so fanciful
formed the substantial basis of the statement which we eventually submitted to the Conference on February 23, 1919.

The summons to Paris came while the Action Committee was
still in session, and I left them to continue their deliberations
while I joined Mr. Sokolow and the other members of our
delegation in Paris, where we were to appear before the
Council of Ten of the Peace Conference: the Council included

Balfour and Lord Milner for Great Britain, Tardieu and Pichon for France, Lansing and White for America, Baron Sonnino for Italy. Clémenceau was present during the early part of the session. The scene is still vivid in my memory, but for the account I make use of the report which I gave my colleagues of the Action Committee on my return to London on March 5.

We were admitted to the Conference chamber at three-thirty on Thursday afternoon, February 23. Mr. Sokolow delivered a very short, concise speech upon the first point, namely, the historic claim of the Jewish people to Palestine, and referred to the favourable declarations which had been made by the various governments on this subject. He described the immemorial attachment of the Jewish people to *Eretz Israel*, and explained how local Jewish questions, in whatever countries, really turned upon Palestine: on these grounds, he continued, we demanded the foundation of a Jewish National Home in Palestine. From where I stood I could see Sokolow's face, and, without being sentimental, it was as if two thousand years of Jewish suffering rested on his shoulders. His quiet, dignified utterance made a very deep impression on the assembly.

After him I dealt with the economic position of the Jewish people. I pointed out that as a group the Jews had been hit harder by the war than any other; Jewry and Judaism were in a frightfully weakened condition, presenting, to themselves and to the nations, a problem very difficult of solution. There was, I said, no hope at all of such a solution—since the Jewish problem revolved fundamentally round the homelessness of the Jewish people—without the creation of a National Home. The third and fourth speakers—five had been allotted to us—were Ussishkin, who spoke in Hebrew, and André Spire, who spoke in French. The last was Sylvain Lévi. His speech might be divided into two parts. In the first he soared to heaven, in the second he came down plumb to earth. He began by describing the foundation of the Jewish colonies in Palestine, the development of Hebrew, the work of the *Choveve Zion*, Baron de Rothschild and the *Alliance Israélite*; he declared that the work of the Zionists was of great significance from the moral point of view: it had uplifted the Jewish masses and oriented them to Palestine. The second part of his speech raised three points: one, that Palestine was a small and poor land, that it already had a population of six hundred thousand Arabs, that the Jews had a higher standard of life than the Arabs and would tend to dispossess them. Two, that the Jews who would go to Palestine would be mainly Russian Jews, who were of 'explosive' tendencies. Three, that the creation of a Jewish National Home in Palestine would introduce the dangerous principle of Jewish dual rights, and this was of especial importance to France as the principal Mediterranean Power.

When M. Lévi ended his speech the rest of us felt profoundly embarrassed; it was not that he had made any great impression on the Conference; it was rather that the astoundingly unexpected character of his utterance—it was not for this purpose that he had been invited as a *Jewish* representative—constituted a *chillul ha-shem*, a public desecration. We held a short consultation among ourselves. Each of us had spoken for five or six minutes, M. Lévi had taken twenty, about as much as the rest of us put together. If we asked permission to refute his arguments we should change the proceedings into a debate between M. Lévi and ourselves—an exceedingly undignified spectacle.

Something in the nature of a miracle came to resolve our dilemma. Mr. Lansing, the American Secretary of State, called me over and asked me: 'What do you mean by a Jewish National Home?' That opened the door to us, and Mr. Lansing's intervention rendered us a very great service. I defined the Jewish National Home to mean the creation of an administration which would arise out of the natural conditions of the country—always safeguarding the interests of non-Jews —with the hope that by Jewish immigration Palestine would ultimately become as Jewish as England is English. I asked Mr. Lansing whether I had made my point clear, and he replied: 'Absolutely!' I then dealt with M. Lévi's remarks, and said that the Zionist task was indeed a difficult one, but it was not more so than the present condition of the Jewish people; the question was not whether Zionism was difficult, but whether it was possible. I gave a brief technical exposition of the point, and took as my example the outstanding success which the French had at that time made of Tunisia. What the French could do in Tunisia, I said, the Jews would be able to do in Palestine, with Jewish will, Jewish money, Jewish power and

Jewish enthusiasm. As far as the question of double allegiance was concerned, there was nothing in our proposals which raised that principle. There were a few Jews who had qualms in this matter, but they were less than five per cent of the Jewish people. It was true that the Russian Jews had lived in an excitable atmosphere, but they were not responsible for that, and the very work which M. Lévi had praised in the first part of his speech had been done by Russian Jews. Mr. Balfour afterwards described my speech as 'the swish of a sword.'

The proceedings ended with this, and we withdrew. Mr. Balfour sent out his secretary to congratulate us upon our success. As we came out of the Conference precincts M. Lévi came up to me and held out his hand. Instinctively I withdrew my own and said: 'You have sought to betray us.' He got the same response from Sokolow.

That was the last time I saw Sylvain Lévi. We had known of course that he was no Zionist, but his behaviour in Palestine had been correct enough, and he gave us no hint of the attitude he would take up at the Peace Conference. To this day I am at a loss to understand why Baron Edmond de Rothschild, a good Zionist, should have supported his candidacy for membership in the delegation; he may have felt that some voice should be heard besides the official one of the Zionists—and quite possibly he had no inkling of the extraordinary performance M. Lévi was going to put up.

We got quite a good press in France—except for the *Journal des Débats*. The evening of the hearing M. Tardieu, French representative on the Council of Ten, issued an official statement, saying that France would not oppose the placing of Palestine under British trusteeship, and the formation of a Jewish State. The use of the words 'Jewish State' was significant; we ourselves had refrained from using them. The only disturbing public note was a rather surprising interview with the Emir Feisal which appeared in the *Matin* and was frankly hostile. Feisal's secretary promptly disavowed it, and a meeting was arranged between the Emir and Mr. (now Justice) Felix Frankfurter, who was a member of the American Zionist deputation, with Lawrence of Arabia present. In a few days the Emir addressed to Mr. Frankfurter the following letter:

HEDJAZ DELEGATION
PARIS
March 3, 1919

DEAR MR. FRANKFURTER:

I want to take this opportunity of my first contact with American Zionists, to tell you what I have often been able to say to Dr. Weizmann in Arabia and Europe.

We feel that the Arabs and Jews are cousins in race, suffering similar oppressions at the hands of powers stronger than themselves, and by a happy coincidence have been able to take the first step towards the attainment of their national ideals together.

We Arabs, especially the educated among us, look with the deepest sympathy on the Zionist movement. Our deputation here in Paris is fully acquainted with the proposals submitted by the Zionist Organization to the Peace Conference, and we regard them as moderate and proper. We will do our best, in so far as we are concerned, to help them through; we will wish the Jews a most hearty welcome home.

With the chiefs of your movement, especially with Dr. Weizmann, we have had, and continue to have, the closest relations. He has been a great helper of our cause, and I hope the Arabs may soon be in a position to make the Jews some return for their kindness. We are working together for a reformed and revived Near East, and our two movements complete one another. The Jewish movement is national and not imperialistic. Our movement is national and not imperialistic; and there is room in Syria for us both. Indeed, I think that neither can be a real success without the other.

People less informed and less responsible than our leaders, ignoring the need for co-operation of the Arabs and the Zionists, have been trying to exploit the local differences that must necessarily arise in Palestine in the early stages of our movements. Some of them have, I am afraid, misrepresented your aims to the Arab peasantry, and our aims to the Jewish peasantry, with the result that interested parties have been able to make capital out of what they call our differences.

I wish to give you my firm conviction that these differences are not on questions of principle, but on matters of detail, such as must inevitably occur in every contact with neighbouring peoples, and as are easily dissipated by mutual good will. Indeed, nearly all of them will disappear with fuller knowledge.

I look forward, and my people with me look forward, to a future in which we will help you and you will help us, so that the countries in which we are mutually interested may once again take their place in the community of civilized peoples of the world.

Yours sincerely,
FEISAL

This remarkable letter should be of interest to the critics who have accused us of beginning our Zionist work in Palestine without ever consulting the wishes or welfare of the Arab world. It must be borne in mind that the views here expressed by the then acknowledged leader of the Arabs, the bearer of their hopes, were the culmination of several discussions. Of equal interest to the critics should be the agreement into which Feisal, as head of the Arab delegation, entered direct with me, on January 3 of that year, before we were called before the Peace Conference, and I think it is proper to say that the existence of that agreement had much to do with the positive attitude towards Zionist aspirations of the Big Four. I quote only paragraphs three and four of that agreement:

In the establishment of the Constitution and Administration of Palestine, all such measures shall be adopted as will afford the fullest guarantees for carrying into effect the British Government's [Balfour] Declaration of November 2nd, 1917.

All necessary measures shall be taken to encourage and stimulate immigration of Jews into Palestine on a large scale, and as quickly as possible to settle Jewish immigrants upon the land through closer settlement and intensive cultivation of the soil. In taking such measures the Arab peasant and tenant farmers shall be protected in their rights, and shall be assisted in forwarding their economic development.

Feisal added a condition to this agreement, a perfectly understandable one as far as he was concerned: 'If the Arabs are established as I have asked in my manifesto of January 4 addressed to the British Secretary of State for Foreign Affairs, I will carry out what is written in this agreement. If changes are made, I cannot be answerable for failure to carry out this agreement.'

Great changes indeed were made, and their results were visited upon the heads of the Zionists. But at the time the general impression in Paris was that our cause was won, though the details remained to be decided. 'Everything,' I told the Action Committee in London, 'now depends upon ourselves.'

A second meeting of the Action Committee was held, also in London, four months later, in June 1919, this time with the participation of an American delegation headed by Justice Brandeis, whom I now met for the first time. I was, in fact, just getting to know American Jewry, through some of its representatives. I was to learn a great deal about it in the future—it has, in fact, been one of the major experiences of my life.

Felix Frankfurter I first met during my mission to Gibraltar in 1917. I had known him by reputation, and certainly was not disappointed when I came face to face with him. He was quick, intelligent, scintillating, many sided, in contrast to myself, who have little interest in affairs outside Zionism and chemistry. He was of great help to us, as we have already seen, in the negotiations with the Emir Feisal. He also helped me a great deal towards understanding the ways and ideas of the American political leaders of that time. During the controversy with Justice Brandeis, described in ensuing chapters, Frankfurter and I drifted apart for some years, but I believe that even during this period our relations did not deteriorate seriously, and I am happy to think that whatever breach there was has been healed, so that there are today stronger mutual bonds of affection and respect.

It is curious that though we did not have any long discussions of our problems, and only exchanged notes on them— that, too, at rare intervals—we almost always discovered an identity of view and interest. These days it is a great joy to me to see him in Washington, enthroned as one of the great Justices, and I never miss an opportunity of getting in touch with him when I am in America.

Stephen S. Wise, too, was one of the great personalities whom I began to know in those days. But of him I must remark that we found our way to each other rather slowly. He belonged to the old school of political Zionists, and for some reason or other we did not find a common language for many years, though I knew him to be devoted to the ideals of the movement and ready to give them of his best.

Wise was of great value to the movement during the time of Wilson, whom he had interested in our purposes about the time of the Balfour Declaration. In later years, as the result of more frequent contacts, Wise and I got nearer to each other, and a friendship developed which was never disturbed by differences of opinion or by any other circumstances. He has always been utterly unsparing of himself in his devotion to the movement and remains till this day one of the significant forces in Zionism and world Jewry.

Justice Brandeis, as I have remarked, I first met at the Action Committee Conference in London, in June 1919. He was on his way to Palestine—his first visit—and could stay in London only a couple of days. He was accompanied by Mr. Jacob de Haas, to whom he referred as his 'teacher in Zionism.'

Justice Brandeis has often been compared with Abraham Lincoln, and indeed they had much in common besides clean-chiselled features and lofty brows. Brandeis too was a Puritan: upright, austere, of a scrupulous honesty and implacable logic. These qualities sometimes made him hard to work with; like Wilson he was apt to evolve theories, based on the highest principles, from his inner consciousness, and then expect the facts to fit in with them. If the facts failed to oblige, so much the worse for the facts. Indeed, the conflicts which developed between Brandeis and ourselves were not unlike those which disturbed Wilson's relations with his European colleagues when he first had to work closely with them.

De Haas, his mentor, had always shown some hostility towards my leadership and that of my colleagues. I had had almost no personal contacts with him before—he had lived in the States—and though I had seen him once or twice at pre-war Zionist Congresses, I did not remember a single passage-at-arms with him. So I was forced to ascribe his opposition to the old division, dating back to Herzl's time, between the 'practical' and the 'political' Zionists. But what was altogether curious now was the fact that De Haas now posed as the 'practical' Zionist. Like Justice Brandeis he was of the opinion

that 'political Zionism' had very little more—if anything—to
do. The political chapter of the movement might therefore be
considered as closed. I pondered this phenomenon in vain, and
sometimes wondered whether De Haas might resent the fact
that a leading 'practical' Zionist, in the original sense, should
have been so closely connected with the major political achievement of the Zionist movement. Perhaps he felt it to be utterly
wrong that I should have had anything to do with the Balfour
Declaration which was obviously not my domain, but his, as
an old Herzlian Zionist. In any case, his views had already
influenced Brandeis to some extent before the Americans
arrived in London.

They found a good deal to criticize about the London office,
which was a very modest establishment. De Haas produced
elaborate plans for the building up of Palestine which seemed
to us both vague and fantastic. But we knew that much would
depend on our American friends, and were anxious not to hurt
their susceptibilities.

I tried to give Brandeis as accurate a picture of Palestine as
I could; above all, I warned him that he would find a poor,
underpopulated, underdeveloped, neglected country, with a
very small Jewish population, ravaged by four years of war,
and almost completely cut off from the outside world. Moreover, the Palestinian Jews were already rather disappointed
by the attitude of their new masters.

Looking back now, I think it may have been uncertainty
that made Brandeis and De Haas more trenchant in their
criticisms than they otherwise might have been—that and the
fact that they did not make sufficient allowance for the difficult
circumstances resulting from the war.

Brandeis's stay in Palestine did not exceed a fortnight, and
could not possibly permit a thorough survey of conditions.
When he returned, he was obliged to generalize on the basis
of the scanty facts he had been able to collect; his views,
however correct theoretically, squared badly with realities. He
was for instance definitely of the opinion that unless a large-
scale 'sanitation' of the country were first undertaken, it would
be wrong to encourage immigration. He supposed that the
Government's first act would be to drain the marshes, clear the
swamps, build new roads, not realizing that no one in authority

had the slightest intention of starting these operations. He repeatedly stated—this was thirty years ago—that Zionist political work had come to a close, that nothing remained but the economic task. These views pointed to a coming conflict between Brandeis and myself, as also between the majority of European Zionists and a powerful group of our American friends. In America itself they were to lead to a breach within the Zionist Organization which was not to be healed for many years.

Mr. Brandeis also made some sweeping and derogatory statements about the few Jewish settlements he had been able to visit. They were mostly the 'old' settlements, since apart from Deganiah, Merchaviah, Ben Shemen and Hulda there was nothing that could be called Zionist colonization; and all the settlements, old and new, were still scarred by the war. It seemed hardly fair to pass judgment on them on the basis of a hurried visit in a period immediately following a bitter war, itself following generations of Turkish occupation.

It was my conviction then, as it is today after the passing of nearly three decades, that constructive work in Palestine cannot be directed from a distance, even by the ablest of men, on the basis of an occasional short visit and of reports. One must not only spend sufficient time on the spot, one must be a participant in some enterprise, one must have the feel of the country and of the institutions. For this reason, among others, I returned to Palestine in the autumn of that year, taking with me my wife, whose first visit it was.

Two queer incidents have stayed in my mind in connection with the journey out. Travelling was still difficult in 1919, and the boat which we eventually got at Marseilles, after a ten-day wait, was filled chiefly with military passengers. One evening, having nothing better to do, I bought a ticket for the 'pool' on the day's run, and then found myself bidding in the auction against a rather blimpish general. I got the number. As luck would have it, my ticket won the pool, which amounted to about a hundred pounds, and I handed the money over to the sailors' fund. Never was it made more clear to me that I had no right to exist, much less to win sweeps and enjoy the popularity—ephemeral as it is—that haloes the winner!

The second incident was more serious. While we were still

on the high seas, General Congreve, Acting High Commissioner in Egypt during Allenby's absence, was informed that a Zionist by the name of Weizmann would shortly be arriving in Alexandria, and as his coming would certainly make trouble, he had better not be permitted to land. My old friend Colonel Meinertzhagen was political officer in Egypt at the time, and it was from him that we learned all the details of the affair. Meinertzhagen got wind of Congreve's intentions and made strong representations to his superior officer that things were not quite like that: in fact I was travelling with the knowledge, and indeed at the request, of high British authorities, and Zionism was a part of British policy. I was carrying with me letters from Allenby and Lloyd George. But Congreve stuck to his guns; he said he knew nothing about Zionism and cared less, and had never heard of me. Meinertzhagen took the drastic step of cabling London over the head of Congreve, and it took direct orders from the Foreign Office and the War Office to dissuade the General from turning us back. When we arrived in Alexandria he called on us at our hotel, primarily, I thought, to make it clear that whatever bees the high-ups might have in their bonnets, *he* at least was not to be taken in. But after this visit, during which he became most affable, he invited us to lunch at the Residency.

We stayed in Jerusalem with David Eder, who was now established in a home of his own. After making contact with the Jerusalem office, now reinforced—as a result of the Action Committee's decisions—by the addition of Mr. Ussishkin, Mr. Robert Szold and Dr. Harry Friedenwald, we devoted some time to seeing the country, particularly Upper Galilee and the north, which I had not visited since 1907. (The Turks still held that territory during my first stay with the Zionist Commission.) We travelled fairly extensively, crossing the Syrian border into Lebanon, and stopping off at some of the outpost settlements. Every hill and every rock stood out like a challenge to me at this time, telling me at every turn of the road how much planning and energy and money would have to be poured into this country before it could be ready to absorb large numbers of people.

Already the pressure from without was beginning to be felt. The first *chalutzim* (or pioneers)—the word was new then: it has since accumulated about itself a great tradition—were arriving from the broken Jewish communities of Poland and other countries of Central and Eastern Europe. Some of them came with a rudimentary training in agriculture: others brought nothing but their devotion and their bare hands. They came by an extraordinary variety of routes: in some instances their trek had lasted for months, even years, and had carried them from the Ukraine to Japan, and back across the Himalayas and India and Persia. Forward-looking men like Arthur Ruppin were immensely heartened by their coming, nor could anyone remain unmoved by this magnificent human material. But what I saw chiefly was that we had no plans for their reception, because we had no budget! Nor was there, on the part of the Palestine administration—with a few notable exceptions—any intention of making easier for us the fulfilment of the Balfour Declaration.

CHAPTER XXIII

PALESTINE—EUROPE—AMERICA

Accumulating Difficulties—Administration Obstructionism—Rich Jews Indifferent—Land Bought in Emek Jezreel—Tension in Palestine—The Tel Hai Tragedy—The Administration Supine—Jerusalem Riots—Jabotinsky Imprisoned—Purpose of the Arab Riots—The San Remo Conference—The Riddle of the Palestine Administration—General Bols's Letter—At San Remo—Balfour Declaration Confirmed—First Large Post-war Zionist Conference—Brandeis Heads American Delegation—Cleavage with the Brandeis Group on Jewish Agency Idea and on Budget—I am Invited to America—Louis Lipsky—I Become President of the World Zionist Organization

I N those days began to emerge the triple field of force in which I had to move for many years. The Jewish Homeland, British and European politics, American Jewry formed a pattern to which my life had to adapt itself. Jerusalem-London-New York became the focal points: at each point there were varying fortunes and special complications.

In Palestine I found myself obsessed by the discrepancy between the desirable and the possible. Occasionally the difficulties—political and economic alike—seemed so formidable that I fell a prey to dejection. Then I would go away alone into the hills for a little while, or down to the seashore near Tel Aviv, to talk with some of the older settlers—men like Abraham Shapiro of Petach Tikvah, or Joshua Chankin, or others of their generation. They would tell me of their own early difficulties, their own impressions when they had first come to 'this desert,' in days when there was not even a Zionist Organization, let alone a Balfour Declaration, when the Turkish blight lay on the land, and a Jew returning to Palestine was looked upon as a sort of religious maniac. They showed me the places that were already cultivated, covered with Jewish orange groves and vineyards: Rehovoth, Rishon-le-Zion, Petach Tikvah: so much had been done with limited means, limited experience, limited manpower, in this country. And then I knew again that Jewish energy, intelligence and will to sacrifice would eventually triumph over all difficulties.

Abraham Shapiro was in himself a symbol of a whole process of Jewish readaptation. He accompanied me on most of my trips up and down Palestine, partly as guide, partly as guard, and all the while I listened to his epic stories of the old-time colonists. He was a primitive person, spoke better Arabic than Hebrew, and seemed so much a part of the rocks and stony hillsides of the country that it was difficult to believe that he had been born in Lithuania. Here was a man who in his own lifetime had bridged a gap of thousands of years; who, once in Palestine, had shed his Galuth environment like an old coat. There were a few others of his type: the Rosoff family in Petach Tikvah, the Levontins, the Grasovkys and the Meirowitzes in Rishon. But they were all too few, and the first obvious task was to see to it that their numbers should be increased as fast as possible.

I went back to London in January 1920, carrying with me the plans which had been prepared by the Jerusalem office—plans for immigration, irrigation, colonization, calling for considerable sums. Little provision was made for land purchase, for we believed, on what seemed sufficient ground, that the Government would shortly place at our disposal stretches of land which were Government property. We were soon to discover that this belief had no basis in fact, and that every dunam of land needed for our colonization work would have to be bought in the open market at fantastic prices which rose ever higher as our work developed. Every improvement we made raised the value of the remaining land in that particular area, and the Arab landowners lost no time in cashing in. We found we had to cover the soil of Palestine with Jewish gold. And that gold, for many, many years, came out of the pockets, not of the Jewish millionaires, but of the poor.

It was an income wholly inadequate for our requirements, but it gave us the opportunity to make our first substantial land purchases, and to take the first tentative steps in organized immigration. Thus, in the summer of 1920, we bought the first Emek Jezreel lands, our one extensive tract up to that date—about eighty thousand dunams (twenty thousand acres). It had formerly belonged to the Sursuk family—typical absentee landlords—and bore only a few half-deserted Arab villages ravaged by malaria. The price we paid was, we then thought, atrociously high, but time has shown it to have been thoroughly justified. We owed it to what was then regarded as the very high-handed action of Mr. Ussishkin, in defiance of the prudent advice of most of his colleagues on the Executive, and particularly of the Americans. I like now to remember that I was among his few supporters in that momentous decision.

I have anticipated a little. My stay in London was a short one; by March 1920 I was on my way eastward again, this time with my elder boy, Benjamin, who was then twelve. We were to spend the Passover with my mother in Haifa. I might not have returned to Palestine so soon had it not been for a meeting with Lord Allenby in Paris on my westward journey. He was uneasy about the workings of the Zionist Commission, and thought I should be in Jerusalem rather than London.

We arrived to find Herbert Samuel already in Palestine. Allenby and Bols (the latter was then Military Governor of Palestine) had invited him in as adviser to the administration. Everyone was relieved to have Samuel there, for General Allenby's premonition had been only too sound: we all felt that things were not going well, that there was tension in the country. There was a great deal of open agitation in Arab circles, and there was no evidence that local administrators were making any effort to avert trouble; on the contrary, there were members of the official hierarchy who were encouraging the troublemakers. I am not alarmist by nature, and I was inclined at first to be sceptical about the reports. But they persisted, and some of our young people who were close to Arab circles were convinced that 'the day' was set for Passover, which that year coincided with both Easter and *Nebi-Musa*— an Arab festival on which the inhabitants of the neighbouring villages assemble in Jerusalem to march in procession to the reputed grave of the Prophet Moses on a near-by hill. Galilee, too, was in ferment owing to its nearness to Syria, whence Feisal was being edged out, and where friction between the English and the French was growing daily. Lawless bands prowled and raided on our northern hills, and as is usual in such cases banditry took on an aspect of patriotism. A month before my arrival Joseph Trumpeldor, one of the earliest and greatest of the *chalutz* leaders, had gone up with some companions to the defence of Tel Hai, an infant colony near the Syrian border; and there he and five companions, two of them women, were killed by marauders. The tragedy had plunged the whole *Yishuv* into mourning.

As Passover approached the tension grew more marked, and by that time some of the more friendly of the British officials—for instance Meinertzhagen (now the Palestine administration's political officer)—were apprehensive. Before leaving Jerusalem to spend Passover with my mother, I called on General Allenby, who was then in the city. I found him with General Bols and Herbert Samuel at Government House, still located in the old German hospice on the Mount of Olives. My representations regarding impending trouble made little impression on them. Bols said: 'There *can* be no trouble; the town is stiff with troops!' I replied that I had had some experience of the atmosphere which precedes pogroms; I knew also that troops usually proved useless at the last moment, because the whole paroxysm was liable to be over before they could be rushed to the field of action. There would be half an hour or an hour of murder and looting, and by the time the troops got there everything would be 'in order' and there would be nothing for them to do but pick up the pieces. However, I could see that I was wasting my breath. I was advised not to worry, and go home to my family for the Passover as arranged. I could feel assured that everything would go off quietly in Jerusalem.

Against my better judgment I went home, though what I could have done after this if I had stayed on in Jerusalem it is difficult to say. Passover in Haifa came and went; and the next morning there was no disturbing news from Jerusalem—no news at all, in fact. I felt uneasy. I tried to telephone, but could get no connection, which naturally increased my anxiety. So I decided—greatly to my mother's disappointment—to go up to Jerusalem and to take Benjy with me. The journey was uneventful as far as Nablus, but there I found a police escort. The Governor of Nablus, who supplied it, dropped a vague hint or two, and I became more and more convinced that 'something' really had happened.

Jerusalem, when we got there, looked deserted. A curfew had been imposed, and there was little movement in the streets except for police and military patrols. We made straight for Dr. Eder's flat in the centre of the city, and found him deeply disturbed. The story he had to tell was one that has since become all too familiar: Arabs assembling at the Mosque of Omar, listening to speeches of violent incitement, forming a procession fired with fanatic zeal, marching through the streets attacking any Jews they happened to meet. In spite of all the rumours which preceded the attack the Jews seem to have been caught completely unawares, and practically no resistance was offered. When one small group of young men, under Captain Jabotinsky, had come out to defend their quarter, they had been promptly arrested. The troops had, of course, arrived when all was over, and quiet now reigned in the city. The situation was 'well in hand.'

In the trials which followed before a military court, Jabotinsky received the savage sentence of fifteen years' hard labour. He was later amnestied (by Herbert Samuel when he became High Commissioner), but rejected the amnesty with scorn, because it included Aref el Aref, the main instigator of the pogrom, Amin el Husseini (the notorious Grand Mufti of later years) and one or two others of the same type. He insisted on making his appeal, and the sentence was in due course quashed.

The impression made on Benjy by the atmosphere in Jerusalem in the days that followed the pogrom terrified me. He was full of questions to which I had no answers: 'How can this happen? Who is guilty? Will they be punished?' I was thankful that we were staying with Eder, where at least the worst of the stories that ran round like wildfire could be kept from him.

All of us felt that this pogrom might have been averted had proper steps been taken in time to check the agitation, had the attitude of the administration been different. The bitterness and incitement had been allowed to grow until they found their natural expression in riot and murder. Philip Graves, no special friend of the Zionist movement, was then in Palestine as *The Times* correspondent under Lord Northcliffe; he admitted, in the account which he published in 1923, that:

The military, having completed the conquest of Palestine, naturally desired a rest after a long and trying campaign, and therefore took the line of least resistance in dealing with the local situation. They were, moreover, jealous of their own official prerogatives, and strongly objected to the manner in which members and employees of the Zionist Commission too often overstepped their functions and attempted, as the soldiers thought, to dictate to them. . . . But the highly disturbed state of the chief Arab countries . . . and above all, the failure of the British Government to furnish the Chiefs of the Administration in Palestine with any detailed instructions, explain the unwillingness of the soldiers to adopt an 'unmistakable and active pro-Zionist attitude.' . . . At the same time it must be admitted that, if most of the accusations brought by the Zionists against the Military Administration as a whole were unfounded, there were cases in which individual officers showed pro-Arab or pan-Arab sympathies. The Arabs, sometimes encouraged, perhaps unwittingly, by such officers, grew more and more petulant.

While suggesting that 'the Zionists have made too much of this pogrom,' and too little of the difficulties of the military, Graves adds:

Mistakes were made by some members of the Military Administration. The Chief of Staff to the Chief Military Administrator appears to have left Jerusalem for a trip to Jericho at a moment when crowds were already gathering in ominous fashion near the Jaffa Gate.

It might seem, to a dispassionate British observer, that we were making too much of this pogrom. (Only six Jews were killed, though there were many serious injuries.) But it is almost impossible to convey to the outside world the sense of horror and bewilderment which it aroused in our people, both in Palestine and outside. Pogroms in Russia had excited horror and pity, but little surprise; they were 'seasonal disturbances,' more or less to be expected round about the Easter and Passover festivals. That such a thing could happen in Palestine, two years after the Balfour Declaration, under British rule ('the town is stiff with troops!'), was incomprehensible to the Jews, and dreadful beyond belief. For those whose facile optimism had led them to believe that all political problems were safely out of the way, and that all we had to do was get on with the 'practical' work, this was—or should have been— the writing on the wall.

There was, of course, something more to the pogrom than

the primitive frenzy of its perpetrators. The instigators, those that had lashed the mobs to blind action, were more far-sighted than their illiterate dupes; they knew that within a few weeks there would be held in San Remo, in northern Italy, the Conference of the Allied Powers at which the fate of the dismembered Turkish Empire would be considered; they knew that the Balfour Declaration would then come up for inclusion in the disposition of Palestine; from being a statement of policy it would be converted—if Zionist hopes were realized —into the substance of an international agreement. And they hoped by their demonstration of force to prevent this con-summation.

I decided that I must return to Europe immediately, to see what could be done. With me travelled Alexander Aaronson (brother of Aaron Aaronson, the discoverer of wild wheat, who had been killed the year before in the London–Paris plane) and Mr. Emanuel Mohl, the representative in Palestine of the American Zionists. We were given a police escort as far as Egypt, and reached Cairo the evening of the same day. We went to the Hotel Continental, where I usually stayed, to dis-cover that a big dance was in progress, and I was painfully surprised to note that a considerable proportion of the guests seemed to be drawn from the Egyptian-Jewish community. A whole world lay between the Jerusalem I had left that morning and the ballroom of the Continental. Disheartened, I went straight to my room and, though the journalists got to work on me soon enough, refused to see anybody. There was only one person I wanted to see, and that was Allenby, and after seeing him I would leave at the earliest possible moment.

I notified Allenby of my presence the next morning, and he invited me to lunch. His first words when we met were: 'I'm afraid you're going to say: "I told you so!"' I answered that I had no intention of saying anything of the sort, but I wanted him to know that we intended to go on with our work, and at a quicker pace than hitherto, because I believed that if we had, say, four hundred thousand Jews in Palestine instead of a miserable fifty thousand, such things would be less likely to happen. (Not entirely accurate as prophecy, I fear, but that was how it looked to me at the time.) Allenby asked what he could do. 'I suppose you would like us to clear out!' I said:

L

'On the contrary! I very much hope that at San Remo it will
at last be definitely decided that the British are to have the
Palestine Mandate, and that a more solid régime will then be
established. I would like to see a civil administration in
Palestine as soon as possible, as I don't think the soldiers
understand what are the problems involved, or how to approach
them.' He pressed his point: 'You don't seem to have much
faith in the military administration.' I said: 'That's putting it
mildly—in fact, I have none whatsoever! The sooner they
leave the better for everyone concerned!'

He took it good-humouredly—one could always talk to
Allenby. The subject was dropped and we turned to future
plans for immigration, land purchase and other practical
matters. He was sceptical; like most of his officers, he did not
really think we could make anything out of this sandy, marshy,
derelict country, though he certainly had far more imagination
than any of his subordinates. I knew it was no use arguing;
only time could show. As I was leaving, he said: 'You are
going to San Remo; can I do anything for you?' I said I would
like a letter from him to Lloyd George, to facilitate my placing
our problems before him. He agreed at once—and the letter
consisted of two sentences: the first saying that he did *not*
share Dr. Weizmann's opinion of his administration, and the
second that he did agree with his practical proposals and would
be most grateful for anything Mr. Lloyd George could do to
further them!

I carried with me another letter—from Colonel Meinertzhagen—describing the pogrom and the period leading up to it,
and stressing the blindness (real or wilfully induced) of the
administration which had refused to see the danger after their
attention had been repeatedly called to it.

As we travelled slowly towards Italy I tried to find an answer
to a question which was to occupy me for the remainder of my
life: Why, from the very word go, should we have had to face
the hostility, or at best the frosty neutrality, of Britain's representatives on the spot? The Home Government at this time was
very friendly, even enthusiastic, about the Jewish National
Home policy. Enlightened British public opinion regarded the
Balfour Declaration—and later the Mandate—as important
and creditable achievements of the peace settlement. The

'misdemeanours' of which we were later accused, and which were the basis of arguments against us, were still in the future: we had bought no land to speak of, hence no 'displaced Arabs' argument; we had brought in few immigrants—hence no 'overcrowding' argument—and Palestine was officially described as seriously underpopulated anyhow; nobody had had any experience with us on which to base praise or blame. Why, then, were we damned in advance in the eyes of the official hierarchy? And why was it an almost universal rule that such administrators as came out favourably inclined turned against us in a few months? Why, for that matter, was it later a completely invariable rule that politicians who were enthusiastically for the Jewish Homeland during election forgot about it completely if they were returned to office? I shall have more to say on this point but, to pose the question at its starkest, I shall quote here a letter which General Louis Bols, whom Allenby left behind him as military administrator, wrote to his chief on December 21, 1919:

DEAR GENERAL

I am sending you this by Dr. Weizmann. He has been out here a couple of months and has done much good work in dealing with all matters in a quiet, impartial way. I think there is little doubt that antagonism to Zionism has been reduced by his action, and my view, after a month as Chief Administrator, is that there will be no serious difficulty in introducing a large number of Jews into the country provided it is done without ostentation. There are a few agitators and of course their cry for an undivided Syria will continue.

The country is in need of development quickly in order to make the people content. . . . The moment the Mandate is given we should be ready to produce a big loan, part of which should be subscribed by the inhabitants. I want Sir Herbert Samuel here for advice on this matter. . . .

With such a loan, say ten or twenty millions, I feel certain I can develop the country quickly and make it pay, and gradually the population should increase from the present 900,000 to $2\frac{1}{2}$ million. There is plenty of room for this. The Jordan Valley should hold a million instead of its present 1,000. . . .

I hope that:

(1) You will send Weizmann back soon.

(2) You will send Sir H. Samuel for a visit.

(3) You will send me a big financial fellow.

(4) Consider the plans for a loan.

If this is done I can promise you a country of milk and honey in ten years, and I can promise you will not be bothered by anti-Zion difficulties. . . .

Sincerely yours,

L. J. BOLS

It was under General Bols's administration, and in the circumstances already described, that the pogrom took place in Jerusalem less than four months later.

We dawdled northward from Brindisi in constant expectation of finding the line cut after the next station, for the Italian railways were in the throes of a general strike. Eventually we reached Rome, and thence San Remo—tired, grimy, hungry, but generally intact.

In the hall of the Hotel Royal I found Mr. Philip Kerr, then one of Mr. Lloyd George's secretaries; and my mood was such that I started in on him straight away with congratulations on the first pogrom under the British flag. (Looking back, I am more than a little sorry for Kerr at that moment; he was a good deal taken aback!) I gave him Allenby's letter and asked for an early appointment with the Prime Minister. In a quiet corner of the lounge there sat, while we talked, Sir Herbert Samuel and Mr. Sokolow, both exquisitely groomed, very calm and collected, absolutely undisturbed. I was very conscious of the contrast we presented, in appearance, background, manner and, above all, frame of mind. So apparently, was Kerr, my personal friend of many years, for he said, glancing towards them: 'When you look a little more like those two, I shall be pleased to fix an appointment for you!' There was much wisdom in that suggestion, though at the time I dismissed it as unwarrantably frivolous.

A week or so passed in Sam Remo while we waited for the Conference to make up its mind about Palestine. As it was almost the last item on the agenda we had little to do except gaze at the sea and discuss things among ourselves. There was always the uneasy feeling that the recent events in Palestine might bring some revision of policy, but Mr. Balfour assured me that they were regarded as without importance, and would certainly not affect policy, which had been definitely set. I was glad to hear that this view was shared by Lord Curzon, who was known to be no particular friend of ours. One of the first things mooted in those days in the corridors of the Conference was the suggestion that Herbert Samuel should be our first High Commissioner in Palestine. Samuel himself was willing, Mr. Lloyd George and Mr. Balfour both approved. It was clear that no one had been put off by the incidents in Palestine; the instigators of the pogrom had failed in their main purpose.

The Conference dragged on interminably, and the decision about the Palestine Mandate was not taken until the last few hours. These found me nervously pacing the hall of the Royal Hotel, waiting for the delegates to emerge from the Council chamber. Suddenly I caught sight of Mr. Balfour, waving impatiently to someone in the distance. I went up to him and asked if he was waiting for the delegates. 'Oh, no,' he answered calmly. 'My tennis partners. They're very late!'

At long last the gentlemen came out, and I made for Philip Kerr and the Prime Minister, both of whom proceeded to congratulate me warmly on the result of the meeting: the confirmation of the Balfour Declaration and the decision to give the Mandate to Great Britain. Mr. Lloyd George was particularly kind, telling me that we now had a very great opportunity and must show what good use we could make of it. He said: 'You have no time to waste. Today the world is like the Baltic before a frost. For the moment it is still in motion. But if it gets set, you will have to batter your heads against the ice blocks and wait for a second thaw.'

Everyone was kind at San Remo, including Lord Curzon, whose attitude I particularly appreciated because I knew him to be far from enthusiastic about the National Home idea. But he was entirely loyal to the policy adopted, and meant to stand by the declaration—as he did, later on, when he became Foreign Secretary.

Even the Arab delegations seemed happy about it all! Anybody entering the dining-room of the Royal that evening would have found the Jewish and Arab delegations seated together at a really festive board, congratulating each other under the benevolent paternal gaze of the British delegation at a neighbouring table. The only man to ignore the whole business was Philip Sassoon, another of Lloyd George's secretaries—and, as it happens, the only Jewish member of the British delegation.

The violence of the shock which the Jerusalem pogrom had created in the Jewish world, the extent of the fear that a revision of the Palestine policy might ensue, could be gauged from the reaction to the San Remo decision. Representatives of the Genoa Jewish community came over the next day to congratulate us, and we soon learned, by cable and from the press, of the general enthusiasm which the decision aroused everywhere. I was deeply moved when, arriving a few days later at Victoria Station in London, I was met by representatives of the community bearing the Torah—the Scroll of the Law.

To complete the pattern of this chapter, in which I am attempting to indicate the triple field of force which constituted my Zionist work, I shall speak briefly of the first large contact with America, which took place early in July of that year; not, however, in a visit to America—that was to come soon after— but through the arrival in London of a large American delegation to the Zionist Annual Conference. Seven years had passed since the last fully representative gathering of world Zionists— the eleventh Congress, held in 1913. Justice Brandeis headed the American delegation, and there at once became manifest those divergences between the American leaders and ourselves —and within the American delegation, too—of which I have spoken in the last chapter.

With a number of my European colleagues I felt that we should lose no time in approaching the great Jewish organizations which might wish to share in the practical work in Palestine, with a view to the creation of some kind of Jewish council. This was the idea which eventually developed into the Jewish Agency. To the American leaders—for convenience I shall, in this connection, speak hereafter of the Brandeis group —it seemed unnecessary to have any kind of double organization: it was their view that people who wished to co-operate in the work of rebuilding the Jewish National Home could join the Zionist Organization.

This was not merely a difference in formal approach; it represented a real cleavage. The Brandeis group envisaged the Zionist Organization as henceforth a purely economic body.

Since, in their view, it had lost its political character by having fulfilled its political function, there was no longer any reason why non-Zionists who were prepared to help in the economic building up of Palestine, but who were not prepared to subscribe to political Zionism, should refuse to become members. But our reason for wishing to keep the Zionist Organization in being as a separate body was precisely the conviction that the political work was far from finished; the Balfour Declaration and the San Remo decision were the beginning of a new era in the political struggle, and the Zionist Organization was our instrument of political action. There were numbers of Jewish organizations and individuals which, with all their readiness to lend a hand in the practical work in Palestine, insisted that they would not be implicated in any of our political difficulties. Their attitude might be illogical, but there it was, and it had to be reckoned with. The question was, then, whether a new organization should be formed for the accommodation of the non-Zionists, or whether the Zionist Organization should be completely reorientated; should, in fact, give up completely its political character.

A complicated and sometimes acrimonious discussion developed round this subject; the proposal of the Brandeis group was defeated by a substantial majority.

A second controversial point was the budget. The European group set this at something in the neighbourhood of two million pounds a year, to which they had to admit that they themselves could contribute very little. The Americans generally—and not only the Brandeis group—were shocked by this 'astronomical' figure, and asserted they could not guarantee more than one hundred thousand pounds a year. Mr. Brandeis contended that this was the utmost that could be got from American Jewry—and this at a time when it was well known that American Jews had acquired and were acquiring considerable wealth.

I found myself explaining that we could not possibly adopt a budget of that order; it was not merely inadequate to the task which faced us, it was derisory: it would damn us in the eyes of friends and enemies alike. I added that if this was all he could find in America, I should have to come over and try for myself.

I doubt if Justice Brandeis ever quite forgave me for that challenge. Eventually the Conference reached agreement with a group of the American delegation—this was the group which was afterwards to lead in the struggle against the Brandeis régime —headed by Louis Lipsky, which invited me to come over to America at the earliest opportunity after my return from Palestine, and to see for myself what could and what could not be done.

I found in Lipsky an unusual combination; he was perhaps the leading theoretician among the American Zionists, but he possessed a remarkable understanding of the European movement. Of him, too, I can say that, although for long periods we did not communicate with each other, we almost invariably reached the same conclusions on important problems. During the period of the construction of the Jewish Agency he was under constant attack by the non-Zionists. When they met him, they discovered in him a man of first-rate mind, of charm and integrity. He is still the pillar of Zionism in America, but like myself he is now trying to put some distance between himself and the daily rough and tumble of the movement. His value as an elder statesman will still be great for many years.

To return to the London Conference: towards its close it elected officers to conduct the affairs of the movement until the first post-war Congress should be able to meet; Justice Brandeis became Honorary President, I became President of the Organization, and Mr. Sokolow became chairman of the Executive. Together with the Action Committee which was then elected, and which met in July, we appointed as departmental heads Mr. Ussishkin, Mr. Julius Simon (representing America) and Mr. Nehemiah de Lieme, of Holland. The Presidium and the departmental heads constituted the Executive.

Thus the movement had once more a constituted, if provisional, governing body, and incidentally I acquired, for the first time, some formal authority. During the greater part of the negotiations in London I had had none whatsoever, though since early in 1917 I had been President of the English Zionist Federation. That, however, was only one of the smaller constituent bodies of the Zionist Congress; its importance had been due only to the fact that it had been at the centre of action when the constituted authorities of the movement—those elected by the pre-war Congress—could not even be consulted. It will be remembered that we had, in fact, severed all connection with the 'Copenhagen Bureau' at an early stage in the war.

One of the highlights of the Conference—and, I must add, one of its few attractive features—was a great public meeting held at the Albert Hall under the chairmanship of Lord Rothschild. This was, I think, the only occasion on which Lord Balfour addressed a great Jewish gathering in England. I dined with him before the meeting at 4 Carlton Gardens, and as we drove from there to the Albert Hall, Lord Balfour was struck by the great crowds of Jews making their way to the West End. In his usual vague manner he asked me: 'But who *are* all these people?' I reminded him of what I had told him in 1906, that there were Zionist Jews enough to pave the streets of Russia and Poland: 'These are a few—a very few—of them!'

When the Conference finally dispersed, my wife and I went for a short rest to Switzerland, returning to London again, via Paris, in the autumn. My thoughts were again turning West, to the American visit which, I was beginning to feel, I had undertaken rather lightheartedly at the Conference. Herbert Samuel's departure for Palestine, as its first High Commissioner, had marked the close of an important chapter in 'political Zionism,' and opened the door, as we then thought, to a great expansion of Jewish effort in Palestine. But the portent of the Annual Conference remained an ominous cloud on the horizon, and I was haunted by the fear that American Jewry would fail to rise to the occasion.

I felt it best to arm myself, as it were, with another visit to Palestine. This time I went with Sir Alfred Mond. We spent January and part of February touring the country, and Sir Alfred showed himself—hard-headed man of affairs that we all took him to be—profoundly susceptible to the more romantic aspects of the work. I remember still the shock of astonishment which went through me when, as we stood watching a group of *chalutzim* breaking stones for the road between Petach Tikvah and Jaffa, I observed how very close he was to tears. They looked to him, those children of the ghetto, altogether too frail and too studious for the job they had in hand. Perhaps he had just realized that these young men and women were building themselves, as well as the road.

Early in March I was back in London, preparing for my first contact with the New World.

L*

CHAPTER XXIV

CLEVELAND AND CARLSBAD

My First Visit to America—Its Purpose—Albert Einstein Joins Our Delegation—New York's Reception of Us—The Deeper Meaning of the Split in American Zionism, 1921—'Private Initiative' versus 'National Funds'—'Washington versus Pinsk'—Break with the Brandeis Group—Cleveland Convention—Fund Campaigning in America—Zionist Educational Work—The Carlsbad Congress—Disappointments in Palestine—Larger Immigration and Colonization Begin—Criticism of our 'Fancy Experiments'—Tug of War between City and Soil

I HAVE so far indicated only the beginning of the divergence between the Brandeis group on the one hand and the remainder of American Zionism, allied with European Zionism, on the other. It had to do with much more than programme and method; its source was a deeper divergence in what might almost be called folkways. It reached into social and historic as well as economic and political concepts; it was connected with the organic interpretation of Zionism. It cannot be described in abstract terms, and its nature will reveal itself gradually as the narrative unfolds.

Some suspicion of this truth was already present in my mind when I made my preparations for the trip to America—for me a *terra incognita*. Shmarya Levin was there, of course; he had been caught by the war and held in the country for four years, during which time he had carried on a great educational campaign among Zionists and Jews at large. His work in those early years was to bear fruit for an entire generation, and I knew that at the time of my first visit in 1921 he was doing everything possible to prepare the ground for us. But I still had misgivings about the magnitude of the task before me, and wished to go armed with as much support as I could find.

The immediate purposes of the trip were two: first to found the American *Keren Hayesod* (Palestine Foundation Fund), as one of the two main instruments of the rebuilding of the Homeland—the other, the Jewish National Fund, I have already described; second, to awaken American interest in the Hebrew University. It seemed to us that the foundation stones had been standing alone on Mount Scopus for quite long enough, and now that we had a civil administration under Herbert Samuel it was time to get on with the job of actually establishing the University. At the back of my mind there was also the intention of taking some soundings as to the prospects of establishing some sort of Jewish council (or agency) with the co-operation of some of the important Jewish organizations engaged in public welfare work.

It was an ambitious programme—more so than I quite realized. But I set about the creation of as strong a delegation as possible. From among my colleagues I enlisted Mr. Ussishkin and Dr. Ben-Zion Mossinsohn, director of the Herzliah Gymnasium in Tel Aviv. I also approached Professor Albert Einstein, with special reference to the Hebrew University, and to my great delight found him ready to help. He brought with him his secretary, Simon Ginsburg, son of Achad Ha-am; my wife and I joined them at Plymouth, to continue the journey on a Dutch boat. Leonard Stein, just released from the army, and recently returned from Palestine, where he had been acting as Military Governor of Safed, came along as my personal assistant. So we were quite a party on the boat.

I remember that we arrived in New York Harbour about noon on Saturday, April 2, 1921, altogether unaware of the extraordinary reception that awaited us. Some half-dozen boats carrying friends and journalists came out to meet us, and for the whole of that afternoon we were subjected to an endless series of gruelling if well-meant interviews. Since it was the Sabbath, we could not land until the onset of evening; we simply had 'to take it.' Einstein was, of course, the chief target; his name was something of a portent in those days, and the journalists were eager to get from him a bright, popular paragraph on the theory of relativity. When they failed in this, they invariably turned to me, saying, 'But you're a scientist, too, Dr. Weizmann.' In the end, in sheer desperation we took refuge in an inconspicuous cabin and waited till it was time to go ashore.

We intended, of course, to proceed straight to our hotel,

settle down, and begin planning our work. We had reckoned
—literally—without our host, which was, or seemed to be, the
whole of New York Jewry. Long before the afternoon ended,
delegations began to assemble on the quay and even on the
docks. Pious Jews in their thousands came on foot all the way
from Brooklyn and the Bronx to welcome us. Then the cars
arrived, all of them beflagged. Every car had its horn and every
horn was put in action. By the time we reached the gangway
the area about the quays was a pandemonium of people, cars
and mounted police. The car which we had thought would
transport us quickly and quietly to our hotel fell in at the end of
an enormous procession which wound its way through the entire
Jewish section of New York. We reached the Commodore at
about eleven-thirty, tired, hungry, thirsty and completely
dazed. The spacious hall of the hotel was packed with another
enthusiastic throng; we had to listen to several speeches of
welcome, and I remember making some sort of reply. It was
long after midnight when we found our rooms.

I was the more anxious to come to grips with my task because
I knew that this magnificent popular reception was only one
part of the story. Before leaving the ship I had received a
printed memorandum brought to me by Judge Julian Mack, in
which the Brandeis group, which constituted the American
Zionist administration, expounded their views and set forth
the conditions on which they would be prepared to support my
mission. The main points dealt with their conception of the new
character of the Zionist Organization and with the economics
of the movement. Henceforth world Zionism was to consist of
strong local federations, so that the old unity which had been
the background of the authority of our Congresses should be
replaced merely by co-ordination. In this there was a reflection of the deeper—and less conscious, therefore less overtly
formulated—feelings of the Brandeis group about the organic
unity of world Jewry. To us who had grown up since childhood
in the movement, Zionism was the precipitation into organized
form of the survival forces of the Jewish people; Zionism was
in a sense Jewishness itself, set in motion for the re-creation of a
Jewish Homeland. The World Zionist Organization, the Congresses, were not just *ad hoc* instruments; they were the expression of the unity of the Jewish people. The propositions of the

Brandeis group, dealing ostensibly with merely formal matters, with organizational instrumental rearrangements, actually reflected a denial of Jewish nationalism; they made of Zionism simply a sociological plan—and not a good one, as I shall show—instead of the folk renaissance that it was. And then there was the attitude of the Brandeis group on the national funds. It became clear that the opposition to the attempt to raise a large budget really did not spring from a conviction that large sums could not be obtained: the Brandeis group stood for emphasis on 'private investment' and 'individual project' methods. My colleagues and I knew that 'private initiative' would not be feasible to any significant extent before the Jewish people, in its corporate, national capacity, had made the financial effort which would create the foundations of the Homeland.

What we had here was a revival, in a new form and a new country, of the old cleavage between 'East' and 'West,' in Zionism and Jewry; and the popular slogan called it, in fact, 'Washington v. Pinsk,' a convenient double allusion to Brandeis and myself, and also to the larger ideological implication.

There was, in fact, a deep gulf; but I was determined to do my utmost towards finding a compromise solution. The memorandum presented me by Judge Mack, as a condition for the co-operation with me of the Zionist Organization of America, I could not accept. It was in the nature of an ultimatum. Its formal provisions dealt with matters on which only the World Zionist Congress could speak authoritatively; I could not agree to changes which I, as President of the World Zionist Organization, had not been empowered to introduce. And still I hoped that some discreet middle road would be found in practice, and that we would face the world as a united group. I was all the time thinking of the people in Palestine whose hopes were centred on this trip, and of the new High Commissioner, so anxious to see large-scale colonization undertaken in the country. We *had* to have maximum results.

We felt—and the event proved us right—that the great masses of American Zionists resented the attitude of their leaders, but the leaders were powerful, and I foresaw that it would be difficult to do anything substantial without their co-operation. For weeks we discussed the possibility of compromise—greatly assisted by Leonard Stein's conciliatory disposition and drafting abilities. We knew he would go to the utmost limit of possible concession, and that if it were possible to find a 'formula' he would find it. On the other hand, there was Ussishkin, who was not prepared to yield a jot on the budget, or on the constitution and functions of the *Keren Hayesod*; at the other end, the Brandeis group was not going to permit us to proclaim the *Keren Hayesod* as a Zionist instrument, and to raise funds for it in America, without an acceptance of the terms of the memorandum.

It was an unhappy situation, with passions mounting on both sides and things being said which added nothing to the substance of the discussion. A whispering campaign was launched against the Executive in Jerusalem, which was accused of consisting of men completely incapable of handling large sums of money: great idealists, of course, but utterly impractical, and given to 'commingling of funds.' And neither they (the members of the Palestine Executive) nor we (the anti-Brandeisists) had any notion of 'American standards'—whatever that might mean. Enough poison was put in circulation to render the collection of any substantial sum of money extremely difficult.

As time went on the ideological controversy also crystallized into a conflict between the mass of American Zionism and a few privileged 'Western' Jews who occupied high positions in American society. There was also implied a struggle for the control of the fate of Palestine, whether it should belong to 'America' or 'Europe'—a struggle which in turn implied a fatal breach in the unity of world Jewry. All this was further complicated by the fact that some non-Zionist American Jews whom I was intensely anxious to win over for the practical work in Palestine (e.g. Mr. Louis Marshall and his friends) disliked the Brandeis group. Marshall himself, as will be seen, was no fanatical opponent of Zionism, and often acted as our disinterested adviser. Another, darker complication developed during our stay in America—the bitter Jaffa outbreak of May 1921, which led Herbert Samuel to suspend immigration temporarily. Everything during those days pointed to the urgent necessity of proceeding with our work and of getting a firm foothold for the Jewish National Home.

All our endeavours to find a compromise formula led to nothing. Samuel Untermyer, the brilliant lawyer and arbitrator, did his best to find a middle ground for us, but in vain. In the end we were compelled to break off relations with the Brandeis group, and I had to issue a statement to the American Jewish public, that, by virtue of the decision of the last Zionist Conference, and of the authority vested in me as President of the World Zionist Organization, I declared the *Keren Hayesod* to be established in the United States. This action provoked violent protest from the other side, mingled with some abuse—all of it played up by the general press, so that the public at large was fully aware of our dissensions. So, of course, was the British Embassy. I remember going to see Sir Eric Geddes in Washington one morning when one of our opponents' pronouncements had appeared in the papers, and he remarked that I had rather placed myself in the position of President Wilson when he appealed to the Italian people over the heads of their constituted Government; he hoped I would not meet with the same fate! I said that my relations with the American Jewish community were, after all, a good deal more organic than Wilson's with the Italians, and I therefore hoped to avoid his failure.

My hope was vindicated when we underwent our formal trial of strength with the Brandeis group. At the twenty-fourth Convention of the Zionist Organization of America—the famous 'Cleveland Convention'—of June 1921, the mass of the American Zionists proved that they understood thoroughly the nature of the issues. The fact was that the American leaders did not want the *Keren Hayesod*, nor did they really want to see the Zionist Organization a world organization. They regarded our political work as ended—this despite the shock of the May riots in Palestine, and Samuel's suspension of immigration— and they had their own views as to the economic building up of the country. All my detailed reports to the American leaders about the attitude of the British administration in Palestine, and about the need for mass colonization, failed to move them. They refused to see the portents, and they insisted that the best plan would be for every separate Zionist federation—the German, the Austrian, the Polish—to undertake some specific task in Palestine, the Executive of the World Zionist Organization having nothing to do but 'co-ordinate' the work. This proposal would have meant, in effect, the reduction of the whole World

Zionist Organization to the status of a technical bureau with
doubtful authority; and the Zionist Congress, which was the
forum of world Zionism, its deliberative and legislative body,
expressing the will and the aspirations of world Jewry, would —
if it did not fall into complete desuetude—become a conference
of 'experts.'

All this was threshed out in Cleveland, in an atmosphere
which I could not re-create even if I wanted to. I attended the
Convention with the rest of the European delegation, but did
not think it proper to take part in the proceedings. The issue was
fought out between the American Zionists: on the one side the
nationally known figures of Judge Mack, Professor Felix Frankfurter, Stephen S. Wise; on the other the relatively obscure but
thoroughly representative figures like Louis Lipsky, Abraham
Goldberg and Morris Rothenberg. The result was that the
administration was defeated by an overwhelming majority. I
am afraid that they did not prove very good losers, for the
whole Brandeis group resigned from the Executive of the
American Organization. Nor did they remain neutral; most of
them entered into active and formidable opposition against our
work. There is little doubt that our efforts in the first few years
after Cleveland—crucial years for Palestine—would have been
much more productive if not for the implacable hostility of most
of our former colleagues.

We declared the *Keren Hayesod* officially established in
America. Samuel Untermyer became its first President, and
the job of organizing and popularizing the fund began. We
divided the work among us as far as possible—I am speaking
now of the European delegation—but I am afraid the lion's
share of it fell on my shoulders; first, because I spoke both
English and Yiddish, while the others, Ussishkin, Mossinsohn and Shmarya Levin, though excellent Yiddish speakers—
Shmarya was, as I have already said, an orator of the very first
order—knew but little English at this time; second, because I
was urged to take the lead. Thus I found myself committed to
visiting most of the principal American Jewish centres.

To anyone who has not actually been through it, it is difficult to convey any idea of what this experience meant. It must
not be confused with the round of a lecturer, and not even with
that of a political campaigner; I was, if you like, both of these,

but I was also out to raise large sums of money. Besides, it was my first visit to the States, and I was completely ignorant of the terrain; I did not know what had to be done or—more important—what could safely be omitted. A typical day's 'stand' in American towns worked out something like this:

One arrived by an early train, to be met at the station by a host of enthusiasts in cars, who formed a sort of guard of honour to escort one through the streets of a still half-sleeping town. All advance requests for the omission of this part of the proceedings, all suggestions that it would be helpful and healthful to have an hour or two to oneself on arrival after a night on a train, were completely ignored; one was repeatedly assured that the parade was an essential part of the publicity campaign—indispensable advertisement of coming events. So one submitted, in order not to upset the elaborate arrangements in which the local workers had taken so much pride.

From the station one proceeded to the hotel or to the city hall, to breakfast with anywhere between twenty-five to fifty local notables, including, usually, the mayor. One listened and replied to speeches of welcome. By the time this was over, it would be about ten o'clock, and the cameramen and reporters would be ready, all looking for some particularly sensational pose or statement. No discouragement could put them off. For some unfathomable reason they always billed me as the inventor of T.N.T. It was in vain that I systematically and repeatedly denied any connection with, or interest in, T.N.T. The initials seemed to exercise a peculiar fascination over journalists: and I suppose high explosive is always news.

One was lucky to be through with the press by eleven or eleven-thirty, and to find time to sneak up to one's room for a bath and change before the formal luncheon, usually timed for twelve-thirty, and seldom starting less than an hour late. This was a long, gruelling affair of many courses and speeches, and the arrangement always was that the guest of honour should speak last, lest the public should be tempted to leave, thus depriving some of the other speakers of their audience. After this performance one was permitted an hour or so of rest, though even this was seldom without its interruptions.

In the late afternoon came the meeting for the local workers, tea—and more speeches; then there was dinner, very like lunch, only more so, and the day usually concluded, officially, with a mass meeting at the town hall or some similar building. From the mass meeting one was escorted by friends and well-wishers to the train, to retreat, with a sigh of relief, into one's sleeper, and one awoke the next morning in the next city on the list, to begin the whole performance all over again.

This went on with astounding regularity for weeks and months, with only minor variations. If I stayed more than a day in any town, I might indeed manage to get a little leisure. Then the local leader was sure to place his car at my disposal 'to drive around a bit and see the sights.' Being inexperienced, I used to accept, in the earlier days, with alacrity. But when the car arrived it usually contained three or four occupants, all grimly determined to entertain me, or to be entertained by me, as long as the drive lasted. And I had hoped for a little blessed solitude, and fresh air!

Intervals between public functions were usually filled in with private talks with 'big donors' (a big donor was anyone whose contribution might be expected to reach about five thousand dollars). Often, alas, the 'prospect' turned out to be a gentleman the indefiniteness of whose knowledge about Palestine was exceeded only by the extreme definiteness of his views about it. I would have to listen then to strange versions of the criticisms levelled at us by the Brandeis group, or by non-Zionists and anti-Zionists, to crank schemes for the overnight creation of a Jewish Homeland, to paternal practical advice from successful businessmen, all of which had to be received attentively and courteously.

They were good, kindly, well-intentioned people, some of them intelligent and informed Zionists, but my endurance was reaching its limit. I thought longingly of the ship that was to take us back to Europe. Yet even in Europe—though I did not know it yet—I was never to be free from the consequences of my work in the States. As soon as the summer invasion began, if I happened to be in London or Paris, I had to face the necessity of meeting the friends who had helped me in Boston or Baltimore or Chicago. It was important to show them every courtesy, lest they become offended and decide to take it out of me when I returned to America. It was not that I minded very much giving umbrage on my own account; but I learned that there were people who, having tried to see me in Europe and failed—I am sure through no fault of mine—went back to the States to cancel their pledges to the *Keren Hayesod*!

In the States a big donor would often make his contribution to the fund conditional on my accepting an invitation to lunch or dine at his house. Then I would have to face a large family gathering—three or four generations—talk, answer questions, listen to appeals and opinions, and watch my replies carefully, lest I inadvertently scare off a touchy prospect. I would sit through a lengthy meal and after it meet a select group of local celebrities, and again listen and answer till all hours of the night. Generally, I felt that I had fully earned that five thousand dollars.

On the whole the response of American Jewry was remarkably good, considering their unpreparedness for the burden thrust upon them, and the secession and active opposition of the Brandeis group. The work was vigorously continued after our departure, and the first year's income was about four times the five hundred thousand dollars which Mr. Brandeis had set as the maximum obtainable from the Jews of America, thus proving the tonic effect of setting a fairly high budget. But we still had nothing near the sum required by the programme of the Annual Conference. However, we could go ahead with some land purchase and with immigration and settlement. The first year or two after the foundation of the *Keren Hayesod* saw the founding of the Agricultural Mortgage Bank, an extremely important institution, the beginning of our payments on the Emek Jezreel purchase, and the founding of Nahalal, the first of our post-war settlements, which became the centre of our activity in the Emek, the draining of its swamps, the combating of malaria, and so on.

As the years passed, and my visits to America were repeated almost annually, a sort of tradition was established and a routine—a policeman's beat between Jerusalem and San Francisco. Gradually the *Keren Hayesod* took hold, became an acknowledged institution, until it was swallowed up in the United Palestine Appeal. The work grew easier, more profitable and more pleasant; visitors began to come to Palestine from America, contacts between the countries became frequent.

But there was something more to all this than political

propaganda and money-raising. All of us regarded our mission as, fundamentally, education in Zionism, both on its practical and on its theoretical side. On the practical side I sought to explain to American businessmen the reasons why their American experience did not always apply to the Palestinian scene. I said: 'When a pioneer comes into Palestine, he finds a deserted land, neglected for generations. The hills have lost their trees, the good soil has been washed into the valleys and carried to the sea. We must restore the soil of Palestine. We must have money to sink in Palestine, to reconstruct what has been destroyed. You will have to sweat and labour and give money on which you will not get any return, but which will be transformed into national wealth. When you drain the marshes, you get no returns, but you accumulate wealth for the generations to come. If you reduce the percentage of malaria from forty to ten, that is national wealth.'

And again: 'You cannot build up Nahalal and Nuris without national funds. The *chalutzim* are willing to miss meals twice a week. But cows must be fed, and you cannot feed a cow with speeches.'

How obvious it all seems now, how new it was then, and for years to come, and how difficult to get the lesson home. I shall show later what a fierce struggle developed in Zionism between what I considered premature emphasis on private enterprise and profits, and the laying of the national foundations. But there was needed, as the background to that understanding which I sought to instil in regard to practical matters, a feeling for the basic elements of the Jewish problem. I said to one meeting:

'Among the anti-Semites none is more interesting than the tender-hearted variety. Their anti-Semitism is always based on a compliment. They tell us: "You are the salt of the earth"— and there are Jews who feel themselves extraordinarily flattered. Yet I do not consider it a compliment to be called "the salt of the earth." The salt is used for someone else's food. It dissolves in that food. And salt is good only in small quantities. If there is too much salt in the food you throw out the food and the salt with it. That is to say, certain countries can digest a certain number of Jews; once that number has been passed, something drastic must happen: the Jews must go.

'They call us not only salt, but leaven. The Jews are not only the salt of the earth, but also a valuable ferment. They produce extraordinary ideas. They provide initiative, energy; they start things. But this compliment, too, is of a doubtful sort. There is a very fine difference between a ferment and a parasite. If the ferment is increased by ever so little beyond a certain point, it becomes a parasitical growth. So that those who wish to be polite call us "ferments"; others, less polite, and less scientific, prefer to call us "parasites."'

I explained part of the reason for the status of the Jew with a simple simile: 'You will always be treated as a guest if you, too, can play the host. The only man who is invited to dinner is the man who can have dinner at home if he likes. Switzerland is a small country, and there are more Swiss outside of Switzerland than in it. But there is no such thing as anti-Swiss sentiment in the sense that there is anti-Jewish sentiment. The Swiss has a home of his own, to which he can retreat, to which he can invite others. And it does not matter how small your home is, as long as it is your home. If you want your position to be secure elsewhere, you must have a portion of Jewry which is at home, in its own country. If you want the safety of equality in other universities, you must have a university of your own. The university in Jerusalem will affect your status here: professors from Jerusalem will be able to come to Harvard, and professors from Harvard to Jerusalem.' This is, in fact, what has happened.

I sought to bring inspiration to them from the past. I said: 'We are reproached by the whole world. We are told that we are dealers in old clothes, junk. We are perhaps the sons of dealers in old clothes, but we are the grandsons of Prophets. Think of the grandsons, and not of the sons.'

It was really moving, the way they listened and took the words to heart. Despite the exhaustion and the discomfort and the occasional tedium, I felt an immense privilege in the work. I told them once: 'I cannot think of any man with whom I would change positions. Here I am, without police, without an army, without a navy, carrying out with a group of fellow-workers a proposition which is really unheard of: trying to build up a country which has been waste two thousand years, with a people which has been waste two thousand years, at a time when one-half of that people, perhaps the best half, has been broken up by a terrible war. And here, at midnight, you are sitting, five or six thousand miles away from Palestine, a country which many of you may never see, and you are waiting to hear me speak about that country. And you know very well that you will probably have to pay for it. It is extraordinary. I defy anyone, Jew or gentile, to show me a proposition like it.'

From my first visit to America I went almost directly to the Congress in Carlsbad, the first since 1913 to bring together representatives of Zionists from all over the world.

Herbert Samuel had been High Commissioner for about a year, but there was already noticeable, in the Congress discussions, the beginnings of the disappointment, and even bitterness, which his régime was to inspire. I myself felt that he had not had a real chance yet, but three things had happened which gave rise to uneasiness.

First there had been his handling of the riots of May 1921, which I have already mentioned. Desirous of starting his work as peaceably as possible, Samuel's reaction to the riots had been to stop immigration, and this decision had been announced at a gathering of Arab notables in Ramleh. Both the decision and the form of its announcement came as a severe shock to Jews everywhere. Immigrants already within sight of the shores of Palestine were not allowed to land. Samuel disregarded the protests of Dr. Eder, and the interdict stood.

Samuel had also amnestied the two principal instigators of the Jaffa and Jerusalem pogroms, and it was largely due to him that Haj Amin el Husseini later became head of the Moslem Supreme Council and Mufti of Jerusalem (or Grand Mufti), with very considerable powers, and control over large funds—and with results too well known to need mention. In spite of the proverb, poachers turned gamekeepers are not always a success. The Arabs soon discovered that the High Commissioner's deep desire for peace made him susceptible to intimidation, and this discovery led to the third of what we regarded as Samuel's mistakes.

An Arab lawyer in Haifa, Wadi Bustani by name, had succeeded in working up a widespread agitation on behalf of certain Bedouin who had frequented the State lands in the Beisan area. They laid claim, through Bustani, to a large tract of irrigable Government land—about four hundred thousand dunams (one hundred thousand acres); and eventually, after a good deal of argument, their demands were granted, and the land was handed over to them for a nominal fee. One of the most important and most potentially fertile districts of Palestine (and one of the very few such districts which were 'State lands') was thus condemned from the outset to stagnation and sterility, and important water resources which could fertilize much larger areas still run to waste today because of the 'Beisan Agreement.' Except for such portions as the Jews have been able to buy piecemeal from individual Arab beneficiaries, the Beisan lands are still, in fact, not under plough. I believe that Samuel himself later realized that the claims put forward through Bustani had no legal foundation; and the British representative who appeared before the Mandates Commission in 1926 could not defend the action on economic grounds; but all this hindsight did not help us to cultivate the Beisan Valley. We, on the other hand, had to struggle for years, and pay heavily, in order to obtain any share at all in the State lands, and then it was only some seventy-five or eighty thousand dunams, much of it consisting of the sand dunes of Rishon-le-Zion—valueless unless large sums are sunk in their amelioration.

The pogrom, the suspended immigration and the lost State lands were on the record at the preliminary meeting of the Action Committee in Prague. But what depressed me more than these was my own feeling of helplessness in the face of the lack of understanding which seemed to prevail, even among responsible Zionists. For instance, the Action Committee adopted a budget of seventeen million five hundred thousand dollars for the coming year, to cover considerable acquisitions of land and the settlement of large numbers of immigrants, as well as of some who had come to Palestine before the war and were still awaiting settlement. But the compilers of this budget unfortunately failed to indicate where the money was to be found. I knew that no such sum was in sight; in the conditions of that time it could not be produced even by superhuman effort. European Jewries had just not got the money; American Jewry had yet to be educated to the assumption of so great a responsibility. True, it was spending a great deal on the relief of distressed Jewish communities in Europe, but there was no sign yet of any readiness to divert even a part of these vast sums to the resettlement of European Jews in Palestine. The Action Committee budget was, of course, severely criticized in Congress as unreal, and eventually cut down to fifteen or twenty per cent of the original figure. But this naturally gave rise to deep disappointment in the ranks of the movement, and we should have known better than to allow such fantastic figures to be dangled before the eyes of our constituents.

The Congress did well to bring the movement down to earth, to some appreciation of the hard facts, and to set our feet on the only path that could lead to success—the path of slow, laborious and methodical work in Palestine. It formally decided to establish the settlements of Nahalal, Kfar Yechezkiel, Ain Harod and Tel Yosef, thus beginning the conquest of the land —and that was worth more than all the rest of the talk. I rejoiced in these decisions because I knew men who were ready and waiting to invade the malaria-infested Emek and establish themselves and their families there, to face all the risks and hardships of a pioneering life. I saw my duty for the next five or ten years very clearly; it was to help these people to make a success of their venture. For their success would be of greater political importance than any so-called 'political' concession which we might obtain, after heart-breaking negotiations from a reluctant Government.

The Congress had opened on a depressed note; it ended on a note of optimism. After all, immigration had begun, at the rate of something like ten thousand a year, and though this was not a very imposing figure it was not negligible either, considering the conditions in the country. We knew that a too rapid increase in this stream of immigration would lead to unemployment, of which there were faint but visible signs already on the horizon, and therefore the stream had to be stemmed and regulated.

But it was bringing with it the first *chalutzim*—that new and heartening phenomenon in Jewry. Keen, eager, intelligent, they had trained themselves to do any kind of physical work in Palestine; they were determined to let no one else perform the duties, however primitive and exacting, which attended the laying of the foundations of the National Home. They would build roads, drain marshes, dig wells, plant trees—and they faced all the physical dangers and hardships joyfully and unflinchingly. Of such were the young men and women I had watched, with Mond, breaking stones on the Tel Aviv road the previous year.

Much was heard before, during and after the Congress of the non-rentability of Jewish National Fund land. There was a good deal of criticism of the first co-operative settlements, which were just beginning their work. Again, I felt that time was too young to afford any basis for judgments; these infant enterprises should be given their chance. We faced the task of converting into peasant farmers an urbanized people, completely divorced from the soil for hundreds, if not thousands, of years, a people whose physical and intellectual equipment unfitted them for the hardships of an outdoor life in a barren land whose soil was exhausted by centuries of misrule and poor husbandry. Moreover, we had not the means to start our agricultural ventures properly, and our heavily cut budget made no provision for the inevitable percentage of failures which occurs in all colonizing work—such as, to take recent instances, the settlement of British soldiers in Canada or Australia. When we compared our results with those of the British Dominions (which had adequate finances, unlimited virgin soil, familiar climates, a friendly population speaking the same language as the immigrant—and no Arab problem) I think we had, even in those early days, no reason to be ashamed of the Jewish experiment.

Still, the Jews grumbled, and the non-Jews criticized mercilessly. British officials and Zionist visitors to Palestine returned to advise us to put an end to 'all these fancy experiments' in agriculture, and concentrate on building up industry and trade —in other words, take the line of least resistance, and relapse into the old Diaspora habit of creating towns to receive an urbanized immigration. I have already said something, and will have more to say, about my views on the subject of premature private enterprise. I resisted all this advice strenuously, and sometimes in my eagerness to defend my point of view I may have been less than just to the lower-middle-class people who came to settle in Jerusalem, Tel Aviv and Haifa, since they too were pioneers, in their own fashion. They built up hundreds of small industries, investing their small lifetime savings, brought with difficulty out of Poland or the Ukraine; and they too were building up the National Home of their people.

Even so, I still believe that the backbone of our work is and must always be agricultural colonization. It is in the village that the real soul of a people—its language, its poetry, its literature, its traditions—springs up from the intimate contact between man and soil. The towns do no more than 'process' the fruits of the villages.

So, for more than a quarter of a century now, it has been given to me to watch, with a deep and growing exultation, the steady development of our village life in Palestine. I have watched the Emek's marshes drying out, and gradually growing firm enough to support more and more clusters of red-roofed cottages, whose lights sparkle in the falling dusk like so many beacons on our long road home. The thought of those spreading clusters of lights in the dusk has been my reward for many weary months of travel and disappointment in the world outside.

CHAPTER XXV

THE STRUGGLE ABOUT THE MANDATE

Drafting the Mandate—'Historic Right' or 'Historical Connection'?—
Arabs and 'Diehards' Attack Us—The Haycraft Commission and Report
—Lord Northcliffe Turns on Us—Beaverbrook Joins the Assault—The
Arab Delegation in Rome, Paris and London—Counteraction—Italy and the
Vatican Have Complaints—'We Fear Your University'—The Remarkable
Italian Jewish Community—I am Mistaken for Lenin—Berlin and Walter
Rathenau—Parliament Debates the Mandate—The Churchill White Paper
—Transjordan Lopped Off—Our Own Shortcomings—The Stage Set for
Mandate Decision—Miracle from Spain—The Mandate is Unanimously
Ratified

B Y the autumn of 1921 I was back in London, having surveyed
the tasks confronting us in Palestine, in America and in Europe.
We were very conscious that though policy had, in principle,
been settled for some time past, the situation in Palestine was
almost bound to be uncertain and unsatisfactory as long as the
Mandate remained unratified by the League of Nations. The
ratification did not take place until July 1922, and in the interval
a good many unforeseen difficulties arose and had to be overcome—at the cost of numerous journeys between London,
Paris, Geneva and Rome. Besides the political work in connection with the Mandate, the other main problem which could
never be lost sight of for a moment was the building up of the
Keren Hayesod, already established in Palestine and America,
but either not established at all, or still in embryo, in most of
the European countries. My travels in the winter of 1921–22
had thus a double object.

Curzon had by now taken over from Balfour at the Foreign
Office, and was in charge of the actual drafting of the Mandate.
On our side we had the valuable assistance of Ben V. Cohen,
who stayed on with us in London after most of his fellow-
Brandeisists had resigned from the Executive and withdrawn
from the work. Ben Cohen was one of the ablest draftsmen in

America, and he and Curzon's secretary—young Eric Forbes-
Adam, highly intelligent, efficient and most sympathetic—
fought the battle of the Mandate for many months. Draft after
draft was proposed, discussed and rejected, and I sometimes
wondered if we should ever reach a final text. The most serious
difficulty arose in connection with a paragraph in the Preamble
—the phrase which now reads: 'Recognizing the historical
connection of the Jews with Palestine.' Zionists wanted to have
it read: 'Recognizing the historic rights of the Jews to Palestine.'
But Curzon would have none of it, remarking dryly: 'If you
word it like that, I can see Weizmann coming to me every
other day and saying he has a *right* to do this, that or the other
in Palestine! I won't have it!' As a compromise, Balfour suggested 'historical connection,' and 'historical connection' it
was.

I confess that for me this was the most important part of the
Mandate. I felt instinctively that the other provisions of the
Mandate might remain a dead letter, e.g. 'to place the country
under such political, economic and administrative conditions
as may facilitate the development of the Jewish National
Home.' All one can say about that point, after more than
twenty-five years, is that at least Palestine has not so far been
placed under a legislative council with an Arab majority—but
that is rather a negative brand of fulfilment of a positive in-
junction. Looking back, I incline to attach even less importance
to written 'declarations' and 'statements' and 'instruments'
than I did even in those days. Such instruments are at best
frames which may or may not be filled in. They have virtually
no importance unless and until they are supported by actual
performance, and it is more and more to this side of the work
that I have tried to direct the movement with the passing of the
years.

As the drafting of the Mandate progressed, and the prospect
of its ratification drew nearer, we found ourselves on the defensive against attacks from every conceivable quarter—on our
position in Palestine, on our work there, on our good faith.
The spearhead of these attacks was an Arab delegation from
Palestine, which arrived in London via Cairo, Rome and Paris
in the summer of 1921, and established itself in London at the
Hotel Cecil. Under the leadership of Musa Kazim Pasha, it

ventilated numerous Arab grievances at the Colonial Office, and also in Parliamentary, press and political circles, and seemed to find little difficulty in spreading the most fantastic stories. The delegation served as a rallying point for elements which we should now describe as 'reactionary' or 'fascist,' but which we then spoke of as 'the diehards.' Joynson-Hicks led them in the Commons; in the Lords they found able spokesmen in Lord Islington, Lord Sydenham, and later Lord Raglan, effectively supported in the press by the Northcliffe and Beaverbrook papers, with the 'Bag-and-Baggage' campaign for reduction of British overseas commitments in the interests of British economy and the British taxpayer. One had the impression that many English people were coming to regard Palestine as a serious liability, a country where Jews rode roughshod over 'the poor Arabs,' and charged the British taxpayer several shillings in the pound for doing it. Along with this type of argument went quasi-impartial statements suggesting that the Jewish enterprise in Palestine was utterly unsound and uneconomic, and that the whole thing was being run by a bunch of impractical idealists who did not know the first thing about colonizing or building up a country.

Well, we were idealists, and we knew we had a lot to learn —and much of it we could only learn by making our own mistakes. But we also saw—as our critics apparently did not— that their two arguments cancelled each other out: if the Jewish National Home was an impractical dream, incapable of realization, it could hardly present any real danger to Arabs or British, and there would seem to be no need to do anything about it except leave it to die of inanition. But nothing seemed further from our adversaries' intentions.

In November 1921 they found fresh ammunition in the Haycraft Report (the report of the local judicial commission which investigated the riots of May 1921) which, while condemning the brutality of the rioters, and denying most of the absurd allegations against the Jews in Palestine (e.g. that they were Bolshevists), contrived to leave on the reader's mind the impression that the root of the difficulty was a British policy with which the Arabs were—perhaps justifiably—dissatisfied. The Haycraft Report also implied that the Zionist desire to dominate in Palestine might provide further ground for Arab

resentment. Again there was a curious contradiction: in dealing
with the actual facts which the Commission was appointed to
investigate, the report frankly admitted, for instance, that the
particularly savage attack on Hedera was mainly due to the
spreading of false rumours by agitators in Tulkarm and neighbouring villages; but it made no attempt to indicate how and
why and through whom these rumours had been spread. Thus
it happened that an important official document could be held
—by those interested in such an interpretation—to support
some of the accusations made against us. It was a situation
which was to recur more than once in the years that followed—
in fact, as often as a commission went out to Palestine to investigate and report upon 'incidents' or complications on the spot.
In a sense, the Haycraft Report contained the germ of very
many of our main troubles in the last twenty-five years.

The report was, of course, a gift for our opponents, and they
made good use of it. So much confusion was created, so many
misstatements of Zionist aims were made, that we felt driven
to issue a full reply. This was drafted by Leonard Stein, who
had by now become our political secretary in London, and was
a most effective piece of work. But I remember feeling at the time
that our opponents were unlikely to pay much heed to the
marshalled facts and to the arguments advanced with such
forceful logic; they were impervious to objective reasoning on
the subject. Now I wonder whether the underlying cause may
not have been a vague anti-Jewish sentiment rather than any
specific anti-Zionist conviction.

Another gift for our attackers was Lord Northcliffe's return
to London after a visit to Palestine 'to see for himself.' His visit
was brief, his criticisms sharp. He had, during the war, been
inclined to support us, but his Palestine experiences seem to
have put him off. He had, it appears, succeeded in impressing
himself most unfavourably on the few Jewish settlers he met,
and the feeling was mutual. It was related that he happened to
arrive in Tel Yosef (then just founded) about lunch-time. Lunch
in a new settlement is apt to be a rather sketchy affair: people
rush in straight from the fields, collect a snack from the hatch,
and dispose of it with small ceremony before rushing back to
their jobs. Lord Northcliffe's presence in the dining-room
passed unnoticed for a time (in itself enough to arouse some

resentment), and when it was announced it evoked no great enthusiasm. Whatever it was, Lord Northcliffe came back with the impression that Jewish settlers in Palestine were mostly Communists and/or Bolshevists—and arrogant, aggressive types into the bargain. Still, he did leave us Philip Graves as *The Times* correspondent in Palestine, and Graves was a man of much more balanced and moderate views, though his cautious mind was often critical, and the series of articles from his pen which appeared in *The Times* about this period often damned with faint praise. We cannot forget, however, that we owe to him a most able and authoritative exposure of the Protocols of the Elders of Zion.

Once back in London, Lord Northcliffe lost no time in making his views known. I received an invitation—perhaps I should say command—to lunch with him. I found him with Mr. Maxse, to whom he was already representing Zionism as a danger to the British Empire, on the grounds that in his opinion it was a matter of five hundred thousand Jews (at most) against fifty million Moslems—and it was lunacy to upset the fifty million Moslems for the sake of the five hundred thousand Jews. It was useless to challenge this over-simplified version of the facts: Lord Northcliffe had been to see for himself —and had returned not to listen, but to talk. After lunch we adjourned to another room containing a number of very comfortable easy chairs, and one super-easy chair, to which Lord Northcliffe promptly gravitated. He placed me on his right and Maxse on his left, and said: 'Now, Maxse represents England; you are a Jew; I am the umpire!' From this we inferred that we were to be asked to state our respective cases— but not at all! Lord Northcliffe proceeded forthwith to tell us all about it. This conception of the functions of an umpire was new to me, and suggested that I was probably wasting my time, so I shortly made my excuses and withdrew. I daresay Lord Northcliffe was not pleased. Anyhow, though *The Times* remained dignified—if mistrustful—on the subject of Palestine, the other Northcliffe papers—the *Daily Mail*, the *Evening News*, and so on—launched out into a virulent campaign against us. In particular a certain Mr. J. M. N. Jeffries succeeded, in a series of savage articles, in presenting a wholly distorted picture of Jewish life in Palestine. His conclusion was that the only thing to do was to annul the Balfour Declaration and scrap the whole British Palestine policy.

The Beaverbrook press was conducting a similar campaign from a slightly different angle. They incorporated Palestine in their 'Bag-and-Baggage' demand for withdrawal from a number of British overseas commitments primarily on grounds of economy. While using roughly the same arguments as the Northcliffe press, they lumped together the cost to Britain of Palestine, Transjordan and Iraq (Palestine's share was, even at this early stage, insignificant—something like five million dollars annually), and thus suggested that the ordinary British taxpayer was being heavily mulcted in order to enable a few East European Jews to oppress and expropriate the Palestine Arabs. In fact, of course, the building up of Palestine as the Jewish National Home was not costing the British taxpayer a penny. About seven million five hundred thousand dollars a year was at that time being spent on maintaining the garrison, but that would in any case have had to be maintained somewhere, and probably cost less in Palestine than it would have in Egypt.

Another tempting target for the arrows of the press was, of course, the 'Rutenberg Concessions' for the harnessing of the Auja and Jordan rivers, which were made in 1921. All sorts of claimants appeared on the scene, and were sure of good publicity. They were mostly people who had secured 'concessions' from the Turkish Government, and felt themselves entitled to have those concessions confirmed by the British. Many of them had friends in Parliament through whom they could bring pressure to bear on the Government on the ground that the Rutenberg Concessions were favours granted to the Jews at the expense of the general interests of Palestine and of Britain. And this, besides holding up the development of Palestine, increased the difficulty of our political task.

Through all this maze we still managed somehow to progress, if with maddening slowness, towards the ratification of the Mandate. We had some good friends, whose help did much to offset the attacks. Among them were Mr. Ramsay MacDonald and Lord Milner, both of whom visited Palestine and returned to speak and write of what they had seen there: Mr. Mac-Donald with enthusiasm of the Jewish communal settlements, and Lord Milner with knowledge and sympathy of the great tasks in agriculture, afforestation, industry, transport, education, and so on, which awaited the Jews in Palestine, and of the way in which the Jewish community was addressing itself to them. Lord Milner, at least, had no fears that the Mandate would involve any noticeable extra burden on the British taxpayer, and felt confident that such burden as there was would very soon disappear.

Opposition to the Jewish National Home policy was not confined to England. On its way to London the Arab delegation had stopped in Rome and Paris, and in both cities had proved, as it was to prove in London, a rallying point for reactionary forces. Pressure on the British Government was therefore to be anticipated from some, at least, of the Allied governments—though they had already given their endorsement of the Balfour Declaration and signified their approval in principle of the Mandate based upon it.

Partly for this reason, and partly in the interests of the *Keren Hayesod*, I found myself committed to visiting a number of European capitals; and since the most serious political opposition to the Balfour Declaration policy seemed likely to emanate from the Vatican, I decided to begin with Rome.

We knew that the Latin Patriarch in Jerusalem, Monsignor Barlassina, was strongly opposed to Zionism, and that for some reason he held us responsible for the unsatisfactory settlement of the question of the Holy Places. It was in vain that we declared that we were completely uninterested in this problem, that we fully realized it to be something to be settled between the Christian powers and the Vatican, and that if these could not reach a satisfactory agreement among themselves it was no fault of ours. When I set out on my round of visits in Rome, therefore, I had it in mind to try and discover what really was the trouble about the Holy Places, and in what manner it could be considered to concern us.

Signor Schanzer, the then Italian Foreign Minister, was a Triestino, and probably of Jewish descent. I remember an odd talk with him in which he urged me to do my utmost to bring about a speedy settlement of the problem of the Holy Places in the sense desired by the Vatican. I protested in vain that it might be, to say the least, a little tactless for a Jew to meddle in

M

such matters, but somehow my protestations seemed unconvincing to him. He was particularly anxious about the *Cenacolo* —the Room of the Last Supper—on the outskirts of Jerusalem. My education in Church history having been deficient, I did not know why the Italians laid such stress on the *Cenacolo*, nor could I understand why Schanzer, presumably representing a purely secular Italian interest, should be such an ardent champion of a cause which one would have imagined to be primarily the concern of the Vatican. Clearly I had a great deal to learn in this field, and I decided to prolong my stay.

In due course I received an invitation to call on the Cardinal Secretary of State, Cardinal Gasparri. He had been very well informed by Monsignor Barlassina, who, as I have said, was no friend of ours. It happened that my first talk with Cardinal Gasparri took place the day after an address of mine at the Collegio Romano, which had been attended by representatives of the Italian and international press, as well as by a number of Italian dignitaries—the mayor of Rome, the chief of police, and so on. I had tried at this meeting to explain what we were doing in Palestine, and what our aims and aspirations were. The next morning a full report appeared in the *Osservatore Romano* (the organ of the Vatican); not an unfair report, on the whole, but with a few pinpricks. For instance, my statement that for the moment we were not buying land in Palestine, as we had reserves of land sufficient for the next ten years or so, appeared in the *Osservatore* something like this:

Dr. Weizmann stated that the Zionist Organization was in possession of vast reserves of land, and would not need to expropriate the Arabs for another ten years.

When I came into His Eminence's room next morning, he said: 'You made a very interesting speech yesterday.' I replied: 'Do you mean my speech at the Collegio Romano, or my speech in the *Osservatore Romano*?' He smiled and said that one must bear with the journalists, who sometimes slipped up, and I said that I thought far too highly of Vatican journalists to attribute to them careless mistakes in reporting. That point dropped, I thought I had better take my opportunity of asking what it was that the Vatican really feared from the Zionist movement; for I remember that Mr. Sokolow had, in audience with His Holiness, given a very full explanation of our aims, and that his explanation had apparently found favour. It gradually became apparent that his Eminence was concerned with matters which had to do with the British administration rather than with the Zionists. He was, for instance, distressed that members of various nursing and teaching Orders, and other Catholic emissaries to Palestine, were finding some difficulty in getting visas. I tried to explain that we had nothing to do with the granting of visas to travellers, but clearly His Eminence still suspected that the Zionist Organization was, in some obscure fashion, a branch of the Palestine Government, and 'could use its influence' if it chose. I spent some minutes trying to make the position clear, but I am not at all sure whether I had any success, either on this point, or on the question of the Holy Places.

At another interview with Cardinal Gasparri, when the talk had been on more general lines, and I had been giving some account of the work we were actually doing and preparing to do in Palestine—agricultural settlement, drainage, afforestation, medical work, education—he indicated that the colonization work, and so on, caused him no anxiety, but added: '*C'est votre université que je crains*' (it is your university that I fear). Which gave me food for thought.

I saw a number of Italian statesmen and officials, including the Duke of Cesaro, Signor d'Amandola (the Minister for the Colonies), Prime Minister Luzzati, Signor Contarini of the Foreign Office. I was received in audience by the King, who spoke appreciatively of his acquaintance with Dr. Herzl (whose photograph stood on his desk). But the question I had come to ask: What exactly was the reason for Italian and Vatican opposition to Zionism? remained unanswered. Nor could I discover to my own satisfaction why the purely religious issue of the Holy Places should arouse so much interest in Italian political circles—and in French ones, too. There were no Holy Places in Palestine to which the Jews laid actual physical claim —except, perhaps, Rachel's tomb, which was at no time a matter of controversy. The Wailing Wall we did not own, and never had owned since the destruction of the Temple; controversy was later to arise over the Jewish prayers conducted there, but at this time there was no suggestion even of that. Yet the resentment felt by the various Christian communities in Palestine—and especially by the Catholic communities—at the choice of a Protestant Mandatory Power lent a special edge to the discussion of the question of the Holy Places, and we could not escape from it. Our disclaimers fell on deaf ears.

I can make a happy digression at this point. My stay in Italy brought me, for the first time, into close contact with the Italian Jewish community, and with Italian Zionism. The latter had always held for me the fascination of mystery. None of the motives for Zionism which held good in other countries applied in the case of the Italian Jews. Jewish emancipation in Italy had been complete for generations. The community was a small one, but its members took an active part in Italian life—political, economic, artistic, scientific—and were to all intents and purposes indistinguishable from their fellow-citizens, except that they went to synagogue instead of to Mass. In metropolitan Italy they numbered no more than some fifty thousand of a total population of forty million or so. Of these fifty thousand, some fifteen thousand lived, curiously enough, in a sort of voluntary ghetto in Rome, spoke a language which was virtually Italian, with some Hebrew and Arabic embroideries, and pursued various minor crafts or kept small shops. But the rest of the community was assimilated to a degree.

Yet, under the influence of Peretz Chayes, the brilliant scholar who later became Chief Rabbi of Vienna, a group of young people had founded an Italian Zionist Organization. They had begun in Florence, where lived a young and ardent prophet of Zionism, Arnoldo Pacifici; and when they formed their society they went the whole way: they spoke Hebrew, they began to prepare themselves for life in Palestine; many of them—including Pacifici himself—became strictly orthodox; they edited one of the best Zionist papers of the day—*Israël*. Numerically insignificant, they were by the depth of their conviction and their absolute sincerity a great moral force. And though at first the community at large was inclined to resent them, they were so tactful, and at the same time so transparently honest in their faith, that even convinced anti-Zionists came to look on them as something in the nature of 'apostles' of the Jewish revival, and to respect, if they could not understand, them.

Early leaders of this group, besides Pacifici, were men like

Dante Lattes, Enzo Sereni, nephew of Angelo Sereni, head of the Rome Jewish community, and David Prato, later Rabbi of Alexandria. With the last named I toured the cities of Italy—Florence, Pisa, Milan, Genoa, Leghorn, Padua. It was a great experience for me to meet ancient Jewish families with a long intellectual tradition (sometimes deriving from Spain), a wide culture, and an exquisite hospitality. Amid all the suffering of the last few years, there is for me a special poignancy in the destruction which has overtaken the Italian Jewish community —though a number of Italian Jews have been fortunate enough to reach Palestine. They had given so much to Italy, and so much to their own people. Before World War I, on my very first visit to Italy, friends had pointed out to me with pride that the Italian Cabinet contained four Jews: Luzzati, Otto-lenghi, Sonnino, and—I think—Titoni. Then the mayor of Rome was also a Jew. The greatest living Italian mathe-matician, Levi Civita, was a Jew: the great Italian firm of contractors which was charged with the maintenance of the harbour of Alexandria was a Jewish firm. In short, the Italian Jewish community seemed to be a community of *sujets d'élite*. And the *élite* of that community, accustomed to enjoy in Italy every material and social advantage a man can ask, were turning their eyes to Palestine. I could not explain it. I could only thank God.

My tour with Dr. Prato was mainly in the interest of the *Keren Hayesod*, but also a little in the hope of winning at least some sections of Italian public opinion over to a more tolerant view of Zionism. I was beginning to attach considerable impor-tance to Italy; I saw it as a leading Mediterranean Power with extensive contacts in the Levant, under a Government which was taking more than a passing interest in our affairs. Gradually it was becoming clear to me that Italian official circles feared that Zionism was merely a cloak for the creation of a British imperial outpost in the Levant: they were thus very ready to press the Vatican contentions with regard to the Holy Places.

We had a rather strenuous few weeks, and afterwards my wife and I took a short rest in Capri. The island was at that time something of a centre for Russian émigrés; they frequented the smaller cafés and restaurants on the promenade, and in many of these the only language commonly heard was Russian.

One morning, as we walked into one of them, I heard a whispered aside: 'Here comes our Minister.' I was not as puzzled as I might have been, for it was not the first time I had been mistaken for Lenin; the same thing had happened not long before in Genoa, during the Economic Conference, the first Western European Conference to be attended by representatives of the Soviet Government. I had been walking with a friend—a high official of the Genoa municipality—when we noticed that our footsteps had for some time been dogged by a policeman. My friend stopped, and asked him why we were being followed. The answer was: 'We have received instructions, sir, not to let the Russian delegation out of our sight. I believe you have M. Lenin with you.' It took quite some time, and all my friend's official authority, to persuade the policeman that I had no connection with Lenin, beyond a remote physical resemblance.

Capri was exquisite, but at the back of my mind were always London and Jerusalem. The reports were disturbing. In London the campaign against the Mandate was in full swing, and from Jerusalem came distressing news of inadequate income, cut budgets, settlers leading lives of incredible hardship—without beds, with insufficient food, without tents in the quagmire that was still the Emek. I had for the time being done what I could on the financial front in America—and anyhow, I could not leave Europe again until the Mandate was ratified. I therefore decided that the *Keren Hayesod* must make a start in the principal European Jewish communities, and my next port of call was Berlin, where a German Zionist Federation was just beginning to make some headway.

My previous contacts with the Berlin Jewish community had been slight, and I was relieved to find a warm welcome, and to hear Herr Dernburg, a former Minister for the Colonies, paying high tribute to our colonization work in Palestine and to the new methods we were developing there. In such an atmosphere I felt that the German *Keren Hayesod* would soon become a real prop to the work—and such, in fact, proved to be the case. From the outset it owed much to the devotion of Kurt Blumenfeld, and to the keen mind and warm heart of Oskar Wasserman.

One of the more vivid impressions I retain of this visit is that of my talk with Walther Rathenau, whom I met one evening at Einstein's house. He plunged at once into eloquent argument against Zionism—much on the lines of his book *Hear O Israel*. The gist of what he had to say was that he was a Jew, but felt entirely German and was devoting all his energy to the building of German industry and the redeeming of Germany's political position. He deplored any attempt to turn the Jews of Germany 'into a foreign body on the sands of the Mark of Brandenburg'—that was all he could see in Zionism. His attitude was, of course, all too typical of that of many assimilated German Jews; they seemed to have no idea that they were sitting on a volcano; they believed quite sincerely that such difficulties as admittedly existed for German Jews were purely temporary and transitory phenomena, primarily due to the influx of East European Jews, who did not fit into the framework of German life, and thus offered targets for anti-Semitic attacks. The 'real' German Jew would be immune, from above, from all that. . . . By no stretch of the imagination could Rathenau be described as an East European immigrant; all the same, not many months were to pass before he fell at the hands of Nazi assassins. Not even then did his Jewish friends and followers see the writing on the wall.

From Berlin we went to Paris, again mainly on *Keren Hayesod* business, though I knew that the proceeds from France would not be very considerable. The Fund there was under the able direction of Professor Hadamard, Dr. Zadoc Kahn, and one or two other leading French Jews—by no means all of them Zionists. The Foundation Fund proved from the beginning a sort of bridge, or halfway house, for Jews who, while interested in Palestine and anxious to help, hesitated to throw their whole weight behind the Zionist movement because of its 'political implications.' They would help to pay for the work, but they were not prepared to assume any responsibility for its political, social or moral outcome. With some of these people, in France as elsewhere, there may also have been the underlying idea that it might be prudent to direct future Jewish immigration away from the Western countries, lest such immigration provoke a recrudescence of anti-Semitism.

For a French fund—French voluntary funds are seldom very successful—the *Keren Hayesod* did fairly well, and I was not unduly disappointed with my visit from the financial point of view. I of course profited from my stay in Paris to see one or two official people—M. de Monzie and General Gouraud among them. With the General I discussed the then vexed question of the northern frontiers of Palestine, though without conspicuous success, since the French tended to regard Palestine as 'southern Syria,' and Syria as a whole as a French sphere of influence, hence to resent the separation of Palestine, and to regard with special suspicion any attempt to modify its northern frontier. I tried to convince General Gouraud of the importance to Palestine of the waters of the river Litani, but could arouse no interest, and came away with the rather depressed feeling that for him, as for the Italians, Zionism was nothing more than camouflage for British imperialism.

From Paris we returned to London, to find debates on Palestine pending in both Houses of Parliament. Lord Sydenham, Lord Islington and Lord Raglan led the attack in the Lords, and in spite of a rather lively debate, their motion for the repeal of the Balfour Declaration won by a substantial majority. In the Commons, with such champions as Mr. Churchill and Major Ormsby-Gore, we had better luck, and a similar motion was heavily defeated. Still, I was greatly distressed by the outcome of the debate in the House of Lords. I went to see Mr. Balfour at Sheringham, and expressed my perturbation. He advised me not to take it too seriously, saying: 'What does it matter if a few foolish lords passed such a motion?'

Against this background, the London Zionist Executive was engaged in correspondence and discussions with the Colonial Office on various matters arising in connection with the final text of the Mandate. The volume of criticism directed against the Mandate policy had convinced the Government of the need for a detailed commentary, and this took the form of a White Paper published in June 1922 (the 'Churchill White Paper'). The main memorandum, we thought, was probably drafted by Sir Herbert Samuel, though it compared none too favourably with some of his Palestine speeches and was clearly dictated by a desire to placate the Arabs as far as possible. It was as little realized in 1922 as it is today that the real opponents of Zionism can never be placated by any diplomatic formula:

their objection to the Jews is that the Jews exist, and in this particular case, that they desire to exist in Palestine. It made, therefore, little difference whether our immigration was large or small: protests were as vociferous over a hundred immigrants as over thousands. This main memorandum was communicated to us in advance of publication, and we were invited to signify our acceptance of the policy defined therein.

The Churchill White Paper was regarded by us as a serious whittling down of the Balfour Declaration. It detached Transjordan from the area of Zionist operation, and it raised the subject of a legislative council. But it began with a reaffirmation of 'the Declaration of November 2, 1917, which is not susceptible of change.' It continued: 'A Jewish National Home will be founded in Palestine' and 'the Jewish people will be in Palestine as of right and not on sufferance.' Further, 'Immigration will not exceed the economic capacity of the country to absorb new arrivals.'

In short, it limited the Balfour Declaration to Palestine west of the Jordan, but it established the principle of 'economic absorptive capacity.' In addition, it was also made clear to us that confirmation of the Mandate would be conditional on our acceptance of the policy as interpreted in the White Paper, and my colleagues and I therefore had to accept it, which we did, though not without some qualms. Jabotinsky, at that time a member of the Zionist Executive, was arriving from America on the very afternoon when we had to signify our acceptance of the statement of policy. A messenger was sent to meet the boat at Southampton with a copy of the document and of our letter of acceptance, in order that his agreement might be obtained in time. I was more than a little nervous about his reaction, but curiously enough he raised no serious objection, merely remarking that the White Paper, if carried out honestly and conscientiously, would still afford us a framework for building up a Jewish majority in Palestine, and for the eventual emergence of a Jewish State. Subsequent events showed his view to have been right: so long as, through immigration and the investment of capital, the Jews were able to develop the country, its 'absorptive capacity' would continue to grow, and immigration would show a steady rise. It was only when the Government interfered with the activities of the community,

M*

with the definite intention of hampering such development, that the growth of the National Home was impeded. We know now, though we were not so sure in 1922, that the principle of 'absorptive capacity' could, if generously applied, have been the key to the rapid and stable expansion of the *Yishuv*; we also know that it was in fact applied in such a spirit as to prove a stumbling block to Jewish enterprise. For 'absorptive capacity' does not grow wild on the rocks and dunes of Palestine; it must be created, and its creation calls for effort, enthusiasm, imagination—and capital.

It follows that in the expansion of 'absorptive capacity' the economic policy of the Government is no less important than its political policy, and in the economic field the motto of the Palestine Government was from the outset 'safety first.' In fairness I must add that, in the early years after the ratification of the Mandate, great opportunities really did open out before us in Palestine, but we could not take full advantage of them while the time served because of lack of really substantial support from the Jews of Europe and America. Two other factors slowed down our early progress in Palestine. First, as I have already said, Russian Jewry had for our purposes ceased to exist, and Polish Jewry was broken and impoverished. Second, our methods of colonization were still in the experimental stage: we were feeling our way by trial and error towards a new system, for it was clear that the colonies of Baron Edmond, and even some of the early Zionist colonies, were insufficient to justify a speedy advance in agricultural colonization. We were hesitating between the *kvutzah* (communal) and the *moshav* (co-operative smallholder) settlements. In the Emek we had started with Nahalal, which is a *moshav*; Ain Harod, which followed shortly afterwards, is a large *kvutzah*.

When the signatures of the Zionist Executive were appended to the letter of acceptance, the stage was set for the formal submission of the Mandate for ratification; but ratification itself was by no means a foregone conclusion. By the League's constitution, Council decisions had to be unanimous, and we were not certain of the attitude of the representatives of some of the states which had seats on it.

In states with a fair number of Jews it was possible to enlist their aid in winning over the sympathy of the governments.

In the case of France, the Jewish population could argue in our favour. We could turn to the Jews of Italy in the same expectation. But there was Spain. There were practically no Jews in Spain. The story of our relationship with Spain is a long and bloody one. The absence of a significant Jewish community in Spain has something to do with it. There was Brazil. Our numbers in Brazil were insignificant. Yet as far as our fate in Palestine was concerned, the votes of Brazil and Spain were each equal to the vote of England.

The Palestine Mandate came up for ratification only on the last day of the League Council meeting (Saturday, July 24, 1922), in London, and up to the last day we were uncertain of what would happen. We weighed every possibility and looked on every side for help. We remembered then that when, in 1918, we laid the foundations of the Hebrew University in Jerusalem, there came a congratulatory telegram from a professor of the University of Madrid. To this man we turned for help; and he brought all his influence to bear on his friends that they might in turn urge the Government to act in our favour.

This Spanish professor was a marrano (a descendant of the crypto-Jews of the time of the Inquisition), and most of the friends he enlisted were also marranos. Suddenly we discovered a great deal of unexpected and—at the moment—inexplicable sympathy in Spain. Members of the learned societies, the higher clergy, prominent members of the Spanish nobility, received the local delegation in the most friendly fashion. Meanwhile, in London, we called on the Spanish representative on the Council, and it chanced that he was to be the President of the session at which our fate was to be decided. We said to him: 'Here is Spain's opportunity to repay in part that long-outstanding debt which it owes to the Jews. The evil which your forefathers were guilty of against us you can wipe out in part.' Whether it was our plea, whether it was the pressure from Madrid, the Spanish representative promised us his help, with Brazil as well as with his own country, and kept his word.

At the eleventh hour the Papal Nuncio tried to get the Secretariat of the League to postpone this item on the agenda. I happened to be in M. Viviani's rooms in the Hyde Park Hotel (M. Viviani was the French representative on the Council) when Signor Ceretti called on him, and asked his help in obtaining the postponement. There was, said Signor Ceretti, an important document due from the Vatican. M. Viviani introduced me and said: 'As far as I am concerned, I have no objection to the postponement, but it is for this gentleman to decide.' I said that there had been delay enough, and if we waited till Monday or later, who knew what differences would arise around the Council table? Signor Ceretti, who did not at all like M. Viviani's trick of making me the responsible party, heard me out, then bounced from the room in high dudgeon. M. Viviani smiled at me and said: '*Quand les prêtres de village se mettent à faire de la politique, ils font des gaffes*' (when village priests take to politics they always make howlers).

So on the Saturday morning Mr. Balfour introduced the subject of the ratification of the Palestine Mandate. Everything went off smoothly, and with the unanimous vote of ratification there ended the first chapter of our long political struggle.

CHAPTER XXVI

TRIAL AND ERROR

Realism and Unrealism in the Zionist Debates—Fred Kisch Enters Zionist Work—Ruppin and the Collectives—Chaim Arlosoroff—The Lean Years—Transforming a People—Agricultural Foundations—The Attack on the Kvutzah—'Capitalist' versus 'Working-class' Immigration—I Warn against Economic 'Ghettoism' in Palestine—Land Speculation—Chalutzim in Tel Aviv for Rosh Hashanah

THE Annual Conference of the World Zionist Organization—the smaller representative gathering which met in the alternate years between Congresses—began its sessions in Carlsbad on August 25, 1922, a month after the ratification of the Mandate. Its debates followed a pattern with which I was to become very familiar in the ensuing years, at Conferences and Congresses.

My report was followed, naturally—and properly—by adverse as well as favourable comment. Criticism of the Churchill White Paper was particularly sharp, but was to a certain extent, I thought, unreal; for it concentrated on its negative and ignored its positive aspects, emphasized the theoretical and minimized the practical. I remember one delegate who compared the White Paper at great length and most unfavourably with 'the charter'—that traditional object of Zionist aspiration in Herzlian days, the international document which was to 'give us' Palestine. I had to point out the basic difference between the two documents, namely, that the White Paper existed, the charter did not. And the White Paper gave us the opportunity for great creative work in Palestine.

In my report I had to devote much space to conditions in Palestine, and these were not commensurate with the political victory we had just scored. In spite of the smallness of our immigration there were already some fifteen hundred to two thousand unemployed in Palestine—a heavy proportion of our population. It was my painful duty to insist that no amount of diplomatic success could neutralize this fact, and that for it we had no one to blame but ourselves. Constructive criticism was needed: not belittlement of the terms of the White Paper, but indication of methods by which those terms could be taken advantage of in order to expand the Jewish Homeland.

There were, fortunately, constructive critics, men like Arthur Ruppin, Shmarya Levin and Chaim Arlosoroff—the last a young rising force of whom I shall have more to say—who emphasized the great possibilities of the moment, and stressed the need for concentrating on the improvement of the financial resources of the movement, and for attracting new forces from among those Jews who had hitherto stood aside. Ruppin put it succinctly as follows: Zionist work rested on three pillars: the sympathy of the enlightened world, an understanding with the Arabs, and the devotion and single-mindedness of the Jewish people itself. While we might have little control over the first two, the last depended entirely upon ourselves.

I left the Conference more than ever convinced that for many years to come my life would be divided between Palestine, where the actual work had to be got under way as soon as possible, and the great Western communities which would have to provide the bulk of the funds for it.

The Palestine Executive was by that time gradually consolidating its position, but it was sadly weak in its contacts with the administration. Until August 1922, our mainstay on this front had been the invaluable Dr. Eder, but he told us at the Conference in Carlsbad that he would shortly have to return to his medical work in London, which he had neglected too long. There, he promised, he would give us such help as he could, and up to the time of his death his wise and experienced mind was at the service of the London Executive. To replace him in Palestine was not a simple matter.

In this difficulty I turned to General Macdonogh of Military Intelligence, a devoted friend of the Zionist movement, in the hope that he might be able to suggest someone shortly to be released from his department. It was General Macdonogh who had arranged my trip to Gibraltar described towards the end of Book One of these memoirs. I explained to him the complicated nature of the proposed assignment: we needed a man belonging to both worlds, English as well as Jewish; and on the Jewish side he had to be willing and able to understand and co-operate with the Eastern Jews who would form the bulk of our immigrants as well as with the Westerners who would supply most of the funds for the work. The General brought up the name of Colonel Fred Kisch, with whom I had had fleeting contact precisely in connection with my Gibraltar trip. During most of the war Kisch had been with the Engineers in Mesopotamia, but during a brief convalescence had been attached to Intelligence. After the war, Kisch was stationed in Paris, and his work was connected with the drafting of some of the peace treaties. Macdonogh recommended him warmly.

In my first long conversation with Kisch I realized at once that his chief had been right in thinking that he had many of the qualities needed. He was completely British in upbringing, but came of a family which already had some connections with Zionism. His father, Hermann Kisch, was an old *Chovav Zion*. He was therefore not entirely a stranger to our problems, even though his life as an engineer officer had so far lain apart from us. I explained frankly to him the scope, the difficulties and the complications of the task which would lie before him if he came to us, and made no secret of the fact that he might easily fall between two stools: the Jews might not accept him because he was too much of an Englishman, while the British might come to regard him—in spite of his distinguished military career —as an Englishman 'gone native.' I told him that he would need a lot of courage, self-discipline and self-sacrifice, and would most probably get little satisfaction out of it. I also advised him not to decide until he had actually seen Palestine and got to know some of the people with whom he would have to live and work for years to come in a rather narrow circle.

Kisch made only one condition: that I should personally initiate him into his work. So it came about that we set out for Palestine together in November 1922, and I was able to watch over his first steps in the new environment. They were very cautious. I soon saw that I had made an excellent choice. Some of his senior colleagues, particularly Mr. Ussishkin, did little to make the job easier for him, but Kisch, once he had seen the country and the people, was so fascinated by the possibilities of the job that he was not to be deterred. Almost his first act on settling in Palestine was to make arrangements for a daily Hebrew lesson, so as to understand the Palestinians and be able to make himself understood without an interpreter. His next was to make a careful survey of the country. He had the advantage of being well acquainted with Sir Herbert Samuel, on whose warm support and encouragement he could count, and thus started on his new career under favourable auspices. For the first few months he served as political officer to the Executive, without formal status, but at the thirteenth Congress, in the summer of 1923, he was elected to the Executive, and continued to serve on it until he resigned in 1931, following my defeat at the Congress of that year.

The story of those nine years he has told for himself in his *Palestine Diary*. They were years of absorbing interest and very considerable difficulty—years of foundation-laying. Kisch showed himself to be devoted, painstaking and resourceful to a degree, and made a great contribution to the development of the Jewish National Home in its early formative stages. As time went on, the Jews of Palestine, and of the movement outside, came to know him and to appreciate him. But in proportion as his authority grew with the *Yishuv*, it diminished at Government House, and, more especially, among the lower strata of British officialdom in Palestine. But this in no way impaired Kisch's morale; he was not to be deflected from his chosen road. After his resignation from the Executive he settled in Palestine, and only left his beautiful home on Carmel to rejoin the Royal Engineers at the outbreak of the Second World War. He served with great distinction as chief engineer of the Eighth Army, and died in the front line before Tunis on April 11, 1943.

Kisch's arrival in Palestine meant much to me personally. For the first time there was somebody with whom to share the work which since Eder's resignation had been my own responsibility; someone who could also go to America and talk to the assimilated Jews there as man to man—and from them get the respect due to an officer high in the British military hierarchy. Indeed, he was better able to talk to them than I was, for he did not bear the stigma of being an East European Jew; and his work with the Western assimilated Jews was always eminently successful.

It was a good thing that it was so, for the years 1923-4 saw the beginning of Palestine's first post-war depression and, as I have already recounted, our travels to America and various European capitals took place against a background—of which we were ceaselessly conscious—of inadequate income, unpaid teachers and officials in Palestine, settlement work held up for lack of funds, settlers short of the most elementary necessities, and the ever-present threat of serious unemployment. Gradually, as the various branches of the Fund got under way, larger amounts trickled in; but the increase in those early years was very slow, and anxiety lest the utmost we could do should prove 'too little and too late' dogged our every footstep.

Another man who carried a heavy burden at that time, and carried it magnificently, was Arthur Ruppin. He helped to found our colonies in a manner which set an example not only for Palestine, but for many other countries. The human problem that faced us was the highly complex one of absorbing into agriculture immigrants who were by nature and training urban, and who had been divorced all their lives, like their ancestors for hundreds of years, from agricultural pursuits and traditions. Our material was, in fact, what our enemies sometimes called 'the sweepings of the ghetto.'

These men and women had to be trained, and prepared to lead new lives in a strange climate, on a soil neglected and abused for centuries. And this had to be done at a time in human history when the prevailing tendency everywhere was in the opposite direction—a marked drift away from the village and into the town. So we were working against the stream—'trying to set the clock back' (another favourite phrase of our opponents). And our income was both limited and uncertain. At best the results of agricultural colonization are slow to mature; faced with the task of the rapid absorption of considerable numbers of people, one would naturally turn to urban industrial development as the easier course. I have already told of the conflict which therefore developed between those of us who thought that the first task of the Zionists was to create industries and develop towns, and those who, like myself, were convinced that without a solid agricultural basis there could be no firm foundation for a Jewish culture, or for the Jewish way of life, or even for a Jewish economy. As immigration into Palestine proceeded, this difference of outlook became more acute; by 1923-4 the debate was in full swing.

It was Ruppin who, undaunted by the storm of polemics which raged about him, and the abuse to which he was subjected, calmly pursued his agricultural programme in the teeth of every difficulty. If today Jewish Palestine can proudly review the sons and daughters of some three hundred agricultural settlements, this is largely due to Ruppin's foresight and obduracy, and his profound understanding of the East European Jew. Himself a Westerner, his sympathetic insight enabled him to find ways and means of adapting the East European mentality to the hard conditions of Palestine agriculture.

It was in the collective settlement, in the *kvutzah*, that Ruppin found the form that best served both as training ground for newcomers to the land and as a unit able to establish and maintain itself in remote and unsettled parts of the country. Roads were few and bad in those early days, and new settlements had to face months and years of virtual isolation. The solitary settler, or the small village of independent farmers, could not have existed in the conditions then prevailing.

But the 'collectives' had to face an extremely hostile section of Zionist and general public opinion. A great deal of nonsense was talked and written about them by opponents, both within the movement and outside it. We were told that they were 'Communist' (i.e. Bolshevist) cells; that men and women were herded together in them, leading lives of sexual promiscuity; that they were irreligious, atheistic, subversive—in short, sinks of iniquity scattered up and down the Holy Land. Such 'criticisms' could only come from people who had never been inside a *kvutzah*, or what was worse, had been inside one for half an hour. With the passing of years, and the gradual increase in the number of people who *had* visited them, ideas began to change. Travellers returning from Palestine had, and have, nothing but praise for the communal villages, the life their members lead, and the work they are doing. These units are based on the principles of co-operative buying and selling, self-labour and the national ownership of land. Fifty years ago all these ideas sounded like dreams; today, in Palestine, they are solid economic reality. The settlements are firmly rooted, conveniently as well as pleasantly designed; the settlers are robust, cheerful, keen on their jobs. They love the country, and are bringing up a young generation proud of their agricultural skill, eager, upstanding, independent—young men and women who have shed all the attributes of the ghetto and acquired those of a normal, healthy, self-respecting peasant class.

The way has not been easy. For lack of funds the work was prolonged and made more costly, and much unnecessary suffering was caused. Often on my early visits to new settlements my heart ached with the knowledge that the settlers were doing their utmost to spare me any real perception of their daily difficulties. I heard no word of complaint, but I read in the eyes of settlers more than they could have put into words. I was particularly touched by the efforts they made—for instance in Nahalal and Ain Harod—to comfort *me*, and to assure me that 'better times would surely come.'

What made things harder still was the accusation that Ruppin and the settlers were doctrinaires, more interested in proving a theory than in getting results. The opposite was the truth; Ruppin was interested precisely in practical results. It was his contention that the *kvutzah* cost less per settler than any other form of colonization. It was also more useful as a training school for men and women new to the land and to village life. It met to a very great extent one of the principal difficulties in adapting town dwellers to rural life, namely, the loneliness in the early stages. It was, in addition, more capable of defending itself when new settlements had to be established in isolated areas. Twenty-five years have proved that Ruppin was right.

With Ruppin worked Elazari Volcani, who is still at the head of the Agricultural Experimental Station in Rehovoth. Between them and their colleagues they elaborated, after many trials and errors, and in the face of innumerable difficulties, the most suitable type of agriculture for Palestine, namely, mixed farming.

There was an organic connection between Ruppin's outlook on practical matters and his association with me in the 'parliamentary' struggle in the Congresses. Shmarya Levin's support of me was equally consistent and effective, but had other roots. In the years which elapsed since my student days in Berlin, I had grown to love and admire his great personality and apostolic devotion to Zionist work. Somehow, without words, without preliminary agreement, we always found ourselves, by instinct, on the same side of the fence. It was so in the days of

the great controversy with Herzl on what was then called
'political Zionism'—and it was so in the Zionist Congress
debates for many years after the ratification of the Mandate. Still
another pillar of strength on our side in this struggle was Eliezer
Kaplan, who in later years became the treasurer of the Jewish
Agency and exercised a powerful influence in the ranks of labour.

Chaim Arlosoroff, whom I have mentioned as another
staunch supporter of my view of Zionist work, was by far the
youngest of us. He was a man of brilliant mind, and he was
particularly fitted to present our philosophy of Zionism to the
younger generation. He did it with great zest and power and
with indefatigable energy. It was a privilege to watch him at
work. He became later the political officer of the Executive—
this was in the time of the Wauchope administration—but
already at the Congresses and Conferences of 1922 and on, he
was one of the leading spirits. He was merciless in his attacks
on the extremist group, which later crystallized into the
Revisionist faction.

Arlosoroff had received an excellent education, and his
Jewish background was solid. He was one of the few who knew
the East and the West equally well, and was therefore most
suitable for the office which he filled. He was fundamentally
good-natured, but did not suffer fools gladly, and was severe
in his attacks on his opponents. But he took as well as gave.
His brilliant career was cut short in 1935 by an assassin. He
was murdered in dastardly fashion late one night on the seashore of Tel Aviv. His death left a gap which has not been
adequately filled until the present.

The controversy had not yet reached, in 1922 and 1923, the
fury which was to characterize it later, but it was already very
lively. The year 1923 saw the beginnings of a change in the
character of our immigration. The early immigrants had been
preponderantly of the *chalutz* type. In 1923 a new regulation
offered settlement visas to anyone who could show possession of
twenty-five hundred dollars—this was called 'the capitalist'
category—and gave a much needed opportunity to many
Russian Jews stranded in Poland after the war. These new
immigrants were permitted over and above those who received
'labour certificates.' And so the immigration figures rose
month by month. So, unfortunately, did the unemployment

figures, though much more slowly. I was uneasy. True, a considerable amount of capital was being brought into the country by these small capitalists, but openings in industry, trade and commerce were as yet limited, and the numerous small shops which seemed to spring up overnight in Tel Aviv and Haifa caused me no little worry. These people were, as I have indicated, not of the *chalutz* type, and some of them were little disposed to pull their weight in a new country. A few, in their struggle for existence, showed anti-social tendencies; they seemed never to have been Zionists, and saw no difference between Palestine as a country of immigration and, for instance, the United States. Many of them had no knowledge of Hebrew, and it was soon being said, rather ruefully, that at this rate Tel Aviv would shortly be a Yiddish-speaking town. Even to the casual observer, the new immigration carried with it the atmosphere of the ghetto. In the end, I felt that I had to give warning. I had to give it many times, in fact; and its character may be gathered from a speech I made in Jerusalem in October 1924.

I said, among other things: 'When one leaves the Emek and comes into the streets of Tel Aviv, the whole picture changes. The rising stream of immigration delights me, and I am delighted, too, that the ships should bring these thousands of people who are prepared to risk their life's savings in the Jewish National Home. Nor do I underrate the importance of this immigration for our work of reconstruction. Our brothers and sisters of Djika and Nalevki'—I was referring to typical ghetto districts of Warsaw—'are flesh of our flesh and blood of our blood. But we must see to it that we direct this stream and do not allow it to deflect us from our goal. It is essential to remember that we are not building our National Home on the model of Djika and Nalevki. The life of the ghetto we have always known to be merely a stage on our road; here we have reached home, and are building for eternity.'

This speech earned me the hatred of a great many Polish Jews, particularly of the *Mizrachi* type—a hatred which I have never lived down. I daresay I might have put it more tactfully, but I felt too strongly to mind. Naturally, such statements got me into hot water; the new immigrants, with their three or four or five thousand dollars each, considered themselves just as good as the men from Deganiah and Nahalal, and I was accused of taking sides, and discriminating between one type of immigration and another. It was not that I did not realize the importance of the small capitalists for Palestine's economy; their industry, diligence and frugality were invaluable assets. But I feared that in the early stages of our growth a too high proportion of them might unduly weight the balance. I feared that too many of them would meet with disappointment in an unfamiliar country, lose their small savings, and be driven to return to Poland or Rumania. And that would have been a catastrophe. In fact, something of the sort did happen, though on a small scale; but small as it was, we were not to escape its dire consequences.

The most vicious of the forms in which the 'ghetto' influence found expression was land speculation. We had to struggle very hard to suppress this type of activity, which cut at the very root of our land system and hence of our whole work. But the prospect of quick gain was a powerful attraction for many people, and the only way to combat it was to concentrate the acquisition of land in the hands of the Jewish National Fund. This, however, meant much more money than the Jewish National Fund had, or could expect, at the time. So we had to stand by and watch the rise in land prices which we knew must inevitably lead to a slump, to failures, to re-emigration, with all the attendant sufferings and difficulties. There were some land speculators who never even came to Palestine. Bogus land companies sprang up, and parcels of Palestine land were hawked on the markets of Warsaw, Lodz and Lemberg, changing hands with bewildering rapidity. We knew that such speculation carried its own nemesis, but it was hard to convince the small man who saw a chance of doubling his life's savings at one stroke. After all, he always knew of someone who had made a fortune that way: why not he?

All this was the more painful to watch because most of the human material of the new immigration was extremely fine. I came again to Palestine in the autumn of 1924, and spent the High Holidays in Tel Aviv, where my mother then lived. This gave me the opportunity to see some of the various small industries which were being created by the new immigration. Often I would go to a dwelling consisting of one biggish room, with an annex. In the big room one would find a loom and the

head of the family—often a man of advanced age—with his
son or daughter, working it. I asked more than once whether
such home industries were providing even a modest livelihood
for the family. The reply was almost invariably something like
this: 'Dr. Weizmann, don't you worry about the economic
side. *We* shall manage to pay our way here. You'll see. What
you have to do is see that more Jews come into Palestine.'
One way or another we came through the period of trial; some
of those little industries are big industries today. The process of
over-expansion was arrested in time, and later we established
a sort of industrial bank to give credits to small shopkeepers
and industrialists in the towns. The Anglo-Palestine Bank also
extended assistance to the same type of immigrant. All the
same, they had, I am afraid, some reason to be dissatisfied with
the Executive and myself. There was a time when the agricultural settlers were getting the advice and support of the Zionist
Organization, while the urban settlers were left to their own
devices. But the fact was that it was impossible to satisfy everybody, and we—particularly I—believed the agricultural side
to be the more important.

The experience of the great festivals of the New Year and the
Day of Atonement in Tel Aviv was a great one for me, and left
a deep impression. The atmosphere was so different from that
of a Russian or Polish town—or even an English one. As soon
as the hour of sunset approached, the Great Synagogue—at
that time still unroofed, and covered with some sort of make-
shift tarpaulin arrangement—began to fill with a mass of
young men who had marched into Tel Aviv from the neighbouring villages. They were sturdy, bronzed, healthy-looking
specimens, in everyday clothes (they had no other), some even
in shorts, but all very clean, and somehow festive-looking. Their
presence in the synagogue belied all the rumours that the people
of the *kvutzoth* were atheists, disregarding all the traditions and
tenets of the Jewish religion. Chaim Nachman Bialik and I
stood watching them throughout the service, thinking the same
thoughts: these were men and women who served God with
spade and pick and hoe on weekdays, and came at the High
Festivals to the synagogue to thank God for permitting them
to do so, for bringing them out of the hell of the ghetto, and
setting them on the threshold of a new life.

CHAPTER XXVII

THE JEWISH AGENCY

Non-Zionist Jewish Leaders and Philanthropists—Anything Rather than Jewish Nationalism—Russian Colonization Plans—Zionist Division on the Agency—Louis Marshall—Felix Warburg—Philanthropy and National Regeneration—Zionist Educational Work Continues—Western Cities— Samuel Zemurray—The Constituent Assembly of the Jewish Agency, August 1929—The Triple Setback

SEVEN years lay between the ratification of the Mandate—, July 1922—and the founding of the Jewish Agency—August 1929. Amid the varying fortunes of the Zionist movement, I did not once, during that period, forget the need for the Agency. I had, in fact, been preoccupied with the idea in preceding years.

Article IV of the Mandate reads: 'An appropriate Jewish agency shall be recognized as a public body for the purpose of advising and co-operating with the administration of Palestine in such economic, social and other matters as may affect the establishment of the Jewish National Home. . . . The Zionist Organization . . . shall be recognized as such agency. It shall take steps in consultation with His Britannic Majesty's Government to secure the co-operation of all Jews who are willing to assist in the establishment of the Jewish National Home.' The words 'Jewish Agency' as used in my narrative mean specifically the Agency in the extended or enlarged form contemplated by the Mandate.

Chiefly, though by no means exclusively, I had in mind the leaders of the American Jewish community, the mainstay of the Joint Distribution Committee. Their philanthropies were manifold and generous, and Palestine might occasionally be included among them as a peripheral interest. They had done and were doing magnificent relief work for European Jewry during and after the First World War, but for one who believed that the Jewish Homeland offered the only substantial and abiding

answer to the Jewish problem, their faith in the ultimate re-
stabilizing of European Jewry was a tragedy. It was heartbreaking to see them pour millions into a bottomless pit, when
some of the money could have been directed to the Jewish
Homeland and used for the permanent settlement of those very
Jews who in Europe never had a real chance. They accused us
Zionists of being doctrinaires, of being more interested in
creating a Jewish homeland than in saving Jewish lives.
Actually the shoe was on the other foot. They were too often
the doctrinaires who gladly supported any worthy cause as
long as it did not involve them in what they called Jewish
nationalism.

An outstanding instance was the project for the creation of
an autonomous Jewish settlement in Soviet Russia, which
began with the Crimea as the chosen area. It was, of course, a
reasonable scheme, though it was confined to Russian Jewry,
and could have no effect on the Jews of Poland, Rumania, etc.
I believe the Crimean scheme was a sincere attempt on the
part of the Russian Government to 'normalize' certain Jewish
elements which did not fit into the reorganized economic life
of Soviet Russia. They consisted of middlemen and small
traders who would be condemned to starvation under the new
régime unless they could change their means of livelihood.
Though the project entailed certain risks, no one would have
felt justified in opposing a scheme so well intentioned. There
was no need for Zionists to support it actively, but there was
equally no need for violent opposition. But for a great many
non-Zionists, at that time at any rate, the peculiar merit of the
Crimean scheme was precisely that it had nothing to do with
Palestine and Jewish nationalism, and could in fact be used to
deflect from Palestine the attention of Jewish groups. This
attitude, in turn, gave a handle to certain Zionist groups which
were not particularly keen—for reasons I shall shortly give—in
seeing the enlarged Jewish Agency materialize.

Nor was it only to Jewish causes that these men were generous
donors—to the practical exclusion of Palestine. Mr. Julius
Rosenwald, of Chicago, for instance, was a universal philanthropist. For a Negro university, for a *Volksmuseum* in Munich,
for a Berlin school of dentistry, his purse seemed bottomless.
But the only Palestinian institutions to share in his benefactions

were the Teachers' Seminary in Jerusalem and the Agricultural Station in Athlit. What seemed odd to me, in these circumstances, was his continued and apparently quite lively interest in all that went on in Palestine. He read most of our material, and his stock remark whenever I met him was: 'If you can convince me that Palestine is a *practical* proposition, you can have all my money.' But nothing could convince him. Personally he was most friendly to me and to Shmarya Levin. To Levin he once said: 'Look, my villa in the suburbs is called "Tel Aviv." What more do you want?' Levin answered: 'Only that you should build a house in the suburbs of Tel Aviv and call it "Chicago."'

In most countries, as I have pointed out, the *Keren Hayesod* provided a sort of bridge for those people who were interested in Palestine and who were ready to help the work as long as it did not commit them in the political field. But this was not enough. The Mandate referred to a 'Jewish Agency' which would in fact speak for all Jews interested in the building of the Homeland. The Fund was an instrument, not an agency. It did not provide for the degree of participation which the phrase in the Mandate contemplated and which I was eager to obtain.

Among the Zionists the opposition to the Agency was of two kinds. There was, it will be remembered, the Brandeis group, which wanted the Zionist Organization to remain as the Agency since, in their opinion, it was no longer essentially a political body, and non-Zionists no longer needed to shy away from it. But since the Brandeis group had more or less withdrawn from organizational work, its opposition was not important. Much more important was the second type of opposition, which sprang from precisely the opposite point of view.

Many of the European Zionists, and some of the American Zionists, did not want to have the rich Jews of America, the so-called 'assimilationsts,' in an Agency which would have a controlling voice in the affairs of the Jewish Homeland. These Zionists were afraid of an emasculating influence in the direction of philanthropy; and I was accused of trying to drag those rich Jews into Zionist work against their will and better judgment. 'If they want to co-operate,' said those Zionists, 'the doors of the Organization are open to them. They can become Zionists.' Which of course begged the question; such men were

not ready to join the Zionist Organization any more than the
P.I.C.A. was ready to give up its individuality and merge with
us. Moreover, the difference between them and the Zionists
was not only political; it was also social.

Among those American Zionists who were strong advocates
of the Agency idea were men like Louis Lipsky—whom I have
already mentioned—the late Jacob Fishman, and Morris
Rothenberg. Fishman, who will long be remembered as one of
the ablest Jewish journalists in America—he was for many
years editor of the *Jewish Morning Journal*, and conducted a
widely read column on current affairs—had a special insight
into the public mind. There were very few in America, or for
that matter anywhere else, to whom I stood nearer, and with
whom I could discuss Zionist affairs in a more intimate way.
He made his paper a powerful influence for good; his calm,
level-headed comments helped to maintain an informed point
of view during times of crisis, like the struggle with Brandeis,
and the struggle round the Jewish Agency. Jacob Fishman died
in harness—attending the Zionist Congress at Basle in 1946.
It was a great loss to the Zionist movement, and to his friends.

Morris Rothenberg belonged to the younger set, and has
played a considerable rôle in many phases of American
Zionism as a clear, cool-headed and judicial mediator between
various contending parties. In spite of this rôle, which often
exposes a man to attacks from both sides, he always enjoyed the
respect of divergent elements. He was, and remains, an
extremely valuable counsellor, especially to one like myself
who only comes for short periodic visits and is likely to commit
grave errors if not loyally guided by advisers fully conversant
with the scene and with the *dramatis personæ*.

The idea of the Jewish Agency was debated at our Action
Committee meetings, our Conferences and Congresses, as
stormily as our relations with Great Britain. But shortly before
I left for America in February 1923, a session of the Action
Committee, held in Berlin, adopted a resolution approving in
general terms the idea of the Jewish Agency, and laying down
as a guiding principle for our negotiations 'that the controlling
organ of the Jewish Agency shall be responsible to a body
representative of the Jewish people.' This beautifully vague
statement, though it left me free to make a start, also left the

door open to the partisans of the 'World Jewish Congress' idea.

There were, it might seem, two ways of drawing into the work of Palestine those Jews who were not prepared to declare themselves Zionists—two ways of creating the Agency. One was to organize a full-fledged 'World Jewish Congress' with elected delegates from every Jewish community. Theoretically this was correct enough; but in practice the calling of a World Jewish Congress encountered insuperable difficulties—foremost among them the fact that the very elements in Jewry which we wanted to bring in would have nothing to do with the idea! So that, even if and when achieved, such a congress would amount to little more than a slightly enlarged Zionist Organization.

There were other grounds for the rejection of the World Congress idea in this connection. To the people whose co-operation we sought, the ultra-democratic machinery of Congresses was wholly unattractive. They were reluctant even to meet the Zionists and discuss with them the possibility of a covenant. It was therefore clear to me that the only practical approach was to invite the various great organizations already at work in other fields to join with us without forfeiting their identity. This second way was the one I proposed and ultimately carried into effect.

It was a curious fact that while the plan was attacked by ultra-Zionists as 'anti-democratic,' the most democratic body in Palestine itself, the labour organization, was wholly in favour of it. At the various meetings of the authoritative Zionist bodies the Palestine labourites stood behind these efforts because they were men of practical experience; they knew how badly we needed new sources of income and new forces in order to get on with the job; and though they may have seen certain dangers in the plan, they agreed with me that it would be a grave mistake to exclude from our work, on grounds of purely formal 'democracy,' those powerful and responsible groups of American Jews.

So much for internal Zionist opposition to the Agency. There remained still 'the party of the second part.' Within the non-Zionist groups too there was opposition to the proposed match. The Joint Distribution Committee suffered, moreover, from a great weakness: it had very few men to give us who could participate in executive work on the level of their Zionist opposites in the Agency. Whereas the Zionist men of the Executive were elected at Congresses after a severe struggle, which more or less assured a high level of quality, the executives of the Joint Distribution Committee were appointees. I do not say that they did not do their work very well, but when the Agency was in fact constituted their position in the mixed Executive was somewhat precarious. And before the Agency was constituted they did whatever they could to prevent the merger, fearing that in it they would lose their privileged position.

My acquaintance with Louis Marshall began in 1919, when he came to Paris as the head of the American Jewish Delegation to the Peace Conference. I saw little of him, for I did not take part in their work; the whole fight for minority national rights seemed to me to be unreal. But I was greatly impressed by Marshall's forceful personality, his devotion to Jewish matters and the great wisdom he brought to bear on the discussions. Although counted among the 'assimilationists,' he had a very clear understanding of and a deep sense of sympathy for the national endeavours of the Jewish communities in Europe who were struggling for cultural minority rights. He had learned Yiddish and followed the Yiddish press closely, showing himself very sensitive to its criticism. Of a naturally autocratic habit of mind, firm if not obstinate on occasion, impatient of argument, he was, I felt, a man who, once convinced of the rightness of a course, would follow it unswervingly. The main difficulty in working with him lay in his tendency to procrastinate—mainly due to his preoccupation with his profession and his various public activities. One had always to be at his elbow to make sure that the particular business in hand had not been snowed under by other urgent duties. This naturally added to the delays in our negotiations—the more so as the opponents of the Agency idea made use of this weakness in Marshall. I countered by maintaining such pressure as I could. Unable always to be in America, I sent out others; once Leonard Stein, and on another occasion Kisch. Morris Rothenberg acted as a sort of permanent liaison officer.

It was a profound mistake to think, as some Zionists did at

the time, that Marshall was not 'representative' because he had not been elected, like members of the Zionist Executive. As one travelled up and down the States one could not but be impressed by the extent and power of his influence. The most important Jewish groups in every city in America looked to him for the lead in communal matters, and his attitude went a long way, in fact was often decisive, in determining theirs.

And yet in one sense he was not representative of his following. He was much nearer to Jews and Judaism; nearer, in fact, than Brandeis, an ardent Zionist, ever was. For Brandeis Zionism was an intellectual experiment, based on solid foundations of logic and reason. Marshall was hot-blooded, capable of generous enthusiasms as well as of violent outbursts of anger—though it was seldom long before his cooler judgment reasserted itself.

I found him at first completely sceptical as to the possibilities in Palestine, knowing next to nothing about the country and about our work. But he had such a great fund of sympathy and was so warm-hearted that it compensated for his ignorance of the subject. I remember how, at the end of a long conversation on our prospects, he suddenly burst out in his temperamental way: 'But Dr. Weizmann, you will need half a billion dollars to build up this country.' To which I calmly replied, 'You'll need much more, Mr. Marshall,' and that completely disarmed him. He was so baffled that he stared at me for a long time, and I said: 'The money is there, in the pockets of the American Jews. It's your business and my business to get at some of it.' I think that from that moment on he began to understand the magnitude—and the appeal—of the problem.

Of an entirely different character was Felix Warburg, whom I did not meet until the spring of 1923. He was a man of sterling character, charitable to a degree, a pivotal figure in the American Jewish community, if not in very close touch with the rank and file. There was something of *le bon prince* about him. But he was susceptible to gossip, and readily believed—or at least repeated—what his satellites told him about Palestine.

Shortly after my arrival in the spring of 1923, I was somewhat surprised to receive an invitation to lunch with him at the offices of Kuhn, Loeb and Company in William Street. Enthroned in one of the more palatial rooms of that palatial

building, I found an extremely affable and charming gentleman, very much the *grand seigneur*, but all kindness. I decided
that my lunch with him was going to be quite as much pleasure
as duty. I judged too soon. We spent about an hour and a half
together, and almost the whole time was occupied by Mr.
Warburg's account of what, according to his information, was
happening in Palestine. A more fantastic rigmarole I have, to
be honest, never heard from a responsible quarter: bolshevism,
immorality, waste of money, inaction, inefficiency—all of it
based on nothing more than hearsay. I listened with what
patience I could muster—it seemed to me then a good deal—
to this tirade, and felt a little embarrassed at the thought of
replying. I could not leave his statements unchallenged, but as
his guest I found it difficult to frame the flat contradictions
which they called for.

I let him talk himself out, and then I said: 'You know,
Mr. Warburg, I am really quite well acquainted with Palestine
and with the work there; I have been there every year since
the end of the war, the last time only a couple of months ago.
I have been present at the inception of almost every enterprise
of ours. But as to these stories which I hear from you—I must
suppose at second, or third, or even fourth hand—I cannot
deny that there may be some particle of truth in the accusations—"no smoke without fire"—and so on—but so far it has
escaped my attention. I think you have not yet been in Palestine yourself, and I am frankly not prepared to accept your
sources as unimpeachable.' I then asked if I might put a plain
question to him: 'What if things were the other way round?
Suppose I came to you with a collection of all the tittle-tattle
and backstairs gossip that circulates, I have no doubt, about
Kuhn, Loeb and Company? What would you do?'

He laughed and answered: 'I should probably ask you to
leave.'

I said: 'I can hardly ask you to leave, for I am your guest.'

He at once realized that he had gone too far, and he was
ready to make amends by offering me a contribution. I forget
whether to the *Keren Hayesod* or the Hebrew University. I did
not accept, saying: 'Mr. Warburg, it will cost you much more
than you are likely to offer me now. The only way you can
correct this painful interview is by going to Palestine and seeing

for yourself. If your information is confirmed at first hand I shall have no more to say, for I must respect your views when based on personal experience.'

To my astonishment he took me up! 'Your suggestion is the right one,' he said. 'I will talk it over with my wife, and if possible go to Palestine at once.' To my further astonishment he was as good as his word, and left for Palestine, with Mrs. Warburg, within a fortnight of this first conversation. I wired to Kisch to show them around.

The next news I had of Warburg was a post-card—still in my possession—in which he wrote that he had been going up and down the country and felt like doffing his hat to every man and every tree he saw! He was deeply moved by every phase of our work, settlements, schools, hospitals, and most of all by the settlers themselves. He and his wife returned to the States—I was still there—eager to help in every way they could. I was again invited to lunch, this time at their home. Again I sat and listened, and what I heard now was nothing but praise of Palestine and of our enterprises. I have seldom witnessed a more complete conversion.

Yet somehow it left me cold. Warburg noticed this, and said I did not seem very pleased. I tried to explain: 'You see, you went to Palestine convinced that of every dollar collected here in America some ninety cents was being wasted. Probably you had a pleasant surprise to discover in Palestine that, as far as you could see, only fifty cents was being wasted. Perhaps, if you take a genuine interest in the work—enough to lend a hand—you may one day discover that not one cent is wasted. We have our difficulties; sometimes the progress is very slow, sometimes it picks up a little speed; but ours is a living organism, afflicted with all the diseases and complications that commonly beset living organisms. If you want to understand it, it will take more than one visit to Palestine. I am sure you will go again, and yet again—and not merely as a tourist; and in the end we shall understand each other.'

This talk was the real beginning, I think, of Warburg's participation in our work. Incidentally it laid the foundations of a lifelong friendship which stood the strain of a good many differences of opinion. These arose from the fact that we looked at Palestine from different angles: for us Zionists it was a movement of national regeneration; for him it was, at any rate in the early stages of his interest, one among the fifty-seven varieties of his philanthropic endeavours—perhaps bigger and more interesting than some others, but not different in essence. His whole upbringing militated against his taking the same view as we did; besides, his co-workers in the innumerable other causes to which he was committed no doubt constantly warned him against the danger of identifying himself too closely with the Zionists. Warburg was one of their most valuable assets in communal work, and they greatly feared to lose him under the impact of a new idea which by its very radicalism might capture his imagination. Particularly was this the case with a certain Mr. David A. Brown, a typical American go-getter with a noisy technique for conjuring millions from the pockets of wealthy American Jews. People used to tell me wistfully that if we could only get for Zionism the whole-hearted support of Mr. David A. Brown, all our troubles would be over.

Warburg made several more trips to Palestine, where he was usually under the guidance of Dr. Magnes or of some member of the Executive. He really learned to know Palestine. The Hebrew University was his chief interest; he contributed large sums to it and became a member of its Board of Governors. Later the Dead Sea project and the Rutenberg development also attracted him.

The weight of Marshall's and Warburg's influence made things easier for me in the States. Even before the Agency was officially founded American non-Zionists began, under this influence, to co-operate in the *Keren Hayesod* and in other instruments for the building of Palestine. The fact that Marshall spoke from the same platform with me on March 13, 1923—it was my first American meeting of that visit—gave the *Keren Hayesod* campaign a new impetus. Subsequently Marshall and Oscar Strauss, the former Ambassador to Turkey, called together a number of their friends with the purpose of founding a new investment corporation for Palestine. They did not achieve this object, but they did bring new support to what is now the Palestine Economic Corporation, which was able greatly to increase its investments in various Palestinian enterprises.

In the autumn of 1923, when I went for the second time that year to America, after attending the thirteenth Zionist Con-

N

gress in Carlsbad, Mr. Warburg initiated a half-million dollar fund for the Hebrew University through the medium of the American Jewish Physicians Committee. A first tentative sketch of the Jewish Agency constitution—half a dozen headings on a few quarto sheets—which we had worked on in the spring was being elaborated; its development and ramifications were to keep us all busy at intervals for the next six years.

During all this period I carried on, throughout my American visits, and side by side with my Agency conferences, my direct Zionist activities, which I have already described. American Jewish communities were not of a uniform pattern. Chicago was a difficult city for us, because of Rosenwald's influence. Still more difficult was Cincinnati, where the community consisted mainly of Jews of German extraction—and assimilated at that. There was a comparatively weak Russo-Jewish colony, and some of its members worked hard to maintain some sort of Zionist movement in the face of stony opposition. Generally speaking our difficulties increased as we moved westward. California was a different world, remote from the Jewish interests of the eastern states, and practically virgin soil from the Zionist point of view.

There were a few clearings, or oases, here and there. In Chicago there were, among others, two able, hard-working Zionists, Albert K. Epstein and Benjamin Harris, whose lives were saturated with Zionist thought and feeling. It was a particular pleasure to work with them because there was more than a coincidence of Zionist feeling; they were both industrial chemists, and they had practical plans for Palestine. Some of these are now being put into effect, and I have a large file of letters from them dealing with both Zionism and chemistry.

I made an unusual 'find' in New Orleans, where lived a very remarkable personality in American Jewry—Samuel Zemurray, the 'Banana King.' I paid my first visit to New Orleans specially to meet him. He had been told of my arrival and postponed his own planned departure from the city for several days—days which I found not only extremely interesting, but also profitable for the Funds.

Zemurray had come to America from Kishinev as a very young man, and his early years in the New World had been filled by all manner of occupations, which somehow had successfully brought him a little further south. His first venture to prove even moderately successful was peddling bananas from a barrow; this had paid his way down as far as New Orleans, where he arrived with a small surplus in hand. He decided to continue in the line which had brought him his first credit balance. By the time I met him he was the 'Banana King'—the owner of vast plantations in Honduras, with their warehouses, packing sheds, and so on, as well as of his own fleet of refrigerator ships. Today he is the head of the United Fruit Corporation, one of the most powerful American produce companies. Throughout all this record of success Zemurray retained his simplicity, his transparent honesty, his lively interest in people and things, and his desire to serve. His chosen studies in leisure hours were mathematics and music, and he got a great deal of satisfaction out of them. It was said of him that his success in the Central American republics was mainly due to the fact that he was deeply concerned for the welfare of the peons he employed—which was by no means the case with most of his competitors. He built schools, hospitals, recreation grounds and model villages, and generally made his work-people feel that he had a genuine interest in their condition. His building operations resulted incidentally in the excavation of some remarkable relics of the Maya culture, and his great collection of these antiquities is now one of the show pieces of the New Orleans University.

Zemurray was one of the highlights of my visit to the States in that year; and I never missed an opportunity of seeing him on later visits. He did not take a public part in our work; but his interest has been continuous and generous. I found him, at the outbreak of the war, depressed by the White Paper of 1939— depressed, yet hopeful of the ultimate outcome. Despite his distress over the White Paper, he handed over the greater part of his fleet of ships to Great Britain at the beginning of the war.

I have said enough, I believe, concerning the obstacles, the delays, the opposition, the internal and external complications which make up the story of the creation of the Jewish Agency. Seven years and more of my life were consumed by it, and the most shattering blow of all was reserved for the hour of our triumph.

In August 1929, immediately after the Zionist Congress of that year, the Constituent Assembly of the Jewish Agency met at last, in Zurich. Zionist opposition had been overcome, external opposition had been soothed: a genuine assembly of Jewish leaders in the non-Zionist world declared its intention to stand side by side with the Zionists in the practical work in Palestine. All sections of the Jewish people were represented and every community of any size. I have described in this chapter only the American scene in the history of the Agency; in Poland, England, Holland, in every country with a Jewish population, the same story had played itself out. And it was not only the wealthy heads of the large philanthropic organizations who had been drawn into the partnership. The Jewish Agency brought together as distinguished a group of Jews as we have witnessed in our time; all classes and fields of achievement were represented, from Léon Blum, the great socialist leader, to Marshall and Warburg on the right; from Lord Melchett, one of England's leading industrialists, to Albert Einstein the scientist and Chaim Nachman Bialik the poet.

At the end of the meeting I had a long talk with Marshall and Warburg. They assured me that now my financial troubles were over; it would no longer be necessary for me to go up and down America and other countries—from city to city, making innumerable appeals and addresses in order to help create the means for the limited budget of the Zionist Organization. This prediction or promise of theirs represented, I am sure, their sincere belief.

A few days after the Constituent Assembly had dispersed amid mutual felicitations, and while Zionists and non-Zionists all over the world were congratulating themselves on the creation of this new and powerful instrument of Jewish action, the Palestine riots broke out on August 23. On September 11, Louis Marshall, the mainstay of the non-Zionist section of the Agency, died after an operation. And within a few weeks there came the great economic crash of 1929, to be followed by the long depression—perhaps the severest in modern history— which struck hard at the sources of support which the Agency had planned to tap.

It would be quite wrong to say that this last series of blows undid the work of the preceding years. To begin with, the educational achievement of the long effort could never be undone. Its effects continued to grow, the breach between the Zionist and non-Zionist sections of public opinion continued to narrow. The very negotiations produced, before the Agency was completed, a more sympathetic response on the part of the non-Zionists. The notion that the building of the Jewish Homeland was a fantastically Utopian dream, the obsession of impractical, Messianically deluded, ghetto Jews began to be dispelled by the participation of prominent men of affairs with a reputation for sober-mindedness and hard-bitten practicality. Today as I write, nearly twenty years after the official founding of the Jewish Agency, the presence of such figures in the work for Palestine is a commonplace. The dark events of recent years have had a good deal to do with winning them over. But the first steps were taken, the pattern was created, during the long period of persuasion and negotiation which I have described in this chapter.

CHAPTER XXVIII

FOUNDATIONS

A Decisive Decade—Progress of the Hebrew University—What were to be its Functions?—Inauguration Set for April 1, 1925—Lord Balfour Agrees to Preside—Preparations—An Unforgettable Ceremony—Balfour Tours Palestine—A Loving Reception—Significance of the Opening of the University—Rising Anti-Semitism in Europe, Political Setbacks in Palestine—The 'Duality' of the Mandate—The Mandates Commission of the League of Nations—Criticism within the Movement—Jabotinsky Founds Revisionist Party—Ussishkin Resigns from Executive—But the Work Goes on, the Foundations are Laid

THE years between 1920 and 1929 were for the Zionist movement and the National Home years of alternating progress and setback, of slow laborious achievement sown with recurrent disappointment, and of the gradual emergence in Palestine of foundations whose solidity was to be demonstrated in the time that followed. For me they were years of hard work and frequent anxiety, of much wandering in many lands, and of continuous effort within the Zionist Organization to keep our activities and methods in line with the views which I have set forth in the preceding pages. Those were also the years that witnessed the rise of the new anti-Semitism in Europe generally and of Nazism in Germany, imparting new and desperate urgency to our task.

One event stands out in the decade of the twenties on which I linger with pleasure, because of both its practical and its symbolic significance, and that is the opening of the Hebrew University. If I give it a special space in these memoirs it is not only because of the peculiar relationship that I had and have towards that institution, but because it represents the fulfilment of my particular dream of the early days of the movement.

The first step towards the realization of the dream, the reader may remember, was the acquisition of Grey Hill House on

Mount Scopus in the very midst of the war. The second was the erection of the library building—the Wolffsohn Memorial— near by, to house the large collection of books already existing in the Jewish National Library in Jerusalem. Our first librarian was Dr. Heinrich Loewe, an old Zionist comrade-in-arms of my student days, who had in the interim become librarian of the Berlin University Library. To Dr. Loewe we owe the establishment of a sound bibliographical organization and tradition. Once the work was launched, we found books pouring in from all corners of the earth; the Oriental section was particularly fortunate, and rapidly assumed real importance in its field. The opening of the School of Oriental Studies followed closely on the completion of the library building, and was for some time accommodated in a private house rented for the purpose.

In 1923 Professor Patrick Geddes was invited to Jerusalem to assist in the replanning of the city. We asked him to undertake the design and layout of the university buildings, and after a study of the site he prepared some magnificent sketches which delighted all of us. Unfortunately none of them has been actually carried out, though the general plan has been followed. And for myself I still hope before I die to see the great assembly hall which Geddes designed rising on the slopes of Scopus.

Grey Hill House was rebuilt completely, to house the two institutes of microbiology and biochemistry, the first under Professor Saul Adler, formerly of Leeds, the second under Professor Fodor, who devoted much time to the acquisition of equipment and the adaptation of the building to laboratory use. The American Jewish Physicians Committee supplied much of the money for this beginning, and covered the budget of the two institutes for the first three years. We now felt that we had at least the nucleus of a faculty of sciences.

Most popular of the faculties was, of course, the Institute of Jewish Studies (endowed by Sol Rosenbloom of Pittsburgh). Baron Edmond de Rothschild, Felix Warburg and other friends took a personal interest in this branch of the University, and, indeed, there was a stage when I felt there was some danger in the enthusiasm which it aroused. There were too many who thought of the institute romantically in terms of a great centre of Hebrew learning and literature; it was placed under the patronage of the Chief Rabbis of London and Paris, and its council included Dr. Magnes. It ran the risk of becoming a theological seminary, like those of London, Breslau or Philadelphia, instead of the school of *literæ humaniores* of a free University. Happily the danger was averted when the council of the Institute of Jewish Studies was merged into the general structure of the University.

Somehow few people in those early days gave much thought to the possibility of developing a great scientific faculty at the Hebrew University. I was repeatedly told that we could never hope to compete with Cambridge or London or Paris or Harvard in chemistry, physics or mathematics. I felt this to be an erroneous conception—anyhow, taking a long view. True, for the first few years we might not amount to anything in this field, but if the University was encouraged to develop freely, who could tell what young new forces we might attract from the scientific world? I felt, too, that the sciences had to be encouraged at Jerusalem, not only for their own sake, but because they were an integral part of the programme for the full development of Palestine, and also because opportunities for Jewish students in the leading universities of Europe were becoming more and more restricted. The last consideration was at the time no more than a vague uneasiness, even in my own mind. Events in recent years have made it only too bitterly specific.

In addition to the institutes already described, we had, in Jerusalem, the great Rothschild Hospital, which we felt might well be used for research, and later on for teaching. We also had a Jewish Agricultural Experimental Station, with quite a number of research workers, and this might make the beginning of an agricultural faculty.

Altogether, we thought all the foregoing a fair start. Everything was of course on the most modest scale, but it seemed to us to contain much promise. We realized that the process of building up a university was bound to be a slow one, even apart from the fact that limited finances (in relation to the task in hand) imposed on us the utmost caution. But I had never believed that such things as universities could spring into being overnight, particularly in a country still struggling to provide itself with the bare necessities of life. Nor did I believe that everything would—or even ought to be—plain sailing for the

infant University. Such institutions, like men, are often none
the worse for having experienced poverty and adversity in
youth: if they survive at all, they are the stronger, the more
firmly rooted, for it.

What seemed important was to make a start with the
materials in hand, and to put them to the best possible use. To
this we applied our minds in 1923 and the following years, to
such purpose that by the spring of 1925 we could look at 'our
University' and feel there really was enough of it to justify a
formal 'opening ceremony.' Of course at that early stage no
students had been accepted, but a body of research workers
was gradually assembling and the various institutes were taking
shape. After much discussion and heart-searching, therefore, we
sent out invitations for an opening ceremony to be conducted
by Lord Balfour on April 1, 1925. I need not say how much
his instant and enthusiastic acceptance of the invitation meant
to us.

I therefore found myself, in the middle of March 1925, setting
forth with my wife and our son Benjy, to join the *Esperia* in
Genoa. On board we found Professor Rappard, permanent
secretary of the Mandate Commission, who was representing
the University of Geneva at the opening. The Balfour party—
Balfour himself, his ex-secretary, Edward Lascelles and Mrs.
Lascelles, Balfour's niece—came on board at Naples; Balfour,
being an indifferent sailor, wished to curtail the sea passage as
much as possible. Other friends—notably the Sokolows—were
also on board, so that there was plenty of company. As far as
Sicily the weather held, but after Syracuse the wind sprang up
and the sea became choppy, and the Balfour party was out of
action for three days. It is rare for the Mediterranean to mis-
behave so late in March, and I suppose more than one of us
muttered '*absit omen*' under his breath. Lord Balfour did not
emerge again until we docked in Alexandria. It was still
blowing half a gale, and a heavy shower of cold rain met us
as we walked down the gangway. Mrs. Lascelles's ironical
remarks about the wonderful weather in the Mediterranean
and the blue skies of Egypt left me with an uncomfortable
impression that I was perhaps being held responsible for the
misconduct of the elements.

The Balfours went on to Cairo, to stay with Lord Allenby,

N*

who came with them a couple of days later to Kantara and accompanied us up to Jerusalem.

The situation in Palestine was at the time somewhat tense, but the security officers assured us that apart from a fairly peaceable demonstration in the form of a strike, and the closing of a few Arab shops in Jerusalem, Haifa and Jaffa, nothing untoward was happening. Which was just as well, as our guests were beginning to arrive in considerable numbers: representatives of universities and learned societies from all over the world, not to mention a great influx of tourists. It was not easy to find rooms for all these people in Jerusalem, for hotel accommodation was still scarce, and not of the best. Still, our reception committee did its work well, and I was not aware that any complaints were made. Every resident who had an appropriate house had placed it at the committee's disposal, and one way or another we managed to see to it that our guests enjoyed reasonable comfort.

The Balfour party and the Allenbys stayed of course at Government House. Kisch, Eder and I lived through some days of rather severe tension, with the responsibility of so many distinguished people on our hands under rather difficult conditions. There was, for instance, only one road from the city to the University on Mount Scopus, and that a narrow one, with little room for cars to turn. Control of traffic was a rather alarming problem, for the number of cars travelling to and fro was a record for Jerusalem at that time. Another purely physical difficulty was the actual site chosen for the opening ceremony. There was as yet no hall which could accommodate anything approaching the number of our guests and visitors—we expected some twelve thousand to fourteen thousand people. The only place, therefore, where we could stage the ceremony was the natural amphitheatre facing a deep wadi on the north-east slope of Scopus. Round this amphitheatre we arranged tiers of seats, following the natural rock formation. Everything was rather rough and ready, but the setting had such natural beauty that no art could have improved on it.

The snag was that, to face the audience in this amphitheatre, the platform had to be on a bridge over the wadi itself. The gorge was deep, sheer and rocky; the bridge was an improvised wooden affair which inspired—in me at least—little confidence.

I was told that it had been repeatedly tested, but my blood ran cold at the thought that something might give way at the crucial moment. . . . The builders, however, were convinced that the platform could safely bear two hundred or two hundred and fifty people. However, two hundred of our sturdiest young *chalutzim* volunteered to dance an energetic *hora* on the contraption. Nothing happened—except a great deal of noise—and I felt a little easier. Minute inspection of the platform failed to reveal any damage.

One final problem remained: the guarding of the tested platform during the night before the opening. Again our young *chalutzim* (members of the Haganah this time) came to the rescue: they established a sort of one-night camp in the wadi, and conducted frequent inspections, the last only a few minutes before the guests began to arrive.

Though the accommodation might be simple, even primitive, the surroundings—the austere magnificence of the landscape which opens out before one from this part of Scopus—more than made up for it. I doubt if anyone who made the pilgrimage to Mount Scopus that day, and the arrivals began before dawn, regretted the non-existence of the Central Hall. Apart from our foreign visitors, people came from all over the country, people of every class and age and type. Only the three or four front rows of the amphitheatre were reserved; the rest were open to the public, and needless to say were thronged hours before the ceremony began. I noted with some pride the discipline and good humour shown by the crowds.

Half an hour or so before the opening time the speakers and other platform guests assembled in the Grey Hill House to don their academic robes; then they passed, a colourful little procession, through the University grove on to the platform. The party from Government House approached direct, from the opposite side. Lord Balfour's appearance set off a tremendous ovation, which was hushed into complete stillness as he took his place on the platform.

The ceremony itself is a matter of historic record, and I need not describe it here. Many of the speakers were deeply moved. One or two of them were, as was only to be expected, rather long-winded. I remember thinking at the time that Bialik (of all people!) was rather straining people's patience: he spoke in

Hebrew, which to many of those present was a strange tongue. Moreover, I knew that at sunset the air would cool rapidly, and I was afraid that Lord Balfour (who was a man of seventy-seven) and some of the others might suffer, since all were bare-headed and without overcoats. However, we did finish before sundown; the crowds dispersed in orderly fashion; the guests departed to rest before the dinner party arranged for the evening; and the various committees responsible for the arrangements heaved a sigh of relief that everything had gone off without a noticeable hitch.

At dinner that evening my wife sat next to Lord Allenby. She was moved to ask him: 'Did you think my husband com-pletely harebrained when he asked your permission for the laying of the foundation stones in 1918?' He thought for a moment and replied: 'When I think back to that day—as I often do—I come to the conclusion that that short ceremony inspired my army, and gave them confidence in the future.' He repeated this statement in the short speech which he made after the dinner.

Before Lord Balfour came to Palestine, it had been our idea to spare him as much as possible. We had planned a short drive through the country to show him one or two places in which we thought he might be specially interested, but nothing at all tiring. We had, however, counted without our guest, who refused to be spared. He liked the look of the country, and wanted to see as much as he possibly could of it. We were also very anxious that he should not speak too much, especially in the open. But here again, when it came to the point, there was no holding him back. He was warmly received wherever we went, and naturally the man in charge would say a few words of welcome (which I tried, with varying success, to keep as few as possible). Lord Balfour clearly liked replying. He said on one occasion that it reminded him of a general election tour —but with everybody on the same side!

The most impressive feature of his trip was to Tel Aviv. I had been a little uneasy about this beforehand. It was a biggish town, and there were bound to be all sorts of people among its crowds. Anyone who wanted to work mischief could easily do so. Security measures were, of course, stringent. We travelled down by car from Jerusalem one morning, and stopped for lunch at Mikveh, the Agricultural School a couple of miles this side of Tel Aviv. There we had a light lunch, and left Lord Balfour to rest, while we went ahead to reconnoitre. The crowds I met both impressed and terrified me. The main streets—Allenby Road and Herzl Street—were lined with solid blocks of people: not only were the pavements a living wall, but every balcony, every window, every roof-top, was jammed to capacity. These crowds had been waiting for some hours. I went to see Mr. Dizengoff, the mayor, who assured me that there was every reason to be satisfied with the measures taken for the maintaining of order, and then we returned to Mikveh to pick up the rest of the party.

So we came into Tel Aviv in the early afternoon, in an open car. The enthusiasm with which Lord Balfour was received was indescribable. In Herzl Street stood a group of Jewish women from Poland, weeping for joy; now and again one of them would press forward and gently touch either the body of the car or Lord Balfour's sleeve, and pronounce a blessing on him. He was obviously deeply affected. The car moved forward slowly; complete order prevailed; and in due course we reached 'Balfour Street,' which Lord Balfour was to open. Here he was greeted by representatives of the municipality, and the short ceremony followed. Then we moved on to the Herzliah High School, where the students staged a gymnastic display which greatly impressed the Balfour party. With one voice they made two comments: 'These boys might have come from Harrow!' And 'Mr. Dizengoff might easily be the mayor of Liverpool or of Manchester!' Both remarks were intended—and taken—as the highest compliments.

After tea we adjourned to the quarters prepared for the party in Shmarya Levin's old house, which had been vacated for the purpose. Everything was ready there, including a staff of servants and a guard, and we left Balfour and his party to recover from a rather strenuous day. I arranged to call on them in the morning.

Later in the evening I thought I would like to see how things were round about the Levin house, and strolled in that direction. But a cordon of young men, on guard, shut off the whole neighbourhood. Even I could not get within three hundred yards of the gate. This was only in part for security reasons; the idea was mainly to keep off the noise of the crowd which showed little disposition to go home to bed. Balfour told me the next morning that he had had a quiet night, so the precautions seem to have been effective.

We set out that day on a short tour of the Judean colonies—Rishon and Petach Tikvah—then turned north to Haifa, where Balfour had another wonderful reception at the Technical Institute (opened almost simultaneously with the University). We went on into the Emek. On the way to Nahalal we passed a hill crowned with a newly erected barracks, round which clustered a number of people who looked like recently arrived refugees. They made a striking group. We discovered that they were *Chassidim* who, led by their Rabbi (the Rabbi of Yablon), had landed in Palestine only a few days before. Many of them had since then been compelled to sleep in the open, which in spite of the light rains still to be expected in April, they were finding a wonderful experience. Balfour alighted from the car and went into the barracks to receive the blessings of the Rabbi. I told him that if he would come again in a year or two he would find quite a different picture: he would find these people established on their own land, content, and looking like peasants descended from generations of peasants.

The tour prolonged itself to include a number of places not originally contemplated. Balfour talked to the settlers everywhere—at least to those who could understand English. He also met some of the Arab sheikhs who came in from near-by villages. He was impressed by the looks and bearing of the settlers: upright, sunburned, quiet, completely self-possessed—entirely different from the nervous deportment of the urbanized Jew. The children, too, were obviously village children, sons and daughters of the soil, simple, modest, without affectation, and of an infectious gaiety. Lord Balfour showed a lively interest in everything and everybody. He wanted to understand these people, their lives, their requirements, their budget, how they managed without money or personal possessions, how they kept their relations with the outside world so simple, how they managed to live in virtually self-contained villages, what sort of intellectual life they had, what music they played, what books they read. Towards the end of the trip he said to me: 'I think the early Christians must have been a little like these men.' He added: 'They fit quite remarkably into this landscape.'

The trip ended in Nazareth, into which we came one glorious evening under a full moon. The Balfour party was leaving the next morning for Syria, and I was returning to Haifa to join my mother for Passover, so this was really farewell. I remember walking that last night with Edward Lascelles along the road out of Nazareth, and our being accosted by two or three Arab youths anxious to offer their services as guides to the city. As it was night, we said we would perhaps meet them the next day. They then entered into conversation with us, and told us in their rather curious English that there had just arrived in Nazareth a very great Jew, Mr. Balfour. We tried to persuade them that they were mistaken in this, but they were quite sure that he was a Jew, and had come to 'hand over' Palestine to the Jews. It was all said quite without bitterness, indeed lightly, and half-banteringly. One could only reflect that Arab propaganda had already made considerable progress.

At dinner that evening a discussion arose as to whether Lord Balfour should go to Damascus by car, or take the train as had been arranged. I protested vigorously against the suggested change. I did not think it safe for him to travel by car to Syria; besides, the French authorities under Sarrail had given every guarantee for the train journey, and the train would be waiting at the frontier. It had been hard enough in Palestine to take all the measures needed for security, and there we had regular co-operation with the authorities, in addition to thousands of young men prepared to maintain order both in the towns and on the roads. Nothing of this applied in Syria. Quite an argument developed between Mrs. Lascelles and me, and once or twice she hinted that I was exploiting her uncle for purposes of propaganda. This was just what I had been doing my level best to avoid. I had all the time been trying to protect him from such 'exploitation'—it was he who had objected to my well-meant efforts at restriction. In the end Mrs. Lascelles appealed to Balfour himself, who had listened to the whole conversation without giving the slightest indication of his own views, and he said: 'Well, I suppose we shall have to obey Weizmann's orders; after all, we must be imposing a great strain on him.' So the original programme was followed.

I had sent my secretary, Miss Lieberman, on to Beirut ahead of the party, to report to me how things were going there. The next morning I heard from her on the phone, and received the whole story of the violent demonstration which brought the Balfour visit to an abrupt end almost before it began: how crowds tried to storm the Victoria Hotel; how Sarrail had had to smuggle the party away, and send it by fast car to the boat.

We were deeply chagrined that the visit which had gone off so harmoniously in Palestine should have closed so unpleasantly in Syria, but were thankful that nothing worse had happened than the cancellation of the party's plans. I went down to Alexandria to meet the *Sphinx* and to tell Lord Balfour how sorry I was about the incidents in Beirut. He replied placidly: 'Oh, I wouldn't worry about that—nothing compared with what I went through in Ireland!' From Alexandria, too, he wrote me a charming letter of thanks for the Palestine visit. In it he said: 'The main purpose of my visit was the opening of the Hebrew University. But the highest intellectual and moral purposes can be only partially successful if, parallel with them, there is not a strong material development. This is why I was particularly happy to see the flourishing Jewish settlements which testify to the soundness and strength of the growing National Home.'

In the weeks that followed I thought over the question of the opening ceremony, and the criticisms which it had provoked, both before and after. Even Dr. Magnes, about to become the head of the University, was inclined to deprecate the ceremony as too much of a 'political act.' I did not see why it was a 'political act' or, if it was, why it should lose any value thereby. It may be that the creation of any great institution in Palestine —or anywhere else, for that matter—is always a political act. The very existence of the Jewish National Home was a political act. But I gathered from Dr. Magnes that the words had a derogatory meaning. Other critics said that there was not enough of the University to justify this 'enormous display' and the 'solemnity' of the inauguration. Up to a point I agreed. In fact, we had not a real university; we had the germ of a university. It was like the Jewish National Home itself: small, but with great potentialities. It had seemed to me that what was needed was some strong stimulus to galvanize the whole thing into new life, and that the formal opening had something of the effect intended was shown by the fact that funds began to flow in very shortly afterwards from all quarters—sometimes from quarters till then indifferent to Palestinian affairs. Externally, too, the opening ceremony made a profound impression. Scientists and scholars from abroad had travelled through the country and seen for themselves what was being done there. Many who had previously been sceptical had revised their views in the face of the facts. Among them were Rappard and Allenby. Though by no means unfriendly, Rappard had on the whole been critical, and it was certainly a surprise to him to find so marked a revival, both of the people and the land, within so short a period. Allenby was, if anything, even more deeply impressed. He had said openly at the beginning that he had been rather against the whole enterprise as impractical; now he had come to believe both in the Jewish National Home and also in its importance to the British Empire.

Again, the ceremony had served as a link with friends, Jewish and non-Jewish, in the Diaspora. Many non-Jewish learned societies held meetings on the same day: in Paris, for instance, a distinguished gathering, headed by Léon Blum, Painlevé and others, sent us messages of greeting; others came from New York, Chicago, Stockholm and—unthinkable as it may seem today—from Berlin, Frankfurt and Leipzig.

Today, less than a quarter of a century after the opening ceremony, we have on Scopus a full-fledged University, comparable in most respects with the ancient homes of learning of Western Europe. It is rapidly approaching completion, in so far as a university may ever be said to approach completion, and if not for the war would already have gained for itself no small reputation. Looking back now, I really believe that this rapid development would not have come to pass without the great impetus given to the idea in April 1925, when Balfour stood, like a prophet of old, on Mount Scopus, and proclaimed to the world that here a great seat of learning was being created—seeing far beyond the few small buildings which then formed the skeleton of the university of the future.

I have said that for me the opening of the Hebrew University was the highlight of a period of labour and anxiety, of alternating

disappointment and achievement, during which the foundations of the Jewish National Home were being laid. The more
dramatic events and the more spectacular achievements of
later years have dimmed the memory of the era preceding 1929
and obscured its significance; but if there is today a powerful
Yishuv in Palestine and a great Zionist movement in the world,
their existence and character can be understood only against the
background of the early struggle.

The first shadows of the eclipse of Jewish life in Europe were
already visible. Hitler made his brief and inglorious début on
the German scene in 1923; in 1924 *Mein Kampf* was published,
with its outright declaration of war on the Jewish people.
Similar stirrings were noticeable in Rumania, Hungary and
Poland. Most of us have since forgotten these earlier manifestations, and few of us gave them their proper evaluation at the
time. But a handful of persons—these mostly in our movement
—gave warning even then. Sokolow's speech at the 1923 Congress was devoted mainly to the rise of the new anti-Semitism,
and we all knew that he was very far from being a scaremonger.

Side by side with these portents there was a general diminution in the political status of the Jewish National Home. In
England the attacks on the Mandate policy for Palestine continued, both in the Lords and in the Commons. The policy
naturally had its defenders, too, but what disturbed us most
was the evidence of a constant tendency on the part of the
British Government to shift the emphasis from the dynamic
aspect of the Mandate to the static. Instead of viewing the
Jewish National Home as an institution in the making it seemed
to be placing increasing emphasis on the *status quo* in Palestine.
The White Paper of 1922, which removed Transjordan arbitrarily from the operation of the Mandate, proposed for Palestine 'a Legislative Council with a majority of elected members.'
Carried out to the full, this would have meant handing over
Palestine to the Arab majority and excluding world Jewry, the
partner to the Balfour Declaration, from a say in the destinies
of Palestine. The legislative council was never set up; but in
1923 we faced another proposal of the same kind. The British
Government offered the Arabs an 'Arab Agency,' presumably
intended as a sort of counterpoise to the 'Jewish Agency'
provided for in the Mandate. It was difficult to see what func-

tions such an agency would discharge, for it would clearly not represent anyone but the Arabs of Palestine (if them), but it may have been felt that it would please the Arabs to feel that they had, at least in name, equal status with world Jewry, in respect to Palestine. The Government had informed us that they would proceed with this offer of an Arab Agency only if both parties, the Arabs and the Jews, agreed to it. As it happens the Arabs turned it down on sight.

In all these actions we were placed in the curious position of seeming to oppose democratic rights to the Arabs. Only those who had some notion of the structure of Arab life understood how farcical was the proposal to vest political power in the hands of the small Arab upper class in the name of democracy. But of this I shall have much more to say further on. What mattered more at the time was the insidious exclusion, by implication, of the relationship between Palestine and world Jewry.

The notion of the 'duality of the Mandate,' of equal weight being given to the Arabs of Palestine as against the entire Jewish people, crept into the reports of the Mandates Commission too. In October 1924 the Mandates Commission issued this statement:

. . . the policy of the Mandatory Power as regards immigration gives rise to acute controversy. It does not afford entire satisfaction to the Zionists, who feel that the establishment of a Jewish National Home is the first duty of the Mandatory Power, and manifest a certain impatience at the restrictions which are placed in the way of immigration and in respect of the granting of land to immigrants. This policy is, on the other hand, rejected by the Arab majority of the country, which refuses to accept the idea of a Jewish National Home, and regards the action of the Administration as a menace to its traditional patrimony. . . .

The implication here is that the policy in regard to Palestine should include only the Arab majority and the Jewish minority confronting each other in the country—a policy which would have completely nullified the Balfour Declaration.

The attitude of the Mandates Commission undoubtedly owed something to its President, at that time an Italian, Count Theodoli, a definite opponent of the Zionist movement, who had married into an Arab family. Of him too I shall have more to say. However, that first report of the Mandates Commission was for us a warning of how little Zionist aims and aspirations were understood even by those called upon to supervise the administration. It was obvious that a special task lay before us, namely, to explain to the League of Nations, its members, and its organs in Geneva, the fundamental principles, political, ethical and historical, which guided the Zionist movement. We decided to open an office in Geneva, under the guidance of Dr. Victor Jacobson. Gradually succeeding sessions of the Mandates Commission were to show traces of its effect. My own contacts with the leading personalities of the Mandates Commission were, I believe, also of value.

These external difficulties were reflected in the internal stresses of the Zionist Organization which, as a democratic institution, gave full play to the possibilities of an opposition. I faced prolonged and often bitter attacks at the Conferences and Congresses; and I used to complain, half-seriously, that, if our movement had no other attribute of a government, it had at least the first prerequisite—an opposition.

Jabotinsky withdrew from the Executive shortly after the issue of the White Paper of 1922, which he denounced, though he had, like the rest of his fellow-members, signed the letter of acceptance. He proceeded to establish the Revisionist Party, which ultimately became the 'New Zionist Organization,' to provide the necessary platform. He attacked me for what he called my 'Fabian' tactics and insufficient energy and enterprise: 'We have always to fight the British Government.' It was rather odd that he should also have attacked me for arranging the opening ceremony of the Hebrew University. He accused me of throwing dust in the eyes of the public, and described it as a tawdry performance—an 'imitation whale made of wood.' It was, according to him, a combination of political arrogance and sickening hysteria. Strong words—but not quite in keeping with the other accusation of lack of energy and enterprise.

Ussishkin too went into opposition. At the Action Committee meeting which preceded the Congress of 1923, he subjected the conduct of our affairs to an extremely critical review, and marshalled a series of facts concerning the attitude of the

British administration in Palestine and the difficulties resulting from it—all of which he laid at my door. Kisch, Sokolow and I could only urge in reply that we were quite as aware of all this as Mr. Ussishkin, and had taken every possible step both in London and Jerusalem to improve matters. Sometimes we had succeeded, sometimes not; but we were certainly not conscious of any sins of omission in this respect. When we asked what Mr. Ussishkin and his friends would have done in our place, the reply was: 'Protest! Demand! Insist!' And that seemed to be the ultimate wisdom to be gleaned from our critics. They seemed quite unaware that the constant repetition of protests, demands and insistences defeats its own ends, being both futile and undignified. I emphasized once more that the only real answer to our difficulties in Palestine was the strengthening of our position by bringing in the right type of immigrant in larger numbers, by acquiring more land, by speeding up our productive work.

I realized, even then, that I had to argue in a vicious circle: in order to get the good will of the Government we had to hasten the work of development; but in order to hasten the work of development we desperately needed the active good will of the Government. This dilemma has faced us, from one angle or another, throughout the last thirty years, and I have often thought how much easier life would be if one had to deal only with single-pronged problems, and not with the twin horns of a dilemma.

The very painful debate with Ussishkin ended in his resignation from the Executive and Kisch's appointment in his stead. We were all deeply sorry about it, and I was much distressed to hear later from Kisch that Ussishkin's comment had been: 'I am going now—but I shall come back as President of the Organization.' This did not in fact happen, but Ussishkin continued to play a prominent part in our councils, and later accepted the Presidency of the Jewish National Fund; as time went on, the breach between us slowly healed.

These, then, were the struggles I faced within the Organization. They centred on relations with England, relations with the non-Zionist groups of the Agency-in-the-making, methods of colonization, the co-operative versus the individualist colonies, private enterprise versus the national funds, urban

versus rural growth. And throughout it all the foundations of
the National Home were slowly being laid. We went through
very hard times in 1926, 1927 and part of 1928. The big influx
of 1925, with its large proportion of small capitalists, produced
the crisis which I had feared and warned against. The signs
were there by the end of that year; by 1926 there were six
thousand unemployed in Palestine, and by 1927 a thousand
more. There were strikes, lock-outs and clashes between employers and workers. And always there was the shortage of
funds, the failure of the wealthier elements in Jewry to respond.
But underneath it all there was a steady organic growth, often
invisible at first. When the economic crisis came to an end in
1928 the Jewish population had tripled since the close of the
war; it stood at close to one hundred and seventy thousand.
Unemployment had vanished. The lands of the Jewish National
Fund had increased until they had the lead over the old, rich
P.I.C.A. The most dreadful feature of the depression had been
a reversal in the migratory movement; in 1927 there were
three thousand more emigrants than immigrants—a startling
portent. By 1928 the stream had again been reversed, and it
continued to swell. We could begin to draw breath.

Our relations with the Arabs were, on the surface at least,
not altogether unsatisfactory. The small upper level which constituted the backing of the so-called Arab Executive continued
its protests and propaganda abroad; within Palestine there was
quiet. Thousands of Arab workmen were employed by Jewish
farmers, and thousands more made a good livelihood selling
produce to the Jews.

Sir Herbert Samuel relinquished his post as High Commissioner in 1925, and was succeeded by Field-Marshal Lord
Plumer, whose prestige and authority did much to discourage
any mischief which the Arab agitators were planning. Typical
of his attitude is the following story.

During Plumer's High Commissionership the Jewish community decided to transfer the regimental colours of the Jewish
Battalion of World War I from London to Jerusalem. The
colours arrived in due course, and permission was granted by
the High Commissioner to carry them in solemn procession to
the Great Synagogue of Jerusalem. As soon as the Arab leaders
heard of this, they became greatly agitated and betook them-

selves in a crowd to see Lord Plumer and to remonstrate with him. His A.D.C. reported to him that there was a biggish crowd of Arabs in the hall, waiting to see him, to which Plumer said: 'Will you kindly tell the Arab gentlemen that I have twelve chairs, and they might elect twelve speakers. Then I could see them in comfort.' This was done, and the speakers entered. In their usual manner the Arab leaders began to protest and threaten, saying that if the procession took place they could not be responsible for order in the city. To which Plumer promptly remarked: 'You are not asked to be responsible, gentlemen; I shall be responsible—and I shall be there.'

It was done in the grand manner, and it was effective. This is how a determined administrator speaks politely and firmly to political mischief makers, and thwarts their intentions without resorting to a display of force. Of course one has to be a Plumer to carry it off, and Plumer remained with us less than three years—all too short a period. He was succeeded by Sir John Chancellor, a man of much smaller calibre.

During all those years I spent the bulk of my time travelling, sometimes accompanied by my wife, sometimes alone, when she did not feel she could leave the children, who resented my constant absences. I was actually at home only for short intervals between trips to America, Palestine, Germany, France, Holland and Belgium, not to speak of my attendance at various international conferences. I was trying to build up the movement, making contacts with governments and Jewish communities, and in the process acquiring a good many friendships in political, literary and scientific circles in different countries. I came to feel almost equally at home in Brussels or Paris or San Francisco. But in the late summer or early autumn of every year there were a carefully engineered few weeks which I spent with my wife and family on holiday.

They were quiet holidays, and always much the same: a village in the mountains of Switzerland or the Tyrol, long walks in the hills among the rocks and glaciers, till I felt I knew almost every stone and rock by name; and then, as the weather in the heights deteriorated, we would go down for a few days to Merano, to a small sanatorium. Merano had an attraction of its own; in those days it was off the beaten track, never overrun with tourists, enjoying an almost perfect climate, especially in the autumn. It was beautiful, too, full of orchards and vine-yards. Moreover, it had admirable funicular railways, by which one could reach altitudes of five or six thousand feet in a short time. So most of my days were spent there walking in the mountains, enjoying the pure air and the wonderful scenery, and returning at sunset to the sanatorium, refreshed and invigorated.

Thus I managed to get a few weeks off for real rest and relaxation with my family every year. Often attempts were made to get me back to London or elsewhere before the allotted time was up, but I always refused to budge. My holi-day was sacrosanct, devoted entirely to my wife and children, and I grudged every interruption, however urgent. I still believe that without these few weeks of absolute quiet I would never have been able to carry the burden during the rest of the year. Very occasionally I would also manage a break of a week or ten days in the winter, spent as a rule in Switzerland; but this, when I got it, was much more subject to interruptions. Most winters I spent in America or Palestine, hard at work.

CHAPTER XXIX

ATTACK AND REPULSE

*The Riots of 1929—Their Political Significance—Death of Louis Marshall
—The Shaw Commission Report Whitewashes the Palestine Administration
—The Simpson Report and the Passfield White Paper—Warburg, Melchett
and I Resign from Jewish Agency—The Struggle with the Colonial Office—
We Receive Strong non-Jewish Backing—Misinterpreting the Mandate so
as to Exclude World Jewry—The Pose of Neutrality—Retraction of the
White Paper in Ramsay MacDonald's Letter—Sir Arthur Wauchope
Appointed High Commissioner—Consequences—Failure of Arab 'Strategy'*

THE first constituent meeting of the Jewish Agency opened in
Zurich on August 11, 1929, and the agreement between the
Zionists and the non-Zionists was signed on the fourteenth.
This meeting followed close on the sixteenth Zionist Congress,
held in the same city; its opening, in fact, coincided with the
close of the Congress, which had lasted from July 28 to
August 11. By the time the last business of Congress and the
Agency had been cleared away I was quite exhausted, for I
had come to Zurich still suffering from the after-effects of a
protracted illness.

I was exhausted but happy. What the founding of the
Agency meant to the Zionist movement, what hopes I reposed
in it, what labour I had put into its creation, has already been
indicated. I looked forward to, and I needed, one of those
holidays which I have described at the end of the last chapter;
and on August 23 my wife and I left Zurich for Wengen, in
the Bernese Oberland, to join our son Michael. I remember
well the happiness which I felt during the three-hour journey,
and the sense of peace and achievement which filled me. I felt
free from care, I anticipated confidently a future which would
witness a great acceleration in the building up of the National
Home.

We reached Wengen in the evening, and for the whole of the
following day I rested. I tried not to think of the hard years

through which we had passed. I did not even look at a newspaper. On the second morning I was awakened by the hotel boy, who brought me a telegram. The envelope was bulky, and I had an instant premonition that it brought bad news. I did not expect any business telegrams. I had separated from my friends less than two days before, and I knew they had all dispersed for their holidays. What could this bulky telegram mean? Only bad news from Palestine. For several minutes I refused to open it, and then I gave way. It began with the words 'The Under-Secretary of State regrets to announce . . .' and brought me the first news of the Palestine pogroms of 1929, in which nearly a hundred and fifty Jews were killed, hundreds more wounded, and great damage done to property.

I was struck as by a thunderbolt. This, then, was the answer of the Arab leadership to the Congress and the Agency meeting. They had realized that our fortunes had taken an upward turn, that the speed of our development in Palestine would soon follow the same curve. The way to prevent that, they thought— wrongly, as we all know now—was a blood bath. The means used to precipitate the riots, the appeal to religious fanaticism, the whipping up of blind mob passions, the deliberate misrepresentation of Zionist aims—on all this I shall not dwell here. It is in the record. In the record too is the story of that mixture of indifference, inefficiency, and hostility on the part of the Palestine administration which had helped to give the Arab leaders their opportunity.

I began telephoning to London, but all my friends were away. I could only reach Mrs. Philip Snowden, wife of the Chancellor of the Exchequer, who tried to comfort me. I felt I could not stay on in Wengen. We made arrangements for the care of the children, and left for London. On the day of our departure we learned that Louis Marshall, who was still in Zurich, was gravely ill and would have to submit to a dangerous operation. Soon after our arrival in London we received the news of his death. This was the second blow.

It is difficult to convey the state of depression into which I was cast. The Colonial Secretary of that time, Lord Passfield (the former Sidney Webb) had shown extremely little sympathy for our cause, and was very reluctant to see me on my arrival in London. I had a conversation, at his house, with Lady Passfield (the former Beatrice Webb), in the presence of Josiah Wedgwood who, in those days, as always, stood staunchly with us. What I heard from Lady Passfield was: 'I can't understand why the Jews make such a fuss over a few dozen of their people killed in Palestine. As many are killed every week in London in traffic accidents, and no one pays any attention.'

When at last I managed to see Passfield and his friends in the Colonial Office I realized at once that they would use this opportunity to curtail Jewish immigration into Palestine. I tried next to see Ramsay MacDonald, the Socialist Prime Minister, but in spite of the efforts of his son, Malcolm, who was extremely sympathetic to our cause until he in turn became Colonial Secretary—a familiar story, this—no interview could be arranged. In fact I did not see Ramsay MacDonald until much later, when he was attending a meeting of the League Council in Geneva.

Meanwhile the machinery was set in motion for the political attack on our position in Palestine. First came the Shaw Commission, sent out to Palestine two months after the riots, to inquire into their 'immediate causes' and to make recommendations for the future maintenance of peace. The report which it brought in some months later merely conceded that the Arabs had been the attackers; but it said nothing about the strange behaviour of the Palestine administration, which during the attacks had issued one communiqué after another representing the riots as 'clashes' between Jews and Arabs. From these communiqués it was made to appear that there were two peoples at war in Palestine, with the British administration as the neutral guardian of law and order. Apart from the gross misrepresentation of the Jewish attitude which such utterances impressed on the world, the implied exoneration of the Arab mobs and their inciters boded ill for the future. I have said that the Haycraft Report of 1921 contained the seed of much of our later troubles. Here were some of the fruits.

Then came the Simpson Report. Sir John Hope Simpson and his commission were sent out to Palestine in May 1930, to look into the problems of immigration, land settlement, and development. But before the report was issued, together with what is now called the Passfield White Paper, the Government declared publicly that it intended to suspend immigration,

introduce restrictive land legislation, curtail the authority of
the Jewish Agency and in general introduce in Palestine a
régime which made the appointment of the Simpson Commission either a superfluity or a propaganda instrument for the
Government's predetermined policy.

I managed at last to see the Prime Minister. My wife and I
had gone to Geneva. During the Channel crossing we met Lady
Astor, whose attitude towards our work was at that time
friendly. I put our case before her, and expressed my desire to
see MacDonald, in the hope of obtaining from him a promise
that the proposed negative legislation should not be put into
effect. In Geneva an interview with the Prime Minister was
arranged, and in a long conversation with him I did obtain
what seemed to be a satisfactory statement. I saw other statesmen in Geneva, Briand among them, and many of them
promised me their support.

There was another meeting with the Prime Minister that
spring, with the late Lord Reading, Lord Melchett, Pinchas
Rutenberg and myself for our side, and Mr. MacDonald, Lord
Passfield and a group of senior officials for the Government. I
came to that meeting with a special grievance, the nature of
which indicated the depth and persistence of Passfield's
hostility. He had promised to have Simpson see me before he
left for Palestine, and then had broken the promise deliberately.
In a very polite way I charged Passfield openly with a breach
of faith. His Lordship never said a word or moved a muscle.
I added one strong sentence. I said: 'One thing the Jews will
never forgive, and that is having been fooled.' The Prime Minister smiled, and it also brought out a broad grin on the faces of
the officials. Thereupon I turned to them and said: 'I can't
understand how you, as good British patriots, don't see the
moral implications of promises given to Jews, and I regret to
see that you seem to deal with them rather frivolously.' The
grin disappeared.

It was curious to see how little the Prime Minister seemed to
realize the inconsistency of the new course with the letter and
spirit of the Mandate. And curious too was the spate of reassurances which he offered us—as he offered them to Mr. Felix
Warburg in a meeting they had at Chequers. If either of us
took those assurances seriously, he was doomed to be bitterly

disappointed. On October 21, 1930, the Government published, simultaneously, the Hope Simpson report and the White Paper.

This is not the place for an analysis of the Passfield White Paper. Suffice it to say that it was considered by all Jewish friends of the National Home, Zionist and non-Zionist alike, and by a host of non-Jewish well-wishers, as rendering, and intending to render, our work in Palestine impossible. There was nothing left for me but to resign my position as the President of the Jewish Agency. In this drastic step I had the complete support of Lord Melchett and of Felix Warburg, who also resigned, the former as the chairman of the Council of the Agency, the latter as a member of the Jewish Agency Administrative Committee.

Then began an intense struggle with the Colonial Office which, having been unable to guarantee the security of the Jewish community in Palestine, having ignored our repeated warnings concerning the activities of the Mufti and of his friends of the Arab Executive, having made no attempt to correct the indifference or hostility of British officials in Palestine, now proposed to make us pay the price of its failure. We realized that we were facing a hostile combination of forces in the Colonial Office and in the Palestine administration, and unless it was overcome it was futile to think of building on the foundations which we had laid so solidly in the previous years.

There were, of course, great protests throughout the Jewish world; they were backed by powerful figures in the non-Jewish world. Stanley Baldwin, Sir Austen Chamberlain, Leopold Amery, General Smuts, Sir John Simon, and a host of others, all from various points of view, attacked the Passfield White Paper as inconsistent with the Mandate which Great Britain had been given in Palestine. Apparently the Prime Minister had anticipated an unfavourable reaction, but not the force and volume of it. A few days before the issue of the White Paper he had, perhaps with the idea of heading off my protests, invited the Jewish Agency to appoint a committee which should consult with a special Cabinet Committee on Palestine policy. We accepted—but that did not prevent my resignation, nor the resignations of Lord Melchett and Mr. Warburg.

On the Cabinet Committee there were, among others, Arthur Henderson as chairman, and Malcolm MacDonald as secretary. On our side, besides myself, were Leonard Stein, Harry Sacher, Harold Laski, James de Rothschild, Professor Brodetzky and Professor Namier. On this joint committee we fought back and forth throughout that winter. There were two major points which we sought to establish as the firm basis of all future action on the part of the British Government. The first was intended to counteract the growing tendency to regard the Mandate as something applying only to the Jews in Palestine as against the Arabs in Palestine. I put it thus: 'If the obligation of the Mandatory Power is reduced to an obligation towards one hundred and seventy thousand people as against seven hundred thousand people, a small minority juxtaposed to a great majority, then of course everything else can perhaps be explained. But the obligation of the Mandatory Power is towards the Jewish people of which the one hundred and seventy thousand are merely the vanguard. I must take issue, as energetically as I can, with the formulation of the obligation of the Mandatory Power as an obligation towards both sections of the Palestine population.' The second point issued from the first, and was directed against the conception that the Jewish National Home could be crystallized at the stage which it had then reached.

A third point might be considered as having been raised by the first. I quote again from the minutes of one of the sessions: 'In paragraph ten of the White Paper,' I said, 'it is stated that "incitements to disorder or disaffection will be severely punished in whatever quarter they may originate."' I saw in that paragraph the influence of the Palestine administration, with its attitude of 'neutrality' between two hostile and two equally guilty sections of the population. I said: 'Obviously the intention of the author of the White Paper was to balance his statements. If anything is said against the Arabs, something must be said against the Jews, or vice versa. I think His Majesty's Government must be well aware that there is only one quarter from which disaffection, disorder, violence and massacre have originated. We do not massacre; we were the victims of a murderous onslaught. Not one Arab leader has raised his voice against the inhuman treatment meted out to the unfortunate victims.'

Lord Passfield was present at some of the committee sessions and proved to be the head and fount of the opposition to our demands. What effect our arguments had on the Government, and how much the change was due to the pressure of an adverse public opinion in England and elsewhere, I cannot say. But on February 13, 1931, there was an official reversal of policy. It did not take the form of a retraction of the White Paper—that would have meant a loss of face—but of a letter addressed to me by the Prime Minister read by him in the House of Commons and printed in *Hansard*. I considered that the letter rectified the situation—the form was unimportant—and I indicated as much to the Prime Minister.

I was to be bitterly attacked in the Zionist Congress of that year for accepting a letter in place of another White Paper. But whether I was right or not in my acceptance may be judged by a simple fact: it was under MacDonald's letter to me that the change came about in the Government's attitude, and in the attitude of the Palestine administration which enabled us to make the magnificent gains of the ensuing years. It was under MacDonald's letter that Jewish immigration into Palestine was permitted to reach figures like forty thousand for 1934 and sixty-two thousand for 1935, figures undreamed of in 1930. Jabotinsky, the extremist, testifying before the Shaw Commission, had set thirty thousand a year as a satisfactory figure.

The first indication that I had of the seriousness of MacDonald's intentions was when he consulted me with regard to the appointment of a new High Commissioner to replace Sir John Chancellor. He said he realized how much depended on the choice of the man, and added, 'I would like to appoint a General, but one who does it with his head, not his feet.' The next High Commissioner for Palestine was Sir Arthur Wauchope, who assumed office in 1931, and under whom the country made its greatest advance.

Two remarks may be added regarding the riots of 1929 and the Passfield White Paper. The riots were the strongest effort made up till that time by the Arab leaders to frighten us, by mob action, from continuing with our work in Palestine. They failed. And if the riots were intended, whatever their effect on our nerves, to overthrow the structure of the National Home, they came too late. We had built too solidly and too well.

Similarly, the Passfield White Paper may be regarded as the

most concerted effort—until the White Paper of 1939—on the part of a British Government to retract the promise made to the Jewish people in the Balfour Declaration. That attack, too, was successfully repulsed. The solid structure of the National Home in the making was paralleled by the solid support we had in public opinion. That there is an organic relationship between the two is the essence of my 'political' philosophy. Had we, in the years between 1922 and 1929, concentrated on obtaining statements, declarations, charters and promises, to the neglect of our physical growth, we should perhaps not have been able to withstand the sheer physical shock of the riots. Then the political assault would have found no resistance either in us or in public opinion. The dismal incidents of 1929 and 1930 were a severe test of our system and methods, which emerged triumphant.

CHAPTER XXX

DEMISSION

*Zionist Congress of 1931—Revisionists and Mizrachi Head Opposition—
Vote of No Confidence—The Meaning of the Struggle—'Short Cut' versus
Organic Growth—Sokolow Elected President—I Return to Science—Richard
Willstätter's Kindness—Scientific Work for Palestine—The Laboratory in
Holborn—No Getting Away from Zionist Work—Colonial Trust in Diffi-
culties—I Accept Presidency of English Zionist Federation—Other Obliga-
tions—Refugee Work and Youth Aliyah—Sir Arthur Wauchope*

I COME now to an incident in my life on which I look back
with little pleasure, and write about with some distaste: my
demission from the Presidency of the Zionist Organization at
the Congress in July 1931.

In spite of the fact that the Ramsay MacDonald letter had
restored our political position and initiated a period of peace,
prosperity and great immigration into Palestine, the excitement originally created by the Passfield White Paper continued to exercise the minds of the Zionists, and particularly of
the Revisionists, led by Jabotinsky. The latter spoke of the letter
contemptuously, in part because it was only a letter; they
demanded British official endorsement of a clear-cut Revisionist
policy, and the acceptance of anything short of that maximum
—which meant a Jewish State on both sides of the Jordan, with
all that this implies—they declared to be political weakness,
cowardice and betrayal. As the Congress of 1931 approached I
became the butt of ever-mounting attacks, and the occasion
for a pernicious extremist propaganda. I held my ground and
continued to point out that in a movement like ours the centre
of gravity is not an exaggerated political programme, but
work—colonization, education, immigration, and the maintenance of decent relations with the Mandatory Power. Important, too, was the enlightenment of public opinion in Britain,
America and the rest of the world as to our aims and aspirations;
this could not result from confusing the issues by impractical
demands which excited the Arabs and helped to precipitate
troubles which affected the attitude of the Mandatory Power.

O

My admonitions were in vain. The politicians at the Congress were determined to initiate a debate on 'the ultimate aims of the Zionist movement' as if that had any relevance at the moment, and as if any sort of declaration would increase our strength or achievements by one iota. It is difficult to say if this debate was meant sincerely, and was the expression of a desire to fix the Zionist programme for all time, and to provide guidance for future generations, or whether it was simply a means to provoke my opposition, and thus facilitate my resignation from office. If the latter, it was the more unjust—I permit myself to say even indecent—in that I announced, in my opening address, my intention of resigning because of the precarious state of my health, which was patent to everybody. My doctors had, in fact, remonstrated with me severely on the dangers of even attending the Congress.

In spite of this, the Congress insisted on going through the motion of passing a resolution of non-confidence in my policy by a roll-call vote, in which the Revisionists under Jabotinsky took the leading part, with the *Mizrachi*, the religious wing of the movement, strongly supporting.

The conflict, which thus reached an unnecessary dénouement, had of course been going on in the movement for years. It was the conflict between those who believed that Palestine can be built up only the hard way, by meticulous attention to every object, who believed that in this slow and difficult struggle with the marshes and rocks of Palestine lies the great challenge to the creative forces of the Jewish people, its redemption from the abnormalities of exile, and those who yielded to those very abnormalities, seeking to live by a sort of continuous miracle, snatching at occasions as they presented themselves, and believing that these accidental smiles of fortune constitute a real way of life. I felt that all these political formulæ, even if granted to us by the powers that were, would be no use to us, might possibly even be harmful as long as they were not the product of hard work put into the soil of Palestine. Nahalal, Deganiah, the University, the Rutenberg electrical works, the Dead Sea Concession, meant much more to me politically than all the promises of great governments or great political parties. It was not lack of respect for governments and parties, nor an underrating of the value of political pronouncements. But to me a pronouncement is real only if it is matched by performance in Palestine. The pronouncement depends on others, the performance is entirely our own. This is the essence of my Zionist life. My guiding principle was the famous saying of Goethe:

> *Was du ererbst von deinen Vätern,*
> *Erwirb es, um es zu besitzen.*

The others believed only in the *Erbe,* and therefore were always claiming their rights; they wanted the easy road, the road paved with the promises of others. I believed in the path trodden out by our own feet, however wounded the feet might be.

I said to the Congress: 'The walls of Jericho fell to the sound of shouts and trumpets. I never heard of walls being raised by that means.'

Of course it was not only a theoretical political opposition which I faced. It was also the disappointment of middle-class groups which really believed that but for me they would quickly have transformed Palestine into a land of golden economic opportunity for themselves and thousands of others. To me this too was utter lack of realism. I said to the Congress: 'I have heard critics of the Jewish Agency sneer at what they call the old "*Chibath Zion*" policy of "another dunam and another dunam, another Jew and another Jew, another cow and another goat and two more houses in Gederah." If there is any other way of building a house save brick by brick, I do not know it. If there is another way of building up a country save dunam by dunam, man by man, and farmstead by farmstead, again I do not know it. One man may follow another, one dunam be added to another, after a long interval or after a short one—that is a question of degree, and determined not by politics alone, but in a far greater degree by economics.' And to those critics I again said: 'Private capital can establish individual enterprises, but it is for national capital to create conditions,' and, 'But for the work of the Jewish Agency and the National Funds there would even now be no suggestion of a "business basis" for the development of Palestine by the operation of natural economic laws, and no prospect of such a development within any measurable period of time.'

At this Congress I found myself in a minority, with only the labourites and a few of the general Zionists understanding me. I sat through the whole performance, until the last man had voted. When it was finished, and some tactless person applauded my so-called downfall, the feeling came over me that here and now the tablets of the law should be broken, though I had neither the strength nor the moral stature of the great lawgiver.

I left the hall with my wife and a handful of close friends and went for a stroll in Basle. I was immediately joined by Bialik, very tense and very depressed. He said: 'I've been watching the hands which were lifted against you. They were the hands of men whom you have not invited to your house, whom you have not asked to share the company of those you cultivate, the hands of people who have not sat at your dinner table—the hands of those who never understood and never will understand the depths that separate you from them. Don't be sad. What they have done will disappear, what you have done will stand for ever.' We parted with a friendly embrace and Bialik added: 'I have nothing more to do in Basle. I leave the city today.'

The curious outcome of the Congress was the election of Sokolow to the Presidency: curious because Sokolow (like Brodetzky and others who were re-elected) had been closely identified with me since 1916, not only in the general line of work but in almost every detail. Jabotinsky had resigned, Dr. Soloveitchik, the Lithuanian delegate, had resigned: Sokolow had co-operated in loyal agreement. To create an antithesis between Sokolow and me was the height of inanity and showed up the artificiality of the set-up. But if I was wryly amused, Jabotinsky was bitterly disappointed. He had always lived in the illusion that I was the one who stood in the way of his ascent to the Presidency. After the vote was taken Jabotinsky sent my wife a little scribble, 'I am proud of my friends,' meaning us both. My wife wrote back on the scribble: 'Thanks for condolences; we are not dead yet.' It was Jabotinsky's belief that if I went down, he would go up. And it must have been galling to him to see the election go to Sokolow, for whom he had very little respect—if he did not actually despise him. It was, I think, the feeling of my opponents that the pliability of Sokolow would make it easier for them to give the movement the direction they had in mind.

The break in my life produced by my demission was not without its blessings. It was not a complete break, as will soon be evident, but it did relieve me of a vast burden of labour. I tried to fill the vacuum as quickly as possible. I directed my attention to other matters; I felt it would be dangerous for me to indulge in contemplation and resentment and become bitter. I fought against such emotions, though they continued to well up in my subconscious.

I was particularly sorry for my children, who took the turn of events as a bitter affront to their father, who in their opinion had given up the whole of his life to the movement, to their detriment. They had become resigned to a situation which deprived them of my company for long stretches every year, but they were deeply shocked by what they regarded as the ingratitude with which I was rewarded; and they were extremely happy when I announced to them my intention of opening a laboratory in London, and going back to my chemistry, which I had neglected for so many years.

It was, by the way, not an easy decision. I was now in my fifty-eighth year. I had not been in a laboratory—except on a chance visit—for about thirteen years. The science of chemistry had made enormous advances in that time, and I had followed the literature only in a desultory fashion. It was a psychological effort to revert to quiet laboratory work after the stormy and adventurous life of the preceding thirteen years. And if I did know something about the latest developments in science, I had lost contact with practical work and had to become accustomed afresh to manipulating chemical apparatus and carrying out the usual operations. It is difficult to explain to a layman how painful and arduous a task it is to restart this sort of professional occupation in one's mature years, and to refind one's way in the literature of the profession, which in the interval had grown to an immense volume.

But, quite suddenly and unexpectedly, there came to my assistance a guide who, by his authority and kindness, made the transition as pleasant and easy as possible.

It happened that at about that time Professor Richard Willstätter, one of the greatest modern chemists, came to London to receive the Gold Medal of the Royal Society. I had met him only once before, and fleetingly. I discovered in him now a delightful companion and a true friend. His knowledge of chemistry and chemical problems was encyclopædic, and as unlimited as the kindness he showed me. I had been told that he was pedantic and rather *geheimratisch*; he did not make me feel that at all, and I confessed to him all my difficulties. After a severe cross-examination of me, he agreed that we should collaborate on a piece of work in a field which was very familiar to him and on which he had done extensive work. I took over only a small corner of this vast field, and was able after a few years to make something practical of it—a vegetable foodstuff which is now being produced on a considerable scale in America and may shortly be produced in other countries.

Willstätter was consistently helpful to me, and his collaboration not only helped to set me on my feet again, scientifically speaking, but enabled me to see him whenever I was in the vicinity of his city, Munich.

There were two factors which urged me on in this change. First, my intrinsic relation to science, which had been part of my life since my boyhood; second, my feeling that in one way or another it had something to do with the building of Palestine. I was already thinking, then, of a research institute which should work in combination with the Agricultural Experiment Station at Rehovoth—and of something larger, and of wider scope too. And it was during the period when I was out of office that the Daniel Sieff Research Institute was founded, to be followed many years later by the Weizmann Institute of Science.

The break, I said, was not a complete one. It could not be, of course. There was only a considerable shift of emphasis. I opened up a modest laboratory at 6 Featherstone Buildings, Holborn, in an old house belonging to a friend who had been my patent agent for many years. The laboratory was not particularly well-fitted out, but it served my purposes, at least at the beginning. I also linked up again with an old friend and assistant, Mr. H. Davies, who had been with me in Manchester and who had worked with me during the first years of World War I. It began to look again like old times. I enjoyed immensely going to the laboratory every day and returning home in the evening. It reminded me very much of my years at Manchester University. My existence was—at least by comparison with the in-between years—unshackled and untrammelled.

The echoes of Zionist problems penetrated only faintly the walls of my laboratory and visitors from the non-scientific world who descended on me there usually got a cold reception. Gradually the useful rumour got around that to visit me in my lab. was not the way to get anything out of me.

However, there were plenty of visits from Zionist friends at our home, and plenty of pressure to keep me at Zionist tasks. Indeed, only a few days after the Congress, when we were resting at Bad Gastein, a delegation of the labourites visited me, and urged me to take up the leadership of the opposition. This I refused categorically. But a plea of another kind I could not turn down.

We had spent about two weeks in Bad Gastein, and had gone with the children on to Karersee, a charming spot in the Italian Tyrol above Bolzano. No sooner had we settled down there than I began to receive alarming telegrams from the directorate of the Jewish Colonial Trust in London, the bank of the Zionist Organization, which indicated that it was in an extremely precarious position. It was the middle of the world depression and the bank had practically no liquid assets; if a run came, it might mean ruin, and the majority of the depositors were poorer Jews of the East End of London.

It was suggested to me that I should go to Paris and talk to Baron Edmond de Rothschild, urging him to extend a helping hand. I felt I had no right to worry the old gentleman, but it was impossible to refuse the plea of the bank for assistance, and there was no one else to turn to! So I left my holiday resort and travelled a long way to Paris. I went in vain. The Baron said: 'All banks are at present in a critical condition. The difference between our bank and others is that ours has no friends to help it through.' He pointed out that when we had come to him two years previously, asking him to help us meet the educational budget in Palestine, he had given us something like £30,000. But he was not prepared to support a financial instrument which was perhaps being mismanaged. All I got from him on this occasion was the advice to sell whatever securities could be sold—for instance some shares of the Rutenberg Concession—and thus increase the liquidity of the bank.

But my visit was not a dead loss. I discovered while in Paris that the Baron's organization, the P.I.C.A., owed the Colonial Trust a sum of £20,000, about which the Trust had completely forgotten! Between that and the sale of some securities a margin of liquidity was created for the bank.

Back I went to my family, and we decided to go to Yugoslavia and see the Dalmatian coast. We started out in our car, and got as far as Abbazia, on the Yugoslav frontier. There I found another series of frantic telegrams, imploring me to return to London and take counsel with the directors—or such of them as were not *hors de combat*; for some had fallen ill and others had lost their heads.

I gave way again, and persuaded my family to abandon the Yugoslav tour and go instead to Spain. We knew of a nice, quite place, Sitges, on the coast near Barcelona. There they would be safe and comfortable, and there I would join them as soon as possible. Meanwhile I set off for London.

There we were able to float a loan on the basis of securities, and another liquid fund of about £60,000 was created which enabled the bank to ride out the depression. Today the Jewish Colonial Trust is more secure than it ever was.

I have put in the foregoing incident as a sort of first corrective for any reader who might be under the impression that stepping out of office meant a repudiation of Zionist responsibilities. Actually I had plenty to do outside the laboratory; and my laboratory work, too, soon suffered long interruptions, to the great distress of my children, who considered my absences as dangerous bits of backsliding.

I found it impossible, in those years of crisis—as in fact I had found it impossible in an earlier crisis, that which followed the Kishinev and other pogroms thirty years before—to abstract myself even temporarily from Jewish life. In those days I had no sooner settled to my laboratory work at Manchester University than I began to seek out the local Zionists. Now, in 1931 and the following years, I had no sooner got into the swing of laboratory routine than I found myself loaded with outside obligations. I could not refuse the request of the British Zionists to accept the Presidency of their federation. Still less was it possible to withhold my assistance from the Central Bureau for the Settlement of German Jews, created by the Jewish Agency. I became the chairman of that body, and President of Youth Aliyah. In the summer of 1932 I interrupted my scientific work for five months in order to tour South Africa for the Zionist

Funds; the Executive was passing through a financial crisis and here again I felt that I could not evade my duty.

Another, shorter interruption occurred the following year. In the spring of 1933 I received a number of urgent telegrams from Meyer W. Weisgal, who was then arranging 'Jewish Day' at the Century of Progress Fair in Chicago, offering me one hundred thousand dollars for the refugee funds. All he wanted in exchange was that I should deliver a single address at the celebrations in Chicago. I was very much tempted, both for the sake of the Funds and out of regard for the man.

Weisgal is the foremost of the younger friends I have in America. A man of outstanding ability and integrity, with a phenomenal capacity for work, he finds nothing too difficult to undertake when there is service to be rendered to the movement. In these enterprises he spends himself recklessly, and his loyalty and friendship are equalled only by his energy. He has been a moving spirit in the Zionist movement for many years, and at present is one of the chief initiators of the Weizmann Institute of Science in Palestine. I accepted his offer in 1933, made the round trip of some eight thousand miles for the sake of a single appearance and returned with the addition of one hundred thousand dollars to refugee funds.

Now I am not going to pretend that all of these assignments were merely chores. Some of them were, of course; others were not. Our visit to South Africa, for instance, to which I devote a brief chapter, had other compensations besides the sums it brought in for the *Keren Hayesod*. Then there were types of work which, being an amalgam of Zionist work, German refugee settlement work and scientific work, could not be wholly described as 'interruptions' of the last of these. Such, for instance, was the creation of the Daniel Sieff Research Institute in Rehovoth, which I shall describe at some length further on.

I took no part in the inner political struggles of the Zionist Organization and did not even attend the eighteenth Congress, that of 1933. I was extremely chary of lending colour to any accusation that I was 'planning a return,' or that I was in any way hampering the activities of the Executive then in power.

It was with a certain discomfort that I even went to see Sir Arthur Wauchope, the new High Commissioner for Palestine, before he left to take up his post in the autumn of 1931, and I

o*

did so only at his invitation. I went to him, and later corresponded with him, in my private capacity as one who had paid more than twenty visits, of varying duration, to Palestine in the preceding thirteen years, and had some knowledge of the country. After 1935, the year of my return to office, our contacts were official; but during the period now under review, 1931 to 1935, I saw him either in a private capacity, or as the head of the Sieff Institute; and it is pleasant, in spite of strong differences which developed between us towards the end of his régime, to pay wholehearted tribute to him. Sir Arthur was a distinguished administrator and scholar, perhaps the best High Commissioner Palestine has had, and I believe a proof of Ramsay MacDonald's serious effort to undo the harm of the Passfield White Paper. I cannot doubt that he was given the right sort of send-off by the Prime Minister, and he happened to be the kind of man who could be influenced in the right direction. In contradistinction to previous High Commissioners, he really tried to understand the moral and ethical values underlying the Zionist movement and the work in Palestine. He was deeply moved by many features of the life there, such as the *kibbutzim,* and even after he left office he gave frequent expression to his feelings in England, praising the *kvutzoth* and *kibbutzim* as a new way of life which should be emulated in other countries, England included, even if it meant adapting it to specific English conditions. He was much attracted by certain leaders in the movement, like young Arlosoroff, and the older Shmarya Levin. He valued greatly the scientific approach to our agricultural programme, and used to be a frequent visitor at the Agricultural Experiment Station in Rehovoth, where he helped to endow a laboratory for plant physiology which bears his name.

I believe that the differences which did develop between him and the Zionists towards the end of his régime were owing to the great deterioration in the general policy of England, and in the increasing tendency towards appeasement which set in with the Abyssinian war in 1935, extended to Spain and then reached Palestine. I do not believe that of his own accord Wauchope would have taken the stand he did in certain matters which will be related in their turn. We remember him in Palestine as a friend, an intellectual, a soldier, an administrator, and a statesman.

CHAPTER XXXI

A STRANGE NATIONAL HOME

Visit to South Africa—Its Jewish Community—The Remark Game Reserve

SOUTH AFRICA was a new experience for my wife and myself. We were attracted by the idea of a visit to the country of Smuts, who had played such a noble part in the first stages of our movement and whose generous interest had, and has, continued unabated. The official attitude towards us was thoroughly cordial. Smuts and Hertzog and their colleagues received us most kindly. Hertzog was perhaps more formal, Smuts—who was not then in power—treated us as old, trusted friends.

I found myself in an unusual Jewish community scattered over a wide sub-continent in small groups, but united in Zionist spirit. South African Jewry was singularly free from the so-called assimilationist taint. There were practically no German Jews in the country, and the few exceptions were mostly diamond or gold magnates who were isolated or had isolated themselves, and had little or no contact with the majority of Jewry. The Jews of South Africa were preponderantly—in fact almost exclusively—from Kovno, or Vilna, or Minsk and the little places in between these Jewish centres. The little town of Shavli seems, for some unknown reason, to have provided South Africa with great numbers of Jews—it was a puzzle to me how such a small place could have produced such a large emigration.

The South African Jews were kindly, hard-working, intelligent people, and what one may term organic Zionists. If Russian Jewry had not had its life interrupted by the advent of bolshevism it would probably have developed on the pattern of South African Jewry. It was a pleasure to watch and hear those Jews. Remote as they were from the great stream of Jewish life, the arrival of a visitor from Europe was a tremendous occasion, and the whole life of the community revolved about the event.

I met many types of modest, quiet workers to whom Zionism was the whole of their existence. There were not too many wealthy individuals, but the average level of prosperity was fair. There were not too many intellectuals among them, either, but the few that one met were genuine and attractive. One found both hospitality and comfort in their company.

From the technical point of view the trip was well organized but extremely trying, as one had to visit small communities scattered over a vast sub-continent. Still, we went religiously through our duties, and at the end were satisfied with the results, which were financially quite considerable.

We had few pauses or relaxations in those five months, but there was one which calls for special and somewhat detailed mention, and that was a visit to the famous game reserve. This is a unique institution. It was founded by Kruger, who had been greatly concerned over the rapid disappearance of the South African fauna due to the habits of the early Dutch settlers, who used to kill wild and tame beasts indiscriminately. He had therefore decided to set aside a territory amounting to something like eight thousand square miles for the preservation of animal life. Within that area the shooting of animals, or their molestation in any way, was forbidden, and they lived a free and unmolested life. And the animals knew their privileges! They walked about in the presence of human beings freely and unconcernedly, and driving through this vast place was one continuous excitement.

Naturally one had to have guides and guns—our guide, and a great expert, was a Lithuanian Jew—but the danger was slight if one did not interfere with the animals. There were no roads in the real sense of the word, but there were so-called summer tracks, and as you drove along casually you could meet anything from a specimen of the famous South African springbok to a python curled up on a tree, or a pride of lions. Or suddenly there would break on your ears the ringing and thundering noise of a herd of elephants on the march. If one was particularly observant one saw something of the social life of the jungle.

So, for instance, I once noticed in passing an old wildebeest, squatting abandoned under a tree. It looked dejected and crestfallen, the very personification—if I may use that word—of melancholy. Struck by its appearance, I asked the guide for the meaning of the phenomenon. He told me that this was an old bull who until a little while ago had been the leader of his herd. He had grown old, and had been ousted by a younger and more energetic successor. He had had to leave the herd, and he lived now in absolute isolation, waiting for the lions to come along and tear him to pieces. It all sounded so human.

We spent three days on the game reserve, and it so happened that during our visit the lions—they were always the high-point of a visit—were making themselves scarce. We travelled about a good bit, but they did not put in an appearance and we thought we were going to be disappointed. I was ready to give up, but my wife was a little more persistent. Late in the third night we were awakened in our hut by a sound of prowling and growling, and at about 4 A.M. excited Kaffir boys crowded about our entrance, conveying the news that lions were in the vicinity.

We promptly put on our clothes, threw ourselves into the car, and drove in the direction indicated. Sure enough, before long, we came across a magnificent-looking lion standing in the middle of the road like a bronze statue, and occasionally throwing a contemptuous glance at our car. We were admonished not to let our rifles protrude from the car—the lions do not like the sight of them. We could not move forward, so we remained still about twenty yards away from the lion and awaited his pleasure.

About ten minutes passed and the lion decided to leave the middle of the road; he went into the grass which screened him almost completely from our sight, its colour being the same as that of his tawny skin. Looking more attentively we suddenly noticed two lionesses crouching there, with the male lion circling about them, looking occasionally in our direction and emitting a growl. After observing this scene for about fifteen minutes we backed away and drove off. We had had a good view of lions and could leave with a clear conscience.

It must be of particular interest—and a source of enormous satisfaction—to a naturalist to spend some time in the reserve and to observe all this animal life, in a state of nature, at close range. As for myself, I could not help reflecting about something else; here were these wonderful animals with a beautiful home reserved for them, with trees, water, grass, food, going about unmolested, as free citizens, establishing their own laws, habits and customs, knowing their way about, probably having their own language, and wise to the natural dangers of their environment. I was told, for instance, that a tiny springbok would approach a lion quite freely when it happened to know—as it could by instinct—that the lion had had his fill, and therefore would not attack it. Not so, however, with the leopard, which kills for the sake of killing, and is therefore always shunned by the springbok. This and more I heard from my guide on the habits of the animals in the reserve.

Here they were, I thought, in their home, which in area is only slightly smaller than Palestine: they are protected, Nature offers them generously of her gifts, and they have no Arab problem. . . . It must be a wonderful thing to be an animal on the South African game reserve!

CHAPTER XXXII

SCIENTISTS—AND OTHERS

The Advent of Hitler to Power—The Tragedy of German Jewry—My Work with the Central Bureau for the Settlement of German Jews—The Ousting of the Scientists among Others—Richard Willstätter Opens Sieff Institute in Palestine, Refuses Post with Us, Returns to Germany—Is Expelled—Fritz Haber's Brilliant Career—His Expulsion—Turns to Us, Too Late—German Jewish Scientists and Palestine—Jewish Tradition and Science—Dr. David Bergmann Joins Us—The German Jews and Palestine—Their Contribution to the Homeland

THE year 1933, the year of Hitler's advent to power, marked the beginning of the last frightful phase in the greatest catastrophe that has ever befallen the Jewish people. We did not anticipate the full horror of the episode; but enough was already happening, and had happened in the preceding years, to spur us to the most strenuous efforts.

When I accepted the chairmanship of the Central Bureau for the Settlement of German Jews, I had no particular qualifications for the work. But the need was so urgent, the human suffering so great, and the men and women who sought help so pathetic in the misfortune which had come over them like a tidal wave, that there could be no question of preparing oneself specifically for the job. One just did the best one could; and I found that my best would be connected with Palestine. So my work was divided into two parts, one general, the other specifically Palestinian. The pressure of need and the development of circumstances brought a welcome unity into the work.

My work ran parallel with that of the Youth Aliyah, which was headed by one of the most remarkable figures in modern Jewish history—Henrietta Szold. She was seventy-three years of age, and her life had been filled with many labours—literary, educational and Zionist. In the founding of *Hadassah*, the American Women's Zionist Organization, she had made an immense contribution to the social and political development

of the Jewish Homeland; and to climax her work and that of
her organization, she had settled in Palestine, where her energy,
wisdom and devotion were an inspiration to the community.
At an age well beyond that of usual retirement from public
life, she undertook and carried through with magnificent
effectiveness the direction of Youth Aliyah, one of the most
important Zionist tasks of the last fifteen years. She carried on
virtually to the day of her death, in 1945.

To return to my particular task in that period of calamity:
The catastrophe in Germany had of course destroyed the
careers of a great many brilliant young scientists who were,
almost at a moment's notice, uprooted from their positions and
thrown into the street. Nor was this true of the younger people
alone. Men of outstanding reputation and achievement, who
had rendered invaluable service to science—and to Germany—
were forced out one after the other; and often it was difficult to
say which was the deeper, the external and physical tragedy,
or the internal and spiritual. Two such men stand out in my
mind, not because their fate was exceptional, but because of
my more intimate contact with them. They are Richard
Willstätter and Fritz Haber.

Of Willstätter's kindness to me in 1931, when I opened my
little laboratory, I have already told. He was by that time no
longer on the faculty of Munich University, but not because
of governmental action. At a meeting of the University senate
some time in 1928 a discussion had arisen about the appointment of a mineralogist. A candidate was proposed, a front-
rank mineralogist by the name of Goldschmidt. As soon as the
name was mentioned a murmur arose in the meeting and
someone remarked: '*Wieder ein Jude!*' (another Jew). Without
saying a word Willstätter rose, collected his papers and left
the room. He never crossed the threshold of the University
again, this despite the repeated entreaties of his colleagues and
of the Bavarian Government. It was felt—this was still 1928—
that he was too valuable a man to lose, that his withdrawal was
a severe blow to the prestige of the University.

It was a tragedy for Willstätter to be deprived of the laboratory in which he had been accustomed to work, but he found a
place in the Munich Academy of Science. Not that he ever
entered that place either! He directed the work from outside,

and, as he told me with a sad smile in 1931, he would be on the telephone with his assistant for between an hour and two hours every day. I could just about see it in my mind's eye. He was extremely exact and attentive to the slightest detail, and although laconic in speech and writing, his explanations were always lengthy because of their completeness. He missed the laboratory work all the more because his manipulative skill was magnificent, just as his methods were interesting, original, exact, and always directed towards the clarification of some important problem. Such was, for instance, his classical research on the constitution and function of chlorophyll in plants and its relation to the hæmoglobin of the blood. Although his reputation was immense, and he was a Nobel Prize winner, he was modest, unassuming and retiring in character; he often reminded me of the old-time venerable type of great Jewish Rabbi.

For a long time Willstätter refused—in spite of his experience in 1928 and his violent reaction to it—to understand what was taking place in Germany. I saw him in Munich, at the end of 1932, and again in Zurich and Paris, in 1933, after Hitler had come to power; but, though deeply disturbed, he would not believe that the German people and government would go any further in their anti-Jewishness. We discussed the Daniel Sieff Research Institute, which was then in process of construction; he was immensely interested and generous with his advice. He readily accepted my invitation to preside at the opening, but to my repeated and insistent pleas that he leave Germany and come to us in Palestine, he turned a deaf ear. He came to the opening of the Institute and returned to Germany (in 1934!). He still felt that he was protected by his reputation and by the devotion of the Munich public.

I was not the only one to plead with him to stay with us. I remember how Sir Simon Marks, among others, urged him to accept the directorship of the new institute, assuring him of a first-class laboratory, all the buildings and apparatus he wanted, and a staff of eager and able assistants. Some of his pupils were already with us. No, he was not to be moved.

The opening of the Sieff Institute coincided with the Passover, and I took Willstätter up to Haifa to attend the Seder at my mother's house. Our Seder was always a rather lively performance, very jolly and unconventional, with some thirty-odd members of the family at table. The celebration reached its critical point when our house was suddenly surrounded by a tremendous crowd of workers, men and women—there must have been over two thousand of them—who had come from their own Seders to greet us for the festival. They filled the whole street, singing Hebrew songs and dancing the *hora*. Willstätter and I were half-pulled, half-carried down from the balcony on which we stood watching, and forced into the dance. Very curious indeed it was to watch the old German professor trying to dance a *hora* surrounded by *chalutzim* and *chalutzoth* singing and clapping their hands. I know he enjoyed the experience. But nothing of all this induced him to change his mind. His last word on the subject was: 'I know that Germany has gone mad, but if a mother falls ill it is not a reason for her children to leave her. My home is Germany, my university, in spite of what has happened, is in Munich. I must return.'

He actually stayed on in Germany until the outbreak of the war in 1939. Then he was expelled, and took up his residence in Locarno, in near-by Switzerland. There he found a small apartment of two or three rooms, and there he lived in complete isolation. I visited him several times. Of his possessions nothing was rescued but his library, which his old housekeeper had carried off to Stuttgart. He occupied himself, during the closing years of his life, with the writing of his autobiography, and died towards the end of the war. His obstinacy in not acceding to our request was a great loss to Palestine and, I think, a great loss to science.

Fritz Haber's was the second case. Haber was a great friend of Willstätter, though by nature and temperament very different from him. He too was a Nobel Prize winner, and responsible for one of the biggest technical successes of the age, namely, the conversion of the nitrogen of the air into ammonia and nitric acid. These two chemicals are essential ingredients in the making not only of explosives, but also of artificial fertilizer, which thus became accessible in large quantities at a low price. Unlike Willstätter, Haber was lacking in any Jewish self-respect. He had become a convert to Christianity and had pulled all his family with him along that road. Long before I met him I had other reasons to feel prejudiced against him. It will be remembered that when I made my first visit to America, in 1921, I had been fortunate enough to enlist the co-operation of Einstein. I learned later that Haber had done all he could to dissuade Einstein from joining me; he said, among other things, that Einstein would be doing untold harm to his career and to the name of the Institute of which he was a distinguished member if he threw in his lot with the Zionists, and particularly with such a pronounced Zionist as myself.

I therefore had no desire to meet Haber; nor was there any occasion of an impersonal kind since his field of chemistry— chiefly that of inorganic materials—was remote from mine. But as it happened Haber's son, who was also a chemist, was employed by my brother-in-law, Josef Blumenfeld, a distinguished industrial chemist in Paris, and once, during a visit to London, Blumenfeld brought the Habers, father and son, to see me. I was already busy—at any rate in my mind—with the founding of the Sieff Institute, and by that time Haber's anti-Zionist prejudices must have been wearing off, perhaps under the influence of developments in Germany. I found him, somewhat to my surprise, extremely affable. He even invited me to visit him at his research institute, which had the high-sounding name of *Kaiser Wilhelm Forschungs Institut*, in Dahlem, which I did towards the end of 1932, on one of my visits to Berlin.

It was a magnificent collection of laboratories, superbly equipped, and many-sided in its programme, and Haber was enthroned as dictator. He guided me through building after building, and after the long tour of inspection invited me to lunch with him at his villa in Dahlem. He was not only hospitable; he was actually interested in my work in Palestine. Frequently, in the course of our conversation on technical matters, he would throw in the words: 'Well, Dr. Weizmann, you might try to introduce that in Palestine.' He repeated several times that one of the greatest factors in the development of Palestine might be found in technical botany. This is a combination of plant physiology, genetics and kindred sciences, which was represented in Dahlem both by great laboratories and by first-class men conducting them. I was comparing in my mind those mighty institutions which served the agriculture of Germany with our little Agricultural Experiment Station at Rehovoth, and hoping that the new Institute which I contemplated might help to fill some of the gaps in our reconstruction.

I left Dahlem heavy-hearted and filled with forebodings, which I remember communicating to my wife on my return to London.

Not long afterwards, I received a telephone call at my home in London from Haber. He was in the city, staying at the Russell Hotel. He had had to leave Berlin precipitately, stripped of everything—position, fortune, honours—and take refuge in London, a sick man, suffering from angina pectoris, not quite penniless, but with very small reserves. I went to him at once, and found him broken, muddled, moving about in a mental and moral vacuum.

I made a feeble attempt to comfort him, but the truth is that I could scarcely look him in the eyes. I of course invited him to the house, and he visited us repeatedly. He told me that Cambridge was prepared to provide him with a laboratory, but he did not think he could really settle down. The shock had been too great. He had occupied too high a position in Germany; his fall was therefore all the harder to bear.

It must have been particularly bitter for him to realize that his baptism, and the baptism of his family, had not protected him. It was difficult for me to speak to him; I was ashamed for myself, ashamed for this cruel world, which allowed such things to happen, and ashamed for the error in which he had lived and worked throughout all his life. And yet it was an error which was common enough; there were many Jews with his outlook—though not with his genius—who had regarded Zionists as dreamers or, worse, as kill-joys, or even as maniacs, who were endangering the positions they had fought through to after many years.

I began to talk to him then about coming out to us in Palestine, but did not press the matter. I wanted him first to take a rest, recover from his shock and treat his illness in a suitable climate.

He went south, and that summer (1933), following my hasty visit to America, we met again in Switzerland. I was staying in Zermatt, at the foot of the Matterhorn, and Haber was somewhere in the Rhône valley and came over to see us. We dined together that evening. I found him a little improved, somewhat settled and past the shock. The surroundings in the Rhône valley had had a beneficent effect on him.

During the dinner, at which my wife and my son Michael were also present, Haber suddenly burst into an eloquent tirade. The reason was the following: the eighteenth Zionist Congress was then being held in Prague. I had refused to attend, not wishing to be involved in any political struggle. During the dinner repeated calls came from Prague, and frantic requests that I leave Zermatt at once and betake myself to the Congress. I persisted in my refusal, and though I said nothing to Haber about these frequent interruptions, except to mention that they came from Prague, he guessed their purport from something he had read in the papers, and he said to me, with the utmost earnestness:

'Dr. Weizmann, I was one of the mightiest men in Germany. I was more than a great army commander, more than a captain of industry. I was the founder of industries; my work was essential for the economic and military expansion of Germany. All doors were open to me. But the position which I occupied then, glamorous as it may have seemed, is as nothing compared with yours. You are not creating out of plenty—you are creating out of nothing, in a land which lacks everything; you are trying to restore a derelict people to a sense of dignity. And you are, I think, succeeding. At the end of my life I find myself a bankrupt. When I am gone and forgotten your work will stand, a shining monument, in the long history of our people. Do not ignore the call now; go to Prague, even at the risk that you will suffer grievous disappointment there.'

I remember watching my young son, as he listened to Haber, who spoke a halting English which his asthma made the more difficult to follow. Michael was literally blue to the lips, so painfully was he affected, so eager was he for me to take Haber's advice, even though it meant my leaving him in the middle of his holiday.

I did not go to Prague, much to Haber's disappointment. But I made use of the opportunity to press upon him our invitation to come out to Palestine and work with us. I said: 'The climate will be good for you. You will find a modern laboratory, able assistants. You will work in peace and honour. It will be a return home for you—your journey's end.'

He accepted with enthusiasm, and asked only that he be allowed to spend another month or two in a sanatorium. On this we agreed—and in due course he set out for Palestine, was taken suddenly ill in Basle, and died there. Willstätter came from Munich to bury him. Some ten years later Willstätter too died in Switzerland, like Haber, an exile from Germany.

These were two of the men whom I sought to attract to our institutions in Palestine, both for their sake and for ours. There were others, of course. I felt it would be a great accession of moral strength and a valuable source of technical knowledge if we could offer to the Hebrew University, or to the Sieff Institute, Albert Einstein the physicist, James Franck of Göttingen, the mathematician Hermann Weyl, the physicist Placzek, the chemist Wiegener, to mention but a few names. But somehow I failed to convince them. Some of them found homes in England, at Oxford, Cambridge, Manchester, Birmingham; others, as we have seen, in America. That was comprehensible; but there were other places chosen in preference to Palestine which were utterly beyond me.

Zurich was the centre which dealt with academic refugees, and thither I went to consult the members of the Swiss committee. There I learned early one morning that James Franck was in the city, a refugee—and that he and his wife were breakfasting with my friend, Professor Richard Baer, the physicist. Without waiting for an invitation I barged in on them and found the two gentlemen and Mrs. Franck immersed in a discussion about the merits of going to—Turkey! Whether Franck was considering the idea for himself, or whether he was recommending it to others, I couldn't make out, but at that moment I entirely lost my good manners. I could not contain myself, and exclaimed: 'I can understand it if you want to go to Oxford, Cambridge, New York or Chicago. But if you go to Turkey you will find the scientific conditions there much worse than in Palestine—you might as well accept our invitation to go to Palestine.' Franck objected that there was no security of tenure in Palestine, to which I promptly replied that tenure in Palestine would be more secure than in most other countries —not excluding the Western ones. 'It is true,' I said, 'our University has not got government support, but if men like you came out, a great physics institute would be built round you, and after a certain time you would not lack for anything.'

It was interesting to watch Mrs. Franck during this conversation. She was a Swedish Jewess, very blonde, and obviously very proud of her 'Nordic' descent. She thought that I was trying to reduce her husband to a condition too awful for words. She kept looking daggers at me, and I had to give up the consultation. I felt then as I had felt in the early days of Zionism. Just as the rich Jews never came to us until we were a 'practical' proposition, so these intellectually rich Jews thought that Palestine would be detrimental to their careers. True, the German catastrophe had greatly altered the situation, and Palestine was absorbing more refugees than all other countries combined; yet the inertia, the weight of prejudice, was such that many of them preferred Turkey to the Hebrew University in Palestine.

I had an opportunity of seeing some of the scientists who went to Istanbul and Ankara when I visited those cities a few years later. They were a sad lot, bewildered, lost, waiting for their contracts to expire, and knowing that in most cases they would not be renewed. To each scientist had been attached a few young Turkish students who were supposed to learn from him the tricks of the trade, so as to replace him at the end of a few years. In this policy, if it can so be called, the Turks of course miscalculated. It is not enough to learn a few facts from a professor in order to become a scientist. It is background that makes a man a scientist, and that is not to be acquired in a few years; it is a matter of tradition and of generations of endeavour. The Turks still had to learn this elementary truth.

It was a truth I had borne in mind when the foundation stones of the Hebrew University were laid. I knew it was not going to be easy to create a model National University with human material which had to be brought together from the various countries of the Dispersion. There is an ancient saying of the Hebrew sages that to make a pair of tongs one needs a pair of tongs. But we at least had had our institutions and traditions. Something of the latter was rescued out of the general destruction in Europe, though when we contemplate our losses we are overwhelmed by their extent. Not only were millions of human beings done to death, but great institutions which were also living organisms. Among the former, who knows how many Einsteins and Habers and Willstätters there may have been; they perished with the centre of learning which would have helped to mould their gifts.

Our great men were always a product of symbiosis between the ancient, traditional Talmudic learning in which our ancestors were steeped in the Polish or Galician ghettos or even in Spain, and the modern Western universities with which their children came in contact. There is, as often as not, a long list of Talmudic scholars and Rabbis in the pedigrees of our modern scientists. In many cases they themselves have come from Talmudic schools, breaking away in their twenties and struggling through to Paris or Zurich or Princeton. It is this extraordinary phenomenon—a great tradition of learning fructified by modern methods—which has given us both first-class scientists and competent men in every branch of academic activity, out of all relation to our numbers.

Now these great places of Jewish learning in Vilna, Warsaw, Kovno, Breslau, Vienna, Pressburg, have been wiped off the face of the earth; the great Jewish archives have been plundered or destroyed, and we have to reconstruct them fragmentarily page by page. We have suffered not only physically; we have been murdered intellectually, and the world scarcely realizes the extent of our affliction. It sounds like a cruel irony when British or American statesmen reproach the remnants of Jewry when they wish to leave the graves in Germany and Austria and Holland and move to Palestine, where they hope to build a new life under more stable conditions; for whatever the aberrations of a few at the top, that is the longing of the great majority of the survivors.

Among the most gifted of the younger scientists who were expelled from their posts with the advent of Hitler was Dr. David Bergmann. He had been the soul of the first university chemical laboratory in Berlin, had had many collaborators, and promised to become one of Germany's leading scientists. I had never met him personally, but I knew of his work. One morning in the spring of 1933 I received a telegram from a friend of mine still working at the Dahlem Institute, telling me that Bergmann had been thrown out. Almost by return of post, and without having any real budget for it, I invited Bergmann and his wife, who was also a chemist, to come over to London and join me. It will always be a deep source of satisfaction to me that I did not hesitate, or wait to obtain a budget, but just took the plunge and brought over this man, who was destined to play such an important part in my life as one of my nearest and most devoted friends, and in the scientific and technical development of Palestine. I did not learn till later that Bergmann was a Zionist, and that he was the son of a Rabbi, that he had received a sound Jewish education, was a Hebrew scholar and a great intellect, and that he lived and worked for Palestine and for Palestine only.

It did not take him long to establish himself on my premises in Holborn. I took another floor in the somewhat ancient house and rigged up a sort of laboratory for him, and there he proceeded to work—for something like eighteen hours a day. He entered with the utmost enthusiasm into my plans for the Sieff Institute. I remember a conversation I had in Paris not long after, with Willstätter and Haber, with Bergmann present. He developed before them his plans for work in the Institute which was then nearing completion. The two eminent scientists listened very attentively, and then Willstätter asked me ironically: 'How many floors has the Daniel Sieff Institute?' To which I replied: 'As far as I know it will have two floors.' 'Well,' said Willstätter, 'you had better build a skyscraper if you wish to carry out the programme Bergmann has outlined to us.'

I happened to be in Palestine when the first stream of German immigrants came in. Here they were, these German Jews, used to a regular and sheltered life, mostly in solid businesses or professional pursuits, altogether unfamiliar with social earthquakes of this kind, which were more or less commonplaces to East European Jewry. They lacked, therefore, the flexibility and adaptability of Russian and Polish Jews; they were more rigid in their customs and habits; they took their tragedy—which in 1932–3 still resembled the old Russian expulsions, and had not yet reached the bestiality of the extermination chambers—more desperately to heart.

I saw them also in Germany as the shadows were closing in on them, and remember with particular vividness an evening late in December 1932, when I went from Willstätter's house to that of my old friend Eli Strauss. Strauss was a Zionist more or less of my generation, the head of the Munich Jewish community, a distinguished and upright man. He was very sick, suffering from cancer of the throat, without, of course, knowing it. He insisted on getting up, receiving me more or less in state, and offering me a meal. All my attempts to dissuade him from undergoing this strain were futile. Not only did we sit out this meal, during which I watched him with great anxiety trying to swallow his food, but in spite of the pain he insisted on talking about the threat hanging over German Jewry and the world at large.

After dinner there arrived a few leading members of the community, and I have seldom lived through such a sad evening. Our host was obviously a dying man, and his condition seemed symbolic of German Jewry generally and of the Munich community in particular. They besieged me with questions. What did I think of the situation? Was it really going to be as bad as they were inclined to think at the moment? Would England try to stretch out a protecting hand over the persecuted? I had no comfort for them. Already the signs of what was later to be called appeasement were in the air. It was heart-rending to see these men—all of whom had built up fine lives, who had taken part in German public affairs, and contributed to the greatness of their country—feeling that the storm was about to break upon them, and at a loss where to turn for comfort and succour. When I parted from these people, I knew I was seeing Eli Strauss for the last time, and that I would never again see a Jewish community in Munich. The tears stood in their eyes as they watched me leave, and all I was able to utter at that moment was, 'May God protect you.'

These were the people who began to stream into Palestine in 1933 and 1934. I knew them, and I had a profound respect for the rôle which all of them had played in the life of their country, and some of them had played in the Zionist movement. But I was somewhat estranged from them by their social rigidity, so different from the life and surroundings in which I had grown up. I came into a Seder ceremony in Haifa, attended by newly arrived German immigrants. They sang the *Hagaddah*, but though the tune was rather a gay one, it sounded like a dirge, and I could see, writ large on the faces of these people, the memory of their homes. These were people who only a little while before had felt secure; they had represented a great moral, social and intellectual force. Now they were uprooted, brought into a country with which few of them had had any physical connection, compelled to build up a new life—some of them at an advanced age—in a climate unsuitable for many of them, in a place lacking the amenities to which they were accustomed. Watching these people one asked oneself: Will they succeed? Will they be able to push new roots into the hard soil of Palestine? Or will they end their lives here in a sort of exile, forever bewailing the past and unable to reconcile themselves to the present?

Remembering that scene, which is ever present in my mind, I think with pride and deep satisfaction of the transformation through which the German Jews have passed in Palestine, and of the distinguished contribution which they have made to the orderliness, discipline, efficiency, and general quality of our work. They exercised a great educational influence on the East European Jews who still form a majority, and who were inclined to look down upon the newcomers, though prepared to give them all the assistance in their power. I could not help thinking of the streams of Russian Jews who used to pass through the German ports of Hamburg and Lübeck on their way to America, in my student days towards the close of the last century; I remembered how they used to be kindly—and patronizingly—received by the committees of German Jewry, guided from the frontier to the ports and given a send-off on the Hamburg-Amerika line. I used to go very often to the central station in Berlin, to see the emigrants and exchange a few words with them in their own language. I did not think then that a similar fate would befall the solid and powerful German Jewry, that they in their turn would be driven from their homes. There was, however, one profound difference between those East European emigrants and these of the nineteen thirties: the latter were coming home! True, their home was still alien to them, but their children adapted themselves swiftly—and the parents followed suit not long after.

It was not easy at first. We faced difficulties of a new character, for this was not a *chalutz* immigration whose nature was familiar to us and to which we could apply known and tested methods. It was a middle-class immigration, not all young people and not all adaptable to hard physical work. We founded for them special types of suburban settlements, in which the family could devote itself to the lighter kind of agricultural work, while the head of the family was within easy distance of the city. Between the garden plot and the occupation, such as it was, of the head of the family, a livelihood could be eked out, and in time the system worked, and yielded good results.

There was a transitional period when we were disquieted by the great increase of the urban population, particularly in Haifa and Tel Aviv, due to the advent of the German immigrants. I had, as the reader now knows, always been fearful of an undue urbanization of the *Yishuv*. The tendency was always there; land settlement is by its nature slower and more difficult, and the acquisition of land in Palestine is fraught with its own problems. It was therefore natural that the drift to the towns should have been accentuated by the stream of German immigrants. We sought to arrest it by the halfway system I have described, and our success was due to the adaptability of the younger generation, which in this as in other respects led the way. The new types of settlement like Ramath Ha-Shavim, and Kiryat Bialik and Nahariah, created in those years, have taken firm root. They are till this day, as they were at the beginning, composed almost entirely of German Jews; they stand as model communities, reflecting great credit both on the founders and on the country.

Thus my four years out of office were filled with laboratory work in London and Rehovoth, fund-raising, visits to America, South Africa and other countries, the founding and launching of the Sieff Institute in Rehovoth, the resettlement of German refugees, and other duties. They were full years, but not happy ones, for the world was darkening towards the eclipse of the Second World War.

CHAPTER XXXIII

RETURN TO OFFICE

*The International World Darkens—The Abyssinian War, a Prelude—
Zionist Illusions—Pinchas Rutenberg and His Great Plan—Premature
Emphasis on Private Initiative in Palestine—The Unwritten Covenant with
the Workers—Chalutzim, Past and Present—The Moral Ballast of the
Movement*

IN 1935 I returned to office as President of the World Zionist
Organization and of the Jewish Agency. I did it reluctantly,
and after long and earnest pleading on the part of my friends,
particularly of the labour movement. I had got into the stride
of my scientific work again, spending more and more time in
the laboratory in the new Institute, among my colleagues. For
several months in the latter part of 1934 and the beginning of
1935 my wife and I had lived in a little bungalow in Rehovoth,
which we had rented from the poetess, Jessie Sampter. And we
had begun to plan our own home, which was completed in 1937
and where we finally settled down. I used to go every morning
to the laboratories of the Sieff Institute, working myself and
following the work of my colleagues. Every week I attended the
meeting of the Zionist Executive in Jerusalem. I went about
the country a good bit, but in general I tried to lead a regular
life, or at least one not as fragmentated as I had led in years
past. I believe that my activities were not without value for the
National Home.

Yet this was not the fundamental reason for my reluctance.
It was rather that I did not see a genuine change of heart in
the movement, or, let me say, of the majority which had ejected
me in 1931. They were asking for me because a certain number
of Zionists were now of the opinion that they had nobody who
could do much better! Sokolow, though respected by the
British as a man of learning and dignity, had not got very far
with them. Curiously enough, those of the general Zionists
who had been my strongest opponents in 1931, namely, the

445

Americans, were now among the most vigorous proponents of my return. I could not help thinking that very soon after taking office I would be faced with the same old troubles. I would again be made the scapegoat for the sins of the British Government. Indeed, I anticipated a harder time than before 1931, for circumstances were becoming more and more unfavourable. After a long threatening, the Abyssinian war finally broke out in the summer of 1935. I said to the Congress: 'The Mediterranean is becoming stormy, and we occupy on its shores one of the key positions.' I regarded the Abyssinian war and the Spanish Civil War as the curtain-raisers of a much greater struggle. Both Mussolini and Hitler were arming at a great pace, while the democracies showed both weakness and lack of foresight. It was not to be expected that our path would be made easier.

The reactionary spirit which was rapidly spreading over the whole world was affecting the Zionist movement too, and this had been evident even in 1931. The change was unhappily fostered by the illusory promises of quick results which were held out by certain prominent people in the movement— promises which played upon the natural impatience of our workers to get on with the job, and led to counsels of despair. It was made to appear that the gap between the desirable and the possible was very easy to bridge, a doctrine which I have always opposed. The encouragement of this error went back to the time of the so-called Brandeis struggle, and it always had, in the strangest way, the support, or promised support, of men who were not Zionists at all. And always, perhaps not so strangely, it was associated with an attitude of hostility to our most characteristic creation in Palestine, the communal colonies, the co-operatives, and the labour movement generally.

The history of the later years of Pinchas Rutenberg provides an apt illustration.

Here was a man whose rôle in Palestinian life as a great builder was outstanding, whose devotion and *savoir faire* were beyond question. Had he confined his activities to his engineering work, he would have achieved even more in his own field. Unfortunately, like a great many people in Palestine, he had political ambitions, and he did not realize that he was by nature and temperament utterly unfit to stand at the head of a complex political organization. He combined, in political matters, a childish naïveté with a colossal self-confidence, and he always dreamed of raising vast sums of money—say of the order of fifty million dollars, which was in fact a vast sum in Zionist work twelve or fifteen years ago—so as to build up a huge land reserve and proceed with colonization on a massive scale.

He did not realize that the privately owned land organization which he projected would have to sell its land to the highest bidder and that, if the enterprise were at all attractive financially, large tracts would pass into the hands of speculators. I was astonished and shocked when I received his first annual report of the activities of the Palestine Electric Corporation, of which he was the manager. It was divided into two parts. The first was devoted to the proper business of the Corporation. The second contained an attack on the national funds of the Zionist Organization, and the outline of a plan whereby the building of the Jewish National Home was to be taken over by the Board of Directors of the Palestine Electric Corporation!

A long and unhappy controversy ensued and again I found myself fighting against men—Rutenberg was one of them—for whom I had both respect and admiration, but whose views on the development of Palestine did violence to my conception of the organic character of Zionism. Whatever form the controversy took, I was always in opposition to the 'quick and easy' way. Today this aspect of the controversy has lost some of its edge; there are at present several investment companies in Palestine which work successfully. They are, I repeat, due to the groundwork done by the National Funds, and done under conditions rendered unnecessarily difficult by the very advocates of private initiative. It was not easy, in America, to explain the basic problem to donors who would have preferred to give their money to those who promised them returns, rather than to a 'philanthropic' organization of which it was freely said that it was incapable of handling finances. Those that spread such rumours, perhaps quite honestly, did not seem to understand that they were undermining their own position. It was my task during my many journeys in America, during my pilgrimages from city to city—some were quite small ones— to counteract these nefarious influences, and to build up, painfully and systematically, good will for a Palestine which was not showing financial returns at the time, but which was increasing its absorptive capacity for those who wished to go and settle there. It was a remarkable fact, which testified to a sound instinct and real patriotism, that just the poor elements responded to such treatment and gave liberally of their substance. It was the richer people who were keen on investment.

Here was the fundamental difference between the two views of Zionism. The views put forward long ago by Greenberg and Marmorek and Nordau, and later by Jabotinsky and the Revisionists, and those held by our group. That impatience, that lack of faith, was constantly pulling the movement towards the abyss; and between the abyss and the actual work in Palestine stood the phalanx of the workers, to whom—though I never identified myself with them—I considered myself attached. Gradually an unwritten covenant was created between the small group of my friends in the so-called General Zionist movement and the great mass of workers in the settlements and factories of Palestine which formed the core of the Zionist movement. This was the guarantee of our political sanity, of our sense of realism and of our freedom alike from Revisionist delusions and methods of violence.

There was something more than a personal bond between me and the labour leaders and the rank and file, the men of Nahalal, Ain Harod and the Emek generally. There was a partnership in effort and in suffering, and but for them I do not think I could have endured the nervous and physical grind of my fund-collecting tours of America and other countries. I always bore in mind that the money would go towards redeeming the Emek, the Jordan Valley and other waste places: and sometimes, when I remembered the workers as I had last seen them, in Nahalal, their eyes glittering with the hunger of weeks and months, greeting me cheerfully and hopefully—I felt I had a part, however small, in their suffering and their achievement.

Much has been written about the efforts of our pioneers, and unfortunately much has been forgotten; and there were many good Zionists who, in the years I am now writing of, were under the impression that the old pioneering days were over in Palestine, and that the great days of the *chalutzim* were for ever a thing of the past. Not only was this untrue of 1935; it is not true in 1947.

One has only to go down these days to the Dead Sea, where the young people who have come out of the Diaspora are leaching the salty earth of Sodom and Gomorrah—earth which for thousands of years has borne nothing but Dead Sea fruit—and with patient effort are bringing it to life again, in order to know that the struggle still goes on. Or one may visit the groups of young men and women who have settled in the Negev desert, in the dangerous outpost positions between Gaza and the Egyptian frontier, rebuilding a part of Palestine on which, with the exception of a few thin strips which the Bedouins have sown with scanty barley, not a blade of grass has grown for thousands of years. I have watched the work for the last three years, and I always approach these settlements with a feeling of awe; and every time I go to bed I cannot help reflecting on those small groups of young men and women—most of them members of the Youth Aliyah, saved from Germany only a few years ago—in the middle of the desert, quite alone, working energetically, gaily, without making a single complaint. For all I know they come from families as good as and better than mine, and grew up in circumstances very different from those they are placed in now. But they have gone through a hardening process, in which they witnessed the destruction of their near and dear ones. I remember the inscription on one of the 'illegal' ships which sailed once into the harbour of Haifa—a streamer prepared for the benefit of the British soldiers and sailors: *Don't shoot, we are not frightened: we made our acquaintance with death long ago.*

Our workers are the moral ballast of the movement today, just as they were in the early days of the Zionist movement, and as they were in the years of which I am writing. It is only of late that a negative relation has sprung up between a few of the urban labour leaders and my group. And again, significantly enough—inevitably, I might say—it is a struggle between those who proclaim that they know how to bring a million and two million Jews into Palestine in three or four years, and those who know the possibilities and accept them.

P

CHAPTER XXXIV

MEDITERRANEAN INTRIGUE

The French Attitude towards Palestine—M. de Jouvenel, High Commissioner of Syria—M. Herriot's Astonishing Speech—Italy and Palestine—Conversations with Mussolini—Count Theodoli, Italian Representative on the Permanent Mandates Commission—Turkey and Palestine—Visit to Turkey, 1938

AMONG the tasks which fell on the shoulders of the President of the Zionist Organization was the maintenance of contacts with the various governments of the Powers which were represented on the League of Nations. Foremost among these were the French, who, besides being England's immediate neighbours across the Channel, were also her Mandatory neighbours in Syria on the northern border of Palestine; and the Italians.

I was therefore frequently in Paris and in Rome—and each city presented its own problem to us.

In Paris I met, I believe, every Premier between the two wars, from Poincaré to Reynaud. Léon Blum had a long record of co-operation with us. In the days when Nahum Sokolow was conducting our negotiations on the Continent he was always kept informed semi-officially of the French situation by M. Blum. In later years M. Blum came to take a real interest in the movement, working closely with M. Marc Jarblum, one of the leaders of the French Zionist Organization. M. Aristide Briand was also quite sympathetic, although a little vague as to what was going on. Briand used to say: 'Palestine must be a wonderful country, and a very impressive one,' and praise the oranges which he used to receive from us every Christmas as the best he had ever eaten. But his sentiments went no deeper than the skin of the oranges. He was a warmhearted man of strong liberal sympathies, and was attracted by the idea of the Jewish renaissance, but he knew little about the moral force of the Zionist movement, and made no effort to find out more.

By far the largest majority of the officials of the Quai d'Orsay were either indifferent or hostile; occasionally they were jealous of our progress. I have remarked already that the French followed the Arab lead in regarding Palestine merely as the southern part of Syria, and when Palestine was given a separate Mandate they felt they had a grievance. The French, moreover, had always considered themselves *the* representatives of Europe in the eastern Mediterranean, and the protectors of the Christians in those parts. English was practically unknown until after Allenby's time. It is too often forgotten in England that it was the Balfour Declaration which brought her to Palestine, and gave her her *raison d'être* there. The French were inclined to look at the revival of Jewish Palestine through Catholic eyes, and as an encroachment on the French tradition.

An exception was M. de Saint-Quentin, whose connection with the Levant went back to the First World War, when he was liaison officer between the French Army and Allenby. He had encouraged me at the time of my visit to Feisal; and later he encouraged me to make several visits to Syria, and to meet the French High Commissioners.

Among these the most interesting, in my opinion, was M. de Jouvenel, who was opposite number to Field-Marshal Lord Plumer. M. de Jouvenel had been the editor of *Le Matin*, one of the most influential French newspapers; he was hostile to the Zionist idea and anything connected with it, and we were never able to get a favourable line in his paper. When I first met him he was not slow, either, in giving expression to his views.

This happened in Beirut, where I was presented to him by some French friends. He made use of the occasion to unburden himself, and I let him go on; then I said: 'Your Excellency really cannot speak of Zionism and Palestine, never having studied the one or seen the other. The latter is right on your Syrian frontier, and if you were to visit it for only a couple of days, you might change your views.'

He agreed, and came over shortly afterwards to stay with the High Commissioner of Palestine, where I met him again. A very queer contrast he made, by the way, with Lord Plumer: the one a sophisticated and gallant Frenchman, the other a staid and serious English aristocrat of the Victorian era. He toured the country, and then I met him again a third time, and the change which had come over his views reminded me a little of the transformation which the first visit to Palestine had wrought in Felix Warburg. M. de Jouvenel not only retracted his previous criticisms; he even reproached the Zionists for never having made any attempt to come and work in Syria!

I was very much startled by his suggestion, and answered that we had plenty to do in Palestine, where we were working under the terms of a Mandate, without coming to Syria, where we had no standing and would be regarded by the Arabs as intruders—the vanguard perhaps of Jewish expansion over the entire Middle East. But de Jouvenel insisted that the Jews were the only people who could develop Syria.

'Of course,' he added, 'I would not want you to work in southern Syria, because immediately after you'd come to Tyre and Saïda you would want the frontier rectified. But I have one great project, and that is the development of the region of the Euphrates. It is of course many hundreds of miles away from Palestine,' and he produced a map on the spot, and showed me where the Euphrates crosses great stretches of desert country with a very thin population, mostly Bedouin. 'Thousands of square miles,' he said, enthusiastically, 'could be irrigated here and nourish a great population.'

He went on to mention that French aviators who had flown over the Euphrates basin had found traces of the ancient canals which had brought water thence to the oasis of Palmyra, where a considerable civilization had flourished in ancient times. 'What has been done in ancient times,' he said, 'can certainly be done in modern,' and he grew eloquent on the possibilities. But the only reply it provoked from me was: 'You know, M. de Jouvenel, we have our own water problem in Palestine, but we shall have to be satisfied with the modest Jordan. Wonderful as the picture is, we can't be tempted by it.' He even pleaded on historic grounds. 'Dr. Weizmann, it is written in the Book of Nehemiah that Tadmor, which as you know is Palmyra, was built by the Jews.'

He raised the subject again when we met later in Paris, and even persuaded Léon Blum of the soundness of the idea. But it had no practical value for us.

A very queer incident sticks in my mind in connection with

my visits to France and my efforts to influence public opinion in our favour. This took place in 1933, when with Hitler's ascent the tide of German refugees was beginning to move towards Palestine.

I received one day a telegram from Mlle Louise Weiss, a French journalist of distinction, who had wide contacts in political circles, inviting me to deliver an address on Zionism and Palestine in the lecture theatre of the Sorbonne. She assured me that the meeting would be held under the most distinguished auspices and would attract an important audience. I hesitated for one reason only. I felt that it would be impossible for me to avoid speaking on the events in Germany; my feelings might perhaps run away with me, and we had too many hostages in Hitler's hands. I would never forgive myself if I made their position even harder than it was. On the other hand this was a unique opportunity to state our case to an influential part of the French public. I weighed the pros and cons, sought the advice of a few friends, and finally accepted.

The meeting was all that Mlle Weiss had promised. The lecture hall was packed. The chairman was M. Martin, an ex-Minister of Finance, and I was informed that there was present *tout Paris*. I recognized in the audience some members of the British Embassy, friends from the Quai d'Orsay, representatives of the Rothschild family, the son of Captain Dreyfus, the Chief Rabbi of Paris, and others.

I tried to speak calmly of conditions in Germany and of the responsibility which rested upon the civilized world towards the victims of German policy. I spoke of the refuge which some of them were finding in Palestine—it was more than a refuge: for the children it was, after a few months, a homecoming. I had seen the German children mixing with the Palestinian and becoming, in a short time, indistinguishable from them. I then dealt with the country itself, which, in spite of its smallness, seemed to be able to expand its capacity as the need presented itself.

The audience followed my statement with intense interest, and when I had ended I was somewhat astonished to hear the chairman say that I ought to repeat the same lecture in the same place the following day. There were, he was certain, numbers of people who would like to hear it again, and a chance should also be given to those who had been unable to obtain admittance the first evening. He stated further that he was quite certain that M. Herriot would be glad to act as chairman for the second evening. I could not but accept.

I spoke again, the next day, before a packed audience, but my chairman was not M. Herriot. He failed to appear, so we went ahead without an official chairman, Mlle Weiss opening the meeting. I was in the middle of my address when M. Herriot suddenly irrupted into the hall. Without paying the slightest attention to me—perhaps he did not even notice me, for I had stopped speaking when he entered—he rushed on to the platform and in a stentorian voice delivered himself of a twenty-minute address on matters which had nothing to do with Zionism, Palestine or the Jews: it was all about the greatness of French civilization, done in magnificent style, but consisting of generalities. He finished as abruptly as he had burst in. The audience was utterly nonplussed by this extraordinary intermezzo, but Mlle Weiss calmly took the chair again, and asked me to resume.

I never met M. Herriot again, and I am quite certain that he had not the faintest notion what the meeting was all about.

Of the attitude of the Italian Government to the Zionist movement I have already spoken in the chapter describing the struggle round the ratification of the Mandate. Italy had been, prior to the advent of fascism, entirely free from anti-Semitism, but a change began to appear shortly after the accession of Mussolini. He himself violently denied any anti-Semitic tendencies, but they were fostered by underlings like Staracci and Federzoni, and the whole fascist press was flavoured with anti-Semitism. From time to time articles appeared attacking Zionism and the participation of Italian Jews in the movement. The Zionists, and the Jews generally, though they did not give loud expression to their views on the subject, were known to be anti-fascist. Enzo Sereni, a member of a very distinguished family—later one of the founders of the co-operative colony Govat Brenner—was marked by the Italian police. A brother of his, a known Communist, was arrested and condemned to the Lipari Islands. He could have obtained his release by recanting. His father, who was the King's physician, pleaded with him to do so. He refused. Later he escaped from the

Lipari Islands and made his way to Moscow. Other Jews were caught smuggling anti-fascist literature from France into Italy, and the position of the community became a difficult one.

All these circumstances made my visits to Rome matters of some importance to the Italian Jews. They felt that my talks with the head of the government, my explanations of the aims of the Zionist movement, would help to ease the situation for them.

I had three conversations with Mussolini, spaced over a number of years. My first took place shortly after the First World War, and he received me in his famous office—a long room, dimly lighted and almost empty of furniture. He sat at a small desk at the furthest corner from the door, so that the visitor had to walk quite a distance to meet him. Before the table stood a hard chair, for the visitor. It was all somewhat theatrical, and in no way contributed—was perhaps not intended to contribute—to putting the visitor at his ease.

However, he greeted me affably enough, shook hands with me, and after the usual exchange of politenesses led off with the remark, in French: 'You know, Dr. Weizmann, not all Jews are Zionists.' To which I replied, 'Of course, I know it only too well, and not all Italians are Fascisti.' He smiled wryly, and did not take it too badly. At any rate, the conversation became very normal and there was no attempt to browbeat or intimidate me. I told him about our plans and intentions, and he was interested in finding out whether much of our immigration went through Italian ports. I explained that Trieste was very important for us and that we had extremely friendly relations with the Lloyd Triestino. We were also using Genoa, Venice and Naples; and we were anxious to cultivate the good will of the Italian people.

Mussolini then spoke of England and insinuated that the Zionists were merely a pawn in Great Britain's power game. I said that I had never seen any particularly sinister intentions behind Britain's Zionist policy; so far England was the only great country that had shown readiness to help us begin actual operations in Palestine. What ulterior motives there may have been in the minds of certain British statesmen I could not know; but as long as these operations were possible, and we could carry on without too many difficulties, we should maintain our relations with England, which I considered essential. He said, suddenly: 'You know, we could build your state *en toute pièce*.' To which I replied: 'I remember that the Romans destroyed it *en toute pièce*.'

He was not particularly pleased with this answer. He probably had expected me to say what I thought the Italian Government could do for us, but I was not going to walk into that trap. He went on to ask whether the Italian language was being taught or spoken in our schools, and I had to answer in the negative. However, I added, there would certainly be a chair of Italian language and literature at the Hebrew University. The Jews had always admired the Italian spirit of freedom and tolerance, and as he knew, many Jews had distinguished themselves in the service of Italy. There might be some disagreement in certain sections of young Jewry on the subject of fascism, but this should not be construed as unfriendliness towards Italy. We greatly admired the Italian civilization.

I felt I was skating on thin ice and wanted to end the conversation as soon as I had spoken my piece on Jews and fascism and Italy, but he kept me for some time, asking me about our various undertakings in Palestine, which were then in the embryonic stage. He was obviously keen that the port of Haifa, which was already being talked about, should be built by Italian firms. He hinted at Jews who were leaders in this field, and I knew that he meant the firm of Almaja. I said I would be glad to know more about them.

I carried away the impression that Mussolini was not hostile to the Zionist idea, or to our work in Palestine; his suspicion and hostility were directed at the British, who in his opinion were using the Jews in the eastern Mediterranean in order to cut across the Italian control of *Mare Nostrum*.

I became acquainted with the Almajas, a very distinguished old family which still maintained the Jewish tradition, and they mentioned their interest in the port of Haifa. I had to answer truthfully that we would not have much say in this matter, and that there were great British firms of ship and port builders, like Armstrong Whitworth. It might be well for the Almajas to get in touch with them.

As fascism became more strongly established in Italy it fell more deeply under the influence of German anti-Semitism, and the attacks in the fascist press increased in number and violence. Mussolini was still hesitating between linking up with the Western Powers and throwing in his lot with Germany. His price—from whichever side he might obtain it—was expansion in Africa, and gains in Europe—Savoy, Nice, Corsica. There was hesitation and uncertainty of direction in the fascist camp. The Germans, as always, were extremely active in Italy. It was not that they considered Italy a particularly valuable ally; they were more concerned with a springboard for action in the Mediterranean, directed against Britain.

We were an insignificant factor in this struggle of the Great Powers; still, there we were, growing, pushing our roots into an important part of the Mediterranean shore, and the Italians did not like it. Their attitude found more than journalistic expression in the Permanent Mandates Commission, where the Italian representative, Count Theodoli, could always be relied on to veto any constructive suggestion in our behalf.

What Count Theodoli's personal convictions on the subject of Zionism were I do not know; but he did have a personal relation to it. He was connected with a great Arab family in Beirut, the Sursuks, who were the absentee landlords from whom we had bought large stretches of land in the Valley of Jezreel. Neither Theodoli nor his relatives the Sursuks could get over the fact that they had sold the land so cheaply— actually they got a very high price for areas which our work made valuable later—and they always threw the blame on Victor Sursuk, a member of the family who kept a great establishment in Alexandria, and whom they accused of Zionist leanings. They should have held on to the land, and they would have got for it five times as much as they did. In vain did I explain to Theodoli and his Arab relatives that what they had sold us was a deadly marsh, and they better than anyone else should have known how the Arab villages in that district had disappeared, and how we had had to sink hundreds of thousands of pounds into drainage and improvement and roads. If the land was so valuable now, it had become so through our work and effort, our sacrifices in blood and money. This, incidentally, is a phenomenon we are constantly running up against in Palestine. Visitors who know nothing about the country and its history are always making the unfounded

P*

charge that the Jews have taken the best land. Actually we took the worst, and made it the best by our efforts. It seems as if God has covered the soil of Palestine with rocks and marshes and sand, so that its real beauty can only be brought out by those who love it and will devote their lives to healing its wounds.

On the Permanent Mandates Commission Count Theodoli, following instructions, posed as the great defender of Arab rights and of the Catholic Church against the imaginary encroachments of the Jews. The Italians were worried by the excessive liberalism of the new Jewish institutions, and helped to spread the legend of the flagrant atheism of the Jewish settlements in the Holy Land. This was a time when the fascists were entering into close relations with the Vatican, and making what political capital they could of the combination.

I paid a second visit to Italy to see Mussolini and to tour the Italian-Jewish communities. The Rome-Berlin Axis had not yet been forged, the issue of Italy's alliance was still in doubt, and I hoped to make some improvement in our relations with the Italians. I believe my second talk with Mussolini was not without value. He said he had been delighted to learn that the Zionists in Jerusalem were on excellent terms with the local Italians; also that our colonies were making good progress. After this second interview a better tone towards us could be observed in the Italian press; the substance of the interview got out, and its friendly character contributed a great deal towards improving the position of the Jewish community. I have a particularly vivid recollection of the second interview with Mussolini because it took place on the eve of *Yom Kippur*.

My third and last interview with Mussolini still fell within the period of Italian indecision; it was the longest of the interviews and the most substantial in content. Count Theodoli arranged it, and on this occasion he showed himself full of good will and friendliness—a Saul changed into a Paul. Mussolini too was extremely affable, and talked freely of a Rome-Paris-London combination, which, he said, was the logical one for Italy. He spoke also of the chemical industry, and of the Italian need of pharmaceuticals, which we could produce in Palestine. He regretted that his gestures towards London and Paris had not met with the proper response.

I repeated the substance of this conversation to my British friends in London, but it had no consequences. Shortly before the outbreak of the war Halifax and Chamberlain visited Mussolini and tried to win him over, but by then it was too late. He was hopelessly in the clutches of the Germans, whom he strongly disliked, always speaking with contempt of their manners and their overbearing character. The contempt was, of course, quite mutual. I do not know whether detaching Rome from Berlin would have prevented the outbreak of the war, but it certainly might have made a great difference to the war in the Mediterranean, might have saved many lives and shortened the agony by many months.

It was not without a certain discomfort that I used to make my views known to British officials. The British Jews were in an awkward predicament. Their hostility to Germany, their manifest unhappiness at seeing British statesmen on friendly terms with our bitterest persecutors, could give the impression that they wanted the British to fight our war for us; the fact that what they sought was consonant with England's interests was thereby obscured.

There was another instance of this kind which occurred much later, in fact only a year before the outbreak of the Second World War. Relations between Jews and Arabs in Palestine were very strained—this was the time of the Arab terror—and I was advised by many friends to see whether I could not persuade the Turkish Government to use its good offices as intermediary between us and the Arabs.

It struck me as a sound idea. It should be borne in mind that although Kemal Ataturk had secularized the Government, Turkey was still viewed by the Arab world as a major Moslem community. Its progressive record, its position as a bridge between Europe and Asia, its standing with the Western world, all helped to enhance its prestige in the eyes of the Arabs. There was no doubt that the good will of the Turks could go a long way in improving relations between us and the Arabs, the more so as the Turks had begun to take an interest in our work. We had put up a pavilion at a Turkish Exhibition in Smyrna, with samples of Palestinian industrial and agricultural products, and the usual statistical tables on education, hygiene and so on. These had made a profound impression on visitors, and Kemal

Ataturk had sent a number of Government representatives to Palestine to see whether our methods could not be applied to the revival of Turkey. We knew, of course, that the Turks would be very careful not to offend the susceptibilities of the Arabs; also that there was much bitterness in Turkey over the fact that the liberated Arabs had taken possession of vast tracts of the former Turkish Empire and were doing nothing to develop them. It would therefore not be plain sailing to get the Turks to act as intermediaries for us; but it was certainly worth trying.

There was another purpose in my visit to Turkey in 1938. One already felt the approach of the war. Germany was doing everything in her power to attach Turkey to the Axis, and anything that might be done to counteract this influence was of value. Although my main interest was Zionist, I kept the British Government informed of my conversations with Turkish officials and of the impressions I gained in regard to general matters.

My wife and I arrived in Istanbul on November 27, 1938. Istanbul made on us the impression of a city almost devoid of life and movement—a vast agglomeration of houses and abandoned palaces, exquisitely beautiful in certain parts, but in a dying condition. The shops of Istanbul were full of German rubbish, evidence of the inroads which German trade had made on the Turkish market.

Ankara made a very different impression. Situated in the interior of Asia Minor, amid picturesque surroundings, in the heart of the agricultural country, it was new, healthy and alive, corresponding to the new spirit of the Turkish people. Very impressive, too, were the 'Gates of Tamerlane,' a great fissure in the rocks dominating Ankara, through which the Tartars are said to have irrupted into Asia Minor on their way to Europe.

We spent a few days in the two main cities and I had numerous conversations with Turkish officials, chief among them Jellal Bayard, the Prime Minister, and Ismet Ineonu, then Finance Minister. I found, as I had expected, a considerable interest in Palestine, but what permanent results the conversations might have had for us it would be difficult to say. The war intervened shortly after. But the secondary aspect of my visit may still be of interest.

The Turkish officials approached me from a single point of view: they wanted to know whether the Jews could help them to obtain a gold loan. Of course I could not hold out any promises. I had, before leaving London, consulted several banker friends (this after a couple of visits to the Turkish Embassy) and all I could suggest was that the Turkish Government invite out a committee qualified to discuss such matters. The proposal, practical as it seemed to me, did not appeal to the Turkish authorities, who were probably under the naïve impression that I was in control of vast fortunes, and was merely putting them off.

I discussed the matter with the British Ambassador, Sir Percy Lorraine, who told me that what the Turks needed was about half a million gold pounds per annum to see them through their immediate difficulties. Astonished at the smallness of the sum, I ventured to suggest that the British might, usefully and without much risk, negotiate such a loan for the Turks, and that it might go a long way to neutralize German influence. My suggestion found no echo, and again I had the feeling that I was suspected of looking at matters entirely from the Jewish point of view; I was not being as careful as British officialdom in taking the feelings of the Germans into account! I do not assert that one could have bought a Turkish alliance with the sum proposed; but I imagine that a gesture of good will on the part of Great Britain would have been of value. In any case, Turkish neutrality during the war cost the Allies a great deal more than the half-million pounds per annum asked.

It was during this visit that I came in contact with the German Jewish scientists who had accepted positions at the Universities of Istanbul and Ankara. They were an unhappy lot. They did not complain of any derogatory treatment, but most of them were faced again by the problem they thought they had solved five years before: refuge. Their contracts were expiring, and there was no prospect of renewal.

CHAPTER XXXV

THE PERMANENT MANDATES COMMISSION

Function of the Commission—Professor William Rappard of Switzerland— M. Orts of Belgium—Lord Lugard of England—Attitude of the Colonial Office

AMONG the many activities which took me periodically out of England was the maintenance of contacts with the Permanent Mandates Commission of the League of Nations. Although we had an office in Geneva to deal with matters in a routine way, there were the special occasions when the members of the Permanent Mandates Commission came together to receive and consider reports. Except for Professor Rappard none of them lived in Switzerland. They therefore had to be kept informed by special and individual contacts between sessions.

Whether the views and criticisms of the Mandates Commission carried much weight with the Mandatory Power is doubtful; but the cumulative effect of those annual reports was not without importance, both for the record and for its effect on public opinion. It was our business to present our case in the best possible way, to bring out the facts in exact and proper form, and to see to it that the reports should not be limited merely to criticism of administrative details, but should give a general picture of our work and the growth of the National Home in the face of the difficulties we encountered.

We were not entitled to appear at the sessions of the Mandates Commission, nor did I consider it dignified or proper to come to Geneva during such sessions and lobby in the antechambers. The members of the commission were very much overworked at those periods, and had as much as they could do to study the reports. To approach them then would have been an imposition, the more so as the Arabs and other interested parties would have followed suit, and an impossible situation would have ensued. It was therefore necessary to see the various members of the Mandates Commission in their respective countries.

On the whole this very distinguished body, which had a unique task to perform, was impartial, honest and industrious in its attempts to get at the truth. Occasionally it was over-impressed by the might of the Mandatory Power, but on the whole we were given a good chance to present our case, and in the course of the years some of the members became thoroughly acquainted with the details of our work in Palestine and with the various aspects of our movement. I am anxious to make it clear that I have never found any bias in any of the members, excepting Count Theodoli of Italy. We had some well-wishers in the commission, but their friendliness did not blind them to the performance of their duties or incline them to view the facts otherwise than with absolute objectivity.

Foremost among the members of the commission was Professor William Rappard, of the University of Geneva. He was well acquainted with the Anglo-Saxon mentality, had lived for many years in America and had been, I believe, one of Woodrow Wilson's favourite secretaries. He was a man of the greatest intellectual capacity, with a deep understanding of the Jewish problem in all its bearings and as deep a sympathy with our hopes and endeavours.

Professor Rappard was a helpful guide to us, and to me in particular, in the inner workings of the League, an intricate labyrinth leading to many dark domains in European and world politics. It is a source of pleasure, and of not a little pride, to recall that our acquaintance, which was purely formal and official at first, crystallized into a lifelong friendship. Whenever M. Rappard came over to England, which happened once or twice every year, we always met if I happened to be in the country, as we did if I happened to be passing through Switzerland when he was there. It was always a delight to converse with this sage and experienced man, in whom I found a peculiar and impressive blend of the intellectuality of the scholar and statesman with the simplicity and solidity of the Swiss peasant.

Another member of the commission who was a commanding personality was the Belgian, M. Orts, a man of great administrative experience, who had occupied a high position in the

Congo. Interestingly enough, this experience had taught him that there is a world of difference between the black Congo and white Palestine, and he understood the incongruity of British attempts to apply the methods of the first to the problems of the second—attempts which, among a sensitive and sophisticated population, often turned the machinery of administration into a sort of Procrustean bed. M. Orts fought against that, sometimes quite effectively. In him too we found a sympathetic and critical appreciation of our efforts, and a deep understanding of the bearing of the Jewish problem on the National Home. He saw the latter not simply as a place of refuge for immigrants, but as a centre of civilization built by a modern people drawing on an ancient tradition in a land hallowed by memories and associations. I used to visit M. Orts once or twice a year in Brussels and spend a long evening with him in his study, sometimes explaining our position to him, sometimes sitting at his feet and learning from his wide experience as a great administrator, statesman and man of the world.

A third leading member of the Mandates Commission was Lord Lugard, the British representative; again a personality of great power, commanding the respect and affection of those whose privilege it was to come in touch with him. One of the most remarkable features in my relations with Lord Lugard was his complete impartiality in dealing with a matter closely affecting the interests of Great Britain. He had been a lifelong servant of British imperial interests, and, like M. Orts, the administrator of a large African dependency. He had been one of the first to try to associate the native population with the administration, and he had made an enviable name for himself throughout the black continent. He was humane in his outlook, sympathizing with the submerged and dispossessed, but at the same time strong in his views and severe in his criticisms. In conversation he always made on me the impression of a great judge called upon to try a complicated case. This manner of his did not disturb me at all; his severe exterior was belied by a pair of kindly and understanding eyes. He felt the Jewish plight deeply, and I always knew that he would put the Jewish case in the best possible light, though he would not say a word about it to me.

It became almost a tradition for me to pay him regular visits at his modest place in Little Parkhurst, near Dorking, in Surrey. Curiously enough, his residence was very close to that of Claude Montefiore, one of the spiritual leaders of English Jewry, but (as the reader may remember from earlier chapters) an avowed and active anti-Zionist. These two men were apparently on terms of close friendship; I never met Montefiore there, but from some hints dropped by Lord Lugard I gathered that they had discussed the Jewish National Home more than once.

It was always an intellectual and spiritual occasion to spend a few hours with Lord Lugard, though it was not without its drawbacks. He was advanced in years and hard of hearing, and I had to make a considerable physical effort to make him understand what I was saying. Now and then I used to meet him in town, at his request, once or twice in the offices of Barclays' Bank, of which he was a director.

These three persons formed the core of the Mandates Commission, and I could easily imagine a clash between them and the rather dry functionaries who came before them to justify the actions of the Colonial Office. These used to complain about the necessity of having to account to a lot of foreigners for the administration of Palestine, asking somewhat ironically what a foreigner could understand of British methods and British mentality. They usually forgot that among the members of the Mandates Commission there was Lord Lugard, an Englishman, and a magnificent administrator who understood their methods only too thoroughly, and did not by any means always approve of them. For that matter, the ways of the Colonial Office were not beyond the comprehension of men like Rappard and Orts, either.

CHAPTER XXXVI

RIOT AND THE PEEL COMMISSION

Appeasement of the Arabs—The Legislative Council—An Undemocratic Proposal—Riots in Palestine, April 1936—The Mufti to the Fore—The Administration Fumbles—Appointment of the Peel Commission—I Give Evidence before It—Partition Comes up—The Twentieth Zionist Congress —Violent Controversy—The Jewish Position Misrepresented

THE beginnings of the strain which developed between us and Sir Arthur Wauchope were to be found in his advocacy of a legislative council, to which he was committed by the Government, but which he himself also favoured. This difficulty, by itself, might have been overcome, for Sir Arthur's sympathies with the National Home were, as I have said, profound and informed.

From the time of his arrival in 1931 Sir Arthur had entered into the problems of the country with great enthusiasm and had realized from the outset that the mainspring of our progress was immigration. By 1935 the annual immigration figure passed the sixty thousand mark, and we thought that if this would only continue for another few years we would be past the difficulties which had given us most trouble. Fate decreed otherwise. We can see now that this period was an oasis in the desert of time.

The Abyssinian war came in 1935, and with it the accentuation of England's policy of appeasement towards the aggressive powers and their possible satellites. Among the latter the Foreign Office placed the Arabs—and here began the deterioration both of our position and of our relations with Sir Arthur Wauchope.

Appeasement of the Arabs did not at first take the form of limitation of Jewish immigration; that, in 1934, 1935 and part of 1936, was more or less regulated by the absorptive capacity of the country. It took, instead, a form which, if allowed to develop, would have led to the complete arrest both of Jewish

466

immigration and of Jewish progress generally: namely, British advocacy of a legislative council with Arabs in the majority.

The idea of a legislative council had been mooted as far back as 1922, in the Churchill White Paper. It was raised again in the Passfield White Paper of 1931. It was contained in the instructions with which Ramsay MacDonald had sent Sir Arthur Wauchope to Palestine, and Sir Arthur had always been favourably inclined to the idea. But he did not begin to press it upon us until he himself was under strong pressure from the Colonial Office. The proposal submitted to us was for a council consisting of fourteen Arabs (nine elected, five appointed), seven Jews (three elected, four appointed), two members of the commercial community of unspecified race (appointed) and five British officials.

Discussions regarding a legislative council had, then, been going on for years. During my out-of-office period Sir Arthur had frequently consulted me on the subject, and I had pointed out that to talk of elected Arabs representing their people was to contradict the democratic principle which it was supposed to further. A legislative council in Palestine would be merely a modernized cloak for the old feudal system, that is, a continuation in power of the family cliques which had held the country in their thrall for centuries and ground down the faces of the poor.

I pointed out what was equally obvious, that official election to power would enable the Husseinis, the Mufti and their group to terrorize the villages even more effectively than before. Sir Arthur may or may not have agreed with me; he pressed his line with increasing insistence from the winter of 1935 on.

It was true that the proposed council would be so constructed that the number of Arabs would be balanced by the combination of Jews, British officials and unspecified members; and it was also true that the granting of certificates of immigration would be reserved to the High Commissioner. But as to the first point, we had had experience enough with the British officials in Palestine to know that we could not rely on them to defend the principles of the Mandate; as to the second, we foresaw that once the council was set up, the next step would be to give the Arabs increasing powers over the reserved subjects, and we would find ourselves confronted by the danger of the premature crystallization of the Jewish National Home. We would not agree to the council; we fought it in Palestine and in London.

Again I must, in fairness, stress the good relationship which had existed between us and Wauchope until that time. His attitude had been positive and helpful ever since his arrival in the country. When I saw a pro-Zionist administrator coming out to Palestine I was full of apprehension, and I usually gave him six to ten months in which to forget his Zionist tendencies and revert to the regulation type of administrator such as may be found on the Gold Coast or in Tanganyika or some other British dependency. We became natives in his eyes, and he resented the difficulties we created for him; we, on the other hand, resented the application of Gold Coast administrative measures to a highly developed, highly differentiated, critical and sceptical society like the *Yishuv* in Palestine. It says a great deal for the intellectual acumen and stamina of Sir Arthur Wauchope that he kept his original ideals for four years, and yielded only under the influence of events which were casting their shadows on the life of the whole world.

Among the various counter-proposals to the form of legislative council urged by the Government was one on which Jews and Arabs would be equal in number, with balance of power held by British officials. This seemed to me to present a possible solution. I knew the dangers inherent in it, but I felt that we might find some compensation in the public opinion of the world; for the position in which we placed ourselves by our refusal to consider the legislative council was, as I have explained, an unfortunate one. The public heard the words 'legislative council for Palestine'; it heard of Zionist opposition; the obvious conclusion was that the Zionists were undemocratic, or anti-democratic! I had a second point in mind: on a council with equal Jewish and Arab representation there would be regular contacts between the two peoples; perhaps by patience and by fair dealing we might diminish the fears which kept the two peoples asunder. Fears are unconquerable by ordinary logic; but they sometimes yield to daily contact.

The council, as we know, was never set up in any form; but the fact that I was prepared to consider it if there was equality of representation was made the occasion for some of the bitterest attacks to which I have ever been subjected. I was called not merely an appeaser, but a British agent—and this accusation was periodically revived whenever I clashed with the extremists of the movement. It is no doubt still current. I can only quote, in this connection, the words of Nietzsche: '*Dem Reinem is alles rein, dem Schweine ist alles Schwein.*'

With the deterioration of the international situation, the rise of Hitler Germany, the Italo-Abyssinian war, the preliminaries to the Civil War in Spain, the lack of policy on the part of the democracies, new and disturbing elements were injected into the picture. France's indecisiveness towards Hitler, who was moving towards the Rhine, England's indecisiveness towards Mussolini, who was sending his warships through the Suez Canal, tended to give the Arabs the impression that with the democracies force alone won concessions. In April 1936 rioting broke out in Palestine, and a new and unhappy chapter opened in Zionist history.

The outbreaks were sporadic at first. In the general spirit of the period, the Government did not act decisively. For a long time no serious effort was made to cope with the rioting so that the Arabs gained the impression that they had in fact chosen the means and the moment well. A month elapsed, and the Arab leaders, encouraged by developments, formed the Arab Higher Committee, headed by the Grand Mufti, and called a general strike.

The connection between the Arab Higher Committee and the rioting was clear enough. Fawzi Kawukji, the Syrian guerrilla fighter who came into Palestine to organize the bandits, was an old friend of the Mufti's. The waylaying and murdering of Jewish travellers, the attacks on Jewish settlements, the burning of Jewish fields, the uprooting of Jewish trees, spread over the entire country. The Palestine Administration, undoubtedly acting on instructions from London, encouraged the intervention of the Arab states, and in August 1936 invited the Foreign Minister of Iraq to negotiate with the Arab Higher Committee, thereby giving a sort of official status to the employers of the Kawukji. It was all in the true spirit of 'appeasement.'

That military action was feeble, and administrative action

unwise, was the opinion of a British staff officer then serving in Palestine under General Dill. In his account of the early months of the riots, *British Rule and Rebellion*, H. J. Simpson writes: 'The delay in obtaining reinforcements, the restrictions placed on the actions of the troops from the outset, and the latitude to the other side to obstruct their movement became of secondary importance in view of the freedom of movement allowed to rebel leaders.' And again: 'The connection between the Arab leaders in Palestine and the armed bands raised in Palestine, as well as those brought in from abroad, seems to be established. The civil authorities persisted in maintaining that there was no connection and persisted in trying to squeeze a public pronouncement against the use of armed force out of the Mufti . . . they refused to act vigorously against the Arab leaders. Why that theory was fixed in their minds remains a mystery.'

It was not much of a mystery to those who looked at Palestine in a larger setting, and saw in it as it were the mirror of events in Spain, at the other end of the Mediterranean, where England and France 'persisted in maintaining that there was no connection' between the rebels and the Axis Powers. Similarly, England was refusing to admit, at least publicly, that Axis encouragement and Axis money were playing a part in the Palestine riots.

Once the situation had been permitted to get out of hand, once the bandits had organized in the hills, the military had a real problem on its hands. An army is always at a disadvantage against guerrilla fighters, especially in a country with the geographic features of Palestine. Fawzi was a skilful fighter, and he managed his small forces well. In particular he trained them to disband, melt into the villages and reassemble. The British troops, with their heavy equipment, could not cope with the light-armed, fast-moving Arabs. Nor was the attitude of the Palestine Administration particularly helpful, as we have seen. The officer in command, General Dill, was a brilliant military leader, as was proved later in the war; but he rather resented, I believe, the awkward situation in which he was placed.

In May 1936 the British Government decided to appoint a Royal Commission to 'investigate the causes of unrest and alleged grievances of Arabs or of Jews.' This was the now

famous 'Peel Commission,' so called from its chairman, Earl
Peel—by far the most distinguished and ablest of the investiga-
tory bodies ever sent out to Palestine. Its members were men
with excellent training and in some cases of wide experience.
There were among them an ex-administrator of a province in
India, a professor of colonial history at Oxford, an ex-Ambassador, a judge of the High Court, and a lawyer of eminence.
The chairman was of ministerial rank. Many of us felt that this
was not only an extremely competent body, but that it would
prove to be both thorough and impartial. The findings of such
a commission, we believed, would go a long way towards
solving our problems.

For my own part, I must state that when the commission
arrived in Palestine—this was not until November 1936—and
the time for the hearings approached, I became deeply convinced that a new and possibly decisive phase in our movement
might now be beginning. Knowing something of the records of
the members of the commission, I had complete confidence in
their fairness and their intellectual honesty. Nevertheless it was
with considerable trepidation that I went up to Jerusalem on
November 25 to deliver my evidence. I remember that, as I
walked between two rows of spectators to the door of the building where the sessions were being held, there were audible
whispers on either side of me '*Ha-shem yatzliach darkecho*' (God
prosper you on your mission), and I felt that I not only carried
the burden of these well-wishers, and of countless others in
other lands, but that I would be speaking for generations long
since dead, for those who lay buried in the ancient and thickly
populated cemeteries on Mount Scopus, and those whose last
resting places were scattered all over the world. And I knew
that any misstep of mine, any error, however involuntary,
would be not mine alone, but would redound to the discredit
of my people. I was aware, as on few occasions before or since,
of a crushing sense of responsibility.

I must confess, further, that the few friendly words addressed
to me in the way of introduction by the chairman, as he asked
me to sit down, meant a great deal to me, and perhaps carried
more encouragement than was intended. In them one felt the
innate courtesy of a gentleman, whose patience and kindliness
at that time were the more remarkable as he was in great

physical pain. Lord Peel was suffering from cancer, and died of it shortly after the publication of his report.

I began my address in slow, measured sentences. I had no prepared text, for I could not on such an occasion have read out a written document. I did, however, have comprehensive notes, which I had worked out with my colleagues, and I kept close to these. Not knowing how patient my auditors would be, I probably attempted to compress too much, but after speaking for perhaps half an hour, I noticed to my deep joy that they were following me with interest. They had moved forward, and I did not have to strain my voice. I went on practically without interruption for about an hour and a half, when I asked for a drink and a short break, as I was feeling a little faint. The chairman offered me something stronger, which I refused. I was now at my ease, and resumed my address, which took up another forty minutes or so.

I believe that the reader who has followed the narrative so far will already have some notion of the contents of my address, into which I sought to put both the permanent principles of the Zionist movement and the immediate urgency of the Jewish problem. I spoke of the six million Jews (a bitter and unconscious prophecy of the number exterminated not long after by Hitler) 'pent up in places where they are not wanted, and for whom the world is divided into places where they cannot live and places which they may not enter.' For them 'a certificate for Palestine is the highest boon. One in twenty, one in thirty may get it, and for them it is redemption.' Seeking to explain how they had reached this condition, I told of the deterioration of Jewish life in Central and Eastern Europe under the impact of new forces. But I sought to go deeper, into more enduring causes. 'When one speaks of the Jewish people one speaks of a people which is a minority everywhere, a majority nowhere, which is to some extent identified with the races among which it lives, but is still not quite identical. It is a disembodied ghost of a race, and it inspires suspicion, and suspicion breeds hatred. There should be one place in the world, in God's wide world, where we could live and express ourselves in accordance with our character, and make our contribution to civilization in our own way, and through our own channels.'

I spoke next of the Balfour Declaration, of which 'it has

sometimes been glibly said, "Here is a document, somewhat vague in its nature, issued in time of war. It was a wartime expedient."' I disproved, I believe, that the Balfour Declaration had been issued hastily and frivolously; and I cited the words of Lord Robert Cecil as to what the Balfour Declaration had been intended to convey: 'Arabia for the Arabs, Judea for the Jews, Armenia for the Armenians.' I spoke finally of what we had achieved in Palestine, which, at the time of the Peel Commission, contained four hundred thousand Jews as against the fifty-five thousand of the time of the Balfour Declaration; pointing, of course, to the general benefits which had accrued to the country from our work.

So much for the opening address; I had an opportunity, on ensuing days, to go into the details of our difficulties, during a long and thorough cross-examination. I was greatly impressed by the seriousness, patience, and relevance of the proceedings. I left Jerusalem and returned to Rehovoth, to resume my laboratory work, but was recalled to Jerusalem on several occasions to appear before the commission.

The subject of the partition of Palestine was first broached to me by the commission at a session which was held *in camera* on January 8, 1937. No colleague was with me. I was asked how the idea struck me, and naturally answered that I could not tell on the spur of the moment, nor would I give my own impressions except after consultation with my colleagues. Actually I felt that the suggestion held out great possibilities and hopes. Something new had been born into the Zionist movement, something which had to be handled with great care and tenderness, which should not be permitted to become a matter for crude slogans and angry controversy. I remember saying not long afterwards to a colleague: 'A Jewish State, the idea of Jewish independence in Palestine, even if only in part of Palestine, is such a lofty thing that it ought to be treated like the Ineffable Name, which is never pronounced in vain. By talking about it too much, by dragging it down to the level of the banal, you desecrate that which should be approached only with reverence.'

The idea of partition was, as I have said, first imparted to me *in camera*. A few days later I replied that this was an impossible position for me. I was the President of a democratic organization, and I could not give the commission my views on such an important subject without having consulted my colleagues.

It was obvious from the beginning that the territory to be 'offered' us would be a small one. Part of it would be the Negev, or southern desert. A possible alternative would be a shift to the north, leaving out the Negev.

Apart from the practical details of a partition plan, there was the fundamental question of partition as such. It had, besides its political and economic problems, its religious aspect. I took the matter up with a number of men for whose religious convictions I had the deepest respect, but men not involved in any way in the politics of the movement, and I did not find too much resistance. I put it to them thus: 'I know that God promised Palestine to the children of Israel, but I do not know what boundaries He set. I believe that they were wider than the ones now proposed, and may have included Transjordan. Still, we have forgone the eastern part and are now asked to forgo some of the western part. If God will keep His promise to His people in His own time, our business as poor humans, who live in a difficult age, is to save as much as we can of the remnants of Israel. By adopting this project we can save more of them than by continuing the Mandatory policy.'

It was my own deep conviction that God had always chosen small countries through which to convey His messages to humanity. It was from Judea and from Greece, not from Carthage or Babylonia, that the great ideas which form the most precious possessions of mankind emerged. I believed that a small Jewish State, well organized, living in peace with its neighbours, a State on which would be lavished the love and devotion of Jewish communities throughout the world—such a State would be a great credit to us and an equally great contribution to civilization.

There were—and are—immediate political considerations which inclined me towards the idea of partition. I saw in the establishment of a Jewish State a real possibility of coming to terms with the Arabs. As long as the Mandatory policy prevails, the Arabs are afraid that we shall absorb the whole of Palestine. Say what we will about the preservation of their rights, they are dominated by fear and will not listen to reason. A Jewish State with definite boundaries internationally guaranteed would be something final; the transgressing of these boundaries would be an act of war which the Jews would not commit, not merely because of its moral implications, but because it would arouse the whole world against them. Instead of being a minority in Palestine, we would be a majority in our own State, and be able to deal on terms of equality with our Arab neighbours in Palestine, Egypt and Iraq. As to our immediate neighbours, the Palestinians, we would have a great many interests in common—customs, harbours, railways, irrigation and development projects; such a community of interests, if properly handled, becomes the basis of peaceful and fruitful co-operation.

My hope that the question of partition would be dealt with on the high level to which it belonged was disappointed. It became the focus of one of the most violent controversies that has ever divided the Zionist movement. The twentieth Zionist Congress, held in Basle in August 1937, in the gathering shadows of the Nazi domination of Europe, broke into the *Ja-sager* and the *Nein-sager*, the opponents and the proponents of partition; not, I am compelled to say, on the merits of the question, but very often on the basis of prejudgments. I pleaded in vain that in the opinion of our most capable experts a Jewish State in part of Palestine would be able to absorb one hundred thousand immigrants a year, and sustain a Jewish population of two and a half to three millions. The divisions of opinion followed familiar lines, and I found myself again opposed by the combination of an American group, the *Mizrachi*, and that section of the Revisionists which had not seceded from the Zionist Organization.

But even the opposition could not wholly ignore the threat which now hung over the Jews of Europe, and the prospects of substantial rescue which a Jewish State held out made impossible outright rejection of partition. The following resolutions, among others, were accepted.

The Congress declares that the scheme of partition put forward by the Royal Commission is unacceptable.

The Congress empowers the Executive to enter into negotiations with a view to ascertaining the precise terms of His Majesty's Government for the proposed establishment of a Jewish State.

In such negotiations the Executive shall not commit either itself or the Zionist Organization, but in the event of the emergence of a definite scheme for the establishment of a Jewish State, such scheme shall be brought before a newly elected Congress for decision.

In this roundabout way the Congress indicated that it was ready to talk partition, and the issue seemed chiefly to be between those who had the courage to say so frankly, and those who wanted to retain a reputation for uncompromising maximalism.

But the battle was fought in vain, at least for the time being. The partition plan put forward by the British Government on the basis of the Peel Report was not followed up seriously. The rumour was started, and gained wide currency, that the Jews were against partition. This was simply not true. Considering the vital departure from the original Zionist programme which partition represented, considering also the internal political by-play of the various parties, the two to one vote of the Congress for the above-mentioned resolutions was very significant. I explained all this to Ormsby-Gore and to members of the Mandates Commission shortly after the Congress. That I had correctly interpreted the Jewish attitude towards partition has been made very clear to the world since that time.

CHAPTER XXXVII

TOWARDS NULLIFICATION

The White Paper of 1937—Surrender to the Arab Terrorists—Letter to Ormsby-Gore—Havlagah in Palestine—Letter to the High Commissioner— Drift towards Chaos in Palestine—My Warnings—The Woodhead Commission—Sabotaging Partition Proposal—The Palestine Administration's 'Neutrality'—Orde Wingate in Palestine—His Personality and His Career

BRITAIN's official offer of a partition plan was contained in a White Paper issued early in July 1937. The offer was accompanied by a series of interim administrative measures—'while the form of a scheme of partition is being worked out'—which struck heavily at the Jewish National Home. These measures were put into effect before Jewish opinion on partition had been tested. They were the first steps towards the nullification of the Balfour Declaration; actual nullification came with the White Paper of 1939. It was the classic technique of the step-by-step sell-out of small nations which the great democracies practised in the appeasement period.

The Government White Paper of 1937 was based on the Peel Report. The latter was an extraordinary document. On the one hand it testified to the achievements of the Jews in Palestine, on the other hand it recommended measures which seemed to us to be in complete contradiction with that testimony. The report put an end to the persistent falsehood that Jewish land purchases and land development had led to the displacement of Arabs; then it recommended severe restrictions on Jewish purchases of land. It asserted that Jewish immigration had brought benefits to the Arab people; then it recommended the severe curtailment of Jewish immigration. And it did this last in a form which was all the more shocking because it practically conceded the point made by the Arab terrorists, and undermined the very foundations of the Mandate.

By the terms of the Mandate, and by the agreement between

the Jewish Agency and Great Britain, Jewish immigration into Palestine was to be controlled by the economic absorptive capacity of the country. This was the safeguard against undue harm to the population of the country. The Jews were in Palestine 'as of right and not on sufferance,' and they came there as the opportunities were created for their employment. It was an arrangement which had worked according to the Peel Commission; Jews had come into Palestine in large numbers—over forty thousand in 1934, over sixty thousand in 1935 —and the Arabs had benefited economically by their coming. Now the Peel Report recommended that in granting immigration permits to the Zionists, 'political and psychological factors must be taken into consideration.' In other words, our entry into Palestine was made conditional on the mood of the Arabs. It was not put so frankly, of course. That last brutal clarification was reserved for the White Paper of 1939. But that was what it amounted to. Arab terrorism had won its first major victory. The Mandate was pronounced unworkable.

The Peel Report and the White Paper were issued simultaneously; and I felt it to be a very bad augury that I could not, almost up to the last minute, obtain an advance copy of the report. I called up Ormsby-Gore, then the Colonial Minister, and angry words passed between us. A day or two later I wrote him at length. The letter follows in its entirety. I make no apology for reproducing it, and one or two others belonging to that time. There has been so much talk about my inability or refusal to stand up to British officialdom ('British agent,' it will be recalled, are words that have been used about me) that I feel myself entitled to the publication of these letters. It might be added, in this connection, that it is easy to hurl denunciations at a government from the platform at a public meeting; it is another matter to carry the fight to the men with whom you are negotiating.

London
July 4, 1937

DEAR ORMSBY-GORE:

I have to thank you for your letter of July 1st. I am extremely sorry that you should have been distressed at my tone and manner over the telephone. It was certainly never my intention to say anything that might give you personal offence, and if I have done so, I sincerely regret it.

You think that I am under some grave misapprehension—namely, that the Cabinet will be taking far-reaching and final decisions of policy before the publication of the Report. This is not the main cause of my present anxieties. I quite understand that it would be impossible for the Cabinet, in so short a space of time, and occupied as it must be with many other very grave problems, to come to a quick and final decision on the Report. I also fully appreciate that time must elapse before the Report can be implemented, either wholly or in part. Still, your refusal to let me have a copy of it for a few days in advance of its publication has rendered more difficult for me an anyhow very difficult situation.

We are now on the eve of events which will shape the destiny of Palestine and of the Jewish people for years to come, and which, as you said, will also prove of vital importance for the British Empire. May I therefore tell you, with perfect frankness, how I see the present situation? I have no desire to indulge in mere retrospect, still less in useless recrimination: but possibly what I have to say may be of value for you in times that lie ahead, when you will have to decide the fate of Palestine.

In the last twenty years, and especially in the last two years since my re-election to the Presidency of the Jewish Agency, I have had ample opportunities to observe the attitude of the Palestine Administration towards us and the Mandate; and the conviction has been forced upon me by my experience that the Mandate for Palestine has hardly had a real chance, and that now as in the past it is being, consciously or unconsciously, undermined by those called upon to carry it out. It was the *leit-motif* of my evidence before the Royal Commission that things should never have been allowed to come to this pass; and that the present situation has not been brought about by any inherent defect in the Mandate (though this may have its weaknesses like all works of man). I understand from you that the Royal Commission, for whose impartiality and judgment I have the highest respect, have condemned the Mandate. I am prepared to accept their judgment of the situation, but with one fundamental reservation; it is not the Mandate that should be condemned, but the people who administered it. Had it been the aim of the Palestine Administration to prove that the Mandate was unworkable, it could be congratulated on the choice of the methods adopted in the past two years. This is the crux of the matter. A situation had been artificially created in which nothing was left for the Royal Commission but to bring in this verdict against the Mandate; and thus their work was vitiated from the very outset. What could they think, coming fresh to Palestine and staying there for a few months, when they found that the country had been in a state of armed revolt for the better part of a year, successfully defying the armed forces of the British Empire? They were inevitably driven to the conclusion that there must be some deep underlying cause, a movement of exceptional magnitude and with wide ramifications outside of Palestine; and naturally the Administration had every interest in persuading them of the existence of such a cause, and in painting the situation in the darkest colours in order to justify its own record. What was that record? Complete inaction; paralysis of Government; surrender to crime; demoralization of the Civil Service—men willing and able to do their duty prevented by the faint-heartedness of their superiors; denial of justice; failure to protect the lives and property of law-abiding citizens, Jewish and Arab; in short, a condition of things unthinkable in any other part of the British Empire. These things fall, to a great extent, into your own term of office. In vain did we appeal to you to see authority re-established in Palestine. Almost a year ago, when Wauchope gratuitously brought the Arab kings upon the Palestinian stage, I pointed out to you the very grave dangers of this measure. For a moment the Government bethought itself, stopped the intervention of Nuri Pasha (a 'force' that faded out overnight), decided to try the strong hand in Palestine and sent out General Dill at the head of an army. But the High Commissioner soon succeeded in frustrating this attempt and turned it into an expensive farce—the military authorities will best be able to tell you this part of the story. Through no fault of theirs, order was not re-established in Palestine, and Wauchope's régime continues, inflicting untold damage on us, and earning no credit for the British Government. The Mufti is still at large, and pandered to by the Administration; under its very eyes he now travels about, organizing armed resistance to the forthcoming recommendations of the Royal Commission, and enlisting the help of destructive elements in the neighbouring countries. The Arab kings are being mobilized once more to impress His Majesty's Government, and especially the Foreign Office, with the bogy of Pan-Islam and the strength of the Arab national movement—a movement which is crude in its nature, which tries to work up the hatred of the British and the Jews, looks to Mussolini and Hitler as its heroes, and is supported by Italian money—you know it all, and still you allow these things to go on.

I take it that you have read the report for 1936 submitted by the Palestine Administration to the League of Nations Council. That report contains a deliberate distortion of the truth. Having failed to discharge the most elementary duty of any civilized government, namely to maintain order and protect the lives and property of law-abiding citizens, the Administration now tries to suggest that we have been guilty of provoking the riots. I enclose a copy of my letter to the High Commissioner, which he has refrained from answering in writing. The blaming of the victims is a procedure with which I am painfully acquainted after pogroms in Czarist Russia, but I never expected to see it adopted by a British Administration. Can you possibly uphold such a report in Geneva?

We shall shortly be asked to acquiesce in a revolutionary plan which would amount to the abolition of the Mandate and a partition of Palestine. Not having seen the report, I am naturally unable to discuss its proposals. But I see that the High Commissioner has been specially summoned from Palestine, I presume to advise the Government on the statement of policy which you are about to issue; and is returning to Palestine to maintain 'order' there if a revolt breaks out. Frankly, considering his record during the past fifteen months, I view the immediate and the more distant future with the gravest apprehension. I understand that, if the scheme of partition is adopted, a period of transition is to intervene before a Jewish State is established. This will be a most delicate and dangerous time. Even the best proposals made by the Royal Commission are liable to suffer the fate of the Mandate, and for the same reasons; and the result will be that after the Mandate has been discredited and scrapped, there will be nothing to take its place.

Q

I am speaking to you frankly, and without any of the circum-locutions usually employed in discussing such matters. The time is too serious and too much is at stake. I see no future for any constructive policy unless there is a complete change of heart and a clean sweep in Palestine. Successive Colonial Secretaries have left us to struggle all these years with an Administration which has been inefficient, unimaginative, obstructive and unfriendly. There have been and undoubtedly are good men among them, but they have not been able to prevail against the dead weight of others of a very different stamp. In spite of these, we have succeeded, and the greater our success, the bitterer they became. The process has reached its culminating point in the last two years, and it was my fate to bear the brunt of it. This is the more tragic for me when I see you at the head of the Colonial Office, you who have helped us whole-heartedly in earlier days; and I trust that even now you have not become 'impartial' in the sense of the Palestine Administra-tion, who refuse to distinguish between right and wrong, and try, in fact, to obliterate the difference between them.

Just before the riots broke out I had an intimate talk with the High Commissioner. He asked me whether I thought troubles were to be expected. I replied that in Czarist Russia I knew that if the Government did not wish for troubles, they never happened. The Palestine Administration did not wish for riots, but has done very little to prevent them; has let things go from bad to worse; has allowed the situation to get out of hand, and the country to sink into anarchy. Perhaps at the beginning of the troubles some officers were not even altogether sorry to see such a reply given to the debates in Parliament which had destroyed their scheme for a Legislative Council, and which they wrongly assumed to have been brought on by us. In the last resort, some of these men, with no faith in the Jewish National Home, can hardly have regretted to see the policy of the Balfour Declaration and of the Mandate discredited and dishonoured.

What hope is there, then, for the future, after twenty years of such an Administration? This is at the root of my very grave anxiety. The account given of the disturbances in the Annual Report of the Palestine Administration to the League is only the last link in a long chain of obstruction and injustice.

You close your letter by urging me not to burn my boats, nor to go off the deep end. I have no boats to burn. You further ask me not to come up with a flourish of trumpets. Can you in the last twenty years point to a single occasion on which I have done so? I have borne most things in silence; I have defended the British Administration before my own people, from public platforms, at Congresses, in all parts of the world, often against my own better knowledge, and almost invariably to my own detriment. Why did I do so? Because to me close co-operation with Great Britain was the cornerstone of our policy in Palestine. But this co-operation remained unilateral—it was unrequited love.

When you speak of 'consultation' you suggest that, were you to consult me on policy with regard to Palestine, you would hardly know where you could stop! I claim that what Palestine is now is due primarily to the work of my people; I have had my share in that work, and I represent them. This was the foundation of my claim, and I leave it to history to decide whether the claim was excessive.

You ask me for some measure of trust; to no one would I be happier to give it, because I remember—and I shall never forget—your old friendship, and the work we did in common in the difficult days now far removed. But however I may feel towards you personally, how can I trust the system with which you have now unfortunately become identified? You want me slowly to 'feel my way.' But I am not an isolated individual, and I ought to be able from the very outset to give a lead to my people. I cannot do so if I receive the Report, which you describe as voluminous and complex, two days before publication, about the same time as it will, I imagine, be given to the Lobby correspondents of newspapers. On my part there will be no flourish of trumpets—that is anyhow not my style—but something which may, in the result, prove very much worse: enforced silence.

The letter to the High Commissioner, above referred to, was addressed to him in London, where he had arrived for consultation with the Colonial Office. The reader will find it self-explanatory; but he should also bear in mind the total background. During those years of Arab violence the Jews of Palestine adopted and resolutely followed, in the face of the utmost provocation, the policy of *Havlagah*, or of self-restraint, which I think may be properly described as one of the great moral political acts of modern times. The *Haganah* remained throughout a defence organization, and the *Yishuv* as a whole did not believe in, did not practise or encourage, counter-attack or retaliation. Yet it is hard to describe the heart-sickness and bitterness of the Jews as they watched the larger Hitler terror engulf their kin in Europe, while the gates of Palestine were being shut as a concession to the Arabs and the Palestine Administration failed to proceed with the necessary vigour against the Arab terrorists.

London
30th June 1937

DEAR SIR ARTHUR:

I have just read the remarkable and peculiar account of last year's disturbances given in the Government's Report to the Mandates Commission. The story of the events at the outset of the disturbances has been made to convey the impression that these were to a large extent provoked by a series of Jewish attacks on Arabs. Further, in the record of the casualties suffered between the 19th and the 22nd April, no indication is given of the fact that not one of the Arabs killed was killed by a Jew. The impression thus given of the outbreak of the disturbances is at variance with your own communiqué of the 19th April, and any unbiased person with a knowledge of the facts must see in this account a calculated distortion of the truth.

In the entire Report, there is not a single reference to, still less a word of praise for, the restraint which the Jews have shown during the long months of violence directed against them by the Arabs. You yourself have, on various occasions, both in public and in private, expressed your admiration for the behaviour of our people. That there should not be a single reference to it in the Report is, I think, an indictment of the authorities themselves.

I am both astonished and pained that such an account should appear in an official record which must be assumed to have received your approval.

The state of affairs in the summer of 1937 may be gathered
from the two foregoing letters. In the months that followed
things went from bad to worse. In Palestine there was a spurt
of military activity which promised for a time to put an end
to the riots—Orde Wingate was then in the country; but the
improvement was more than offset by the apparent indifference
which the British Government manifested towards its own
partition plan. Here I was, exerting myself to break down the
resistance to the plan in our ranks, while the Government
seemed to grow increasingly cool towards it. On the last day
of that year I wrote to Sir John Shuckburgh, Permanent
Under-Secretary for the Colonies:

. . . Nearly six months have elapsed since the Report of the
Royal Commission and the White Paper were published, yet
nothing has been done to advance matters. This inactivity of
the Government in the political sphere is largely neutralizing
the good effect produced by the active measures adopted by it
in regard to security. There is utter confusion as to the political
intentions of His Majesty's Government, which is doing infinite
harm to the economic life of the country, to the authority of
the Government and to the prospects of an eventual settlement. . . . The atmosphere of doubt and suspense thus engen-
dered provides an ideal ground for every schemer and
intriguer, self-appointed or foreign-paid, to try his hand at
advertising alternative 'solutions.' All these schemes have one
and the same object: the liquidation of the National Home
and the virtual handing over of the country to the clique of
so-called Arab leaders who organized the disturbances of last
year and from their hiding places are now running the terrorist
campaign. . . . The terms are always the same: liquidation of
the Mandate and Jewish acceptance of minority status, the
Jewish position to be protected by that invaluable instrument
of 'minority rights' of which we have had such instructive
experience in Eastern Europe. Let there be no mistake about
the action of the representative bodies of the Jewish people to
any of these schemes. Jews are not going to Palestine to
become in their ancient home 'Arabs of the Mosaic Faith' or
to exchange their German or Polish ghetto for an Arab one.
Whoever knows what Arab Government looks like, what

'minority status' signifies nowadays, and what a Jewish ghetto in an Arab state means—there are quite a number of precedents —will be able to form his own conclusions as to what would be in store for us if we accepted the position allotted to us in these 'solutions.' It is not for the purpose of subjecting the Jewish people, which still stands in the front rank of civilization, to the rule of a set of unscrupulous Levantine politicians that this supreme effort is being made in Palestine. All the labours and sacrifices here owe their inspiration to one thing alone: to the belief that this at least is going to mean freedom and the end of the ghetto. Could there be a more appalling fraud on the hopes of a martyred people than to reduce it to ghetto status in the very land where it was promised national freedom?

Those who advance these schemes know perfectly well that there is no prospect of their acceptance by the Jews. Their purpose is not to find a solution which would meet our ever more urgent need for a National Home but, on the contrary, to strangle our effort of national reconstruction. The same forces which last year used every device of violence and blackmail to destroy the Mandate are busy, now that they believe that object to have been essentially achieved, in undermining partition, which, they perceive, might still offer a chance of realizing the Jewish National Home even though in a much reduced area.

So, month after month, the technique of keeping a promise to the ear and breaking it to the heart was applied to us. The offer of partition was stultified, first by delay, second by the manner in which the British Government approached it practically. Another commission was appointed, the Woodhead Commission, to suggest actual plans. But the instructions given it—the terms of reference—were such as to foredoom any sort of plan. For what was bound to emerge was a Jewish territory so small that there would hardly be standing room for the Jews who wanted to come; development and growth would be out of the question. Plans would be offered only for the planned purpose of being rejected.

Meanwhile the ground was burning under our feet. We saw the Second World War advancing inexorably, and hope for our millions in Europe diminishing. And the frustration was all the more unbearable because we knew that in the coming struggle the Jewish National Home could play a very considerable rôle in that part of the world as the one reliable ally of the democracies. It was quite fantastic to note the ingenuity and inventiveness which England expended, to her own hurt, on the shelving of that ally. But was not this the essence of the appeasement panic? I have already mentioned the assiduous spreading of the report that the Jews were opposed to the idea of partition as such. To make assurance doubly sure, the partition plan was finally put forward in obviously impossible form. Then, on top of that, quite a discussion developed in England on the strategic unimportance of Palestine as compared with Cyprus. In the letter to Sir John Shuckburgh, above quoted, I said:

Allow me to say one word on the strategical question which is so much in the fore of the discussion at the present. It would be presumptuous for a mere layman like myself to express any opinion as to the relative strategical values of Haifa and Cyprus, but there are some crude facts which even a plain chemist can understand. The pipeline, the aerodromes and the Carmel cannot be removed to Cyprus, nor the railway to Egypt, or the connection with the Suez Canal and the corridor to Baghdad. More I would not presume to say on this point.

To Ormsby-Gore I wrote a little later, in April 1938:

We could form a force of something like 40,000 men now and with increased immigration into the future State area such a force would rapidly grow. I do not wish to overstate my case in any way, but I would like you and your colleagues to know it. The position is analogous to that of 1914–17, if anything much more serious for everybody concerned and for us in particular. This again is another very urgent reason for speedy action. I have had some conversation on this subject with General Georges of the French General Staff, and found him very understanding indeed.

The futility of these arguments, and of all the practical considerations behind them, is only too well known. The British

Government had simply made up its mind to crystallize the Jewish National Home, and if not for the stubborn resistance of the Jews, who refuse to be trifled with in this matter, they would have succeeded.

In Palestine the Arab terror continued, with ups and downs which reflected not so much the fortunes of war as the fluctuations in British determination. In the autumn of 1936 there was vigorous action against the Arab terrorists, with good results. Numbers of Jews were enrolled as *ghaffirim*, or supernumerary police, for the defence of the colonies. The country was comparatively quiet during the presence of the Peel Commission. In the summer of 1937 the unrest intensified. Between April 1936 and March 1937, ninety-three Jews were killed and over four hundred wounded. Damage to Jewish property amounted to nearly half a million pounds; but this does not take into account the heavy losses due to the diversion of men from productive work to defence, the disruption of communications and the economic deterioration due both to terrorism and the uncertainty of the political future.

In September the military again acted with energy, and again there was a lull in the terrorism; in October it again flared up. In the early months of 1938 the guerrillas in the hills were particularly active. In 1938, sixty-nine British were killed, ninety-two Jews and four hundred and eighty-six Arab civilians. Over one thousand rebels were killed in action. The disturbances did not die down until September 1939, when the war began.

During the entire period of the rioting the Jews of Palestine exhibited that moral discipline of *Havlagah*, or self-restraint, which, following the highest traditions of Zionism, won the admiration of liberal opinion all over the world. The consistency with which this policy was maintained was the more remarkable when we consider that violence paid political dividends to the Arabs, while Jewish *Havlagah* was expected to be its own reward. It did not even win official recognition. Sir Arthur Wauchope's report—the subject of my letter to him, on p. 484 —illustrates the point. The Jews followed their tradition of moral discipline, the Palestine administration followed its tradition of bracketing Jews and Arabs 'impartially' in the 'disturbances.' It looked very much like incitement of Jews to terrorism, and the human thing happened when a dissident Jewish minority broke ranks at last in the summer of 1938, taking its cue from the Arabs—and from the administration. But it was still a very small minority. The *Yishuv* as a whole, then as now, stood firm against Jewish terrorism.

The darkness of those years is relieved by the memory of the strange and brilliant figure mentioned a few pages back—Orde Wingate, who has sometimes been called 'the Lawrence of Judæa.' He won that title not only for his military exploits as the leader of the Jewish groups which were organized against the terrorist activities, but for his passionate sympathy—one might say his self-identification—with the highest ideals of Zionism.

Of his gifts as a soldier, especially as the organizer and leader of the famous Chindits in Burma, there are several brilliant descriptions in contemporaneous literature, and it is not for me to pass judgment on them. But I can testify that he was idolized by the men who fought under him, and that they were filled with admiration for his qualities of endurance, courage and originality. There are hundreds who recall how, having to cope with the Arab guerrillas who descended on the Haifa-Mosul pipeline from time to time, destroyed a section of it, and retreated as fast as they had come, Wingate created a special motor-cycle squad to patrol the whole length of the line, and by matching speed against speed, eliminated the threat. The Jews under his command were especially feared by the Arabs. Wingate used to tell me that when, at the head of a Jewish squad, he ambushed a group of raiders, he would hear a shout: 'Run! These are not British soldiers! They are Jews!'

I met Wingate and his beautiful young wife, Lorna, at Government House in Jerusalem. I was immediately struck by his powerful personality and by his spiritual outlook not only on problems in Palestine, but on those of the world at large. He came often to my house in Rehovoth, travelling alone in his little car, armed to the teeth. From the beginning he showed himself a fanatical Zionist, and he had come to his views not under any personal influence or propaganda, but by the effect of Zionist literature on his deep and lifelong study of the Bible. In this his superiors—Wingate had the rank of captain in the Palestine intelligence service—were entirely out of sympathy

Q*

with his views: he in turn chafed under the command of men he considered intellectually and morally below him.

His two great intellectual passions were military science and the Bible, and there was in him a fusion of the student and the man of action which reminded me of T. E. Lawrence. There were other reminders in his personality: his intenseness, his whimsicality and his originality. I thought of Lawrence more than once when Wingate sat opposite me, arguing fiercely, and boring me through with his eyes; and I did not learn until many months after we had met and become friends that he was in fact a distant blood relative of Lawrence's.

To complete his Zionist education Wingate used to repair for days at a stretch to some of the settlements—Ain Harod being his favourite—and there he would try to speak Hebrew with the settlers and familiarize himself with their outlook and their way of life, to which he was greatly drawn. He was often very impatient with me and with what he called my cunctatorial methods. He was as critical of the Government as of his superiors, and preached the doctrine that unless one forced it, the Government would never do anything for us; the Palestine Administration, in his opinion, consisted almost without exception of enemies of the Zionist movement.

He said, more than once: 'You must find your way to Downing Street, go up to the Prime Minister and tell him that everything is wrong, the Government is letting you down, is behaving treacherously. And having said that, don't wait for an answer, leave the room.'

To which I usually replied, 'I won't have to leave it, if I follow your advice. I shall be thrown out.' Much as I admired and loved Wingate, I did not think that his diplomatic abilities in any way matched his military performance or his personal integrity. Shortly before his death he wrote me from the Far East, and in this, his last letter to me, he admitted that my policy was the right one, the only one that could be pursued with any hope of success. He apologized for having chivvied me so often on my methods; the apology was not necessary— I knew in what spirit his reproaches had been made. My wife and I both loved and revered him.

Perhaps his own life taught him towards the end. He was a man who did not suffer fools gladly, was trenchant in his criticism of our betters, and was always in hot water with his superiors. General Wavell writes of him, after praising his brilliant work in Abyssinia: 'When it was all over he sent to my headquarters a memorandum that would almost have justified my placing him under arrest for insubordination.' When Wingate was on leave in London, during the war, he would get hold of all sorts of people and preach Zionism to them. Amongst others he hit on Lord Beaverbrook. In the course of the argument which developed, Beaverbrook tried to rebut Wingate saying, 'I think thus and thus,' and Wingate interrupted with: 'What you think doesn't matter a damn; what matters is what God thinks, and that you don't know.'

After the Abyssinian campaign Wingate, desperately sick with malaria, and almost constantly drugged with quinine, became so embroiled with his superior officers that he fell seriously ill, and was hospitalized in Cairo. On returning to London he was shoved into an obscure job training raw recruits in some small place near London, being adjudged too unbalanced to command men in a responsible capacity. Had this continued for a longer time, it would have meant his moral and physical collapse. He turned to me for advice. I was ignorant of military procedure, and though I was anxious to help him hardly knew where to begin. Then it occurred to me that I might put his case before Lord Horder, a leading London physician and a very enlightened and sympathetic person. To him I recounted briefly the facts of Wingate's career, and asked him to go before the Army Medical Council and testify, if he thought fit, to Wingate's reliability and sense of responsibility. He did this, and before long Wingate received an appointment —again under Wavell—to India, where he organized his famous Chindits for the Burma campaign behind the Japanese lines. His achievement in this enterprise has become one of the war's legends. He was killed in an aeroplane accident when he insisted on flying to an outpost in the jungle against the advice of the pilot. His body was not found until some three years later.

Wingate's death was an irreparable loss to the British Army, to the Jewish cause, and to my wife and myself personally. While he was commanding the Chindits in Burma, Churchill learned of his exploits and recalled him to London to attend the Allied Conference in Quebec. On his return to London he was promoted to the rank of major-general, and it was vouchsafed us to see him for a few days, happy to have found recognition at last, and modestly resplendent in his new uniform. He left soon after for his command in the Far East, and this was the last his friends saw of him.

He had one consuming desire which was not fulfilled: he wanted to lead a British army into Berlin. When, after long negotiation and discussion, the Jewish Brigade was agreed upon and actually formed, I applied for the services of Wingate, but this request was, for obvious reasons—as I think—refused. The idea of a Jewish fighting force was never popular with the pundits of the War Office; and to have had such a unit headed by an arch-Zionist like Wingate was just too much for the generals in Whitehall. The refusal was definite and complete.

CHAPTER XXXVIII

THE WHITE PAPER

*Partition Torpedoed—The Tripartite Conference, February-March 1939
—The Days of Berchtesgaden and Godesberg—The Coffin Boats on the
Mediterranean—The* Patria*—Lord Halifax's Astounding Proposal—How
the White Paper was Prepared—The Betrayal of Czechoslovakia—Jan
Masaryk's Tragic Visit—Negotiations in Egypt—Last Warning to
Chamberlain—His Infatuation with Appeasement—The White Paper
Debated in Parliament—The Jews Unanimously Reject the White Paper*

AT the time it issued the Peel Report, in 1937, the British
Government began to set up the Woodhead Commission, which
was to submit a partition plan. The Commission did not proceed to Palestine until April 1938; and in October of that year
it published a report stating that it had no practical partition
plan to offer. The following month the Government rejected
the idea of partition. It looked as though the Commission had
been appointed merely to pave the way for a predetermined
course of action for which no commission was necessary.

The same may be said of the Tripartite Conference—British,
Arabs, Jews—which the Government now proceeded (December 1938) to call. Just as the Government of that time could
and would have done what it did about partition without the
gesture of a new commission, so it could and would have done
what it did about nullifying the Balfour Declaration without
the gesture of the St. James's Conference of February-March
1939. The reader must bear the period in mind: in October
1938 the Sudetenland had been handed over to Hitler as a
result of the Munich Conference; in March 1939 Hitler annexed
the rest of Czechoslovakia; and Mr. Chamberlain still believed,
or pretended to believe, that by these concessions he was pur-
chasing 'peace in our time.' What chance had the Jewish
National Home with such a Government, and what likelihood was there that commissions and conferences would deflect
it from its appeasement course?

493

Nevertheless the Jews and Arabs were duly invited—Jews representing all sections of opinion, and Arabs representing Palestine and its neighbours, Egypt, Iraq and so on—and the Conference was opened with much solemnity in St. James's Palace on February 7, 1939. The dignity of the occasion was somewhat marred by the fact that Mr. Chamberlain's address of welcome had to be given twice, once to the Jews and once to the Arabs, since the latter would not sit with the former, and even used different entrances to the Palace so as to avoid embarrassing contacts.

The proceedings were usually conducted by the Colonial Secretary, Malcolm MacDonald, supported by a staff of high-ranking officials of the Foreign and Colonial offices; they were attended from time to time by the Foreign Secretary, Lord Halifax. Towards the end, for reasons which will appear, they lost any appearance of purpose or intelligibility which may originally have been imparted to them. I did not attend the closing session. But during the Conference I exerted myself—as indeed I have always done—to maintain contacts with the most influential figures in and about the Conference, and with leading personalities generally, among them the Prime Minister (Mr. Chamberlain), Lord Halifax, Mr. Malcolm MacDonald and Mr. Winston Churchill.

The atmosphere of utter futility which dominated the Conference was, of course, part of the general atmosphere of the time. Those were the days of the Berchtesgaden and Godesberg 'conferences.' The atmosphere was not peculiar to England; the French were as assiduous in their attendance on Hitler. I remember Léon Blum telling me at that time: 'There is a wild hunger for physical safety which paralyses the power of thought. People are ready to buy the illusion of security at any price, hoping against hope that something will happen to save their countries from invasion.' My conversations with Halifax, Chamberlain and Malcolm MacDonald were vitiated from the outset by this frightful mood of frustration and panic. They were determined to placate the Arabs just as they were placating Hitler. That, of course, did not prevent me from carrying on until the last moment—and after.

My personal relations with Lord Halifax were of the best. I had made his acquaintance through an old friend, the late

Victor Cazalet, one of the few members of the House of Commons who never failed to speak up in defence of Zionism, and who did whatever he could to keep our case before the public eye. He was, in fact, chairman of the Parliamentary Pro-Palestine Committee. Through Cazalet's willing offices—he was an intimate friend of Halifax—I was able to meet the latter more frequently and a little more informally than might otherwise have been the case. The character of some of these private meetings may be indicated by the two following instances.

Some time before the issue of the White Paper, when immigration restrictions were already in force, the desperation of the Jews fleeing from the coming destruction began to rise to its climax; the efforts to reach the safety of Palestine led to the tragic phenomenon of the coffin boats, as they were called, crowded and unseaworthy vessels which roamed the Mediterranean in the hope of being able ultimately to discharge their unhappy cargoes of men, women and children in Palestine. Some sank in the Mediterranean or the Black Sea. Some reached Palestine either to be turned back or to have their passengers taken off and interned or transhipped to Mauritius.

One of the worst cases—that of the *Patria*—occurred during the war under the Colonial Secretaryship of Lord Lloyd; and on hearing of it I went to him, in despair rather than in hope, to try and persuade him to give permission for the passengers to be landed. I was met with the usual arguments about the law being the law, to which I retorted: 'A law is something which must have a moral basis, so that there is an inner compelling force for every citizen to obey. But if the majority of citizens is convinced that the law is merely an infliction, it can only be enforced at the point of the bayonet against the consent of the community.'

My arguments were wasted. Lord Lloyd could not agree with me. He said so, and added: 'I must tell you that I've blocked all the approaches for you. I know you will go to Churchill and try to get him to overrule me. I have therefore warned the Prime Minister that I will not consent. So please don't try to get at him.'

But it seemed that Lord Lloyd had not blocked the approach to the Foreign Office, so I went to see Lord Halifax. Here again I had to rehearse all the arguments about law and ethics and the immorality of the White Paper which was not really a law but a ukase such as might have been issued by a Russian Czar or any other autocrat engaged in the systematic persecution of the Jews. I saw that I was making no dent in Lord Halifax's determination. Finally I said: 'Look here, Lord Halifax, I thought that the difference between the Jews and the Christians is that we Jews are supposed to adhere to the letter of the law, whereas you Christians are supposed to temper the letter of the law with a sense of mercy.' The words stung him. He got up and said: 'All right, Dr. Weizmann, you'd better not continue this conversation. You will hear from me.' To my immense relief and joy I heard the next day that he had sent a telegram to Palestine to permit the passengers to land. I met Lord Lloyd soon after, and he said, quite unresentfully: 'Well you got past me that time. I thought I'd blocked all the holes, but it seems I'd forgotten Halifax.' I was convinced in my heart of hearts that Lloyd was not displeased to have the incident end thus.

An interview of quite another kind with Lord Halifax sticks in my mind. During the Saint James's Conference he called me in and addressed me thus: 'There are moments in the lives of men and of groups when expediency takes precedence over principle. I think that such a moment has arrived now in the life of your movement. Of course I don't know whether you can or will accept my advice, but it would be desirable that you make an announcement of the great principles of the Zionist movement to which you adhere, and at the same time renounce your rights under the Mandate and under the various instruments deriving from it.'

At first I did not quite appreciate the full bearing of this proposal. I paused for a few moments, then asked: 'Tell me, Lord Halifax, what good would it do you if I were to agree, which in fact I won't and can't? Suppose, for argument's sake, I were to make such an announcement; there could be only one effect, that I would disappear from the ranks of the Zionist leaders, to be replaced by men much more extreme and intransigent than I am, men who have not been brought up in the tradition I have been privileged to live in for the last forty years. You would achieve nothing except to provoke the Zionist movement to yield to its most extremist elements.'

I added: 'So much for the movement. And what of myself?' I briefly recounted to him the history of Sabbathai Zevi, who, in the seventeenth century, had been a successful leader of the 'Return,' who had gathered round him a mass following from all over the world, and who stood at the gates of Constantinople, constituting some sort of menace to the Sultan. The Sultan felt helpless in the presence of this mystical and dangerous assembly, and sent for his Jewish physician, who advised him as follows: 'Call in this Jewish leader, and tell him you are prepared to give him Palestine on condition that he embrace Islam.' Sabbathai Zevi accepted the proposal and became a Moslem, with the result that his adherents, who amounted to hundreds of thousands, melted away; and of his movement nothing remains except a small group of Turkish Jews who call themselves Dumbies, the descendants of the few apostates who followed Sabbathai Zevi into Mohammedanism. I wound up: 'You do not expect me, Lord Halifax, to end my career in the same disgraceful manner.' With that we parted.

Lord Halifax was strangely ignorant of what was happening to the Jews of Germany. During the St. James's Conference he came up to me and said: 'I have just received a letter from a friend in Germany, who describes some terrible things perpetrated by the Nazis in a concentration camp the name of which is not familiar to me,' and when he began to grope for the name I realized it was Dachau he was talking about. He said the stories were entirely unbelievable, and if the letter had not been written by a man in whom he had full confidence he would not attach the slightest credence to it. For five or six years now the world had known of the infamous Dachau concentration camp, in which thousands of people had been tortured and maimed and done to death, and the British Foreign Secretary had never heard of the place, and would not believe that such things could go on; only the fortuitous circumstance that he had received the letter from a man in whom he had 'full confidence' had arrested his attention. It is difficult to say whether this profound ignorance was typical of the British ruling class, but judging from its behaviour at that time it either did not know, or else it did not wish to know because the knowledge was inconvenient, disturbing, and dangerous. Those were Germany's 'internal affairs,' and they should not be permitted to interfere with friendly relations between two Great Powers.

It was astounding to meet this bland surprise and indifference in high places. When the great burning of the synagogues took place, after the assassination of vom Rath in Paris, I said to Anthony Eden: 'The fire from the synagogues may easily spread from there to Westminster Abbey and the other great English cathedrals. If a government is allowed to destroy a whole community which has committed no crime save that of being a minority and having its own religion, if such a government, in the heart of Europe, is not even rebuked, it means the beginning of anarchy and the destruction of the basis of civilization. The powers which stand looking on without taking any measures to prevent the crime will one day be visited by severe punishment.'

I need scarcely add that my words fell on deaf ears. British society was falling over itself to attend the elegant parties given by Ribbentrop in the German Embassy; it was a sign of social distinction to receive an invitation, and the Jewish blood which stained the hands of the hosts was ignored though it cried out to heaven. I believe that the Duke of Devonshire never accepted any of von Ribbentrop's invitations.

It should be remembered, however, that things were not much better in France, where the walls were being chalked with the slogan *Mieux vaut Hitler que Blum*, though there the relationship with Germany was less amiable than in the case of England. Well, they got their Hitler, and no doubt the taste of it will remain with the French people for a long time. But whether those who used the slogan so widely have been cured of their affection for Hitlerism is much to be doubted.

In those days before the war, our protests, when voiced, were regarded as provocations; our very refusal to subscribe to our own death sentence became a public nuisance, and was taken in bad part. Alternating threats and appeals were addressed to us to acquiesce in the surrender of Palestine. On one occasion Lord Halifax said to me: 'You know that we British have always been the friends of the Jews—and the Jews have very few friends in the world today.' I need hardly say that this sort of argument had on us the opposite effect of what was intended.

That the tide was running heavily against us was obvious

from the beginning of the Conference, but exactly what the Government would do was not so clear at first. In the early days of the Conference we gave a party at our house for all the members as well as the representatives of the Jewish organizations. Lord Halifax, Malcolm MacDonald and all the high officials accepted. Later the atmosphere was not so cordial. The debates and conversations meandered along, and the Government was reluctant to formulate a programme. It limited itself to generalities and bided its time. But the Government had made up its mind. It was only waiting for the most favourable moment for the announcement of its plan.

One day, when the Conference was fairly advanced, we received an invitation to a lunch to be given by His Majesty's Government, and we of course accepted. The lunch was to take place on a Monday. On the Saturday preceding this Monday I received a letter from the Colonial Office, addressed to me obviously by a clerical error—it was apparently meant only for members of the Arab delegation. There, in clear terms, was the outline of what was afterwards to be the White Paper, submitted for Arab approval: an Arab State of Palestine in five years; a limited Jewish immigration during these five years, and none thereafter without Arab consent! I could scarcely believe my eyes. We had, indeed, begun to feel that the discussions had become meaningless for us; and after what had happened to Austria and Czechoslovakia nothing should have surprised us. But to see the actual terms, in black and white, already prepared and communicated to the Arabs while 'negotiations' were proceeding, was utterly baffling.

I happened to remember, when I had finished perusing the extraordinary document, that most of my Zionist friends were at a party being given by Harry Sacher in his home, which was only a few doors from mine. I went over, and we managed to get Lord Reading and Malcolm MacDonald to join us. A heated and extremely unpleasant discussion ensued. We told MacDonald freely what we thought of the document and asked him to cancel our invitations to the luncheon: we would not break bread with a Government which could betray us in this manner. MacDonald was very crestfallen and stammered some ineffective excuses, falling back always on the argument that the document did not represent the final view of His Majesty's Government, that it was only a basis for discussion, that everything could still be changed, that we should not take it so tragically—the usual twaddle. The meeting lasted a long time; its only value, I suppose, was that our delegation was forewarned and the British Government clearly informed of the mood and temper of the Jews. If it was waiting for us to facilitate its publication of the document it was waiting in vain.

After the outbreak of the war I was to learn how elaborately and how far in advance the Government had been preparing the White Paper, and how meaningless the St. James's Conference had been. I was in Switzerland on a special mission, and called on the British Minister at Berne, who received me very cordially with the words, 'Oh, you're the man I've been waiting to see for quite a time, to get the other side of the story.' I asked him to explain and he went on: 'I was in on the White Paper. So were most of the Ambassadors and Ministers. Their opinion of it was asked in advance. Well, you know that most Ambassadors and Ministers take on the colour of the countries to which they are assigned, and the views we presented were all one sided. That is why I would like to hear your side of the story.' My reply was obvious: 'It is too late—and too early—for you to listen to the other side. Had you listened a year ago, the verdict might possibly have been different. Now we are in the midst of the war, and we are trying for the time being to forget the White Paper. Perhaps when the war is over you may still be inclined to listen to the other side.'

The disclosure to us of the Government document which was to become the White Paper coincided roughly with Hitler's unopposed and unprotested invasion of Czechoslovakia and the occupation of Prague. I remember that day well, because Jan Masaryk came to dinner with us. Between Masaryk and us there was, until the end, a deep friendship, both on personal and general grounds. There has always been a great affinity between the Masaryks and Zionism—Jan's father, the founder and first President of the Czechoslovak Republic, had been a strong supporter of the Balfour Declaration—and now, in the days of the White Paper, the representatives of the Czechoslovak Republic were beginning to be treated by the Great Powers as if they were Jews.

Neither the Jews nor the Czechs will forget the words of Chamberlain on the occasion of Hitler's occupation of the Czech capital. Why should England risk war for the sake of 'a far-away country of which we know very little and whose language we don't understand?' Words which were swallowed down by a docile Parliament many members of which must have known very well that the Czech Republic was a great bastion of liberty and democracy, and that its spirit and its institutions had all the meaning in the world for the Western Powers. It was, apart from everything else, a colossal insult to a great people. And I remember reflecting that if this was the way the Czechs were spoken of, what could we Jews expect from a Government of that kind?

When Jan arrived at our house that evening he was almost unrecognizable. The gaiety and high spirits which we always associated with him were gone. His face was the colour of parchment, and he looked like an aged and broken man. My wife, my children and I felt deeply for him—perhaps more than anyone else in London—and without saying too much we tried to make him comfortable. For a while he was silent, then he turned to us and, pointing to the little dog he had brought with him, said: 'That's all I have left, and believe me, I am ashamed to look him in the eyes.' Once he had broken the silence he went on talking, and what he told us was terrible to listen to. He had had a conversation that morning with the Prime Minister, and had taxed him with the deliberate betrayal of Czechoslovakia. 'Mr. Chamberlain sat absolutely unmoved. When I had finished he said: "Mr. Masaryk, you happen to believe in Dr. Beneš, I happen to trust Herr Hitler."' There was nothing left for Masaryk but to get up and leave the room.

A great democratic country, a magnificent army and a superb munition plant had been delivered to the future conqueror of Europe, and a people which had fought valiantly for its freedom was betrayed by the democracies. It was cold comfort to us to reflect that the misfortunes which had befallen Czechoslovakia were in a way more poignant than those we faced—at least for the moment. We could not tell what the future held in store for us; we only knew that we had little to expect in the way of sympathy or action from the Western democracies.

However dark the outlook, however immovable the forces arrayed against us, one had to carry on. We explored the possibility of some sort of understanding with the Arabs. One or two meetings—more or less unofficial—were arranged between us and some members of the Arab Delegation. They served no immediate purpose, but they did help to bring about a kind of relationship. Mr. Aly Maher, the Egyptian delegate, was personally friendly. Some of the Iraqi people were inclined to discuss matters with us, and not merely to stare at us as the invaders and prospective destroyers of the Middle East. The most intransigent among the non-Palestinian Arabs was the Iraqi Premier, Nuri Said Pasha. His attitude was stonily negative, but the probable explanation is illuminating. Iraq is immensely interested in finding an outlet to the Mediterranean; it would therefore look with favour on a greater Syria consisting of Iraq, Syria, Transjordan and Palestine. Within the framework of such a union Iraq would probably concede the Jewish National Home, with certain limited possibilities of expansion and immigration. Opposition, therefore, to a Jewish National Home had much more to do with particular Iraqi ambitions than with the rights and wrongs of the Jews and Arabs; but under the circumstances Nuri Said Pasha was adamant.

His colleagues, however, were not so firm in their opposition. Neither did I think the Saudi Arabia delegates entirely inaccessible to reason on our part. It seemed to me that however discouraging the prospect was, it ought to be pursued for whatever it was worth. We left London for Palestine on March 25, and stopped in Egypt on the way. There Aly Maher, who had arrived before me, arranged a meeting between me and a number of leading Egyptians, among them Mahommed Mahmoud, the Premier. We talked of co-operation between Egypt and the Jews of Palestine, in the industrial and cultural field. The Egyptians were acquainted with and impressed by our progress, and suggested that perhaps in the future they might serve to bridge the gulf between us and the Arabs of Palestine. They assumed that the White Paper (it was of course not yet in existence as such) would be adopted by England, but its effects might be mitigated, perhaps even nullified, if the Jews of Palestine showed themselves ready to co-operate with Egypt.

There was a ray of encouragement in these talks, especially after the dismal atmosphere of the St. James's Conference. I felt again, as I have so often before and since, that if the British Government had really applied itself with energy and good will to the establishment of good relations between the Jews and the Arabs, much could have been accomplished. But whenever we discussed the problem with the British they found its difficulties insuperable. This was not our impression at all. Of course one had to discount, in these unofficial conversations, both the usual Oriental politeness and the fact that private utterances are somewhat less cautious than official ones.

On my brief visit to Palestine in April 1939, I was able to confirm at first hand what I already knew from reports—that the Jews would never accept the death-sentence contained in the Government proposals. I wrote to many friends in England —Leopold Amery, Archibald Sinclair, Lord Lothian (newly appointed Ambassador to the United States), Sir Warren Fisher, Lord Halifax, among them—to apprise them of this fact. I cabled the Prime Minister:

> Feel it my solemn duty to warn H.M.G. before irrevocable step publication their proposals is taken that this will defeat their object pacification country surrender to demands terrorists will not produce peace but compel Government use force against Jews intensify hatred between Jews and Arabs hand over peaceful Arab population to terrorists and drive Jews who have nothing to lose anywhere to counsels of despair in Palestine. . . . Beg you not underestimate gravity this warning.

It had been my original intention to stay in Palestine for several months—perhaps until the forthcoming Congress which was to be held in Geneva that August. I did not believe that anything more could be done in London at the moment. I was tired out by the physical and nervous strain of the past few weeks, and I felt that it would be a sort of rest to resume my work in Palestine. But my friends insisted that I return to London and make a last-minute effort to convince the Prime Minister in person of the frightful harm which the publication of the White Paper would do to us and to the prestige of England. I was convinced that it was useless, and I told my colleagues so. But still they insisted that the effort be sustained until the last moment.

It was not easy for me to leave my wife in Palestine that spring of 1939. She fortunately did have, for company, Lorna Wingate, staying with us at the house. There was also, as visitor, a young boy of twenty-two by the name of Michael Clark, a charming youngster who was a schoolmate and great friend of my younger son, Michael. Michael Clark had come to Palestine by motor-cycle, making his way alone across Europe and Turkey, over the Balkan and the Taurus mountains. With these young people staying at the house in Rehovoth I should have felt more or less easy in mind; but I could not get rid of a feeling of depression when I took my leave. As it turned out, my forebodings were justified. Young Michael had the habit, in spite of the unrest in the country, of travelling about alone on his motor-cycle. My wife pleaded with him repeatedly not to expose himself in this reckless fashion, but he gave no heed to her expostulations. Then one day the poor boy was shot from ambush by an Arab near the railway line where it passes through Rehovoth. He was buried in the military cemetery at Ramleh. I was already in England when this happened, and my wife was so shaken by the dreadful incident that I cabled her to come to London by plane. Meanwhile I had the melancholy task of breaking the news to his mother. I met my wife in Paris, and found her shaken and depressed. We had both been deeply attached to Michael.

In spite of the hopelessness of the prospect, I again made arrangements to see Mr. Chamberlain, and again I travelled the *via dolorosa* to Downing Street. I pleaded once more with the Prime Minister to stay his hand and not to publish the White Paper. I said: 'That will happen to us which has happened to Austria and Czechoslovakia. It will overwhelm a people which is not a state unit, but which nevertheless is playing a great rôle in the world, and will continue to play one.' The Prime Minister sat before me like a marble statue; his expressionless eyes were fixed on me, but he said never a word. He had received me, I suppose, because he could not possibly refuse to see someone who, at my age, had made the exhausting flight from Palestine to London just to have a few minutes with him. But I got no response. He was bent on appeasement of the Arabs and nothing could change his course. What he gained by it is now a matter of history: the

Raschid Ali revolt in Iraq, the Mufti's services to Hitler, the famous 'neutrality' of Egypt, the ill-concealed hostility of practically every Arab country.

Much has been written of Mr. Chamberlain's infatuation with his idea of appeasement, and of his imperviousness to anything which might modify it. I have only one more illustrative incident to add. Some time before the St. James's Conference I happened to receive through secret channels an extraordinary German document which I was urgently requested to bring to the attention of the Prime Minister. It had been prepared and forwarded, at the risk of his life, by Herr Gördeler, the mayor of Leipzig, who shortly before the end of the war was implicated in the unsuccessful plot to assassinate Hitler, and executed. The document was a detailed exposé of conditions in Germany, and wound up with an appeal to Mr. Chamberlain not to be bluffed into further concessions when he went to meet Hitler in Godesberg or Munich.

I showed the document to a friend of mine in the Cabinet, and asked him to get Mr. Chamberlain to read it. He failed. I then went to see Sir Warren Fisher, one of the heads of the Civil Service, a close friend of Mr. Chamberlain's, with a room adjacent to his in Downing Street. I showed him the document, and explained that undoubtedly Herr Gördeler had risked his life several times over to accumulate the information it contained. Sir Warren Fisher opened his desk and showed me an exact copy of the document. 'I've had this,' he said, 'for the last ten days, and I've tried and tried again to get Mr. Chamberlain to look at it. It's no use.'

The St. James's Conference came to its undignified end, the Government proceeded with its preparation of the White Paper, and the time approached for the debate in the House of Commons. We knew that the vote would go against us, such was the temper of the House, which had behind it the record of Vienna and Prague. Our appeals to public opinion were in vain. Shortly after my return from my brief visit to Palestine, I met Winston Churchill, and he told me he would take part in the debate, speaking of course against the proposed White Paper. He suggested that I have lunch with him on the day of the debate. I reported the appointment to my colleagues. They were full of ideas of what Churchill ought to say, and each one told me, 'Don't forget this thought,' and 'Don't forget that thought.' I listened respectfully, but was quite certain that a speaker of Mr. Churchill's calibre would have his speech completely mapped out, and that he would not wish to have anyone come along with suggestions an hour or so before it was delivered.

There were present at the lunch, besides Mr. Churchill and myself, Randolph Churchill and Lord Cherwell. I was not mistaken in my assumption. Mr. Churchill was thoroughly prepared. He produced a packet of small cards and read his speech out to us; then he asked me if I had any changes to suggest. I answered that the architecture of the speech was so perfect that there were only one or two small points I might want to alter—but they were so unimportant that I would not bother him with them. As everyone now knows, Mr. Churchill delivered against the White Paper one of the great speeches of his career. The whole debate, indeed, went against the Government. The most important figures in the House attacked the White Paper; and I remember particularly Mr. Herbert Morrison shaking a finger in the direction of Malcolm Mac-Donald, and reminding him of the days when he was a Socialist; declaring, further, that if a Socialist Government should come into power, it would not consider itself bound by the terms of the White Paper. This last statement, delivered with much emphasis, was loudly applauded by the Labour benches.

The Government answer, delivered by Mr. MacDonald, was a clever piece of sophistry which could carry conviction only to those who were ignorant of the details of the problem. As for those with whom the question of conviction was secondary in that time of panic, nothing that was said mattered. But it is worth recording that even in that atmosphere the Government victory was extremely narrow. There were two hundred and sixty-eight votes in favour, one hundred and seventy-nine against, with one hundred and ten abstaining. As a rule the Government obtained over four hundred votes for its measures. As I left the House with my friends I could not help overhearing the remarks of several Members, to the effect that the Jews had been given a very raw deal.

One consolation emerged for us in those days: the firmness and unanimity of the Jewish delegation. On it were represented

all the major Jewish communities of the world, and every variety
of opinion from the stalwart and extremist Zionism of Menachem Ussishkin to the cautious and conciliatory philanthropic
outlook of Lord Bearsted and Lord Reading. At a meeting in
the offices of the Zionist Organization the question was put to
a formal vote whether the White Paper could be considered as
forming a basis for discussion. The unanimous decision, without
a single abstention, was in the negative.

CHAPTER XXXIX

WAR

Mandates Commission Rejects White Paper—Twenty-first Zionist Congress—We Pledge Co-operation with England in War—Paradox of Our Position—Paris in the Second World War—Difference from 1914—The Young Men who Denounced Chamberlain now Enlist

AN atmosphere of unreality and irrelevance hung over the twenty-first Zionist Congress which sat in Geneva from August 16 to August 25, 1939. We met under the shadow of the White Paper, which threatened the destruction of the National Home, and under the shadow of a war which threatened the destruction of all human liberties, perhaps of humanity itself. The difference between the two threats was that the first was already in action, while the second only pended; so that most of our attention was given to the first, and we strove to assume, at least until the fateful August 22, when the treaty was signed between Germany and Russia, that the second might yet be averted, or might be delayed. But on that day, when Hitler was relieved of the nightmare of having to wage war on two fronts, even the most optimistic of us gave up hope. The Jewish calamity merged with, was engulfed by, the world calamity.

The Congress debates pursued their usual course. Every party had its say, every resolution was fought out in traditional fashion. The record was scrutinized and criticized, the administration attacked and defended. But in the lobbies of the Congress, and outside the walls of the Geneva Theatre where it met, knots of delegates discussed the latest bulletins, and then escaped from the realities by taking refuge within. We went through all the gestures, but felt that nothing said or done at such a moment could have meaning for a long time to come.

Of course we rejected the White Paper unanimously. We declared it illegal; or, rather, we drew attention to the fact that the Mandates Commission, after examining the White Paper, and after having listened to Malcolm MacDonald's defence of it, had declared it illegal, stating explicitly: 'The policy set out in the White Paper is not in accordance with the interpretation which, in agreement with the Mandatory Power and the Council, the Commission has placed upon the Palestine Mandate.' We took note of the fact that hardly a statesman of standing in the House of Commons had failed to declare the White Paper a breach of faith: and we felt that not we, in opposing the White Paper, were the law-breakers, but the British Government in declaring it to be the law. Now, with war upon us, the decision of the Mandates Commission would not for a long time—if ever—come before the Council of the League. Our protest against the White Paper ran parallel with our solemn declaration that in the coming world struggle we stood committed more than any other people in the world to the defence of democracy and therefore to co-operation with England—author of the White Paper. Such was the paradox of our position, a paradox created not by us, but by England.

After August 22 the Congress hastened its pace, the discussions were curtailed, the resolutions adopted with greater speed. The Executive was re-elected, and on the evening of the twenty-fourth, a day before the closing, I took my leave of the Congress. It was a painful leave-taking in which personal and general forebodings were mingled, and hopes expressed that these forebodings might come to naught. I turned to the Polish delegates in particular, saying: 'God grant that your fate be not that of the Jews in the neighbouring land'—and all of us felt that this indeed was the only prayer we could offer up for them. Most of our Polish friends we never saw again. They perished, with over three million other Polish Jews, in the concentration camps and the gas chambers or in the last desperate uprising of the Warsaw ghetto.

We drove that night towards the Swiss frontier, my wife, Mrs. Blanche Dugdale and I, in one car, another car with our baggage following. Very vividly my wife and I recalled how, twenty-five years before, almost to the day, we had been making our way back to England from Switzerland on the outbreak of the First World War. But on that first occasion the war was already several weeks old, and it had come with incredible suddenness: now it was just looming over the horizon, and had been approaching for years. We found the frontier closed; to our expostulations that war had not yet been declared, that we were British citizens going home, that if we had taken the train instead of travelling by car we would certainly have got through, the gendarme kept repeating: '*On ne passe plus.*' The illogicality and confusion of war was already upon us. After endless repetition of the arguments on our side, and of the formula on the other side, the gendarme sent for his superior officer; we went through the whole rigmarole again, and were finally permitted to pass into the neutral zone dividing the province of Savoie from Switzerland.

We spent the night in the charming little summer resort of Divonne-les-Bains, which was filled with excited French and British holidaymakers all intent on getting out as fast as possible. Early in the morning we came to the frontier of the neutral zone—and once more the ritual began. There was no passing —until the officer in charge, seeing that we had an extra car for our baggage, asked us if we would not take his son along to Paris, where he had to report for mobilization. Of course we were happy to oblige. How other people got through, I do not know.

We travelled all day long, avoiding the central artery which was blocked by tens of thousands of vehicles. We reached Paris in the evening, and were joined at the hotel by our two sons, who had been in the south of France, and whom we had telegraphed to before leaving Geneva. It is strange to recall that in those closing days of August 1939, there were still people in high places who believed that war might yet be averted. M. Reynaud, whom I saw the morning after my arrival, and M. Palevski, his *chef de cabinet*, a man of great intelligence, did not think the political situation entirely hopeless. I did not share that view; but I decided nevertheless to risk another couple of days in Paris to see my friends and acquaintances, and to obtain some sort of picture of the public state of mind.

The mood was altogether unlike that which I had found in the war days twenty-five years before. Then, although the Germans had advanced deep into French territory, and were already at Amiens, Paris had been in an exalted and confident mood. There was in the air a religious fervour and an unshakable belief in ultimate victory, however distant it might be. The young men were gone from the city, which looked beautiful and sad; many women were already in mourning; but Paris was proud and confident. Now, although mobilization was in progress, one sensed neither enthusiasm nor depression: there was only a spiritless facing up to an unpleasant fact. There were complaints, of course: two such wars in one lifetime was too much. '*Il faut en finir*' was the cry. Other remarks were heard, *sotto voce*: 'The war isn't necessary. . . . Means must be found of coming to terms with the enemy. . . . Chamberlain's method is the right one. . . . One has to persevere in it. . . . There are people enough in the country who know and understand the régime in Germany, and who can mediate for us. . . .' I must confess that though I heard these voices all around me, and very often in the most unexpected places, I did not appreciate to the full the danger which they represented. It seemed to me that Reynaud and his Government were determined to fight to the end; and undoubtedly they were; but they too do not seem to have appreciated the extent to which the fascist evil had eaten into French life and led to the demoralization of the army.

I came back to England, and that happened in my home which happened in thousands of others—the young generation which had been so outraged by the policy of the Chamberlain Government forgot its grievances and came to the defence of the country as one man. It might have been amusing if it had not been so tragic. I remember how, soon after Munich, a group of young students, mostly from Oxford and Cambridge, friends of my sons, Benjy and Michael, were gathered in the house in Addison Crescent, and with what indignation they denounced Chamberlain, asserting that on no account would they enlist in the army if the disgraceful behaviour of the Government brought on a war by its encouragement of Hitler. All of them —young scientists, students of medicine and law—were agreed on that point. And all of them enlisted when the crisis came. Our younger son, Michael, enlisted in the R.A.F., and was as eager to get into action as he had been in his denunciation of the Government. Our elder son, Benjy, joined an artillery battery commanded by my friend Victor Cazalet, and stationed in the south of England.

CHAPTER XL

THE FIRST WAR YEARS

Gates of Palestine Closed—Our Offers of Help Brushed Aside—Friendly Talk with Churchill—First Wartime Visit to America—America's Touchy Neutrality—First Incredible Rumours of Planned Extermination of Jews—Talk with Roosevelt—Benjy and Michael in the Army—War Work Again—Rubber and High-octane Fuel—Vested Interests—I Propose a Jewish Palestinian Fighting Force to Churchill—A Story of Frustration— Second Wartime Visit to America—Mr. Sumner Welles—State Department and Palestine

THE paradox which was revealed with the opening of the war deepened with the passing of the months. In the fight against the Nazi monster no one could have had a deeper stake, no one could have been more fanatically eager to contribute to the common cause, than the Jews. At the same time England, then the leader of the anti-Nazi coalition, was keeping the gates of Palestine closed against the unhappy thousands of men, women and children who were making the last desperate effort to reach the safety of the National Home. It had been our hope that when at last there was no longer the ignominious need to appease Nazis and Arab leaders, there would be a relaxation of the anti-immigration rulings for Palestine. Nothing of the sort happened. The coffin boats continued to wander over the Mediterranean, unable to discharge their human cargoes. The pressure within Europe intensified. And yet we were determined to place all our manpower, all our facilities in Palestine, at the disposal of England and her Allies. What else was there for us to do?

Perhaps the bitterest touch of irony in the situation was the failure of certain British circles to understand how inevitably, White Paper or no White Paper, we had to work for the victory of Britain and her Allies. Either that, or else those sections of the Government would rather forgo the not inconsiderable assistance we could offer than let the Jews acquire 'credits' for what they had done during the war! Often I was offended by unintelligent remarks I heard in British circles which apparently could not appreciate that a Hitler victory would mean the obliteration of the Jewish people, and that this consideration completely overrode, until Hitler's defeat, all other considerations.

I took the offer of help which the Congress in Geneva had sent to the British Government literally and personally. About a month after the declaration of war I went on a special mission to Switzerland, to try and find out what substance there was in the rumours that the Germans had prepared new methods of chemical warfare. I did not obtain much information, but I did gather the impression that the rumours of tremendous preparations for the destruction of whole cities by gas attacks were without foundation. I so reported to the Government. Incidentally, this was the occasion which brought me in contact with the British Minister at Berne who wanted 'to hear the other side of the story.'

A period of mingled suspense and indecision ensued—the period which was to become known as 'the phony war.' A number of people actually believed that there was going to be no real struggle. I remember vividly how Hore-Belisha, our War Minister, then on an official visit to the French Government, made the curious statement, widely reported in the press: '*Pour moi la guerre est finie*' (as far as I'm concerned, the war is over). I thought it not only an irresponsibly light-hearted statement, but one calculated to bring aid and comfort to those sections of French public opinion which did not want to see a showdown between Hitlerism and democracy. On the other hand it was, for Hore-Belisha himself, a prophetic statement. He ceased, soon after, to be War Minister, and has hardly been heard of since.

In that general atmosphere the impulse to do something constructive and helpful faced frustration everywhere. I began to think of a trip to America, the country which, I already felt, would be later the centre of gravity and the centre of decision in the world struggle. I had nothing too specific in mind. It was to be an exploratory trip, for the purpose of getting my bearings. I was, in a sense, merely laying the groundwork for later trips.

R

I had been seeing a good deal of the higher administrative officials since my return from Switzerland, among them Lord Halifax, the Duke of Devonshire and Sir Edmund Ironside, of the Imperial General Staff. We had already discussed the idea of a Jewish fighting force, though nothing definite was yet suggested. We had also talked of the possibilities in America. When I advised Mr. Churchill, who was back in the Admiralty —exactly where he had been when the First World War broke out—that I was thinking of going to America, he expressed the desire to see me, and on December 17, three days before my departure, I called on him at the Admiralty.

I found him not only cordial but full of optimism about the war. Almost his first words after he had greeted me were: 'Well, Dr. Weizmann, we've got them beat!'

I did not quite think so, and did not say so. I turned the subject instead to our own problem, and thanked him for his unceasing interest in Zionist affairs. I said: 'You have stood at the cradle of the enterprise. I hope you will see it through.' Then I added that after the war we would want to build up a State of three or four million Jews in Palestine. His answer was: 'Yes, indeed, I quite agree with that.'

We talked of certain land legislation, very unfavourable to us, which was being proposed for Palestine, and of the port of Tel Aviv. Mr. Churchill asked for a memorandum on these subjects, which were to come up before the War Cabinet. He also asked that someone be assigned to keep in touch with him during my absence in America. Gradually one perceived that his optimism was not that of a man who underrated the perils confronting England; it was more a long-range confidence which went with coolness in planning and attention to details. It was particularly encouraging to find him, at such a time, mindful of us and our problems.

The trip to America—the first of a series my wife and I made during the war—gave me a glimpse of the disorganization and demoralization which were setting in in Europe. I planned to go by air via Paris and Lisbon—the latter city had already become the fire-escape to the west—but in Lisbon the trans-atlantic flights were cancelled, and we sat about for ten wretched days in an atmosphere of international intrigue, spying, rumours and secrecy. There was no one to speak to, and if there had been one did not dare to speak. It was an extremely ugly little world.

By the turn of the year some seventy or eighty air passengers for America had accumulated, and Imperial Airways made arrangements with the Italian steamship *Rex* to take us over. The trip was, if anything, more unpleasant than our stay in Lisbon. Italy was not yet at war, but we were treated practically as enemy nationals. The Italians were arrogant towards all the English passengers; they were confident of an early Axis victory and of England's downfall and ruin. The charges both for the trip and for services on board were exorbitant—and they refused to take English money! We would have had a doubly bad time of it if we had not met in Lisbon an old friend of ours, Mr. Siegfried Kramarsky, a Dutch banker and a good Zionist, for whom, queerly enough, I had been instrumental in obtaining a Canadian visa a few months earlier. He and his family travelled with us to America; they were among the very few Dutch Jews who managed to escape before Hitler invaded Holland.

We found America in that strange pre-war mood which it is now so difficult to recall. Pearl Harbour was still two years off. America was, so to speak, violently neutral, and making an extraordinary effort to live in the ordinary way. One had to be extremely careful of one's utterances. As I said in one of my addresses: 'I am not sure whether mentioning the Ten Commandments will not be considered a statement of policy, since one of them says: Thou shalt not kill.' I was frustrated both in my Jewish and my general work.

On the Jewish side the position recalled pre-war England, when mention of the Jewish tragedy was associated with warmongering. It had been bad enough in the days of the 'cold pogrom' of concentration camps, economic strangulation, mass expulsions and humiliation. Now for the first time rumours began to reach us of plans so hideous as to be quite incredible —plans for the literal mass extermination of the Jews. I received a letter from an old Zionist friend, Richard Lichtheim, who lived in Geneva and had good sources of information in Germany, warning us that if Hitler overran Europe Zionism would lose all its meaning because no Jews would be left alive. It was like a nightmare which was all the more oppressive because one had to maintain silence: to speak of such things in public was 'propaganda'!

On the general side there was the same frustration. One did not dare to say that England's cause was America's cause; one did not dare to speak of the inevitable. One did not dare to discuss even the most urgent practical problems facing England in the life and death struggle. There was, for instance, rubber, the supply of which from the Far East had been cut off. I had been interested in the chemistry of rubber substitutes since the time of the First World War. But I found it difficult to start any sort of practical discussion with American manufacturers. They were neutral. They were not ready for a great war effort until Pearl Harbour—and even for some time after.

I had a talk with President Roosevelt early in February 1940. He showed a lively interest in the latest developments in Palestine, and I tried to sound him out on the likelihood of American interest in a new departure in Palestine, away from the White Paper, when the war was over. He showed himself friendly, but the discussion remained theoretical. Before I left he told me with great gusto the story of Felix Frankfurter's visit, some time before, to a Palestinian colony where a magnificent prize bull was on show. Frankfurter asked idly what they called the bull, and received the answer: 'Franklin D. Roosevelt!'

I spoke at Zionist meetings in New York, Baltimore, Chicago, Detroit and Cleveland, always with the utmost caution, seeking to call the attention of my fellow-Jews to the doom hanging over European Jewry and yet avoiding anything that might be interpreted as propaganda. I could only stress our positive achievements in Palestine, and express the hope that the end of the war would bring with it the annulment of the White Paper and a new era of progress, on a hitherto unprecedented scale, for the National Home.

All in all, this first American trip, which lasted three months, was not a satisfactory one. There was, however, one considerable gain to record. It was during this visit that I made the closer acquaintance of two of the younger New England Zionists, Dewey Stone and Harry Levine, of whose activities I had heard for some time, but with whom I had had few contacts. Early in 1940 they added to their general Zionist work a special and sustained interest in the Sieff Research Institute, and later they were to take a leading part in the development of the Weizmann Institute of Science. They made, and still make, a rather remarkable team, a sort of Damon and Pythias combination, in their devotion to these special projects. Their co-operation is all the more welcome in that it is guided by a large view and a wide understanding of the future needs of Palestine. With them worked older friends of the scientific development of Palestine, such as Lewis Ruskin, of Chicago, who has been extremely helpful since the time of the founding of the Sieff Institute, and who continued his support throughout the war years. Of Albert K. Epstein and Benjamin Harris, also Chicagoans, I have already spoken in connection with our Rehovoth scientific enterprises.

But, as I have said, the artificial atmosphere of America during that first period of the war was an uncomfortable one, and it was a genuine relief to get back to the realities of England where, if the truth was harsh, it was at least being faced. The symbol of England's awakening to reality was Chamberlain's retirement and Churchill's assumption of office as Prime Minister. The illusions of 'the phony war' were gone; Europe was being overrun by the Nazis, and England knew that, for a time at least, she would be standing alone.

Our two boys were on active service. Benjy, the elder one, was with his anti-aircraft artillery group on an aerodrome in Kent, in the path of the invasion. The battery was often under fire for days at a stretch, and during such periods the men went without sleep or food or drink for thirty-six and forty-eight hours at a stretch. Many of them were so shattered by the bombardments that they ran away into the near-by woods, and had to be collected. After about half a year of service Benjy passed several months in the hospital, suffering from shell-shock. Then he was invalided out of the service.

Benjy had married, in 1937, Maidie Pomerans, who comes of an excellent family of Russian Jewish origin living in Leicester. Maidie studied medicine at London University, and it was in London that they met. Today she practises in the suburbs, running a number of children's clinics. She combines with her professional ability exceptional domestic skill, and maintains a modest but extremely attractive home. She is a charming hostess, reads widely on general subjects and keeps abreast of all developments in her own field. Young and lively, she is loved and respected by all who come in contact with her. Benjy and Maidie have one child, our grandson, David, a bright spark—almost too intelligent— who must constantly be kept back in order that he may not develop into a so-called prodigy. He does admirably at school, and fortunately does as well at games as in his studies, so there is every chance that he will not develop into the overgrown intellectual type with which we meet so often in modern Jewish society.

I return to the story of the war years. Our younger son, Michael, became an officer in the Air Force, and he devoted himself to his duties heart and soul. He was a physicist by training; he had taken his tripos in Cambridge, and engineering at the City and Guilds in London. He was deeply interested in aeronautics and electronics, and in spite of repeated offers from leading physicists at the research stations of the Air Ministry to come and work with them, he insisted on active service. It was his view that one could do research properly only after a long period of operational flying, and only those who had engaged in actual warfare knew what combinations of scientific and practical knowledge would bring the best results.

His work consisted of patrol duty in two directions, one south-ward across the Bay of Biscay, down to Gibraltar, the other westward almost as far as Iceland. He was practically always on night service, and whenever we went to bed we thought of our son flying somewhere over the ocean, dodging enemy planes, bringing in ships with food and ammunition from America to the western approaches of England, always alone, always in danger.

He came on short leaves from time to time, and his visits were a great joy and sadness. It seemed that no sooner did he arrive than the twenty-four or forty-eight hours were over, and we had to part. I always used to accompany him into the blackout, until he said good-bye and disappeared into the unknown.

Meanwhile life in England moved into its wartime grimness. The air attacks on London were intensified until they came with almost mathematical regularity every night. Food became scarce, sleep almost impossible, and we reached a stage when we never went down to the shelter in our hotel—the Dorchester —but remained fatalistically in our rooms. Also it seemed to us that if it came to the worst we preferred to die in our own bed rather than be cooped up in a cellar where, to the danger of immediate death from explosion, was added the danger of suffocation. In our rooms we at least had air and a certain amount of comfort.

Shortly after my return from America I was appointed honorary chemical adviser to the Ministry of Supply, headed by Mr. Herbert Morrison, and was given a little laboratory in 25 Grosvenor Crescent Mews, where I set to work with a small group of chemists. The laboratory was not much more than a large matchbox with a great number of glass windows, and I was always much more apprehensive of the shattering effect of a near-by explosion than of a direct hit. We were not permitted to work in our laboratory until we had an air-raid shelter available in the vicinity, and we found one in the back entrance to the Alexandra Hotel in Knightsbridge, and thither we used to run when the alarm was sounded. But the attacks became so frequent that work proved to be impossible, so we arranged with the air-raid warden to give us a special whistle only when it looked as though the planes were coming over-head. Soon, however, he was whistling so often that we might just as well have listened to the siren; so we threw precaution to the winds and made up our minds to go on working through the air raids. Oddly enough, our particular shelter suffered a direct hit during one of the raids, and fourteen or fifteen people were killed; our lives were probably saved because we had gone on working. The only time when we were compelled to suspend work was when a delayed-action bomb fell near the entrance to the laboratory, and the area was cordoned off until the bomb was removed.

The laboratory was conveniently situated across Hyde Park, a few minutes' walk from the Dorchester Hotel. I found it a great comfort in this time of personal and general stress to have a serious occupation which absorbed a great deal of energy and attention, and gave one the feeling of making some sort of contribution to the national effort.

Early in the war, during my visit to Switzerland, already

told of, I had stopped in Paris and talked with M. de Monzie, then French Minister of Armaments, of the possibility of making use of a certain process which we had worked out in Palestine at the Sieff Research Institute: the process is called aromatization, and is a sort of catalytic cracking of heavy oil leading to good yields of benzine, toluene, and so forth. My assistant, Dr. Bergmann, scientific director of the Research Institute, was invited to France by the Ministry of Armaments and set up a pilot plant for the aromatization of one kilogram of petroleum per hour. The work was then turned over to two French scientists who proved to be pro-German and anti-war. Dr. Bergmann returned to Palestine; not long after he and Dr. Benjamin Bloch, managing director of the Sieff Institute, came to London to discuss with me a programme of pharmaceutical production in Palestine. When I was appointed chemical adviser to the Ministry of Supply I persuaded Dr. Bergmann to remain with me, and we worked on our problems together.

The outlines of our war work may be of some interest to the general reader. Apart from the aromatization process already mentioned, we investigated the fermentation of molasses by mass inoculation, the fermentation of wood and straw hydrolysates, and the preparation of methyl-butinol and its transformation products, especially isoprene. This last was of interest in view of the approaching rubber crisis. We also worked on ketones and their use in high-octane fuels. It was becoming obvious that aviation would develop, during the war, to hitherto undreamed of proportions, and there would be a shortage of high-octane aviation fuel.

We soon discovered that our greatest difficulties would lie outside the laboratory. In our efforts to transfer results from the laboratory to mass production we ran up against vested interests in the chemical field, which were strongly opposed to the entry of 'outsiders,' in spite of the national emergency. I had the support of a number of important people, among them Lord Mountbatten and Geoffrey Lloyd, but things moved very slowly. In the end it was decided that since the source of heavy oil was in any case America, our processes should be tried out there rather than in England. This was the reason for my long visit, from April 1942 to July 1943, to America.

Absorbed though I was in scientific work, I at no time could forget the danger which faced the National Home. That the war would spread to the Mediterranean was a foregone conclusion. In August 1940 I wrote to Mr. Churchill asking for an interview, and adding:

In a war with the magnitude of the present one, it is impossible to say what the strategic disposition of the British fleets and armies may be before victory is attained. Should it come to a temporary withdrawal from Palestine—a contingency which we hope will never arise—the Jews of Palestine would be exposed to wholesale massacre at the hands of the Arabs, encouraged and directed by the Nazis and the Fascists. This possibility reinforces the demand for our elementary human right to bear arms, which should not morally be denied to the loyal citizens of a country at war. Palestinian Jewry can furnish a force of 50,000 fighting men, all of them in the prime of their strength—no negligible force if properly trained, armed and led.

In September 1940 I again discussed the matter at some length at a lunch with Mr. Churchill at which there were also present, among others, Mr. Brendan Bracken and Mr. Bob Boothby, a close friend. Mr. Churchill was friendly about the idea, and was interested in the details, and we worked out there and then a five-point programme, the outline of which I had brought with me and which I was to submit immediately in a memorandum to Lieutenant-General Sir John Dill, Chief of the Imperial General Staff.

The first point on the programme called for 'recruitment of the greatest possible number of Jews in Palestine for the fighting services, to be formed into Jewish battalions or larger formations.' The third point (I shall return to the second) called for 'officers' cadres, sufficient for a Jewish division in the first instance, to be picked immediately from Jews in Palestine, and trained in Egypt.' The fourth point dealt with a Jewish desert unit, the fifth with the recruitment of foreign Jews in England.

The second point was ominous for us, if only as an indication of the difficulties we were to encounter in being permitted to serve. 'The Colonial Office insists on an approximate parity in

R*

the number of Jews and of Arabs recruited for specific Jewish and Arab units in Palestine. As Jewish recruitment in Palestine is certain to yield much larger numbers than Arab, the excess of Jews is to be sent for training to Egypt or anywhere else in the Middle East.' On this point Mr. Churchill yielded to the Foreign Office; on all others he was unreservedly co-operative. I was, on the whole, satisfied with the results; so were the others at the luncheon. Spirits were high, Mr. Churchill being in infectiously good humour. Towards the end of the lunch Mr. Boothby turned to me with a burst of laughter and said: 'That's the way to handle the P.M., Dr. Weizmann, between the cheese and the coffee!' I answered that I would make a note of it for future reference.

The military authorities, unfortunately, were not so easy to handle. Mr. Churchill's consent to the above programme was given in September 1940. Exactly four years were to pass before, in September 1944, the Jewish Brigade was officially formed! Its history does not form part of this record, and I will not go into further detail in regard to the negotiations. I believe enough has been said to provide some notion of the frustration we encountered here, as elsewhere, in our offers of co-operation.

In the spring of 1941 I broke off my work in London for a three-month trip to America. I went at the request of the British Government, which was concerned at the extent of anti-British propaganda then rife in America, but I also gave a good deal of attention to Zionist questions. It was not easy for me to explain away to Jewish audiences the humiliating delays in the formation of a Jewish fighting force, the less so, in fact, as American Jewry, like English and Palestinian Jewry, was wholeheartedly with England. It was my impression that two-thirds of the sums collected in the Bundles for Britain campaign came from Jews!

Among the top political leaders in America I found real sympathy for our Zionist aspirations. I have mentioned my first interview with Mr. Roosevelt. I saw Mr. Sumner Welles several times during my American visits. He was well informed and well disposed towards us. The trouble always began when it came to the experts in the State Department. The head of the Eastern Division was an avowed anti-Zionist and an outspoken pro-Arab, and this naturally affected the attitude of his subordinates and associates. There was a definite cleavage between the White House and Mr. Sumner Welles on the one hand, and the rest of the State Department on the other, a situation not unlike the one we faced in England.

And, again as in England, I was to meet with a certain type of interested resistance to war work which had nothing to do with the Jewish question. This developed during my third visit, and I shall speak of it and of related matters in the next chapter.

CHAPTER XLI

AMERICA AT WAR

Called to America on Rubber Problem—Michael Missing—Talk with Churchill—Big Promises—Third Wartime Visit to America—Science and Politics in America—Critical War Days—Touch and Go in North Africa—Palestine on Brink of Invasion—Zionist Work in America——Hostile Attitude of Near Eastern Division of State Department—Impenetrable Intrigue

EARLY in 1942 I received a call from Mr. Winant, the American Ambassador to Great Britain. When we met, he informed me that President Roosevelt had expressed the wish to have me come over to the United States in order to work there on the problem of synthetic rubber. Mr. Winant advised me earnestly to devote myself as completely as possible to chemistry; he believed that I would thus serve best both the Allied Powers and the Zionist cause. I promised Mr. Winant to follow his advice to the best of my ability. Actually, I divided my time almost equally between science and Zionism.

My wife and I had arranged to fly to New York on February 13, and on February 12 we were in Bristol, where we spent the night. Early the next morning we were already in the car which was to take us to the aerodrome when I was called to the telephone, and our friend Simon Marks, speaking from London, gave me the terrible news that our son Michael had been posted missing on the night of the eleventh. I came slowly down the stairs, completely shattered. My wife only asked: 'Is he killed or missing?'

To proceed with our journey was utterly impossible. We turned back to London and I do not remember in all my life a bitterer or more tragic journey than ours that day from Bristol to London. Throughout all of it we did not say a word to each other. We were met at the station by our son Benjy, his wife, Maidie, and our lifetime friend, Lady Marks, and we proceeded silently to the hotel. There we learned something of the circumstances surrounding Michael's disappearance. He had come down off the coast of France, not far from St. Nazaire, on the night when the *Gneisenau* and the *Scharnhorst* made their dash through the English Channel. All available planes were engaged in the chase, and Michael's signals to the station, repeated several times at intervals of twenty minutes, went unheeded. No plane could be spared to go to his rescue.

It was only when our friends were gone that the tears at last welled up in my wife's eyes, and it was a certain relief to see her shaken out of the stony silence of her grief. Then we talked, and we had the same thought, and the same hope. Perhaps Michael had come down safely after all; perhaps he was even a prisoner in the hands of the Germans, and we would not learn of it for a long time because he would not give his real name. Perhaps, then, some day we would hear from him again. It was a vain hope that pursued us for years, and it died completely only with the ending of the war.

The last time we spoke with Michael was on the night of February 10, 1942. He was usually quite cheerful when he phoned, but this time he sounded disconsolate, and I was rather startled by his tone. I tried to cheer him up, telling him that we would soon win the war, and got in reply a sad laugh. It still rings in my ears. It seems he had a premonition.

We left for America on March 11, and on the day of our departure I dropped in at 10 Downing Street to say good-bye to Mr. John Martin, Mr. Churchill's private secretary, with whom we had been on friendly terms since he had been the able chief secretary of the Peel Commission. I had already taken farewell of him when he suddenly said: 'The P.M. is in the other room. He has a few minutes' time, and I think I'll bring you in to him.' And then a strange brief colloquy took place—or I should say monologue, for I hardly did more than say good-bye to Mr. Churchill. He, however, packed a great deal into those few minutes which we passed together, standing on our feet.

He first wished me luck on my American trip, on which he was, of course, fully informed. 'I am glad you are going,' he said, 'and I am sure you will find a great deal of work to do there.' Then, without any questioning or prompting on my part, he went on: 'I want you to know that I have a plan, which of course can only be carried into effect when the war is over. I would like to see Ibn Saud made lord of the Middle East—the boss of the bosses—provided he settles with you. It will be up to you to get the best possible conditions. Of course we shall help you. Keep this confidential, but you might talk it over with Roosevelt when you get to America. There's nothing he and I cannot do if we set our minds on it.'

That was all. But it was so much that I was rather dazed by it; and the truth is that I would not have taken it all quite literally had it not been for a rather extraordinary circumstance which had puzzled me for some time and which only now became meaningful for me. A few months before I had met St. John Philby, the famous traveller in Arabia and confidant of Ibn Saud. We had talked about Palestine and Arab relations, and he had made a statement which I had noted down, but which had seemed incomprehensible to me coming from him. He had said: 'I believe that only two requirements, perhaps, are necessary to solve your problem: that Mr. Churchill and President Roosevelt should tell Ibn Saud that they wished to see your programme carried through; that is number one; number two is that they should support his overlordship of the Arab countries and raise a loan for him to enable him to develop his territories.' I now fitted together St. John Philby's 'offer' and Mr. Churchill's 'plan.'

I had been asked by Mr. Churchill to keep the contents of the interview confidential. I have already said that I dislike these commitments to secrecy in matters which are of concern to the Zionist movement. Under the peculiar circumstances attending the talk with Mr. Churchill—we were on our way to the train which would take us to the airport—complete secrecy was quite impossible. I had with me at the time Mr. Joseph Linton, our political secretary and one of the most devoted and faithful servants of the movement. I told him, when I came out, what had happened, and said: 'I shall be on the plane very soon. I'm going to make a brief note of this conversation, and you will put it in a sealed envelope and hand it to our friend, Mr. Sigmund Gestetner. He lives in the country, and his place is more or less free from bombing dangers. Should anything happen to me on this journey, or in America, you will open this envelope and disclose its contents to the Zionist Executive.'

I did not discuss Mr. Churchill's plan with President Roosevelt on my arrival in America. Our interview was very brief, in fact little more than a friendly welcome. America had been in the war just about three months. At the moment Mr. Roosevelt saw in me only the scientific worker, and I remembered Mr. Winant's advice to me—to concentrate as much as I could on war work; I would serve the Zionist cause more effectively that way.

My first lead was a letter from Mr. Roosevelt to Mr. Vannevar Bush, then the head of war research. I am afraid that it did not do me much good, for I soon discovered that if I was going to do effective work, I would have to play the politician more than the scientist, a prospect which I found repugnant. The main question was not going to be one of process and production, but of overcoming the vested interests of great firms—particularly the oil firms. I occasionally met with extremely unpleasant treatment on the part of some of the representatives of these firms who were attached as experts to various Government departments.

My proposal, which I made officially to Mr. William Clayton, Under-Secretary of State for Economics, was to ferment maize—of which millions of bushels were available in the United States and Canada—and convert it into butyl alcohol and acetone by my process, which was established and working on a large scale in various parts of America. The butyl alcohol could without difficulty be used for the making of butylene and the butylene easily converted into butadiene, the basis for rubber. I knew that large quantities of butadiene were already being made out of oil, but the trouble was, as far as I could gather, that the butadiene so produced was not pure, and the purification was slow and costly, whereas the butylene produced by my process was chemically pure, and would lend itself more easily for conversion into a purer form of butadiene. But I had come too late, or at any rate very late; the Government had already engaged the oil companies, and to initiate a process which had not the approval of the oil companies was almost too much of a task for any human being.

However, I did have as supporters of my process Mr. Henry A. Wallace, the Vice-President, and the National Farmers' Union. One result was that I became, to my intense distaste, the centre of an argument which took on a political character; it was the Farmers' Union versus the oil companies. A more welcome result was the ultimate switching of a good deal of the production to alcohol and its derivatives. Some time later Mr. Wallace was kind enough to write of my war work in America in the following terms: 'The world will never know what a significant contribution Weizmann made towards the success of the synthetic rubber programme at a time when it was badly bogged down and going too slowly.'

I have given above only one aspect of the war work in which I was engaged. It must be borne in mind that butylene is also needed for the production of high-octane fuel. There was, moreover, another aspect of the rubber problem which was vitally affected, and that had to do with isoprene. Now whether one produces butadiene from oil or from alcohol there is no difference in the final character of the rubber, which, when processed, is hard and is best used only for the outside parts of the tyre, rather than for the guts or soft inner tubing. I had answered this problem by another process—namely, the condensation of acetone and acetylene. I produced thereby an isoprene which is polymerized into isoprene rubber and gives a soft, malleable product which blends well with the butadiene rubber; so one could use pure butadiene rubber for the hard outer tube and a combination of the two rubbers for the soft inner tube.

Here too I must record a long history of delay and opposition. The Government appointed an important committee to go into the matter. Originally a member of the Supreme Court was to head the committee, and Mr. Justice Stone was proposed by the President. Through some administrative blunder Justice Stone refused the appointment, and Mr. Bernard Baruch took his place. Two important members of the committee were Professors Compton and Conant. Professor Conant was sceptical from the outset. He said that he too had been trying to synthesize isoprene from acetylene and acetone, and it seemed to him a tedious and expensive method. I answered, in some astonishment: 'But you don't know what my process is!' I later submitted my findings in an elaborate report, but did not get much further. Colonel Bradley Dewey, assistant director of the Rubber Board, did express great interest in our process when Dr. Bergmann and I and some assistants produced several litres of synthetic isoprene; but when it came to mass production, he could not see his way to setting up a big plant, although Commercial Solvents, the firm which had been handling my processes for years, was prepared to go into it. It was the more puzzling as we had asked for no remuneration and formulated no demands.

To go ahead with our process we should have had to find a private firm, which would work without the assistance of the Government. This would have been doubly difficult, because it was not easy to get licences and permits for supplies and machinery. The struggle was long and tiring, but I would not give in. I achieved some partial success, as is evidenced by Mr. Wallace's letter; but the vested interests were too powerful to permit of a quick break-through. In the end I handed over my processes to a firm in Philadelphia, which began to apply it during the war, and continues to do so now.

The frustration which I felt during the early part of my third visit to America was intensified by the increasing sense of urgency connected with the war generally and with the Mediterranean war in particular. That summer Rommel was making tremendous strides towards Tobruk and Egypt and both the military communiqués and the newspaper reports were utterly depressing. One correspondent who had just flown in from Cairo and Palestine came specially to see me, and told me a shattering story. The Egyptians were preparing to receive the 'conquerors' in great style. Mussolini was ready to fly over at a moment's notice, and a beautiful white charger was to carry him into Cairo, where, like Napoleon, he would address his armies at the foot of the pyramids. I saw in my mind's eye the mountebank posturing in imitation of his great hero, and the picture was a little revolting.

Equally serious, if without the touch of the grotesque, was the news the correspondent brought from Palestine. There, he said, the Arabs were already preparing for the division of the spoils. Some of them were going about the streets of Tel Aviv and the colonies marking up the houses they expected to take over: one Arab, it was reported, had been killed in a quarrel over the loot assigned to him. The correspondent further reported that General Wavell had called in some of the Jewish leaders and told them confidentially how deeply sorry he was that the British Army could not do any more for the *Yishuv*: the troops were to be withdrawn towards India, the Jews would have to be left behind, and would be delivered up to the fury of the Germans, the Arabs and the Italians. The correspondent had also heard that the Jewish leaders had held a meeting and made decisions of despair: they were to be divided into two age groups: the members of the older group would commit suicide: the younger ones would take to the hills to fight their last battle there and sell their lives as dearly as possible: thus the National Home would be liquidated.

There was enough to be heartsick about without taking all this literally, for what could be the fate of the Jews of Palestine if Rommel broke through, after what was happening to the Jewish communities of conquered Europe? In those days, when it was touch and go with the African war, every effort was being made to induce America to send the maximum number of planes and tanks to that theatre. I too added my plea, for what it was worth. Mr. Henry Morgenthau Jr. introduced me to General Marshall, and to the American Chief of Staff I explained what faced us if the needed munitions did not reach the British in time. General Marshall listened gravely and attentively, said very little, made notes of what I told him, and thanked me for the information. The story of how the supplies were rushed across the Atlantic and Africa, of how they arrived in the nick of time, of how the tide was turned at the last moment, has been told many times. But perhaps no one remembers those agonizing days more vividly than the Jews of Palestine, for whom that near-miraculous rescue of the Homeland from complete annihilation still has in it a Biblical echo, recalling the far-off story of the destruction of Sennacherib within sight of the gates of Jerusalem.

For the first few months of my visit I was almost completely absorbed by my chemical work and its attendant problems. When the summer had passed, and with it the immediate military danger to Palestine, and when I had a grip on my war assignment, I permitted myself some Zionist activity; not very much, to be sure, for I still bore in mind Mr. Winant's advice, but enough to maintain contact with external and internal developments.

As to the first, I have already mentioned that in my earlier interview with President Roosevelt we talked only of my scientific work. Later I began to sound out leading Americans on the kind of support we could expect for Zionist demands which we would formulate after the war. But our difficulties were not connected with the first-rank statesmen. These had, for by far the greatest part, always understood our aspirations, and their statements in favour of the Jewish National Home really constitute a literature. It was always behind the scenes, and on the lower levels, that we encountered an obstinate, devious and secretive opposition which set at naught the public declarations of American statesmen. And in our efforts to counteract the influence of these behind-the-scenes forces, we were greatly handicapped because we had no foothold there. The Americans who worked in the Middle East were, with few exceptions, either connected with the oil companies or attached to the missions in Beirut and Cairo. For one reason or another, then, they were biased against us. They communicated their bias to American agents in their territory. Thus it came about that all the information supplied from the Middle East to the authorities in Washington worked against us.

Nor could we ever really find out what was happening behind the scenes. One story will illustrate the queer, obscure tangle of forces through which we had to find our way. I have told, in another part of this chapter, how Mr. St. John Philby, the confidential agent of Ibn Saud, brought us an 'offer,' which seemed to coincide with the 'plan' which Mr. Churchill put so hastily before me a few hours before my departure for America. In America I met a Colonel Hoskins, of the Eastern Division of the State Department, whom I understood to be the President's personal representative in the Middle East. Colonel Hoskins was not friendly to our cause: on the other hand, he was not as hostile as his colleagues of the Eastern Division: in fact he was by comparison rather reasonable. In his opinion, something could be done in Palestine if the Jews would, as he called it, 'moderate their demands.' He spoke of bringing half a million Jews into Palestine in the course of the next twenty years, quite a 'concession' for one who was opposed to Zionism.

Colonel Hoskins left for the Middle East, and when I saw him on his return his tone was very different. He said he had visited Ibn Saud, who had spoken of me in the angriest and most contemptuous manner, asserting that I had tried to bribe him with twenty million pounds to sell out Palestine to the Jews. I was quite staggered by this interpretation put on a proposal which I had never made, but a form of which had in fact been made to me by Ibn Saud's representative—St. John Philby. Colonel Hoskins reported further that Ibn Saud would never again permit Mr. Philby to cross the frontiers of his kingdom. Some time later I told St. John Philby of Colonel Hoskins's report. Philby dismissed it as 'bloody nonsense.' The truth was that the relations between Philby and Ibn Saud had never been better, and these relations, I might add, remain unchanged at the time of writing.

What was one, what is one, to make of all this? Did Ibn Saud deliberately misrepresent his position to Hoskins? Or had he said something which could be interpreted as a complete reversal of his previous position? And to whom else besides myself did Hoskins give this account of the conversation with Ibn Saud? And what effect did it have in the State Department? How was one to get at the truth—if there was a truth?

Nothing came of the 'plan,' as we know today: what prospect of realization it at one time had it is hard to say. Of further negotiations and of other conversations with President Roosevelt and Mr. Churchill I shall speak in the next chapter.

CHAPTER XLII

PEACE AND DISILLUSIONMENT

High Hopes and Deep Disappointment—Roosevelt's Affirmative Attitudes on Palestine—British Labour Party's Repeated Promises—Friendly Reassurances from Churchill—All Come to Nothing—Moyne Assassination—My First Visit to Palestine since 1939—Vast Changes—Frustrations—The Terror—British Labour Comes to Power—Repudiates its Palestine Promises—Bevin's Attitude—Earl Harrison's Report and President Truman's Recommendation—The Anglo-American Commission—The First Postwar Zionist Congress

D U R I N G the latter years of the war two themes were dominant in the minds of the Jewish people, one of despair and one of hope. The tragedy of European Jewry was revealed to us slowly in all its incredible starkness. It was not only a tragedy of physical suffering and destruction, so common throughout the world though nowhere so intensively visited as upon the Jews. It was a tragedy of humiliation and betrayal. Much of the calamity was unavoidable; but a great part of it could have been mitigated, many thousands of lives could have been saved, both in the period preceding the war and during the war itself, had the democratic countries and their governments been sufficiently concerned. This is recalled not in a spirit of recrimination; the tragedy is too deep for that. It is recalled in order that the Jewish position may be understood. As in all tragedies, the feeling that had people cared it might have been different made the anguish less bearable.

The hope which was the counterpart of this despair and anguish was born of the impending defeat of Nazi Germany and of the belief that now, at last, with the coming of peace, the victorious democratic world would bethink itself; less preoccupied with its fears and insecurities, it would realize what had happened to the Jewish people, and give it its chance at last.

The period immediately following the war was, for the Jewish people and the Zionist movement, one of intense disappointment. True, ours was not the only disillusionment; but there were few demands as well founded as ours, and fewer still which represented so bare a minimum of sheer need. All that we asked for was simply the opportunity to save, by our own efforts, the remnant of our people. This was the sum total of our hopes.

It cannot be made too clear that our hopes were not merely general, and based only on the prevailing mood of optimism. They were based equally on specific private and public assurances. Their disappointment was all the more shocking and unexpected because they had been deliberately nurtured by those who could have fulfilled them, promised to do so, and did not. On this the record is painfully clear.

I had taken with me to America, when I went there in 1942, the assurance of Mr. Churchill that he had a 'plan' for us, that together with Mr. Roosevelt he could carry out the plan, and that the end of the war would see a change in the status of the Jewish National Home; the White Paper, which Mr. Churchill had so bitterly denounced in 1939, would go. Towards the end of my stay in America—a stay almost entirely devoted, as the reader may remember, to war work—I had a long interview with President Roosevelt, in the presence of Mr. Sumner Welles. The attitude of Mr. Roosevelt was completely affirmative.

He was of course aware of the Arab problem, and spoke in particular of Ibn Saud, whom he considered fanatical and difficult. I maintained the thesis that we could not rest our case on the consent of the Arabs; as long as their consent was asked they would naturally refuse it, but once they knew that Mr. Churchill and Mr. Roosevelt both supported the Jewish National Home, they would acquiesce. The moment they sensed a flaw in this support they would become negative, arrogant and destructive. Mr. Roosevelt again assured me of his sympathies, and of his desire to settle the problem.

Throughout this interview I was supported by Mr. Welles, who had been somewhat cautious and reticent in our private conversations, but on this occasion was outspoken in his desire to see my proposals materialized. Mr. Welles expressed the belief that America would be prepared to help financially in the setting up of the Jewish National Home. We did not go into details, but Mr. Welles had read my article in *Foreign Affairs*, in which I had outlined my views, and he was in agreement with them. Mr. Roosevelt, to whom I repeated the substance of Mr. Churchill's last statement to me, asked me to convey to the latter his positive reaction.

It must not be supposed that our negotiations were confined to groups, parties and individuals in power, and that the encouragement of our hopes flowed from these alone. Our appeal for justice was not a party matter, and we addressed ourselves to all men of good will. Since the Jewish Agency was a recognized public instrument in the administration of Palestine, we were naturally in more frequent contact with the British Government; but my colleagues and I were constantly pressing our case in other circles. In 1943 and 1944 I discussed the question of the Jewish National Home with men like Archibald Sinclair, Creech-Jones, Ernest Bevin, Hugh Dalton. Berl Locker, one of the outstanding labour leaders in the Zionist movement, was active in British Labour circles. At the Conference of June 1943, the British Labour party reaffirmed its traditional support of the Jewish National Home. In the report of the Labour Party National Executive Committee, issued in April 1944, measures were recommended which in respect of the Arabs went beyond our own official programme.

The report read in part: 'There is surely neither hope nor meaning in a Jewish National Home unless we are prepared to let the Jews, if they wish, enter this tiny land in such numbers as to become a majority. There was a strong case for this before the war, and there is an irresistible case for it now, after the unspeakable atrocities of the cold-blooded, calculated German-Nazi plans to kill all the Jews of Europe. . . . Let the Arabs be encouraged to move out as the Jews move in. Let them be compensated handsomely for their land, and their settlement elsewhere be carefully organized and generously financed.'

I remember that my Labour Zionist friends were, like myself, greatly concerned about this proposal. We had never contemplated the removal of the Arabs, and the British labourites, in their pro-Zionist enthusiasm, went far beyond our intentions.

Again I received friendly assurances from Mr. Churchill at

a brief meeting in September 1943; and yet again, in greater detail, at Chequers, where I lunched with him and a small party, including his brother John Churchill, Mr. John Martin and Major Thompson, on November 4, 1944. Mr. Churchill was very specific in this last conversation.

He spoke of partition, and declared himself in favour of including the Negev in the Jewish territory. And while he made it clear that no active steps would be taken until the war with Germany was over, he was in close touch with America on the matter of the Jewish National Home. Hearing that I was going to Palestine shortly, he recommended that I break my journey in Cairo to see Lord Moyne who, he said, had changed and developed in the past two years. He asked me whether it was our intention to bring large numbers of Jews into Palestine. I replied that we had in mind something like one hundred thousand a year for about fifteen years. I spoke also of the large numbers of children who would have to be brought to Palestine; Mr. Churchill commented that it would be for the governments to worry about the children, and mentioned financial aid. I answered that if the political field were clear, the financial problem would become of secondary importance.

At one turn the conversation touched on oppositionist Jews, and Mr. Churchill mentioned Mr. Bernard Baruch, among others. I said there were still a few rich and powerful Jews who were against the idea of the Jewish National Home, but they did not know very much about the subject.

I asked myself at the time, as I have often done, why men who had given so little attention to an intricate problem like Zionism should take it upon themselves to speak disparagingly on the subject to men in high places, on whom so much depended. I had seen Mr. Baruch several times in America, in connection with my chemical work. Knowing his attitude, I had taken great care not to touch on the Jewish problem; nor had he shown any disposition to question me on it. Yet he had undertaken to state his negative views to Mr. Churchill. But I ought to add that later on, and especially during the period of the struggle for partition before the United Nations, Mr. Baruch changed a great deal; he was helpful to us in many respects, and used his influence freely in our favour.

When the lunch was over, Mr. Churchill took me into his

study and repeated the points he had made in the general conversation. He seemed worried that America was more or less academic in its attitude on the question. He also added that he did not have a very high opinion of the rôle the Arabs had played in the war.

It was, on the whole, a long and most friendly conversation; it was also one of the rare occasions when Mr. Churchill did not do practically all of the talking. I left the meeting greatly encouraged, and shortly after gave a detailed report of it to my colleagues.

So much for the background of our hopes during the closing period of the war. I turn now, briefly, to part of the personal record.

I had not been in Palestine since the spring of 1939, in the hectic days preceding the issue of the White Paper. During the early war years I had oscillated between England and America, occupied by Zionist and scientific duties. All this time my wife and I had hankered after the country, and after our home in Rehovoth, which we had managed to build after such long planning and which we had occupied so little. As my seventieth birthday approached, in the autumn of 1944, we made up our minds that we would spend it nowhere but in Palestine. The war was still on, but its outcome was clear. We felt we had earned a respite. America beckoned again; there were warm and pressing invitations to go there, and promises of great rewards in the shape of funds for the Jewish institutions. We did not accept. We needed a rest, and the place for it was our own home.

The journey began under an ominous cloud. On November 6 (1944), two days after my interview with Mr. Churchill, and five days before we set out, Lord Moyne was assassinated in Cairo. I wrote the next day to the Prime Minister:

I can hardly find words adequate to express the deep moral indignation and horror which I feel at the murder of Lord Moyne. I know that these feelings are shared by Jewry throughout the world. Whether or not the criminals prove to be Palestinian Jews, their act illumines the abyss to which terrorism leads. Political crimes of this kind are an especial abomination in that they make it possible to implicate whole communities in the guilt of a few. I can assure you that Palestine Jewry will, as its representative bodies have declared, go to the utmost limit of its power to cut out, root and branch, this evil from its midst.

There is not a single word in this letter which I have ever wanted to retract, even in the days of our bitterest disappointment. I shall have more to say of this utterly un-Jewish phenomenon. Here I only wish to observe that the harm done our cause by the assassination of Lord Moyne, and by the whole terror—this apart from the profound moral deterioration involved—was not in changing the intentions of the British Government, but rather in providing our enemies with a convenient excuse, and in helping to justify their course before the bar of public opinion.

The reception accorded me by the Jews of Palestine after my absence of more than five years was warm, generous and spontaneous. It was a wonderful home-coming, all that the heart could wish; or rather, it would have been if there had not been certain phenomena which caused me grave concern. Since 1939 the Homeland had undergone great changes; and once at least, when Rommel stood at Alamein, it had passed through the valley of the shadow of death. There had been moments when a frightful premonition of ultimate disaster had haunted us, and we had had nightmares of the Germans and Italians marching into Palestine, and our cities and colonies, the tenderly nurtured achievements of two generations, given over to the same pillage and destruction as German and Polish Jewry. It had not happened, and the Homeland had come through, stronger than ever. The war years had knit the community into a powerful, self-conscious organism, and the great war effort, out of all proportion to the numerical strength of the *Yishuv*, had given the Jews of Palestine a heightened self-reliance, a justified sense of merit and achievement, a renewed claim on the democratic world, and a high degree of technical development. The productive capacity of the country had been given a powerful forward thrust. The National Home was in fact here—unrecognized, and by that lack of recognition frustrated in the fulfilment of its task. Here were over six hundred thousand Jews capable of a vast concerted action on behalf of the remnant of Jewry in Europe—to them no impersonal element but, in thousands of instances, composed of near and dear ones—capable of such action, frantically eager to undertake it, and forbidden to do so.

Side by side with these developments, in some ways linked with them, and in part arising from the bitter frustration of legitimate hopes, there were the negative features I have referred to: here and there a relaxation of the old, traditional Zionist purity of ethics, a touch of militarization, and a weakness for its trappings; here and there, something worse—the tragic, futile, un-Jewish resort to terrorism, a perversion of the purely defensive function of *Haganah*; and worst of all, in certain circles, a readiness to compound with the evil, to play politics with it, to condemn and not to condemn it, to treat it not as the thing it was, namely, an unmitigated curse to the National Home, but as a phenomenon which might have its advantages.

Sometimes it seemed as though the enemies of the Jewish Homeland without were determined to encourage only the destructive elements within. Long before the end of the war the last excuse for the White Paper—pacification of the Arabs, who incidentally were not pacified by it—had disappeared. By 1944, and even by 1943, the victory which the Arabs had done so little to help us obtain was in sight. The moral authority of the democracies was then supreme, and a declaration for the Jewish Homeland then would have had irresistible force. A new excuse replaced the old one: one had to wait for the end of the war. This was the pretext advanced to me in private conversation by Mr. Churchill, and offered by him to the House of Commons on February 27, 1945, after the Yalta Conference. The European war ended in May 1945; no action was taken.

In July of that year came the General Election in England, with a Labour triumph which astonished the whole world and delighted all liberal elements. If ever a political party had gone unequivocally on record with regard to a problem, it was the British Labour Party with regard to the Jewish National Home; within three months of taking office, the British Labour Government repudiated the pledge so often and clearly—even vehemently—repeated to the Jewish people. Today it is clear from the course of events that the promises and protestations of friendship, the attacks on the White Paper in the House of Commons, by those who were to form future governments, the official resolutions of the British Labour Party, lacked character and substance; they did not stand up to the pressure of those forces which, behind the scenes, have always worked against us.

It was on November 13, 1945, that the Labour Government officially repudiated the promises of the Labour Party and offered us, instead of the abrogation of the White Paper, and relief for the Jews in the detention camps—a new Commission of Inquiry. The extraordinary spirit in which this declaration of policy was conceived may be understood from the opening. The British Government 'would not accept the view that the Jews should be driven out of Europe or that they should not be permitted to live again in these countries without discrimination, contributing their ability and talent towards rebuilding the prosperity of Europe.' The British Government, in other words, refused to accept the view that six million Jews had been done to death in Europe by various scientific mass methods, and that European anti-Semitism was as viciously alive as ever. The British Government wanted the Jews to stay on and contribute their talents (as I afterwards told the United Nations Special Committee on Palestine) towards the rebuilding of Germany, so that the Germans might have another chance of destroying the last remnants of the Jewish people.

With such an exordium, the rest of the document can easily be guessed at. Instead of the mass movement of Jews into Palestine which the British Labour Party had repeatedly promised, there was an offer of a trickle of fifteen hundred refugees a month; instead of the generous recognition of the original purposes of the Balfour Declaration, a reversion to the old, shifty double emphasis on the obligation towards the Arabs of Palestine as having equal weight with the promise of the Homeland to the Jews. The let-down was complete.

Mr. Bevin, who, as the new Foreign Secretary, issued the declaration of policy on behalf of the Labour Government, was apparently determined to make it clear that, at any rate as far as he was concerned, no doubts should be entertained anywhere as to his personal agreement with the worst implications of the declaration. At a press conference following the issue of the declaration he said, apparently apropos of our demand for the fulfilment of the Balfour Declaration and the promises of the Labour Party: 'If the Jews, with all their suffering, want to get too much at the head of the queue, you have the danger of another anti-Semitic reaction through it all.'

I thought the remark gratuitously brutal, even coarse, but I cannot say that it surprised me. My personal contacts with Mr. Bevin have been unfortunate: that is, where Jewish matters have been concerned. His tone was hectoring. I first went to see him, in his capacity as Foreign Secretary, with regard to certificates for refugees. We had been offered a ludicrously small number—a remnant, it was stated, unused under the White Paper—which we could not offer the unhappy, clamouring inmates of the D.P. camps without a feeling of shame. We refused the certificates. Mr. Bevin's opening remarks to me were: 'What do you mean by refusing certificates? Are you trying to force my hand? If you want a fight you can have it!' There was not the slightest effort to understand our point of view; there was only an overbearing, quarrelsome approach. An earlier contact with Mr. Bevin, when he had been Minister of Labour during the war, had been somewhat happier; but then Mr. Bevin had wanted my services.

Thus, in the two and a half years which followed my visit of 1944 to Palestine, no positive response came from British or world statesmanship to the pleas and protests of the great constructive majority of Jewish Palestine and the Diaspora. Every objective study of the immediate and long-range problem of European Jewry pointed to one solution: mass evacuation, as fast as economic absorption would permit, into Palestine. Every objective report on Palestine confirmed the claim of Palestinian Jewry, that it was capable of handling the problem. But nothing was done.

In the autumn of 1945 Mr. Earl Harrison, after personal investigation on the spot, reported to President Truman that there was no solution for the problem of the majority of European Jews other than Palestine; President Truman then suggested to the Prime Minister, Mr. Attlee, that one hundred thousand Jews be admitted immediately to Palestine; and President Truman's suggestion was followed by Mr. Bevin's declaration above referred to. This was the origin of the Anglo-American Commission of 1946.

Profoundly disappointed though we were, for we had had our fill of inquiries and investigations, we co-operated loyally with the commission. Its personnel was of high calibre, and included a number of excellent men like Bartley Crum of California, Frank Buxton of Boston, Richard Crossman M.P., James G. Macdonald of New York and Judge Hutchison of Texas.

With these and others I established friendly relations, and did what I could to place the facts before them. But though the commission held sessions in America and in Europe before it proceeded to Palestine, I would not appear before it except in the latter country. I considered that the proper setting, and I wanted the members of the commission to see the Homeland with their own eyes first. I pleaded then once more for the radical solution of the Jewish problem—the evacuation to Palestine of the remnant of European Jewry; and on the basis of our achievements, which they could survey for themselves, and of careful reports prepared by our experts, I submitted practical plans. The commission was favourably impressed; it issued positive though cautious recommendations, among them the admission of the one hundred thousand 'displaced persons,' as suggested by President Truman. It produced no effect, except to prove that the British Government had never intended to take affirmative action. The whole device had been nothing but a stall. The White Paper remained in force, our immigration was still limited to the tragically derisory figure of fifteen hundred a month.

The frustration of our creative impulses in Palestine, with all its demoralizing effects, had its repercussions on the Zionist movement everywhere. The ravages which the war had wrought on the Jewish people, and the political betrayal which had followed the war, were mirrored in our first postwar Zionist Conference, held in London in August 1945, at the time of the British General Election. It is true that the Labour Government had not yet reversed the decision of the Labour Party; but the Government of Mr. Churchill, in which places of leadership were held by men who had denounced the White Paper in 1939, had already failed us; and the effect, added to the calamities of the war, was to depress the tone of the movement, and to encourage counsels of despair. Even more marked, of course, was the effect by the end of 1946, when the first post-war Zionist Congress was held in Geneva. Since this second gathering was the larger, the more official, and the more elaborately prepared, it will suffice to deal with that alone.

It was a dreadful experience to stand before that assembly and to run one's eye along row after row of delegates, finding among them hardly one of the friendly faces which had adorned past Congresses. Polish Jewry was missing; Central and South-east European Jewry was missing; German Jewry was missing. The two main groups represented were the Palestinians and the Americans; between them sat the representatives of the fragments of European Jewry, together with some small delegations from England, the Dominions and South America.

The American group, led by Dr. Abba Hillel Silver, was from the outset the strongest, not so much because of enlarged numbers, or by virtue of the inherent strength of the delegates, but because of the weakness of the rest. The twenty-second Congress therefore had a special character, differing in at least one respect from previous Congresses: the absence—among very many delegates—of faith, or even hope, in the British Government, and a tendency to rely on methods never known or encouraged among Zionists before the war.

These methods were referred to by different names: 'resis-tance,' 'defence,' 'activism.' But whatever shades of meaning may have been expressed by these terms—and the distinctions were by no means clear—one feature was common to all of them: the conviction of the need for fighting against British authority in Palestine—or anywhere else, for that matter. My stand on these matters was well known; I made it clear once more at the Congress. I stated my belief that our justified protest against our frustrations, against the injustices we had suffered, could have been made with dignity and force, yet without truckling to the demoralizing forces in the move-ment. I became, therefore, as in the past, the scapegoat for the sins of the British Government; and knowing that their 'assault' on the British Government was ineffective, the 'activists,' or whatever they would call themselves, turned their shafts on me.

About half of the American delegation, led by Rabbi Silver, and part of the Palestinian, led by Mr. Ben-Gurion, had made up their minds that I was to go. On the surface it was not a personal matter; the debate hinged on whether we should or should not send delegates to the Conferences on Palestine which were to be resumed in London towards the end of January 1947, at the instance of the British Government. By a tiny majority, it was decided not to send delegates—and this was taken as the moral equivalent of a vote of no confidence in me. What happened in the end was that my election as President having been made impossible—no President was elected—the delegates went to London by a back door.

I left the Congress depressed, far more by the spirit in which it had been conducted than by the rebuff I had received. Perhaps it was in the nature of things that the Congress should be what it was; for not only were the old giants of the movement gone—Shmarya Levin and Ussishkin and Bialik, among others—but the in-between generation had been simply wiped out; the great fountains of European Jewry had been dried up. We seemed to be standing at the nadir of our fortunes.

In the early spring of 1947 we returned to Palestine and settled again in our home in Rehovoth. Here I busied myself with scientific work, with the building of the new scientific institute which was founded for my seventieth birthday—as described in the next chapter—and with the dictation of most of these memoirs. The United Nations Special Committee on Palestine, and the deliberations of the United Nations on the Palestine problem at Lake Success, were still to come.

CHAPTER XLIII

SCIENCE AND ZIONISM

Oil and World Politics—The Need to Break Oil's Monopolistic Position—Possibilities of Fermentation Industries—Other Enterprises—Palestine's Possible Rôle—Work Done at Rehovoth—The Daniel Sieff Research Institute—Scientific Pioneering in Palestine—Special Problems—Our Rôle in the War—The Weizmann Institute of Science

T H E reader of these memoirs has long been aware in what an organic fashion my Zionist and scientific interests have been interwoven from my earliest years. This is not, I believe, a purely personal phenomenon. It is, rather, the reflection of an objective historic condition. The question of oil, for instance, which hovers over the Zionist problem, as it does, indeed, over the entire world problem, is a scientific one. It is part of the general question of raw materials, which has been a preoccupation with me for decades, both as a scientist and a Zionist; and it had always been my view that Palestine could be made a centre of the new scientific development which would get the world past the conflict arising from the monopolistic position of oil. Not that our scientific work would be dedicated solely to that purpose; but it would certainly be one of its main enterprises.

During my last and longest war visit to America the struggle between oil and other interests had again been made abundantly manifest. The same problem, in other forms, confronted England. I referred, in the last chapter, to a friendly meeting with Mr. Ernest Bevin—one in which he sought my services. It occurred in the midst of the war, when the British Government sent out to West Africa a small commission to investigate the short- and long-range possibilities of new sources of raw material, with fuel chiefly in view. Walter Elliot and Creech-Jones were on the commission, and I had several subsequent meetings with them.

I suggested that they try to determine whether various types of starches could not be grown easily in West Africa. It is known that Central or tropical Africa produces a great many root starches, like manioc and tapioca; also cane sugar. I was of the opinion that if one could grow abundant supplies of these commodities, one could introduce a fermentation industry into that part of the world, with a large yield of ordinary alcohol, both for power and for the production of butyl alcohol and acetone. These three materials, in large quantities and at a low price, could form the basis of two or three great industries, among them high-octane fuel, and would make the British Empire independent of oil wells.

The commission went out for a survey, and so far nothing has come of it. I am still of the opinion that the plan is feasible. Its most attractive feature is, perhaps, that it is not tied to a geographic point, like an oil supply, but is applicable wherever the substances I have mentioned can be grown. It is, moreover, part of what I believe to be a necessary and probably inevitable shift in a great sector of modern industry. Butyl alcohol, acetone and ethyl alcohol are the bases of many products besides fuel and plastics. The acetylene chemistry derivatives start with methyl butinol, which is itself prepared from acetylene and acetone. Methyl alcohol is made from carbon dioxide and hydrogen, which are yielded as by-products from the fermentation of butyl alcohol; the methyl alcohol can easily be reconverted into formaldehyde, one of the best disinfectants. It is, moreover, widely used in synthetic chemistry. Methyl butinol, again, leads to the formation of certain amino-alcohols, which are most valuable constituents of dyestuffs.

It is on these lines that my collaborators and I have been working for a number of years. The programme is still in its initial stages, and to elaborate it would require quite a number of chemists and a certain amount of time; but enough has been done—in Philadelphia, London and Rehovoth—to indicate the lines of research on which we should move at present.

Another piece of work which has been occupying our attention for the last few years leads to the production of cheap but digestible and valuable nutritive products. It may be briefly described as the attempt to up-grade materials which are used as cattle food, converting them into human food. The materials are peanuts or peanut cake—after the oil has been extracted— soya beans and similar substances. This product has been tested in many hospitals as nutrition for patients, and for people with ulcerated stomachs, and it has proved very beneficial. It is, moreover, cheaply produced, and is within reach of the poorest populations, such as the coolies of India or China. It is entirely of a vegetable nature, is highly nutritive, and without containing a particle of meat has a meaty taste. It should be of particular benefit to those eastern countries in which meat is either too expensive or is prohibited for religious reasons.

This enterprise was worked out in its technical aspect by a group of capable workers in America, and has already produced results. My colleagues and I have been occupied with the chemical side since 1935, aided at the beginning by Willstätter, who was a great authority on the chemistry of proteins.

A third branch of research has occupied my attention in recent years, and in this Dr. David Bergmann and one or two others have participated to a considerable degree. In its early stages it was carried out at the Sieff Institute, later it was transferred to London. It is a process for converting the crude residues obtained after the distillation of oil into aromatic substances like benzine, toluene, xylene, naphthalene and certain gaseous substances like butylene, isobutylene, and so on. Our purpose was to create reserves of toluene, for we remembered our sad experiences in the last war, when we ran out of toluene, the basis of T.N.T. The process proved, however, to have wider value. It was taken up by a private firm to which the Manchester Oil Refinery belongs; a company was formed with a capital of two million pounds, the Government participating to the extent of fifty per cent in view of the national importance of the process.

The ideas set forth in brief outline in the foregoing pages were germinating in my mind for many years. I followed closely the literature on the subject, and discussed it with scientists, particularly with Haber and Willstätter, whenever I could. It was my idea, as I have said, that Palestine might be one place where work of that kind might be initiated. Although it is not a country rich in the necessary raw materials, it is sufficiently near to Africa to enable one to survey the field without too much difficulty. It also has the advantage of standing on the borderline of two great zones, the tropical and the temperate, so that the climatic conditions are especially favourable.

Within Palestine, Rehovoth seemed to me the right place for a beginning. It was the seat of the Agricultural Experimental Station; we would have on the premises botanists and plant physiologists who were already well acquainted with the country. There remained the question of means—and of getting together a group of scientists.

With regard to the first, I approached my friends of the Sieff and Marks family, and asked them if they would not be prepared to build such an institute as I had in mind as a memorial to young Daniel Sieff, who died prematurely, and had been very much interested in scientific problems. They responded at once. With regard to the second, the reader will recall how, in the early Hitler years in Germany, large numbers of first-rate scientists were driven from the German universities. Some of them, like Dr. David Bergmann, his brother Felix and other chemists of distinction, joined our group. With these, and with my old colleague Mr. Harold Davies, with whom I have now been working for over thirty-five years, we began the work. This has been an especially interesting, instructive and, I believe, valuable chapter in the history of the Jewish National Home.

The whole experiment of setting up a research institute in a country as scientifically backward as Palestine is beset with pitfalls. There is, first, the risk of falling into the somewhat neglectful habits of Oriental countries; a second danger is that of losing a sense of proportion because of the lack of standards of comparison. One is always the best chemist in Egypt or in Palestine when there are no others. Also, if one turns out a piece of work which in America or England would be considered modest enough, one is apt to over-evaluate it simply because it has been turned out in difficult circumstances. The standard and quality of the work must be watched over most critically and carefully. Many of the publications issued by scientific institutions in backward countries are very much below the level required elsewhere, but the contributors to these publications are very proud of them simply because the local level is not high. I made up my mind that this sort of atmosphere should not prevail in the Sieff Institute, and that it should live up to the highest standards.

There were several ways of combating the dangers I have

indicated. First there was the proper selection of the staff, and the infusion into it of the right spirit—that of maintaining the highest quality. Every member was enjoined to take his time over his piece of work, and not merely have publication in view.

Second, it became our policy to keep the workers in the Institute in touch with what was being done in Europe and America, not merely by providing a good library, where they could read of the researches of others in scientific journals, but by arranging personal contacts. We made it a rule to invite scientists from other institutes to come and lecture in Rehovoth, spending a few weeks in the laboratories, sharing their experiences with us, and criticizing the efforts of the young research workers. In the years preceding the war we had visits from Professors Henri of Paris, Errera of Brussels, Wurmser of Paris, and others of their standing. Unfortunately the war interrupted this practice, which we are trying to renew at present, and already Professors Louis Fieser of Harvard, Herman Mark of the Brooklyn Polytechnic Institute, and Dr. Ernest Chain of Oxford, among others, have visited the institute since the end of the war.

We also worked in the reverse direction, sending our workers abroad, to the universities. Out of eleven senior workers four have been out in Paris, Ottawa, New York, Chicago and Berkeley. As one returns, another leaves, and so continuous contact is maintained with the great scientific world.

The building and organization of the Sieff Institute was, even for Palestine, a unique case of pioneering. Apart from the psychological difficulties of maintaining a high standard, there was the physical difficulty of scientific organization. When, during the war, we undertook to manufacture certain drugs which till then had been a monopoly of the Germans, we lacked both apparatus and raw material. The former we had to improvise, the latter to manufacture for ourselves. We got a small quantity of raw material from the Middle East supply centre at Cairo, but always with great difficulty. It is almost impossible to develop a pharmaceutical industry unless one has at hand all the necessary raw materials. Pharmaceutical products of a certain complexity are so to speak the crown of the industry, the last stage of several chemical processes. Each of these requires the greatest care, because of the high standards of purity necessary in the end product. We could always handle the last stages, but without a great organic and inorganic chemical industry behind us, the early stages presented enormous difficulty. Thus, for instance, there was—and still is—a lack of sulphuric acid, without which almost nothing can be done. There is no local production of benzine or aniline or similar products. All these had to be obtained at very high prices—when they were obtainable—from sources which were not always ready to encourage the creation of a chemical industry in Palestine.

There were problems of another kind. When the Institute was built, on the premises of the Experimental Station, it looked at first as if we were going to sink in a sea of sand. The buildings of the station were quite neat, as far as their external appearance was concerned, but there was not a tree or a blade of grass to adorn the vast courtyard in which the two institutions were housed, and I had before my eyes the green lawns of English and American universities and scientific academies, and thought that we would be showing a lamentable lack of æsthetic feeling if we merely planked down the buildings and did nothing with the surroundings.

I therefore set about building roads to connect one part of the institution with another, to plant trees and lay out lawns, and in general to indicate through externals that this was an agricultural station. Colours, flowers and creepers began to appear very soon, for we have plenty of water, and the soil is light and easily responds to good treatment. After two or three years of care, the whole was transformed into a garden which delights the eye, and every visitor and worker feels the effect.

There are certain human trifles which are of great importance. The people who came to visit us, brought here by their chauffeurs, did not show what I considered proper respect for a public building. They had to be taught not to litter the place with cigarette and cigar ends, pieces of paper and other refuse. At first the injunctions against this practice met with a sceptical shrug of the shoulders, especially on the part of the critical chauffeurs. There were many ironical remarks at my insistence on tidiness; but soon it became known that such people would not be allowed to enter the premises; by now every chauffeur in Palestine knows that the Sieff Institute is one place in Palestine where one does not throw cigarette ends on the floor, but in the receptables provided for that purpose.

A particular feature in the life of the Institute was the erection of a little club. We are outside the settlement of Rehovoth, and it would take time for the workers to go home for their midday meals; in the heat of the summer it would also mean quite an effort. We organized the club for the purpose of supplying cheap and wholesome meals. It is also a place where the workers can rest, read newspapers, hold meetings and arrange lectures and musical evenings. When I mentioned the idea of the club to Professor Willstätter, he said: 'I hope you will set it up. Believe me, it is more important than one or two more laboratories.'

The Sieff Institute has gradually won a good name for itself, both in the scientific and Jewish world, during the thirteen years of its existence. I believe we have done good practical work. The pharmaceutical company which we created during the war has turned over its experience and good will to a serious concern which will continue the manufacture and distribution of its products. In this way an industry requiring much skill and care has been created, and will carry on, I hope, with increasing effectiveness. Other problems which we have tackled have also led to practical results. I feel that on the whole the standard of our publications is high, and our papers have always been accepted in the best journals of England and America. The name of Rehovoth is familiar to every research chemist in these countries, and we receive quite a few applications from scientists who wish to come and work with us.

The Sieff Institute has proved to be only a beginning. On the occasion of my seventieth birthday a group of my American friends conceived a more ambitious project—a scientific centre which would embrace not only organic chemistry, but physical chemistry and other branches on a much larger and more important scale. Those who had been active for the Sieff Institute in years past, Dewey Stone and Harry Levine of New England, Albert K. Epstein, Benjamin Harris and Lewis Ruskin of Chicago, were joined by new forces, like Edmund I. Kaufmann of Washington, who became President of the American Committee, and Sam Zacks, President of the Zionist Organization of Canada. Under the energetic guidance of my friend Meyer W. Weisgal, this larger project moved forward very rapidly, so that on the third of June, 1946, the cornerstone of the main building of the new institute could be laid. There were present at the ceremony, among others, Professors Fieser of Harvard, David Rittenberg and Chaim Pekeris of Columbia University, Hermann Mark, Kurt G. Stern and Peter Hohenstein of the Brooklyn Polytechnic Institute and Dr. Yehudah Quastel, F.R.S., of University College, Cardiff. Several of these eminent scientists have agreed to accept permanent posts at the Institute, which is to bear the name of the Weizmann Institute of Science, as soon as research can be begun.

There was not a little in that ceremony of the summer of 1946 to remind us of that earlier ceremony, in the summer of 1918, when the cornerstone of the Hebrew University was laid. True, we were no longer in the midst of a general war, and the Jewish National Home to which we were dedicating the new enterprise was substantially in existence. But it was a time of stress and difficulty, when men's minds were little occupied with this type of activity. It was the time of the 'terror,' a time of bitter political disappointment and of impending struggle. Like the laying of the cornerstone of the University on Mount Scopus, this was an act of faith: and it has been a continuous act of faith to carry the work forward.

By the summer of 1947 the central building was completed, and it is now—in the autumn of 1947—being supplied with first-class modern equipment. I think this will be not only an institution of great practical usefulness, but also a source of pride and satisfaction to all of us.

It is gratifying, too, that the new Institute has not remained the 'hobby' of a small coterie. In various parts of the world increasing numbers of far-sighted individuals are evincing a sustained and creative interest in the enterprise. In Palestine, burdened as it is with enormous and pressing material problems, substantial contributions have been made to the Institute. In England, the Marks-Sieff family, the original sponsors of the Sieff Institute, now seconded by my friend, Sigmund Gestetner, are the centre of an active group. In the United States the friends of the Institute are too numerous to list here; but I cannot refrain from mentioning the Philadelphia group, headed by Fredric R. Mann, Walter Annenberg, Simon Neuman and

Judge Louis I. Levinthal, as well as a few individuals scattered throughout the country, like Harold Goldenberg of Minneapolis, Paul Uhlmann of Kansas City, William S. Paley, Abraham Feinberg and Rudolf Sonneborn of New York, Charles Rosenbloom of Pittsburgh, and my old friend Samuel Zemurray of New Orleans.

I have spoken, in an early chapter, of the frightful spiritual and intellectual losses we have suffered in the last war. The creation of scientific institutions in Palestine is essential if we are to ensure the intellectual survival of the Jewish people. It may take us as much as fifty years to regain our strength in this field, and the only hope is that the men of high qualification who come to us will influence the young generation of Palestine in the direction of skill, discipline, order and high-quality performance.

These men will no doubt bring with them their own scientific problems. Many of them are engaged in modern physical, chemical, electronic and isotope researches, and no doubt will continue this work in the new Institute, which will be equipped accordingly. But it will be the business of those charged with the guidance of the Institute not merely to imitate work which is going on in other places, perhaps with superior effectiveness, but to concentrate on problems which are peculiarly Middle Eastern or Palestinian, like genetics, the introduction of new varieties of plants and fibres, and the exploitation of certain resources in the country which at present may not represent any considerable value but which if properly worked can become of great interest. These are matters which will have to be carefully examined when the scientists are assembled, and when they have discussed and distributed their tasks. It is a fascinating problem to the tackling of which I look forward with great eagerness, even though, personally, I can only listen and chime in occasionally, for owing both to my age and eyesight disability I cannot take part in the actual performance.

We must leave it to time to determine the actual lines of development. All that one can do at present is make the preparations as adequate as one can. The initiative of the scientists will make maximum use of the conditions which they will find in the new country, and I have no doubt that their devotion and skill will lead them into the solving of many problems connected with the future growth of the Homeland.

s*

CHAPTER XLIV

THE DECISION

England Refers the Palestine Problem to the U.N.—The Special Committee on Palestine (U.N.S.C.O.P.)—Restatement of My Views—The Significance of the Terror—The British Work against Us in the U.N.—Oil Interests and the Political Stability of the Near East—Decision Approaches in U.N.—Helping Hands—Henry Morgenthau, Jr.—President Truman and the Negev—The U.N. Declares a Jewish State

THE final phase in the struggle for the establishment of the Jewish State may be said to have begun with Britain's decision in the spring of 1947 to refer the whole problem of Palestine to the United Nations. By that time the Anglo-American Commission, and the London Conference of January 1947, had been revealed as delaying devices. The same spirit motivated, I believe, the resort to the U.N. It was not in Mr. Bevin's plans that the U.N. should express itself in favour of the creation of a Jewish State, which it did, by more than the requisite two-thirds majority, in its historic decision of November 29, 1947.

The first action of the U.N. was the creation of the United Nations Special Committee on Palestine, the U.N.S.C.O.P., which proceeded to that country in the summer of 1947 to study the problem on the spot. Its recommendation of partition, the subsequent deliberations of the United Nations Ad Hoc Committee on Palestine at Lake Success, in October and November, and the decision of the Assembly, are recent history. A brief account of my part in these events will bring my life record to a close.

I appeared before the U.N.S.C.O.P. in Jerusalem at the request of the *Vaad Leumi*, or Jewish National Council, and before the Ad Hoc Committee at Lake Success at the request of the Jewish Agency. The official spokesmen of the latter body were Dr. Abba Hillel Silver and Mr. Moshe Shertok. I was no longer President of the Zionist Organization and Jewish

Agency. I felt, nevertheless, that I spoke the mind of the over-whelming majority of Jews everywhere, and that I could, without immodesty, after more than half a century of activity, claim to speak for the spirit of the Zionist movement. The account which follows is not in strict chronological order; its chief purpose is to summarize the substance of my views on the Zionist situation as a whole.

It was, as I said before the Ad Hoc Committee at Lake Success, a moving experience for me to appear before the United Nations at this turning point in Jewish history, and I added: 'My mind goes back something like twenty-five years to the time when, in the Council Chamber of the League of Nations, a somewhat similar discussion took place, and as a result of it there was the emergence of our programme for the reconstitution of the Jewish National Home in Palestine.' But my mind went back much further. I sought to restate, before the two committees, the fundamentals of the movement, its ethical and national meaning, and its historical character, as well as its position in regard to immediate problems. I went back not only a quarter of a century, but half a century and more. I presented, to the best of my ability, a total picture of the meaning of Zionism.

Much of what I had to say to the committees the reader will have gathered from my life story. If I advert briefly to some points which are already familiar to the reader, it is because even the most immediate of our problems must be viewed against that background.

The environment I was born into, and grew up in as a child, the upbringing which I received, made Jewishness—the Jewish nation, nationalism, as others term it—an organic part of my being. I was never anything but Jewish, I could not conceive that a Jew could be anything else. It was very strange for me to hear Mr. Jamal Husseini, speaking for the Arab side at Lake Success, declare that Jews were not Jews at all; they were Khazars, or Tartars, or God knows what. I answered, simply: 'I feel like a Jew and I have suffered like a Jew.'

'To feel like a Jew' meant for me, as for all of those who have had that upbringing, to be a Zionist, and to express in the Zionist movement the ethical as well as the national spirit of our Jewishness. All this was already implicit in the early *Chibath*

Zion movement, when the Russian Jewish masses were stirring under the promptings of Pinsker and Achad Ha-am. The coming of Herzl was an event of enormous importance, but not an unnatural one. It was no revolution; it was a fulfilment. But, as I have said, his creation of the Zionist Organization meant much more for us than his writing of the *Judenstaat*. It was not necessary to supply us with theories of Zionism; we had always had them. What we needed was a means and a way.

And that was what the Zionist Organization became for us. We watched it growing in strength from Congress to Congress. Sometimes we were compelled to fight certain destructive and reactionary forces which intruded into it. It seemed to me that these forces were seeking to increase the membership of the Zionist Organization at any cost, and were ready, for the sake of tempoɪary assistance, to barter away the purity of its basic principles. The pressure of need has always spurred certain elements among the Jews to accept what I have so frequently called the fallacy of the short cut; and sometimes the results have been deeply disturbing. What was the terror in Palestine but the old evil in new and horrible guise? I said before the U.N.S.C.O.P. in Jerusalem: 'The White Paper released certain phenomena in Jewish life which are un-Jewish, which are contrary to Jewish ethics, Jewish tradition. "Thou shalt not kill" has been ingrained in us since Mount Sinai. It was inconceivable ten years ago that the Jews should break this commandment. Unfortunately they are breaking it today, and nobody deplores it more than the vast majority of the Jews. I hang my head in shame when I have to speak of this fact before you.'

In this case, as in all others, a deviation from fundamental principle is not only a denial of ethics; it is self-defeating in its purpose. I have never believed that the Messiah would come to the sound of high explosives. The dissident groups which sprang up in Palestine, and which terrorized the Government and to some extent the Jews, and kept up an unbearable tension in the country, represented to my notion a grave danger for the whole future of the Jewish State in Palestine.

I permit myself a digression at this point. What I said before the U.N.S.C.O.P. and the Ad Hoc Committee about the organic character of Zionism, and my detestation of the terror, was necessarily a brief summary of my views on those subjects.

I believe that they should be treated at somewhat greater length here. There is a tendency to say that it was the activities of the *Irgun* which largely succeeded in drawing the attention of the world to the Palestine problem and in bringing it before the international forum of the United Nations. How the world was affected by the terror in Palestine it is difficult to gauge. We received more publicity than Herostratus, and I do not think that it is desirable to attract attention in that form.

I have said that the terrorist groups in Palestine represented a grave danger to the whole future of the Jewish State. Actually their behaviour has been next door to anarchy. The analogy which is usually drawn between these groups and what happened in Ireland or South Africa presents only a half-truth. It leaves out of account that one fundamental fact with which the Jews have to reckon primarily: namely, that they have many hostages all over the world. And although Palestine is the primary consideration, it must not, it has no right to, endanger the situation of Jews outside Palestine. Apart from which it must be remembered that after all the building of Palestine will depend to a large extent on the good will of Jews outside.

To return now to my addresses before the United Nations Committees. I dwelt at some length on our relations with the Arabs. I reiterated my belief—which I still hold strongly in spite of all that has happened—that co-operation with the Arabs would come about only if we enjoyed a status equal to theirs. This, the reader may remember, was one of the important reasons which moved me to accept partition when the Peel Report first mooted the idea a decade ago. I continued to advocate it when 'prudent' Zionists either treated the suggestion with great caution, or gained an easy popularity by attacking it. I pleaded for partition at the meetings of the U.N.S.C.O.P. in Jerusalem when no one could foresee that this would be its recommendation by an overwhelming majority. It seemed to me then—a great many others see it now—that the creation of a Jewish State, even within diminished boundaries, was the only way out of the impasse, particularly in our relations with our Arab neighbours.

It is also the only way to begin restoring those relations between ourselves and Great Britain which have deteriorated so sadly since the time of the Balfour Declaration. Even in the tense days of the summer and autumn of 1947 I was compelled by the feeling of historic justice to declare, both before the U.N.S.C.O.P. and the Ad Hoc Committee, that the Jewish people would be eternally grateful to Great Britain for the inauguration of that policy which the Balfour Declaration embodied. We must not, I insisted, permit ourselves to be blinded to the fact that the Mandate was inspired by high purposes, worthy of all the exertions and sacrifice which the Jewish people could bring to its implementation.

I said it at a time when the British Government, and its representatives in Palestine, were doing their best to turn the decision of the U.N.S.C.O.P. and the Ad Hoc Committee against us; at a time, I might say, when they were resurrecting arguments which had long since been disproved. I was, for instance, particularly struck by the complaint of the Palestine Administration, in a document prepared for the United Nations Special Committee, that our achievements had 'set up disparities' between us and the Arabs. Once upon a time we were accused of harming the Arabs by displacing them from the land, or by creating unemployment in their midst. This form of the accusation had been thrown out of court by the Peel Commission; the Palestine Administration now revived it in another form. We were not harming the Arabs directly; it might even be conceded that we were bringing them benefits; but there were 'disparities.'

I contended, I think rightly, that these disparities were much smaller than those which exist between the backward population and the so-called master race in many civilized and powerful countries. One might very well ask these rich and powerful countries what they have done for their backward populations. In my opinion it falls far behind the benefits which the Arabs have derived from the Jewish population of Palestine. If more should have been done for the Arabs—and it should—that was the primary business of the Government, and not of the Jews.

But the so-called question of these 'disparities' opened up a much wider field of discussion. The stability of the Near East has long occupied the attention of statesmen: there is a general fear that a political or social collapse in the Arab subcontinent will have grave consequences outside that area. But the most notorious social feature of the Arab subcontinent is the shocking gap between the small layer of the over-rich and the vast base of the submerged and miserable population. Nor is anything of consequence being done, by those who profess to fear the consequences of this evil, to diminish its dangers. Where are the vast royalties from the oilfields going? What fraction of these sums which are being handed over to Arab potentates is applied to bettering the condition of the masses of the population? Only a minimal proportion is actually being used for the founding of schools, or the improvement of hygienic conditions.

One was sometimes driven to the painful conclusion that there was an unwritten covenant between certain elements among the European and Anglo-Saxon powers, and the Middle-eastern Arabs, which ran on something like the following lines: 'We are adherents of non-intervention. Whatever happens in the interior of your country is your business. You can go on dealing with your populations as you think fit. We want peace in order to tap the oil resources and keep the lines of communication open.' But once again so-called 'realism' defeats itself. These elements are the very ones who fear unrest in the Near East. They refuse to understand that this idyllic state of affairs cannot last very long under any circumstances; and therefore they dread the example and influence of the Jewish Homeland. Instead of applauding this example and influence, which has already in Palestine produced a considerable improvement in the condition of adjacent Arab communities, they wish to see it removed; they consider the Jews dangerous not because they exploit the *fellaheen*, but because they do not exploit them. They have not learned, perhaps in their anxiety for immediate profit they are unable to learn, that stability is not to be obtained by the dominion of the few over the many, but by the more even spread of wealth through all the levels of the population.

This, in brief, was the substance of some of the arguments which I submitted to the U.N.S.C.O.P. and the Ad Hoc Committee. But there was much to be done in the way of explanation and exposition apart from my public appearances. Both in Palestine and America I placed myself at the disposal of members of the committees, or of United Nations delegates, who were anxious for more detailed information. My activities were, so to speak, on the sidelines, rather than in bearing the brunt of the public political discussions. In Palestine my house was open at all times to members of the committee. In America I was in frequent attendance at the sessions. If things were going slowly during the rather feverish days preceding November 29, 1947, if unexpected difficulties arose, I was asked to come down to see some group of delegates—the French, the Bolivian, the American and so on.

The official pleading of our cause before the United Nations was conducted with great skill and energy by Mr. Moshe Shertok, the head of the Political Department of the Jewish Agency for Palestine, and Dr. Abba Hillel Silver, the head of the American Section of the Jewish Agency, but many American Jews who until recently were remote from the Zionist movement took a keen interest in the United Nations discussion and helped us in the work. There was a welcome and striking change in the attitude of the American Jewish Committee, under the leadership of Judge Joseph M. Proskauer. Mr. Bernard Baruch and Mr. Bayard Swope, particularly the latter, who visited me frequently, were helpful among the various delegations. Among the younger men there were George Backer and Edward M. Warburg, of whom the latter has inherited from his father a deep interest in Jewish affairs, and has come very close to the Zionist ideology. Of particular assistance was Mr. Henry Morgenthau Jr., with whom I had been privileged to come in contact some years before, when he was a member of the Roosevelt administration. This contact continued after he left the Cabinet and was strengthened when he became chairman of the United Jewish Appeal—a responsibility which he took very seriously, like everything else to which he devotes his attention. All these names, and many others which could be added, make up an astonishing demonstration of the unity of American Jewry with regard to the Jewish National Home; it is in reality a fulfilment of what I had striven for in my old plans for the Jewish Agency.

There were many tense moments preceding the final decision on November 29, and these had to do not only with the probable votes of the delegates. There was, for instance, the actual territorial division. When this was discussed some of the American delegates felt that the Jews were getting too large a slice of Palestine, and that the Arabs might legitimately raise objections. It was proposed to cut out from the proposed Jewish State a considerable part of the Negev, taking Akaba away from us. Ever since the time of the Balfour Declaration I had attached great value to Akaba and the region about it. I had circumnavigated the gulf of Akaba as far back as 1918, when I went to see the Emir Feisal, and I had a notion of the character of the country. At present it looks a forbidding desert, and the scene of desolation masks the importance of the region. But with a little imagination it becomes quite clear that Akaba is the gate to the Indian Ocean, and constitutes a much shorter route from Palestine to the Far East than via Port Said and the Suez Canal.

I was somewhat alarmed when I learned, in the second week of November, that the American delegation, in its desire to find a compromise which would be more acceptable to the Arabs, advocated the excision of the southern part of the Negev, including Akaba. After consultation with members of the Jewish Agency Executive, I decided to go to Washington to see President Truman and to put the whole case before him.

On the morning of Wednesday, November 19, I was received by the President with the utmost cordiality. I spoke first of the Negev as a whole, which I believe is destined to become an important part of the Jewish State. The northern part, running from Gaza to Asluj or Beersheba, is beautiful country. It needs water, of course, which can either be brought from the north, as projected in the Lowdermilk scheme, or provided locally by desalting the brackish water which is found in abundance in these parts. We are, in fact, busily engaged in our Rehovoth Institute in experiments on the second alternative, and have succeeded in producing drinking water at an economic price; the question of larger quantities for irrigation still needs study. The settlements which are already receiving water from a pipe-line are showing remarkable results. Mr. Henry A. Wallace, who had recently returned from a visit to the Negev, was struck by a great plantation of carrots, which had been preceded on the same soil by a good crop of potatoes, while near by there was a plantation of bananas. All this seems fantastic when one takes into account that there has not been a blade of grass in this part of the world for thousands of years. But it is, as I told the President, in line with what the Jews have done in many other parts of Palestine.

I then spoke of Akaba. I pleaded that if there was to be a division of the Negev, it ought to be vertical and not horizontal; this would be eminently fair, giving both sides part of the fertile soil and part of the desert. But for us it was imperative that in this division Akaba should go to the Jewish State. Akaba is at present a useless bay; it needs to be dredged, deepened and made into a waterway capable of accommodating ships of sizable dimensions. If Akaba were taken away from us, it would always remain a desert, or at any rate for a very long time to come. As part of the Jewish State it will very quickly become an object of development, and would make a real contribution to trade and commerce by opening up a new route. One can foresee the day when a canal will be cut from some part of the eastern Mediterranean coast to Akaba. It is not an easy undertaking, but it has already been adumbrated by American and Swedish engineers. This would become a parallel highway to the Suez Canal, and could shorten the route from Europe to India by a day or more.

I pleaded further with the President that if the Egyptians choose to be hostile to the Jewish State, which I hope will not be the case, they can close navigation to us through the Suez Canal when this becomes their property, as it will in a few years. The Iraqis, too, can make it difficult for us to pass through the Persian Gulf. Thus we might be cut off entirely from the Orient. We could meet such an eventuality by building our own canal from Haifa or Tel Aviv to Akaba. The project has a great many attractive possibilities; and the mere fact that such a thing could be done would probably serve as a deterrent against closing the road to India for the Jews. I was extremely happy to find that the President read the map very quickly and very clearly. He promised me that he would communicate at once with the American delegation at Lake Success.

At about three o'clock in the afternoon of the same day, Ambassador Herschel Johnson, head of the American delegation, called in Mr. Shertok of the Jewish Agency in order to advise him of the decision on the Negev, which by all indications excluded Akaba from the Jewish State. Shortly after Mr. Shertok entered, but before the subject was broached, the American delegates were called to the telephone. At the other end of the wire was the President of the United States, telling them that he considered the proposal to keep Akaba within the Jewish State a reasonable one, and that they should go forward with it. When Mr. Johnson and General Hilldring emerged from the telephone booth after a half-hour conversation, they returned to Mr. Shertok, who was waiting for them, tense with anxiety. All they had for him was the casual remark: 'Oh, Mr. Shertok, we really haven't anything important to tell you.' Obviously the President had been as good as his word, and a few short hours after I had seen him had given the necessary instructions to the American delegation,

This decision opened the way to the vote of the General Assembly on November 29, when, by a majority of thirty-three to thirteen, the United Nations declared: 'The Mandate for Palestine shall terminate as soon as possible, but in any case not later than August First, 1948. . . . Independent Arab and Jewish States, and the specific international régime for the City of Jerusalem . . . shall come into existence in Palestine two months after the evacuation of the armed forces of the Mandatory Power has been completed, but in any case no later than October First, 1948.'

CHAPTER XLV

THE CHALLENGE

The Problems of the Jewish State—Immigration—Defence—American
Help in Finance and Human Resources—Constitution of the New State—
Justice—The Arab Minority—One Law for All—A Unified School
System—Industry and Technology—Quality Goods—Rural Foundations—
Religion and the State—Relations with Arabs and Neighbouring States—
The Bridge between East and West—Building a High Civilization

I WRITE this on the day following the historic decision of the
United Nations.

As the year 1947 draws to a close, the Jewish people, and
particularly the Zionists, face a very great challenge. Before
another year is over we must found a Jewish State; we must
prepare a constitution, set up a government, organize our
defences and begin to reconstruct the present National Home
so as to make it capable of absorbing, according to the plan,
some six to eight thousand immigrants a month.

This last item alone is a tremendous task. Seventy to a
hundred thousand immigrants a year represents an increase of
over twelve per cent in a community of six hundred and fifty
thousand. But the numbers express only a part of the problem.
In past years immigration included a large class of people who,
if not rich, certainly could not be classified as paupers. The
majority of them had some worldly possessions; they were in
good health, some had a little capital, others brought their
machinery with them, nearly all of them had a trade. The
financing of this immigration was a difficult but not unduly
heavy task. The immigrant who comes in today is completely
destitute. He has been robbed of everything. In many cases he
is morally and physically sick and must undergo a long process
of rehabilitation and adjustment before he can become productive. This task alone will tax to a very high degree the financial
powers of Jewry; and as European Jewry is today small in
numbers, and, apart from a few Western communities, quite

impoverished, the burden of this operation will fall on the American Jewish community.

To the foregoing must be added the requirements for defence, which, as I hear now, are mounting to something like £6,000,000 a year, but will probably increase. We must also undertake a number of necessary technical improvements, like the renovation of means of communication, roads, rolling stock and harbours. A large number of new buildings will be required. All this will put before us the necessity of raising a loan and of introducing taxes as quickly as possible. In short, we face the difficult and complex problem of the financing of the new State.

Nor is it by any means solely a question of finance. It is proper to ask whether we have all the men needed for our task. Without wishing to reflect on the men who have carried the burden hitherto, I believe we would do well not only to seek financial assistance from the American Jews, but to draw on the human resources of that country. There are many young people sympathetic to the movement who have had vast experience in running important state services, and who are willing to help. There are numbers of such persons in England. It will be a very severe test for the Zionists; they must show that they can divest themselves of their legitimate desires to become high public servants and to occupy positions which they may have deserved because of their activities. They must recognize that it is in the interest of the State to bring new forces and new points of view to bear on the whole situation.

A great deal will also depend on the constitution. It would be regrettable if the constitution of the new republic were to be fashioned in the image of that of the Zionist Organization. The latter is based on the principle of proportionate representation, which necessarily leads to the existence of a great many parties. We must try to avoid a repetition of the elections to the *Vaad Leumi*—the representative body of Palestinian Jewry hitherto. I think it would be sounder to have a constitution like the American, or almost no constituion, like the British, at any rate for the beginning, and to feel our way for the first few years before laying down hard and fast rules.

But all these matters, whether in the realm of finance or of constitutional arrangements, really deal with the externals of the situation. As the State is merely a means to an end it is necessary to envisage the end; or, to change the figure, the State is merely a vessel into which the contents still have to be poured, and it is necessary to know what the contents are likely to be.

Now the first element in such contents, and in my opinion the very lifeblood of a stable society, is justice; and not merely as an abstract principle, but as carried out in the law courts and by the judiciary. It must be quick, it must not be expensive—so that everyone has access to it—and it must be equal for everyone. There must not be one law for the Jew and another for the Arabs. We must stand firm by the ancient principle enunciated in our Torah: 'One law and one manner shall be for you and for the stranger that sojourneth with you.' In saying this, I do not assume that there are tendencies towards inequality or discrimination. It is merely a timely warning which is particularly necessary because we shall have a very large Arab minority. I am certain that the world will judge the Jewish State by what it will do with the Arabs, just as the Jewish people at large will be judged by what we do or fail to do in this State where we have been given such a wonderful opportunity after thousands of years of wandering and suffering.

It is such an extraordinary phenomenon that it will no doubt be the sensation of the century, and both our friends and our enemies—the latter more than the former—will be watching us carefully. Palestine has always been a powerful sounding board; it will become much more so when the Jewish State has been formed. Our security will to a great extent depend not only on the armies and navies which we can create, but on the internal moral stability of the country, which will in turn influence its external political stability.

But justice, though the first, is only one of the elements in the contents of the State. We shall be faced with an important reform in the whole system of education, and particularly in our elementary and secondary schools. We have at present a system based on class divisions. I think it is essential to see that we have a unified school system for which the State as a whole is responsible, and not some political party which tries to shape the mind of the child almost from the cradle. Party control of education makes for inefficiency and produces a bias in the mind and soul of the child from the very start. It will weaken, and not strengthen, the State. Instead of partisanship there must be citizenship, which of course transcends party interests.

Our technical and higher education has to be brought up to date and expanded with the new needs of the State. We shall need railway engineers, harbour engineers and shipbuilders. We shall now have the opportunity of introducing new industries; to this end we must enlarge greatly the available technical skill, increasing it in quantity and improving it in quality and efficiency. This again is a matter of schooling, beginning sometimes with the early years of the child. So, for instance, there is in Switzerland a very long course—six or seven years—in the watch-making school, which turns out skilled workmen and foremen. This is why Swiss watchmaking has taken such a high place in world industry. The same principle is applicable to all other industrial enterprises.

Palestine will have to produce quality goods; only in this way can it compete with larger and more powerful countries which swamp the market with mass-produced goods. Now the production of quality goods is not merely a matter of skill. It is also based on an honest relationship to the task in hand, on a desire to do justice to the product, to allow only the best to come out of the workshop, and to avoid shoddiness. It is in this way that a name and reputation are acquired, which is a very substantial part of the economic battle.

Into the same category fall honesty and frank relationships with the world outside; in the long run these are also profitable. One may be tempted to get rich quickly by producing shabby stuff which may find an initial sale, particularly in backward countries; but this sort of production corrupts the producer, who in the end becomes unable to improve himself, and remains on a low level in the industrial world. Therefore integrity in commercial and industrial relations, efficiency and the desire to produce the best and the most beautiful, are the essential props on which a great industry can be built even in a small country. Again and again I should like to quote the example of Switzerland. The nature of the industry differs from country to country, depending on climate, geographical position, availability of this or that raw material; but the principles behind the fashioning of the product out of the raw material are the same. One may, indeed, speak of moral industrial development.

Happily we have made an excellent beginning in our agricultural colonization. I believe we have, through our system of land nationalization and co-operatives, avoided many mistakes from which old and powerful states suffer in their economy today. We have no 'poor whites,' and we also have no feudal landlords. We have a healthy, intelligent, educated smallholder, who cultivates his land intensively, in a scientific way, is able to extract sustenance in a dignified fashion from a comparatively small plot, have a house and hearth, and even economize a little for a rainy day. So much has been written and said about this side of our life that I need not expatiate on it here. I would only like to add that if I had to begin my life over again, and educate my children again, I would perhaps emulate the example of our peasants in Nahalal or Deganiah.

There is now an opportunity to acquire more land, create more and more of these settlements, and establish again a sort of balance between the town and the village. Civilization is based more on the village and on God's earth than on the town, however attractive certain features of our town life may be. It is in the quiet nooks and corners of the village that the language, the poetry and literature of a country are enriched. The stability of the country does not depend so much on the towns as on the rural population. The more numerous and the more settled the latter, the wider and more solid is the basis of the State. We do not need, in our case, to fear the conservatism or backwardness of the Jewish peasant, or the emergence of a *kulak* type. This cannot happen any more under our system. One would like to see an offset against the rapid growth of towns like Tel Aviv and Haifa. One should strive towards decentralization of the urban population, and not towards the creation of monster cities as we see them in Europe or America. These monster cities are of necessity composed of slums and something like luxurious dwellings, not to say palaces. We have still time to avoid these extremes in our city and village planning. A village in Palestine can have all the advantages of the town because of its nearness to the latter, and all the amenities of a village life, distances being very small.

Many questions will emerge in the formative stages of the

State with regard to religion. There are powerful religious communities in Palestine which now, under a democratic régime, will rightly demand to assert themselves. I think it is our duty to make it clear to them from the very beginning that whereas the State will treat with the highest respect the true religious feelings of the community, it cannot put the clock back by making religion the cardinal principle in the conduct of the state. Religion should be relegated to the synagogue and the homes of those families that want it; it should occupy a special position in the schools; but it shall not control the ministries of State.

I have never feared really religious people. The genuine type has never been politically aggressive; on the contrary, he seeks no power, he is modest and retiring—and modesty was the great feature in the lives of our saintly Rabbis and sages in olden times. It is the new, secularized type of Rabbi, resembling somewhat a member of a clerical party in Germany, France or Belgium, who is the menace, and who will make a heavy bid for power by parading his religious convictions. It is useless to point out to such people that they transgress a fundamental principle which has been laid down by our sages: 'Thou shalt not make of the Torah a crown to glory in, or a spade to dig with.' There will be a great struggle. I foresee something which will perhaps be reminiscent of the *Kultur-kampf* in Germany, but we must be firm if we are to survive; we must have a clear line of demarcation between legitimate religious aspirations and the duty of the State towards preserving such aspirations, on the one hand, and on the other hand the lust for power which is sometimes exhibited by pseudo-religious groups.

I have spoken of the problem of our internal relations with our Arab minority; we must also face the arduous task of achieving understanding and co-operation with the Arabs of the Middle East. The successful accomplishment of this task will depend on two important factors. First, the Arabs must be given the feeling that the decision of the United Nations is final, and that the Jews will not trespass on any territory outside the boundaries assigned to them. As to the latter, there does exist such a fear in the heart of many Arabs, and this fear must be eliminated in every way. Second—and this links up with our internal problem—they must see from the outset that their brethren within the Jewish State are treated exactly like the Jewish citizens. It will be necessary to create a special department dealing with the non-Jewish minority. The object of the department shall be to associate this minority with all the benefits and activities which will grow up in the Jewish State.

The situation requires tact, understanding, human sympathy and a great deal of political wisdom; but I believe that if we follow the lines indicated, the much-desired co-operation will come about, even if slowly. But we must also turn our face to the Oriental countries beyond the Middle East. It was my good fortune during those fateful days of the United Nations sittings to come in close contact with the Indian delegation, which contained a number of highly distinguished men and women. We had many talks with them, and it was they who took the initiative in proposing, first, that I should visit India; second, that we should send a group of Jewish scientists and engineers to India in order to propose new developments; third, the Indian students should come to the Jewish places of learning in Palestine. These men look upon Palestine as an outpost of Western civilization in relation to the Orient. Here is a mighty opportunity to build a bridge between the East and the West, which is one of the most attractive rôles which the Jewish State in Palestine can play. It is a task which by itself is of a magnitude which calls for the efforts of many able men. Do our people, in their present mood of victory, realize all the implications of this new state of affairs, and have we the personnel capable of implementing the possibilities after they have been weighed correctly?

I have spoken of the East. There is also a Western region of Mediterranean countries with which good neighbourly relations will have to be established: Greece, Italy, the Mediterranean islands, as far as Gibraltar. There is Turkey, which also looks upon Palestine as an outpost of European civilization. Our commercial and industrial development will depend to a great extent on our relations with these countries. Given the right relations, Palestine can become a modern Phœnicia, and her ships can trade as far as the coasts of America.

It is not the purpose of these closing pages to outline the full programme of the Jewish State. An enormous amount will have to be left to trial and error, and we shall have to learn the hard way—by experience. These are merely indications and sign-posts pointing along the road which in my opinion must be followed if we are to reach our goal. This goal is the building of a high civilization based on the austere standards of Jewish ethics. From these standards we must not swerve, as some elements have done during the short period of the National Home, by bending the knee to strange gods. The Prophets have always chastised the Jewish people with the utmost severity for this tendency; and whenever it slipped back into paganism, whenever it reverted, it was punished by the stern God of Israel. Whether Prophets will once more arise among the Jews in the near future it is difficult to say. But if they choose the way of honest and hard and clean living, on the land in settlements built on the old principles, and in cities cleansed of the dross which has been sometimes mistaken for civilization; if they centre their activities on genuine values, whether in industry, agriculture, science, literature or art; then God will look down benignly on His children who after a long wandering have come home to serve Him with a psalm on their lips and a spade in their hands, reviving their old country and making it a centre of human civilization.

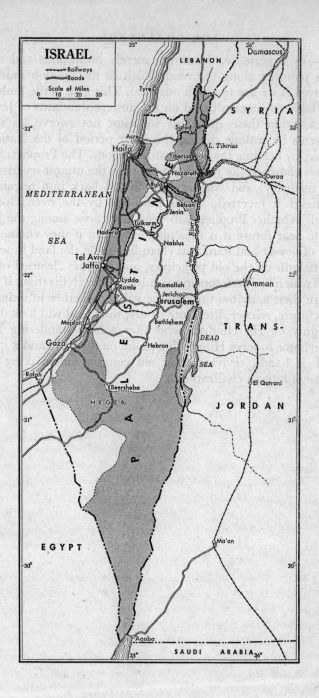

EPILOGUE

SOME nine months have passed since I wrote the last chapter of these memoirs. I believed then that my task was ended and that the long—perhaps too long—record was complete. But the events which have filled the interval have been of a character which compels me, both on personal and general grounds, to add another word. I have made no change in what I wrote up to November 30, 1947, even where the record 'dates': what follows here is a brief review of the extraordinary developments which have intervened.

We accepted the United Nations resolution of November 29 for what it was—a solemn international decision. We assumed —perhaps without thinking very deeply about the matter— that in so far as United Nations action might be needed to implement the decision, such action would be forthcoming; but we also assumed—and here we were on firmer ground—that the main responsibility for implementation would rest with ourselves. For my own part, I felt that the sooner I was in Palestine, the better, and made my preparations accordingly.

For family and other reasons we decided to pay a short visit to London, en route, and we were back at our old apartment in the Dorchester on December 23, 1947. There was, it seemed, little political work to be done in England, for the British Government had announced its intention of abiding loyally by the United Nations decision. We settled down to enjoy the company of our children and of a few friends; I attended to some long-neglected business affairs. I addressed a meeting at Palestine House, and a small dinner party in aid of the Joint Palestine Appeal; these were my only public engagements. We booked an air passage to Palestine for January 25.

. Within those few weeks, however, a disturbing change came over the situation at Lake Success, a result of the deteriorating position in London and Palestine. It soon became evident that the British Government placed a peculiar interpretation on its 'loyal acceptance' of the United Nations decision. The Assembly of the United Nations had appointed a Committee of Five—known later as the 'Five Lonely Pilgrims'—to proceed to Palestine and begin the implementation of the decision. A Jewish militia was to be created and a Provisional Council of Government set up. If, on the withdrawal of the Mandatory Power, Arab opposition developed, the Security Council was to establish an international force; in the meantime the Mandatory was responsible for the maintenance of order. But when, a few days after the meeting of the Security Council, there were Arab attacks on Jewish transports, the Mandatory took no steps. It appeared that the British Government regarded the mere protection of Jewish life as an implementation of partition, and 'loyal acceptance' of the United Nations decision did not call for that. The disturbances, which could easily have been suppressed by prompt action, were permitted to spread—a familiar story, this. The Jewish defence forces were at that time still 'underground.' They had no access to the arms markets of the world. Such arms as they possessed were liable to seizure when discovered. Itself refusing to protect the Jewish community, the Mandatory did not acknowledge the right of the community to protect itself. *Haganah* convoys were searched, *Haganah* fighters arrested in the act of defending Jewish lives. 'Loyal acceptance' of the decision became, in effect, a process of sabotage.

Nor was it all passive. The Mandatory Power refused the United Nations Committee entry into Palestine, refused to permit the organization of a Jewish militia to take over defence, refused to comply with the Assembly's recommendation to open a port of immigration, refused to hand over any of the Government services to an incoming Jewish successor; it expelled Palestine from the sterling *bloc*, dismantled the equipment of Administration without handing any of it over, and simultaneously allowed the Government services to disintegrate. But while Palestine was closed to the Committee of the United Nations, its frontiers were open to the invasion of irregular Arab forces, which came across the Allenby Bridge on the Jordan, an easily guarded point. Under these circumstances it is not to be wondered at that Arab attacks multiplied. The Arabs now felt that what they could not obtain by argument in the court of the United Nations, they could compel by force of arms.

They were encouraged in this view by the apparent effect of their lawlessness on opinion in the United States and the United Nations. The Jews of Palestine, whose hands were tied by the Mandatory Power, were hastily and superficially adjudged incapable of defending themselves, and the cry arose in certain quarters that only armed intervention by the United Nations—a contingency which became remoter with every passing day—could save the November decision. The Jews were openly accused of having exaggerated their own strength, while underestimating the military power of the Arabs, and of having thus obtained the grant of statehood by what was nothing more nor less than a bluff. On top of all this the United States had established an arms embargo for the entire Near East, an action which seemingly placed Arab aggressors and Jewish defenders on the same footing. Thus a wholly synthetic situation was created which enabled the enemies of the Jewish State to make a last desperate attempt to force a revision of the United Nations decision.

Towards the middle of January, I was besieged in London by letters, telegrams and telephone calls from friends in the United States. The Executive of the Jewish Agency sent me a formal invitation to return to New York and to co-operate with it in the gathering crisis. I was reluctant to accept. I still nourished the hope that things would somehow straighten themselves out, and I believed I could be more useful on the Palestinian scene. But as the time for our departure approached the telephone calls from New York became more numerous and more urgent, as one responsible friend after another pleaded with me to change my course. One day before the plane was due to leave we cancelled the flight, and succeeded in obtaining passage on the *Queen Mary* for January 27. The last two days in London were something of a nightmare. We had arranged to give up our flat at the Dorchester on the twenty-fifth, and the moving man moved in promptly. He chased us from room to room taking carpets from under our feet, cushions from behind our backs, pictures from over our heads, till what had for nine years been our London home dissolved before our eyes and reverted to the hotel suite it really was. And all the while there was a constant stream of telegrams and telephone calls. It was in a thoroughly exhausted condition that my wife and I reached the boat train on the twenty-seventh.

We arrived in New York again on February 4, and on the same day I issued a statement to the press in which I said, among other things: 'I am well aware that the implementation of the United Nations resolution raises many difficulties, but these difficulties are as nothing compared with the dangers which would arise if the United Nations policy were to be altered by force. If that were to happen, which I do not believe it will, one result would be the decline of the United Nations and a grave blow to the very idea of international authority. Another would be the prolongation of conflict in Palestine. . . . The interests of America lie in the strengthening of the United Nations, in the curtailment of conflict in the Near East, and in the strictest fidelity to the policies to which they are pledged. . . . The steadfast courage of the Jews of Palestine fills me with the greatest pride. They have a right to expect that the civilized world which has endorsed their title to national independence will not leave them in the lurch in the face of a murderous attack which is being openly prepared against them by forces of extremism and violence in the Arab world. . . . The urgent task now is to convince Arab opinion by tangible facts that the Jewish State cannot be prevented from coming into existence. . . .'

The truth is, as all can now see plainly, that these facts really existed, but were being deliberately obscured in a political play. I was profoundly convinced that not only were the Jews of Palestine thoroughly capable of defending themselves, but that the much-touted danger of complete administrative chaos in Palestine, following on the British withdrawal, was an illusion, chiefly created by the British course of action, but belied, in fact, by the soundness of the structure of Jewish life. But it was not easy, in those days, to convince people that the realities of the Palestinian situation were being misrepresented. In Washington it was already being taken for granted that, in deference to the 'facts,' a fundamental revision would have to take place, and the November decision, if not actually reversed, deferred—perhaps *sine die*. When the Security Council began to discuss the problem at the end of February, the United States leadership was weak. Of the Powers which had supported the November decision, only the Soviet Union still insisted on the assertion of the United Nations authority. The Security Council failed to adopt any resolution for backing up the decision of the General Assembly.

Under these circumstances I obtained an interview with the President of the United States. Unfortunately it was delayed for many reasons, one of them being my ill-health, brought on largely by the strain and pressure of events. By the time I arrived in Washington, on March 18, the adverse tide had apparently become irresistible. The President was sympathetic personally, and still indicated a firm resolve to press forward with partition. I doubt, however, whether he was himself aware of the extent to which his own policy and purpose had been balked by subordinates in the State Department. On the following day, March 19, Senator Austin, the United States representative in the Security Council, announced the reversal of American policy. He proposed that the implementation of partition be suspended, that a truce be arranged in Palestine, and that a special session of the General Assembly be called in order to approve a trusteeship for Palestine, to take effect when the Mandate ended, i.e. on May 15. In spite of all the forewarnings, the blow was sudden, bitter and, on the surface, fatal to our long-nurtured hopes.

The notion of a new trusteeship for Palestine at this late date was utterly unrealistic. Palestine Jewry had outgrown the state of tutelage. Moreover, everything that had made the Mandate unworkable would be present in the trusteeship, but aggravated by the recollection that only a few months before we had been adjudged worthy of statehood. To have accepted this decision would have meant to make ourselves ludicrous in the eyes of history.

In a statement to the press I said, on March 25: 'The plan worked out by the Assembly was the result of a long and careful process of deliberation in which the conflicting claims of the various parties were judged in the light of international equity. In order to achieve a compromise between Jewish and Arab national claims, the Jews were asked to be content with one-eighth of the original area of the Palestine Mandate. They

T

were called upon to co-operate in a settlement for Jerusalem which set that city's international associations above its predominantly Jewish character. We accepted these limitations only because they were decreed by the supreme authority of international judgment, and because in the small area allotted to us we should be free to bring in our people, and enjoy the indispensable boon of sovereignty—a privilege conferred upon the Arabs in vast territories. . . .

'Now some people suggest that the partition decision be shelved because it has not secured the agreement of all parties! Yet it was because the Mandatory Power itself constantly emphasized that the prospect of agreement was non-existent that it submitted the question to the United Nations. . . . Whatever solution may be imposed will require enforcement. A sustained effort should be made on behalf of a solution twice recommended by distinguished commissions—the Royal Commission and U.N.S.C.O.P., and now reinforced by the Assembly's authority. I have spent many years labouring at this strenuous problem, and I know there is today no other practical solution, and none more likely to achieve stability in the long run—certainly not the Arab unitary state which the conscience of the world has rejected, or the so-called federal formula which is in fact nothing but an Arab state in another guise, or an impossible effort to impose trusteeship and arrest the progress of the Palestinian Jews towards their rightful independence.

'But for the admission into Palestine of foreign Arab forces no problem of security would have arisen which the local militia envisaged by the Assembly's decision could not have controlled. I shall never understand how the Mandatory Government could allow foreign Arab forces to cross freely by bridge and road into Palestine and prepare at leisure and with impunity, to make war against the Jews and against the settlement adopted by the United Nations. I have always paid high tribute to the great act of statesmanship of Great Britain in inaugurating the international recognition of our right to nationhood. But in exposing everything and everybody in Palestine to destruction by foreign invaders the Mandatory Government has acted against its own best tradition and left a tragic legacy to the country's future. . . .

'The Jews of Palestine will have the support of Jews the world over in those steps which they will deem necessary to assure their survival and national freedom when the Mandate ends. I would now urge the Jewish people to redouble its efforts to secure the defence and freedom of the Jewish State. . . .'

In a private letter to the President of the United States, written on April 9, I elaborated these views in detail, adding, in view of the widespread rumours that Palestine would be left by the Mandatory in a state of chaos: 'Jews and Arabs are both mature for independence, and are already obedient in a large degree to their own institutions, while the central British Administration is in virtual collapse. In large areas Jews and Arabs are practically in control of their own lives and interests. The clock cannot be put back to the situation which existed before November 29. I would also draw attention to the psychological effects of promising Jewish independence in November and attempting to cancel it in March. . . .

'The choice for our people, Mr. President, is between statehood and extermination. History and providence have placed this issue in your hands, and I am confident that you will yet decide it in the spirit of the moral law.'

In the swift movement of recent events a great part of the public may already have forgotten how dark the picture looked for us only a few months ago, and how completely it was dominated by the curious notion that the Zionists were 'through.' Shortly after the reversal of policy in the United Nations the United States delegation, consisting of Senator Austin, Professor Jessup and Mr. Ross, called on us at my hotel and tried to enlist my support for the trusteeship proposal. I must have astonished as well as disappointed them, for I declared bluntly that I put no stock in the legend of Arab military might, and that I considered the intention of Palestine Jewry to proclaim its independence the day the Mandate ended thoroughly justified and eminently realistic. M. Parodi, the representative of France, came to dinner, and renewed the arguments of the American delegation. I had the same answer for him. I added that, given half a chance, the Jews of Palestine would render the world a service by exploding the myth which had been built up round the Arab aggressors. M. Parodi was polite, but obviously incredulous. A few months later, when the issue had been joined and decided, he informed the Jewish representative at Lake Success: 'What I thought was Dr. Weizmann's propaganda appears to be the truth.'

My strongest protestations I reserved for Mr. Creech-Jones, the British Colonial Secretary, who visited me while I was on my sick-bed. Great Britain was in an anomalous position: largely responsible for the failure—up to that point—of the partition decision, but showing no enthusiasm for the alternative proposal of trusteeship. The British view seemed to be that Arabs and Jews should be left to themselves for an unavoidable period of blood-letting. The British clearly anticipated that the Arabs would make substantial inroads on the territory allotted to the Jews, and on the basis of the situation thus created a new solution would be reached, favourable, both politically and territorially, to the Arabs. It is an astonishing reflection on the relationship of the British to Palestine that they, who had been on the spot for the last thirty years, should have made so false an appraisal of the factors. For either they were really convinced that the Arabs would overwhelm us or else—and this betrayed an even profounder misreading of the realities—they believed that we would ignominiously surrender our rights without so much as a test. Mr. Creech-Jones pleaded that the invasion of Palestinian soil by 7,500 Arabs had taken the Mandatory Power unawares, but there they were, and the Jews had to reckon with them. My answer was that we had no intention of evacuating any of the territory allotted to us. It was with the deepest pain that I saw the Mandate coming to an end under circumstances so unworthy of its beginnings, but the fault was not ours. The British had declared that 'as long as they are in Palestine they insist on undivided control of the country.' One could quite understand that a Great Power should be jealous of its prestige, but Great Britain had not been jealous enough to keep out the Arab invaders. Was that an enhancement of Britain's prestige? And how did it accord with Britain's good name to leave the country in a state of organized chaos? On these points Mr. Creech-Jones was extremely evasive.

The General Assembly of the United Nations reconvened in mid-April. By that time we had something more than protestations to offer, for the realities had begun to emerge. The so-called liberation army of Fawzi Kawukji had been soundly trounced at Mishmar Ha-Emek. In some parts of the country the Jewish forces had assumed the offensive. In an admirable display of discipline and initiative, the *Yishuv* was beginning to erect the pattern of an effective state on the ruins of the Mandatory régime. It was creating departments of centralized government in areas which the British were progressively evacuating. It was clear that while the United Nations was debating trusteeship, the Jewish State was coming into being.

It had been anticipated that the trusteeship plan would be adopted without difficulty; but within the two months since its proposal, the situation had again altered radically. The session of the Assembly was made notable by the remarkable address of the New Zealand representative, Sir Carl Berendsen, who demanded that the United Nations take a stand on its own decision. 'What the United Nations needs,' he said, 'is not resolutions but resolution.' His view won support from Australia and from the countries of Eastern Europe, and from the ever gallant defenders of the Jewish cause from South America, including Professor Fabregat of Uruguay, and Dr. Granados of Guatemala, with both of whom I was in close contact. It was at this time, too, that I made the acquaintance of the Secretary-General of the United Nations, Mr. Trygve Lie, who, within the powers granted him by the Charter, zealously asserted the Assembly's authority. During those crucial days we had many defenders in the public press, foremost among them Mr. Sumner Welles, who wrote a number of impressive articles in the *Herald Tribune*. The *New York Times*, which at best had been always cool to the Zionist programme, strongly criticized the United States reversal, and urged that partition be given a chance.

Still, it was hard going. When it became clear in the Assembly that the trusteeship plan could not be adopted, another delaying formula was devised—a 'Temporary Truce'; both parties were to cease fire, no political decision was to be taken, a limited Jewish immigration was to be permitted for a few months, and in exchange for this transient and dubious security the Jews were to refrain from proclaiming their State in accordance with the November decision. The proposal was to all appearances a harmless one; at bottom it was profoundly

dangerous, if only for the reason that every refusal to face the
realities of the situation weakened the authority of the United
Nations and encouraged in the enemies of the Jewish State the
belief that its creation could be prevented.

I was of course in intimate consultation during this period
with Mr. Shertok, our chief spokesman at the United Nations,
and his colleagues. They were thoroughly aware of the dangers
which lurked in the truce proposal; but they were also aware
that it made a strong appeal to the less determined elements in
our own ranks. Perhaps the most telling argument against us
was that in proclaiming a Jewish State, in the face, apparently,
of American disapproval, we should be alienating a powerful
friend. Moreover, it needed a certain moral courage to decline
a truce when our nascent army in Palestine was still so ill-
equipped and the issue apparently still in doubt. Mr. Shertok,
Dr. Nahum Goldmann and their colleagues felt that at this
point my views on the situation would have a considerable
effect both within and without our ranks.

On the issue of this truce, as on that of the trusteeship, I was
never in a moment's doubt. It was plain to me that retreat
would be fatal. Our only chance now, as in the past, was to
create facts, to confront the world with these facts, and to build
on their foundation. Independence is never given to a people;
it has to be earned; and having been earned, it has to be
defended. As to the attitude of the United States Government,
I felt that many of those who were advising us to ignore the
United Nations decision in our favour, and to let our independence go by default, would respect us more if we did not accept
their advice. I was convinced that once we had taken our
destiny into our own hands and established the Republic, the
American people would applaud our resolution, and see in our
successful struggle for independence the image of its own
national liberation a century and three-quarters ago. So
strongly did I feel this that at a time when the United States
was formally opposed to our Declaration of Independence I
already began to be preoccupied with the idea of American
recognition of the Jewish State.

Many friends and colleagues thought I was being somewhat
less than realistic, and tried to dissuade me from encouraging
a step which in their opinion could only end in retreat and

disaster. They expressed astonishment at what they called my unwonted intransigence. In Palestine, where the doubts and hesitations which reigned at Lake Success found no echo, there was no thought of relinquishing the rights conferred on us, and by a suicidal act of self-denial refusing statehood; or, if there was any doubt, it was connected with our intentions in America rather than with those of the Palestinian Jews. In the general breakdown of British Administration, there was a period when communications between America and Palestine were irregular and unreliable. Our views at the American end were not at all clear to the *Yishuv*. Mr. Ben-Gurion, the chairman of the Jewish Agency Executive, was trying, without success, to ascertain exactly where I stood. In the early part of May, Mr. Shertok left for Palestine to clear matters up, and in the second week of that month I strengthened our contacts with our friends in Washington, and affirmed my intention of going ahead with a bid for recognition of the Jewish State as soon as it was proclaimed. On May 13 I addressed the following letter to the President of the United States:

DEAR MR. PRESIDENT:

The unhappy events of the last few months will not, I hope, obscure the very great contributions which you, Mr. President, have made towards a definitive and just settlement of the long and troublesome Palestine question. The leadership which the American Government took under your inspiration made possible the establishment of a Jewish State, which I am convinced will contribute markedly towards a solution of the world Jewish problem, and which I am equally convinced is a necessary preliminary to the development of lasting peace among the peoples of the Near East.

So far as practical conditions in Palestine would permit, the Jewish people there have proceeded along the lines laid down in the United Nations Resolution of November 29, 1947. Tomorrow midnight, May 15, the British Mandate will be terminated, and the Provisional Government of the Jewish State, embodying the best endeavours of the Jewish people and arising from the Resolution of the United Nations, will assume full responsibility for preserving law and order within the boundaries of the Jewish State, for defending that area against external aggression, and for discharging the obligations of the Jewish State to the other nations of the world in accordance with international law.

Considering all the difficulties, the chances for an equitable adjustment of Arab and Jewish relationships are not unfavourable. What is required now is an end to the seeking of new solutions which invariably have retarded rather than encouraged a final settlement.

It is for these reasons that I deeply hope that the United States, which under your leadership has done so much to find a just solution, will promptly recognize the Provisional Government of the new Jewish State. The world, I think, will regard it as especially appropriate that the greatest living democracy should be the first to welcome the newest into the family of nations.

Respectfully yours,

CHAIM WEIZMANN

On the fourteenth of May the President and his advisers were in constant consultation on the Palestine issue. The Assembly of the United Nations had neither revoked nor reaffirmed its resolution of November 29. In Palestine the British Mandate had only a few more hours to run.* On the same day a historic assembly of the representatives of the *Yishuv* was convoked in Tel Aviv, and proclaimed to the world the rightful independence of the Jewish State, to take effect as of the hour of the termination of the British Mandate.

At a few minutes past six o'clock, American time, unofficial news reached Lake Success that the Jewish State had been recognized by the Government of the United States. The delegates were incredulous, which perhaps was natural at a time when many wild rumours were running through the corridors of the United Nations building. The United States delegation was unaware of any such decision. Finally, after much confusion, Professor Jessup rose to read the following statement issued from the White House:

This Government has been informed that a Jewish State has been proclaimed in Palestine, and recognition has been requested by the

* It should be borne in mind that Palestine time is seven hours in advance of Washington time.

Provisional Government itself. The United States recognizes the Provisional Government as the *de facto* authority of the new State of Israel.

This historic statement must be regarded not only as an act of high statesmanship; it had a peculiar and significant fitness, for it set the seal on America's long and generous record of support of Zionist aspirations.

On May 15 a great wave of rejoicing spread throughout the Jewish world. We were not unmindful of the dangers which hung over the new-born State. Five Arab armies were at its frontiers, threatening invasion; our forces were not yet properly organized; we were cut off from international support. But the die was cast. The demoralizing illusions of trusteeship and truce were behind us. We were now face to face with the basic realities, and this was what we had asked for. If the State of Israel could defend itself, survive and remain effective, it would do so largely on its own; and the issue would be decided, as we were willing it should, be, by the basic strength and solidity of the organism which we had created in the last fifty years.

May 15 was a very full day. Recognition was extended to the State of Israel by the Soviet Union and Poland, to be followed shortly by several countries of Eastern Europe and South America. Great Britain remained silent, and I received reports that Mr. Bevin was bringing pressure to bear on the British Dominions and Western Europe to withhold recognition. However, I bethought myself of one surviving author of the Balfour Declaration and addressed a cable to General Smuts. This was closely followed by South African recognition.

On this same day, amidst the avalanche of messages reaching me from Tel Aviv, there was one signed by the five Labour Party leaders in the Provisional Government, David Ben-Gurion, Eliezer Kaplan, Golda Myerson, David Remez and Moshe Shertok:

On the occasion of the establishment of the Jewish State we send our greetings to you, who have done more than any other living man towards its creation. Your stand and help have strengthened all of us. We look forward to the day when we shall see you at the head of the State established in peace.

T*

I answered:

My heartiest greetings to you and your colleagues in this great hour. May God give you strength to carry out the task which has been laid upon you and to overcome the difficulties still ahead. Please accept and transmit the following message to the *Yishuv* in my name: 'On the memorable day when the Jewish State arises again after two thousand years, I send expressions of love and admiration to all sections of the *Yishuv* and warmest greetings to its Government now entering on its grave and inspiring responsibility. Am fully convinced that all who have and will become citizens of the Jewish State will strive their utmost to live up to the new opportunity which history has bestowed upon them. It will be our destiny to create institutions and values of a free community in the spirit of the great traditions which have contributed so much to the thought and spirit of mankind.'

CHAIM WEIZMANN

Two days later, when I was resting in my hotel from the fatigue of the preceding weeks, a message reached me that, according to one of the news agencies, the Provisional Council of State had elected me as its President. I attached no credence to the report, thinking it unlikely that the Council of State, absorbed with a thousand urgent problems, of which not the least were the dangers of the invasion, would have been giving thought to this matter. A few hours later, however, the same message was repeated over the radio and was picked up in the adjoining room where my wife was entertaining friends. Almost at the same moment Aubrey Eban, then one of our younger aides at the United Nations, and at this time of writing the brilliant representative of Israel before that body—and I might add, one of its most distinguished members—came in with some friends from Madison Square Garden, where the Jews of New York were celebrating the establishment of the Jewish State at a mass rally which I could not attend because of ill-health. They brought definite confirmation of the report. That evening my friends gathered in our hotel apartment, and raised glasses of champagne in a toast to the President of Israel.

The next day I received a more detailed report of the proceedings in Tel Aviv. The Minister of Justice, Dr. Felix Rosenblüth, had proposed my election. Mr. Ben-Gurion, Prime Minister and Minister of Defence, had seconded it. He did not conceal the many differences of opinion which had divided us in recent years. He went on, however, to say: 'I doubt whether the Presidency is necessary to Dr. Weizmann, but the Presidency of Dr. Weizmann is a moral necessity for the State of Israel.' I quote these words, at the risk of incurring the charge of immodesty, only as an indication of the essential unity of purpose which underlay all those struggles of ideology and method which formed part of our movement. But I will not deny that the occasion was one which filled me with pride as well as with a feeling of deep humility. Replying to the notification of my election, I cabled Ben-Gurion:

Many thanks your cable May seventeenth. Am proud of the great honour bestowed upon me by Provisional Council of Government of State of Israel in electing me as its first President. It is in a humble spirit that I accept this election and am deeply grateful to Council for confidence it has reposed in me. I dedicate myself to service of lands and peoples in whose cause I have been privileged to labour these many years. I send to Provisional Government and people of Israel this expression of my deepest and most heartfelt affection, invoking blessing of God upon them. I pray that the struggle forced upon us will speedily end and will be succeeded by era of peace and prosperity for people of Israel and those waiting to join us in construction and advancement of new State.

My first official act as President of the State of Israel, and my last on American soil, was to accept the invitation of the President of the United States to be his guest in Washington and to take up the usual residence at Blair House. I travelled from New York to Washington by special train, and arrived to find Pennsylvania Avenue bedecked with the flags of the United States and Israel. I was escorted to the conference at the White House by representatives of the United States Government and by Mr. Eliahu Epstein, whom the Provisional Government had appointed as its envoy to the United States. In the course of our interview, I expressed our gratitude to the President for the initiative he had taken in the immediate recognition of the new State, and as a gift symbolizing the Jewish tradition, I presented him with a scroll of the Torah. We passed from ceremonial to practical matters and discussed the economic and political aid which the state of Israel would need in the critical months that lay ahead. The President showed special interest in the question of a loan for development projects, and in using the influence of the United States to ensure the defence of Israel—if possible, by preventing Arab aggression through United States action, or, if war continued to be forced upon us, by ensuring that we had the necessary arms.

The following day I set sail for Europe. It had been my original intention to go again to England for personal and family reasons. I now felt that I was no longer free to do so. Arab armies were attacking Israel by land and from the air; the spearhead of this aggression was the Arab Legion of Transjordan, equipped by British resources, financed by the British Treasury, trained and commanded by British officers. By a particularly bitter twist of historical irony, the main operations of this force were directed against the Holy City. The Hebrew University and the Hadassah Medical Centre were under bombardment; Jewish shrines in Jerusalem, which had survived the attacks of barbarians in medieval times, were now being laid waste. Liberal opinion throughout the world, and especially in the United States, was profoundly shocked. I had always believed that an anti-Zionist policy was utterly alien to British tradition, but now an atmosphere had been created in which the ideals of the State of Israel, and the policies of Great Britain, under Mr. Bevin's direction, were brought into bloody conflict. I had no place in England at such a time, and I felt it to be a bitter incongruity that I should not be able to set foot in a country whose people and institutions I held in such high esteem, and with which I had so long and so stubbornly sought to link the Jewish people by ties of mutual interest and co-operation. I decided to arrange my affairs in France; for that country, my wife and I, accompanied by Mr. Ivor Linton, Political Secretary of the London Office of the Jewish Agency, set sail on May 26. From France we proceeded to Switzerland, where I planned to take a much-needed rest before going on to Israel to assume my duties.

Here, in the quiet of Glion, I write these closing lines to the first part of a story which is not yet half-told—is, indeed, hardly begun. Of the crowded events of the last few months, of the first struggles and triumphs of the infant State of Israel, of truces

and renewed attacks, of mediation and of old solutions in new
guise, I will not speak here. These matters are too close to be
evaluated. All that is written here is by way of introduction—
one of the many prefaces that may yet be written—to the New
History of Israel. Its writing has been for me a labour com-
pounded of pain and pleasure, but I am thankful to lay it aside
in favour of more active and practical pursuits. If anything I
have said should lead the reader to look more understandingly
and more kindly on the early chapters of our new history, now
in the making, I shall feel amply rewarded.

GLION, SWITZERLAND
AUGUST 1948

INDEX